# Business Ethics

## A contemporary approach

*Business Ethics: A contemporary approach* introduces students to ethical issues and decision-making in a variety of contemporary contexts. It develops an awareness of the many ways in which ethical considerations can manifest in commercial domains, thereby helping prepare students for their professional careers.

*Business Ethics* shows how theory works in practice. It includes hundreds of real-world examples that will help engage students. Examples draw on recent and emerging concerns, such as the moral implications of social media and the enforcement of codes of behaviour within industries. The book also addresses corporate social responsibility, stakeholder management and sustainability, reflecting the broad scope of business ethics today.

Comprehensive online resources are available at www.cambridge.edu.au/academic/business-ethics. Student resources include additional review questions and case studies, with answer guides, to help students reinforce learning and prepare for assessment tasks. Instructor resources include an extensive set of tutorial exercises, PowerPoint slides and a test bank of assessment resources.

*Business Ethics* will equip students with the individual and organisational strategies to analyse and improve the ethical climate in workplaces, professions and commercial life in general.

**Gael McDonald** is President, RMIT University, Vietnam.

# Business Ethics

**A contemporary approach**

**Gael McDonald**

CAMBRIDGE
UNIVERSITY PRESS

# CAMBRIDGE
## UNIVERSITY PRESS

477 Williamstown Road, Port Melbourne, VIC 3207, Australia

Cambridge University Press is part of the University of Cambridge.

It furthers the University's mission by disseminating knowledge in the pursuit of education, learning and research at the highest international levels of excellence.

www.cambridge.org
Information on this title: www.cambridge.org/9781107674059

First published 2015

Cover designed by Tanya De Silva-McKay
Typeset by Newgen Publishing and Data Services
Printed in Singapore by C.O.S Printers Pte Ltd

*A catalogue record for this publication is available from the British Library*

*A Cataloguing-in-Publication entry is available from the catalogue of the National Library of Australia at* www.nla.gov.au

ISBN 978-1-107-67405-9 Paperback

Additional resources for this publication at
www.cambridge.edu.au/academic/businessethics

To my husband Collin and children James and Tess –
my world is so much better because of you.

# Contents

# Preface

After the popularity of the movie *The Bucket List*, starring Jack Nicholson and Morgan Freeman, a lot of people, shall we say in the 'older age bracket', started making up bucket lists. Activities, usually involving travel to exotic locations, featured prominently on these lists. I also made up a bucket list but, intriguingly, on mine was that I'd always wanted to write a textbook on business ethics, which has been my preferred research area for more than 25 years. So, when Cambridge University Press approached me, I was rather reluctant to turn the task down as I knew that if I didn't do it then it would probably haunt me in the future.

When initially conceptualising the project, I was cognisant of and guided by various models of moral behaviour, with the intention of delivering on four key dimensions that I wanted the text to develop:

- **Moral sensitivity** – the ability to recognise that a moral dilemma exists, to interpret the circumstance and assign recognition of what ethical issues are contained in the situation.
- **Moral motivation** – the ability to prioritise moral values in relation to other personal values.
- **Moral judgement** – the ability to make a morally justifiable decision and judge whether an action is morally right or wrong.
- **Moral action** – the ability to provide, in the face of situational pressure, an ethical outcome.

More specifically, I wanted to:

- examine the current factors which are driving an increased awareness of business ethics in today's business environment
- provide some clarity to the lexicon of business ethics and related terminology
- engage with current issues in the business environment and society at large, as presented in the media
- investigate ethics in a variety of functional areas of business including information technology, human resource management, marketing, accounting, entrepreneurship and international business
- present ethical principles which are of relevance in these key functional areas
- review the theoretical foundations of ethics
- provide guidelines to assist with ethical decision-making
- discuss the strategies that can be used to strengthen the ethical climates of organisations.

Given the extensive theoretical foundations and ever-changing landscape of current ethical issues evident in the business environment, the difficulty of writing a textbook on business ethics is not what one puts in but, rather, what one leaves out. A strict word limit for each chapter meant that we created an approach that puts as much content as possible in the chapter itself, and subsequently refers the reader to the book website for material that is usually found at the end of book chapters. The website is, therefore, a significant complementary resource, and contains a range of materials:

- Student and tutor resources, including answers to exercises from the book, and assessment items
- Ethics on video: Relevant multimedia material
- Ethics in print: A list of current texts relating to the topics discussed
- Ethics at the movies: Films with related themes
- Ethics on the web: Website and web material of interest.

A book of this nature has two audiences – students and their lecturers. Wherever possible, I have resisted the temptation to write as if I were speaking to tutors (those with prior knowledge of ethics) or even reviewers (who are experts in the field). Instead, the book has been written intentionally for those with little or no prior exposure to ethics. While it would be ideal if the book was read sequentially, the chapters have deliberately been written with the possibility that a student may prefer to dip in and out of chapters in random order.

The text itself is, essentially, divided into four parts. Part 1 (Chapters 1 and 2) contains introductory chapters which walk the reader into business ethics and related terminology, as well as discussing the drivers promoting an increased awareness of ethics. Part 2 (Chapters 3 to 9) goes into specific functional areas and looks at the issues that are currently being experienced, for example, in the areas of IT, human resource management, marketing management, accounting and finance, entrepreneurship and small business, and international business. Part 3 (Chapters 10 and 11) deviates from the norm in that ethical theory is presented *after* an awareness of ethical issues has been addressed, rather than as a preliminary chapter as is usual in a text of this kind. Naturally, the theory is used as a lens to be applied in the decision-making process, and once students have covered this material it is hoped they will start tackling some of the larger cases in relation to each chapter, and build up their expertise in ethical analysis. Part 4 contains just one chapter (Chapter 12) and takes the reader from the perspective of developing their own personal ethical decision-making to the responsibilities of building an ethical culture in one's own business context; here, we discuss strategies as to how one might enhance the ethical climate from an organisational perspective.

For tutors, the text is to be used in conjunction with lectures, and I anticipate that chapters will be assigned as they occur within the course format, so tutors should feel free to take the chapters out of sequence to suit their course plan. The website also has tutor resources, which contains:

- tutorial experiential exercises, cases, online discussion and additional teaching materials
- PowerPoints for each chapter
- assessment questions for each chapter, a written assignment and overarching cases, which act as a buffet from which tutors can choose a range of assessment options.

The philosophy of the book is reflected in the title – we take a contemporary approach to business ethics. While we do mention some of the better recognised historical ethical cases, our focus is on current examples and recent developments. The downside of this currency is that this content may date over time, so it is hoped that in future editions the text will contain examples from a number of contributors, through crowdsourcing or something similar, of recent ethical and unethical business activity from around the world. We hope that tutors will also be able to share their teaching cases, exercises and favourite web references.

In research, we are always trained to entertain and articulate the limitations of a study. For this text, I have received considerable input from reviewers, which I particularly appreciate, and that feedback has resulted in constructive changes. I am also rather prone to extensive rewriting, while realising that, if we constantly twiddled, the text would never be published. However, there is one piece of reviewer feedback we would like to address here; a niggling concern raised by a reviewer who stated that there was 'an absence of enough material on how managers can enact their moral values in organisational contexts. It is good to talk about issues and provide detailed decision models, but ethics is about enactment. Students need to be given opportunities to learn how to convince others as to what should or shouldn't be done. That is, skills in arguing for particular courses of action'.

I have to say, I agree entirely with this statement. This type of enactment is, however, easier to achieve in experiential exercises but a tad harder to do in a written text – hence the section on moral courage in Chapter 11. I have also referenced, with her permission, Mary Gentile's book, *Giving voice to values: How to speak your mind when you know what's right*, and I encourage further exploration of her work. I do, however, implore readers and tutors to consider seriously not just the content of the issues provided in this book but also what it means to be in the thick of the many ethical dilemmas discussed in the text, as well as the considerable pressures a person can come under, and how they might demonstrate integrity in the face of such pressures. This involves both voicing concerns and enacting one's values – skills that we need to be constantly developing.

# Acknowledgements

The saying goes that 'it takes a village to raise a child' – well, it takes a small troupe to produce a book. Previously, when I have written a book, it was a relatively simple process, but in today's digital world there is as much need for web-based material as there is for chapter content. To accommodate the increased workload I was superbly assisted by a number of fabulous people, whom I would like to sincerely acknowledge and to thank for the tremendous support and significant contribution they provided to me.

Dr Jade McKay, who filled the research holes where needed and so capably stewarded the project to completion. Kim Findlay, who, among many other tasks managed the permissions, embellished the PowerPoints and text with wonderful graphics and lent her talent as a case writer. Teo Yiong, who assisted with assessment items, reviewing the learning objectives and provided the mind maps.

Natalie Gallagher, or 'nimble fingers Nat' as she is called because of her incredible keyboard skills, supported the creation of chapter notes while Karlie Matthews, my Executive Assistant, assisted when asked and kept the office humming in her usual efficient way. Lynn Spray did a superb job, as always, with the academic proofreading of the various drafts both before and after review.

At Cambridge University Press, Bridget Ell was the initial Commissioning Editor and David Jackson took the reins for the vast majority of the journey. David has been encouraging throughout the project and demonstrated a subtle hand in endeavouring to keep me to task and the timetable, supported by Jessica Pearce as Publishing Assistant. In the later stages of the project, Managing Editor Jodie Fitzimmons, Development Editor Tara Peck and Development Editor Vilija Stephens provided considerable support, and Katy McDevitt did a great job as copyeditor of the book and web materials. However, the real star of the Cambridge team has been Amelia Fellows, Academic Project Editor, who took the reins in the final stage.

My thanks also go to the many academic chapter reviewers, both in Australia and internationally, who provided comments and constructive input to the material.

In closing, my heartfelt gratitude goes to my supportive family, and particularly to my husband Collin and our twins, Tess and James, who sacrificed a significant amount of family time over many months to enable me to complete this book.

Once again, thank you all so much for your support. I most certainly could not have done this without you.

# Acronyms

| | |
|---|---|
| AAA | American Accounting Association |
| ACCA | Association of Chartered Certified Accountants |
| ACCC | Australian Competition and Consumer Commission |
| ACIG | Australian Content Industries Group |
| AHRI | Australian Human Resource Institute |
| AI | Amnesty International |
| APRA | Australian Prudential Regulation Authority |
| ASIC | Australian Securities and Investment Commission |
| ASX | Australian Securities Exchange |
| ATTAC | Association for the Taxation of Financial Transactions for the Aid of Citizens |
| AUSTRAC | Australian Transactions Reports and Analysis Centre |
| BITC | Business in the Community |
| BOP | Base of the Pyramid |
| BSR | Business for Social Responsibility |
| CDM | Clean Development Mechanism |
| CERC | Certified Emission Reduction Credit |
| CERES | Coalition for Environmentally Responsible Economies |
| CERT | Computer Emergency Response Team |
| COPPA | Children's Online Privacy Protection Act (US) |
| CPA | Certified Practising Accountants |
| DDOS | Distributed Denial of Service Attack |
| DOS | Denial of Service |
| DOJ | Department of Justice (US) |
| EBNSC | European Business Network for Social Cohesion |
| EEOC | Equal Employment Opportunity Commission (US) |
| EFTA | European Fair Trade Association |
| EPA | Environmental Protection Agency (US) |
| FBI | Federal Bureau of Investigation (US) |
| FCPA | Foreign Corrupt Practices Act (US) |
| FERC | Federal Energy Regulatory Commission (US) |
| FOFA | Future of Financial Advice (Aus.) |
| FLA | Fair Labor Association |
| FLO | Fairtrade Labelling Organisations International |
| GEM | Global Entrepreneurship Monitor |
| GRI | Global Reporting Initiative |
| HRW | Human Rights Watch |
| HSBC | Hong Kong Shanghai Banking Corporation |
| IAASB | International Auditing and Assurance Standards Board |
| IAESB | International Accounting Education Standards Board |

| IBLF | International Business Leaders Forum |
| ICAA | Institute of Chartered Accountants Australia |
| ICAC | Independent Commission Against Corruption |
| ICANN | Internet Corporation for Assigned Names and Numbers |
| IESBA | International Ethics Standards Board for Accountants |
| IFAC | International Federation of Accountants |
| IFAT | International Federation for Alternative Trade |
| ILM | Institute of Leadership and Management |
| ILO | International Labour Organisation |
| IMF | International Monetary Fund |
| IOE | International Organisation of Employers |
| ION | InterOrganizationNetwork |
| IPA | Institute of Public Accountants (Aus.) |
| IPSASB | International Public Sector Accounting Standards Board |
| ISO | International Organization for Standardization |
| ITC | Independent Television Commission (UK) |
| ITSA | Insolvency Trustee Service Australia |
| IUCN | World Conservation Union |
| LEAD | Leadership, Employment and Direction |
| LGBTI | Lesbian, Gay, Bisexual, Transgender and Intersex |
| LIBOR | London Inter-Bank Offered Rate (UK) |
| MES | Multi-dimensional Ethics Scale |
| MLM | Multi-level Marketing |
| NBES | National Business Ethics Survey |
| NC3Rs | National Centre for the Replacement, Reduction and Refinement of Animals in Research (UK) |
| NOHSC | National Occupational Health and Safety Commission (Aus.) |
| NSA | National Security Agency |
| OECD | Organisation for Economic Co-Operation and Development |
| PEIR | Personal Environmental Impact Report (US) |
| PIPA | Protect Intellectual Property Act |
| PwC | PricewaterhouseCoopers |
| RIAA | Recording Industry Association of America |
| RSPCA | Royal Society for the Prevention of Cruelty to Animals (UK) |
| SAI | Social Accountability International |
| SEC | Securities and Exchange Commission (US) |
| SFO | Serious Fraud Office |
| SOPA | Stop Online Piracy Act |
| SRI | Socially Responsible Investing |
| TBL/3BL | Triple Bottom Line |
| TPB | Tax Practitioners Board |

| | |
|---|---|
| UNCTC | United Nations Centre for Transnational Corporations |
| UNGC | United Nations Global Compact |
| USAID | US Agency for International Development |
| VGT | Virtual Global Taskforce |
| WBCSD | World Business Council on Sustainable Development |
| WFTO | World Fair Trade Organization |
| WHO | World Health Organization |
| WIPO | World Intellectual Property Organization |
| WRI | World Resources Institute |
| WTO | World Trade Organization |
| WWF | World Wide Fund for Nature |

# PART 1

# Business Ethics Overview

# Chapter 1

## Introduction to business ethics

'It takes 20 years to build a reputation and five minutes to ruin it.'
Warren Buffett, 1930–,
American investment entrepreneur

## Chapter aim

To provide an introduction to business ethics and enable the development of a clear understanding of the numerous factors that enhance ethical awareness in business.

## Chapter objectives

1. Gain an appreciation of the range of industry sectors in the business environment that are experiencing ethical challenges.
2. Critique current attitudes to business ethics.
3. Describe the four levels on which business ethics operates.
4. Clarify the concepts of legality, morality, personal character and values in relation to ethics.
5. Differentiate moral relativism from moral absolutism, and extrapolate Kohlberg's Theory of Moral Development to organisations.
6. Identify which market, government and social drivers are currently operating to increase ethical awareness in business.

# Ethics in the media: Personal reputation

Reputation.com provides a technological service that protects and polishes the online image of people who want to protect their personal reputation. It has 1.6 million customers, each of whom pays US$99 a year for the service, which monitors when a person is mentioned online and alerts them if it comes across anything sensitive ('The price of reputation' 2013).

## Introduction

In what has been described as the worst industrial accident in South Asia since the Bhopal disaster in 1984, the collapse of an eight-storey garment factory at Rana Plaza in Dhaka, Bangladesh, resulted in the deaths of more than 1100 people and a greater number of injuries ('Disaster at Rana Plaza' 2013). In the past, this type of event would have been viewed as a tragic incident culminating from poor construction and lack of ongoing maintenance in a localised context, but, in today's business environment, the circumstances take on a larger and more global perspective in regard to ethical responsibility and culpability.

The owners of the factory clearly violated their duty of care and refused to take action, although the local police and industry associations had notified them that the building was unsafe. However, blame and ethical accountability has extended beyond the owners of the factory. Labour lobbyists have critiqued the actions of the international companies who commission work through such factories and extensively utilise low-wage manufacturing sites. Consumers are also now becoming cognisant of how their purchases may be contributing to unethical practices, especially where low-cost items purchased in one country may come at a human cost in another. Increasingly, we are seeing ethical responsibility becoming far more pervasive with vicarious responsibility being demanded throughout the supply chain and encompassing the ultimate consumer. In recognition of this responsibility, the multinational corporations (MNCs) who sourced from the Dhaka factory have promised compensation to victims and their families. Walmart has launched a fire safety training academy in Bangladesh, while Gap have announced plans to help factory owners upgrade their plant. However, these gestures could be deemed reactive rather than proactive as the companies involved attempt to cover up a lack of ethical oversight.

The business world is littered with the consequences of ethical failures, as is evident from the banking disasters in the recent global financial crisis (GFC) and the collapse of organisations such as Enron, WorldCom and Lehman Brothers in the United States, Satyam in India, Akai Holdings in Hong Kong and HIH Insurance, Storm Financial and Centro in Australia, as well as global firms such as Arthur Andersen. All these company collapses have been sobering and important reminders of the consequences of ethical failure. However, those are only the companies that have failed – many more are fully operational but grappling with key ethical issues.

# Ethics on reflection: The Enron scandal

For an insightful clip about the Enron scandal see <www.youtube.com/watch?v=2GdvKh3Gr3E>. What were the major ethical shortcomings in this company?

## Ethical issues in industry sectors

Here is a challenge – have a look at today's media, either online or a hard copy newspaper, and see if you can spot an ethical issue in business. You will probably find an issue with remarkable ease, as scarcely a week goes by without a company coming under attack for wrongdoing. While some industry groups feature more predominantly, notice that ethical issues are evident in all sectors.

**The banking and finance sector** – particularly since the GFC has received a lot of attention, and, in 2013, the European Union (EU) fined six of the world's top financial institutions a record €1.7 billion for rigging financial benchmarks. The penalty was the largest fine to date imposed by the European Commission (EC) (*Top banks in record fine* 2013). In the United Kingdom, a parliamentary committee published a long-awaited report into the failings of the British banking system, and recommended the creation of a new criminal offence for reckless misconduct by banks' management teams ('The world this week' 2013).

# Ethics in the media: Financial scandals

For a full report on the EU's fine of the world's top financial institutions, see 'Top banks in record fine' (2013) at <http://nz.finance.yahoo.com/video/top-banks-record-fine-154825136.html>.

A US federal investigation was initiated into the hiring practices of JP Morgan throughout Asia, focusing on South Korea, Singapore and India, where it appears that flagrant cases of **nepotism** occurred. The Security Exchange Anti-Bribery Unit began investigations into the bank's practice of hiring the children of China's elite in order to win business with anonymous sources, indicating that the bank went so far as to create a formal sons and daughters program (Silver-Greenberg 2013).

**nepotism** – where an employee hired, promoted or favoured is a member of the manager's or supervisor's family.

**The retail industry** – has been lobbied extensively in regard to safety and labour practices in its supply chain, with big retailers being named. Marks and Spencer were accused of selling clothes made by child labour. Similarly, Walmart and Walt Disney have, historically, been the focus regarding labour abuses in Bangladeshi factories, and Nike have for some time now responded to public pressure and produced a Memorandum of Understanding to be signed with every factory that produces Nike shoes.

**The automobile industry** – implicated for lack of duty of care and defective products. Firestone tyres used on a Ford Explorer were found to be faulty and potentially lethal. A jury ordered Ford to pay more than US$61 million to the family of 17-year-old Lance Crossman, who was killed in an accident when his friend fell asleep while driving an Explorer. Ford were found liable in the accident because they knowingly sold a vehicle that handled poorly and was not stable.

**The food and drink industry** – Starbucks have been challenged in the UK for their tax minimisation strategies, and, previously, anti-globalisation protesters have criticised Starbucks over labour standards in their retail outlets, which they have subsequently endeavoured to address. As a result of consumer dissatisfaction, Starbucks announced in December 2012 that for the next two years they would voluntarily pay extra tax in Britain to the tune of around £10 million per year more than their official tax obligation ('Wake up and smell the coffee' 2012).

**The hotel industry** – responding to growing public concern about the environmental and social impact of some of its holiday resort developments, hotel giant, Six Continents, which own brands such as Holiday Inn, Intercontinental and Crown Plaza, published their first environmental and social report in 2002.

# Ethics in practice: Ethical crises

For a discussion of ethical crises, view the video, *The ethics of business: Where and why it can go wrong* (2013), available at: <www.youtube.com/watch?v=vKWNFAiQHG8>.

The organisations caught up in these wrongdoings have often suffered financial and reputational damage, and, as Edson Spencer, a former Chairman of Honeywell, has concluded, it takes many years to build a good reputation, and one bad move can destroy it overnight (Cialdina, Petrova & Goldstein 2004). Environmental factors, such as deregulation, liberalisation, international competition and demands for profit performance, are undoubtedly creating pressures on business behaviour. The possibility that ethical and commercial considerations will conflict has always faced those who run companies; it is not a new problem. The difference is that wider and more critical interest is being taken in decisions and the ethical judgements which lie behind these decisions (Cadbury 1987).

Some companies appear to be primarily motivated by the strategic need to manage their reputation and risk, rather than recognising their ethical accountability. Smart companies are, however, increasingly seizing the chance to take an ethical stance and to demonstrate responsibility, while remaining understandably cautious of ethical positioning in case they put themselves on a pedestal from which they might fall.

# Ethics in the media: The 12 least ethical firms

What happens when an organisation is not concerned with creating an ethical climate and culture? *The Huffington Post* recently reported on the findings from research carried out by Swiss research firm, Covalence, which identified the 12 least ethical companies in the world (Riser 2010). A slideshow of these 12 companies and their wrongdoings can be found at: <www.huffingtonpost.com/2010/01/28/the-least-ethical-compani_n_440073.html?slidenumber=0ZHHXzV%2FaPE%3D&slideshow>.

## Current views about business ethics

Many believe that the term business ethics is an oxymoron, with 'Business' and 'Ethics' being at the opposing ends of a continuum, much the same as jumbo shrimp and military intelligence (Ketz 2006).

As Neville Cooper, the former chairman of the London-based Institute of Business Ethics has commented, in relation to business ethics the points of view range from the hard-bitten cynic, who might state that business ethics is an oxymoron, through to the pragmatist who indicates that business is difficult enough without adding ethics into it. Concern for ethics in business can range from being uninterested to motivations to protect the brand, right through to the more committed that see ethics as being synonymous with good business.

Published every two years, the Ethics Research Centre's National Business Ethics Survey (NBES) is a recognised barometer of workplace ethics. A survey conducted in 2011 found ethics in business is at its weakest point since 2000, and that in the previous two years, 45% of US employees observed a violation of the law or ethics standards at their places of employment. Curiously, reporting of this wrongdoing was at an all-time high – 65% and 20% of whistleblowers saw retaliation for their actions (Ethics Resource Centre 2011).

How does this compare to the UK? It appears that three out of five managers in the UK have felt pressure to behave unethically at work, according to research from the Institute of

Leadership and Management (ILM) and Business in the Community (BITC). The report found that 9% of managers have been asked to break the law at some point in their career, while one in 10 have left their jobs as a result of being asked to do something that made them feel uncomfortable. In the survey of 1000 managers across the public and private sectors, 93% said their organisation had a value statement, but over 43% had been pressured to behave in direct violation of it. Encouragingly, 77% of managers believe that since 2008 the general public expectations of UK organisations' ethical behaviour have risen (Ethical Performance 2012a).

## Generational attitudes

Recently there has been some interesting research into whether there are generational differences when it comes to views on business ethics. The Ethics Resource Centre (2013) published a study titled *Generational differences in workplace ethics: A supplementary report of the 2011 National Business Ethics Survey*, which examines the differences in attitudes towards ethical issues among four generational groups (**Traditionalists**, **Baby Boomers**, **Gen X**, and **Millennials/Gen Y**). The study found that the Millennials (born 1981–2000), who are the youngest workers, are significantly more likely than their older colleagues to feel pressure from others to break ethical rules, with pressure easing as workers spend more time in the workforce and learn ways of coping with their work environment.

**Traditionalists** – born between 1925 and 1945; hardworking, respectful of authority, and value loyalty.

**Baby boomers** – born between 1946 and 1964; hardworking, idealistic, and committed to harmony.

**Gen X** – born between 1965 and 1980; entrepreneurial, flexible and self-reliant, and comfortable with technology.

**Millennials/ Gen Y** – born between 1981 and 2000; tech-savvy, appreciative of diversity, and skilled in multi-tasking.

Generational attitudes: Millennials (© shutterstock.com/Andre Adams)

Another finding in the generational study was that younger workers observed more ethical misconduct in the workplace during the previous 12 months than their older colleagues, with Millennials observing more instances than any other generation. The types of misconduct observed include:

- personal business on company time: 26%
- lying to employees: 22%
- abusive behaviour: 21%
- company resource abuse: 21%
- discrimination: 18%.

# Four levels of business ethics

It should be noted that business ethics can be examined from a number of levels as depicted in Figure 1.1.

- **Personal level** – at the individual level, each of us must routinely engage in ethical decision-making as we grapple with what is the right thing to do in a range of business circumstances.
- **Organisational level** – at the organisational level, we are looking at the ethical actions of the firm, recognising that circumstances of corporate wrongdoing are usually the result of ongoing and aggregate inappropriate decision-making. This level evokes a fundamental discussion of **corporate moral agency**, where it has been argued that corporations, while not possessing human embodiment, are moral agents with accompanying rights and are accountable in much the same way as individuals (French 1984).
- **National level** – at the national level, ethics focuses on the collective expectations of society; that is, the shared norms and values that guide ethical business behaviour, as well as the end-state effects on a country as a result of corporate behaviour and what is deemed appropriate and inappropriate by society. For example, an ethical issue at this level is the presence of **corruption** and **bribery**.
- **International level** – at the international level, we are seeing coordinated efforts across national boundaries to address issues that arise as a result of globalisation, as well as prominent societal concerns. Prompted by directives such as the millennium goals, interagency agreements and cooperation are required to coordinate efforts and achieve outcomes. Notable examples are international sustainability efforts, tax minimisation and **Fair Trade**.

**Figure 1.1** Four levels of business ethics

**corporate moral agency** – corporations, while not embodied in the way humans are, are moral agents with accompanying rights, and are accountable in the same way as individual people.

**corruption** – misuse of entrusted powers for private gain.

**bribery** – the offering, accepting or soliciting of an inducement (gifts, donations, services) for an action.

**Fair Trade** – engaging producers, distributors and consumers in the eradication of exploitation and the pursuit of trading conducted fairly and in accordance with Fair Trade practices.

# Ethics in the media: National bribery

In Guatemala, more than 15% of respondents to a national survey reported that they had paid a bribe in order to reconnect to the public water system. In Bangladesh, 64.5% of citizens responded that they had paid a bribe when interacting with law enforcement agencies (Transparency International 2009a).

# Ethics in the media: Violating international sanctions

Standard Chartered Bank agreed to pay a staggering US$340 million to settle claims made by the New York State Financial Regulator that the bank had possibly contravened American sanctions on Iran.

The bank which appears to have put profit before legislative requirements, at the risk of losing their New York operating licence ('The world this week' 2012).

## Defining business ethics

**business ethics** – rules, standards, codes or principles that provide guidelines for morally right behaviour in specific business situations.

In an aptly titled paper, 'Defining business ethics: Like nailing jello to a wall', Lewis (1985) reflected on the difficulties of defining business ethics but arrived at the conclusion that **business ethics** is comprised of rules, standards, codes or principles that provide guidelines for morally right behaviour in specific business situations. **Unethical behaviour** has also been defined as acts of omission, or commission, by individuals, groups of individuals, and organisations, which violate socially constructed norms, regulatory and/or legal structures (Khan, Tang & Zhu 2013). The question, of course, is whose constructed norms they are referring to. Are they the norms of one's ethnic group or subculture, national culture, or the organisational climate in which an individual is operating? In this context, socially constructed norms are deemed to be higher order social norms such as honesty, transparency and avoiding conflicts of interest.

**unethical behaviour** – acts of omission or commission by individuals, groups of individuals or organisations, which violate socially constructed norms, regulatory, and/or legal structures.

## Differentiating business ethics

In order to build our understanding of what is business ethics, we need to differentiate between the capacious concept of ethics and related terminology.

### Legality and ethics

On 3 December 1984, an accidental leakage of Methyl Isocyanate gas in the Indian city of Bhopal killed some 2400 residents and injured a further 200 000; yet, given inadequacies in the legislative framework, apparently no law was violated. It seems that the company involved, Union Carbide, were morally responsible if not legally culpable. Conversely, an activity may be legal but ethically questionable, as we see in the examples of Apartheid in South Africa, animal testing, and labour abuses in developing countries.

# Ethics on reflection: Rules versus public good

In certain circumstances, the law may get in the way of public good. For example, a Melbourne driver witnessed an accident involving a suspected drug-affected driver. The witness parked in a loading zone to report the accident, and received a traffic violation for infringing the traffic regulations. In court, the Magistrate upheld the guilty conviction, but dismissed the AU$141 fine (Donnelly 2013).

**Question:**
1. What are your thoughts on the ticket and the fine?

In business, legal transgressions are commonly viewed as the result of unethical behaviour and frequently come under the category of **white-collar crime** – which is described as any non-violent act committed for financial gain, regardless of one's social status (Brightman 2009). It is not unusual to see the terms 'financial crime', 'white-collar crime' and 'fraud' used interchangeably, although financial crime generally describes a multiplicity of crimes involving the unlawful conversion of property belonging to another to one's own personal benefit. Crimes include fraud, bribery, corruption, money laundering, embezzlement, insider trading, tax violations, and cyberattacks (Henning 2009).

**white-collar crime** – any non-violent act committed for financial gain.

White-collar criminals are often found to be wealthy, highly educated, socially connected, and typically employed in legitimate organisations (Gottschalk 2011). Interestingly, it has been noted that, when explaining criminal intentions, people do not label their own actions as committing a crime; rather, they seek to redefine the circumstance and see the risk of being fined as just one of many imperfect regulations of business conduct (Rousseau & Telle 2010).

The **law** attempts to ensure social stability and embodies the ideals that it considers should not be violated. Although law is codified and written down, a recognised limitation of the law is that you cannot codify every social problem or enforce every rule which seems desirable (Shrader-Frechette & Westra 1997). Law, therefore, provides the minimum of what is acceptable. Above this threshold there is a grey area where often the law runs out, and it is up to individual decision-making to determine what is ethical and what is not. Not every wrong can be addressed by the law, and ethics is, therefore, generally viewed as doing right even when not required to by law. For a diagrammatic representation of the relationship between legality and ethics, see Schwartz and Carroll (2003).

**law** – codified statements that ensure social stability and embody ideals that are considered those that should not be violated.

## Morality and ethics

In his book *Death in the afternoon*, Ernest Hemingway quipped that morality is judged by how you feel after the event. The linguistic ancestries of morals and ethics are quite different.

**morality** –
principles of
right and wrong.
Morality consists
of what a person
ought to do in
order to conform to
society's norms of
behaviour.

**ethics** – the
philosophical
reasoning for,
or against, the
morality society
has stipulated.

Morals derive from the Latin *moralis*; ethics derives from the Greek work *ethikos*. **Morality** refers to principles of right and wrong. Morality consists of what a person *ought to do* to conform to society's norms of behaviour, while **ethics** is the philosophical reasoning for, or against, the morality that has been stipulated by society.

Morality is comprised a number of components, as represented in Figure 1.2. **Moral principles** that are general rules such as rights, justice and utility that are used to establish moral norms (for examples of moral principles, see Table 1.1). **Moral norms** are expectations of behaviour that require, prohibit or allow certain behaviour, such as showing respect and being honest. Moral norms are generated from a number of different sources and can come from one's family, society, church or even organisation. **Moral standards** are derived from these moral norms and are supposed to override self-interest, but, given emotional considerations, they are the criteria that individuals use to guide their decision-making.

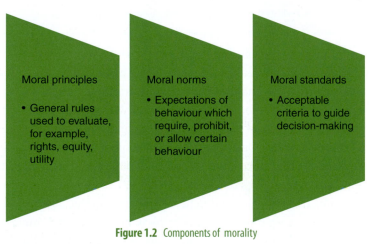

**Figure 1.2** Components of morality

**moral principles**
– general rules,
such as rights,
justice and utility,
which are used
to establish moral
norms.

**moral norms** –
expectations of
behaviour that
require, prohibit
or allow certain
behaviour, such as
showing respect
and being honest.

**moral standards**
– derived from
moral norms, they
are the criteria
individuals use
to guide their
decision-making.

**Table 1.1** Examples of moral principles

| Moral principle | Definition |
| --- | --- |
| Honesty | Being truthful. For example, being candid and not covering up mistakes. |
| Fidelity | Keeping promises, such as providing warranties and guarantees. For example, Goretex guarantees to keep you dry – see <www.gore-tex.co.uk/remote/Satellite/content/our-guarantee>. |
| Reparation | Setting wrongs right; that is, paying for damages resulting from actions of the firm. For example, BP's Deepwater Horizon Accident – see <www.bp.com/en/global/corporate/gulf-of-mexico-restoration/deepwater-horizon-accident-and-response/compensating-the-people-and-communities-affected.html>. |
| Gratitude | Providing appropriate honour and recognition. For example, extending appreciation to long-serving employees, or publicly recognising a job well done. |
| Justice | Ensuring consistency and fairness. For example, giving all staff an opportunity for professional development and promotion. |
| Beneficence | Making things better for others, such as appropriate payment of tax, and acts of charity and philanthropy. For example, personal commitments from wealthy individuals – see <http://givingpledge.org/>. |
| Non-maleficence | Not harming others. For example, ensuring all products and work environments are safe. For example, the clothing brand Icebreaker – see <http://us.icebreaker.com/on/demandware.store/Sites-IB-US-Site/en/Page-Show?cid=what-is-our-supply-chain>. |

(Adapted from: Cottrell & Perlin 1990)

Morality could be viewed as the foundation on which ethics rests. Ethics, however, is more proactive and seeks to critique moral principles as time passes. For example, racial segregation has, in the past, been an acceptable (and legal) norm of human conduct, but has, fortunately, been modified and deemed inappropriate through the process of ethical reasoning, particularly with reference to equity and justice (gay marriage is also undergoing a similar revision in some countries).

Ethics is the discipline of actually dealing with what is good and bad, right and wrong, with moral duty and obligation. Ethics is the more pragmatic side of morality where norms and values are put into action. Through **ethical reasoning,** which is the rationale and thinking process that a person engages in when dealing with an ethical dilemma, justification and review occurs, and conduct is open to scrutiny and can be defended or rejected. Ethics can therefore be described as the practice of morality, and business ethics is morality as it applies to business behaviour.

While individuals make moral decisions within a business, the business itself is also seen as a moral entity. As such, Goodpaster (1983) summarises why **corporate morality** is not necessarily the same as the personal morality of its top executives. As he notes, having a conscience in the running of a business does not necessarily translate into running a conscientious business. Rather, running a conscientious corporation necessitates the *institutionalisation* of specific values – not simply the possession of those values.

> **honesty** – being truthful.
>
> **fidelity** – keeping promises.
>
> **reparation** – setting a wrong, right.
>
> **gratitude** – providing appropriate honour and recognition.
>
> **justice** – ensuring consistency and fairness.
>
> **beneficence** – making things better for others.
>
> **non-maleficence** – not harming others.

**ethical reasoning** – the thinking process that a person engages in when dealing with an ethical dilemma.

**corporate morality** – institutionalisation of moral values.

## Moral relativism and moral absolutism

At the core of **moral relativism** (sometimes called **cultural relativism**) is the question: Do moral principles apply universally or are all values and ethical judgements relevant to their context, particularly the cultural context? The advocates of moral relativism indicate that moral standards differ between groups, within a single culture, between cultures, and across time. The theory of ethical relativism is supported by the recognition of historical, cultural and individual diversity, as witnessed by variations in moral customs around the world. Relativism, therefore, asserts that there is no consistency in moral beliefs because moral principles are relative to individual persons and cultures. What is right or wrong depends on the context. At its extreme, for example, the act of allowing defective new babies to die in impoverished nations with little or no health support structures would, therefore, carry a different moral weight, given the context in which the circumstance exists.

**moral relativism/ cultural relativism** – the belief that moral standards differ between groups, within a single culture, between cultures and across time.

Business Ethics

**moral absolutism/ universalism** – the belief that all ethical standards and actions could be rooted in common universal moral standard(s).

Those in international business have been critical that ethical relativism has been used as a form of moral sanctuary and, as a consequence, acts are then justified, given their existence in specific locations and the perception that the actions are immune from moral criticism. Relativists claim that there are no ultimate universal ethical principles, and that all value judgements are relevant to particular cultural contexts.

**Moral absolutism** does not negate the existence of multiple moral standards actually in use and employed around the world. It recognises that despite these variables, all ethical standards and actions could be rooted in common universal moral standard(s). These common, universal, moral standards are based on our requirements as human beings and are a necessity of long-term survival. Ethical absolutism has also been referred to as **universalism**, in which an omnipresent standard should apply universally, being equally valid in all places and times. So, certain ethical moral norms such as honesty, integrity, self-discipline, loyalty and compassion are perceived as basic moral standards, and are widely proclaimed as part of many societies despite the variance in adherence to those standards. Ethical absolutists consider that what people *think* is right varies in different countries and times, yet, what *is* right is everywhere and always the same. In doing so, absolutists recognise the frailty of individuals and accept that despite the presence of common moral standard(s), there will be variations in how individuals actually behave.

# Ethics in practice: Morals and values test

For questionnaires that provide personalised feedback about your morals and values, go to YourMorals.Org (n.d.), <www.yourmorals.org/explore.php>.

## Personal character and integrity

Think about the best boss you have ever had. What were the top five personal characteristics of that individual? Now think of the worst boss you have ever had and list their top five personal characteristics. Right Management Consultants (2013) asked a similar question of 570 full-time white-collar employees in the US, to find out what they thought was the most important trait for the leader of a company. Creativity, decisiveness, attention to detail are the responses you might expect, whereas in fact, these were among the five least important traits. Out in front were the traits of integrity, morals, ethics, caring, compassion, fairness and creating good relationships with employees, including listening and being approachable.

"Hurry with the balloons!
We must get a more festive atmosphere!"

Differentiating business ethics: Personal character and integrity (© shutterstock.com/Cartoonresource)

**Personal character** denotes the moral qualities distinctive to an individual and the personal attributes exhibited by those you work with, your superiors and colleagues, as well as the behaviour that you yourself exhibit. Demonstrating **integrity** means consistently adhering to strong moral principles. Building on Cottrell and Perlin (1990), it should be recognised that being ethical is not just possessing moral principles and values; these also need to be supported and, consequently, there are four dimensions of one's ethical self:

1. Holding values, and a concern for those values (moral claims).
2. A capacity to reflect (which also entails self-criticism).
3. A sense of community and a belief in a public good (not pure self-interest).
4. A willingness to act consistently on those values (moral courage).

> **personal character** – the moral qualities distinctive to an individual.

> **integrity** – consistently adhering to strong moral principles.

# Ethics in practice: Integrity and work ethics test

For an integrity and work ethics test, see PsychTests AIM Inc. (2013), <www://testyourself.psychtests.com/testid/3090>.

## Values

**Values** are deeply held beliefs as to what is important and highly valued. They can be either individual values, in other words, those held in high esteem by a person, or, they could be organisational values which are endorsed and promoted by a specific company. For example, an organisation that values creativity, collegiality or honesty, and, in doing so, would actively seek to hire individuals who possess those characteristics and to reward individuals who demonstrate those behaviours. In the same way, an organisation that valued ethics would

> **values** – deeply held beliefs as to what is important and highly valued.

communicate frequently about what behaviours they believe are morally appropriate and wish their employees to exhibit.

## Ethics on reflection: Personal values

What things do you personally value? What character traits do you admire in yourself? What are ones that you would like to improve? (To identify your personal values go to <www.mindtools.com/pages/article/newTED_85.htm>.)

## Ethics on reflection: Organisational values and culture

For an example of an organisational statement of its values, see the Wells Fargo website at <www.wellsfargo.com/invest_relations/vision_values/5>.

## Ethics in the media: Trust

According to a recent Monash University study, the one-child policy that has operated in China since 1979 has not only prevented an estimated 400 million births, but has also made those only children less trusting, less trustworthy, more risk averse, less competitive, more pessimistic and less conscientious than individuals born just before the policy was introduced. ('One child policy raises multiple issues' 2013.)

## Ethics on reflection: Is good ethics good business?

Reflect on the question of whether good ethics is good business and the importance of personal character and reputation. See Kevin Byrne, <www.youtube.com/watch?v=M6fGTz1hok0>.

## Kohlberg's theory of moral development

**Kohlberg's theory of moral development** was initiated using the Heinz dilemma. See <www.youtube.com/watch?v=5czp9S4u26M> for an interactive animation that explains the ethical dilemma, and the choices or reasoning Heinz could make as a consequence of the dilemma.

This dilemma was used in the research by Kohlberg, who was not interested so much in the answer to the question of whether Heinz was wrong or right, but in the *reasoning* for each decision as made by the participants in his study. The responses were then classified into various evolutionary stages of reasoning in his theory of moral development (see Table 1.2).

**Kohlberg's theory of moral development** – a cognitive ethical theory which describes the ethical reasoning process, which becomes progressively more sophisticated as individuals move through three broad categories (similar to childhood, adolescence and adult thinking) of moral development, which are further classified into six stages.

**Table 1.2**  Kohlberg's stages of moral development

| Pre-conventional (Child) |
| --- |
| **Stage 1**<br>Avoidance of punishment, obedience to authority and fear. |
| **Stage 2**<br>Motivated by self-interest, what's in it for me, or an expectation of reward or satisfaction. |
| **Conventional (Adolescent)** |
| **Stage 3**<br>Awareness of others, seeking approval of group norms. |
| **Stage 4**<br>Loyalty and belonging and a justification of 'everyone does it'. |
| **Post-conventional (Adult)** |
| **Stage 5**<br>A broader view of right and wrong, not depending on the norms of the group, but concerned for standards of society. |
| **Stage 6**<br>Broad ethical principles are in place, with universal reasoning. Decisions are based on conscience. |

The theory, although it has been criticised, still resonates today in our understanding of the reasons for variations in the morality of individuals and their approach to ethical decision-making. Kohlberg's theory was developed from the finding that people advance from concern for self to higher order principles of universality. In Kohlberg's theory of moral development, ethical reasoning becomes increasingly more sophisticated as individuals move through three broad categories of moral development, which are further classified into six stages. Progress is made over time and in a linear fashion towards moral maturity, and the three stages are not dissimilar to the human stages of childhood, adolescence and adult thinking.

While not intended, the theory could also have a useful application when we look at organisations and how they may be identified on a continuum of moral maturity and commitment to developing an ethical culture (see Table 1.3).

**Table 1.3** An organisational perspective of Kohlberg's theory of moral development

| Pre-conventional (Defensive) |
| --- |
| Stage 1<br>Motivated to be ethical for fear of being sanctioned or prosecuted. |
| Stage 2<br>Motivated to be ethical solely because of the positive reputational and brand effect. |
| **Conventional (Developing)** |
| Stage 3<br>Motivated to be ethical because of the need to adhere to professional/industry codes of conduct. |
| Stage 4<br>Motivated to be ethical because of broad industry standards and ethical norms/expectations. |
| **Post-conventional (Integrated)** |
| Stage 5<br>Motivated to be ethical because of expectations from society and a broad group of its members, that is, lobby groups, customers etc. |
| Stage 6<br>Committed to ethical principles being in place, irrespective of what others are doing, because of a conscientious and internalised belief that is how it should be. |

# Ethics in practice: Personal ethical decision-making

Sally, an accountant, was promoted to partner and shortly afterwards two senior members of the accounting team revealed to her some of the deception that had been occurring in financial documents. Sally was mortified as she had signed off on these documents and was now legally culpable. In considering her situation, she realised that if she came clean it would damage her career, and, in all likelihood, undermine her role as a new partner. She decided, therefore, to think about what was happening and take stock. She was well aware what her professional responsibilities entailed, but her personal situation was overriding her decision-making (adapted from Cottrell and Perlin 1990).

**Questions:**
1. What stage of moral development is Sally exhibiting?
2. You are a friend of Sally's. What would you advise her to do, and why?

## Power and politics

In considering people's ethical behaviour, it is important that we take into account the many pressures on a person that may adversely affect or erode their ethical judgement. One of these pressures may be the power that others within the organisation have over them.

There are countless examples where ethicality has been compromised when it collides with power and politics in organisations. Power is seen as the capacity to influence others – particularly those who are in positions of dependence (Johns & Saks 2004) – and it is often held by those in higher levels. Politics is viewed as the practice and theory of influencing others, and thus the two terms are inextricably linked. When people are in positions of power over others in an organisation this may result in them having influence over the behaviour of others and the more power one has, the stronger the influence.

The link between power and ethics has been explored for centuries. Plato proposed that power is a necessary aspect of 'the good' and Aristotle adopted a similar view of power and its influence on ethical behaviour (Jurkiewicz & Brown 2000). In contrast, the Romans saw power and ethics as unrelated, and others (see Friedman 1970; Ladd 1981; Werhane 1980) have since maintained that the exercise of power in an organisation is amoral (Jurkiewicz & Brown 2000).

According to Jurkiewicz and Brown (2000), power and ethics are so comprehensively intertwined that it is virtually impossible to consider one without the other, particularly when we seek to understand the behaviour of leaders within organisations and how individuals in positions of dependence act in response to that power. We must therefore consider the extant power relationships within an organisation when attempting to introduce an ethical climate and culture (Jurkeiwicz & Brown 2000).

# Ethics on reflection: Power and politics

Considering the power and politics that operate in organisations, what types of pressure might individuals experience that could erode their ethical behaviour (for example, fear of losing a job or missing out on promotion; pressure from partners; being excluded from an old boys' club)? What effects might these pressures have on individuals?

As well as the influence of those holding the power within an organisation, many other factors may impact on a person's ethicality and behaviour. Some of these pressures are depicted in Figure 1.3.

**Figure 1.3**  Pressures for unethical practices

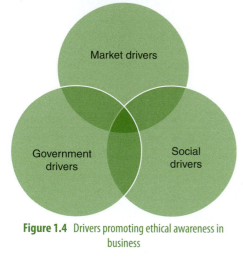

**Figure 1.4**  Drivers promoting ethical awareness in
business

# Drivers promoting ethical awareness in business

There are several drivers promoting ethical awareness in business today and they can broadly be delineated as market drivers, social drivers and government drivers, as shown in Figure 1.4. Each driver has a number of associated factors that are further encouraging greater consideration of the importance of ethics in business.

## Market drivers

**Market infrastructure** – the importance of market infrastructure and the maintenance of the integrity of that infrastructure is pertinent in relation to the banking and finance sector, which came perilously close to a market infrastructure meltdown during the GFC. The International Monetary Fund (IMF) calculates that the GFC produced total bank losses of US$2 trillion, and also led to a collapse of trust in business and politicians ('Companies' moral compasses' 2013).

"Sales, profits and impatience are growing."

Market drivers (© shutterstock.com/Cartoonresource)

**Consumers** – consumers are one of the most significant factors promoting increased ethical awareness, as they exert their expectations on business in relation to the quality of products and how products are sourced, both in relation to raw materials and manufacturing, and the ethical and environmental behaviour of the firm. Consumers are also demanding redress for ethical failure. In a 2003 global survey by Wirthlin Worldwide, 80% of people indicated that they decided to buy a firm's goods or services partly based on their perception of the company's ethical position ('The hidden costs of unethical behavior' 2004). The Fair Trade movement has been largely generated through consumer demand, and now significantly influences the trade of coffee, bananas and diamonds, to name a few.

**Investors and owners** – there appears to be a relationship between the ethics of a company and the stock price, and it has been found that investments in unethical firms earn abnormally negative returns for prolonged periods (Long & Rao 1995). Verschoor (1998) in the US found a relationship between overall financial performance and an emphasis on ethics. In the UK, Webley and More (2003) also observed that financial performance (market value added, economic value added and price/earnings ratio) for those companies with a code of ethics outperformed a similar size group that had no code. It was further observed that companies without a code experienced more price earnings volatility, and showed a decline in average return on capital employed. There is also an active group of institutions and individuals seeking **socially responsible investments**; that is, investments that meet specific social and environmental criteria.

**socially responsible investments** – investments that meet specific social and environmental criteria.

**Shareholders** – shareholder activism is alive and well and becoming an increasingly compelling force in urging top management to do the right thing. For example, Xstrata was forced to amend its pay deals for bosses following objections by shareholders ('Business' 2011), and, in a rather famous incident, a group of shareholders in America launched a lawsuit against News Corporation's board for dragging down the company's share price by rubberstamping all of Rupert Murdoch's requests ('News Corporation' 2012). In Germany, a prominent businessman, Gerhard Cromme, resigned as Chairman of the Supervisory Board of Thyssen-Krupp, after shareholders revolted due to several investment failures and price-fixing scandals. Remarkably, Mr Cromme had earlier overseen the drafting of Germany's Corporate Governance Code in 2002 ('Cromme comes a cropper' 2013).

# Ethics in the media: Defamation claims

Australian resource companies''head honchos' are taking legal action over defamatory remarks made by small shareholders in public forums and correspondence. Legal action was initiated by Cudeco's founder, Wayne McCrae, in 2010. Empire Oil & Gas and now Korab Resources' Andrej Karpinski have also taken similar actions (Burrell 2013).

**Employees** – where there is competition for skilled labour, employers are conscious that their ethical brand (i.e. the ethical connotations associated with their brand) which is just as important as their market brand i.e. the market positioning of their brand, for attracting good employees. Employees are also becoming critical of their employers. In what could be a disturbing trend, websites such as Glassdoor and its Australian equivalent InsideTrack are examples of job sites where staff are able to comment on employers and hold employers to account ('Honestly unvarnished' 2012).

**Other stakeholders** – the commonly recognised major stakeholders of an organisation are the individual investors, institutional investors, employees, consumers and suppliers. The other business stakeholders are the competitors, regulators, non-government organisations, and the immediate community. Some go so far as to say that the environment and future generations are also key stakeholders, although they are hampered by a limited voice. Each of these groups has ethical concerns and is applying pressure to have them resolved.

## Social drivers

**International lobby groups** – numerous international lobby groups are urging more ethical responsibility on business. Currently labour organisations, that are prominent among international lobby groups are shining a light on unsafe and abusive practices. For example, in India, girls as young as 11 are sold into bonded labour and compelled to work for three years on the promise of a lump sum payment of 50 000 rupees (AU$850). Child rights campaigners estimate that as many as 200 000 girls may be enslaved in such work schemes even though such bonded labour violates numerous Indian laws. Western consumers are ignorant of the abuse and exploitation that may exist within the supply chain (Doherty 2013). When thinking of lobby groups, a historical case worth examining is the intervention of Greenpeace as they frustrated Shell's attempts in 1995 to dispose of the Brent Spar platform in the North Sea. Greenpeace were remarkably effective in raising concern about the proposed disposal and, today, are active in a variety of environmental problems on a global scale.

**National advocates** – advocates can also be country-specific. Starbucks in Britain has been brought to task by Uncut, a UK group that campaigns against corporate tax avoidance. Since Starbucks first came to Britain in 1988, they have only paid £8.7 million in corporate income tax, due to low, secret rates of tax negotiated with subsidiaries in The Netherlands and Switzerland ('Wake up and smell the coffee' 2012).

**Individual activists** – although individuals have less clout than groups, they can still influence others. In 2000, a Paris-based activist launched a media and judicial attack on Yahoo, specifically in relation to the sale of Nazi items on the auction site (Le Menestrel, Hunter & De Bettignies 2002).

**Local community** – usually prompted by a specific issue, the weight of local communities, once rallied, can be brought to bear on organisations, as experienced by McDonald's Australia, who faced unanticipated opposition in the Victorian township of Tecoma, where 90 000 people signed a petition calling on McDonalds to back off. With support from celebrity chef Jamie Oliver, who lent his public profile to the cause, high-powered lawyers offering their services and protesters were charged with offences related to disrupting development, and the situation turned quite volatile (Rintoul 2013).

**Mainstream media** – the media is unrelenting in its pursuit and publicity of wrongdoing, as it makes for good copy. In the past, Nike, Nestlé and Union Carbide have all been embarrassed by the media in relation to their practices in developing nations. However, media attention can surround both large and small organisations, and the media appear indifferent to the ethical or environmental programs that exist in those firms. For 20 of the largest oil companies in the United States, researchers have determined each firm's level of environmental stewardship using a metric which scored firms based on their environmental strength. Using text mining software to scan the news stories for positive and negative language, the researchers found that companies with high environmental strength scores received just as much negative publicity as companies with low scores ('CSR offers no "halo effect"' 2012).

**Social media** – social media is now a powerful influence in the corporate environment and affects even those who are only marginally aligned. After failing to get Facebook to remove pages glorifying violence against women, feminist activists waged a digital media campaign that highlighted marketers whose ads were found alongside these pages. Nissan and several smaller advertisers subsequently removed their ads from the site. This type of vicarious pressure demonstrates how there can be a spillover effect through consumer or interest group backlash, as concern for brand tainting is fairly evident (Vega & Kaufman 2013).

# Ethics in the media: Social media

Under proposed changes to US national privacy laws, employers would be restricted from demanding access to job seekers' Facebook pages and other social media accounts. The proposed changes to privacy legislation would allow people to sue employers for invasion of privacy. Currently, it is illegal to ask potential employees for social media passwords in 13 US states (Witbourn 2013).

**Business and professional associations** – where an industry or profession depends heavily on maintaining reputation and trust, there is often a strong push for a collective statement of ethical intent, or code of conduct, to cover areas of critical concern to the business association or profession. The accounting profession has been internationally active in ensuring that a high level of ethics operates in the profession. See Table 1.4 for the seven ethical principles commonly found in professional codes of conduct.

**Educational institutions** – often driven by international accreditation of business schools, the numbers of business and society courses and courses in business ethics are

**Table 1.4** Fundamental principles of professional conduct

| Fundamental Principles | Description |
| --- | --- |
| Public interest | A duty to safeguard and advance the interests of the public before others. |
| Competence | The attainment and maintenance of a level of knowledge from formal education, training and continual professional development. |
| Confidentiality | Ensuring that information acquired in the course of one's work is not disclosed to a third party without express authority. |
| Due care | Pursuit of excellence in the provision of professional services and acting in the best interest of those who rely on it. |
| Integrity | Being honest and sincere and withstanding pressure from significant others to impair integrity. |
| Objectivity | Exhibiting an impartial attitude and not being subject to undue influence. |
| Professional behaviour | Behaving in a manner that is consistent with the good reputation of the profession. |

(Source: Dellaportas et al. 2005, p. 79)

increasing and moving to become compulsory. An indicator of this change is that between 2001 and 2011, MBA programs increasingly required students to take courses dedicated to business and society, with the percentage of students studying the courses increasing from 34% to 79% (Samuelson 2013).

**Non-government organisations (NGOs)** – strong NGOs can be motivators and supporters for the improved ethical performance of business. An excellent example of business–NGO cooperation comes from Lipton Tea, the largest global tea brand owned by Unilever, which accounts for 12% of the black tea market. Unilever have partnered with the Rainforest Alliance to set standards and certify sustainable agricultural methods. Unilever also engage the Rainforest Alliance to respond to consumer concerns about sustainable agriculture (Lacy, Haines & Hayward 2012).

## Government drivers

**Formal legislation** – new or revised laws can have both a push and pull effect on ethical awareness. On the push side, legislation usually stems from mounting disquiet about wrongdoing. For example, the Victorian State Government in Australia is pushing for a crackdown on airbrushed advertising, amid fears that digitally-altered images are contributing to anorexia and anxiety in young people, and is advocating for truth in advertising in order to tackle the trend of young people being influenced by false media images. In 2003, the cosmetic giant, L'Oréal, were forced to pull an advertising campaign that featured the movie star Julia Roberts and supermodel Christy Turlington, after the UK advertising watchdog upheld complaints that the images were too heavily airbrushed (Tomazin 2013).

On the pull side, one of the primary motivations for the development of ethical programs has been to avoid or reduce punishments. The US introduced its **Federal Sentencing Guidelines** in 1991 to bring more uniform consequences for those who violate federal laws. Since corporations cannot be incarcerated (although their managers can), some consistency regarding penalties for corporations was required. The sentencing guidelines require a judge to not only determine whether an organisation, or an individual, is guilty, but also to establish an organisation's **culpability score;** culpability being determined by the actions taken by the company prior to the offence. Essentially, having an ethics programmer heavily promoted by those in senior management and early self-reporting of any wrongdoing would lower a firm's culpability score and can reduce a sentencing outcome (Calhoun, Olivero & Wolitzer 1999).

**Federal Sentencing Guidelines** – US guidelines created to bring more uniformity of consequences for those who violate federal laws.

**culpability score** – part of the US sentencing guidelines. A culpability rating is determined by the actions taken by the company prior to the offence, such as ethics compliance programs.

At last he had found the Regulatory Guidelines.

Government drivers (© shutterstock.com/Cartoonresource)

## Ethics in the media: Judicial outcome

A US$13 billion settlement was reached in 2013 between the Justice Department and the bank giant, JPMorgan Chase & Co, for their involvement in the 2008 housing market crash. JPMorgan Chase were not the only financial institution to knowingly bundle toxic loans and on-sell them (Hall 2013).

**Regulatory bodies** – regulatory bodies come in a variety of forms. In industry, for example, the Association of Chartered Certified Accountants (ACCA) are a global body for professional accountants; the Hong Kong Independent Commission against Corruption (HK ICAC) are a national example; and internationally there is the World Health Organization (WHO). Each body acts as an ethical driver. As a result of the *Dodd–Frank Act 2010* in the US, employees, suppliers and clients are now actively encouraged, and financially rewarded, for offering high-quality original information leading to a US Securities and Exchange Commission (SEC) enforcement action that results in sanctions of more than US$1 million (Pavlo 2013).

## Ethics in the media: Marketing harmful products

In 2012, Australia unveiled a scheme to force cigarette manufacturers to sell their product in logo-free packets, adorned with gruesome images of mouth cancer and other smoking-related illnesses. The plan accords with the WHO's guidelines and the results will be closely watched by international tobacco companies ('The world this week' 2012).

# Conclusion

There is a saying that ethics in business is a bit like a fire extinguisher: Everybody ignores it until there is an emergency. Not a day would go past when you don't read or hear of an ethical issue surrounding an individual, an organisation or an industry. Some of these ethical violations are high profile – large organisations that were believed to be too big to fail – companies like Enron, WorldCom and Global Crossing, whose unethical actions resulted in insolvency; while others have lived on, but had their reputations tarnished.

While a lot of the discussion surrounding ethics is about unethical practices, it is important to note that ethics in business is about good business practice, and we should be looking at what is done well, as well as what is being done badly. Consider Aflac, the number one provider of supplemental insurance in the US and Japan, which have been selected to appear in Ethisphere's 2013 annual list of the World's Most Ethical Companies (WME). Aflac are the only insurance company to appear on the prestigious list for seven consecutive years. Their appearance on the WME list was seen by the company as an endorsement of their belief that ethics and profits should and can exist side by side (Aflac 2013).

Making business ethics a priority is not just about an organisation functioning with integrity or being credible and competitive; it is also about optimising the efficiency and the functioning of the organisation. Fundamentally, focusing on ethics is linked to good management practices. Research from the Ethics Resource Centre (2013) demonstrates that strong ethics and compliance and ethical cultures result in elevated standards, lower levels of observed misconduct, increased rates of reporting unethical conduct, and decreased levels of retaliation against people reporting unethical conduct.

**shared value** – stresses that the creation of social value can help a commercial business to create economic value.

More recently, business ethics has been broadened to include the concept of **shared value**, which stresses that business should reconnect the success of the company with social progress; and that the creation of social value can help a commercial business to create economic value in a virtuous cycle so that, rather than shared value being an adjunct to a business, it is part of a business's core ('Capitalism with a value-added face' 2012). It is clear that the focus on business ethics is not going to ease and, in all likelihood, expectations of ethical and social responsibility will continue to increase. It is, therefore, worth exploring the issues, concepts and theory in more detail.

# Ethics in the media: Company culture

The company SAS were ranked number one employer in 2010. In addition to generous employee packages, and an industry-low turnover rate of 2%, the defining feature of the company culture was a commitment to trust between employees and the employer (Lotich 2011).

# Ethics in practice: Differentiating business ethics

You are an account director at a marketing research agency working with a newly acquired and potentially lucrative client. The client is quite clear that the results must support a decision that has already been made.

**Questions:**

1. Would you 'fudge' the results to meet the client's request?

2. What if you were the managing director and principal of the agency?

3. What if the research involved qualitative techniques that allowed you to 'steer' the responses of the participants?

4. What if the client wasn't potentially lucrative? (Used with permission: Charles Areni.)

## Ethics on video

**Importance of ethics** – *Ethics: Why bother?* 2011, YouTube, Dr Roger Walsh, <www.youtube.com/watch?v=UPPAWNL8CTs&list=PLFF4C629B957B05A5>.

**Introduction to ethics** – *An introduction to ethics* 2012, YouTube, Institute of Chartered Accountants Australia (ICAA), <www.youtube.com/watch?v=w9Kro5GwrlA>.

See web material for more videos.

## Ethics at the movies

Some movies have ethical content in relation to introduction to business ethics, and you may find these ones relevant to this chapter:

**The Method** – a Spanish movie in which a major corporation interviews for a new executive using dubious testing methods. *The Method* 2005, motion picture trailer, Arrojo, RG, Herrero, G, Ramos, F & Tellería, A, <www.youtube.com/watch?v=xn4_DMUCghk>.

*\* The Wolf of Wall Street* – based on the true story of stockbroker Jordan Belfort and his infamous, unethical work practices. *The Wolf of Wall Street* 2013, motion picture trailer, Scorsese, M, <www.youtube.com/watch?v=idAVRvQeYAE>.

\***Author's pick**

See web material for more movies.

# Ethics on the web

**Business Ethics**, a webpage by Sharon Stoerger with articles, case studies, and additional business ethics resources, <www.web-miner.com/busethics.htm>.

**The Center for Business Ethics, Bentley University**, the objectives of the centre are to inspire ethical leadership, collaboration and knowledge through thought and action, <www.bentley.edu/cbe>.

See web material for more web references.

# Student exercises

See web material for answers to student short answer questions.

## Short answer questions

1. What are some of the more topical ethical issues in discussion in the media today? List at least eight ethical issues.
2. Consider what you have learnt in this chapter about what ethics is. By extension, what would you say that ethics is not?
3. Who are commonly listed as the major stakeholders for an organisation?
4. Contrast moral relativism with moral absolutism.
5. Name factors that are promoting ethical awareness in business.
6. Of all the factors coalescing to drive an increased awareness in business ethics, which three do you believe are currently the most influential, and why?
7. Select three or four ethical issues and find examples of cases which typify the issue.
8. Do you agree or disagree with the statement that 'One's ethical values are formed in childhood and do not alter'?
9. The US Federal Sentencing Guidelines cover mitigating factors that might enable a fine to be reduced. What are these mitigating factors?
10. All of us are faced with ethical dilemmas, and we may respond to them in inappropriate ways depending on our choice of outcomes. Regrettably, it is often the pressure of the circumstance that dictates our response. What different approaches can you suggest to help resolve ethical dilemmas?
11. What are the ethical issues in relation to lobbying?
12. Undertake research to ascertain what might be the benefits and costs associated with the ethical tone of an organisation.
13. Investigate the criticisms of Kohlberg's theory of moral development.
14. In a seven-page recruitment form, the energy company Chevron asked applicants whether they had ever been pregnant, had an abortion or had

a stillborn child, and required details about the health of their children, including whether any of the children had birth defects. Do you believe that these questions were legal or appropriate?

15. News that the product Lyprinol, extracted from the green-lipped mussel, had the potential to cure cancer was released from an Australian university days before Lyprinol was launched on the New Zealand market in July 2000. New Zealanders rushed pharmacies and reportedly spent NZ$2 million in one day on the $49.95 packets of 50 capsules of the unapproved product. Was this an astute marketing attempt or a legal issue?

16. In an effort to promote ethical behaviour, some MBA programs have set a requirement for their students to undertake an MBA oath on completion of the course – see <www.MBAoath.com>. The oath requires to the student to pledge their contribution to the wellbeing of society and promise to create sustainable economic, social and environmental prosperity worldwide (MacDonald 2010). Do you think that the MBA oath is a good idea?

## Experiential exercises

1. Please go to <http://personality-testing.info/tests/MFQ.php>, and take the interactive Moral Foundations Questionnaire, which has 32 questions and measures five foundations of morality (harm, fairness, loyalty, respect and purity). It will take approximately four minutes to complete the questionnaire.

2. Review the web and current media to identify an individual or organisation that is currently embroiled in an ethical scenario. What are the key features and facts of the circumstance?

3. Some researchers have linked the personality concept of Machiavellianism to a propensity for unethical behaviour in individuals. Investigate this concept. For fun, you may wish to test yourself on this trait at <http://personality-testing.info/tests/MACH-IV.php>.

# Small case

## Case: Legality and ethics

In 2009, two News Limited journalists were fined for refusing to cooperate with authorities who wanted them to divulge confidential details about their informants. They refused as the request contravened a fundamental journalistic ethical code. More recently, five Australian journalists are facing criminal convictions, fines and jail terms for maintaining their ethical responsibility to protect their sources. These journalists are facing court actions brought by two leading businesspeople, in two different actions, where they are being asked by the court to present

their sources (Willingham 2013). For video coverage see, <www.theage.com.au/victoria/five-journalists-facing-charges-make-plea-on-source-protection-20130402–2h4dr.html>.

**Questions:**

1. What is the distinction here between what is ethical and what is legal?
2. What are your views on the circumstances described in this case?

# Large case

## Case: When private gain leads to social cost – The case of natural gas fracking in Central Pennsylvania

For the citizens of Central Pennsylvania, preserving the natural environment for future generations has a special meaning. The Susquehanna River flows through the heart of Central Pennsylvania, from its source in upstate New York through Pennsylvania into the Chesapeake Bay. Dozens of tributaries, fed by mountain streams and surrounded by lush forests, offer a vast ecosystem for humans and the natural environment.

In addition to its lush forests, the Susquehanna River Valley includes rich deposits of coal. More recently, estimates of trillions of cubic feet of natural gas beneath the Marcellus Shale region (www.depweb.state.pa.us 2011), stretching from West Virginia through Pennsylvania to upstate New York, has further attracted attention to the natural resource wealth of the Susquehanna River Valley.

This has ushered in a governance conflict involving private acquisition of wealth versus social and environmental cost. In the 19th century, forests along the Susquehanna River were clear-cut by firms that then continued a westward quest, leaving behind soil erosion in the Susquehanna which, ironically, provided transport of the logs south to the Chesapeake Bay. Subsequently, coal mining became a dominant industry in Central Pennsylvania from which long-abandoned mines continue draining acid into the streams and rivers of the basin. The Pennsylvania Department of Environmental Protection estimates the total cost to clean up the acid mine drainage at US$15 billion (Susquehanna River Basin Commission 2010 Report 2010). Thus, to many citizens of the Susquehanna Valley, the prospect of natural gas fracking creating a third degradation of the natural environment has led to growing public activism.

## What is natural gas fracking?

Extracting natural gas from the Marcellus Shale formation requires horizontal drilling and a process known as 'hydraulic fracturing' or 'fracking', which uses far greater amounts of water than traditional natural gas exploration. Drillers pump large amounts of water mixed with sand and other proponents into the shale formation under high pressure to fracture the shale around the well, which allows the natural gas to flow freely. Once the hydraulic fracturing process is completed, the used water, often referred to as 'frac fluid', must be treated to remove chemicals and minerals (www.dep.state.pa.us, 2011).

A *Vanity Fair* article by Christopher Bateman (2010) notes that 'while hydraulic fracturing has been in use for decades to increase production when a well starts to run dry, its use in unconventional types of drilling, such as shale gas, is relatively new … It is an energy – and resource-intensive process, with every shale gas well that is fracked requiring between three and eight million gallons of water'.

## What is sustainability governance?

The sustainability of the Susquehanna River Valley ecosystem lies at the heart of the conflict between stakeholders favouring the use of 'fracking' in drilling for natural gas and NGO groups concerned about the responsible use of natural resources in the region. While corporate governance, in the Anglo-American tradition, involves managers acting as agents in order to control and protect the private property of its shareholders, ecosystem governance involves managing dynamic relationships between humanity and the natural environment in order to preserve 'the commons' for future generations (Heuer 2011). Ecologists suggest that individual organisations should not view themselves as becoming sustainable so much as contributing to a large system in which

sustainability may or may not be achieved (Jennings & Zandbergen 1995, p. 1025). Consistent with that governance philosophy, numerous coalitions formed in the Susquehanna River Valley in response to soil erosion from agriculture, pollution of streams and tributaries flowing into the Susquehanna River from acid mine drainage, and ecological impacts on fish and other wildlife. One example is the Susquehanna River Heartland Coalition, comprised of a diverse network of concerned citizens, academics, local businesspeople, farmers and sports enthusiasts. Generally speaking, the Heartland Coalition serves as an informal hub for a decentralised network of people who value the Susquehanna River for different reasons, all of whom are joined by a passion for its beauty and concern for its wellbeing. With the rapid increase of natural gas fracking and a concern that a third wave of outside economic interests might create another environmental disaster for the next generation to deal with, the Heartland Coalition, along with other coalitions such as the Responsible Drilling Alliance (see <www.responsibledrillingalliance.org>), the Riverfront Coalition, and Organizations United for the Environment (see <www.ouenews.org>), have become advocates for resisting the spread of this drilling practice.

Groups supporting natural gas fracking have also become active, including the Marcellus Shale Coalition, which has as its stated purpose 'the responsible development of natural gas from the Marcellus Shale geological formation and the enhancement of the region's economy that can be realised from this clean-burning, Pennsylvania-based energy source in an environmentally sound manner' (Marcellus Shale Coalition 2011).

The legitimacy of the opposing governance approaches involves not only economic and ecological perspectives, but also conflicting social and political positions. With unemployment remaining chronically high throughout Central Pennsylvania (although lower than the current national average), job creation has become a major factor in legitimising opposing viewpoints. Both sides agree that natural gas development has produced new jobs for labourers at well sites, truck drivers to haul equipment and waste water, and even engineers and accountants (Maher 2011). The Marcellus Shale Coalition claim that 72 000 jobs were created last year, using data based on new hires rather than conventional new job figures, in order to achieve optimistic results. Meanwhile, the Pennsylvania Department of Labor estimate that 13 000 jobs were created last year in industries related directly and indirectly to natural gas. The Keystone Research Center, who receive funding from foundations and labour unions, cite 6649 jobs created last year, while emphasising emphatically that the positive impact of the industry on the Pennsylvania economy is overstated (Maher 2011).

From a social perspective, the national profile developed around Dimock, Pennsylvania, serves as a symbol of painful social externalities caused by fracking, as up to 8000 gallons of Halliburton-manufactured fracking fluid leaked from faulty pipes, seeping into wetlands and causing environmental damage. Cabot Oil and Gas were fined US$360 000 by the Pennsylvania Department of Environmental Protection for contaminating Dimock's groundwater. Moreover, Dimock is now notorious as the town where one woman's water well spontaneously combusted (Bateman 2010). More commonly, residents in small towns routinely complain about the influx of out-of-state workers and the convoys of large trucks hauling away wastewater, all of which overburdens rural roads and other infrastructure.

From a political perspective, three US Members of Congress from Pennsylvania (two Democrats and one Republican) recently urged President Obama to expand Marcellus Shale drilling in the US as a way to promote energy independence. The three argued that shale gas recovery 'does not pollute our Nation's water supply' and implored President Obama not to pursue further environmental regulation of the industry (Edgerton 2011). Under a 2005 law passed by the U.S. Congress, natural gas fracking was exempted from major federal environmental laws such as the Clean Air Act, Clean Water Act, and the Safe Drinking Water Act, thus limiting federal oversight. However, in July 2011, President Obama's Environmental Protection Agency (EPA) released proposed regulations to address air quality issues resulting from natural gas fracking.

At the state level, legislative and regulatory action has been limited. The natural gas industry contributed more than $7 million to Pennsylvania candidates and Political Action Committees from 2000 through the end of 2010, and the current Pennsylvania Governor Tom Corbett accepting more than $640 000 from the natural gas industry during the last half of 2010 during his election campaign. Pennsylvania remains the only state among the top 15 natural gas producing states not to impose a severance tax on the industry (Boehm 2010), with Governor Corbett on record as continuing his opposition during his term as Governor.

## What are the political governance implications of this industry support?

Josh McNeil of Conservation Voters of Pennsylvania summed it up as follows*:

> We know that natural gas drilling is a serious threat to the safety of our air and our drinking water, but it's becoming clear that the gas industry checkbooks pose an equally dangerous threat to our democracy. When our Governor and our legislative leaders ignore the overwhelming public support for a fair tax on gas drillers, how can they ask us to believe that six-figure contributions aren't playing a part in their decisions? (Conservation Voters of Pennsylvania 2011).

**Questions:**
1. Which levels of business are apparent in this case?
2. Which organisational perspectives of Kohlberg's theory of moral development does the case outline?
3. What are the ethical issues?
4. Which drivers are promoting ethical awareness?

*(Used with permission from: Heuer, MA 2012, 'Where private gain leads to social cost: The case of natural gas fracking in Central Pennsylvania', in P Wells & J Mueller (eds), *Contemporary challenges in corporate governance*, RossiSmith Academic Publishing, Oxford, pp. 181–185. Available for purchase on Amazon at <www.amazon.com/Contemporary-Challenges-Corporate-Governance-Learning/dp/0986459763/ref=sr_1_1?ie=UTF8&qid=1387450871&sr=8–1&keywords=Contemporary+challenges+in+corporate+governance>).

See web material for:
- answers to short answer questions
- additional student cases
- tutor resources (tutor password required)
- additional material including Ethics at the movies, Ethics in print, Ethics on video and Ethics on the web.

# Chapter 2

## Ethical terminology

'A business that makes nothing but money is a poor kind of business.'
Henry Ford, 1863–1947,
American industrialist

## Chapter aim

To clarify terminology related to business ethics.

## Chapter objectives

1. Explain what the theoretical foundations of corporate responsibility are in relation to agency, social contracts and integrated social contracts theory.
2. Outline the essential tenets of stakeholder management.
3. Delineate the four levels of social responsibility.
4. Critique the relationship and activities that differentiate environmentalism from sustainability.
5. Describe the key dimensions of corporate governance.
6. Identify the reporting expectations in relation to the triple bottom line.

## Ethics in the media: Sustainability

Water scarcity is a recognised global problem, with demand for water projected to exceed supply by 40% by 2030 (Hales 2013).

# Introduction

A decade ago, Coca-Cola were banned from soft-drink production in South India after the government and several non-government organisations (NGOs) objected strongly to their water consumption (the company uses water not just in the drink itself but also in the manufacturing process, and making 1 litre of Coke consumes more than 3 litres of water). In response, Coca-Cola developed a strategy for sustainable water stewardship and established joint projects with USAID and relationships with previously adversarial non-profits, such as Greenpeace and the World Wildlife Fund for Nature (WWF), resulting in the company now using only 2 litres of water to produce 1 litre of Coke, and being 52% of the way to meeting their 2020 target for water neutrality (Lovegrove & Thomas 2013). Coca-Cola is not the only beverage company pursuing a more sustainable approach. The Florida Ice and Farm, a beverage bottler based in San José, Costa Rica, with revenue in excess of $500 million and a compound annual growth of 25%, met their goal of becoming water neutral in only four years (Haanaes et al. 2013).

Miller Coors, America's second-largest brewer, are also using less water to brew their beers according to their 2013 *Sustainability Report*, and decreased water usage by 6.1% to a record low of 3.82 barrels of water (by comparison, some brewers use as much as 6.62 barrels of water). The CEO indicated that employees, and not consumers, were the driving force behind sustainability efforts (Ethical Performance 2013b).

Not to be outdone, the brewers Stella Artois and Anheuser-Busch (maker of Budweiser beer) have been ramping up their environmental commitment with seven new global goals that aim to improve water management. In addition, the Belgian beer company, for the first time, have set global goals on packaging materials' reduction and eco-friendly purchases (Ethical Performance 2013a).

In describing the actions of these companies a number of phrases come to mind, such as being ethical, socially responsible and environmentally conscious, a good corporate citizen, and a sustainability leader. Coca-Cola have also been referred to as demonstrating **tri-sector leadership**; that is, bridging the chasm of culture incentives across government, business and not-for-profit organisations (Lovegrove & Thomas 2013), and **responsible capitalism**, a term that describes the existence of an unwritten social contract that obliges organisations to act responsibly without affecting society detrimentally.

For organisations acting in an ethically responsible manner, the descriptors continue, such as being a mission-driven company, a hybrid organisation, an authentic organisation, a company with a conscience and a social enterprise (Nazarkina 2012). Problematically, it has been observed that more than 100 concepts have been proposed on how ethical issues in business should be defined. This explosion of concepts and definitions has inadvertently increased the vagueness and ambiguity of ethics (Van Narrewijk 2003) and the terms have often been used interchangeably.

**tri-sector leadership** – bridging the chasm of culture incentives across government, business and not-for-profit organisations.

**responsible capitalism** – the existence of an unwritten social contract that obliges organisations to act responsibly without affecting society detrimentally.

(© shutterstock.com/Everett Collection)

Despite good intentions, we often see terminology start to coalesce, particularly in the use of such terms such as business ethics, corporate social responsibility (CSR), stakeholder management, governance, sustainability, accountability, triple bottom line, corporate citizenship, and even philanthropy. The general media does not help with its synonymous use of these terms and frequently intermingles them when reporting. Further understanding is needed in relation to business ethics and other ethics-related concepts, and, rather than feeling uncomfortable about the overlapping terminology, it is useful to take a broader perspective and consider that the ultimate intent of all of these concepts is that of creating a better organisation.

In this chapter, we will endeavour to unpack and clarify some of the key terminology related to business ethics, but first it is appropriate to establish a theoretical foundation in relation to the responsibilities of organisations.

## Ethics on reflection: Ethical lexica

Clearly, clarification is needed in relation to business ethics and other ethics-related concepts, but do you think we are dealing with a single field with various labels, or an entirely fragmented range of activities that have little in common?

# Theoretical foundations of corporate responsibility

## Agency theory

**agency theory** (sometimes referred to as **principal agency theory**) – the relationship between the principal (owners or shareholders) and their agents (managers and administrators).

**Agency theory** (sometimes referred to as **principal agency theory**) describes the relationship between principals (usually the owners or shareholders of a company) and their agents (usually the managers and administrators of the company). Principals need to delegate to agents but, in doing so, there is an inevitable loss of control, with the risk that administrators and managers (agents) may not always act in the best interest of owners or shareholders (principals). Principals should therefore be suspicious of agents making decisions that will benefit themselves at the cost of the principal, thus appropriate controls should be introduced.

Given such apprehension, the separation between ownership and control through shareholder investment may result in managers exploiting this separation, and indifferent shareholders may amplify the situation. These activities have resulted in a new class of companies, **trust companies**. These companies are overseen by a board of trustees who are trusted with balancing the needs of all stakeholders, not just shareholders, thus ensuring that companies live up to their corporate values. Voting rights are linked not just to how many shares one owns, but also how long the shares have been held ('Companies' moral compasses' 2013).

## Social contract theory

Social contract theory broadens the relationship between principals and agents to other entities and society. **Social contract theory** proposes that an implied contract exists between a business and the state regarding rights, responsibilities and expectations of behaviour. An implied social contract allows a corporation to be formed and, in return, its managers are ethically obliged to pursue corporate profit but only if it increases societal welfare above what it would be in the corporation's absence, and without violating basic rules of justice (Donaldson 1982).

Thomas Hobbes (1603–1679) was the first to promote social contract theory. He indicated that without social contracts, disorder and anarchy would result, therefore, moral rules are required to maintain relationships between individuals and the rules should be enforced. Jean-Jacques Rousseau (1712–1778) further developed the theory by identifying the difficulties in creating rules to ensure safety and property rights, while also enabling individuals to have an element of freedom. The determination of rules is, therefore, made by members of the community and all members of the community are obligated to adhere to the rules.

In summary, there is an implicit contract between the members of society and business in which the members of society recognise business as a legal entity, grant businesses authority to acquire and control resources, that is, to hire employees, in return for certain benefits. The benefits to society are an increase in the welfare of the society through the production of goods and services and by compensation for employment.

## Integrated social contract theory

Social contract theory has been extended even further with **integrated social contract theory**, which recognises that through explicit contracts, and informally through implicit agreements, ethical rules develop. These obligations are based on both theoretical macro social contracts between economic participants and micro social contracts among members of specific communities (Donaldson & Dunfee 1994). The more a business knows about the expectations of these communities, the better it is able to deliver on social contracts, which leads us to

**trust companies** – companies overseen by a board of trustees who are trusted with balancing the needs of all stakeholders, not just shareholders, and ensuring that the companies live up to their corporate values.

**social contract theory** – an implied social contract or agreement between business and society, and an expectation of behaviour that surrounds this agreement.

**integrated social contract theory** – recognises that explicit and implicit agreements are the basis for developing ethical rules.

an investigation of who these communities or stakeholders are and to an exploration of the related term of stakeholder management.

Rules are the foundation of corporate responsibility (© shutterstock.com/Krasimira Nevenova)

# Stakeholder management

**stakeholder theory** – emphasises that a company is part of the social system, therefore, it cannot only recognise shareholders as stakeholders, but must also recognise a variety of internal and external groups of importance to the company.

Stakeholder theory emphasises that a company is part of the social system and recognises a variety of internal and external groups of importance to the company, not just shareholders. **Stakeholder theory**, therefore, moves the maximising of returns for shareholders (principals) to a wider constituency of interested parties of which the business needs to be cognisant. The term 'stakeholder' is a deliberate play on the words 'stockholder and shareholder' to signify that other parties have a stake in the organisation.

Stakeholder theory originated at the Stanford Research Institute in 1963 and, following seminal work by Freeman (1984), was subsequently supported by Donaldson and Preston (1995). Stakeholder theory proposes that regardless of the potential for improved financial performance, a firm should find the ideal balance among all important stakeholders without violating the rights of any one stakeholder (Morris et al. 2002).

There can be a myriad of different stakeholders. Stakeholders can be employees, customers, suppliers, investors, owners, banks, interest groups, the community, media, government, society and even competitors, and they can be classified as primary or secondary stakeholders (Clarkson 1995). See Table 2.1.

Stakeholder groups can be categorised as either profit or not-for-profit organisations. For example, the Salvation Army are a not-for-profit organisation that provide services and welfare programs to people in crisis, in Australia, and

**Table 2.1**  Primary and secondary company stakeholders

| Primary stakeholders | Secondary stakeholders |
|---|---|
| Employees | Competitors |
| Customers | Media |
| Suppliers | Trade associations |
| Community | Special interest groups |
| Government and other regulatory bodies | |
| Unions | |

(Adapted from: Clarkson, MBE 1995).

worldwide. The key stakeholders that have been identified for the Salvation Army (adapted from Kenny 2013) are:

- Salvation Army officers/the church
- employees and volunteers
- donors
- alcohol and gambling companies
- other faiths/other NGOs
- clients
- families
- client representatives or advocates
- funding bodies.

# Ethics in practice: Stakeholder groups

For each stakeholder group for the Salvation Army, map out the stakeholder expectations associated with each group.

More recently, the list of stakeholder groups has been extended to include the less immediate stakeholders with the inclusion of future generations as a constituent for whom the corporation is responsible, particularly in regard to environmental stewardship. When we reflect on the stakeholder groups for multinational corporations the picture becomes even more complex as we include NGOs, national and international bodies of influence. The general proposal is that a diligent consideration of each of these stakeholders forms the basis of a more personal and socially responsive approach to business, as each stakeholder group will have potential ethical issues of concern to them (see box).

# Selected stakeholder ethical issues

- Competitors – deceptive gaining of competitor information, predatory tactics, and price collusion.
- Government – disregarding rules and regulations, tax avoidance, bribery and corruption.

*cont.*

*cont.*

- Customers – unsafe products and services, deceptive marketing and labelling, invasion of privacy and the inappropriate use of customer information.
- Employees – discriminatory practices in relation to recruitment, promotion, training, compensation. Labour abuses and unsafe work environments.
- Investors – conflict of interest, provision of accurate information, violation of duty of care in relation to money invested, and market manipulation.
- Future generations – waste management, carbon reduction, avoiding pollution and environmental damage, and ensuring future sustainability.

# Ethics in practice: Stakeholders

The company you work for has produced jam for more than 50 years. There is a suggestion, as yet unconfirmed, that one batch of your strawberry jam product may be contaminated. The source of the contamination is not known but you do know that the result is probable gastric illness. You propose waiting until further cases are reported.

**Questions:**

**1.** Who are the key stakeholders of your company?

**2.** What do you think about the proposed action of waiting until further cases are reported?

It has been suggested that it is impossible to develop an effective set of strategies for an organisation without first identifying its key stakeholders, that is, those groups that have, or could have, a major impact on an organisation's future. Mitchell, Agle and Wood (1997), however, suggest that not all stakeholders are equal and their importance could be viewed according to:

- their power to influence the firm
- the legitimacy of the relationship to the firm
- the urgency of the claim on the firm.

Similarly, Jawahar and McLaughlin (2001) insist that in different stages of an organisation's life cycle, certain stakeholders will be more important than others, and the strategy an organisation employs to deal with each stakeholder depends on their importance to the organisation relative to other stakeholders. By assessing each stakeholder's potential to threaten, or cooperate with, the organisation, managers may identify where the stakeholder sits with respect to the degree and level of support they provide (Savage et al. 1991).

# Corporate social responsibility

Another influential concept in the lexicon of business ethics is that of **corporate social responsibility (CSR)**. Bowen (1953) wrote the seminal book, *Social responsibilities of the businessman*, and since then there has been a shift in terminology from the social responsibility of business to CSR. Unfortunately, an agreed definition of CSR has proved elusive since beliefs and attitudes regarding the nature of exactly what these responsibilities are tend to fluctuate with the topicality of the issues. However, CSR is described as the interrelationship, including obligations and duties, that exists between institutions and society (Steiner 1972). These relationships are 'social contracts', and the individual or institutions with whom these social contracts are made are, naturally, the organisation's stakeholders.

CSR, therefore, goes further than merely identifying the organisation's stakeholders and their critical concerns (which is largely done through **stakeholder analysis**), but actively recognises that organisations have obligations, duties and social contracts to fulfil in relation to stakeholders. There are, effectively, additional responsibilities now placed on an organisation, which it can decide whether it will, or will not, meet. With the original conceptualisations of CSR there is still a discretionary element on the part of the organisation as to whether it will actively engage in socially responsible behaviour, but the expectations remain.

The CSR movement is premised on the belief that business is intertwined with the rest of society and has responsibilities to be profitable, lawful, ethical and philanthropic (Carroll 1991). The four components of CSR begin with the basic building-block notion that economic performance underpins all else – although, at the same time, business is expected to obey the law (because the law is society's codification of acceptable and unacceptable behaviour) and to be ethical (this is the obligation to do what is right, just, and fair, and to avoid or minimise harm to others). Business is also expected to be a good corporate citizen, which is captured in the philanthropic responsibility level, where business is expected to contribute financial and human resources to the community and to improve quality of life. For example, during Hurricane Katrina, Walmart mobilised to provide meals, emergency supplies and cash, and apparently no internal debate was needed as such actions were obviously seen as the right things to do (Dach 2013). Figure 2.1 presents one view of the components of CSR.

This later stage, while initially restricted to charitable distributions, has moved to community development, societal problem-solving and **corporate citizenship (CC)**, which call for more active involvement and functioning as societal citizens by corporations. In the global context, this would have multinationals participating in the communities in which they operate, assisting with societal governance, promoting civil and social rights and collective problem-solving (Moon, Crane & Matten 2005). CC becomes particularly important when operating in developing nations where civil and social rights may not be afforded to the same extent as in other geographic locations. Firms in these circumstances, consistent with their citizenship, would be expected to uphold and protect civil and social rights.

**corporate social responsibility (CSR)** – generally accepted relationships, obligations and duties between major institutions and people.

**stakeholder analysis** – identification of the key stakeholders of influence to an organisation.

**corporate citizenship (CC)** – the recognition that corporations have moral responsibilities just as human citizens do.

**Figure 2.1** Pyramid of corporate social responsibility (Adapted from Carroll 1991)

Moon (2013) suggests that today CSR has progressed sufficiently so that there are now:

- CSR associations (e.g., Business in the Community; ASEAN CSR)
- indexes/standards of CSR performance (e.g., Dow Jones Sustainability Index, FTSE4Good, ISO 26000; Equator Principles)
- CSR consultants (with over 100 alone in the UK)
- specialist media (e.g., Ethical Corporation, Ethical Performance).

**social obligation** – corporate behaviour conforming only to legal requirements and competitive pressure.

**social responsibility** – corporate behaviour congruent with the prevailing norms, values and expectations of society.

## Four levels of social responsibility

Building on the work of Sethi (1979), four levels of social interaction in CSR can be observed (see Figure 2.2).

1. **Social obligation** – corporate behaviour directed at conforming only to legal requirements and competitive pressure, however, the law merely specifies the lowest common denominator of acceptable behaviour. Legality is therefore not the main criterion for judging acceptable business behaviour.
2. **Social responsibility** – corporate behaviour congruent with prevailing norms, values and expectations of society and responding to the needs of a wide range of stakeholders.
3. **Social responsiveness** – corporate behaviour that takes preventative action in relation to stakeholder concerns, and anticipates future requirements beyond current expectations

or principles. Socially responsible organisations are those that do not just react to stakeholders, but have institutionalised policy and structure to proactively cope with social change. These organisations anticipate the needs and act accordingly.

4. **Social impact** – also referred to as **corporate social performance (CSP)**, social impact is corporate behaviour that looks for specific outcomes and redresses adverse social phenomena; that is, it uses the organisation's core competencies for financial as well as social ends. CSP is less interested in rhetoric or glossy statements of intent from corporations, but rather in the actual impact or effects achieved to remedy societal concerns.

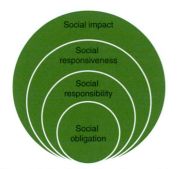

**Figure 2.2** Four levels of social responsibility

An example of how business can impact on a social problem is provided by the mining giant Anglo America, which have taken on the mammoth task of attempting to address the AIDS crisis in South Africa. The company encourages employees to take a voluntary HIV test, with HIV-positive staff being given access to company-funded drug therapy. The HIV test results are used to monitor safe sex practices, with results indicating lowered infection rates. In 2005 rates were 2.1 in every 100, lowering to 0.63 by 2013. Some, however, may argue that the motivation is not altruistic, given the significant impact that HIV illnesses have on productivity and turnover ('Sex, drugs and hope' 2013). Other examples of entrepreneurs with businesses focused on social impacts are: James Green, founder of One Night Stand, which sell premium nightwear and bedding and use the profits to tackle homelessness in Australia; Julian Lee, founder of Food Connect, Sydney, which deliver boxes of sustainable seasonal produce in the city and pay a fair price to local farmers; and Simon Griffith, founder of Who Gives a Crap, a toilet paper company that use their profits to build toilets in the developing world (Fitzsimmons 2013).

**social responsiveness** – corporate behaviour that takes preventative action and anticipates future requirements beyond current expectations.

**social impact** (also referred to as **corporate social performance** or **CSP**) – corporate behaviour, looking for specific outcomes and redressing adverse social phenomena; that is, using the organisation's core competencies for financial and social ends.

Corporate social responsibility (© shutterstock.com/Chatchawan)

# Ethics in practice: Corporate social performance

SABMiller, the brewing company, have an active program to reduce HIV infection rates. Undertake internet research on SABMiller's program.

# Ethics on reflection: Social responsibility

A beer company in New Zealand sold bottles of beer at sporting events, but they were very conscious that the bottles could be broken resulting not only in unsightly littering and extra cleaning costs for venue owners, but also the risk of injury from broken glass. The company therefore proactively spent a considerable amount of time and money on developing a plastic bottle for use at sporting events (beer and plastic is not usually a good combination and reduces the shelf-life of the product). The bottles are also being used during public holidays near popular beach locations.

**Question:**
1. What level of social responsibility does this represent?

## Benefit organisations

**benefit organisations** (also referred to as **B organisations** or **B Corporations**) – a new class of corporations designed to create benefit for all stakeholders, not just shareholders.

In recent years the current legal framework has been deemed to be outdated and not equipped to accommodate for-profit entities whose social benefit purpose is central to their existence. As a consequence, a new classification of business organisation is gradually being introduced through legislation called **benefit organisations** (also referred to as **B organisations** or **B Corporations**). The legislation provides legal clarity on the duties of directors (previously firms faced the risk of litigation if they failed to maximise shareholder value), and creates a new class of corporations designed to provide benefit for all stakeholders, not just shareholders (Clark et al. 2013). Today, there are approximately 600 Certified B Corps across 15 countries, including more than 60 industries working together towards the shared goal of redefining success in business (GIIRS 2012).

# Ethics in practice: B Corporations

For more information on B Corporations, view B Corporations' YouTube clip: <www.youtube.com/watch?v=99vksspg2Gl>.

## Corporate social responsibility in India

CSR is also being advocated on an international scale. In India, the government is endeavouring to mandate CSR with a new law that came into effect in 2013. It has implemented ground rules for CSR, with a requirement that companies with a net worth of more than Rs 500 crore, or revenue of more than Rs 1000 crore, or net profits of more than Rs 5 crore, spend at least 2% of their annual net profit on CSR. Although the law does not stipulate penalties for non-compliance, it is anticipated that expenditure will be in areas such as education, rural skill development and sport (Malik & Jenkins 2013). As a consequence, companies are starting to take CSR more seriously. Coal India have signed a MoU with Tata Institute of Social Sciences to carry out needs assessment on projects, and have streamlined their CSR team to be more efficient in monitoring project work. Tata Steel have placed greater emphasis on sustainability in and around their plants, particularly in the area of waste management related to their steel manufacturing, with 83.16% of their waste being recycled. Curiously, the biggest problem is reported to be finding sustainable issues in smaller towns and cities to work on, particularly in areas like education, healthcare, entrepreneurship, ecology protection and the safeguarding of heritage sites (IndiaCSR 2013).

## Corporate social responsibility standards

Accompanying increased CSR activities are a raft of advocated standards. Painter-Morland and Ten Bos (2011, p. 264) suggest that CSR standards can be differentiated into three types:

1. **Principle-based CSR standards** – provide business with broadly defined principles that can be used as guidance, such as those launched in the United Nations Global Compact (UNGC) in 2000. The 10 principles cover human rights, labour standards, the environment and anti-corruption.
2. **Reporting-based CSR standards** – provide an indication of performance expectations that can be used for reporting, such as the Global Reporting Initiative (GRI) Guidelines, which utilise economic, environmental and social standards as content category guidelines.

**principle-based CSR standards** – standards, such as the United Nations Global Compact (UNGC), which utilise broadly defined principles to be used as guidance.

**reporting-based CSR standards** – an indication of performance expectations that can be used for reporting, such as the Global Reporting Initiative (GRI).

3. **Certification-based CSR standards** – provide compliance targets and audits that evaluate company performance against these targets, such as, Social Accountability (SA) and Audit (SAA) has developed SA8000, AccountAbility (AA1000), and the ISO 26000, as well as sector-specific certification initiatives. Companies can also use third-party certification such as organic, Fair Trade, Energy Star, Green Seal and LEED, and the Forest Stewardship Council.

The ISO 26000 standard is one of the more popular CSR standards and is intended to:

- develop an international consensus on what social responsibility is and the issues that organisations need to address
- provide guidelines on translating principles into effective actions
- distil the best practice, as evolved, and disseminate it worldwide for the good of the international community.

ISO certification is an index of corporate social responsibility (© shutterstock.com/ValentinT)

## Dimensions of CSR

Eccles and Serafeim (2013) and Eccles, Ioannou and Serafeim (2012, 2013) have provided the most complete picture to date of the broad parameters of CSR, including a number of dimensions (within each of which there are further sub-areas of attention). They have proposed five dimensions to which CSR now relates:

1. **Environmental** – i.e. carbon emissions reduction policies, environmental accidents, the efficiency of energy and water usage, green supply chain policies, transportation, pollution.
2. **Social capital** – i.e. community engagement, strategies to improve customer health and safety, ethical market development of new products, disclosure and ethical labelling of products, considering access to services and customer privacy.
3. **Human capital** – i.e. achieving diversity and equal opportunity, labour relations and compensation, internal promotions, training and development, staff retention, health and safety of employees, ensuring human rights criteria are met.

4. **Business models and innovation** – i.e. long-term viability, product considerations are innovative research and development, societal value of the product, product life cycle impact, product packaging and pricing, and the quality and safety of the product.
5. **Leadership and corporate governance** – i.e. regulatory and legal challenges, shareholder engagement, policy standards, codes of conduct, business ethics, board structure and executive compensation functions using sustainability metrics, competitive behaviour, sourcing of raw materials, supply chain management, and transparency of political contributions and lobbying.

# Environmentalism

Admittedly, environmentalism has a narrower focus than CSR, but, as a compelling force on business today, it should be examined. Interbrand's *Best Global Green Brands Report* examines the gap between a corporation's environmental practices and consumer perceptions of those practices; as reported, car brands dominated the 2013 report, with Toyota coming top for the third year running, Ford second and Honda third. Nestlé was fourth, and Nokia ninth (see Ethical Performance 2012b).

Many companies are anxious to do the right thing from an environmental perspective. For example, the information technology (IT) company, Dell, are stepping up their environmental efforts by setting itself a 100% waste-free packaging scheme by 2020. Dell will ensure that their packaging is sourced from sustainable materials, and that materials used are also either recyclable or compostable (Ethical Performance 2012c).

**Environmentalism** provided the origins and foundations of what has become sustainable development, being primarily concerned with pollution prevention and waste minimisation (Rainey 2006). More recent attention has been given to ways of mitigating climate change, notably by reducing carbon production, and a commitment to renewable energy. Parties to the United Nations' Framework Convention on Climate Change have largely reaffirmed the Kyoto Protocol, which is intended to limit carbon emissions, as well as strategies to achieve climate change below two degrees Celsius.

Worth mentioning is the **Clean Development Mechanism (CDM)**, which was set up under the Kyoto Protocol to assist developing countries in reducing their carbon emissions. The mechanism allows for projects that reduce greenhouse gas emissions in poor countries to earn a **Certified Emission Reduction Credit (CER)**, which can be sold to firms in rich countries obliged to cut their emissions. Unfortunately, with an oversupply of credits comes a collapse of carbon prices, particularly since Europe, previously the main source of demand for credits, has reduced pollution while also having a generous carbon quota ('Complete disaster in the making' 2012).

**environmentalism** – provides the origins of what has become sustainable development, with primary concerns for pollution prevention and waste minimisation.

**Clean Development Mechanism (CDM)** – set up under the Kyoto Protocol to assist developing countries in reducing their carbon emissions.

**Certified Emission Reduction Credit (CER)** – projects that reduce greenhouse gas emissions in poor countries to earn credits that can then be sold to firms in rich countries who are obliged to cut their emissions.

## Ethics on reflection: Green issues

For some fascinating and colourful depictions of current green issues and a guide to green symbols available, see <www.easywaystogogreen.com>.

## Ethics in the media: Environmentalism

The Los Angeles City Council approved an ordinance to outlaw plastic supermarket bags, which came into effect in 2014. This is by far the biggest city in America to do so. A 10-cent charge will be applied on paper bags for shoppers who do not bring their own reusable ones ('The world this week' 2013).

Can you build a business on the back of environmentalism? It appears so. The Australian businessman, Anthony Pratt, was sent to the United States in 1990 by his late father to work with the company's US operations. Pratt Industries has since risen to fifth place (up from 45th position) in the corrugated box market, posting US$1.5 billion revenue in 2013. The US business is unique in that the American empire has been built on the cornerstone of recycling, not sourcing its raw materials from forests. An underlying principle is the use of waste as an energy source, and, rather than burning the waste, an alternative method to incineration is gasification. Given that the World Bank expects the 1.3 billion tonnes of waste produced in major cities to double by 2025, this would appear to be an admirable solution (Heathcoat 2013).

The environmental business model is not just about business practices though, as companies are seeing rising demand for products and services that help business-to-business customers, and the end consumer, to reduce their own environmental impact. The British department store chain John Lewis are trialling a new product labelling scheme that informs consumers of the lifetime electricity cost of whitegoods, rather than the traditional kilowatt hours of energy use per annum that is currently used (Smithers 2013). Similarly, Siemens report that their environmental product portfolio showed the strongest growth, generating €23 billion revenue, nearly a third of Siemens' total annual revenue (Lacy, Haines & Hayward 2012).

## Ethics in the media: Environmentalism

Data collected by scientists tracking global emissions (Global Carbon Project) demonstrate that global greenhouse gas emissions are at their highest level in human history, and are projected to surge higher (Arup 2013).

## Ethics in the media: Environmentalism

America is unveiling an 'I want to be recycled' public service advertisement, which will target the 62% of Americans who actively avoid recycling ('First public service ad campaign in forty years targets recycling' 2013). See <http://ethicalperformance.com/news/article/7833>.

## Ethics in practice: Business tools

Review what specific business tools are available to organisations to achieve environmental improvements at the International Institute for Sustainable Development website, <www.iisd.org/business/tools/bt.aspx>.

# Sustainability

Sustainability is very much a value-based symbol, and follows trends of democracy, capitalism and sustainability as central themes from the past 20 years, and economic growth as a trend 20 years before that. In a UNGC survey of nearly 100 countries and 25 industries, CEOs' views reinforced sustainability as a key ingredient to future business success, and recognised the need to integrate environmental, social and governance issues into core business (Lacy et al. 2012).

While the term initially referred to predominantly environmental issues, our idea of sustainability has broadened and now incorporates activities that:

- extend the longevity of organisations
- maintain and renew the biosphere and protect all living species
- enhance society's ability to maintain itself and solve its major problems
- maintain appropriate levels of welfare for present and future generations.

The literature tends to prefer the term **sustainable development** rather than sustainability to indicate the ongoing nature of the task; however, for ease, we will use the term sustainability.

**sustainable development** – a term used in the literature to indicate the ongoing nature of sustainability.

## Phases in sustainability

There are six successive phases, through which many organisations pass as they move towards **strategic sustainability** and ultimately towards becoming **sustaining corporations**. They represent a set of ideal types that can be used to help organisations define where they currently are on the sustainability path and to chart the way ahead (Dunphy, Griffiths & Benn 2003).

The phases, also shown in Figure 2.3, are:

**strategic sustainability** – sustainability is now an important part of the organisation's business strategy.

1. **Rejection** – the organisation holds a strong belief that organisations exist to maximise profit and that the environment is a free good to be exploited.
2. **Non-responsiveness** – there is ignorance or a lack of awareness rather than active opposition to a corporate ethic that is broader than financial gain.
3. **Compliance** – the focus is on reducing the organisation's risk of sanctions for failing to meet minimum standards.
4. **Efficiency** – a growing awareness by managers that there are real advantages to be gained by proactively instituting sustainable practices.
5. **Strategic sustainability** – sustainability now becomes an important part of the organisation's business strategy.
6. **The sustaining corporation** – there is a strong internalised ideology of working for a sustainable world.

**sustaining corporations** – a strong internalised ideology within organisations of working for a sustainable world.

This is not intended to be a strictly linear model; that is, not all organisations move through all phases and they may move back and forth between them. A change in CEO, for example, may lead to a significant shift and a company leapfrogging certain stages.

**Figure 2.3**  The phases of sustainability
(Adapted from: Dunphy, Griffiths & Benn 2003)

# Ethics in practice: Sustainability

The Warehouse, a large New Zealand retailer, undertook a 10-year energy-saving program, which led to a 50% reduction in costs and $4 million in annual savings.

**Question:**

1. What phase on Dunphy, Griffiths and Ben's (2003) sustainability scale does this suggest?

**Sustainable business development (SBD)** is also relevant as it is perceived as a subset of the broader concepts of sustainability and sustainable development. SBD advocates the achievement of social, economic and environmental objectives to protect human kind and the natural world (Rainey 2006).

A good example of phase 5, and the building of strategic capability, is Intel Corporation, which set themselves a goal to reduce their global warming greenhouse gas footprint by 20% between 2007 and 2012. Intel have achieved IT sustainability benefits thus far by developing the four following key capabilities:

1. **Strategy and planning** – aligning IT sustainability with core corporate sustainable goals.
2. **Process management** – reinforcing sustainable principles and practice in everyday actions and decision-making.
3. **People and culture** – encouraging a sustainable culture with creative involvement in innovation by all employees.
4. **Governance** – establishing consistent policies to meet current and future sustainability objectives (Curry et al. 2012).

**sustainable business development** – articulating and achieving social, economic and environmental objectives to protect human kind and the natural world.

# Ethics in practice: Sustainability at McDonald's

To explore the issue of sustainability in the case of McDonald's, view the video <http://amatv. marketingpower.com/ama-tv-mcdonald%e2%80%99s-sustainability-new-year-new-career-marketing-like-never-before-more>.

## Ethics in the media: Sustainability

Marks and Spencer, the UK's biggest clothing retailer, have initiated a '**shwopping**' (the combination of shopping and swapping) campaign. Through a partnership with Oxfam, Marks & Spencer are encouraging their 350 million customers to select a clothing item from their closet to recycle before purchasing a new item. Marks & Spencer facilitate this through 'shwopping drops' in their stores ('A new social movement. Marks & Spencer' 2013).

## Sustainability in developing nations

**shwopping** – a campaign that encourages customers to select a clothing item from their closet to recycle before purchasing a new item.

Rapidly developing economies tend to lag behind in regard to sustainability due to their priority being to raise their citizens out of poverty rather than protecting the environment. Other restraints are their weak regulatory bodies, resentment of pressure from industrialised nations and a hesitation to restrict newly liberalised markets (Haanaes et al. 2013). There is, however, a unique opportunity for companies in developing nations to assist with sustainability efforts, and, in 2010, the Boston Consulting Group, in conjunction with the World Economic Forum, identified 1000 companies ranging in size from US$25 million to US$5 billion and from a wide array of markets and industry sectors, with effective sustainability practices operating in the developing world (Haanaes et al. 2013).

## Sustainable sourcing

**sustainable sourcing** – sourcing of materials that takes into account social and environmental responsibility as well as enhancing supplier capabilities.

**Sustainable sourcing** originally meant ensuring that the products being sourced were created in safe facilities by workers who received good treatment, received fair wages and worked legal hours. It also implies that the supplier is respecting the environment during the production and manufacture of the products (Life Without Plastic Wholesale 2014). More recently, the term has widened from sourcing of materials that takes into account labour issues, social and environmental responsibilities and the minimisation of resource depletion (Consumer Goods Forum 2012), to firms taking a more proactive approach not just to source sustainably but to actively enhance the viability and performance of their suppliers. For example, the American food company, General Mills, are significantly involved with sustainable sourcing, with a new US$1.1 million program in the US, aimed at helping small artichoke farmers in Peru. The program focuses on training farmers in crop management and post-harvest practices, as well as offering them micro-loans (Ethical Performance 2013c).

## Ethics in the media: Sustainable sourcing

By Dell using wheat straw (sourced from Jiangsu Province, China) in the manufacture of many of their cardboard boxes, 180 tonnes of $CO_2$ emissions will be eliminated annually, as the straw, a by-product of wheat harvesting, is usually burnt (Ethical Performance 2012c).

## Ethics in practice: Sustainable sourcing

Currently, more than one-third of the raw material used to make Unilever products is sourced sustainably. However, Unilever aim to increase the content to 100% by 2020. View this video for more details: <www.youtube.com/watch?v=-eSJKNXsvwI>.

## Sustainability divestment

With a strong emphasis on sustainability, commitment is now extending to what has been called **sustainability divestment**. Essentially, an organisation not only looks at how it can improve its environmental impact through its own enabling policies and processes, but also at where the organisation currently invests, and whether its investments are enhancing or hindering sustainability. For example, the managed funds that companies invest in can include fossil fuel companies, and fossil fuels are the largest contributors to global climate change. Pressures are, therefore, appearing for organisations to divest themselves of investments that contradict the organisation's sustainability objectives.

**sustainability divestment** – organisations divesting themselves of investments and, specifically, managed funds that include contributors to global climate change.

## Corporate governance

Historically, governance was thought of as being focused primarily on board member performance, the relationship between the board and senior management, and the overarching internal control and reporting systems of an organisation that ensure compliance and functional performance. Corporate governance, however, has a broader mandate – the creation of processes that are used to direct and control the corporation (Painter-Morland & Ten Bos 2011). A more expansive view of **corporate governance** in business covers the procedures for how private sector organisations are directed, managed and controlled, including the relationships between, and responsibilities and legitimate expectations among, different stakeholders, the board of directors, management, shareholders and other interested groups (Transparency International 2009a). This broader definition alludes to the social and environmental demands, in addition to financial performance expectations.

**corporate governance** – processes by which corporations are directed and controlled and hold the balance between economic, social goals and environmental goals and between individual and communal goals.

Risk is just one aspect of corporate governance (© shutterstock.com/iQoncept)

## Dimensions of corporate governance

There are eight common dimensions of corporate governance:

1. **Ethical standards** – the setting, communication, support and enforcement of the organisation's ethical expectations.
2. **Board composition and performance** – the formation of boards, diversity and capability of board membership and avoidance of conflicts of interest.
3. **Board committees** – the structure of subcommittees, their functionality and their performance.
4. **Reporting and disclosures** – the timely meeting of external reporting requirements, the accuracy and honesty of the representation of financial position and risk.
5. **Remuneration** – the equitable, but not excessive, remuneration of board members, and senior executives relative to other personnel.
6. **Risk management** – the meeting of compliance requirements and the ongoing monitoring of risk.
7. **Auditing** – the effective stewardship of financial and non-financial resources, ethical and social audits and appropriate reporting.
8. **Shareholder and stakeholder relations** – the attention given to shareholder interests, provision of investor returns and the meeting of stakeholder expectations.

The following structural components of governance are essential to enable us to move away from the rhetoric of governance and concentrate on a full integration of its dimensions:

- Setting expectations and standards
- Ensuring that operating processes are functioning
- Monitoring performance
- Accurately reporting outcomes.

# Ethics in the media: Corporate governance

An intriguing observation and empirical finding in corporate governance is a correlation between the post-GFC banks that got into the most trouble and shareholder-friendly executive pay and governance arrangements (Fox 2013).

# Ethics in the media: Corporate governance

The Asian Corporate Governance Association watchdog downgraded Japan to fourth in Asia for corporate governance in 2012, tied with Malaysia. This is on the back of a report from the Japan Association of Corporate Executives that highlighted existing problems in Japanese boardrooms that will require a revolution to improve them ('Back to the Drawing Board' 2012).

## Board management

Although several dimensions are involved in governance, as mentioned above, there is still a fascination and focus in the governance literature in relation to boards, particularly the connections between boards and board composition.

Social network theory examines the connections between companies through board membership and ownership, with the suggestion that through multiple board memberships a network develops, in which board membership is based not on individual attributes but on who knows whom (Dellaportas et al. 2005).

**social network theory** – examines the connections between companies through board membership and ownership, indicating a relatively small and networked group of individuals.

**co-determination** – opening up company boards to full representation.

**Co-determination** involves opening up company boards to full representation with the genuine belief that a board performs better when there is diversity of thought and experience at the table, and that employees should also be an active part of the process. The co-determination model can go even further when there is both a supervisory board and a management board. Co-determination has been attributed to economic development in Germany; however, one of the barriers to implementation of this model is a resistance by managers to give employees direct input into the management and governance of the company.

# Ethics in practice: Governance

You have a friend who has just become President of the local sport club. This is a voluntary role, but the club is a fairly large organisation that employs 10 staff and coordinates a small army of volunteers. Your friend is wanting to improve board performance that in the past, from his experience, has been somewhat dysfunctional. Your friend has asked you to undertake research to determine the current thoughts and best practices exhibited by effective boards, and how he might improve the governance of the club.

**Question:**

1. What recommendation would you make?

## Women on boards

While governance does involves multiple facets of considerable focus, in the area of governance there has been a lack of discussion around women on boards. It has been determined that women directors average about 12% on boards, ranging from 0.1% in Saudi Arabia to 40.1% in Norway ('Research needed on women on boards' 2013). Only 13.7% of board members of large firms in the EU are women, up from 8.5% in 2003, with female presidents and chairwomen even rarer, just 3.2% of the total now compared with 1.6% in 2003 ('Women in business' 2012).

In the US, the InterOrganization Network (ION) released its eighth annual status report on women directors and executive officers of 100 public companies in 14 regions of the United States. It identified that among the Fortune 500 companies in 14 regions, Massachusetts reported the highest percentage of women directors, at 20.7%. Three regions – Kansas, Missouri and New York metropolitan region – reported a decrease in the number of all-male boards. Of all the regions, Florida made the biggest strides, with a reported 5% increase of women executives over the past year; however, 42 of Florida's 100 public companies still have no women directors and women occupy only 9.3% of board seats (ION 2013).

In the US, it has been found that where companies have higher levels of women in senior leadership positions, companies are more likely to be socially responsible than companies with fewer women in these roles ('Women of influence' 2012). Interestingly, it also appears that women are more philanthropic. According to the report *Gender and corporate social responsibility: It's a matter of sustainability*, Fortune 500 companies with no women directors contributed an average of US$969,000 to charitable causes in 2007, compared with US$27.1 million by those with three or more women on the boards. The report finds that each additional woman on the board equates to a US$2.3 million increase in giving (Soares, Marquis & Lee 2011).

A number of countries are actively seeking to address the lack of women on boards by using quotas, with Norway making enormous gains, from 9% in 2003 to 40% in 2012. France is aiming to increase the number of women on boards from 20% of board seats by 2014 to 40% by 2017; while Belgium's goal is slightly lower at 33% representation ('Women in business' 2012). These quotas are a prelude to the new European Commission's (EC) legislation, which requires European companies to achieve greater gender equity on boards by requiring 40% of non-executive board positions to be filled by women by 2020, a significant increase from the existing 15% of non-executive positions held ('Europe launches "board ready" database' 2013).

## Ethics in practice: Quotas for women on boards

The EC is imposing specific quota rules in the European Union for women in senior roles and on boards. Some question whether quotas will work as there is a feeling the women should be able to rise naturally to senior executive roles, and that quotas are an artificial elevation. A significant impediment to women rising to such positions is the time commitment; as a 2007 McKinsey study notes, 54% of senior women executives surveyed were childless, compared with 29% of the men (Schumpeter 2012).

**Question:**
1. What do you believe could be done to increase female representation on boards?

## The triple bottom line (TBL or 3BL)

**Triple bottom line** accounting has organisations working on, and reporting on, their performance in the three areas of social, environmental and economic outcomes, which have also been called people, planet and profit (see Figure 2.4). The concept was first described by John Elkington (1994) and has since gained momentum. From 2005, quoted UK companies have been producing operating and financial reviews that also take into account their social and environmental performance. Nearly 80% of the 250 largest corporations issue reports on non-financial information, which is up from 50% in 2005 (KPMG 2009).

**triple bottom line** (also known as **TBL** or **3BL**) – organisations working on and reporting on their performance in the three areas of social, environmental and profit.

# Ethics in practice: Measuring the TBL

Consider how you would actually go about measuring an organisation's triple bottom line. For a simple explanation, see <http://toolkit.smallbiz.nsw.gov.au/part/17/84/363>.

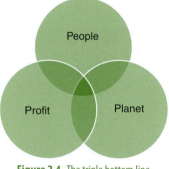

**Figure 2.4** The triple bottom line (Adapted from Powell 2011)

## Measuring the triple bottom line

The difficulty is not in defining TBL, but in measuring it and deciding how one would go about actually calculating the triple bottom line. Slaper and Hall (2011) have suggested three approaches:

1. Monetising all the dimensions of the TBL, including the social and environmental elements. While that would have the benefit of creating a common unit – dollars, for example – it is difficult to find the right price for, say, lost wetlands or endangered species.
2. Calculating TBL in terms of an index. Examples of indexes that compare a country's performance are the Transparency International Corruption Index, or the Indiana Business Research Centre's Innovation Index. The drawback with indexes is that they are subjective.
3. Using individual indicators and measures where each sustainability measure stands alone. The downside to this approach is the proliferation of metrics that may be germane to measuring TBL.

The latter approach is more commonly in use, although there are no universally accepted standard indicators that cover each of the TBL categories. It has been noted that this could be a good thing, as it allows for adaptation to meet the needs of different entities, projects and geographic boundaries. With these differences driving the decisions about what measures to include in the TBL score card, however, Table 2.2, does provide some recommendations. For a more detailed list, see Slaper and Hall (2011).

In practice, deciding on the indicators is usually achieved through the company identifying what its key indicators are in each of the three domains – profit, planet and people. It is important that the indicators are measurable, as target goals are established for each indicator and are incorporated into the strategic planning process. Initiatives are implemented and the key metrics associated with the key indicators are assessed and reported on in the company's TBL report.

In an example of TBL reporting, Nestlé have, for more than a decade, been profoundly aware of the link between the company's long-term profitability and the health of the agricultural communities from whom they source product, as well as water resources and consumer expectations. Consequently, every country manager is expected to craft a business plan that delivers progress on these issues, and includes profits for shareholders. An outcome of this process is that Nestlé launched Maggi Masala-a-Magic, a micro-nutrient-reinforced spice product, priced for low-income consumers in India. Through research, the company discovered that 70% of children under the age of three, and 50% of women in India suffered from anaemia. They then visited 1500 poor households to understand cooking customs and diets. As a result of this research, they realised that the most commonly used item, spice, offered a vehicle for hiding the bad taste of the critical micro-nutrients iron, iodine and vitamin A. They then set about developing and upgrading manufacturing lines before launching the product. In just three years, the company sold 138 million servings, using both existing and non-profit distribution channels. The product is priced at a manageable 3 rupees. The company has been financially rewarded for recognising and responding to a social problem in an environmentally conscious manner (Pfitzer, Bockstette & Stamp 2013).

The triple bottom line (© shutterstock.com/visioner)

**Table 2.2** Common indicators for triple bottom line reporting

### Environmental

Greenhouse gas emissions

Waste reduction

Waste recycling

Air quality

Water consumption

Energy generation

### Social

Life expectancy

Childcare provision

Maternal and child heath

Quality of life

Investment in the arts

Charitable contributions

Educational attainment

Adoption of innovation

### Economic

Revenue generated

Profit

Tax contribution

Personal income improvement

Reduction in unemployment

Jobs generated

# Conclusion

Despite its historical roots in normative philosophical thought, the field of business ethics is evolving, and it is important that we are able to clarify related ethical constructs and terminology. There are currently increasing numbers of associated concepts, which overlap with business ethics and which are undoubtedly causing confusion – terms such as CSR, stakeholder management, corporate governance, sustainability and corporate citizenship, to name a few. The lexicon is broadening and is being claimed by familiar, but conceptually expanding notions, and, while is not uncommon to treat each term as a distinctive and separate topic and highlight potential differences between them, such an approach ignores their inherent similarities.

To recap, social responsibility is grounded in agency, social contracts and integrated social contracts theory, which reminds us that an implied contract exists, which grants businesses the right to operate if they generate benefits to society. This has created the foundation for stakeholder management where the firm moves from maximising returns, not just to principals such as shareholders, but also to a wider group of stakeholders. CSR has been described as generally accepted relationships, obligations and duties between major institutions and their stakeholders. It should not, however, be confused with creative expenditure of the marketing budget in order to promote the organisation's brand, or purely philanthropic endeavours and charitable giving. In recognising that there are differing levels of social responsibility, von Weltzien Høivik and Shankar (2011) have reiterated a move that the adoption of CSR should be shifting from a reactive defensive strategy, used to reduce risk and costs to shareholders, to a new level with a more fundamental driver to create additional value not necessarily pure profit. This value is naturally much broader than financial results as, interestingly, no overall correlation exists between financial results and social responsibility (Hansen, Ibarra & Peyer 2013). Fortunately, many companies have demonstrated that both sustainability and financial performance can be achieved successfully and, in fact, sustainability can provide a company with reinvention opportunities (Haanaes et al. 2013).

Today's corporations are larger than ever; just 1000 businesses now account for half of the total market value of the world's 60 000 public companies. Their sustainability strategies will have a significant impact (Eccles & Serafeim 2013). Building on earlier forms of environmentalism, however, sustainability is a complex area as it requires new technologies, changes to production processes and modifications of lifestyles and consumption patterns, as well as changes in the business models on which organisations operate (Wells 2013).

Corporate governance, another common ethical concept, was for too long constrained by the more popular dimensions of board composition and board performance. However, it has now been recognised for its broader mandate, which includes established ethical expectations, appropriate operating procedures (particularly those that manage risk), as well as monitoring and accurate reporting. And, in relation to reporting, the TBL has been a well-established requirement of a number of stock exchanges which wish potential investors to be fully informed on not just the financial, but also the non-financial dimensions of the environmental and social performance of firms.

In closing, we suggest that you think conceptually of business ethics as an umbrella term, which has the overarching role of gathering associated terminologies and sheltering the development and evolution of related concepts. We also encourage you to look at the similarities rather than the differences in the lexis relating to business ethics.

## Ethics on video

**Citizenship** – *Corporate citizenship* 2012, YouTube, Deutsche Bank Group, 11 October, <www.youtube.com/watch?v=YPPFjoeykmM>.

**Sustainability strategy** – *Build a strategy for sustainability* 2009, YouTube, HarvardBusinessReview, 23 July, <www.youtube.com/watch?v=K_usAROt9bc>.

**Triple bottom line** – *Seminar: The triple bottom line: The business case for sustainability* 2013, YouTube, Thayer School of Engineering at Dartmouth, 31 January, <www.youtube.com/watch?v=4BtoN3RUUbk>.

See web material for more videos.

## Ethics at the movies

Here are a few movie suggestions that have ethical content in relation to ethical terminology:

**An Inconvenient Truth** – a documentary showing Al Gore's campaign to educate people about climate change. *An Inconvenient Truth* 2006, documentary, David, L, Burns, SZ & Bender, L.

*****Erin Brockovich** – A small law firm takes on big business after uncovering the illegal dumping of toxic waste and the ramifications for a small town. *Erin Brockovich* 2000, motion picture movie, DeVito, D, Sher, S, Shamberg, M, Lyon, G & Hardy, J.

*****Author's pick**

See web material for more movies.

## Ethics on the web

**ANZSOG Institute for Governance**, an organisation that operates from the University of Canberra to focus on governance research and professional development – see <www.governanceinstitute.edu.au>.

**United Nations Global Compact**, a strategic policy initiative, which encourages businesses to support universally accepted principles around human rights, labour, environment and anti-corruption, ensuring economies and societies benefit from globalisation – see <www.unglobalcompact.org>.

See web material for more web references.

## Student exercises

See web material for answers to student short answer questions.

### Short answer questions

1. The difficulty is not in defining a triple bottom line, but in measuring it. How would you go about calculating the triple bottom line?
2. Articulate what might be the main criticism of the corporate citizenship approach.
3. Compare the stakeholder groups for accountants versus doctors. Which profession has the larger group of stakeholders?
4. What efforts are being undertaken to revive the European carbon market?
5. What is sustainable divestment?
6. Outline some of the international initiatives to encourage adoption of CSR.

### Experiential exercises

1. Provide some examples of large ethical businesses.
2. Investigate a company that is using the triple bottom line approach and identify what are the specific indicators that they are using in relation to the three key dimensions of the TBL.

# Small case

## Case: CSR at BHP Billiton

CSR – BHP Billiton 2012, 'BHP Billiton case study: the forum on corporate responsibility', *BHP Billiton*, retrieved 13 February 2013, <www.bhpbilliton.com/home/aboutus/sustainability/reports/Documents/2012/TheForumOnCorporateResponsibility.pdf>.

# Large case

## Case: Bangladesh factory conditions – the cost of low-price garments

### Background

Bangladesh is the second-largest garment exporter, with the garment industry providing 80% of export earnings (Mukherji & Rickling 2013), and 80% of these workers being women (Evans 2013). The growth of this market has come about through low regulations and low wages; the trade-off is that retailers negotiate hard for low prices per garment. Until recently, labour unions in Bangladesh had trouble gaining traction to fight for improved working conditions for employees. Before a trade union could be formed, at least 30% of the workforce had to sign up to join the union; that list of employees was handed in to the government; and the government in turn forwarded the list to the factory owners. At this stage, some owners prevented the union forming (Greenhouse & Yardley 2013). Recent government changes mean that, thankfully, the owners will no longer receive the list, which should hopefully assist in the formation of unions (Greenhouse & Yardley 2013).

On 13 May 2013, the Bangladesh Government approved other labour law changes that aligned their law with international labour standards – the changes still require parliamentary approval to go ahead (Greenhouse & Yardley 2013). Workers, and particularly women, feel that being a garment worker gives them a voice and rights, despite the rampant exploitation, and for these women, such work is a way to rise up from the lowest rungs of society and poverty; a way to provide for their family (Evans 2013).

### The Rana Plaza tragedy

On 24 April, Rana Plaza, the site of an eight-storey clothing factory, collapsed in Dhaka, killing 1100 people (Hansegard & Lahiri 2013; *Fashion victims: Four Corners* 2013). This tragedy followed another factory fire six months earlier near Dhaka, which had killed another 117 people. The world was stunned by these developments, and wondered how such disasters were able to occur with building regulations in place.

### Ethical considerations

Part of the problem relates to existing government regulations not being enforced. This may have something to do with around 24 factory owners being Members of Parliament, which creates a conflict of interest, due to their positions of power and privilege. The other complication is that, if Bangladeshi factory building regulations are enforced, the cost of garments will increase and retailers will source the garments from other cheaper locations ('Avoiding the fire next time' 2013).

For a managing director of a manufacturing exporter in Bangladesh, Ms Huq, the problem lies with the price squeeze retailers put onto manufacturers, who are already working on very tight margins (Huq 2013; *Fashion victims: Four Corners* 2013). Other factory owners back up this claim, saying their profit margin is 5% of each item sold (Uddin & Newland 2013), and that this low margin prevents them from improving the minimum levels of compliance. Not only would factory upgrades be expensive, around $138 000 per factory, there is a very real chance retailers may pull their orders in favour of a cheaper manufacturers, resulting in a huge outlay for a factory owner, with no chance of repaying the loan (they already pay 10-year bank loans at 18% interest). She believes the only way the industry can jump this hurdle is for retailers to acquiesce to higher garment prices to subsidise the cost of factory upgrades, and to commit to long-term trade agreements, giving factory owners security to invest the sums of money required to undertake factory upgrades (Huq 2013; Uddin & Newland 2013).

Foreign companies are concerned that other tragedies may affect their international reputation, and also that the exiting frameworks in place for auditing their supply chain are not particularly effective ('Avoiding the fire next time 2013), and that keeping track of supplier subcontracting is a difficult task. Nike and Gap concede any problems highlighted in factory audits require closer relationships with factory owners to ensure the problems are attended to ('Avoiding the fire next time' 2013), and H&M have increased the number of unannounced factory visits to increase oversight (Hansegard & Lahiri 2013).

Despite calls for Western government intervention to place pressure on Bangladesh, but there has been even more pressure on the *global* clothing industry to come up with a solution, including signing up to a binding agreement to upgrade factory conditions ('Avoiding the fire next time' 2013). The introduction of the Accord on Fire and Building Safety in Bangladesh worried some retailers because of its legally binding nature, which could make retailers liable in US court proceedings (Banjo, Zimmerman & Kapner 2013). The Accord works with international trade unions, Bangladeshi trade unions and companies to ensure the Bangladeshi readymade garment industry is safe and sustainable over the next five years (Accord on Fire and Building Safety in Bangladesh 2013). The agreement will result in 5000 factory inspections over a two-year period with the results made public, as well as retailer and union representation. The Accord is being seen by the consumer and labour groups as a good development, provided there is general industry consensus to signing up (Greenhouse & Yardley 2013). H&M, an enormous user of the Bangladesh garment industry, joined the Accord in the early stages, pledging to work with the factories to improve

standards (Hansegard & Lahiri 2013), and were instrumental in encouraging other retailers to join.

Not all apparel and retail companies have agreed to sign up to the Accord, with some (particularly American-based companies) opting instead to join the Alliance for Bangladesh Worker Safety (2014), supported by the US State department (Biron 2013). The Alliance is a binding agreement for a five-year period. The Alliance shares knowledge between Alliance members, makes contributions to a safety fund, and will provide low-cost capital to assist factory owners with factory improvements (Alliance for Bangladesh Worker Safety 2014). There are fundamental differences between the two organisations, with the Accord providing stakeholder engagement with trade unions and a five-year commitment to place orders with Bangladesh. The Alliance is deemed to be a watered-down version of the Accord.

Better regulations and enforcement of the regulations in place might have prevented the Rana Plaza disaster. However, it is encouraging that there has been a global response to the tragedy, which may help prevent such an event recurring. Certainly, better oversight by retailers will go some way towards this; however, the Bangladeshi Government, factory owners, workers and trade unions are all important stakeholders in rectifying the long-term problems. It will be interesting to see what benefits the Accord and Alliance bring to the working conditions of these workers.

## Questions:

1. Which theory (social contract theory or integrated social contract theory) have the retailers applied in their response to the Bangladesh factory disasters?

2. Who are the stakeholders and what ethical issues are involved?

3. Which level of CSR are the garment retail industry working from? What factors give you this impression?

4. From a sustainability perspective, what are the benefits to the Bangladesh factory owners of receiving support to upgrade their factories? What factors complicate this perspective?

See web material for:
- answers to short answer questions
- additional student cases
- tutor resources (tutor password required)
- additional material including Ethics at the movies, Ethics in print, Ethics on video and Ethics on the web.

# PART 2

# Business Ethical Issues

# Chapter 3

## Ethics in information technology

'You have zero privacy (on the internet) anyway. Get over it.'
Scott McNealy, 1954–,
former CEO of Sun Microsystems, 2009

## Chapter aim

To identify current ethical issues, predominantly within the information technology (IT) and information systems (IS) domains.

## Chapter objectives

1. Recognise current and emerging ethical issues in IT.
2. Understand the ethical principles most relevant to IT.
3. Describe organisational, personal and societal ethical issues in IT.
4. Conduct further exploration into key issues of interest.
5. Analyse contrasting positions that underpin ethical issues in, for example, the freedom of information.
6. Formulate views in relation to current ethical issues that may affect you personally.
7. Review the common content of current Codes of Conduct for IT professionals.

# Ethics in the media: Hacking

Facebook's shares are soaring, but are shareholders concerned about Mark Zuckerberg's ethics? At the age of 19, he hacked a website to ascertain what was being written about him, and called social network members 'dumb f**ks' for sharing private information (Hastings 2012).

## Introduction

Our interactions with technology are contradictory. We are often excited about new technologies and what they can do for us. Having a phone with the ability to communicate, photograph, store data and search the web is liberating but often, once new technologies have been developed and adopted, ethical issues in regard to their use are raised and need to be deliberated. Once an ethical issue in relation to IT has been raised and starts to firm up, legislation may begin to wrap itself around the issue and parameters for control or protection are introduced. However, given the speed at which technology is developed, the extent of the consideration needed to be given to these issues and the slowness with which legislation is introduced, unresolved ethical issues abound.

Advances in technology are providing us with huge benefits and the tools to tackle some of our more significant societal problems. For example, in California, participants in the Personal Environmental Impact Report (PEIR) program willingly allow, via their mobile devices, a continuous location trace. The ongoing personal monitoring of a participant every few seconds, allows the system to determine their location and, subsequently, infer their most likely mode of locomotion, whether it be by foot, car, or bus. The participant's travel profile is then correlated with Southern California air quality and weather data, allowing PEIR to estimate the participant's carbon footprint, as well as their exposure to air pollution. The accuracy of the data gives an unprecedented look into the environmental harm people create and also suffer (Pimple 2011).

However, with the benefits also come risks and, in this situation alone, some may be understandably concerned about how continuous monitoring could be used in a negative context. Taking searches to a new level, researchers at the University of Glasgow are developing a new kind of web search for more complex enquiries in relation to location-specific individuals, or advanced location queries, such as, 'What is the traffic like on the Monash Freeway near Burke Road?' Even more scarily, 'Where is my girlfriend?' This request could be answered by using social network accounts, cross-referencing findings and facial recognition software. Interestingly, people readily agree to social networking terms and conditions, yet these same provisions are not available for public security and surveillance situations (Maiolo 2012).

Technology's capabilities and, more importantly, the application of technology, are increasing exponentially and, while largely providing positive outcomes, there is also disquiet in regard to the abuses and unintended consequences of some technological developments. The ethical problems that arise range from outright fraud and censorship of the internet, through to invasion of **privacy**, and extend to the chilling consequences when technology goes awry, for example, the malfunctioning of expert systems such as medical equipment.

These issues will not dissipate as we are increasingly enamoured with technology. The downside is that we are now more exposed not only to our dependence on functioning technology but also to the abuse of the huge amount of personal and business-related data now swirling in cyberspace that can be relatively easily caught in electronic nets for alternative illegitimate purposes. It has been observed that as technology usage increases we are encountering tools that are beneficial to the general public but, in the wrong hands or inappropriately used, can create great controversy, breaching our basic right to privacy, respect and free will (Danish, Muhammad & Ali 2011). Twitter can be used for inane social purposes, such as psyching out Olympic athletes, but, more recently, political movements such as the Arab Spring and Occupy Wall Street have come about through the use of social media platforms (Campbell 2012).

A further complication is the speed at which ethical dilemmas arise with technological changes. The recency of developments leaves us struggling to deal with emerging scenarios to which we have had little prior exposure, whether they are in relation to cyberterrorism, inappropriate use of computing resources, or sharing of information. Novel computing applications create policy 'holes' from which ethical issues arise (Moor 1985). The holes, or ethical vacuums, also occur in other fields as a result of technology advancements. Art Caplan, as Head of the Bioethics Centre at the University of Pennsylvania, illustrated this when he said his mother taught him all he needed to know as a child, but she never taught him about foetal transplants (Donaldson 2001). Alternatively, it has been suggested that new developments in technology and, specifically, IT, do not actually produce new ethical issues at all. Instead, innovations simply force people to look at old ethical issues in new ways (Goree 2007).

**privacy** – the security of personal data and the erosion of anonymity which can come in two forms; the first is through the sharing of sensitive information, and the second is through tracking technologies.

"Guide us, oh Webmaster."
© shutterstock.com/Cartoonresource

# Ethics in the media: Cyber-security

On 23 April 2013, an Associated Press Twitter account was hacked. A fake tweet announced that the White House had experienced an explosion with Barack Obama being injured.

This tweet resulted in a temporary stock market crash where US$130 million was wiped off the stock market index Standard & Poor's 500 ('#newscrashrecover' 2013).

## Defining ethics and technology

**information systems** (IS) – Interrelated hardware, software, infrastructure on personnel in support of organisational processes.

Before we embark on a discussion of ethical issues in relation to IT and **information systems** domains, it is appropriate to mention here that the lexicon is full of related terms which are all used for describing the increasing importance of computerised information and communication technologies, terms such as: digital era, information society, knowledge, network, virtual world, and cyber-society. For Gorniak-Kocikowska (2007), the abundance of terms reflects the confusion we are currently experiencing. The general term, information communication technology, or ICT, is said to be slippery as, literally, ICT would refer only to technologies that detect signals, and transmit, store, process and present them (McDonald 2012). The more commonly used term **information technology** (IT) refers to both ICT as well as data (text, sound and images) (Quinn 2012).

**information technology** (IT) – devices used in the creation, storage, manipulation, exchange and dissemination of data, including text, sound and images.

The numerous ethical issues propagated by the technology age have also been described by terms such as computer ethics, internet ethics, cyber-ethics and information ethics. While it is permissible for a technology novice to treat these terms as synonymous, there are subtle distinctions between them. Tavani (2007) has assisted with differentiating the terminology by proposing the term computer ethics to connote ethical issues associated with computing machines and their users. **Computer ethics** might, therefore, suggest a field of study that is concerned exclusively with the ethical issues involving computer use as they relate to computer professionals. Computer ethics is the set of moral principles that regulate the use of computers (Christensson 2013). Computer ethics also refers to ethical problems exacerbated, transformed or created by computer technology and, by inference, the internet. Moor (1985) indicates computer ethics analysis is the interplay of **social impact** and nature and the ensuing formulation of policies for the ethical use of technology. Gotterbarn (1990) has intimated that the term 'computer ethics' should be restricted to the ethics of the profession and should not seek to cover all unethical acts committed using technology. This view, however, is probably too restrictive if we are to fully consider a range of ethical issues in IT.

**computer ethics** – moral principles that regulate the use of computers.

**social impact** – the negative impact on society of IT, for example, using computers as a means of blackmail, allowing children to watch or play violent games.

Specifically, ethical issues restricted to the use of the internet are referred to as **internet ethics**. Tavani (2007) has indicated a preference for the term **cyber-ethics** which he believes is a closer description than computer or internet ethics, and more appropriate and comprehensive given that the ethical issues are broader than those relating specifically to internet and computer usage. The challenge for cyber-ethics is to discuss principles of morality that can guide human action so that people are empowered to establish a sustainable, participatory global information society. Cyber-ethics is, therefore, about meta-norms that moderate behaviour within cyberspace (Spinello 2003). The overarching term, however, that is commonly used to embrace ethics in relation to all activities associated with information usage (creation, storage, manipulation, exchange and dissemination) is **information ethics**. Information ethics is a convergence between the internet, the media, libraries, information science, management information systems, business, and computer ethics (Froehlich 2004).

So, what are the broader ethical issues beyond the use of the internet and computers? Ethical issues in IT include a wide array of activities encompassing inappropriate use of computing resources, inappropriate sharing of information, and even extend to cyberterrorism. Ethical issues in IT exist in relation to the more obvious areas of computer crime, **intellectual property** (IP), professional ethics, and health and wellbeing; as well as the traditional areas of privacy, software piracy, network security and freedom of expression, and the newer areas of security risks of cloud computing, green computing, social networking, and the digital divide.

# Ethical principles in IT

Pierce and Henry (1996) observe that ethical decisions related to technology and computer use are subject to three influences: the individual's own personal code; any informal code that exists in the workplace; and exposure to formal codes of ethics. The interplay of these influences is investigated in Peterson's study (2002b) which indicates that individuals with strong universal moral rules displayed high ethical intentions regardless of their organisation's guidelines around computers. In contrast, individuals with lower universal moral rules, but strong company guidelines, were likely to exhibit positive ethical intention outcomes.

The key ethical principles that are of most relevance to those involved with IT are in relation to:

- **honesty and accurate representation** – for example, the number of circumstances where deception could occur in the accuracy of web content and plagiarism
- **respect for privacy** – for example, ensuring confidentiality and security of databases that hold information on company personnel or customers; privacy can, however, be eroded through such practices as installing keyboard readers, embedded links, the generation of lists for spamming, cyberbullying and identity theft
- **respect for IP rights** – for example, in regard to the issue of cybersquatting and internet domain name control, and the use of unlicensed software
- **avoiding harm** – for example, which could occur as a result of computer hacking, viruses, worms, denial of service attacks, excess computer usage, violence in games, **internet addiction** and the potential for personal harm through interaction with social sites
- **respect for the environment** – for example, as commonly mentioned in relation to green computing.

**internet ethics** – ethical issues restricted to the domain of the internet.

**cyber-ethics** – ethical issues in cyberspace. The term cyber-ethics is deemed to be more appropriate and comprehensive given that the ethical issues are broader than those relating specifically to the internet and computer usage.

**information ethics** – the ethics in relation to all activities (creation, storage, manipulation, exchange and dissemination) associated with information usage.

**intellectual property** – property that has legal ownership attached to it. Abuses of IP rights are, for example, using unlicensed software, plagiarising from the internet, copying licensed software.

## Ethics on reflection: Ethical IT issues

Which ethical IT issue currently worries you the most, and why?

## Ethics in the media: Cyber-security

The IT security company NCC Group report that in the first quarter of 2012, the UK accounted for 2.4% of hacking attempts, and reports cyber-attacks are at record levels on the cyber-crime league table ('UK – the world leader in cyber-crime' 2012).

**internet addiction** – heavy users of the internet exhibit harmful outcomes and impulse control difficulties, problems particularly associated with adult entertainment, playing games and chatting on the internet.

**cyber-security** – technologies, processes and practices to protect networks, computers, programs and data from damage through unauthorised access.

# Organisational ethical issues in IT

## Cyber-security

The body of technologies, processes and practices designed to protect networks, computers, programs and data from attack, damage or unauthorised access is referred to as **cyber-security** (Rouse 2010). The elevated rates of serious violations of IT security and data protection are currently sitting as the primary ethical concerns for most organisations (Perry 2012) and with the adoption of **cloud computing**, where a third party is introduced, data security is further complicated (Karena 2012). In 2011, the Australian mining companies Rio Tinto and BHP Billiton were the targets of cyber espionage, thought to have originated in China (Smith 2012a), and Shell Australia and the Australian resource company Woodside have noted attacks from China, Eastern Europe and Russia (Kerr 2012).

It is one thing when a computer hacker infiltrates an organisational system, but it is truly another when hackers target key areas with the intention of adversely affecting a wider population or destabilising a country.

- In 2012, Saudi Arabian hackers attacked Israel's stock exchange and national airline. In response, Israeli hackers disrupted Abu Dhabi's stock exchange and attacked two bank websites (Smith 2012a). The Australian Securities Exchange (ASX) has in recent years detected an increase in malicious cyber-activity, resulting in cyber-security being one of ASX's top priorities.

- In 2007, in Queensland, Australia, a computer hacker released raw sewerage from a government sewerage plant into public waterways (Schenker 2003).
- Allegedly, hackers left infected USB drives in the parking lot of the Pentagon in the US. Employees purportedly used the flash drives and, in doing so, allowed the hackers access to confidential information (Kerr 2012).

**cloud computing** – third-party computing resources that can be scaled up and down as needs change.

A hacker (© shutterstock.com/IkazNarsis)

Cyber-assaults, such as those described above, provide an indication of just how vulnerable the internet, corporations and government are to attack. With automated tools little computer knowledge is required to spread havoc, increasing the possible pool of vandals (Schenker 2003). Attacks can be costly; for example, in 2011 Sony experienced personal and confidential data losses for more than 77 million of their customers (Perry 2012).

# Ethics in the media: Hackers

Amid fears of cyberterrorism, hackers are increasingly being treated with trepidation. Kevin Nitnick was arrested in 1995 on hacking related charges, and detained as a pre-trial detainee for four years before going to trial (Best 2006).

Chess, Palmer and White (2003) observe that most systems routinely use tools such as firewalls, passwords and access control to prevent intrusion of external parties. However, such preventive measures are no longer enough, as it is now difficult to deploy a fully secure system because of inevitable design and implementation flaws. As a consequence, malicious software, or **malware** as it is often called, supports a multi-billion dollar

**malware** – unwanted or malicious software installed on a computer. It usually comes through an email that contains suspect links or attachments.

industry, with two sides to the coin; those who steal information and subvert computers on one side, versus those who devise, sell or test digital protection ('Computer viruses: a thing of threads and patches' 2012).

# Ethics in the media: Cyber-weapons

The American and Israeli governments worked together to develop Stuxnet software, a cyber-weapon which was used against Iran to disrupt centrifuge operations at a nuclear site (see 'Cyber warfare seek and hide' 2012).

## Hacking

**hackers** – those who break into network systems for various reasons; can be criminal, ethical, a learning exercise etc.

**ethical hackers (white hats)** – consultants used to test the security and penetrability of the IT systems of companies.

Public opinion about hacking, which originated in the 1950s, has changed significantly. **Hackers**, once considered the heroes of the computer revolution and troublemakers (Levy 1984), are now presumed to be delinquents and criminals, capable of destabilising crucial networks economically and socially. Conversely, a hacker's intentions may be tamer, aiming to expose security issues and improve their own hacking skills (Best 2006). Even more benign are **ethical hackers** (also known as **white hats**). Ethical hackers are highly paid professionals with a legitimate status and access to systems. They are employed to deliberately hack into systems to clearly identify flaws. In doing so, they are able to minimise the risk of an actual malicious hacking attack by understanding the current weaknesses of the system and the likely impact from an attack. Ethical hackers, essentially, explore vulnerabilities beforehand to minimise risk (Danish, Muhammad & Ali 2011).

Hacking can be both a criminal and an ethical issue; criminal in that there are penalties attached to hacking, and ethical in that the outcomes of hacking can have considerable ethical implications, given the harm that they cause. The views on hackers are as mixed as are the motivations that propel them to hack into systems. The motives of those who perpetrate computer crime can range considerably, from a demonstration of their programming skills, the desire for financial gain, the intention to cause organisational or social harm, to promotion of a particular ideology or the gaining of competitor information. Unfortunately, some skilled hackers share their expertise through networks such as Usenet and FidoNet. They use their abilities to harm society by finding vulnerabilities in companies' systems and attacking them, usually by creating and distributing virus-containing codes. Others consider that their motives are purely positive; the hackers merely wish to highlight flaws in existing systems and indicate that hacking is wrong for any gain, financial or personal. Meanwhile, there are anarchist hackers who wish to ensure free access to IT (Best 2006).

# Ethics in the media: Cyber-attacks

In 2012, following an internationally coordinated effort, the US Federal Bureau of Investigation (FBI) charged six hackers from various countries, allegedly involved with the computer hacker group Lulz Security (LulzSec), who claimed to have taken the website of the Central Bureau of Intelligence offline through cyber-attacks (see 'The world this week' 2012).

Although hacking is painted as destructive and antisocial in the eyes of the mainstream media, some hackers seek to reclaim it and its meaning as a harmless, if not socially beneficial, activity. So, we have the doves and the hawks, so to speak, with the distinction inspired by their commitment to the **hacker's ethic**, the code by which 'ethical' hackers abide.

**hacker's ethic** – the code by which 'ethical' hackers abide.

# Types of hacker

**Crackers** – individuals who access networks illegally, possibly just because they can.

**Hacker gangs** – groups that hack into each other, and into websites and companies.

**Hacktivists** – hackers who are motivated by a social or political cause.

**Criminal hackers (black hats)** – those motivated to hack with the goal of obtaining money or doing harm.

**Cyberterrorist hackers** – violent extremists who are using hacking as a terrorist tool.

**Nation state hackers** – are employed by national security agencies in order to defend national interests or infiltrate other governments' networks.

# Ethics in practice: The hacker's ethic

Undertake an internet search and outline the key tenets of the 'hacker's ethic'.

**Question:**

1. What are the normative ethical principles upon which the hacker's ethic rests? (You may want to look at Levy 1984.)

# Ethics on reflection: Hackers and privacy

NDS Group, a pay TV software company, have denied they paid hackers to search competitor systems for improper reasons, and claim they were making a point about privacy (see 'News Corporation' 2012).

**Question:**
**1.** What are your thoughts on the action by NDS?

# Ethics in the media: Hacking

In 2012, one of the most infamous hacking groups, called 'Anonymous', took down the Vatican's website. The group's leader alleges the purpose was to expose the 'corrupt' Catholic Church (see 'Vatican website attacked' 2012).

# Ethics in the media: Hackers and privacy

Some hackers, such as Dr Chris Soghoian, are 'activist technology researchers'. They set out to expose corporate online security flaws to demonstrate how corporations like Facebook and Google can compromise and violate privacy ('A knight in digital armour' 2012).

**viruses** – programs that make copies of themselves on as many computers as possible, often with a specific malicious intent such as deleting files or sending information off-site.

## Malware

In 1999, a Taiwanese student developed *Chernobyl*, a virus which corrupted and deleted data from some 700 000 computers (Spinello 2000). Further investigation of ethical issues such as the *Chernobyl* virus requires us to go a little deeper into the likely tools used. The more general term used to describe these tools is malware – where entrance is usually gained through infected emails or links, which then proceed to install malicious programs on the target's computer and result in a malware infection (Pryor 2012). Malware comes in many different forms and all usually do harm in a variety of ways that commonly corrupt or delete data or deface a website. It is, therefore, worth examining the types of malware:

- **Viruses** – programs that make copies of themselves on as many computers as possible, usually with a specific malicious intent such as deleting files or sending information off-site (State Services Commission 2000). Viruses are usually sent via email attachments and activated when the attachment is opened, or via shared media such as USB drives. They are small pieces of code attached to a legitimate program and a responsible signifi-cant system and file destruction (Janssen n.d.). Viruses are not just the domain of rogue hackers, governments have also been implicated.

- **Spyware** – any technology that aids in gathering information about a person or organisa-tion without their knowledge (Rouse 2011). Spyware is relatively easy to install; the recipi-ent is tricked into downloading spyware when the software is hidden inside a benign exte-rior, for example, an email promising photos of the latest celebrity, or is sent wrapped in an e-greeting card, and programmed to install itself when the card is opened (Cohen 2001).

- **Adware** – a type of spyware, and a code that tracks a user's personal information and passes it on to third parties without the user's authorisation or knowledge (Rouse 2011).

- **Trojan horse** – an infectious code within an imbedded program. A Trojan is often dis-guised as something entertaining, such as an email, but is a program that also steals pass-words (State Services Commission 2000). A variation is a **logic bomb** where the imbed-ded program is activated by a specific action or event (Quinn 2012).

- **Internet worm** – malicious software that replicates and distributes copies of itself through the internet by exploiting vulnerabilities that can be found in legitimate software. Unlike Trojans or other viruses that require user intervention, worms can replicate on their own (Janssen 2012a). On 25 January 2003 at 5.30 a.m., an internet worm called Slammer attacked, corrupting credit card networks, automatic teller machines and telephone traf-fic worldwide, and took five days to contain (Schenker 2003).

- **Denial of service (DoS)** – a mode of attack in which a target, which can be either a per-sonal, business or government site, is overwhelmed by a large volume of requests it can-not meet, thus crashing the website (State Services Commission 2000).

- **Distributed denial of service attack (DDoS)** – is where a site is swamped with requests that result in the dominant activity becoming automated responses, leaving legitimate users unable to access the site and the site collapses (Quinn 2012). The distinction between DDoS and DoS is in the impact and connectivity. With DDoS, more attacks are made and more computers are involved. In February 2007, Yahoo, Amazon, ebay, Buy.com and CNN were all hit with DDoS attacks (Best 2006). Hackers can extort money to restore normal service. DDoS is possibly one of the more worrying types of attacks on the internet; eliminating the threat requires considerable cooperation among different internet service providers globally, while the attack is underway. **Computer Emergency Response Team (CERT)** is an organisation which monitors IP security problems and assists with recovery from attacks. The original CERT is based in Carnegie, US, but now has a number of bases worldwide (State Services Commission 2000).

---

**spyware** – technology that aids in gathering information about a person or organisation without their knowledge.

**adware** – a code that tracks a user's personal information and passes it on to third parties without the user's authorisation or knowledge.

**Trojan horse** – an infectious code within an imbedded program.

**logic bomb** – a variation of the Trojan horse virus, which activates an embedded program triggered by a specific action or event.

**internet worm** – malicious software that replicates and distributes copies of itself through the internet by exploiting vulnerabilities that can be found in legitimate software. Unlike Trojans or other viruses that require user intervention, worms can replicate on their own.

**denial of service (DoS)** – a mode of attack in which a target, which could be personal but commonly are business and government sites, is overwhelmed by a large volume of requests it cannot meet, leaving it effectively unavailable.

- **Rootkit** – this software is a hidden file that, when opened, enables administrative level (backdoor) access to a computer or network. **Key logger** software may also be used to steal sensitive data (Janssen 2012b).
- **Botnets** (also known as **zombies**) – currently considered the greatest threat to the internet, as once bots have infected a computer, they allow the attacker to take control of the affected computer (Merritt 2013) and can forward transmissions, spam and other viruses to other computers (Rouse 2012) without the owner's knowledge. A group of infected machines are known as a 'botnet zombie army' (Merritt 2013).

**distributed denial of service attack (DDoS)** – where a site is swamped with requests that result in the dominant activity being automated responses, leaving legitimate users unable to access the site.

# Ethics in the media: Malware

As malware's sophistication increases, so does the damage they can cause. Frankenstein, a self-camouflaging malware virus, scans Microsoft Windows operating systems for 'gadgets' (chunks of code) and then through algorithms proceeds to infect new machines ('Computer viruses: a thing of threads and patches' 2012).

**Computer Emergency Response Team (CERT)** – an organisation which monitors IP security problems and assists with recovery from attacks.

**rootkit** – software that is a hidden file that, when opened, enables administrative level (backdoor) access to a computer or network.

# Ethics in practice: Malware

In 1999, the Melissa virus plagued email servers. It used Microsoft Outlook and, through the use of a macro, forwarded the virus to the first 50 people from the address book. Although it did not destroy data, it did produce volumes of emails that debilitated email services (Spinello 2000).

**Questions:**
1. To demonstrate the fragility of the internet, search the media and internet for any current examples of computer viruses or worms.
2. What was the name of the virus or worm you identify? How did it operate, and what was its impact?

**key logger** – software used to steal sensitive data.

**botnet** (also known as a **zombie**) – a computer bot that has infected a computer and allows the attacker to take control of the affected computer.

## Violation of IP

Intellectual property (IP) has been described as a tool for economic growth because attaching property rights to knowledge-based goods and services is seen as a means for economic growth (Kuppuswany 2009). Historically, IP protection is based on the **labour theory of property**. This theory traces its origins to the 17th-century philosopher, John Locke, who argued that when a person mixes his or her labour with land, that person is entitled to the fruits of his or her labour. So, if a person tends and plants crops on a section that is not already owned by another, that person has a right to claim ownership of the crops (Tavani 2007). Critics of the labour theory argue that a rationale for granting property rights should not be confused with an individual's labour, that is, you do not necessarily have to toil to own something. **Rights of ownership**, or **property rights**, are better understood as conventions instituted by the state (Tavani 2007), with the protection of innovation, providing the motive for more innovations.

A difficulty with IP protection is in relation to IT and the need to be current. For example, Chinese copyright law was written in 1991 and is now outdated, making it difficult for infringements to be enforced (Sujuan 2012). A further complication is that while IP within one jurisdiction is easily contemplated, extending it on an international scale is clearly a more complex matter. Managing this complexity is the focus of the World Intellectual Property Organization (WIPO). In addition, the World Trade Organization (WTO) has responsibility for promoting the protection of IP rights. IP protection has a number of ethical domains, including trademark infringement, product piracy or the access and use of competitor information. In this instance, however, we are restricting the discussion to IT, which has other more critical areas of concern:

- **Copyright infringement** – where a company inadvertently or deliberately uses property, such as code that has been developed by another organisation. For example, Google was found to be guilty of infringing IP by copying nine lines of code and the Android Operating System from Java software. Fair use infringement was not clear to jurors, hence Oracle's damages were limited to US$150 000, far below the US$1 billion it hoped to claim ('Not very evil' 2012). Copyright, of course, extends beyond software and relates to all protected material where it is internet-based, such as music, where song writers are protected, although not always. Apple has a global, uniform, profit-sharing system to protect copyright holders. However, in China, content providers are less disciplined and often upload without notifying or paying copyright holders (Sujuan 2012). The move to cloud computing will strengthen international copyright protection, although Canada, Britain, Ireland and Australia are limiting copyright damages for non-commercial breaches ('Copyright and the internet' 2012). While, conversely, the provision of web content free of intellectual copyright protection, without having to pay or ask, is gathering momentum with creative commons.
- **Reverse engineering** – where software re-uses existing code that has been developed and protected in another program (Reynolds 2012). This problem is alleviated by the use of open-source software.
- **Internet piracy** – where copyrighted material is illegally reproduced and distributed on the internet ('internet piracy' n.d.). According to the lobby group, the Australian Content Industries Group (ACIG), there are 20 illegal downloads for every one song bought legally on iTunes (Bleby 2012), with Australians being the worst culprits (measured per head of population) (Zuel 2012).
- **Domain name usage** – in 2011, there were 22 suffixes in use, the most common being the .com suffix. However, in 2012 the Internet Corporation for Assigned Names and Numbers (ICANN) allowed applications for new suffixes. This naturally will create difficulties with protecting existing IP. For example, 'Disney' may be assigned to Disney

**labour theory of property** – the theory that when a person mixes his or her labour with land, that person is entitled to the fruit of his or her labour. So, if a person tends and plants crops on land that is not already owned, that person has a right to claim ownership of them.

**rights of ownership** or **property rights** – artificial rights or conventions devised by the state to achieve certain practical ends.

**copyright infringement** – use of the copyrighted material of another.

**reverse engineering** – where a software developer uses the code of the current database programming language to recover the design of the information system application.

**internet piracy** – illegally reproducing and distributing copyrighted material on the web.

**domain name usage** – the registration of a domain name with the Internet Corporation for Assigned Names and Numbers (ICANN), which is responsible for the assignment of internet addresses in cyberspace.

**cybersquatting** – registering domain names of other people and then selling them with the intent to profit from a trademark which belongs to someone else.

**cyber-pirates** – internet users who access unauthorised sites and services.

**use of hyperlinks** – established by web designers to link related material, enabling the user to hop from one page to another.

**data mining** – the indirect gathering of personal information through an analysis of implicit patterns discoverable in data.

**computer matching** – combining information from several databases to look for patterns; the purpose is to identify fraud or criminal activity.

**expert systems** (also known as **autonomous systems**) – systems (often machines) that have been designed to replicate the decision-making process that would normally be undertaken by humans.

Corporation, but what about 'Disneyexperience'? ICANN indicates there are 751 applications for 230 domain names, which will undoubtedly lead to disputes (Battersby 2012). The sheer volume of requests to be processed could result in time delays of up to three years, giving rivals an unfair advantage.

- **Cybersquatting** – cybersquatting is using goodwill created by another trademark to register traffic or use a domain name for profit (Rouse 2009). Before most businesses fully understood the value of the internet, **cyber-pirates** bought famous domain names with the express intention of selling them to the companies when the companies realised their true value (Maury & Kleiner 2002). One notable cybersquatter was Dennis Toeppen, who registered almost 250 domain names, such as eddiebauer.com and deltaairlines.com, anticipating that the original owners would one day wish to register their own domain names.

- Unauthorised **use of hyperlinks** – hyperlinks are frequently established by web designers to link related material, essentially enabling the user to hop from one page to another. Organisations have objected to the use of hyperlinks without permission, as the hyperlink facilitates the transition to a page not nominated by the site owner. In doing so, the internet user has not entered the site as they would normally, via the front page, and, as a consequence, has not been exposed to the banner advertising on the site that has been paid for. Thus, the web links have avoided and circumvented exposure to the paid advertising.

- **Data mining** – data mining involves gathering personal data through analysing implicit patterns in data (Tavani 2007). The issues around data mining relate to the challenges of secondary uses of information, that is, where information is being used for a second time and not as it was originally intended, nor with the permission of the provider (Quinn 2012).

- **Computer matching** – searching for patterns using data from several databases (Shrader-Frechette & Westra 1997). Usually the purpose is to identify fraud or criminal activity, therefore, computer matching is where data have been mined then matched with data from quite separate databases. For example, the listing of individual taxpayers from the tax department's database of those who have paid tax below a certain level is matched to motor vehicle registrations for luxury cars in order to identify people for tax audits. The databases can be quite separate. For example, in 2000, the internet advertising agency, Double Click, was one of a number of organisations criticised for matching up its cookies with data from an online marketing company that had names, addresses and phone numbers of 88 million Americans, thus enabling the company to create personal profiles of individuals and their web usage habits. Recently, data matching has extended from government use to private institutions, such as banks (Shrader-Frechette & Westra 1997).

- **Expert systems** (sometimes called **autonomous systems**) – are systems (often machines) that have been designed to replicate the decision-making process that would normally be used by humans, but the process is instructed through codified computer software that embodies expert knowledge to generate best outcomes (Forester & Morrison 1990). It can, however, result in harm. A devastating example of an expert systems computer failure is the much-publicised Therac-25. The computerised radiation therapy machine was directly related to six known incidents involving massive radiation overdoses that resulted in deaths and serious injuries. The occurrences, between June 1985 and January 1987, have been described as the worst series of radiation accidents in the 35-year history of medical accelerators using autonomous systems (machines that make choices without human intervention). The difficulty arises, therefore, in assigning responsibility to a system or a robot when things go wrong – is it the system or robot, or those who designed it to blame? The temptation to shift blame is inevitable. Therefore, specific statements about moral responsibility are necessary even when there are circumstances of complicated causality (Pimple 2011). Apportioning blame or responsibility is not just about liability for the issue but can also be a motivator for future harm-minimisation.

## Ethics in practice: Autonomous systems

Look up the paper by Leveson and Turner (1993), entitled 'An investigation of the Therac-25 accidents'. The paper makes disturbing reading but provides an extensive summary, including timelines, associated with the computer-related incident of the Therac-25. This excellent paper explores the issues regarding the ethical issues associated with expert systems.

**Questions:**
1. How many people died?
2. What practices should have been in place?

## Ethics in practice: Autonomous systems

With their increased use and 'intelligence', machines will be making life and death decisions, giving machines moral agency ('Morals and the machine' 2012). This situation becomes problematic when trying to apportion liability. In a hypothetical case, a doctor uses a machine codified with expert knowledge, however, there is a programming error, and as a result, a patient dies (Forester & Morrison 1990).

**Question:**
1. With whom do you think the liability rests – the doctor, the programmer, or someone else?

## Ethics in the media: Peer-to-peer file sharing

In 2011, the Recording Industry Association of America (RIAA) made a claim against LimeWire, a peer-to-peer file-sharing service company, seeking compensation of US$150 000 per illegal download of copyrighted songs. A judge ruled the amount claimed was excessive. They ultimately settled the case for US$105 million (Bleby 2012).

## Personal ethical issues in IT

Having looked at organisation-related issues in IT, it is appropriate to turn our attention to the critical ethical issues that affect individuals.

### Privacy

Privacy is concerned with the security of personal data and the erosion of anonymity. Privacy concerns include identity theft, company and public surveillance, as well as issues regarding the security of personal information, consumer data and profiling (Reynolds 2012). Erosion of privacy takes two forms: (1) personal invasions that share sensitive information; and (2) tracking technologies, such as cookies, web beacon, web bugs (Sar, Al-Saggaf & Zia 2012), and everyware.

**cookies** – embedded code used to monitor a consumer's online activity.

Today there is a multi-million dollar industry around the use of biometric identification technologies (often called biometrics). These technologies include fingerprint scanning, facial recognition, and iris scanning and aim to protect individuals against illegal activities (van der Ploeg 2012). In addition, there are subtle data-collection systems embedded in our everyday IT usage, such as **cookies**, which monitor a consumer's online activity, **beacons** and **web bugs**, which are software that allow webpage tracking of mouse movement (Reynolds 2012), and typing (Sar, Al-Saggaf & Zia 2012).

**beacons** and **web bugs** – small pieces of software that run on a webpage and are able to track what a viewer is doing.

**Ambient intelligence** and **everyware** are commonly used terms for the increasing presence in our everyday lives of information and communication technologies that are too small to notice. They are so well-integrated into appliances, automobiles, or aspects of services that they are invisible to users, so we use them willingly (Pimple 2011). Almost the stuff of spy movies, data capture is becoming increasingly more sophisticated. For example, a security firm has developed a small listening device which, when activated by a SIM card, enables the receiver to listen in from a mobile device for up to four hours, longer if plugged into a computer. This would be long enough to listen in, for example, to a takeover strategy meeting (Kerr 2012) and gain competitor information.

**ambient intelligence** (also known as **everyware**) – the increasing presence in our everyday lives of information and communication technologies that are too small to notice.

Further erosion of privacy occurs with active engagement on social network sites and online purchasing, where vast amounts of personal data are available. As a consequence, an astute person ably assisted by appropriate software, can very quickly unearth information about you for their financial gain or to your personal detriment.

# Ethics in practice: Ambient intelligence

Your social network have updated their privacy conditions and, without any action on your part, can now use your name and pictures in any of their advertisements.

**Question:**
**1.** How does it make you feel?

Social network sites were launched in 1997 but did not gain mass popularity until the advent of Facebook and LinkedIn (Sar, Al-Saggaf & Zia 2012). In an ever-shrinking world, Facebook analysed its 721 million users and found that there are actually 4.7 degrees of separation via their SNS ('Six degrees of mobilisation' 2012).

# Ethics in practice: Privacy

We are starting to see an increasing encroachment of business into all aspects of people's lives as well as exploitation of the amounts of data being collected, analysed and shared. In 2012, there were 1.6 billion online users, however, the number is anticipated to grow to 3 billion users by 2016 ('The value of friendship' 2012). Along with the growth there are concerns about privacy. In 2011, the US Federal Trade Commission (FTC) received complaints that

Facebook was making data available about its users. As a result of the investigation, Facebook was forced to agree to two-yearly external audits of its privacy policies and practices.

**Questions:**
**1.** In your view, is the exploitation of data ever ethical? Explain your reasons.
**2.** Under what conditions might exploiting data be ethical?

Facebook's biggest threat is the increasing introduction of legislature designed to protect citizens from having their personal information exploited by companies ('The value of friendship' 2012). But what about other people accessing this information? Lallo (2012) claims that too often people do not realise the dangers associated with Facebook or Twitter. Too many personal details are divulged including addresses and holiday plans or the uploading of photos from smartphones that have **geotag** locators (which give the location the photo was taken). This information can, potentially, be used by burglars and stalkers.

**geotag** – the ability to automatically locate the precise latitude and longitude where a photo has been taken.

# Ethics on reflection: Metadata

Think about the approach of social network sites to its users' personal data.

**Question:**

1. What are your views about whether it is right to have a business model based on selling personal data without the full knowledge of consumers?

Dimensions of privacy encompass: what is required to maintain privacy (the right not to be intruded upon); the right to privacy (the right to be left alone, whether we choose to or not); the loss of privacy (we have privacy only if we have control over the circumstances, such as information about ourselves); and the violation of privacy (where there is deliberate invasion of our privacy) (Tavani 2000).

# Ethics in the media: Privacy

Worldwide condemnation has been expressed regarding the deliberate invasion of privacy of more than 800 phone-hacking victims by *The News of the World*, including celebrities in London ('Email destruction policy revealed in hacking case' 2012).

Although British laws are not stringent, they provide some protection to family and private life through Article 8 of the European Convention of Human Rights ('Press regulation' 2012).

# Ethics on reflection: Privacy

Concerned about the potential for abuse in their homes, some working parents have installed nanny cams, which secretly video babysitters.

**Question:**

1. What are the ethical issues surrounding the use of such a device?

Parrish (2010) has recognised that social networking sites and technology have affected how people live their lives, causing new ethical dilemmas. The changes require us to reconsider existing social contracts, and to use the following four guiding principles when using social networking sites and sharing information: privacy (one needs to consider not only one's own privacy but also the privacy of others), accuracy (verification of information), property (care as to who owns the information and the inability to retract information that has been provided), and access (authentication of fellow users).

## Personal profiling

Although surfing the internet may seem innocuous, it equates to a loss of privacy. Stein (2001), a commentator on internet privacy, observed that he often looks at real estate websites when in a new city and, within 24 hours, Amazon would be recommending interior design books. As the saying goes, no app is free – you pay for them with your privacy.

By now, all users should be aware that when they log on they are subject to having their privacy invaded and their actions recorded. Companies such as Flurry Analytics are devoted to tracking the user data of approximately 1.4 million people using apps per day, and selling on to companies the resulting market segment data, including the demographic, geographic and interest data (Chadwick 2012). **Metadata** are the collective records of people's calls and emails which, when collated by software, extract a detailed analysis of a person and their habits ('Little peepers everywhere' 2012). The downside is that not only has there been an invasion of privacy without consent but, for example, a person with a great credit history could be denied a loan on the basis that they identify with a risk group or category discovered by data mining.

**metadata** – the records of people who call and email, amassed on a significant scale and then run through software in order to extract a detailed portrait of a person and their habits.

Personal profiling (© shutterstock.com/VLADGRIN)

# Ethics on reflection: Privacy

SpectorSoft, a spyware manufacturer, initially marketed their product to parents and employers, but sales soared when they began marketing to aggrieved romantic partners. Installing the spyware allows people to virtually watch someone's internet and chat room usage; in the process, screenshots are taken and recorded for review at a later date (Stein 2001).

**Question:**

1. What would you think if your ex-girlfriend/ex-boyfriend did this to you?

# Ethics on reflection: Privacy

Before issuing laptops, a Pennsylvania school district added tracking software to assist locating stolen laptops. The software also enabled laptop cameras to be remotely turned on. This proved useful when the thief was identified through the photos; however, an unintended consequence was that it became known that the district had captured 36 000 photographs from unaware students (Bowker & Knobel 2011).

**Questions:**

1. Was the school district justified in its use of tracking software?
2. What if you were one of the people covertly photographed at a time when you were doing something embarrassing?

# Ethics on reflection: Privacy

In the US, property records are increasingly being put online. The information includes the home value and a floor plan. Advocates say the initiative is a boon for open access to government records, but detractors have likened it to being a thief's handbook (Stein 2001).

**Question:**

1. What is your view? Have governments gone too far in making data available online?

## Personal security

With the inclusion of global positioning system (GPS) capabilities in personal devices, it is now possible to keep up to date with friend's locations on social networks, although some apps are designed to distort users' locations, for example 'Tall Tales' and 'Google Latitude' (Bowker & Knobel 2011). Data brokers believe the background information they provide to employers and creditors is ethically legitimate, but there are many which sell private information to any person willing to pay the fee, including identity thieves and stalkers (Stein 2001).

The ever-growing presence of social networking sites, although primarily used for sharing of information and opinions, also have the potential for the content to become offensive. More direct negative repercussions could also come in the form of cyberbullying via text messages, blogs or Facebook. Even more serious, and at the sinister end of the scale, is cyber-stalking, where the interaction is unwanted. For example, after a woman rejected the advances of a man, he took out personal ads posing as her, describing a home invasion fantasy and her home address. As a result, over a five-month period, six men appeared at her home. The man who posted the ad was the first person jailed for cyber-stalking (Stein 2001).

Personal security concerns are:

- **Flaming** – giving someone a verbal lashing in public usually via an electronic medium (Rouse 2005).
- **Sexting** – the sending of salacious texts or images via SMS. In 2012, the increase in sexting prompted the Victorian Parliament's Law Reform Committee to conduct an enquiry into sexting, which they described as the creating, sharing, sending or posting of sexually explicit messages or images via the internet, mobile phones or other electronic devices by people, especially young people. According to a US survey, in 2009, 20% of teens said that they have sent or posted nude or semi-nude pictures or videos of themselves (Kidder 2009).
- **Trolls** – people who hide behind the anonymity cyberspace provides and use open platforms to deliver vitriolic abuse (Short 2012). Public figures are particularly susceptible to trolls, and one Australian media personality, Charlotte Dawson, was urged to suicide in a tirade of abusive tweets (Short 2012). She died in 2014. Why are trolls an increasing presence and menace on the internet? It has been suggested it is based on what could be called the **theory of interaction**. This phenomenon is evocative of sociological research on small and large town interactions. In small towns, through repeated interactions, people have certain standards of behaviour; however, these are lowered in large towns, like New York, as there are fewer 'repeat plays', allowing people to be nastier (Donaldson 2001). Anonymity therefore escalates menacing behaviour.
- **Cyberbullying** – a cyberbully is someone who communicates electronically in a repeated, hostile way with the intention of causing emotional distress to another. **Outing**, that is, revealing someone else's secret online is a type of cyberbullying (Carter 2009).

Cyberbullying can, tragically, lead to people committing suicide (Lowe 2012a). Surprisingly, research indicates nearly 20% of young people engaged in cyberbullying have no empathy for their targets and would not change their behaviour (Brady 2012). To combat cyberbullying, governments are increasingly introducing laws, cyber-safety education is being made compulsory in some schools (Lowe 2012b) and software like ProtectaChild is being developed to track social media activity (Lowe 2012b).

- **Cyber-stalking** – an extension of physical stalking. Cyber-stalking uses electronic mediums to pursue, harass or contact another in an unsolicited fashion. A difference between cyberbullying and cyber-stalking is that in cyber-stalking often (but not always) the stalker is unknown to the person being stalked. There is also the more severe threat of physical harm.
- **Internet vigilantes** – people who actively crusade against an individual, groups or a cause. Technology can further advance vigilantism using techniques such as computer worms and viruses which can dig through files on your hard drive. For example, the virus VBS. NoPED.A@mm invades computers and searches for child pornography. If it finds picture files with suspect-sounding names, it notifies the police and emails some of the files to them, as well as sending copies of itself to the addresses in the victim's address book. Besides posing privacy concerns, one of the issues is that NoPED is not always right (Stein 2001).
- **Exploitation of children** – a study by Consumer Reports found that 5.6 million children under the age of 13 in the US were already using Facebook (although children under 13 years old are specifically excluded), with the major area of concern being that young

**flaming** – giving someone a verbal lashing in public, usually via an electronic medium.

**sexting** – sending of salacious texts or images via SMS.

**trolls** – people who hide behind anonymity and use the free publishing platforms to hurt their victims with hateful vitriol.

**theory of interaction** – anonymity that escalates menacing behaviour.

**cyberbullying** – a communication intended to coerce, intimidate, harass, or cause substantial emotional distress to another person using electronic means.

**outing** – revealing someone's secret online; also a form of cyberbullying.

**cyber-stalking** – using electronic mediums to pursue, harass or contact another in an unsolicited fashion.

**internet vigilantes** – people who actively crusade against an individual, groups or a cause.

**exploitation of children** – there is concern that children under 13 years of age lack the maturity to cope with social networks and other internet users.

children lack the maturity to cope with social networks. There is also the worry that network sites will find devious ways to make money from naïve children. As a consequence, there is concern as to how adequate protection can be given to children under 13 from other internet users. The Children's Online Privacy Protection Act (COPPA) in the US attempts to protect children under 13 who are using the internet ('Kid gloves' 2012).

Trolls and cyberbullying (© shutterstock.com/Nlshop)

**fraud** – gaining another person's assets, usually by deception, a common practice in business scams.

**social engineering** – posing as an insider or technician on the telephone to gather passwords or other sensitive information.

**phishing** – sending fraudulent emails that result in recipients being conned into providing personal information. If it is a text message on a phone, it is called **smishing**, and on voicemail it is **vishing**.

**password sniffing** – a technique for harvesting passwords that involves monitoring traffic on a network to pull out information.

# Fraud

**Fraud** (sometimes called cyber-crime) occurs in various forms such as credit card fraud, social security fraud, identity theft and IP theft. Fraud is the gaining of another person's assets, usually by deception, and is commonly practised in business scams.

A few notable examples of scams are:

- Some Bank of America customers were tricked into divulging financial details when they accidentally went to 'wwwbankofamerica.com' (domain name, minus the dot after www). However, the Bank of America managed to get the website taken down (Stein 2001).
- In 2012, Global Payments, a payment processor for both Visa and MasterCard, had 1.5 million credit card account details stolen. This breach was fairly minor in comparison to that experienced in 2008 by Heartland Payment Systems, where in excess of 100 million credit card accounts were stolen. As a result of the breaches and concern from the US Privacy Rights Clearing House, the White House has enacted a national data breach reporting law (Elliott 2012).

How is fraud perpetrated? Here are some common methods:

- **Social engineering** – posing as an insider or technician on the telephone to gather passwords or other sensitive information (State Services Commission 2000).

- **Phishing** – the sending of fraudulent emails that result in recipients being conned into providing personal information. Often the email can look like an official document. If it is a text message on a phone, it is called **smishing**, and voicemail is **vishing**. Naturally, these practices are inhibiting legitimate call centre operations, which are now finding respondents are resistant to engagement because of concerns that calls may be a phishing activity (Reynolds 2012).

- **Password sniffing** – harvesting passwords by monitoring network traffic and retrieving relevant information (Smith 2012b). This process is accomplished either manually or by using software code such as Firesheep and Wise Shark (Pash 2011).

- **Identity theft** – pretending to be someone else in order to either steal or gain benefit. Examples of identity theft include obtaining and using someone's credit card details illegally, or obtaining an entire identity in order to conduct illegal business under that name (ACCC 2013a). It is estimated 500 000 Americans were victims of identity theft in 2001 (Stein 2001), and statistics from 2010 showed this figure rise enormously to 8.1 million people (Finklea 2012). The US Privacy Rights Clearing House, which works with victims of identity theft, has indicated that it takes an average victim two years to clear their credit rating. However, in a worst-case scenario in which the identity thieves have gone on to indulge in further criminal activity, victims could be left with a criminal record that is difficult to expunge.

> **identity theft** – stealing money or gaining other benefits by pretending to be someone else.

## Ethics in the media: Fraud

Technology advances have facilitated increased counterfeiting, particularly of ID cards. To combat this eventuality, Britain has developed Touch2ID which encodes fingerprints and proof of age in smart stickers on mobile phones. To prove their age and be served in a bar, phones must be swiped over a chip reader ('Fake ID cards, identity crisis' 2012).

## Plagiarism

Still in the domain of ethical IT issues that can affect us personally, an area which could have been mentioned under violation of IP but is better addressed here, is plagiarism. Regrettably, plagiarism appears to be on the increase. In 2011 in the UK, nearly 8500 university applications were thought to be copied and the incidence of plagiarism of personal statements tripled in just one year (Kershaw 2012). Interestingly, research findings indicate that personality traits such as agreeableness, conscientiousness and emotional stability are significantly and negatively correlated with unethical internet behaviour in university students. By unethical internet behaviour, they are referring to such activities as plagiarism and misuse of facilities (Krim, Zamzuri & Nor 2009).

Plagiarism (© shutterstock.com/Sielan)

The growing popularity of online courses has prompted concerns about how assessment can be manipulated and how students can cheat. The issue of online cheating will become increasingly prominent as more institutions embrace online courses, and as institutions try new systems of educational badges, and certifying skills and abilities learnt online. The reproducibility, that is, the ease of replication and distribution of material on the internet, supports plagiarism and highlights the ethical issue it presents (Weckert 2000). Some universities are turning to plagiarism-detection tools such as Turnitin Software; however, Shaw (2012) suggests that is unlikely to be a deterrent. The internet is also being used by writers who sell their services to facilitate custom-written assignments. To overcome this problem, research is being undertaken based on the underlying premise that people's writing has a unique signature or style fingerprint. We could, therefore, create a document fingerprint for each student when they turn in their first assignment. The system would then produce an alert if future papers differed significantly in style. In addition to electronic fingerprinting, other security measures being explored are a combination of face recognition software utilising laptop webcams or, at the extreme level, products such as secure exam remote proctor, which scans fingerprints and captures a 360-degree view around students (Young 2012).

A further control on plagiarism is the **doctrine of fair use**, which balances the rights of copyright owners with the interests of society. It allows limited-impact copying, where small sections of text are used in the context of news, student work, teaching and research and publications (Tysver & Mawhood 2000). In the Australian context, however, the term that is more favoured is 'fair dealing' (see <www.copyright.org.au/find-an-answer/browse-by-a-z>).

Traditional examples of fair use include:

- a small excerpt from a book which may be used in a book review
- using quotations from a speech when making a news report
- quoting a paragraph from a book in an academic paper
- using some elements of a work in order to make a parody (Tysver & Mawhood 2000).

**doctrine of fair use** – allows copying in circumstances that are deemed to be important or will have limited impact. Copyright, therefore, is not deemed to be infringed in certain circumstances where small sections of text are used in the context of news, student work, teaching and research, and publications.

# Societal ethical issues in IT

The third dimension of ethical issues in information technology relates to those that do not just affect business organisations or individuals, but society as a whole and, as a consequence, tend to be broader in nature. Key societal issues are covered in this section.

## Freedom of information

**freedom of information** – the ability to access and distribute information without impediment.

**free speech** – the ability to communicate without restriction.

Inherent in the principle of **freedom of information** is the ability to access and distribute information without impediment. This concept is obviously held in high regard by the media. However, ownership of and control over information has become an important source of political power in society (Brey 2000). **Free speech** is the ability to communicate without restriction. This is considered an essential right of a functioning democratic society and as the philosopher, John Stuart Mill, argued – truth is much more likely to spring from a free flow of ideas and contested debate (Johnson 2000). Information technology can greatly assist with the dissemination and critique of alternative views, and it has been suggested that was the case with the Arab Spring where technology was used to garner national and international support (Short 2012). But what happens when this information dissemination is restricted and the dissenting voices silenced? In an interesting duality, some argue it could be an efficient tool for enabling autocratic or totalitarian behaviour (Gorniak-Kocikowska 2007).

## Ethics in the media: Freedom of information

In June 2012 Google revealed that 45 countries had asked them to block content in the last six months of 2011. Apparently, this was up from only four countries in 2011 ('Internet freedom' 2012).

Key questions in the discussion of freedom of speech and IT's role in promoting or curtailing this freedom are:

- What if access to alternative political ideologies undermines the prevailing ideology?
- To what extent should there be a proliferation of variant views?
- What role do governments have to play in restricting access to information? For example, in the interests of national culture and to protect the people, all forms of internet and television ownership were banned until 1999 in Qatar (Weckert 2000).
- What information should be made public for the betterment of society, and what should be kept secret?

The last of these questions is particularly topical when considering WikiLeaks and its founder Julian Assange. In 2010, Assange released hundreds of thousands of classified US documents, including a video showing US forces killing Iraqi civilians and journalists whom they mistook for insurgents. At the end of 2010, another 250 000 classified US State Department cables were released, purportedly destabilising US global diplomacy (Satter 2012). WikiLeaks has been described as the most challenging journalistic phenomenon to have emerged in the digital era, and it has provoked anger and enthusiasm in equal measure (Beckett & Ball 2012).

## Ethics on reflection: Freedom of information

As a protest, on 18 January 2012, more than 7000 websites, including Wikipedia and Google, turned black to protest against the proposed Stop Online Privacy Act (SOPA).

**Question:**

1. Given our reliance on the web for free information, consider how a closure of the web might affect you?

# Ethics on reflection: Freedom of information

Consider, when does freedom of information go too far? Should sexting, that is, the sending of salacious texts or photographs, be included in our freedoms? What, if any, information should society be protected against?

# Ethics in practice: Freedom of information

In a bid to protect themselves, and also to reduce student reliance on university resources, some universities are blocking student access via filters to websites containing material such as pornography, drugs, bomb-making, terrorism, and sex. Unfortunately, this restriction also stops access to sites which encourage safe sex practices, as well as some sites needed for research.

**Questions:**
1. Do you think that filtering inhibits freedom of speech or expression?
2. How would you view a university storing pornographic materials in an effort to provide open access to these sites for research (Johnson 2000)?

# Ethics in practice: Freedom of speech

Go to <www.google.cn> and search with the English option for key terms such as 'Tibetan uprising', 'democracy' and 'freedom of speech'. Contrast this with a Google search in your own country location.

# Ethics in the media: Freedom of speech

Google seems, at times, to be a champion of free speech, such as when they refused to remove YouTube content that Brazilian authorities said breached their electoral laws. Conversely, two weeks earlier, they blocked eight Muslim countries from watching a film trailer that may have incited violence, repudiating their stand ('Internet freedom' 2012).

While governments are frequently seen as a source of the control of freedom of information, thought could also be given to other entities of control. For example, The City University of Hong Kong took the unusual decision to block student access to some information (Beckett & Ball 2012). If internet censorship could be viewed as any constraint on freedom of information, could it, therefore, also include internet filters such as Net Nanny parental controls, CyberPatrol and Cybersitter? As freedom of information has to do with any restriction, it could also relate to grunge sites, defamation sites, hate speech or even corporate blogging. There are several related areas of interest to freedom of speech:

- **Grunge sites** (also known as **cyber-griping**) – where the commentary has become defamatory, or could also be blatantly inaccurate and the outcomes have significant effects on personal and/or brand reputations. In one instance in Hong Kong, a businessman who claimed guests suffered food poisoning at Sun Hung Kai Properties registered a domain name <www.sunhungkai.com> in order to complain about his experience (Wu 2002).
- **Mobile activism** – the use of mobile technology, usually text messages, to advocate for social and political change (Pickert 2012). Planned Parenthood used text messages from an imaginary mobile phone baby to demonstrate the demands of an unplanned pregnancy by sending the 'parent/s' messages simulating a real baby, regularly alerting them to the baby's needs (Pickert 2012).
- **Collective activism** – where key organisations group together for a cause. In a show of solidarity, Yahoo, Microsoft and Google have joined the **Global Network Initiative**, and agreed to support free expression and online privacy, thereby limiting their involvement in authoritarian countries ('Internet Freedom Plus ça Change' 2012).
- **Matthew effect** – named after a line in the gospel of St Matthew (25:29), 'For to everyone that has shall be given, and he shall have abundance: but from him that has not shall be taken away even that which he has'. The Matthew effect is concerned with the algorithms search engines use which then decide what access to knowledge is available, and tend to privilege Western content, thereby also affecting where information is sourced from. For example, a search for 'Cameroon' is unlikely to yield any sites that relay information from a Cameroon perspective until the fourth search results page (Bowker & Knobel 2011). The difficulty therefore arises when the information received from a search may be biased and inadequate, or is not from an original source.

## Public surveillance

Technology is now facilitating even greater surveillance of citizens than has been possible in the past. According to recent reports, the rate of government requests to companies to yield information about citizens has been growing. Verizon, a US mobile service provider, has reported a 15% increase over five years ('Data privacy out of shape' 2012); and Google reports receiving 27% more requests between July and December 2011 than the year before, with 93% of the requests coming from US officials ('Government surveillance' 2012).

In the US, the *Patriot Act 2001* has allowed requests to be served on internet service providers (ISPs) requiring them to provide details of both the sender and recipient of emails, the size

**grunge sites** (also known as **cyber-griping**) – sites where the commentary has become defamatory or offensive in nature, or is inaccurate.

**mobile activism** – the use of mobile phone technology, mainly text messaging, to disseminate information, raise money and advocate for political and social change.

**collective activism** – where key organisations group together for a cause.

**Global Network Initiative** – a group of organisations that have agreed on principles of free expression and online privacy.

**Matthew effect** – a specific concern in relation to search engines, particularly the algorithm that provides almost universal access to knowledge, but also unwittingly suppresses knowledge.

of the email file and their web browsing habits ('Government surveillance' 2012). In the US, intelligence agencies eavesdrop on communications between Americans and people overseas without a probable cause warrant, due to increased technological capabilities and lagging laws. Warrants are required to get a wiretap and do a physical property search; however, capturing online data is not subject to the same judicial review process ('Data privacy out of shape' 2012). What can be found by security agencies as they scan Facebook pages is quite alarming.

Public surveillance (© shutterstock.com/RedDaxLuma)

## Ethics in the media: Public surveillance

In 2012, a New York judge ordered Twitter to provide three months of messages from a protester involved in the Occupy Wall Street movement (accused of disorderly conduct). Twitter argued against the request, asserting that its users have a reasonable expectation of privacy. The judge, however, disagreed ('Government surveillance' 2012).

## Ethics on reflection: Public surveillance

Explore the trade-off between security and privacy in relation to the government. Most national security agencies want to maintain loopholes that allow them to pursue lines of communication, whereas individuals are increasingly seeking privacy within cloud computing where search queries cannot be traced to an individual user or IP.

**Question:**
**1.** What is your view on this trade-off?

# Ethics on reflection: Metadata

Phone companies are approached by government agencies to provide data from tower dumps, where large amounts of information are taken from a mobile tower and involve a significant number of people, whether relevant to the case or not ('Little peepers everywhere' 2012).

**Question:**

**1.** How would you feel if you found you had been caught in a tower dump?

It is not just telephones and email that are the main instruments of public surveillance; **face recognition software** is becoming increasingly more sophisticated. In recent years, face recognition technology has advanced significantly and, rather than acquiring a still photo capture, face recognition is now able to be applied to a large number of moving individuals. Face recognition software is not just being used for border control but also in jails, at sporting events and on street surveillance cameras, which are increasingly present in most major cities.

**face recognition software** – the electronic ability to capture photos of faces and to match them against databases.

## Vigilantism

Vigilantism is where an individual subverts legal practice and process and takes the law into his or her own hands in order to seek redress. Previously, public citizens relied on the skills of the police to investigate and correct wrongdoing, but now, with a wealth of data and systems at hand, citizens can become vigilantes and take action. For example, a man whose iPad was stolen from a suburb in ACT, Australia, used the Find My iPad app and a GPS to locate his device. Once his suspicions were confirmed, he notified the police, who searched the property and located the iPad ('Tracking of iPad illegal' 2012).

## Societal cyber-security

Cyberterrorism has already been touched on in relation to organisational issues, but it is worth briefly mentioning again in relation to national cyber-security. Such threats are undoubtedly a concern for society, not least because of the potential financial burden of the economic damage a malicious code can cause (Taylor 2002). Significant protection is required. In 2002, New Zealand ordered a program of work to improve protection for New Zealand's critical infrastructure from cyber-crime and other IT-based threats, particularly such menaces as computer hacking and viruses. According to the State Services Commission (2000), the program was aimed at anticipating risk, improving protection, and guarding against IT-based risks that could have an impact on New Zealand's national welfare or international standing. This is consistent with initiatives taken by most developed countries. As with the New Zealand government, the programs usually entail the establishment of an independent unit to monitor IT security and risks on a day-to-day basis, providing advice and training on securing infrastructure from cyberattacks, applying **patches** (a small change to software readily distributed to fix an IT problem) as they become available to maintain security of computer systems, participating in global initiatives to curtail DOS attacks, and considering potential improvements to law. The key areas at risk from an IT threat for most countries are in: finance and banking; transport; electric power; telecommunications, the internet; oil and gas; water; and critical state services that support national safety, security, and income (State Services Commission 2000).

## Digital divide

The **digital divide** (sometimes called the **digital split**) has been described as the gap, or perceived gap, between those who have and those who do not have access to information technologies and the ability to use the technologies and related tools (Compaine 2001). These gaps are evident nationally as well as globally. The digital divide is not just about access to the internet, and the cost and quality of connections, but is also about issues of connection speeds, internet penetration, broadband adaption and mobile usage ('The digital divide, ICT and the 50 x 15 initiative' 2012).

An example of the transformative capability of technology is evident in Africa, where mobile phones have been used to improve many sectors, including banking, education and agriculture (Drencheva 2012). Leonard Waverman found that for every 10% increase in mobile phone penetration in a developing country, 0.6% of economic growth can be expected (Drencheva 2012).

## Green computing

**Green computing** (sometimes called **sustainable computing**) is concerned with the environmental problems associated with the use and disposal of computers and computer-related products at a personal and business level. An example of a company adopting green computing principles is Intel Corporation, which utilises a three-phase roadmap that highlights how sustainability affects existing projects; attempts to reduce the carbon footprint; and has developed sustainable IT practices (Curry et al. 2012).

# Ethics on reflection: Green computing

Count the number of computers and electronic devices you have had in your lifetime, and consider also how much power and possibly paper you have used.

**Question:**
**1.** How were these computers disposed of – was it in an environmentally safe manner?

# Ethics on reflection: IT issues

Suggest new or contemporary issues in technology not already discussed in this chapter. What are the ethical concerns with this new issue?

# Conclusion

Ethical issues in IT are currently one of the more challenging areas in business ethics, especially given the ever-changing landscape. The intention of this chapter was, therefore, to identify and discuss current ethical issues in the IT sector regardless of the fact that, in just a few years, new challenges may supersede these issues.

This chapter initially defined ethics and technology, before moving on to examine organisational ethical issues and IT. The organisational ethical issues encompass, for example, cyber-security, hacking, use of malware, and violation of IP and expert systems. Personal issues in IT were then investigated with the focus on privacy, personal profiling, personal security, fraud, and plagiarism. A third dimension of societal ethical issues in IT was then presented, examining freedom of information, public surveillance, vigilantism, societal cyber-security, the digital divide and green computing.

To conclude, the concerns surrounding ethics in information technology are not only about the mechanics, that is, what the technology can do, but also the consequences of the technology such as the potential to do harm. Advances in technology are constantly creating new issues needing evaluation. The enormous speed at which these issues are presented leaves us with the lingering feeling that we are often out of step, or in a vacuum, when confronted with new technology and what it offers. It has previously been noted that the intellectual progress of humans 'often outstrips their moral and ethical development' (Shrader-Frechette & Westra 1997, p. 3), possibly because we concentrate on the economic benefits associated with technology, but pay little attention to the ethical costs, such as the impact on the environment, health and wellbeing, and the possible threats to life.

# Ethics on video

**Robotics** – *The Ethical Robot* 2011, YouTube, uconn, 15 June, <https://youtube.com/watch?v=pajCoSTGvas>.

**Violating privacy** – *The Ethics of Internet Privacy* 2010, YouTube, null154, 6 December, <https://youtube.com/watch?v=tD4_gJwfCMM>.

See web material for more videos.

# Ethics at the movies

Here are a few movie suggestions that have ethical content related to IT:

\*I, Robot – explores at what point a robot becomes a human, covering a range of issues surrounding robotics, technology and ethical concerns raised by technological advancements. *I, Robot (Trailer)* 2004, motion picture, Davis, J, Godfey, W, Dow, T & Mark, L.

\*The Social Network – from the perspective of the founder of the social networking site, Facebook. The film explores the creation and resulting lawsuits between those involved in its invention. *The Social Network* 2010, motion picture, Chaffin, C, Brunetti, D, Rudin, S & De Luca, M.

*Author's picks

See web material for more movies.

# Ethics on the web

**Ethics in computing**, a comprehensive website about ethical issues in computing, <http://ethics.csc.ncsu.edu>.

**The hacker crackdown: law and disorder on the electronic frontier**, a free e-book from Project Gutenberg, <www.mit.edu/hacker/hacker.html>.

See web material for more web references.

# Student exercises

See web material for answers to student short answer questions.

## Short answer questions

1. Which ethical principles are relevant in IT?
2. What are the three influences impacting ethical decisions related to computer technology and use?
3. How would you know if your computer has been infected with spyware?
4. Undertake an internet search and outline the key tenets of the 'hacker's ethic'.
5. In 2012 LinkedIn updated their privacy conditions without any action from your side and can use your name and picture in any of their advertisements. How can you protect yourself?
6. Match the personal security issues to the appropriate definition.

| Personal Security | | Definition |
|---|---|---|
| 1. Sexting | ___ | Giving someone a verbal lashing via electronic medium |
| 2. Cyberbullying | ___ | Sending salacious texts or images via SMS |
| 3. Cyber-stalking | ___ | People who crusade against individual, groups or causes |
| 4. Internet vigilantes | ___ | Using electronic mediums to pursue, harass, or contact another |
| 5. Flaming | ___ | Communicating electronically in a hostile way to cause distress to another |

## Experiential exercise

Choose a topic from the list below and develop a PowerPoint presentation that provides the definition of the term chosen, the societal issues involved and an example of how it impacts on you personally.

- freedom of information
- public surveillance
- vigilantism
- societal cyber-security
- digital divide
- green computing

# Small case

## Case: Big brother

The British writer Ben Elton's 2007 novel *Blind Faith* points to our current fixation with social media. In his book, the extreme case of no privacy is explored. Not only is the state in full control of information, but its citizens are also fully aware of the actions of others given the requirement to stream the most intimate details to social network sites.

### Question:
1. Where did the term 'Big Brother' come from and discuss this case through the invasion of personal privacy through technology?

# Large case

## Case: Edward Snowden and the NSA secret document leaks… whistleblower or traitor?

### Background

Edward Snowden was 29 years old when he blew the whistle on the National Security Agency's (NSA) PRISM program (Cassidy 2013). Snowden comes from a military family and initially joined the army as a special forces recruit in 2003; however he was discharged after he broke both his legs. From there he went to work for the CIA, and then as an infrastructure analyst for a defence contractor, Booz Hamilton, within NSA. His final post was based in Hawaii, where he lived with his girlfriend (Starr & Yan 2013).

Before Snowden's PRISM revelations, Thomas Drake and Bill Binney (also NSA whistleblowers) exposed a $2 billion NSA facility being built in Utah, which has the capacity to house 100 years of humanity's collective electronic data (Rosenbach, Stark & Stock 2013). In December 2012, some US senators – particularly Senator Wyden – raised concerns about the ability to make informed decisions over the renewal of the FISA Amendments Act for another five-year period. He argued it would give continued expansive power to NSA without adequately outlining the benefits (Aid 2012), and without fully disclosing NSA's existing or planned role. Despite Senator Wyden's concerns, the FISA Amendments Act was passed in December 2012.

## Snowden

On 5 and 6 June, *The Guardian* began leaking details from a whistleblower that outlined some of the data gathering capabilities used in PRISM by NSA. Of particular concern were the claims around NSA's lack of transparency and oversight, and the fact information obtained by NSA was indiscriminate and collected in bulk (Greenwald 2013a). By 9 June, Edward Snowden revealed his identity as the whistleblower during an interview with Greenwald, while holed up in a Hong Kong hotel room.

Outraged by Snowden's data releases, on 21 June the United States Government filed espionage charges against Snowden and attempted to get him extradited from Hong Kong; although due to an apparent paperwork discrepancy from the US, the Hong Kong Government allowed Snowden's passage to Moscow. On 23 June, Snowden arrived in Moscow en route to Ecuador; however, he became stranded in Moscow as the US cancelled his passport and pressured intermediary countries to thwart Snowden's trip to Ecuador (Alpert & Sonne 2013). On 28 June, Ecuador revoked the safe passage pass it had given Snowden, resulting in Snowden applying for asylum in 20 or more countries. The US made it known that any country offering Snowden asylum would likely have sanctions imposed on them (Kuddus 2013). As more countries declined Snowden's application for asylum, or agreed to asylum only if he could get to their country (which

without a passport was effectively a decline), it became likely that Snowden's only alternative would be Russia. The US continued to simultaneously cajole and send veiled threats to Russia, having assured them that Snowden would not be tortured or sentenced to death if returned to the US.

Snowden's father, Lon Snowden, preferred Snowden to return to the US to face federal charges if suitable trial conditions could be negotiated (Knowlton 2013); however, this did not seem to mirror his son's goals.

On 12 July, Microsoft's cooperation with NSA ensured that the new Outlook.com portal allowed NSA to circumvent encryption and gain easier access to its cloud storage service, SkyDrive. Additionally, Microsoft's purchase of Skype allowed NSA to triple the capability of video collection for PRISM (Greenwald et al. 2013).

On 31 July 2013, Greenwald (2013b) released another Snowden leak. This leak exposed NSA's XKeyscore program to access by unauthorised analysts, who mined metadata and email content and activity (e.g. browser history) from agency databases for specific information. Even the director of National Intelligence, James Clapper, admitted that this presented an overreach of legal interpretation by NSA.

Snowden was granted asylum in Russia on 2 August, and finally left the Sheremetyevo International Airport, where he had been holed up since 23 June; that is, for a total of nearly six weeks (Arutunyan & Stanglin 2013).

On 9 August, President Obama announced plans to limit government surveillance programs by changing Section 215, governing metadata collection, through the US's anti-terrorist legislation, *Patriot Act 2001*. President Obama said that the plans for change were not related to Snowden's media releases (ABC News 2013). On the same day, Ladar Levenson, owner of Lavabit, the service Snowden was using, defiantly shut down the email encryption service rather than comply with secret US court orders. Silent Circle follows suit (Greenwald 2013c).

## Ethical considerations

There is dissenting opinion regarding Edward Snowden's actions in his attempt to alert the public to the NSA's global movements. Some are against his whistleblowing, suggesting that Snowden was obliged to keep 'mum' on the surveillance topic because of loyalty and legal contractual commitments. Others, such as Norman Bowie, take a middle road, suggesting there is a *prima facie* employee duty of loyalty that can only be broken in extenuating circumstances – such as in supporting a public good (Duska 2007) – and it is likely that Bowie would concede that Snowden's actions were extenuating. John Cassidy of *The New Yorker* seems to agree with Bowie that the breach of trust Snowden committed was a necessary public service to reveal the extent of the eavesdropping by NSA, and he further points out the information released by Snowden was carefully selected; in sharp contrast to the information 'dump' by Bradley Manning (Cassidy 2013). Duska, on the other hand, contends that whistleblowing is necessary, and even to be expected, as a vehicle to alert society to company misdeeds; however, he wonders whether there is a moral imperative to do so given the likely retribution whistleblowers receive. Edward Snowden may have wondered if Duska (2007) has a point, yet it seems from the interview he gave to *The Guardian* in his Hong Kong hotel room that he knew the difficulties that would lie ahead of him, and nonetheless felt compelled to blow the whistle.

Peter Singer (2013), rather than taking a fixed position on whistleblowing, agrees that the public need to take a stronger position with regard to their points of view on the subject, as part of being in a democracy demands that the public understand and vote for the government of choice based on transparency. The NSA's actions seem to undermine the core tenets of democracy, as does pursuing the prosecution of Julian Assange, Bradley Manning and now Edward Snowden. He

questions why there is not more concern from the public regarding the misleading comments made by the Director of National Intelligence, James Clapper, to the US Congress in March 2013, and presumably why the focus is on Snowden rather than on democratic rights.

It is curious that the surveillance revelations have not created a public outcry; demanding answers regarding the lack of oversight from Foreign Intelligence Surveillance Act Court (Cassidy 2013), and the missteps from James Clapper and General Keith Alexander (Cassidy 2013). Clapper indicated that PRISM had significant oversight from the Justice Department's Inspector-General, Congress, the Attorney-General, and the Director of National Intelligence compliance reports (Joye 2013); yet Julian Assange at a WikiLeaks press conference (2013) said NSA was 'violating United Nations agreements, American Law and the laws of other countries and is doing so in secret' (p. 13). Is this data regulated from an international perspective? It seems that espionage activities are a law unto themselves, and not only in the US. From an Australian perspective, NSA intelligence is used to brief the Prime Minister, and was critical to Australia winning a seat on the United Nations Security Council (Joye 2013). Does the benefit received from the data outweigh the democratic rights which are cancelled to receive it?

The WikiLeaks (2013) press conference dated 24 June outlined Snowden's applications for asylum, based on the Refugee Convention, which protects whistleblowers from 'being persecuted for political opinion' (p.2), and 'trumps any efforts to extradite Edward Snowden' (p.2). Wikileaks further refuted the US Secretary of State's claim that Edward Snowden was a traitor, countering that Snowden was a whistleblower, and pointed out the prosecution the US was seeking was part of 'the Obama Administration's war on whistleblowers' (p. 4). Part of WikiLeaks' concerns are the way the Obama Administration are interpreting the *Espionage Act*

*1917*, hoping to define journalistic sources as spies and intending to hold news organisations criminally liable in an attempt to eliminate the current mechanism utilising the press to keep government accountable. The concern is that, by diluting the media's presence at a time when the government's national security sector is becoming more powerful, a lack of public accountability will lead to tyrannical behaviour. Assange concludes that Snowden is in fact an American patriot, and that his actions show a deep concern for the American people. In fact, this echoes Snowden's claims to date. The US is intent on pursuing Snowden and prosecuting him as a traitor. Even if Snowden is extradited the answer may not be clear, as at the heart of this matter is an ethical dilemma that each person will interpret differently, based on their personal value system.

## Timeline of Snowden scandal

| | |
|---|---|
| December 2012 | Some US senators raise concerns over the renewal of the *FISA Amendments Act 2008* for another five-year period, which would give NSA expansive power. |
| 20 May 2013 | Snowden goes to Hong Kong. |
| 5 June 2013 | *The Guardian* leaks a court order compelling Verizon to turn over millions of US customers' records (Greenwald & MacAskill 2013). |
| 6 June 2013 | *The Guardian* releases documents outlining NSA's direct access to Google, Facebook, Apple, etc. via PRISM which can occur without abuse checks or intermediary control (Greenwald & MacAskill 2013). |
| 9 June 2013 | Snowden identifies himself as the whistleblower through an interview. |
| 21 June 2013 | Espionage charges filed against Snowden by the US (Zakaria & Hosenball 2013). |
| 23 June 2013 | Snowden arrives in Moscow. |
| 25 June 2013 | Obama vows to extradite Snowden; and Putin is asked to hand Snowden over to the US. |
| 28 June 2013 | *The Huffington Post* reports *The Guardian* website has been blocked by the American Army, to ensure personnel do not see classified information (Mirkinson 2013). Ecuador revokes Snowden's safe conduct pass. |
| 29 June 2013 | Ecuador reveals the US vice-president asked Correa to refuse Snowden's asylum claim |
| 1 July 2013 | Snowden applies for asylum in Russia and 20 plus other countries. |
| 2 August 2013 | US places economic and political pressure on all countries considering giving Snowden asylum (Drape 2013). |
| 2 July 2013 | Lon Snowden (Snowden's father) and his lawyer send Edward Snowden an open letter via *The Guardian*. |
| 12 July 2013 | Microsoft's cooperation with NSA outlined (Greenwald et al 2013). |
| 26 July 2013 | The US advise Russia they will not seek the death penalty or torture Snowden if he is extradited to the US. |
| 31 July 2013 | NSA's XKeyscore program exposed (Greenwald 2013b). |
| 2 August 2013 | Snowden granted one year's asylum in Russia. |
| 9 August 2013 | President Obama announces plans to limit government surveillance programs (ABC News 2013). Lavabit shuts down email encryption service (Greenwald 2013c). |

**Questions:**

1. Do you think NSA's surveillance is reasonable given the threats posed by terrorism to the US, even if this opposes the Constitutional right to privacy (Morici 2013)?

2. What do you think about Assange's claims that the NSA is violating UN agreements, American Law, and the laws of other countries?

3. What ethical issues are raised by Snowden's actions?

4. Do you think the Refugee Convention's protection of whistleblowers is applicable to Snowden? Explain.

5. What impact does big data capture by national governments have on you?

See web material for:
- answers to short answer questions
- additional student cases
- tutor resources (tutor password required)
- additional material including Ethics at the movies, Ethics in print, Ethics on video and Ethics on the web.

# Chapter 4

## Ethical issues in human resource management

'Treating people with respect will gain one wide acceptance and improve the business.'
Second Business Principle of Tao Zhu Gong (500 BC),
Assistant to the Emperor of Yue

## Chapter aim

To identify current ethical issues in human resource management (HRM).

## Chapter objectives

1. Identify the dominant ethical principles that relate to HRM.
2. Contrast the rights and duties of employees with those of managers.
3. Describe the variety of workplace contexts within which discrimination can occur.
4. Identify specific ethical issues during recruitment and selection, compensation, engaging in the work environment, health and safety and separation from an organisation.
5. Describe the characteristics of a 'just' work environment.

# Ethics in the media

In 2011, American retailer JC Penney found that a third of their headquarters' bandwidth usage was due to employees watching YouTube videos ('Mayer culpa' 2013).

## Introduction

For most organisations, employees are their largest resource and the most significant financial investment. Consequently, good managers are attentive to ethical issues in relation to human resources and have an overarching concern for fair and proper treatment. **Fair treatment** involves treating people with respect and upholding their rights. Ethical issues in HRM involve not only the rights and expectations of employees, but also the rights and expectations of the employer. So, for example, while there is undoubtedly a duty of care required of employers, there is also the expectation that employees will provide a meaningful contribution for the reward of pay.

**fair treatment** – treating people with respect, not only as a means to an end, and upholding their rights.

Ethical issues involving employees range considerably, from actions such as favouritism in employment through to issues relating to sexual harassment, unfair dismissals, and violence in the workplace – where the impact on individuals can be significant. In exploring these topics further and identifying the ethical issues that arise in HRM, we will utilise some common categorisations of human resource activities. Additionally, we will identify specific ethical issues during: recruitment and selection; compensation; engaging in the work environment; health and safety; and separation from the organisation.

We will investigate numerous areas, such as fraudulent recruitment practices and discrimination in selection. Compensation is dominated by discussion on gender and executive pay differentials, and the need for equitable rewards. 'The work environment' is a rather general heading, pertaining to unethical work practices such as employee surveillance and the need for workplace flexibility. 'Workplace health and safety' encompasses a myriad of issues such as ergonomics, mental health, bullying, sexual harassment, and workplace violence. The last category, separation, describes the variety of circumstances by which a person leaves an organisation – such as dismissal, layoff or voluntary departure – and the ethical issues associated with these forms of departure.

# Ethics in practice: Human resources policies

**Questions:**

**1.** Think about your current work environment (you may be working part time or full time). Discuss an area in which you believe your organisation could significantly improve. What human resource policies or processes do you think need changing?

**2.** What unethical human resource activities have you observed in the workplace? Describe the circumstances.

# Ethical principles in HRM

In most countries, human resources (HR) professionals are governed by a professional code of ethics. In Australia, this code has been developed by the Australian Human Resource Institute (AHRI 2013). As with many professional associations, the ethical and professional conduct guidelines are grouped around ethical principles (see the AHRI website at <www.ahri.com.au>). A review of codes of conducts around the world will indicate similarities in wording and ethical principles; however, ethical expectations do not just apply to human resource professionals, but also to managers and organisational agents in general.

Several common ethical principles relate to HRM:

- **Rights of employees** – obligations of employers to employees which include for example: the right to a safe working environment, the right to fair compensation, the right to be informed, the right to consultation and to express one's view, the right to fair treatment, the right to confidentiality and privacy, as well as the right to equity and fairness.
- **Duty** – a moral obligation applying to the duties of both employees and managers, such as the duty of care in relation to occupational health and wellbeing for managers, and the expectation of honesty and integrity for employees.
- **Respect** – ensuring that for all employees the organisation demonstrates consideration, esteem and dignity, and that staff are not subject to inequitable treatment or discrimination.
- **Due process** – ensuring adherence to appropriate procedures and processes. For example, all incidences of wrongdoing and any subsequent disciplinary action will be dealt with promptly, thoroughly, and confidentially.
- **Justice** – ensuring equity and fairness in the workplace. For example, a person against whom an allegation has been made has the right to transparency and to know what is

alleged against them, the right to put their case in reply, the right for any decision to be made by an impartial decision-maker, and the right to an appeal against a decision.

- **Environmental awareness** – the pursuit of sustainability in human resource practices. For example, the keeping of electronic rather than paper copies of HR records and policies.
- **Confidentiality** – upholding the confidentiality of information and processes to protect privacy. For example, complaints should be treated with confidence, and where confidentiality cannot be guaranteed, this must be clearly indicated (Victoria Legal Aid 2012).

# Ethics in practice: Codes of conduct

**Questions:**

1. Select four countries and undertake an internet search to identify whether there is a Human Resource Institute or relevant professional organisation in each country.

See whether you can locate a professional code of ethics associated with that organisation.

2. Having identified at least three codes of conduct from various countries, undertake a comparison of the similarities and differences.

Ethical principles underpin human resource practices and assist with the many ethical issues that can arise in relation to the administration of personnel; however, they can also create tensions between the rights of employees and those of the organisation. There are numerous rights that employees can morally draw on, including the right to:

- be respected and valued
- equitable compensation
- due process
- privacy
- be informed
- representation and organisation
- freedom from discrimination
- a healthy and safe work environment
- be heard
- not be victimised for making a complaint.

Each of these rights translates into duties; for example, the right to due process entails practices whereby the employer has a duty to ensure an employee is consulted and has the opportunity to express his or her view, receive fair treatment and not be discriminated against (employees also have duties pertaining to their roles and responsibilities). Conversely, employers have rights such as the right to manage, as well as duties such as adherence to organisational policies and processes, and a duty of care in relation to the work environment, health, safety and quality of work.

There are always tensions between the expectations of employees and those of employers; for example, the need for job security on the part of employees and the need for flexibility in workforce planning on the part of organisations, the need for information pertaining to a person's potential for the job and the privacy of an applicant, or the need for drug and alcohol testing in order to create a safe environment. Such tensions need to be reconciled in an appropriate and ethical manner. Some countries have enshrined legal protections, the details of which vary from country to country, but even where legislative requirements are not imposed there are also standards of good practice in relation to fair, just, and equitable treatment of employees, leading to ethical and healthy work environments.

The terms 'fair' and 'just' arise frequently when trying to ensure the ethical treatment of employees in the work environment; so, it is worth expanding on them further. By 'just', what we mean is that justice prevails in all activities. Ethical treatment of employees is underpinned by the concept of organisational justice, although it has been suggested (Fazey 2012) that there are actually three components of organisational justice (see Chapter 10 for further discussion):

- **distributive** – the fair allocation of remuneration and rewards
- **procedural** – fair and consistent decision-making
- **interactional justice** – treating all employees with respect and dignity.

## Ethics on reflection: Unfair treatment

Describe circumstances in which you or someone you know has been subjected to unfair treatment in the workplace. What was the form of unfair treatment (e.g. discrimination, abusive boss, violation of privacy)?

# Ethics in recruitment, selection and promotion

## Deceptive applicant information

Although we have focused initially on the unethical practices of employees, it is surprising (though not uncommon) for job applicants to provide false or deceptive information during the recruitment and selection process. Usually, this is done by embellishing their experience, or telling outright lies about their work experience or qualifications. According to research from talent assessment company SHL, a significant 32% of applicants lie on their résumé. Other findings were that 17% of workers made up or exaggerated their work experience, and 6% got a friend or partner to act as an employer referee (SHL 2010). Lying on a résumé is not only deceptive, but also fraudulent.

**deceptive applicant information** – the provision of false or deceptive information by job applicants.

It is noted that some information is relatively easy to verify. For example, dates of employment or whether someone has a university degree. However, it is harder to assess intangible attributes relating to experience and skills, such as management of a team, financial stewardship and project management (Dent & D'Angelo Fisher 2012).

"Are you sure your resume is accurate?"

Deceptive applicant information (© shutterstock.com/Cartoonresource)

# Ethics in the media: Deceptive applications

After five months in the role as CEO at Yahoo, Scott Thompson stepped down because he had lied about his qualifications in his résumé (see 'The World this Week' 2012).

**soliciting unwarranted information**
– seeking information believed beneficial to inform decision-making but that has no relationship to the decision or to an applicant's future performance on the job; such a search may constitute an invasion of privacy.

## Soliciting unwarranted information

During the recruitment and selection process, employers will naturally wish to seek information that will inform their choice of the best applicant. Their choices should be made using valid selection criteria. Regrettably, however, inappropriate selection criteria may be used, which bear no relationship to job performance, thus restricting the access of certain people to the job. It is therefore important that the selection criteria used should truly reflect the role being filled (Mauboussin 2012).

# Ethics on reflection: Selection criteria

Consider the consequences for both applicants and the organisation if inappropriate selection criteria are used.

Not only could the selection criteria be invalid but requests for information could also be considered an invasion of privacy – such as a request by the recruitment officer to 'friend' the applicant, in order to get access to their Facebook page. As far back as 2008, a study revealed that 20% of employers searched social networking sites in order to screen potential candidates and, of those employers, one-third had found information that caused them not to consider a candidate. Why do employers do this? Apparently, 41% of managers considered information relating to alcohol and drug used to be the top concern, and they were also looking for evidence of a candidate's poor communication skills; inappropriate activities caught on camera; and disparaging comments about former employers or colleagues (Havenstein 2008).

# Ethics on reflection: Interview practice

Do you consider it a questionable interview practice to view an applicant's Facebook page or is it now the norm (see Valdes 2012)?

## Genetic testing

Genetic testing in the workplace is relatively uncommon but has its origins in 1938, when the geneticist JBS Haldane observed that not all workers exposed to a particular occupational hazard became symptomatic. He postulated that the difference in response to toxic exposures was at least in part, genetically determined. If we could be assured that individuals who were genetically susceptible to certain diseases were steered to other occupations, it was reasoned, we could reduce the number of people who became ill. In this context, genetic screening in workplaces was regarded as justified for reasons of public health (Murray 1997).

**genetic testing** – the collecting of genetic data as part of workplace screening in order to determine job eligibility.

**discrimination**
– when employees receive preferential/ less preferential treatment on grounds not directly related to their qualifications and performance on the job.

**preferential discrimination**
– favourable or preferred treatment that is blatantly unfair.

**favouritism**
(often referred to as **cronyism** or an **old boys' network**) – a situation where a supervisor or manager either openly or covertly favours one or more employees over others.

**nepotism** – where an employee hired, promoted or favoured is a member of the manager or supervisor's family.

# Ethics on reflection: Genetic testing

The ethics of discriminating according to genetic predisposition are complex. Imagine being refused a position you fervently desire as a consequence of compulsory genetic testing. How might this impact upon you?

## Discrimination

In the business context, **discrimination** occurs when preferential (or sometimes non-preferential) treatment is bestowed on employees on grounds other than their qualifications or job performance (Crane & Matten 2010). Discrimination is most evident during the recruitment and selection process but can also occur with promotions, as well as opportunities for training, or selection for beneficial assignments. Discrimination can occur in two forms: preferential discrimination and a tautological discriminatory discrimination.

**Preferential discrimination** results in favourable or preferred treatment that is blatantly unfair. It can come in the form of **favouritism** (often referred to as **cronyism** or an **old boys' network**) and is the circumstance where a supervisor or manager either openly or covertly favours one or more employees over others. Where that employee is actually a member of the manager or supervisor's family, it is called **nepotism**.

"I see we're split between those who like my new tie, and those who welcome unemployment."

Discrimination (© shutterstock.com/Cartoonresource)

## Ethics in the media: Applicant favouritism

After a course application by a close relative of the Vice-Chancellor of the University of Queensland received special treatment, a nepotism scandal erupted. As a result, the Vice-Chancellor and his deputy were forced to resign (Woodward 2011).

**discriminatory discrimination** – the unjust or prejudicial treatment of different categories of people. This can come in many forms including age, gender, race, disability, and pregnancy; as well as the stage of one's life cycle.

**Discriminatory discrimination** is the unjust or prejudicial treatment of different categories of people. Discrimination can occur because of: age, gender, race, disability, pregnancy or stage of life. Equal opportunity and anti-discrimination legislation, as well as affirmative action programs, are all intended to protect against inequality and unfairness occurring in the workplace. Discriminatory practices can be overt or covert (see Table 4.1). **Overt discrimination** is where the criteria established for the job are unrelated to the job; for example, all tellers working in the bank must have blue eyes (clearly, how a person will perform in the job has nothing to do with the colour of their eyes). **Covert discrimination** is more subtle. This occurs where selection criteria are so specific they automatically reduce the pool of applicants, while giving the impression of being objective (Crane & Matten 2010). For example, the need to work after 6 p.m. or to travel extensively could rule out parents who have significant childcare responsibilities and do not have the flexibility to be away from their home for extended periods of time. It is generally considered to be illegal to discriminate in the hiring of staff on the basis of sex, race, religion, disability or national origin, unless the criteria for selection are bona fide occupational qualifications.

**overt discrimination** – obvious discrimination, i.e. where the criteria established for the job are unrelated to the job.

**covert discrimination** – discrimination can often surface in an objective form, i.e. definitions of job criteria that automatically make the job beyond the reach of certain applicants.

## Ethics in the media: Gender discrimination

An American airline in the 1980s was found to discriminate against men by choosing to hire only attractive women ('Hiring hotties' 2012).

**Table 4.1** Types of discrimination

| | |
|---|---|
| Sex or gender discrimination | When you are treated differently because you are a woman or a man. |
| Age discrimination | When you face discrimination because your employer thinks you are too old or too young. |
| Impairment/mental disability discrimination | When you are intimidated, ridiculed, insulted, or not allowed to work, given lesser duties, laughed at or ostracised because of your injury, disability, or circumstances. |
| Marital/parental discrimination | When you are treated differently because of your marital status, or are given fewer tasks and opportunities to expand your career because of your obligations as a parent. |
| Racial discrimination | When comments are made about your race or ethnicity; you are sacked because of who you are (for example, your family's cultural background); or you receive different treatment in the organisation compared to people of other ethnicities. |
| Pregnancy discrimination | When you are moved to lesser duties or lose your seniority, are sacked, made redundant while on maternity leave, or are not given a reasonable adjustment of hours on return to the workplace after maternity leave. |
| Religious discrimination | When you are asked to do things that go against your religious beliefs, or are discriminated against in any way because of your beliefs. |
| Sexual orientation discrimination | When your employer treats you differently because of your sexual orientation or preferences. |
| Industrial activity discrimination | When you are sacked or made redundant because you are a member of a trade union, participated in trade union activities, or acted as a rep for a union. |

(Adapted from: 'What is unlawful discrimination?' 2013)

# Ethics in practice: Examples of discrimination

Search the internet for a recent court case in which an employer has been found guilty of discrimination (you can search print media, official media sites and court records). Summarise the details in a paragraph as an example of a real situation in which discrimination has arisen.

There are several common types of discrimination:

**age discrimination** – employment bias on the basis of age.

**Age discrimination** – age discrimination is more pronounced for older, rather than younger, workers. In Australia, despite efforts by the Federal Government to get more over 55s into the workforce, age discrimination still appears to be prevalent. The greatest roadblocks are employers who do not wish to hire older employees despite older workers' greater skills and experience. People over the age of 55 take 63 weeks on average to find a new job. At the age of 30, it is just 24 weeks (Smith 2012a). It has been suggested that companies that ignore mature applicants or retire staff early miss out on the talent, mentoring, and wisdom benefits that age-blind employers enjoy (Smith 2012a). While it is less common, young people are not immune to age discrimination. At 23, Fatima was promoted to store manager of a retail outlet. After a disagreement with the store owner she was dismissed, with the owner advising she was too young for her role. After mediation with the owner, Fatima received $1500 compensation (Australian Human Rights Commission n.d.).

# Ethics in the media: Age discrimination in Spain

In Spain, where more than 50% of young people are unemployed, they are getting desperate in their efforts to find work. Organisations have been found to be taking advantage of young people, making them work long hours or without pay (see Kassane 2012).

**Gender discrimination** – is extended to men and women; although more often it is women who are most affected. In 2011, in Australia, 57% of new graduates were female (Australian Bureau of Statistics 2012). Despite the high number of female graduates entering the workforce, women's careers are not progressing in line with men's, as evidenced by the lower percentage of women in leadership roles.

> **gender discrimination** – employment bias on the basis of gender.

Gender discrimination can occur not only during selection, but also in relation to advancement and pay.

- On average, women working full time earn 17.4% less than men working full time (Workplace Gender Equity Agency 2012b).
- Female graduates entering the workforce earn $5000 a year less than their male counterparts (Workplace Gender Equity Agency 2013).
- As their careers progress, men gain far greater pay increases than women do.
- Only 12.3% of directors of the top 200 companies are women.
- Only 0.02% CEO positions in the ASX200 are held by women.
- Some 61.5% of the top 200 firms have at least one woman on their board (Workplace Gender Equity Agency 2012a).

In Austin, Texas, the Forte Foundation is aiming to address the low number of women on boards by creating a repository of board-ready women nominated (or self-nominated) from 33 US business schools. It is hoped this list will raise the number of women on boards from current low levels ('Identifying women for corporate boards' 2012).

# Ethics in the media: The importance of appearance

It seems looks are important to prospective employers. Good-looking men are more likely to get an interview when attaching a photo to their résumé; however, the opposite is true for good-looking women. They are less likely to get an interview, presumably as HR are largely staffed by women ('Don't hate me because I'm beautiful' 2012).

# Ethics in the media: Discriminatory discrimination

Demonstrating the voracity of equal opportunity provisions, a well-known coffee house chain in the US was investigated by the US Equal Opportunities Commission for discrimination for hiring only young, female staff ('Hiring hotties' 2012).

**marital/parental discrimination** – employment bias on the basis of marital or parental status.

**maternal wall bias** (also known as **family-based discrimination**) – bias against caregivers, particularly mothers.

**Marital/parental discrimination** – affecting both men and women, marital or parental discrimination is when, as a result of child or caring responsibilities, an individual is disadvantaged in the workplace. For example, an inability to travel for extended periods may affect a person's career progression. **Maternal wall bias** (sometimes called **family-based discrimination**) is bias against caregivers, particularly mothers. In the US, working mothers have become increasingly more likely to sue employers for parental discrimination. The filing of lawsuits in relation to family discrimination has increased by 400% from 1998 to 2008, with roughly two-thirds of plaintiffs who sue prevailing (Williams & Cuddy 2012).

The Gender Bias Learning Project (2013) states that mothers are, in comparison to women without children:

- 79% less likely to be hired
- 100% less likely to be promoted
- offered US$11 000 less salary, on average, for the same position
- held to higher performance and punctuality standards.

Intriguingly, it has been revealed that fathers were actually held to lower performance and punctuality standards, and were more likely to be hired and promoted than childless men with identical qualifications (Butler & Skattebo 2004).

# Ethics in the media: Family-based discrimination

In a 2009 verdict of *Lopez v. Bimbo Bakeries USA Inc.*, Lopez was awarded US$3.34 million after Bimbo Bakeries' human relations department violated the California Fair Employment and Housing Act by sending Lopez home on leave when her pregnancy was announced, rather than reviewing her job (Fenwick & West LLP 2009).

A male maintenance worker won US$11.6 million against his employer who penalised him for taking family leave to care for his ailing parents (Williams & Cuddy 2012).

Maternal wall bias can take different forms: subtle, severe and no bias (see <www.genderbiasbingo.com/maternal-wall.html> for further, interactive, details).

## The glass ceiling

When an otherwise qualified person reaches an invisible barrier that prevents promotion or salary increases, they are said to have reached the **glass ceiling** (Grace & Cohen 2010). Commonly, it refers to an individual being denied promotion on criteria not related to the job. An even more subtle approach is where valid criteria exist, but by virtue of those criteria certain individuals are disadvantaged. For example, individuals from lower socio-economic backgrounds are less likely to gain qualifications from prestigious universities, and are therefore rejected for jobs in companies that favour qualifications from those universities.

> **glass ceiling** – an invisible barrier that prevents qualified people from rising above a certain level of rank or salary in business organisations.

"You said if I wore more makeup I would be taken more seriously."

Glass ceiling (© shutterstock.com/Cartoonresource)

## Affirmative action programs

The premise of affirmative action is that due to power imbalances caused by ingrained discrimination, injustices cannot be remedied without radical intervention to support disadvantaged groups (Grace & Cohen 2010). As a result, affirmative action programs have been introduced in the past. **Affirmative action** can be imposed in both the public and private sector to ensure all segments of society experience the full benefits of citizenship (Adams & Maine 1998). The most common strategy used in an affirmative action program is the use of quotas for recruiting of specific under-represented groups. Affirmative action programs were popular in the United States in the 1970s, but in recent years have lost favour, as they are deemed in themselves to be discriminatory.

Affirmative action programs were criticised as being unfair, with the unintended consequence of reverse discrimination. **Reverse discrimination** occurs where affirmative action policies designed to favour minority groups, result in inequity and unfairness for the dominant or majority groups.

Many organisations now have diversity programs in place, rather than affirmative action programs, as they attempt to alleviate inequities and increase representation of minority groups, particularly in regard to women in senior positions.

> **affirmative action** – a body of social programs in both the public and private sectors, intended to ensure that certain segments of society have the opportunity to participate fully in the workplace.

> **reverse discrimination** – where the affirmative action policies and processes have a discriminatory effect, resulting in the majority, or dominant group experiencing inequity and unfairness.

## Diversity programs

**diversity** –
the pursuit
of recruiting,
including and
incorporating
people of all types
and backgrounds
throughout an
organisation.

The goal of **diversity** is to ensure an organisation recruits to reflect the broad spectrum of society (Goree 2007). The emphasis of diversity programs has been on ethnic diversity but with varying degrees of receptivity. In a study on Leadership, Employment and Direction (LEAD) conducted by Leadership Management Australasia (2012), two-thirds of the 2000 people surveyed in the Australian and New Zealand workforce see ethnic diversity as positive for their organisation. Interestingly, only half of the leaders believe diversity brings benefits (Leadership Management Australasia 2012).

**LGBTI** – an
initialism that refers
to people who
identify as lesbian,
gay, bisexual,
transgender or
intersex.

In recent years, diversity has expanded to include a wide range of employees with the common use of the initialism **LGBTI**, which refers to people who identify as lesbian, gay, bisexual, transgender or intersex. For example, the research by Pride in Diversity (2012) annual workplace equality index, found that 34% of employees who completed the survey identified as lesbian, gay, or bisexual; and of that cohort, only 62% felt that they could be themselves at work. These individuals wanted increased recognition and acceptance in the workplace, an inclusive culture where diversity is acknowledged and applauded, and where there is zero tolerance of discriminatory and homophobic behaviour.

# Ethics on reflection: Quotas

Businesses tend to reject the notion of imposing quotas to ensure boards include women, saying this would result in tokenism and perhaps result in the appointment of less qualified individuals. Without quotas, though, will the number of women on boards ever reflect the diversity they represent in the workforce? ('Women in Business' 2012).

**Questions:**
1. What is your view in regard to the setting of targets over a period of years in an effort to redress apparent inequities in representation of key groups, such as women?
2. Should targets be voluntary, a binding directive, or a legislative requirement? Why?

# Ethics in compensation and reward

It is the aim of compensation and reward schemes that any compensation determination process be transparent, linked to qualification, experience and/or performance and accountable. However, this is not always the case. Some of the ethical issues surrounding compensation and reward are:

## Imbalances in pay

There is a large body of research that shows that widespread stereotypes, for example, the notion that women are less productive than men, often shape behaviour subconsciously, even in people who disagree with them (Benard 2012). As a consequence, there is the potential for differences in pay between men and women in the same job, with women commonly receiving lower salaries and being less likely to complain. Disparities in pay have also been noted, not only for gender, but also for race. The 2012 *GradStats* report by Graduate Careers Australia (2012; see Table 4.2) indicated that the gender pay gap for graduates has increased, with median full-time employment starting salaries for men being $55 000 (up from $52 000 in 2011) and for women being $50 000 (no change from 2011). The gender pay gap increased from $2000 to $5000 in 2012. Men's earnings have increased over the year while those of women have not. Across all occupations, the gender pay gap for starting salaries was 9.1%, which is up 5.2% from 2011 (Workplace Gender Equality Agency 2013).

**Table 4.2** Pay differences between women and men by industry – graduate degree holders

| Occupations where men earned more than women in 2012 | Male ($000) | Female ($000) | Gender pay gap (%) | Change from 2011 |
| --- | --- | --- | --- | --- |
| Architecture and building | 52. | 43 | 17.3 | 3.3 |
| Dentistry | 92. | 77.6 | 15.7 | 9.4 |
| Optometry | 82 | 75 | 8.5 | 5.8 |
| Law | 55 | 50.7 | 7.8 | 4.0 |
| Economics, business | 50 | 47 | 6.0 | 4.0 |
| Art and design | 42.5 | 40 | 5.9 | 1.1 |
| Accounting | 50 | 48 | 4.0 | 0.2 |
| Mathematics | 58.1 | 56 | 3.6 | 3.6 |
| Veterinary science | 46 | 45 | 2.2 | 6.8 |
| Paramedical studies | 53 | 52 | 1.9 | 2.0 |
| Social work | 50.9 | 50 | 1.8 | 3.8 |
| Psychology | 49.5 | 49 | 1.0 | 5.0 |
| Agricultural science | 50.5 | 50 | 1.0 | 3.2 |

(Source: Graduate Careers Australia 2012)

# Ethics in practice: The gender pay gap

Conduct literature and internet searches to obtain data to support the notion of whether pay inequities exist in your country.

## Problematic 'pay for performance' schemes

In **meritocratic pay systems**, superior performers receive higher raises and bonuses than mediocre workers. **Performance-related pay** is linked to an index or indices of job-related performance. Performance-related pay is intended to match reward with specified job performance criteria. It is therefore important that the criteria used are relevant, identifiable and measurable. Ethical concerns arise where the individual may have little or no control over the outcome of the indices, but is being judged and remunerated accordingly.

Frey and Osterloh (2012) have observed that pay for performance, or **variable pay schemes** as they are sometimes called, suffer from flaws. Specifically, the criteria may not be appropriate, and all elements of the job may not be covered. Additionally, there can be a manipulation of the performance criteria, with a focus on meeting the criteria rather than a holistic view of the role, which can detract from a person's intrinsic enjoyment of their role.

## Excessive executive pay

Compensation packages to senior managers that are deemed large relative to compensation paid to other workers in the company, or comparative jobs in other sectors are described as **excessive executive pay**. According to a study by Australia's Productivity Commission (2009), remuneration for executives of larger companies has increased significantly since the early 1990s. In the largest companies, executive salaries purportedly increased by 300% between 1993 and 2007. In the US, the average wage of a chief executive is US$10 million, while the UK reports the average as being equivalent to US$7 million (see 'Money for nothing' 2012), considerably higher than the average worker's wage. How has this disparity come about? In addition to market demand, high executive salaries have been attributed to an **agency problem**, in that executives (agents) are more likely to ensure their own interests are looked after rather than pursuing those of the owners (James 2012). Some contend that the solution to this situation is to ensure managers are given monetary incentive to care about the company's interests as well as their own (James 2012). This may be a valid suggestion, but what cannot be denied is the gross inequity between executive pay and the average employees' pay. For example, in the US, the S&P500 ratio of average CEO pay to average employer salary went from approximately 40:1 in the 1970s to 325:1 in 2010 (Frey & Osterloh 2012).

**meritocratic pay systems** – where superior performance receives higher raises and bonuses than work of a lower standard.

**performance-related pay** (also called **variable pay schemes**) – where the pay is linked to some index or indices of job-related performance.

**excessive executive pay** – compensation packages to senior managers that are deemed large relative to compensation paid to other workers in the company or comparative jobs in other sectors.

**agency problem** – when agents (managers) are likely to pursue their own interest at the expense of the owners.

Excessive executive pay (© shutterstock.com/Cartoonresource)

# Ethics in the media: Executive pay

In the UK, in the past 15 years an alarming disparity in salaries between executives and average workers has been noted ('Bosses under fire' 2012).

It is difficult to determine accurate levels of management remuneration, as compensation varies according to the type and size of the company (Productivity Commission 2009), the industry, and the company's performance. However, there is a lot of pressure to unlink pay from performance as a result of mounting evidence that pay for performance is ineffective, and may actually induce executives to take significant risks that adversely affect the companies they manage. It is also suggested that there are better ways to motivate employees, which yield equivalent or better results with smaller outlays (Frey & Osterloh 2012).

# Ethics on reflection: Excessive salaries

Public outrage has been expressed when CEOs have received exorbitant salaries or bonuses. In two notorious Australian cases, the CEOs of Qantas and the Commonwealth Bank of Australia controversially received such excessive compensation packages (Wilson 2012).

**Questions:**
1. What are your initial impressions of the significant pay packages awarded to executives?
2. What are the arguments for remuneration packages of this level?
3. What other methods of reward could be used?

# Ethics in practice: Management remuneration

Imagine you are the Chair of a Board of Directors. A proposal is on the agenda of your forthcoming board meeting to significantly raise the CEO's remuneration level. The proposal is largely driven by the desire for parity with the rest of your company's industry sector, but you have concerns that there may be a backlash from the union when the compensation package is made known.

**Question:**
1. Make a list of the critical issues and questions surrounding this dilemma.

# Ethics in practice: Penalty rates

Australians generally believe that if required to work on a Saturday, and particularly a Sunday, they should be paid overtime. However, in this 24/7 world, companies are increasingly creating flat rates of pay (see D'Angelo Fisher 2012a).

**Questions:**

1. What are your views on removing penalty rates for Saturday and Sunday work? Are they an outdated relic in a 24/7 economy?
2. What might be the consequences of an employment contract between two people, determined without reference to national laws?

## Ethics in the work environment

### Unethical work practices by employees

The term unethical work practices is broadly used to describe a range of activities that could include: misuse of company time and property; concurrent employment; employee interference and misappropriation. In relation to misuse of company time, studies have shown employees spend approximately 7 billion hours a week playing video games at work – which includes 300 minutes of Angry Birds play per day (McGonigal 2012).

**employee fraud** – misappropriation of company assets by employees.

The more severe unethical work practices are those that involve **employee fraud**. The reasons for misappropriation are not always clear and could be due to financial need, sheer greed for financial gain, or a desire to redress an inequity in compensation. Most cases deal with disgruntled employees who ask for raises and then commit fraud when their requests are denied, while there are also employees who steal vital information from their company to start their own company. Some **employee sabotage** entails deliberate and wilful acts of destruction out of malice, such as the *Encyclopaedia Britannica* employee who entered the database for the new edition and changed references from Jesus Christ to Allah. In the electronic age, sabotage usually involves some form of hacking, with 90% of cyberattacks being carried out by rogue employees – thus posing an internal organisational threat (Willison 2006; Danish, Muhammad & Ali 2011). Silent saboteurs are individuals in the workplace whose subversive activities, politics and manipulation can damage working relationships, productivity, trust and job satisfaction (Bennett 2003).

**employee sabotage** – entails deliberate and wilful acts of malice or destruction.

# Ethics in practice: Outside work

You have just had a coffee with a friend from work, who has revealed to you that she has recently started an internet-based business selling children's clothing and related products. You are not surprised by this endeavour as your friend has always struck you as quite entrepreneurial. However, your friend has indicated that the business will grow. At present, she is running the business on the weekend and in the evenings, but anticipates that the business will soon require significantly more effort as sales rise which will encroach on her working day.

**Questions:**
1. How appropriate is your friend's outside work, in your view?
2. Should the employee inform their employer of this internet-based business?
3. At what point does outside work begin to erode the current work environment?

## Employee surveillance

Surveillance systems now enable continuous monitoring of employees using audio, video, and electronic means. Technology can easily analyse keystrokes, email and internet usage; however, there are contrasting views on the ethics of employee surveillance. Employers have the right to ensure that their employees are working satisfactorily, safely, and honestly. They also have the right to identify high-performing and low-performing employees for reward or removal. To do this, employers have the right to monitor employees to ensure safety and improve productivity, thereby possibly reducing costs, enhancing profit and reducing pricing of products. A further benefit of **employee surveillance** is the control of crime in the workplace, especially theft and financial fraud (Miller & Weckett 2000). However, in addition to the obvious concerns of violation of privacy, it appears that there are further negative consequences of monitoring employee computer use, including poorer health, increased stress and decreased morale (Miller & Weckett 2000).

So, to what extent should an employer be able to monitor employees, and what of an employee's right to privacy, confidentiality and a level of independence? The notion of privacy has both a descriptive and a normative dimension. Privacy involves actions to ensure a person is protected and not interfered with; privacy can also be seen as a moral right or good (Miller & Weckett 2000).

**employee surveillance** – monitoring of employees to ensure they are working satisfactorily, safely and honestly.

Employee surveillance (© shutterstock.com/Cartoonresource)

# Ethics in the media: Surveillance in Japan

Organisations sometimes go to great lengths to keep an eye on their employees. In Japan, for example, some companies use face recognition software to assess employees' smiles ('I spy, with my big eye' 2012).

Tavani (2007, p. 316) has suggested there are arguments for and against computer monitoring, shown in Table 4.3.

**Table 4.3**  Arguments for and against computer monitoring

| Arguments in favour of monitoring |
| --- |
| • Helps to reduce employee theft |
| • Helps to eliminate waste |
| • Helps employers to train new employees |
| • Provides employers with a motivational tool |
| • Improves competitiveness |
| • Saves the company money |
| • Guards against industrial espionage |
| • Improves worker productivity and profits |
| **Arguments against monitoring** |
| • Increases employee stress |
| • Undermines employee trust |
| • Reduces individual autonomy |
| • Invades worker privacy |
| • Focuses on quantity, rather than quality of work |
| • Creates an electronic sweatshop |
| • Provides employers with an electronic whip |
| • Reduces employee morale and overall productivity |

(Adapted from: Tavani 2007, Ethics and Technology: Ethical Issues of Information and Communication Technology, 2nd Edn, Copyright © 2007 by John Wiley & Sons, Inc. Used by permission of John Wiley & Sons, Inc.)

The key feature for managers to consider in regard to collection and disclosure of personal data – whether this is of employees, customers, or merely interested parties – is the concept of consent. For this to occur, certain provisions must be met. For ease of recall, we can call them the '**four Cs of consent**'. For consent to be deemed true consent, and permission granted, the individual providing the consent must be:

- **considered** – the person is informed and has fully considered all the ramifications
- **consensual** – the provision of consent is done on a voluntary basis
- **capable** – the person has the mental capacity to provide consent
- **current** – the consent is relatively recent and within an appropriate time frame.

> **four Cs of consent** – the granting of permission providing the consent must be considered, consensual, capable and current.

## Ethics on reflection: Monitoring students

The University of Kentucky monitors students' social media accounts, and staff are notified when students use certain terms (e.g. 'porn', 'beer' or 'bong'). Some states have introduced legislature to prevent universities from forcing students to disclose their social media user names, calling it a violation of privacy (Marcus 2012b).

**Question:**

1. What is your view regarding the University of Kentucky's monitoring of students' social media activities?

## Workplace flexibility

Given the cost of office space and the increasing desire for flexibility, teleworkers (or tele-commuters as they are sometimes called) are on the increase. However, in early 2013, Yahoo's then recently appointed President and CEO Marissa Mayer introduced initiatives to curtail teleworking, possibly concerned about employee abuse of flexible working arrangements.

Research from the Australian Institute of Management (2012) into flexible work arrangements suggests that many employers are still reluctant to introduce flexible options as they are viewed by many as a privilege, a nuisance, or an unnecessary cost. Flexible arrangements also have an impact on promotion opportunities, and inflexible workplaces are contributing to the under-representation of women in senior management, as women opt out of employment when inflexibility occurs.

However, as an ethical consideration, people who work from home are less likely to be promoted and companies still reward being present. It appears that visibility creates what has been called 'the illusion of value'; that is, the positive impression employers have of employees who work late, even if those employees are using Facebook rather than working ('Out of Sight, Out of Mind' 2012). In contrast, those who take up the offer of flexibility are often viewed less favourably ('Out of office' 2012), as some managers associate a person's work schedule with their level of commitment and treat those who work in flexible arrangements as lacking in dedication. This can result in **flexibility stigma**, and in some departments of the Australian Federal Government, women working part time are still barred from management roles. Research finds that flexible work arrangements result in poorer performance and salary reviews, and men who seek to use 12-week family leave are seen as poorly organised and 'feminine' compared to other men (Williams & Cuddy 2012).

**flexibility stigma**
– when employers penalise those who take up the offer of flexibility.

Research, however, has shown many benefits for people who work away from the office, including increased productivity and creativity. Granting employees more autonomy in their lives can assist in achieving a work–life balance, contributing to greater overall happiness. Allowing employees to work from home also has additional societal benefits, increasing the participation pool by allowing parents who have primary caring responsibilities to work, allowing carers access to more work hours, and encouraging older workers to continue working (Australian Institute of Management 2012). Further benefits are that teleworking apparently drives different organisational behaviour, including increased levels of trust, tighter managerial processes, and stronger leadership engagement.

## Ethics in practice: Flexibility

Undertake research into teleworking. Identify a company that has introduced teleworking and describe the perceived benefits associated with their flexible work arrangements.

## Ethics in workplace health and safety

Organisations have an ethical duty of care to employees. There is the expectation that managers will create a safe and respectful working environment. In order to ensure this is achieved, employees have rights which are enshrined in legislation, company policy and practice, in order to afford employees a significant amount of protection from unsafe work places and exploitation. Where this duty of care is not present, the consequences of illness, accidents, disease or fatalities can have significant and detrimental effects on both the individual, families and the organisation.

Looking specifically at fatalities in the workplace, the Australian National Occupational Health and Safety Commission (NOHSC) conducted two comprehensive studies into work-related injuries and deaths in Australia. The first study covered the period from 1982 to 1984, while the second collated data collected between 1989 and 1992. The groups of people studied were

**Table 4.4** Most dangerous industries

| Forestry | 93 deaths |
|---|---|
| Fishing | 86 deaths |
| Mining | 36 deaths |
| Transport and storage | 23 deaths |
| Agriculture | 20 deaths |
| Construction | 10 deaths |

(Source: Better Health Channel 2012)

workers injured while performing paid duties, bystanders killed by the working activities of another person, and others including volunteers, students, homemakers, and farm workers. Deaths caused by disease and suicide were not included. Between 1989 and 1992, work-related accidents claimed the lives of 3627 Australians. This equates to nearly 16% of all deaths during this time period. Of those killed, 2389 were fatally injured while working or commuting. People aged between 25 and 34 years were over-represented. The majority of deaths occurred during the day, with mid-morning and mid-afternoon peaks. The bulk of the people killed were men (around 90%); whose death rates were, on average, 10 times higher than those recorded for women across all categories (Better Health Channel 2012; see also <www.betterhealth.vic.gov.au>).

Some industries are more dangerous than others. The average annual death rates per 100 000 people for the most hazardous industries in Australia are shown in Table 4.4. In Australia, the average annual death rates per 100 000 people for the most hazardous occupations include those shown in Table 4.5. The most common places for work-related deaths include those shown in Table 4.6.

In addition to the more chilling concerns regarding workplace fatalities, and in an effort to act responsibly, managers are becoming increasingly aware of issues that are now being incorporated into the health and safety remit. These issues are worth mentioning given their implications for ethical management.

**Table 4.5** Most dangerous occupations

| Commercial pilots | 197 deaths |
|---|---|
| Fishermen and fisherwomen | 117 deaths |
| Forestry labourers | 116 deaths |
| Drilling plant operators | 72 deaths |
| Mining labourers | 66 deaths |
| Ships' pilots and deck officers | 54 deaths |
| Structural steel labourers | 43 deaths |
| Truck drivers | 41 deaths |
| Excavation and earthmoving machinery operators | 39 deaths |

(Source: Better Health Channel 2012)

**Table 4.6** Most dangerous places

| Public roads | 33% |
|---|---|
| Farms | 19% |
| Industrial or construction areas | 13% |
| Mines or quarries | 8% |
| Trade or service areas | 8% |

(Source: Better Health Channel 2012)

**ergonomics** – the study of efficiency of individuals in their workplace, primarily used in today's context as referring to workplace layout in order to prevent injury and promote wellbeing.

## Ergonomics

Broadly speaking, **ergonomics** studies individuals' working environment efficiency (Visser et al. 2008). Ensuring an ergonomically appropriate workstation involves assessment of key features such as equipment, chairs, avoiding eye strain, temperature, lighting, and others. Long-term damage to employees, such as repetitive strain injury, can occur if individuals' ergonomic needs are not appropriately assessed.

## Stress and mental health

Mental health issues and mental illness are an increasing issue in the workplace, and are among the greatest causes of reduced employee productivity. The Australian Bureau of Statistics (2008) indicates that there is a 20% chance of Australians having mental health issues. A known antecedent to mental health issues is the level of stress that an employee may be facing, and this is further compounded by the fact that workers report rising stress levels. In what is named the **Sisyphus effect**, many employees feel this effect in regard to their jobs where the email box fills up and is cleared – only to find the next day it has refilled again.

**Sisyphus effect** – named after the son of Aeolus, punished in Hades in Greek mythology, who was condemned by the gods to roll a boulder uphill, only to repeat the exercise the next day. Many employees feel this way in regard to their jobs.

Work becomes a grind and there is no work/life balance ('Stress levels rising' 2012). A poll by Essential (Carl 2012) found that:

- 49% of full-time workers do not have enough time to keep in touch with family and friends
- 51% agree with the statement: 'I find it difficult to balance work and other responsibilities'
- 63% of full-time workers feel stressed from juggling work and other responsibilities.

Allowing people greater choice and flexibility in the workforce could help to alleviate these stressors.

Stress and mental health (© shutterstock.com/file404)

## Sexual harassment

**sexual harassment** – unwelcome sexual advances, requests for sexual favours and verbal and physical contact of a sexual nature in the workplace.

For many years, **sexual harassment** was tolerated in the workplace, and incidents that we would consider outrageous today were trivialised or accepted as an unfortunate consequence of men and women working together. According to the Australian Human Rights Commission (2012), 25.3% of women and 16.2% of men have experienced sexual harassment in the past five years. Sexual harassment involves unwelcome sexual advances (either verbally or physically) and, in the more extreme form, there is an implicit or explicit understanding that an employee's employment circumstances hinge on whether they submit to or reject the advances. These advances can lead to an employee's work performance being impeded as a hostile, uncomfortable, and intimidating workplace ensues (Adams & Maine 1998). The most common type of harassment is sexually suggestive comments and jokes. Most people who are sexually harassed will either resign or not make a complaint; however, where a complaint is made, there is usually a cash settlement.

In a summary of studies on factors affecting the perception and judgement of sexual harassment, Adikaram, Gunawardena and Perea (2011) note that:

- male and female perceptions of sexual harassment differ, in that females tend to view more behaviours as sexual harassment than men
- tolerance of sexual harassment seems to decrease as a person ages
- the higher a woman's level of education, the broader her understanding of sexual harassment

- the more exposure a person has to sexual harassment, the wider their definition of sexual harassment tends to become
- participants find it easier to identify circumstances of sexual harassment where there is a power imbalance, than in relationships with peers
- sexual harassment by a man is seen as more stigmatised in a work setting than in a social setting.

Regrettably, when the recipient of unwanted behaviour perceives their organisation as more tolerant of sexual harassment, there is less chance of behaviour being labelled as sexual harassment (McCabe & Hardman 2005). Internationally, a number of countries have laws against sexual harassment; however, these laws now also include a **positive duty on sexual harassment**, which means that businesses now need to be proactive, take steps to eliminate sexual harassment, and to regularly assess their organisation's compliance (Victorian Equal Opportunity & Human Rights Commission 2012). The number of harassment cases is said to be rising and this may be due to the fact that victims are more likely to report it ('Nasty, but rarer sexual harassment' 2011). Not all such cases, however, are necessarily valid, and many high-profile cases have turned out to be unfounded (see Schneiders 2012).

**positive duty on sexual harassment** – businesses now need to be proactive and take steps to eliminate sexual harassment, and to regularly assess their organisation's compliance.

# Ethics in the media: Harassment in the ADF

The Australian Human Rights Commission Report on the review into treatment of women at the Australian Defence Force indicated sexual discrimination and sexual harassment were commonplace and viewed as part of the culture of the organisation (Australian Human Rights Commission 2012).

# Ethics in practice: A question of appropriateness

You are friends with a colleague as you both started on the same day and went through the company induction program together. Your friend recently confided in you that he has been admiring another co-worker for some time. As a result of this affection he has approached the co-worker via LinkedIn, and also on Facebook. She has accepted the former, but rejected the latter. Your friend has been sending a series of occasional emails which are flirtatious in nature and he often follows up with the odd phone

*cont.*

*cont.*

call. More recently, he has been dropping small gifts on her desk, and whenever they are in meetings he finds it difficult to take his eyes off her. Whenever the opportunity presents, he tries to sit himself next to her in meetings and occasionally brushes up against her.

**Questions:**

1. Would any of this behaviour constitute sexual harassment?

2. What is your opinion of the behaviour's appropriateness if the female colleague reciprocates?

3. What is your view of the behaviour's appropriateness if the female colleague has no interest in your friend?

# Ethics in practice: Office romances

Office romances may be frowned on or even prohibited by some organisations because of the ethical issues that can develop. The couple may practise deception in conducting their relationship, and such romances can create potential biases that could develop in the workplace. Also, clearly there is more potential for favouritism between individuals who are romantically involved, and thus they could be compromised in their office dealings.

**Question:**

1. What guidelines, if any, do you believe should be put in place in regard to office romances and to protect against conflicts of interest that may arise?

## Bullying

**workplace bullying** – persistent, unwelcome behaviour; mostly using unwarranted or invalid criticism, finding fault, exclusion or isolation.

**Workplace bullying** has been defined as persistent, unwelcome behaviour, mostly using unwarranted or invalid criticism, finding fault, exclusion or isolation. Instances of workplace bullying have the deliberate intent of causing physical and psychological distress and can include behaviours that intimidate, offend, degrade or humiliate a worker, possibly in front of co-workers, clients or customers (Victoria Legal Aid 2012). Bullying in the workplace can also have tragic consequences (see Victoria Legal Aid 2012). Table 4.7 highlights the characteristics of bullies and bulling and the common reasons why people are bullied, while Table 4.8 presents the effects of bully on the individual and the organisation.

**Table 4.7**  Workplace bullying

Bullying in the workplace can take place between:
- a worker and a manager (or supervisor); 1 in 5 US workers are bullied
- co-workers, including trainees; 14% of bullies work at the same level
- a worker and another person in the workplace (e.g., a client or a student).

Characteristics of bullies:
- 84% of bullies are female
- 81% of bullies are bosses
- low self-esteem; the psychologist, Nathaniel Brandon, suggested that the higher one's self-esteem, the more likely we are to treat others with respect, kindness and generosity
- most were childhood bullies.

The characteristics of bullying:
- ongoing; targets endure bullying for almost two years before filing a complaint
- common; bullying is three times more prevalent than sexual harassment
- covert; bullying is often invisible and occurs behind closed doors without witnesses
- endorsed; even when bullying is witnessed, team members usually side with the bully.

Reasons targets are bullied:
- they stand up; 58% are targeted because they stand up to unfair treatment by the bully
- envy; 56% because the bully envies the target's level of competence
- just nice; 49% are targeted simply because they are nice people
- have ethical standards; 46% are bullied because they are ethical
- just because; 39% are bullied because it was just their turn.

(Based on: Cade 2011; Bully Busters 2011; Brunner & Costello 2003; Kieseker & Marchant 1999; Namie & Namie 2000; Namie 2003; Becker 2012; Victoria Legal Aid 2012)

**Table 4.8**  Effects of bullying

Effects of bullying on an individual:
- severe psychological distress, sleep disturbances and feelings of anxiety; 41% of bullied individuals were diagnosed with depression
- physical symptoms, ill health; over 80% reported health effects such as severe anxiety, loss of concentration, sleeplessness
- incapacity to work; reduced output and performance
- loss of self-confidence, self-esteem and sometimes suicidal thoughts; 31% of female and 21% of male victims suffered from post-traumatic stress disorder.

Effects of bullying on the organisation:
- lower productivity and efficiency
- high staff turnover; 82% of bullied individuals leave their jobs
- higher recruitment and induction costs
- increased absenteeism and sick leave
- workplace trauma; as many as 10% of suicides may be related to workplace traumatisation
- time dealing with complaints; however only 13% of bullies are ever punished or terminated
- cost of counselling; in 51% of cases HR did nothing to help the victim despite requests (in 32% of cases HR supported the bully by reacting negatively to the victim)
- effect on co-workers
- stress-related costs
- compensation claims
- early retirement costs, counselling costs
- costs of litigation.

(Based on: Cade 2011; Bully Busters 2011; Brunner & Costello 2003; Kieseker & Marchant 1999; Namie & Namie 2000; Namie 2003; Becker 2012; Victoria Legal Aid 2012)

# Ethics in the media: Extreme bullying

In a horrific bullying case, a labourer alleged he was hit with a 30-centimetre piece of wood, had a nail gun fired at him without being told it was unloaded, and was docked pay for taking a work mate to hospital (Schneiders 2010).

In Australia, WorkPro (2008) found that 24% of employees have been bullied or discriminated against, and further, that 44% of people have witnessed workplace bullying. In June 2012, the Federal Government launched an inquiry into bullying, and it found that the absence of a single, nationally accepted definition of workplace bullying makes the problem difficult to police and subsequently prosecute. The inquiry also noted that the distinction between home and workplace bullying was becoming blurred with the introduction of new technology. The accessibility of text messages and social media means that people can be bullied anywhere, anytime (see C Lucas 2012).

# Ethics on reflection: Experiences of bullying

**Questions:**

1. Have you experienced bullying at school, university or the workplace? Describe the circumstances surrounding the bullying.

2. What are the usual antecedents for bullying to occur in the workplace?

Bullying is a significant health and safety issue, for which employers are being held responsible. As a consequence, they have a moral and legal obligation to remain vigilant against bullying in the workplace. Protection of bullies is particularly problematic when the individual is the CEO or a high-achieving member of the team. Sometimes there is a tendency to overlook bad behaviour and bullying because the individual is performing well and achieving results for the organisation (Smith 2012b).

Essentially, bullying is aggressive behaviour deliberately intended to cause physical or psychological distress to others (Kieseker & Marchant 1999). It is also perceived as an abuse of power. Behaviour is defined as bullying if a reasonable person observing the situation would consider it to be bullying. A reasonable person is an objective third party. The key is a consistent pattern of behaviour. It is sometimes easy to confuse petty disputes and concerns about workload with bullying. A review of the 2080 bullying complaints lodged with Worksafe Victoria in 2010–2011 revealed that more than two-thirds of these claims were unsubstantiated. Only eight cases were considered serious enough to justify potential prosecution (Guilliatt 2011b).

## Ethics in practice: Bullying criteria

Bullying will generally meet the following four criteria (Victoria Legal Aid 2012):
- It is repeated.
- It is unwelcome and unsolicited.
- The recipient considers the behaviour to be offensive, intimidating, humiliating or threatening.

- Based on the available information, the behaviour would be considered offensive, intimidating, humiliating or threatening to the individual it is directed at, or, for that matter, others who are witness to or affected by it.

**Question:**
1. Create a hypothetical bullying case that meets all four criteria.

## Violence in the workplace

On 24 August 2012, Jeffrey Johnson, a laid-off women's handbag designer, created mayhem at his former workplace, Hazan Corp, with his 0.45 calibre pistol before dying in a gunfight with police. **Going postal** is a commonly used term in the US for employees who assault or kill fellow workers. The phrase was coined after multiple shootings in the late 1980s and early 1990s at US postal services (Berling, Dupré & Kelloway 2009). An unsafe environment at its extreme can result in violence in the workplace and, although relatively rare, the outcome can be tragic when a disgruntled employee attacks another individual and then, commonly, turns on themselves following the attack (Adams & Maine 1998). Workplace violence is clearly a significant issue for Occupational Health and Safety. Characteristically, these individuals have significant grievances against their employer as a result of perceived injustices or unfair treatment (Grove 2012), for which organisations may need to take some responsibility.

**going postal** – a commonly used term in the US for employees who initiate violence in the workplace.

# Ethics in the media: Bullying and violence

Bullying can and does lead to violence. In April 1999, Pierre Lebrun, an employee of OC Transpo in Ottawa, Canada, went on a shooting spree, killing four people before he committed suicide. Lebrun's colleagues had subjected him to incessant bullying and ridicule about a speech impediment and facial tic that he had. At the coroner's inquest the jury made 77 recommendations about preventing and responding to workplace violence, paying particular attention to psychological violence, which it defined as 'bullying, mobbing, teasing, ridicule or any other act or words that could psychologically hurt or isolate a person in the workplace' (Bernardi n.d., p. 3).

## Ethics in separation

Separation of an employee from their organisation can come in many forms. These can be:

- a voluntary departure, usually for another job
- retirement following a period of service
- layoff as a result of technological, structural or financial considerations
- dismissal as a result of poor performance or disciplinary action.

### Voluntary departure

**voluntary departure** – where separation from the workplace by an employee is consensual between employer and employee.

As the separation is consensual in a **voluntary departure**, it is associated with relatively few ethical issues. One consideration, however, is the form and content of a letter of reference that the departing employee may request. For a manager, the ethical issue is of honesty in their assessment of the former employee, and their willingness to communicate this assessment, particularly in writing, to a third party. To alleviate this concern, some organisations have a policy of only providing information in writing, and then only stating the duration of the employee's tenure and their job title.

# Ethics in the media: Employee departure

Given the cost of hiring and replacing employees when an employee does leave an organisation, this should prompt a moment of reflection as to why the person is leaving. The Government of Western Australia's Public Sector Commission (2009) believes exit interviews allow for data to be collected to affect change in common areas of dissatisfaction, for example lack of training and development (D'Angelo Fisher 2012b).

## Retirement

Compulsory **retirement** at a set age does exist in some industries (e.g. in airlines). This can be problematic for employees who feel they are too young to retire and want to continue employment; however, in many organisations retirement is at the discretion of the employee. Ethical issues can arise around compulsory retirement and the company's responsibility to provide the employee with all the retirement benefits to which they are entitled. Issues can also arise when an employee should retire but does not want to do so.

> **retirement** – withdrawing from one's workplace, usually as result of advanced age.

## Layoffs

In recent years, layoffs are frequently prompted by **downsizing**, which is rationalisation of the workforce due to closing operations or relocating operations to lower wage environments (Visser et al. 2008). When downsizing, there are several ethical issues to consider, and the first is in relation to the selection process of those who will be laid off. Just as in the recruitment phase, it is important that the organisation uses relevant and appropriate criteria; further that the process for selection is fair and that the subsequent departure process is handled respectfully. It has been noted that downsizing can be destabilising in an organisation and that can cause temporary harm (Adams & Maine 1998). The Swiss Bank, UBS, in an extensive cost-cutting exercise, shed 10 000 jobs. The difficulty of job loss was compounded by the fact that many staff turned up to work to find they no longer had access to the building – which is definitely not a respectful way to handle layoffs ('Business this week' 2012b).

> **downsizing** – reducing the workforce due to rationalisation, closure or relocation of operations.

The guideline is that employees should be informed, consulted and compensated. Informed means they should be told in advance of the likelihood of workplace change and the outcome of that change. They should be consulted on the processes in an effort to identify alternative resolutions, and remunerated to help compensate the loss of income. Some organisations go further and provide **outplacement** opportunities, which are support activities, in the form of training and counselling, to assist in the transition from the current working environment to a new job.

> **outplacement** – support mechanisms to assist in the transition from the current work environment to a new job.

**open book management** – the frequent sharing of a firm's financial data with employees, thus creating transparency in relation to the operation of the firm.

It has been suggested that greater transparency can assist in the separation process. **Open book management** advocates the frequent sharing of a firm's financial data with employees, thus creating transparency in relation to the operation of the firm and impeding losses. Some companies, such as Ford Australia and King Arthur Flour, used this management style during the global financial crisis (Schumpeter 2012b).

# Ethics on reflection: Computerisation and robotics

Where a computer process has taken over the role that was normally performed by an individual, the outcome is the **de-skilling** of various job holders, and, while unfortunate, it is an inevitability of technological progression and often another reason for layoffs (Tavani 2007). As robots are integrated into the workforce, there are implications for workers with some roles becoming defunct, e.g. bomb disposal experts now oversee the process, rather than being on the frontline (Borenstein 2010).

**Questions:**
1. Identify three jobs that you think will become redundant in the near future as a consequence of computerisation and robotics.
2. In highly skilled roles, such as surgeons, are robotics putting lives at risk?

**de-skilling** – decrease in the quality/range of skilled labour, particularly as a result of new technologies.

## Dismissal

Ethical issues surrounding dismissals are intricately woven around the cause of the dismissal. That is, is the dismissal consistent with policy, and has due process been undertaken in the investigation and the ultimate decision to dismiss an employee? Court decisions are littered with findings that have deemed that an employee was unfairly dismissed due to the nature of the circumstance or where an organisation did not adhere to its own policies.

# Ethics on reflection: Unfair dismissal?

There are now cases of people being dismissed for criticising an employer on social networking sites (Havenstein 2008). Do you think such dismissals are fair?

## Ethics in practice: Cases of dismissal

Look up two recent cases of unfair dismissal and relate the circumstances.

For a dismissal to be valid, it must be consistent with stated policy that has been clearly articulated to employees. An **immediate dismissal** is for an offence deemed to be significant and warrants immediate departure, for example, for an action that is blatantly unsafe or illegal. A more routine dismissal is usually for poor performance and involves a process of several stages, through which an employee is made aware that their performance is inadequate and efforts are made to rectify the situation. Naturally, issues of equity will also surface if two or more employees are guilty of the same circumstance that has resulted in a dismissal.

**immediate dismissal** – where the offence is deemed to be significant and warrants immediate departure.

Most unfair dismissal claims do not get to court. In Australia in 2012, a review of the *Fair Work Act 2009* found that only 4% of the 6759 cases brought forward actually went to tribunal. The majority were resolved before, during or through the process of mediation ('Go away payments' 2012). Claimants may be liable for their former employer's costs if their claim is found to be vexatious; there has also been a reduction in the deadline for adverse claims, with employees only allowed 21 days to realise they have been unfairly dismissed (Fair Work Commission 2013).

## Ethics in the media: Unfounded claims

Sometimes employees cause problems in the workplace. Indeed, many cases have occurred where the employee has claimed harassment or discrimination, yet the courts have found these claims to be unfounded. In one such case, the judge found that the employee had used the complaints system as an instrument of intimidation (see Guilliatt 2011a).

# Ethics in practice: A dismissible offence?

Your company has a policy of random alcohol and drug testing, and this morning, recreational drugs were detected on two employees. In accordance with your policy, this is a dismissible offence, and action was taken immediately. However, the affected employees have approached union representatives, who have pointed out that the detection was a result of the taking of recreational drugs many days beforehand, and that nobody had taken drugs in the workplace.

**Question:**

1. What would be your response as the HR manager to the union?

# Conclusion

Fazey (2012) indicates that from an HR perspective, there are two ethical dimensions. The first relates to employment practices and the way that individual employees in the workforce are managed. The second dimension is to do with the long-term promotion and sustainability of an ethical business culture. Within this chapter, we have been focusing on the first dimension, but later in the text we will be examining how one develops an ethical culture within the organisation.

As we have seen, there are some dominant ethical principles that apply in workplaces, and that create a 'just' work environment. They primarily relate to:

- respectful treatment of individuals
- recognition of the rights of employees
- ensuring that the duties of the organisation are clear
- fairness and equity in the management of employees
- confidentiality and privacy in all dealings
- adherence to due processes
- justice in the treatment of individuals
- transparency and honesty
- environmental awareness and sustainability in relation to HR practices
- integrity in relation to the actions of individual employees and the organisation.

As noted, recruitment and selection can bring up a whole host of concerns surrounding equity and avoidance of discrimination in its various forms. For example, mature job seekers are being left on the employment sidelines as employers spurn them in favour of younger candidates (Adage 2013). In Australia, there are numerous laws intended to protect individuals in the workplace and in public life from discrimination. There is also growing intolerance for discriminatory practices, and it has been observed that, increasingly, juries are taking the side especially of women who face workplace discrimination (Williams & Cuddy 2012).

Similarly, compensation and reward considerations must also be mindful of the potential for unfairness. In regard to the work environment itself, many ethical principles come into play; for example, honesty and integrity in relation to fraudulent activities and sabotage, privacy in relation to employee surveillance, fairness in relation to workplace flexibility, and the right to due process where an action has been taken against an employee, or where there has been some form of capricious or arbitrary decision-making.

Workplace health and safety evokes recognition of the duties of an organisation, particularly as employers have a duty of care to provide a safe work environment. For an environment to be safe, consideration also needs to be given to not only physical wellbeing but also mental health issues. The work environment should be free from intimidation, ridicule, harassment, exploitation, manipulation or abuse of power. Abuse of power can take many forms such as sexual harassment or the more common incidences of workplace bullying. The 1999 Morgan & Banks Australian *Job Index Survey* reported that 10% of employers believe that workplace bullying was increasing. Workplace bullying encompasses a spectrum of behaviour from malicious rumours to verbal and physical intimidation, and even violence (Hanley 2003). If an employee is bullied, harassed or discriminated against, this would clearly violate the duty of care and, consequently, an employer could vicariously be liable for the conduct of a manager or supervisor.

To conclude, the final stage of the relationship between the employee and organisation is when the employee leaves. The departure may be voluntary or involuntary. Transparency should be evident during both dismissal and redundancy processes. For example, employees have the right to know that their job is being considered for redundancy and by what process the selection will be made; this applies not only to redundancies, but also to other forms of separation. Traditionally, unless their dismissal is summary or instant, an individual will have received warnings before dismissal, as a result of performance management.

## Ethics on video

**Excessive executive pay** – *Millionaire CEOs in America. Are they overpaid?* 2008, YouTube, MiCasaMiDinero, 17 July, <www.youtube.com/watch?v=8iiN-eiJXqw&feature=related>.

**Gender imbalances in pay** – *Discrimination in the workplace* 2010, YouTube, Press TV Melbourne, 28 October, <www.youtube.com/watch?v=8wRfqAWPDaU>.

See web material for more videos.

## Ethics at the movies

Here are a few movie suggestions that have ethical content related to HRM:

**Philadelphia** – starring Tom Hanks, typifies the discrimination experienced by the gay community, and those affected by AIDS. *Philadelphia* 1993, motion picture trailer, Demme, J. & Saxon, E.

*  **The Devil Wears Prada** – starring Meryl Streep as a boss who exhibits chronic bullying behaviour, as evidenced by her unrelenting and unreasonable demands on her staff. *The Devil Wears Prada* 2006, motion picture trailer, Finerman, D.

*  **Author's pick**

See web material for more movies.

## Ethics on the web

**Australian Human Rights Commission**, a guide to Australia's anti-discrimination laws, <http://humanrights.gov.au/info_for_employers/law/index.html>.

**Fair Work Ombudsman**, a HR employment guide from the Commonwealth of Australia, <www.fairwork.gov.au/Pages/default.aspx>.

See web material for more web references.

# Student exercises

See web material for answers to student short answer questions.

## Short answer questions

1.  What are the potential ethical issues around office romances?
2.  What are some current statistics on bullying?
3.  When an individual behaves inappropriately, unprofessionally or unethically at work, it is often picked up during the performance management process, or alternatively an independent conversation is undertaken by the staff member and their supervisor. These conversations are never easy. How might one approach this situation and what recommendations can you give for having these difficult conversations?
4.  What are some of the current myths about bullying?
5.  Meritocracy is promoting an individual because of their value and contribution to the company versus being promoted by how long the person has been with the company. The latter method is commonly favoured by unions as it creates a degree of certainty; whereas companies tend to promote people on the basis of worth. What are the ethical issues associated with each of these approaches to promotion?

## Experiential exercise

Take a self-test at: <http://bullyfreeatwork.com/blog/?page_id=2>.

## Small case

### Case: Discrimination

A member of your sales team has recently revealed that he is a practising homosexual. He is involved in considerable client contact in an industry, which has a particularly masculine culture. You are afraid that his homosexuality might affect your business. You propose to release this individual from your company sometime over the next few months.

**Question:**

**1.** Discuss the ethicality of this proposed action.

# Large case

## Case: Rivers Australia and sexual harassment

### Background

Rivers are a discount clothing and footwear merchant with 150 stores Australia-wide (Hadfield 2011). Rivers have operated for 85 years as a family business, with a sole director and shareholder, currently Harry Fieldman. Between 2011 and 2013, two female ex-employees lodged sexual harassment claims against Mr Fieldman. The employees had worked for Mr Fieldman at different times, yet their accounts were remarkably similar.

### The case

Ms Robin, then aged 32, was a designer who had been employed at Rivers. She alleged that she experienced sexual harassment from Mr Fieldman from September 2009 to July 2010, and that the harassment ceased only when she left the company. She claimed that Mr Fieldman groped her bottom and breasts, made sexual comments to her, and forced her to model lingerie. When she initially lodged the claim, the matter was dismissed, as it was felt that the sexual harassment was unsubstantiated and her pre-existing mental conditions negated the claim. Undeterred, Ms Robin started proceedings with the Magistrate's Court, at which point the case was settled (Heard 2011). Ms Robin's lawyers indicated they would pursue a common law claim of aggravated damages against Mr Fieldman. During court proceedings on 2 September 2013, Justice Debbie Mortimer ruled that two other ex-employees of Rivers, making similar allegations, would be able to testify to assist her in assessing both parties' version of events (Portelli 2013).

One of the other ex-employees allowed to corroborate Ms Robin's claim was Ms Adamo, who had also worked for Rivers, although she left the company in 2007, after 14 years' employment there. Claims were made that in 1999 Ms Adamo was asked to wear a catsuit and appear as Pussy Galore in a Rivers advertisement. When she refused, she claims Mr Fieldman starting calling her 'Pussy'. He also called her various other names: 'Madam Lash', 'the Boss' and 'the Queen', while telling her he loved her and wanted to marry her. Ms Adamo lodged a sexual harassment civil action claim in the Federal Court under the *Australian Human Rights Commission Act 1986*, as since leaving Rivers' employment she had suffered depression and post-traumatic stress. Ms Adamo was due to give evidence at Ms Robin's case, but instead settlements for both Ms Adamo and Ms Robin were reached on 3 September 2013. The third employee never brought a case against Mr Fieldman or Rivers.

### Ethical considerations

In determining sexual harassment, the following considerations will be made: was the conduct broadly sexual; was the attention unreciprocal (Redrup 2013); and would a reasonable person have anticipated the interaction would make the person humiliated, harassed, offended or intimidated? The nature of the relationship will be taken into account, as well as the power structure of the relationship; age, position, and gender are all issues that relate to power and have a bearing on the assessment (Monash University 2003).

*cont.*

*cont.*

## Timeline of events

| | |
|---|---|
| 1993–2007 | Ms Adamo employed by Rivers. |
| 1999–2007 | Ms Adamo alleges that Mr Fieldman spoke inappropriately to her during her employment at Rivers, with the inappropriate behaviour beginning in 1999. |
| September 2009– July 2010 | Mr Fieldman allegedly makes unwelcome sexual advances toward Ms Robin. |
| July 2010 | Ms Robin resigns from Rivers. |
| November 2011 | Ms Robin's sexual harassment accusation against Mr Fieldman leads to a confidential settlement, with Workcover's intervention. Her lawyers indicate that they will pursue a common law claim against Rivers, as they believe Ms Robin's post-traumatic stress disorder was caused by the bullying she experienced at Rivers (Heard 2011). |
| February 2013 | Ms Adamo lodges a Federal Court civil action claim seeking damages for mental illness and post-traumatic stress suffered while working for Rivers. |
| 2 September 2013 | Justice Debbie Mortimer rules in favour of hearing Ms Adamo' and another ex-employee's testimony to help her reach a decision about the case. |
| 3 September 2013 | Settlements reached for both the Adamo and Robin cases against Mr Fieldman and Rivers. |

**Questions:**
1. After two sexual harassment claims at the one company, how could the company culture be changed, particularly when the owner is the single shareholder?
2. Given the reasonable person's 'test' for sexual harassment, discuss this case in terms of ethical issues in work place health and safety.

See web material for:
- answers to short answer questions
- additional student cases
- tutor resources (tutor password required)
- additional material including Ethics at the movies, Ethics in print, Ethics on video and Ethics on the web.

# Chapter 5

## Ethical issues in marketing

'Price is what you pay. Value is what you get.'
Warren Buffett, 1930–,
American investment entrepreneur

## Chapter aim

To identify current ethical issues in marketing.

## Chapter objectives

1. Identify the dominant ethical principles that apply to ethical decision-making in relation to marketing practices.
2. Recognise some of the key ethical concerns that apply to the product mix.
3. Describe within the pricing mix which ethical practices are at play.
4. Relate the main ethical criticisms of promotion using the five components of promotion.
5. Illustrate ethical issues that can arise in the course of distributing products or services.
6. Discuss ethical issues in relation to the people dimension of marketing.
7. Distinguish between cause-related marketing and social marketing.

# Ethics in the media: Healthcare fraud

In 2011, the US Department of Justice ordered pharmaceutical giant GlaxoSmithKline to pay US$3 billion in criminal and civil liabilities in the largest healthcare fraud settlement in US history.

GSK were caught promoting several drugs for unapproved uses, failing to report safety data, paying kickbacks to physicians, and reporting inaccurate pricing (Skeptical Raptor's Blog 2013).

## Introduction

**Marketing** is an activity and processes that create, deliver, exchange and communicate value offerings for customers, clients and society (American Marketing Association 2013a). Marketing is considered a critical function of business but it is not without criticism. The more vehement critics have blamed marketing for all the ills of contemporary capitalism through its use of what they see as ruthless targeting of neurological pathways and the assumption that we, as consumers, are being manipulated and exploited. Whether it is cupcakes or Angry Birds we are apparently unaware that we are stumbling into a state of dependent consumerism (Thompson 2012).

However, the aim of marketing, whether in the 'for-profit' or 'not-for-profit' context, is to add value, differentiate products and services from those of competitors, and to create a competitive advantage. To achieve this marketing, practitioners engage in a number of activities, some viewed as appropriate and some inappropriate. **Marketing ethics**, therefore, entails 'the societal and professional standards of right and fair practices that are expected of marketing managers in their oversight of strategy formulation, implementation and control' (Laczniak & Murphy 2006, p. 159). When examining 'right and fair practices' there are moral principles that apply to and influence marketing decision-making. When these principles are not applied, ethical lapses tend to occur.

## Ethical principles in marketing

There are several ethical principles that are relevant to marketing:

**Duty of care** – companies have a duty of care to ensure products are not only effective but are also safe (healthy is another issue) and will not cause harm. For service providers, it means they fully meet their service requirements and what is expected of them.

**Rights** – the area of **consumer rights** is topical and essentially refers to a consumer's expectation of entitlement to, for example:

- the right to safety
- the right to expect a product to perform

**marketing** – the activity, set of institutions, and processes for creating, communicating, delivering and exchanging offerings that have value for customers, clients, partners and society at large.

**marketing ethics** – an examination of moral principles and the societal and professional standards of right and fair practices as they apply to marketing decision-making.

**duty of care** – ensuring that products and services are not only effective but are also safe and will not cause harm.

**rights** – expectations of entitlement.

**consumer rights** – expectations of entitlement for consumers such as: the right to safety, the right to redress if something is wrong, the right to be accurately informed, the right to choose, the right to be heard.

- the right to redress if something is wrong
- the right to be accurately informed
- the right to choose
- the right to be heard
- provide feedback.

While we frequently speak of consumer rights, it should also be remembered that consumers also have obligations, for example, to dispose of unwanted packaging and products responsibly, and to provide honest information when appropriately requested (e.g. not to make fraudulent claims on insurance).

**respect** – acknowledging the basic human dignity of all stakeholders, which would include customers, suppliers, distributors and competitors.

**Respect** – acknowledging the basic human dignity of all stakeholders, who include customers, suppliers, distributors and competitors. This could entail: responding promptly to consumer needs, not engaging in blatant anti-competitive behaviour, valuing individual differences, avoiding stereotyping customers or depicting demographic groups (e.g., gender, race, sexual orientation) in a negative way (American Marketing Association 2013b) and responding respectfully when complaints are made.

**honesty** – ensuring accurate representation of products or services.

**Honesty** – ensuring accurate representation of the product or service, identification of risks linked to usage, and any additional costs and research associated with the product or service. This relates to circumstances such as false and misleading advertising and sales promotions, manipulative sales practices and deceptive pricing practices. With deceptive pricing this may be: false price comparisons, misleading selling prices, omitting conditions of the sale, or making low price offers available only when other items are purchased (Marion 2001). It is purported that over 43% of internet sites misrepresent information or contain errors (Goree 2007). A simple example of the provision of potentially deceptive information is the use of meta tags, which are words used in the construction of a web page, that can be identified by search engines. The descriptors; however, may not represent the content of the site, but are used, effectively, to drive traffic to the site (Tavani 2007).

**accepting responsibility** – acknowledging the consequences of decisions and strategies.

**Accepting responsibility** – acknowledging the consequences of marketing decisions and strategies, by such actions as: serving the needs of customers, avoiding coercion, acknowledging obligations to stakeholders, recognising commitments to vulnerable market segments such as children, seniors and the economically impoverished, protecting the environment and taking immediate action in relation to risks (for example, in a product recall situation).

**transparency** – engaging in the spirit of openness.

**Transparency** – promoting a spirit of openness in marketing operations. This entails unrestricted access to information and full disclosure on circumstances that could affect customers' perceptions. Transparency is not always apparent and it appears that the pharmaceutical industry does not always publish the truth about whether their new drugs work, whether the drugs are better than drugs already on the market, and whether the side effects are a price worth paying (Goldacre 2012).

**equity and fairness** – balancing justly the needs of buyers with the interests of the seller.

**Equity and fairness** – justly balancing the needs of the buyer with the interests of the seller. The areas of focus include: the equitable treatment of customers, avoidance of deceptive communication, appropriate complaint handling, rejecting customer manipulation that could harm customer trust, avoiding conflicts of interest and not engaging in questionable pricing practices. Fairness, for some, also involves the promotion of fair trade.

Organisations that engage in ethical marketing behaviour, such as The Body Shop, engender trust and loyalty. In contrast, organisations that exhibit unethical behaviour erode the confidence of consumers and key stakeholders and can ultimately threaten the viability of the organisation through the imposition of greater control, or loss of profitability. For the benefit of simplicity, we will use the well-known '5 Ps' of marketing – product, price, place, promotion and people – to structure the chapter's discussion, as we investigate the many areas in which organisations may face ethical challenges.

# Products

The product dimension of the marketing mix can cover many areas; for example, when packages are intentionally mislabeled as to contents, size, weight, or use information (this constitutes deceptive packaging), selling hazardous or defective products without disclosing the dangers, failing to perform promised services, and not honouring warranty obligations (Marion 2001). The issue of product piracy and intellectual property theft will be examined in Chapter 8 on international business; however, let us look first at some of the key ethical concerns in relation to the product mix.

## Questionable products

**Questionable products** are products that may be deemed to be unsafe, harmful or questionable given their potential impact. One immediately thinks of tobacco, alcohol and gambling, but there are other mainstream products that could be considered. For example, in the US, Amber Alert GPS (2012) market a tracking device that also carries a microphone to enable parents to eavesdrop on their children. This product could clearly have an impact on people's privacy. The overarching ethical issue is the extent to which marketers take responsibility for the negative impact of products or services.

**questionable products** – products that are unsafe, harmful or of questionable value, given their potential impact.

## Product recall

When a product is known to be defective or unsafe, a company has the responsibility to take back and correct, or discontinue, the product to avoid any further harm. Regrettably, this has not always happened with the degree of urgency that it should and consumers and others have suffered. Both the short- and long-term costs to a firm can be considerable. In 2010, Toyota, having already halted sales and production of eight of their top-selling cars in the US, recalled more than 9 million cars worldwide, leaving the company with the prospect of billions of dollars in charges and operating losses. The Toyota brand, once synonymous with high quality standards, took a heavy hit (Connor 2010). Not all companies take the transparent approach, as was the case in a 'phantom recall' conducted by McNeil Consumer Healthcare in early 2009 (see Tennyson 2012).

**product recall** – the taking back, correcting or discontinuing of a product known to be defective or unsafe.

## Ethics in practice: Product recall

History is littered with situations of product recall, some of which have been handled better than others. Undertake a literature search on three well-known product recalls: Johnson & Johnson's recall of their painkiller Tylenol; the recall of the Ford Pinto; and the Toyota recalls.

**Question:**

**1.** What key lessons can be taken from these experiences?

## Ethics in the media: Defective products

In June 2012, Sandoz, a unit of Novartis, recalled 10 lots of Introvale birth-control pills because a 13-week blister package of Introvale birth-control pills displayed the placebo pills in the incorrect order. This marked the fourth major birth-control pill recall in the same year ('Sandoz recalls some Introvale birth control pills' 2012).

**planned obsolescence** – when a product is deliberately designed with a limitation to its functional life span.

## Product obsolescence

The practice of **planned obsolescence** is when a product is deliberately designed with a limitation to its functional life span. Despite significant advances in technology, planned obsolescence is topical because of the emphasis on continuous product improvement and environmental consequences (Guilti 2009), to say nothing of the additional burden on the consumer. An example of this is Monsanto's role in the agricultural seed market and the use of biotechnology. Robert Shapiro, CEO of Monsanto, insists they have not developed 'terminator' seeds (seeds which 'switch off' certain genes after use, sterilising the seed); however, Shah (2001) suggests development of this technology was put on hold due to activist and protest support, as well as the existing Monsanto business strategy, which only licences farmers to use their seeds for one crop rotation, creating the same effect.

## Ethics on reflection: Planned obsolescence

Many companies have the technology to make products last longer, and choose not to use it. The products wear out faster and consumers have to buy them more often. Is that a responsible way to achieve profitability (Thornton 2010)?

## Animal testing

The use of animals to measure product toxicity, or for in-vivo testing in the cosmetics and pharmaceuticals industries, continues to outrage many. In May 2012, legislative proposals in the UK were introduced. Under the new rules, UK scientists must strive to reduce the number of animals they use in research as well as limiting their suffering. A key organisation in these proposals is the UK National Centre for the Replacement, Reduction and Refinement of Animals in Research (NC3Rs) (Gibney 2012). The Royal Society for the Prevention of Cruelty to Animals (RSPCA) in the UK has developed a farm and animal welfare labelling scheme that gives consumers the opportunities to purchase meat, poultry and dairy products from monitored farms. These products are labelled **freedom food**. The ASPCA in Canada and the RSPCA in Australia both have similar food monitoring systems (Floyd 2012).

**animal testing** – the use of animals for measuring product toxicity.

**freedom food** – a label applied to products like meat, poultry and dairy to indicate to consumers that the product is from a farm that uses animal welfare labelling.

He didn't even remember signing up for the taste test.

Animal testing (© shutterstock.com/Cartoonresource)

## Genetic modification

The exploration of biotechnology to change the genetic make-up of an organism, for many, is viewed with considerable disdain. The website <www.truefoodnow.org> contains lists by brand and category, indicating whether they contain genetically modified (GM) ingredients, or are GM-ingredient free.

**genetic modification (GM)** – the use of biotechnology to change the genetic make-up of an organism.

## Deceptive labelling

Product labelling is another means by which a firm can communicate its key promotion messages to consumers, but if the messages are exaggerated or untrue then the firm has participated in deceptive labelling. The line is, however, not always clear to see. The Australian Competition and Consumer Commission (2009) has provided some good examples:

**deceptive labelling** – when the information provided in the product labelling is exaggerated or untrue.

- In 2004, Cadbury Schweppes' advertising of two products was misleading and deceptive as they showed real fruit being used rather than flavoured cordial concentrate.
- The Outback Juice Company advertised to have 100% fresh, squeezed daily orange juice in 2003; however, tests showed that sugar cane and preservatives were added.

# Ethics in the media: Misrepresentation

In China, 63 traders were allegedly arrested for dyeing mink, fox and rat meat and selling it as lamb meat in Shanghai ('Food' 2013).

# Ethics in practice: Deceptive labelling

A woman took out insurance as part of a financial plan. Years later, she lodged a claim for a non-malignant brain tumour in the carotid artery, which required surgery. The insurer rejected the claim as invalid, although the wording of the policy stated that it covered a 'brain tumour' but without specifying particular locations in the brain (Parker 2012).

**Question:**
**1.** What ethical issues are involved in this case?

**product waste** – when purchasers of products are left with a considerable amount of unwanted packaging, which can have an environmental impact.

**green marketing** – environmentally sensitive organisations that apply environmental principles in their marketing practices.

**green labelling** – the practice of marking products to indicate their eco credentials.

## Product waste

It has been said that the late Steve Jobs of Apple spent as much emotional energy on the packaging of his products as he did on the product itself. This was because he felt that the packaging indicated to potential consumers what experience to expect with the product. The downside of such an approach, and not only with Apple products, is that purchasers are left with a considerable amount of unwanted packaging, which can have an environmental impact. It is not just occasional items that are a worry. It is claimed that if everyone in the US tied all of the plastic bags they used in a year end to end in a giant chain, the chain would reach around the Earth's equator 776 times (Samala 2012).

Green practices in manufacturing, and particularly the consumer disposal of products, are the primary interests of environmentally sensitive organisations. In a marketing context, this is referred to as **green marketing.** It has, however, been pointed out that while global warming and carbon emissions have gained international attention, consumers are still unclear about what they encompass and how they relate to their purchasing behaviour (Polonsky et al. 2012). **Green labelling** is the practice of marking products to indicate their eco credentials; however, there are now more than 400 eco-label systems in 25 countries, which creates a lack of consistency and confuses consumers ('Eco-labels can muddle the message' 2013).

## Ethics in practice: Facebook and marketing leverage

Two business school academics are leading an investigation into whether Facebook users should be paid for the role they play in the success of the social networking site. Christopher Land and Steffen Böhm of the University of Essex Business School consider that updating one's status, 'liking' a website or becoming someone's 'friend' creates Facebook's basic product. They argue that activity on Facebook also creates marketing data about users, which the company can then leverage for marketing and research purposes. Professor Böhm said that company profits were 'only possible because of the time and labour we, as users, invest in Facebook, so why don't we get paid for it?' (Marcus 2012a).

**Question:**
**1.** Do you think Facebook users should be paid?

## Pricing

## Ethics in the media: Price-fixing

In a blatant example of price-fixing, Singapore Airlines Cargo in 2008, and Cathay Pacific in 2009, were fined $23 million in penalties by the ACCC (2012b) for allegedly engaging in cartel conduct in relation to fuel and other surcharges applied to the carriage of airfreight in 2003.

The pricing of products and services is a sensitive topic, and pricing strategies can elicit strong reactions from consumers. For example, because of concern regarding Elsevier's business practices, in 2012 academic staff in Australia refused to act as referees or editors or to publish in their journals in protest at the 'cost of knowledge' which was keeping information out of the public domain (Blackwell 2012).

Within the pricing mix, the following unethical practices are at play:

### Price-fixing

**Price-fixing**, where firms collude on price (also referred to as **price collusion** or **price-setting**), is an illegal practice for which firms can be fined. It is considered to be anti-competitive as well as unethical. In December 2012, LG, Phillips and Samsung had fines imposed for operating a price cartel ('The World This Week' 2012). Price collusion is where a firm agrees with competitors to set prices in a market to the detriment of competition and consumers (Riley 2012). The agreement does not need to be conducted in person. Any form of communication with a competitor

**price-fixing** – where firms collude on pricing (also known as **price collusion** or **price-setting**).

where proceeds are discussed is problematic, particularly where there has been disclosure of list prices, terms of financing as well as available price deals and adjustments. Businesses may also have agreed to divide specific customers, suppliers or territories among themselves.

Price-fixing has the negative consequence of inhibiting free and fair competition for which the consumers suffer. In 2006 in South Africa, a cartel between three producers, Premier, Tiger and Pioneer, was uncovered. The cartel agreed to increase the price of bread, fix distributor prices, and not poach each other's independent distributors. The effect was increased bread prices, slashed distributor discounts and diminished distributor choice (Mokoena 2008).

## Ethics in the media: Price-fixing scandals

The US Justice Department sued Apple and five publishers in April 2012, alleging a conspiracy to raise prices and limit competition for e-books through suppliers such as Amazon, and thereby attempting to strangle pricing freedom for book retailers (Agence France-Presse 2012).

In Australia, a Senate inquiry was told of concerns about price-fixing and collusion in the milk industry following both Coles and Woolworths concurrently dropping the price of their milk to $1 per litre. The inquiry was also told that people who deliver milk had been intimidated after raising their suspicions about price collusion (ABC News 2011). The Indonesian airline, Garuda, was investigated for alleged price-fixing in their freight division, and the ACCC have already successfully prosecuted 10 other airlines for price-fixing, with Qantas and British Airways paying $25 million in fines (Fullerton 2009).

Samsung has had a high profile in the past because of their price-fixing activities. Samsung are the world's largest maker of memory chips as well as producing other electronic items. In the US in 2009 the company pleaded guilty to price-fixing and agreed to pay a US$300 million fine ('Samsung slapped for price-fixing' 2009). The penalty is the largest anti-trust fine in history. In 2013, Samsung were among six companies who conspired to manipulate prices for LCD panels. The price-fixing was achieved during 53 meetings from 2001 to 2006. The six companies have been fined and ordered to pay back revenue (Kan 2013).

We often think of price-fixing in the consumer context but it also occurs in business-to-business tendering, where it is known as **bid-rigging**. In Queensland, the ACCC took legal action when three construction companies undertook bid-rigging during the tender process. The 'cover pricing' is where one company colludes with another to put an elevated tender in, allowing the initial company to 'genuinely' win the contract based on price alone (ACCC 2009).

**bid-rigging** – price collusion occurring in the tendering process.

# Ethics in practice: Bid-rigging

Imagine that you are the manager of a newly formed construction company that has just started up in Brisbane and you have been approached by a representative of a long-standing construction firm. He has enquired about whether you will be tendering for the building of a school in a new suburb and, upon hearing that the project is a bit too big for you at this stage, the representative is encouraging you to put in a high tender anyway, thereby increasing the chances of his company getting the bid. Consider what your response to him might be.

So, essentially, price-fixing practices include:

- competitors fixing prices
- competitors sharing markets or limiting production in order to raise prices
- imposing minimum prices on distributors, such as shops
- competitors fixing supplier purchase prices
- cutting competitors out of the market by selling below cost (Riley 2012).

## Bait and switch

In a **bait and switch**, a product is advertised at a very low price; however, it is only stocked in minimal numbers in the hope of getting customers to buy an upgraded item (Goree 2007).

> **bait and switch** – advertising at a low price to entice customers, and then switching them to another product.

## Price gouging

When an organisation increases prices on specific products to profit from unfortunate circumstances, this is known as **price gouging**. An example of this would be selling generators at significantly higher than normal prices during a power interruption. In Australia, between October 2011 and February 2012, Polaris Solar Pty Ltd and ACT Renewable Energy Pty Ltd alleged carbon pricing would increase electricity prices by 20%. The Australian Competition and Consumer Commission boss, Rod Sims, said companies 'misleading' consumers face penalties of up to A$1.1 million (ACCC 2012a).

> **price gouging** – increasing the price of specific products to profit from a current circumstance.

Price gouging (© shutterstock.com/johnkworks)

## Predatory pricing

**predatory pricing** – pricing below cost.

**Predatory pricing** is pricing below cost, usually with the intention of gaining market share and harming competition.

## Deceptive pricing

**deceptive pricing** – pricing where consumers are unaware of hidden costs associated with a product or service.

**Deceptive pricing** is where a consumer is unaware of hidden costs associated with a product or service. This was not uncommon when purchasing an airline ticket which was promoted at one price but turned out to be an entirely different price once a variety of taxes were added. In 2009, the European Union concluded an 18-month crackdown, which found that misleading advertisements and unfair practices had occurred on 137 airline websites in 15 EU member states. The main issues related to deceptive 'headline' prices, which disguised hidden extra costs such as taxes and charges (European Commission 2009).

# Ethics in the media: Deceptive pricing

In 2012, American Express were fined US$27.5 million for deceiving and overcharging Blue Sky card program users, indicating they would receive US$300, which was never paid; charging illegal late fees; not reporting consumer disputes to credit bureaus as required; and giving misinformed financial advice (AAP 2012).

## Price discrimination

**price discrimination** – when a firm charges a different price to different groups.

**Price discrimination** occurs when a firm charges a different price to different groups, whether consumers or distributors, for an identical good or service, and where the price is not associated with costs. Price discrimination is considered anti-competitive when it is used to create a barrier to entry to the market, or to force competitors from the market (Clarke 2012).

Invariably, companies attempt to charge what the market will bear, and, potentially, consumers may be willing to pay higher prices to protect the environment. We all know, too, that there are considerable variations in prices for certain products and services. These differences may be early-bird pricing, or peak versus off-peak pricing. However, price discrimination occurs when the price differential is not justified, for example, when a company produces two brands of artificial sweeteners where there is absolutely no difference in the base product, just a variation in branding, yet one is marketed at a premium and the other not.

## Ethics in practice: Airlines and price discrimination

The next time you are on a commercial flight, you may wish to ask your fellow passengers what price they paid for their ticket on exactly the same flight, and observe the variations.

## Ethics in the media: Google and fair pricing

In January 2013, after a 19-month investigation by the US Federal Trade Commission, Google consented to signing a decree requiring that the company charge a 'fair, reasonable and non-discriminatory' price to license hundreds of patents deemed essential to the operation of mobile phones, tablet computers, laptops and video game consoles (Associated Press 2008).

## Ethics in the media: Price-fixing in Korea

In Korea in 2010, the Fair Trade Commission (FTC) detected more than 3500 cases of price-fixing; however, only 66 fines were issued. Of those fines, the average penalty amounted to just 2.3% of the unfairly earned revenue ('Let them eat cake' 2012).

# Promotion

Promotional activity has the tricky task of encouraging consumers to buy without deceiving or manipulating them. The main criticisms of promotion and the many forms of marketing communication are that it is inherently untruthful, deceptive, unfair, manipulative and offensive (Eagle 2009). Promotion practices are deceptive when the seller intentionally misleads consumers about how a product is constructed or performs (Marion 2001). The five components of promotion, commonly called the **promotion mix**, are made up of: advertising, sales promotion, direct marketing, personal selling and a catch-all category of public

**promotion mix** – the promotion mix comprises advertising, sales promotion, direct marketing, personal selling, public relations, sponsorship and branding.

relations, sponsorship and branding. These components of the promotion mix will be used to structure our discussion.

## Advertising

**advertising** – securing the attention of the public in relation to a product or business through various means (broadcasting, print, etc.). Used to promote goods and services.

While promotional strategies entail a large number of activities, **advertising** is often viewed as the most prominent. In a review of all complaints lodged with the Australian Advertising Standards Board and New Zealand's Advertising Standards Authority for the period 1999 to 2004, the majority of complaints related to television advertising and, specifically: violence, health and safety, discriminatory portrayal of people, sex/sexuality and nudity, as well as profane language and causing distress to children (Jones & Hall 2006). Ethical issues in advertising usually refer to practices such as the following:

**misrepresentation** – misleading customers; this can range from fraudulently untrue to subtle deception.

**Misrepresentation** – advertising is rarely outright fraudulent and untrue; it is more often subtle in its misrepresentation. This could relate to the wording, the promises made, as well as any pictures used. In most countries, misrepresentation comes with a hefty fine. For example, in a commercial for Skechers, Kim Kardashian dumped her personal trainer for a pair of Shape Up sneakers that would supposedly tone her body without exercise. As a result, the company paid US$40 million to settle charges that they had deceived consumers with unfounded claims about the product's benefits (Federal Trade Commission 2012).

# Ethics in the media: Deceptive marketing of cigarettes

In 2008 the US Supreme Court handed down a decision which encourages future law suits alleging deceptive marketing of 'light' cigarettes (Associated Press 2008).

**offensive advertising** – advertising that is inappropriate, or discriminatory.

**Offensive advertising** – advertising that is offensive can relate to both the content of the advertisement, that is, overtly sexual, demeaning to women, promoting stereotypes, being disrespectful etc., and also to the products themselves, for example, alcohol, tobacco, pharmaceuticals and adult products etc. By way of example, in 2011, India's Information Ministry instructed TV channels not to air sexy deodorant advertisements indicating that the ads offended good taste and decency, and that the depiction of women in the ads was overtly sexual (BBC News South Asia 2011). The advertisements can be viewed by searching 'The Axe Effect'.

**comparative advertising** – advertising that contains negative messages about competitors.

**Comparative advertising** – as with all promotional activity, the aim is to differentiate the product or service from those of the competitors; however, this can be taken too far when negative messages about competitors are used as the main thrust of the advertising campaign.

In a study of four professional groups, Marks and Moon (1995) found that all professional groups believed that a hypothetical example of comparative advertising was unethical, and expressed strong reservations about using this format of advertising; see also Montero (2012) for infamous cases of comparative advertising in the US. For example, Pepsi Challenge versus Coke in the 1980s, Apple's Mac versus personal computer (PC) campaign that ran between 2006 and 2009, Samsung's challenge of Apple in the smart-phone market when promoting its Galaxy SII, as well as Audi versus Mercedes.

In countries that permit comparative advertising, in recent years the advertisements have become less overt comparisons of product A against product B, and appear to be more subtle and implied, as the advertisers try to position themselves on specific attributes that contrast with their competitors' products, without actually naming the competitors. They are, nevertheless, still comparative advertisements.

**Stereotyping** – gender and racial stereotyping has been identified for some time as a key concern in marketing and warrants further research (Hyman, Tansey & Clark 1994). Stereotypes are generalisations of qualities which are assigned (and may not necessarily be accurate) to groups of people related to their race, nationality and sexual orientation, which may result in over-simplification and discrimination (Nittle 2013).

In a critique of power and stereotypes in advertising, Maldonado (2012) highlighted two recent examples in the US of stereotyping: Burger King came under fire due to a leaked commercial promoting their new crispy chicken wraps as the ad invoked and promoted black stereotypes. Also in 2011, the new diet drink, Dr Pepper 10, was sold with the tagline 'it's not for women', and used a variety of masculine stereotypes (Maldonado 2012). In the UK in 2007, the confectionery company Cadbury pulled their advertisement for Trident gum after it was ruled that the campaign showed harmful stereotypes of Caribbean people (Dugan 2009).

In Australia, a 2005 study of television commercials observed that people from culturally diverse backgrounds are not only under-represented, but they are also misrepresented in television advertising (Higgs & Milner 2005). In a further study of the portrayal of males and females in Australian television advertisements, Mazzella et al. (2009) found strong evidence of differences in the presentation of males and females.

**stereotyping** – gender and racial stereotyping in marketing messages.

Stereotype advertising (© shutterstock.com/Stokkete)

# Ethics in the media: Honest advertising

One of the best examples of truth in advertising was an ad placed in the London papers in 1913 that read: 'Men wanted for hazardous journey. Small wages, bitter cold, long months of complete darkness, constant danger, safe return doubtful. Honour and recognition in case of success. Ernest Shackleton' (*The Antarctic Circle* 2011).

**false testimonials** (including **fake tweets**) – when the content of testimonials or tweets has been generated by the company or someone paid by the company.

**Deceptive advertising using social media** – it is estimated that US$5 billion worth of goods were sold via a social marketing platform in 2011, with Facebook leading the pack. Social media platforms provide a powerful sales pitch where friends' recommendations become sales opportunities (Blackwell 2012). User-generated comments are significantly on the rise; however, it does present problems to marketers and notably brand managers who want to protect the brand, but also ensure open dialogue with customers. **False testimonials** and **fake tweets** are where the content is being generated by the company itself or by someone paid by the company. Too many positive comments tend to alert consumers to over-crafting of responses and potential for scepticism to be attached to the brand if it is seen as disingenuous and lacking in authenticity.

# Ethics in practice: Social media and advertising

Marketers now need to be concerned about their engagement with social media. The Advertising Standards Board considered Smirnoff, the Vodka brand, used Facebook as a marketing communication tool, and suggested the Advertising Standards Code continues to apply in cyberspace, although the Code was not breached in this instance (Advertising Standards Board 2012). Similarly, the ACCC suggests that consumer protection laws are in place in social media, and the onus is on the company to ensure that all information on social media sites is accurate, irrespective of the author of the comments (ACCC 2013b).

**Questions:**

1. Comment on the criticism that rulings by regulatory bodies in relation to user-generated comments are commercially naïve and not in keeping with the ethos of social media. Or, is it appropriate that companies are held responsible for the accuracy of comments regarding their products or services?

*cont.*

*cont.*

**2.** In an effort to ensure that consumer-generated comment is not misleading, brands are provided with an excuse to delete unsavoury and unwanted comments. What are your thoughts regarding the appropriateness of deleting user comments from social media?

**3.** Automated software is now able to pick up comments containing words such as profanities or that matches specific rules and delete them before they go up on Facebook. This is called pre-moderation as opposed to post-moderation, which is after a posting has been made and is then required to be checked. Does this erode the honesty and information provided?

# Ethics in the media: False advertising in Australia

An Australian solar panel provider was accused of making false and misleading claims about the source of its rooftop panels and posting fake testimonials on the internet. The panels were imported from China and not made in Australia as asserted ('Solar stoush' 2013).

## Direct marketing

**Direct marketing** targets a marketing message and activities at specific customers. It is a key tool when coupled with selective segmentation. However, when the approach by the marketer is unsolicited and unwelcome, the marketer has effectively crossed the line into unethical behaviour. We all know how annoying a telemarketer can be and direct marketing approaches can be even more problematic in our electronic age where customers are more accessible through mobile phones, text messaging, social media and the internet. In India in 2011, where regulators estimate 10 billion unsolicited calls are made annually, in an effort to restore some rights to privacy, a 'do not call register' was created to prevent unsolicited calls and text messages from telemarketers (Raman 2011). In 2012, further restrictions were imposed to ensure that no one could send more than 100 texts a day and barring commercial calls between 9 p.m. and 9 a.m. to avoid late calls and harassment. Perhaps the most insidious of direct mail activities is spamming, which is legislated against in many countries, starting with the *CANN Spam Act 2004*. There are criminal penalties associated with spamming and it requires opt-in and opt-out parameters. For a comprehensive review of ethical issues associated with direct marketing involving marketing claims, telemarketing, mobile marketing, email marketing and consumer data protection, see the Australian Direct Marketing Association website: <www.adma.com.au>.

**direct marketing** – the selling of goods to consumers through such methods as mail order, the internet, door-to-door selling, and so on, instead of using retailers.

# Ethics in practice: Ethical sales practices

You are a salesperson in an apparel store. Your supervisor instructs you to favour one brand over another because the manufacturer is paying a 'spiff' (promotional incentive) to retail staff for each unit sold. A customer with whom you have a relationship asks for a recommendation.

**Questions:**

1. Would you recommend the promoted brand?
2. What if you felt the brand was inferior?
3. What if you didn't know the customer?
4. What if the promotional incentives were being kept by the store and not passed on to you? (Areni 2010–2011.)

**personal selling** – when a business uses its sales people (through their attitude/ appearance/ product knowledge) to sell its products, usually face-to-face, for example, sales people found in a department store.

**deceptive sales practices** – where a consumer is manipulated into a purchase.

**referral for fee schemes** – undertaken in the legal profession, where a law firm pays a generous fee in return for being passed the contact details of someone who might be interested in their services.

## Personal selling

A well-known **deceptive sales practice** is where a consumer is manipulated into purchasing a product or service. There are many techniques that can be utilised to manipulate customers. A common one is to have them believe they have won a valuable prize. However, it is merely a mechanism to entice the customer to enter the door, whereby the individual delivers the 'prize', then begins a sales pitch. Also, if a company says it is giving a free vacation, they actually need to do it. It is also possible that the method by which salespeople are remunerated could, in fact, be promoting unethical action. Commission structures for salespeople are directly related to the amount of product they sell, thus, the more product sold, the more commission earned. This creates an unhealthy environment in which sales are pursued no matter what the cost, and the product or service that provides the greatest commission is the one that is pressed. In a comprehensive review of the literature on personal selling and sales management research, McClaren (2012) mentions deception, inappropriateness, spying, manipulation and poaching of customers as the common ethical issues relating to sales.

Deceptive sales also occur in the professions. For example, described as the legal industry's dirty little secret, **referral for fee schemes** are intensely controversial and involve a law firm paying a generous fee in return for being passed the contact details of someone who might be interested in their services. The deals are usually between lawyers and insurance companies, but estate agents and trade unions also refer their customers on to law firms, as well as to middlemen who buy contact details and then sell them on. Few of us realise when we buy insurance that an agreement is often buried in the policy's terms and conditions which enables the insurer to pass on our details in the event of an accident. Obviously, selling personal details without a customer's permission is questionable and, in some jurisdictions, is illegal. Many people object to being contacted by lawyers or claims managers touting for business, and, if they have recently been involved in an accident, these approaches will often be particularly unwelcome (Watkin 2011).

## Sales promotion, prizes and competition

In 2000, the UK Independent Television Commission (ITC) upheld complaints about a TV ad that guaranteed free prizes to anyone buying a National Lottery ticket and an instant scratch card together. The ITC ruled that this had been ambiguous and misleading ('Watchdog criticises lottery prize advert' 2000). In many countries the fair trading legislation has oversight of the appropriateness of marketing competitions and, generally, the obligations are:

* **disclosure** – 'disclosing special terms and conditions which must be met before the gift or prize is made available to the consumer'
* **transparency** – 'not disguising the cost of the 'free' gift or prize by including it in the selling price of the advertised goods'
* **fulfillment** – 'supplying gifts or prizes the same as those offered' (© State of New South Wales through NSW Fair Trading 2012).

**sales promotion** – achieving sales through the use of contests, demonstrations, giveaways, discounts, etc.

## Ethics in the media: Lottery tickets

An Oxfordshire pensioner received a letter in the mail informing him of a £1.7 million lottery jackpot. He was told that, to claim his prize, he needed to respond to the sender and send a small amount of money. Six years, 20 000 letters and £30 000 out of pocket later, he was admitted to hospital ('Oxfordshire pensioner spends life-savings on junk mail' 2012).

## Public relations, sponsorship and branding

**Public relations** refers to the role and reputation of the public relations profession in maintaining a favourable image of the organisation with its 'public' (stakeholders), while balancing the company's integrity and gaining the public's trust (PRSA 2009–2013). Unfortunately, backlashes can occur in relation to public relations efforts.

**Sponsorship** is a powerful promotional tool but organisations can come unstuck if the personality to whom they attach their brand acts unethically and is perceived unfavourably by the general public. This was the circumstance with the golfer Tiger Woods and the cyclist Lance Armstrong, both of whom lost their sponsorships due to personal indiscretions (Business 2012).

**Branding** is not usually a contentious issue, but the US Equal Employment Opportunity Commission (EEOC) has carried out several reviews of Abercrombie & Fitch's 'Look Policy'. In 2005 they received a $40 million racial discrimination ruling against them; in 2008 they were scrutinised for religious discrimination for refusing to hire prospective employees wearing head scarves (EEOC 2010); and, in 2013, the CEO received criticism for his comments about not promoting his clothes to 'uncool' and 'fat' people (EEOC 2010).

**public relations** – the role of public relations is to ensure a favourable image of an organisation with its 'public' (stakeholders).

**sponsorship** – when organisations attach their brands to a certain personality in order to promote their product/business.

**branding** – when a distinctive name or trademark is used to identify a product or business.

Public relations, sponsorship and branding (© shutterstock.com/My Life Graphic)

## Distribution

The marketing mix element of distribution centres on all activities, whether they are physical or electronic connections between the product or service and the consumer. Ultimately, this may involve many entities who are intermediaries in the distribution process.

## Ethics in practice: Manipulating customers

You are a consultant with expertise in environmental psychology and retail design. A client asks you to recommend changes in background music, lighting, colour schemes and merchandise layout that will make customers 'stay longer and spend more money'.

**Questions:**
1. What is your view of this work?
2. What if you knew of research showing that consumers are aware that retailers deliberately manipulate music, lighting, colour and merchandise displays to induce shoppers to buy?
3. What if the client was a casino operator? (Areni 2010–2011).

**pyramid schemes** – schemes whereby profits are generated through the addition of new participants and the money they bring, not from the sale and distribution of real products to persons.

## Pyramid schemes

**Pyramid schemes** are deliberate scams designed to benefit the originators while taking advantage of later recruits. Pyramid schemes are a sales technique in which a person is recruited into a plan and then expects to make money by recruiting other people (Kaliski 2001). These schemes operate on the basis that members receive commissions for recruiting new members; however, the scheme inevitably collapses, leaving most participants out of pocket (Rolfe & Lentini 2011). Schemes such as these generate profits through the addition of new participants and the money that they bring, not from the sale and distribution of real products or services to people who actually use or consume them. The scheme essentially involves an internal redistribution of wealth from new entrants to the promoters (Direct Selling Association of Malaysia 2013). Pyramid selling should be distinguished from **multi-level marketing (MLM)**, which is a type of direct selling that involves the distribution, sale and supply of products or services through various independent agents such as contractors and distributors (Koehn 2001).

**multi-level marketing (MLM)** – in marketing, the practice of distributing, selling, supplying products or services through various levels of independent agents.

Pyramid scheme (© shutterstock.com/Daisy Daisy)

## Channel coercion

**Channel coercion** is a broad term that essentially relates to power manipulation and coercion within the distribution channel, usually through exclusive dealer arrangements, franchiser manipulation and territorial protection. For example, monopoly or large chain distributors can dictate the terms of arrangements including mark-ups and product placement, and pressurise vendors to take more stock than they need. Coercion can also occur with manufacturers, for example, where a dominant producer may place pressure on distributors not to stock a competitive product, as was experienced in the early days with Ben and Jerry's ice-cream. Tensions may also exist because of a power differential that prevails with franchisees and their franchiser, and a perception that the franchisees are not getting a fair deal for their franchise fee.

**channel coercion** – relates to power manipulation within the distribution channel.

# Ethics in the media: Google's unfair practices

In 2012, the American Federal Trade Commission investigated claims that Google was unfairly promoting their own services; potentially preventing consumers getting the best deals by favouring their own specialised vertical website searches; trapping online advertisers from transferring campaigns; and limiting standardised technologies to their platform (Federal Trade Commission 2013).

## Ethics in the media: Misrepresentation by MAC cosmetics

In Australia in September 2011, Target removed MAC cosmetics from their shelves, after Estée Lauder claimed the MAC make-up was fake. Testing confirmed the cosmetics were counterfeit; however, on further investigation, the agents that sourced the cosmetics vanished, leaving Target with supply chain questions, as well as the ensuing court cases (Grennblat 2013).

## Ethics in the media: Accuracy of information

Fearing accusations of deceptive and fraudulent practices, in 2012, eBay banned the sale of 'supernatural goods and services' from their website. Craigslist are, however, allowing love and money spells but does caution that they are for entertainment value only (Hsu 2012).

## Web marketing

**web marketing** – using the web to market, promote and distribute products/business.

With the move from pure retailing and the embracing of the internet, the web is now seen as a dominant feature of most firms' distribution strategy and, as a result, ethical issues arise:

- **Accuracy of information** – as with any form of communication that comes from a firm, considerable care needs to be given to the accuracy of information provided and the assurance that the information is not exaggerated, inaccurate or misleading. One area of concern is the unethical practice of using false testimonials or online reviews of, for example, apps, books, films, hotels and restaurants. False reviews have been found to appear on websites such as Amazon, Urbanspoon and TripAdvisor (see Moses 2012).

**spyware** – software that employs a user's internet connection without their knowledge or permission.

- **DataSpyware** – **spyware** is where an internet connection is used as a backchannel (in the background), without the user's knowledge or permission. Using software on the internet in this way is classified as spyware and is theft (Rouse 2011).

**keyword stuffing** (or **cloaking**) – the overuse of links to gain traffic to a website.

- **Misleading search engine optimisation** – techniques, such as the overuse of key words, which is called **keyword stuffing** (or **cloaking**) is where content is misleadingly presented, and there is overuse of links to get traffic to a website and a deliberate creation of duplicate content.

- Inappropriate hyperlinks are frequently established by web designers in order to link related material, so the user, essentially, is able to hop from one page to another. Some organisations have objected to the use of hyperlinks without permission as the hyperlink has facilitated transition to a page not nominated by the site owner. In doing so, the internet user has not entered the site as they would normally, via the front page, and has, as a consequence, not been exposed to the banner advertising that advertisers on the site have paid for. These web links, therefore, avoid and circumvent exposure to paid advertising (Tavani 2007).

# People

It has been proposed that marketers who are concerned to act ethically put all stakeholders first, including employees, customers and suppliers, and that they treat those people with respect, not just as cogs in the marketing system (Laczniak & Murphy 2006). Certain areas associated with this approach warrant mention here.

"The cow mooed, the pig oinked, the
chicken clucked, I baaed and then we adjourned."

People are at the centre of ethical issues (© shutterstock.com/Cartoonresource)

## Market research

Market research is the function that links the consumer, customer and public to the marketer through information. This information is used to: identify and define marketing opportunities and problems; generate, refine, and evaluate marketing actions; monitor marketing performance; and improve understanding of marketing as a process (American Marketing Association 2013c). The ethical problems posed in market research relate to the duties of the researcher (e.g., the duty of honesty in soliciting information, and the protection of anonymity where it has been promised) and the rights of the information provider (e.g., to informed consent, confidentiality and not to be harmed).

According to Akaah and Riordan (1990), an erosion of these duties and rights can jeopardise public confidence and willingness to participate in market research. In their empirical investigation, they delineate unethical practices affecting three groups:

- **Respondents** – for example, concealing the purpose and name of the sponsor, switching to a sales pitch, and not protecting respondents' anonymity.
- **Clients** – for example, violating the confidential client-agency relationship, and conflict of interest.

> **market research** – the function that links the consumer, customer and public to the marketer through information.

- **The general public** – for example, inappropriate methodology, data falsification and misrepresentation of results (Akaah & Riordan 1990).

In Australia, Segal and Giabobbe (2011) investigated the perceived seriousness of unethical practices in market research, and determined that issues that were both serious and frequent related to: results not accurately reflecting findings; non-protection of respondent confidentiality; and client identity. The use of research to generate sales and promotional leads was a mid-ranking priority, as was concern about respondents not being notified if recording devices were being used.

# Ethics in practice: Marketing research

Since 1954, the National Institute of Infant Nutrition and the Research Institute of Mother and Child Care have maintained databases on whether mothers breastfeed or use formula for their newborns; however, neither of those institutions exist. They are both fronts for a marketing survey for Similac, a brand of baby formula (Edwards 2011).

**Question**:
1. What are the ethical dimensions of this revelation?

# Ethics in the media: The ethicality of clinical trials

Pharmaceutical firms' clinical trials have been known to engage in unethical behaviour such as 'burying' or 'massaging' bad results for products they are marketing, running trials on small numbers of under-represented patients, aborting trials and using under-the-counter advertising campaigns to persuade doctors to prescribe a specific company's drug (Goldacre 2012).

# Ethics in practice: Ethics in research

As a diligent and socially responsible consumer researcher, you are studying people who overspend, and you are bound to treat the interview confidentially. However, one respondent admits that overspending can result in him 'cutting loose' on his child. Legally, you must report child abuse yet you are bound by confidentiality (Sojka & Spangenberg 1994).

**Question:**
1. What do you do now?

# Data mining

Through the course of not only market research, but in general interaction with consumers, a company can amass a significant amount of data (particularly digital data). How this data is collected, stored in a (**data warehouse**) analysed/mined, disseminated, used, and possibly shared, are central concerns in relation to **data mining**. The most prevalent data management undertaken is online through web analytics, with the outcome being very sophisticated consumer profiling in order to better target marketing efforts (see 'Very personal finance' 2012).

> ## Ethics in the media: Data mining and Facebook
>
> Facebook is well known for their approach to data mining. The company is able to mine the data of their users, tracking information about their likes and dislikes so as to more effectively target them with ads ('A fistful of dollars' 2012).

**Web analytics** facilitates the collection of customer data, through cookies or embedded javascript code (tagging) (Kenny, Pierce & Pye 2012), as they interface with an organisation. Customer user data is sent to third-party web analysers where the captured data can be analysed to enable the organisation to offer personalised direct marketing campaigns tailored to customers' individual preferences. This practice is entirely automated and, therefore, extremely efficient. While group analytics has been promoted as improving customer relations management, there are undeniable ethical issues associated with these direct marketing efforts in relation to privacy, the potential for discrimination and fairness. Price and marketing discrimination can also be a key concern of data mining, where the same goods are sold at different prices based on the consumers' buying habits (Danna & Gandy 2002); where entirely different products are offered; or where certain products are not offered at all. This is the case with **web lining**, which determines the availability of products according to where the consumer lives (Danna & Gandy 2002); for example, a consumer may be denied credit based on their low-income neighbourhood. Considerable resources are currently being directed towards business analytics software, data mining and data warehousing resources.

> ## Ethics in practice: Banks and data mining
>
> Banking institutions, through data mining, use predictive models to assess customers' value and then approach high-value customers with deals to retain them. For example, they may offer a
>
> *cont.*

**data warehouse** – a database containing historical data that utilises the integration of new data and is subjected to analysis, with the intent of developing trend information for business decision-making.

**data mining** – the collection, storage, analysis and dissemination of customer data.

**web analytics** – the analysis of captured data in order for the organisation to offer more personalised and direct marketing campaigns that can be tailored to a customer's preferences.

**web lining** – categorisation and subsequent discrimination of consumers in the market place.

---

*cont.*

high-value customer a lower interest rate, while informing the low-value customer of increased fees (Danna & Gandy 2002).

**Questions:**

**1.** What is your view of the equity of this situation?

**2.** Role-play this situation, with one person representing the consumer and another representing the bank.

---

# Ethics on reflection: Microsoft and tracking consumers

In May 2012, Microsoft indicated that Internet Explorer 10 would set Do Not Track (DNT) as a default for web browsing. With web tracking off, advertisers' ability to track individuals and send them behavioural ads will be limited; however, the Digital Advertising Alliance believes this may limit consumer choice (Mastria 2012).

**Questions:**

**1.** Should advertisers assume that people are happy to be tracked and sent behavioural ads, or should they have explicit permission?

**2.** Many people give scarcely a thought to being electronically snooped on as they browse, but some furiously object. Where do you stand on this?

---

**marketing to vulnerable groups** – marketing that targets certain groups within the population that may not have the maturity or skills necessary to be able to critically evaluate marketing strategies and, thus, may potentially be harmed. Includes teenagers, children and the elderly.

The ongoing tracking of individuals in public is clearly a concern as individuals lose their anonymity. In January 2012, Google got rid of more than 60 of their privacy policies and replaced them with one policy that they indicated was a lot shorter and easier to read. In what seems to be a somewhat circular statement, Google's privacy policy states that by using Google's service you agree to them using your personal data and privacy protection in accordance with their privacy policies.

## Marketing to vulnerable groups

As we have seen, marketing techniques and subsequent marketing strategies have become very sophisticated, and with them come concerns that certain groups in the population may not have the maturity or skills necessary to critically evaluate marketing strategies and, thus potentially, may be harmed. Collectively, these groups are referred to as vulnerable groups (another rather distasteful description is 'market illiterates'), which include the following (see also Table 5.1 on page 173):

- **Teenagers** – for example, given possible self-esteem issues, painfully thin models may not be the best role models to portray in promotional material directed at teenage girls.
- **Financially disadvantaged** – for example, low income groups being targeted with financial repayment schemes which provide access to goods and services but create further long-term financial hardship.
- **The elderly** – for example, with possibly diminishing cognitive function they are unable to defend themselves against deceptive marketing, aggressive personal sales, or to evaluate sophisticated pricing structures or resist financial scams.
- **Children** – for example, junk food promotion in children's sports, violence in video games, peer pressure for product purchases, promotional use of popular personalities, and inappropriate content or terminology are controversial marketing tools (Bakir & Vitell 2009).

# Ethics in the media: Campaigns targeting children

Companies have been criticised for marketing unhealthy products to children in recent years. They use toys, games and movies to sell their products to vulnerable groups; however, McDonald's now try to market ethically, having come under fire for past marketing campaigns targeting children (Gough 2012).

The ethical guidelines for dealing with the people dimension of the marketing mix, whether they are customers, employees, suppliers, distributors, or some other stakeholder, therefore cover the need to:

1. be aware and sensitive to cultural issues, superstitions or themes that could cause fear
2. be respectful, transparent and honest in the information provided
3. avoid stereotyping and what could be perceived as offensive, and ensure decency particularly relating to sex or violence
4. avoid denigrating other companies' products, or competitors
5. be sensitive to vulnerable groups, such as the elderly and children.

# Ethics on reflection: Companies and their right to block

A Metro train commuter's Twitter account was blocked after a series of allegedly indiscriminate and offensive remarks about Metro trains. This indicates that Metro were unclear about how to respond to tweets outside of legitimate complaints and feedback (Hastings 2013).

# Cause-related marketing

**cause-related marketing (CRM)** – a co-alignment of marketing strategy and corporate philanthropy.

**Cause-related marketing (CRM)** refers to the alignment between a company's marketing strategy and philanthropy (Varadarajan & Menon 1988), in a for-profit organisation or a non-profit or charitable entity. The term was apparently coined by American Express after a campaign in conjunction with the restoration of the Statue of Liberty in New York, where American Express donated a dollar for every new account and a 'penny' for every credit card transaction (Ross, Stutts & Patterson 1991). CRM is therefore a specific marketing strategy whereby, for mutual benefit, a firm offers and provides dollars or effort to a designated cause following a customer engagement.

The closer the alignment between the product or service and the sentiments of the purchaser (for example, Bendon bras and breast cancer), the better the prospects for a cause-related campaign. A 2010 study by Cone Communications (2012), an agency that focuses on CRM, found that 69% of Americans were more likely to buy from a company if they felt their purchase demonstrated their support for a good cause. CRM can, unfortunately, backfire. With its 2010 'Buckets for the Cure' campaign, KFC announced they would use pink buckets and donate 50 cents for every bucket of chicken sold to 'Susan G Komen for the Cure'. Detractors criticised both KFC and Komen as they associated deep-fried chicken with carcinogens linked to causing breast cancer ('Think before you pink' 2012). A critical question in CRM is whether the firm is motivated by an altruistic rationale or is acting from self-interest.

**social marketing** – the application of marketing techniques in the pursuit of social outcomes such as reducing smoking.

Another term worth clarifying is **social marketing**, which is where marketers apply their techniques solely in the pursuit of social outcomes (for example, reducing workplace accidents or reducing obesity). What differentiates social marketing from traditional marketing is not the relative size of their budgets, as has been suggested; while many social marketers have small budgets to work with, large accounts do exist, as in transport safety (Andreasen 2003). The distinction is more to do with the nature of the marketing effort and the intended outcomes. Social marketing tends to deal with social problems such as reducing drink driving or smoking, or encouraging behaviours such as water conservation and immunisation.

The main ethical issue in social marketing is the way the message is delivered – that is, the thematic execution – as the use of fear can play on human insecurities, causing anxiety. Conversely, the use of humour can offend. See, for example, the 'Dumb ways to die' Metro trains public service advertisement <http://dumbwaystodie.com>, a campaign that is both humorous and offensive. Additional issues surround the potential inequities of targeting one group over another, and whether the action being promoted restricts the rights of users or others.

**Table 5.1**  Guidelines for advertising responsibly to children

**Principle 1 – All advertisements should be prepared with, and observe, a high standard of social responsibility to consumers and to society.**

1(a) Advertisements should not undermine the role of parents in educating children to have a balanced diet and be healthy individuals.

1(b) Children should not be urged in advertisements to ask their parents, guardians or caregivers to buy particular products for them.

1(c) Advertisements for treat food, snacks or fast food should not encourage children to consume them in excess.

1(d) Advertisements for treat food, snacks or fast food should not encourage children to consume them in substitution for a main meal on a regular basis, nor should they undermine the Food and Nutrition Guidelines for Healthy Children.

1(e) Advertisements for food should not portray products as complete meals unless they are formulated as such.

1(f) The quantity of the food depicted in the advertisement should not exceed serving sizes that would be appropriate for consumption by a person or persons of the age depicted.

1(g) Benefits of foods as a nutritious diet should not be exaggerated and should not imply that a single food should replace a healthy diet, nor undermine the importance of consuming a variety of foods.

1(h) Nutrient, nutrition and health claims (when permitted) should comply with the requirements of the Food Standards Code. Such claims should not mislead or deceive the consumer.

1(i) Advertisements should not promote inactive or unhealthy lifestyles nor should they show people who choose a healthy active lifestyle in a negative manner.

1(j) Advertisements for slimming products or foods sold as an aid to slimming should not be directed at children.

**Principle 2 – Advertisements should not by implication, omission, ambiguity or exaggerated claim mislead or deceive or be likely to mislead or deceive children, abuse the trust of or exploit their lack of knowledge or, without reason, play on fear.**

2(a) Advertisements should be clearly recognisable as such by children and separated from editorial, programmes or other non-advertising content.

2(b) Advertisements should take into account the level of knowledge, sophistication and maturity of the intended audience.

2(c) Care should be taken to ensure advertisements do not mislead as to the nutritive value of any food. Foods high in sugar, fat and/or salt, especially those marketed to and/or favoured by children, should not be portrayed in any way that suggests they are beneficial to health.

2(d) Food advertisements containing obvious hyperbole, identifiable as such by the intended audience, are not considered misleading.

2(e) Advertisements should not claim or imply endorsement by any government agency, professional body or independent agency unless there is prior consent, the claim and the endorsement are verifiable and current and the agency or body named. An endorser represented as an expert should have qualifications appropriate to the expertise depicted.

2(f) Care should be taken with advertisements promoting a competition, premium or loyalty/continuity programme to ensure that advertisements do not encourage frequent repeat purchases of foods high in fat, salt and sugar.

2(g) Advertisements for foods high in sugar should not claim to be 'low fat' or 'fat free' which could mislead the consumer to believe the food is low in energy or beneficial to health.

2(h) Advertisements for food high in fat should not claim to be 'low in sugar' or 'sugar-free' which could mislead the consumer to believe the food is low in energy or beneficial to health.

**Principle 3 – Persons or characters well known to children shall not be used in advertisements to promote food in such a way as to undermine a healthy diet, as defined by the Food and Nutrition Guidelines for Healthy Children.**

3(a) Persons or characters well known to children may present factual and relevant statements about nutrition and health.

3(b) Persons or characters well known to children should not be used to endorse food high in fat, salt and/or sugar.

(Source: Advertising Standards Authority New Zealand 2010)

## Conclusion

Consumers can become resentful if they believe they have been deceived or ripped off. Unethical conduct can have long-term negative consequences to both a brand's reputation and the profitability of an organisation. It is for this reason that organisations need to be aware of potential ethical pitfalls and endeavour not only to avoid the pitfalls but also to strive for improvements.

## Ethics in practice: Cause-related marketing

Undertake research on cause-related marketing, and respond to the following questions.

**Questions:**

1. Provide an example of a successful campaign and, if possible, the impact on the company's brand.
2. Identify an unsuccessful campaign.
3. What are the possible negative impacts of cause-related campaigns through overuse or misuse?

## Ethics on video

**Advertising to children** – *Killing Us Softly 3: Advertising's Image of Women* 2006, documentary, ChallengingMedia, 4 October, <www.youtube.com/watch?v=_FpyGwP3yzE>.

**Comparative advertising** – *When brands brawl: five digital ad wars* 2012, mixed media article, iMediaConnection, 9 March, <www.imediaconnection.com/printpage/printpage.aspx?id=31182>.

See web material for more videos.

## Ethics at the movies

Here are a few movie suggestions that have ethical content related to Marketing:

* **The Joneses** – stealth marketing and product placement. *The Joneses* 2009, motion picture trailer, Mankoff, D, Zea, K, Spaulding, A & Borte, D.

**What Women Want** – a chauvinistic advertising executive gains insight into what women want. *What Women Want* 2000, motion picture trailer, Cartsonis, S, Davey, B, Matthews, G, Meyers, N & Williams, N.

* **Author's pick**

See web material for more movies.

# Ethics on the web

**Advertising Standards Authority of New Zealand**, the self-regulation body for advertising in New Zealand, <www.asa.co.nz>.

**Australian Association of National Advertisers**, sharing best practice and innovation in marketing, <www.aana.com.au>.

See web material for more web references.

# Student exercises

See web material for answers to student short answer questions.

## Short answer questions

1. Visit the American Marketing Association website at <www.marketingpower.com/AboutAMA/Pages/Statement%20of%20Ethics.aspx>, and locate what strategies one might use to check whether a marketer is adhering to the ethical values. List the six ethical values and provide at least three implementation strategies for each.
2. Do you think lip-syncing in the music industry is ethical?
3. Provide a high-profile example of deceptive labelling.
4. Provide a list of the main criticisms of advertising. What might the counter-arguments against these criticisms be?
5. 'While all stereotypes are generalisations, not all generalisations are stereotypes.' What is meant by this statement?
6. What are some of the potential ethical issues in relation to loyalty programs?

## Experiential exercise

### Marketing to vulnerable groups

Find an example of print or multimedia advertising aimed at vulnerable groups and explore the ethical dimensions of this example by identifying the vulnerable group being targeted (teenage, elderly, children or financially disadvantaged) and, referring to the marketing chapter of your textbook, use the five ethical guidelines provided earlier in this chapter in relation to marketing to vulnerable groups to critique the advertisement.

# Small case

## Case: Distribution – Gaining competitor information

You have heard that a competitor has a new product feature that will make a big difference in sales. The competitor plans to have a hospitality suite at the annual trade show and unveil this feature at a party thrown for dealers. You propose sending someone to this meeting hiding the fact that they work for you and pretending to be a potential client in order to gain valuable information.

**Question:**

1. Would you go ahead with this plan? Why or why not?

# Large case

## Case: Abercrombie & Fitch – Public relations, sponsorship and branding: The cost of an exclusive brand is exclusion

### Background

Abercrombie & Fitch (A&F) are a high-end, aspirational clothing brand delivering products aimed at the 18–22 year old 'cool' demographic, although the company's other brands are targeted at people from their mid-teens to mid-30s. The flagship 'cool' demographic of A&F is white, ripped, preppy boys. Astonishingly, other than one glitch in 2004, they have seen earnings increase for 52 straight quarters, excluding one quarter in 2004 (Denizet-Lewis 2006). Since Mike Jeffries took over as CEO, they have a history of ethically controversial approaches to HRM and marketing, with the two seemingly being inextricably linked.

In 2003, a class action lawsuit was brought against A&F, in which there were allegations of racially discriminatory hiring practices, including the hiring of sales staff who looked 'classically American' for front-of-store roles, while hiring people of colour to work in the stock rooms. The lawsuit was brought in 2003, after the release in 2002 of an ethnically targeted T-shirt range (including the slogan, 'Wong brothers laundry service – two Wongs can make it white'). The case was settled for US$40 million in 2005 (see <www.mhlearningsolutions.com/columbia_southern/0078134536/ch6.PDF> for more details about this case). Later comments by Jeffries suggest A&F did learn from this lawsuit, and have worked harder to embrace diversity in their workforce (Denizet-Lewis 2006).

### Mike Jeffries

In 2013, Jeffries came under fire for discriminatory remarks he had made in *Salon* in 2006, where he reinforced the A&F brand as cool and casually superior, specifically outlining who his brand excluded; the fat, the ugly and the undesirable. Jeffries unapologetically explained that the A&F brand was exclusive for cool kids, and therefore that sizes XL and XXL were not available in their stores for women, although larger sizes were available in men's sizes to target larger athletes (Levinson 2013).

Although these comments have not endeared Jeffries to the general public, R Dooley of *Forbes* (2013) believes that his comments have further entrenched loyalty to the A&F brand of existing clients, reinforcing the brand – which was exactly what Jeffries wanted to achieve – staying authentic to the target audience and at the same time communicating the brand's 'hotness' as a marketing tool (Levinson 2013). The goal was to create an 'us and them' mentality when people think of the A&F brand, bringing an aspirational element to the brand.

## Ethical considerations

A&F's controversial marketing tactics have caused consternation among some, who immediately took to boycotting the products, and there was even a moral movement started to attempt to re-brand the brand as being synonymous with homelessness, '#Fitchthehomeless' (Ralph 2013). This in itself has moral implications, as it further entrenches the 'us and them' framework upon which the brand is modelled.

So, is the ethical dilemma that A&F's marketing strategy is extremely focused and targets its brand narrowly to a niche? It seems unlikely, as many companies use such a strategy to create a successful brand. Or is the problem rather that the marketing strategy openly, and proudly, insults and discriminates against certain people (Kirpich 2013)? In the interim, profits for A&F have increased annually, counter to downward economic trends.

**Questions:**

1. As a business student, how do you think A&F's exacting marketing plan can be reconciled with ethical marketing principles?
2. Do you believe there is a case to be made for unethical conduct in the 2013 'too cool for A&F' comments and deliberately excluding fat, ugly and undesirable people? What are your reasons for your viewpoint?
3. What ethical issues are evident when considering the 2003 lawsuit, and the 2013 marketing controversy?
4. Who are the main stakeholders affected in the marketing controversy, and how might they have been affected by it?
5. What changes could the company make to improve stakeholder outcomes, and at what cost (social and economic) to the company?

See web material for:
- answers to short answer questions
- additional student cases
- tutor resources (tutor password required)
- additional material including Ethics at the movies, Ethics in print, Ethics on video and Ethics on the web.

# Chapter 6

## Ethical issues in accounting and finance

'Earnings can be pliable as putty when a charlatan heads the company reporting them.'

Warren Buffett, 1930–,
American investment entrepreneur

## Chapter aim

To identify current ethical issues in accounting and finance.

## Chapter objectives

1. Recognise the dominant ethical principles that relate to accounting and finance.
2. Describe some of best known recent corporate collapses and evaluate them from the perspective of ethical mismanagement.
3. Identify the primary areas where misrepresentation and inaccurate reporting often occur.
4. Compare the various forms that fraud can take.
5. Discuss insider trading from the perspective of fairness.
6. Understand how conflict of interest and objectivity relate to each other.
7. Clarify the distinction between tax minimisation, tax avoidance and tax evasion.
8. Describe the key features of a Ponzi scheme.
9. Identify what investments are commonly avoided in socially responsible investments.

# Ethics in the media: Tax evasion

A UK Finance lecturer helped his student, a bankrupt businessman, run a tax scam by falsely claiming $2.8 million in VAT and film tax credits when making a Hollywood blockbuster movie. Suspicion was raised by the $1 million low-budget film made to conceal their fraudulent activities, which, ironically, received a festival award ('The Week in Higher Education' 2013).

## Introduction

The information accountants provide is vital to aiding managers, investors and others in making rational economic decisions. As such, ethical improprieties by accountants can be detrimental to society, resulting in distrust by the public and, on a broader scale, disruption of efficient capital markets (Williams & Elson 2010). When reporting financial data, accountants act as intermediaries in the capital markets and are expected to exercise their primary obligation to the public interest. But on occasions it is not public interest, but self-interest that prevails.

When we think of accountants we think of those belonging to professional associations and bound by professional standards and codes of ethics. However, if we were to take a broader view, ethics in accounting and finance also relates to those who do not belong to the accountancy profession but are individual managers and employees both directly, and indirectly, involved in this functional area, as well as, individuals that are in associated regulatory or stakeholder organisations such as: banks, auditors, lending agencies or trading houses.

There is no doubt that the public has been surprised and dismayed by recent financial debacles (Brooks & Dunn 2012). While it is tempting to depersonalise the incidences involving fraud, investment scams, insider trading and misrepresentation of financial data, to problems relating to firms, however, these fiascos relate squarely to individuals, the actions they have taken and their financial mis-dealings. Organisations such as Enron, WorldCom, Bearings Bank, Livent Royal Ahold, Tyco, Adelphia, US Savings and Loan, and in the Australasian context HIH Insurance, One. Tel, and Ansett Airlines, all imploded largely because of financial mismanagement by the leaders and employees within these organisations. See Table 6.1 for more examples of financial scandals.

Closer examination indicates that there are three levels on which we can view these financial scandals (see also Figure 6.1):

1. **The individual level** – individuals that were in key organisational positions and the ethicality of the decisions they made.
2. **The corporate level** – the collective responsibility of all employees as well as the governance structures, systems and processes (essentially checks and balances) that operated within the organisation in an attempt to rein in inappropriate behaviour.

**Table 6.1** Financial fiascos

| Financial fiasco | Company involved | Company's country of origin |
|---|---|---|
| Misrepresentation and inaccurate financial reporting | Olympus Corporation | Japan |
| | Banksia Securities | Australia |
| | Evergrande Real Estate Group Ltd. | China |
| | Australian Wheat Board | Australia |
| | Centro | Australia |
| | Bristol-Myers Squibb | USA |
| | Fannie May | USA |
| | Hanover Compressor | USA |
| | Rent-Way | USA |
| | Rite-Aid | USA |
| Accounting Frauds | Olympus Corporation | Japan |
| | Aegis Media plc | UK |
| | Pescanova | Spain |
| | Satyam Computer Services | India |
| | Peregrine Systems | USA |
| | Lernout & Hauspie | Belgium |
| | The Baptist Foundation of Arizona | USA |
| | Hanover Compressor | USA |
| Insider trading | Galleon Group (USA) | USA |
| | Rene Rivkin (Australia) | Australia |
| | Lonsec Stockbroking Service | Australia |
| Rogue traders | Hogan and Partners Stockbrokers Pty Ltd | Australia |
| | Lewis Charles Securities | UK |
| | Fanny Mae | USA |
| | Freddie Mack | USA |
| Conflict of interest | Cascade Coal | Australia |
| | Arthur Andersen/Enron | USA |
| | Goldman Sachs | USA |
| Tax minimisation and tax evasion | Google | Australia |
| | Dolce & Gabbana | Italy |
| | Purti Group | India |
| | Ernst & Young | |
| | KPMG | |
| Money laundering | HSBC Holdings plc | UK |
| | Standard Chartered plc | UK |
| Investment scams | Stanford International Bank, Allen Stanford | USA |
| | Bernard L. Madoff Investment Securities LLC | USA |
| | Practical Property Portfolio | UK |
| | Frankel International, Barry Tannenbaum | Republic of South Africa |
| Bankruptcy | Satyam Computer Services | India |
| | Mid-Staffordshire NHS trust | UK |
| | Dynegy Holdings | USA |
| | Lernout & Hauspie | Belgium |
| | Enron Corporation | USA |
| | HIH Insurance | Australia |
| | WorldCom | USA |
| | Lehman Brothers | USA |
| | Sunbeam Products, Inc | USA |

(Adapted from: Brooks & Dunn 2012; Stuart & Stuart 2004)

3. **The regulatory level** – the interconnected organisations, such as auditors, bankers and other financial institutions that were found to have colluded in the ongoing deception of the true company performance. For example, as the auditor of companies (for example, Waste Management, Sunbeam, Global Crossing and WorldCom) with accounting transgressions, Arthur Andersen were naturally blamed for these scandals, lost their reputation and were indicted for obstruction of justice (Ketz 2006).

**Figure 6.1** Three levels of accounting scandal

# Ethics on reflection: Investor loss

Imagine you are a significant investor in one of the recently bankrupted organisations. Or alternatively, an employee whose retirement/superannuation fund was used in the last few months of operation to shore up the financial position of the business. You have just been informed the company has gone into receivership and it is unlikely that you will receive anything more than 20 cents in the dollar that you have with the company. It may also be at least two years before a cheque will be received.

**Question:**
1. What would you like to say to the managers of the company?

# Ethics in practice: Corporate collapses

Select one of the following organisations and undertake an internet search to gain an appreciation of the effect the demise these companies had on a large number of people: Enron, WorldCom, Bearings Bank, Livent Royal Ahold, Tyco, Adelphia, US Savings and Loan, HIH Insurance, One.Tel, or Ansett Airlines.

# Ethics in the media: Deceiving analysts

Former top Enron executives were apparently personally involved in stage-managing a fake trading room to impress analysts. Jokingly referred to as 'the sting', secretaries and other staff posed as busy energy traders in an unused trading room as part of the charade (Duska & Duska 2003).

Concerns for ethics in accounting and finance, and to whom one assigns moral responsibility, are not new. The 1892 *Chambers' Encyclopaedia* was scathing about limited liability public companies, as having vastly reduced the integrity of business by separating ownership from behaviour, responsibility and the need for transparency ('On public companies, trolleyology, written knowledge' 2012). Today businesses, and particularly financial institutions, are vulnerable to shareholder activism, investigation, prosecution and litigation from every direction; however, this has not deterred unacceptable practices.

In this chapter, there are a number of approaches which could be taken; we could look at ethics in accounting and finance from the perspective of the accounting profession and it is here that the big professional associations such as ACCA and CPA have a lot to say in regard to the ethical expectations of members of their profession. One appreciates that the higher a profession is held in regard, the greater the likelihood that the profession will retain its integrity and therefore it is within the interest of these professional bodies to support the adherence to ethical standards. But not everyone dealing with ethical accounting and financial issues is a certified or practicing accountant, and so another perspective is to look at ethics in accounting and finance from a broader discipline focus. This is the approach that we will take. While making reference to professional expectations we will examine ethical issues in accounting and finance; whether someone is an accountant, an entrepreneur, an employee or manager in a large organisation.

We also tend to think of financial ethical misdemeanours being those associated with the CEO, the CFO or the COO. However, rank and file employees are just as likely to succumb to unethical pressures. Therefore, it would be remiss to focus solely on the behaviours of managers. For example, in the educational documentary *Crossing the line: Ordinary people committing extraordinary crimes* (see <www.youtube.com/watch?v=QIwH5E7nX-A>), Dr Kelly Richmond-Pope chronicles the lives of five white-collar criminals who have been engaged in different types of financial manipulation at some stage in their careers; one started by mistakenly charging a personal trip on her corporate credit card; another by taking small accounting liberties to make his business unit's quarterly numbers; yet another accepted a lucrative new client despite qualms about the nature of his business. Each story realistically portrays the circumstances where a person moved into an unethical arena irrespective of their professional affiliations, organisational role or level in the organisation.

# Ethical principles in accounting and finance

Before examining specific ethical issues let us first examine the common ethical principles that relate to accounting and finance for which we can be guided by international standards. It should be noted that internationally, considerable thought has gone into what ethical principles apply to the accounting profession. In Australia, CPA Australia, the Institute of Chartered Accountants Australia (ICAA) and the Institute of Public Accountants (IPA) have all joined together in order to speak with a united voice in relation to ethical standards. The fundamental principles of the professional code relate to integrity, objectivity, professional competence and due care, confidentiality and professional behaviour (Joint Accounting Bodies: CPA, ICAA & IPA 2013).

For the purposes of our discussion and the larger capture of professionals and non-professional accounting and finance personnel, the following ethical principles are seen as most relevant:

**Integrity** – to exhibit behaviour and actions consistent with a set of moral or ethical principles and standards embraced by individuals as well as institutions (Transparency International 2009a).

**Confidentiality** – to respect the confidentiality of information acquired as a result of professional and business relationships and, therefore, not disclose any such information to third parties without proper and specific authority, unless there is a legal or professional right or duty to disclose (International Federation of Accountants 2012).

**Objectivity** – avoidance of conflicts of interest, bias, or undue influence of others to override or impact on business decisions. In addition to self-interest, one area that has the potential for eroding independence and objectivity is the receiving of gifts and hospitality from a client, potential client or related business associate. The potential for future compromise is present, although naturally it depends on the cost and the nature of the gift or hospitality offered. A useful guideline is to consider how a third party might perceive the gift or hospitality.

**Honesty** – to be truthful, candid and straightforward in all dealings. After the collapse of Enron and WorldCom, the *Sarbanes–Oxley Act 2002* was introduced in the US in a bid to ensure company honesty. The Act requires senior executives to certify their company accounts, keep an arms' length relationship with auditors, and pay back bonuses if the financials are reworked ('In search of honesty' 2002).

**Fiduciary duty** – a legal obligation by one party to act in the best interest of another party; either based on loyalty or due to being entrusted with a duty of care, which usually

**integrity** – exhibiting behaviour consistent with a set of moral standards.

**confidentiality** – respecting the confidentiality of information acquired as a result of professional and business relationships and, therefore, not disclosing information to third parties without authority.

**objectivity** – avoiding conflicts of interest, bias, or undue influence of others to impact on business decisions.

**honesty** – to be truthful, candid and straightforward in all dealings.

**fiduciary duty** – a legal obligation where one party acts in the best interest of another party due to loyalty or duty of care.

encompasses money or property (Businessdictionary.com 2013). Fiduciary responsibility is commonly in relation to: an employer's resources, client funds and trust accounts.

**Duty of care** (also known as **professional competence**) – maintaining knowledge and skill to ensure that a client or employer receives competent service based on current developments in practice, legislation and techniques, and acting diligently (International Federation of Accountants 2012).

**No maleficence** – avoiding or doing no harm to others (Baron 1996). The Japanese company, Olympus, commenced proceedings for damages against their current and former directors in 2012. These directors were accused of neglecting their duties in an accounting scandal and causing harm to the company ('The world this week' 2012a).

**Trust** – confidence and faith in the reliance and ability of another; an element that is amplified when codified. Trust represents an issue in the financial planning industry where there is not a level commercial playing field, in that some of the financial planners are accountants and ethically and professionally bound by a code of ethics, while some financial planners are not (Brown 2011).

> **duty of care** (also called **professional competence**) – maintaining knowledge and skill to ensure that a client or employer receives competent service.

> **no maleficence** – avoiding or doing no harm to others.

> **trust** – expressing confidence and faith in the reliance and ability of another.

# Ethics on reflection: Professional ethics

Differentiate between personal ethics and professional ethics.

While numerous ethical issues might be examined here, we will focus on the more topical and significant ones: misrepresentation and inaccurate financial reporting; accounting fraud; insider trading; conflict of interest; tax avoidance and tax evasion; money laundering; and investment scams.

## Misrepresentation and inaccurate financial reporting

In July 2007, New Zealand company, Bridgecorp, collapsed owing NZ$460 million to 14 500 investors, having misstated their liquidity after missing principal and interest payments. The three directors were charged with making untrue statements in investment prospectuses (this carries maximum penalties of five years in prison and fines of up to NZ$300 000) (Mace 2012).

In their text *Corporate collapse: Accounting, regulatory and ethical failure*, Clarke, Dean and Oliver (2003) represent a critical voice on the ethical issue of deception, and problems in the reporting of accurate financial information. Chronicling corporate collapses of the 1960s, they suggest that contemporary accounting practices along with managers colluding, have resulted in misrepresentation and an inability to give the full truth about impeding failures. Clarke and Dean (2007) more recently captured the anguish both the commercial and general public experience when misleading financial disclosures of public corporations lead to unexpected collapses, which are largely as a result of misrepresentation and inaccurate financial reporting.

Inaccurate financial reporting and associated misrepresentation are clearly both ethical and legal issues. Under the *Corporations Act 2001* in Australia, misleading and deceptive statements can lead to criminal prosecution. As indicated, a fundamental feature of financial reporting is the accuracy of the information provided, given that investors rely on this information in order to guide their investment decisions. If the information is fraudulent through either misstatement or omission, then investors have the right to take action (Laux & Stocken 2012). The consequence of misrepresentation is that potential buyers, or investors, do not get a true representation of what the business is actually worth; this can lead to inappropriate decisions, poor investments and inevitable reductions in the value of the business ('The world this week' 2012b).

Misrepresentation and inaccurate financial reporting primarily occurs in five areas:

1. **Inappropriate recognition of revenue.** In July 2002, America Online, a unit of AOL Time Warner, was reviewed in relation to 'unconventional' ad deals that increased revenue to meet the expectations of Wall Street analysts (Stuart & Stuart 2004). Albert Dunlap, the CEO of Sunbeam Products, increased net income by fraudulently reporting US$62 million of sales. The company ultimately went into bankruptcy protection in 2001 (Brooks & Dunn 2012). It is not just large organisations that come unstuck. For example, in order to sustain cashflow, some internet companies have been engaging in ethically questionable accounting practices, such as prematurely recognising revenue, treating barter as revenue and investing in companies that are also a company's main advertisers (Maury & Kleiner 2002). These practices have caused the US Security Exchange Commission (SEC) to request an investigation.

2. **Inappropriate recognition of expenses.** WorldCom, one of the world's largest telecommunications companies, acknowledged accounting improprieties relating to line cost expenses. The former financial controller indicated in a court hearing that he was instructed on a quarterly basis by senior management to reduce WorldCom's reported actual costs and thereby increase their reported earnings (Stuart & Stuart 2004).

3. **Misstatements of earnings.** In 2002, Microsoft settled a case in which the SEC alleged the company had misstated their earnings between 1994 and 1998 by US$900 million through manipulation of reserve accounts and either over- or under-reported earnings (Ward 2002); however, Microsoft have neither admitted nor denied wrongdoing. Also in the US, Fannie Mae had an accounting re-statement that resulted in their income reducing by US$9 million (Ketz 2006). Other cases include Xerox, Sunbeam and WorldCom (see Ward 2002).

4. **Understatement of liabilities and overstatement of assets.** It was discovered that Enron were selling assets to Special Purpose Entities (SPEs). These were limited to partnerships, most of which were under Enron's control. An SPE required only 3% to be owned by people or organisations independent of Enron. This allowed Enron to 'have its cake and eat it too', and the deceptive practice allowed Enron to show gains of US$63 million even though they still owned a majority share of the assets and liability which they had not really sold (Duska & Duska 2003).

5. **Hiding losses.** The Japanese camera manufacturer Olympus got into hot water when it was revealed that they had been involved in buying overinflated businesses which were intended to hide losses ('Big trouble in Tokyo' 2011).

But what about the small business owner or entrepreneur, who does not necessarily have the same oversight by interested investors as a larger company? Research reveals that entrepreneurs are more optimistic than investors about the chances that their business ideas will succeed, and even when entrepreneurs bear the damages of this optimism out of their own pocket through legal penalties, this does not necessarily lead to more truthful reporting. In fact, it may lead to more misreporting (Laux & Stocken 2012).

## Ethics in the media: Accounting improprieties

In November 2012, Hewlett-Packard announced that they were writing down the value of Autonomy, a British software company and recent investment by Hewlett-Packard, due to accounting improprieties, disclosure failures and misrepresentations. The write-down was valued at US$8.8 billion ('Accountable' 2012).

## Ethics in the media: Misleading the stock exchange

Mining magnate Travers Duncan, one of Australia's wealthiest businesspeople, was accused of dishonesty and deliberately misleading the Australian stock exchange. Travers Duncan, and other investors, stood to make AU$50 million when they tried to sell their private company, Cascade Coal, to White Energy, a public company (McClymont 2012).

Another more subtle form of inaccurate reporting, which can result in an overstatement of profits and is a problem for internet companies, is a technique called **grossing up revenue**. For example, Priceline.com added gross booking revenues for accommodation, airline costs and car rentals, listing them as their revenue, and then deducted the selling costs of some as product costs to portray gross profit, which in reality was their actual revenue (Maury & Kleiner 2002).

Financial manipulations can occur not only at the corporate level, but also at the national level. In 2001, Greece was intent on joining the European Monetary Union, but was not eligible due to the requirement that its debt-to-GDP ratio be less than 60%. This was not possible given the levels of US and Japanese debt on the country's books. Goldman Sachs assisted the Greek government to manipulate its eligibility by arranging two types of hedges to reduce the reported Greek debt by €2.367 billion, and this allowed Greece to access unreported off–balance sheet financing (Brooks & Dunn 2012).

> **grossing up revenue** – reporting revenue at the full value or 'gross booking' rather than the actual amount received, resulting in an overstatement of profits.

# Accounting fraud

A report from the Association of Certified Fraud Examiners, which covers 94 nations, indicated surprisingly consistent patterns of fraud and fraudulent activity, regardless of legal jurisdiction. Businesses with fewer than 100 employees are most likely to suffer from financial damage with a medium loss of AU$147 000, while larger organisations, with between 1000 and 10 000 employees, incurred losses of AU$100 000 (Douglas 2012). A similar survey by PricewaterhouseCoopers, called *Cybercrime: Out of obscurity and into reality, 6th PwC Global Economic Crime Survey*, has been conducted biennially since 1999, revealing some interesting findings in relation to **accounting fraud** (sometimes called **economic crime**). In addition to identifying the rising threat of cyber-crime, there had been an increase in Australian respondents – 47% – who reported that their organisation had experienced at least one incidence of economic crime in the past year. From the organisations that experienced at least one incident of economic crime, more than 50% reported more than 10 economic crime infractions in the last 12 months, with their organisations losing more than AU$100 000 during the past 12 months. It was also found that 16% of organisations lost more than AU$5 million. Most of these crimes of fraud were perpetuated from internal members of the organisation (PricewaterhouseCoopers 2012).

> **accounting fraud** (sometimes called **economic crime**) – theft involving the use of deception to obtain a financial advantage from an employer or client.

Accounting fraud is defined as 'theft committed by a member of an organisation or professional practice involving the use of deception to obtain a financial advantage from their employing organisation or client such as money, property or information' (Dellaportas et al. 2005, p. 188). Naturally, a variety of activities come under the category of fraud, and as the corporate examples already discussed in this chapter show, all of these circumstances are violations of a fiduciary duty.

**embezzlement**
(also referred to as **misappropriation**) – when a person holding office dishonestly appropriates, uses, or traffics, the funds they have been entrusted with.

**falsifying documentation** – altering or modifying documents, such as tax returns, ID cards and business records, for the specific purpose of deception.

**fraudulent billing** – false invoicing.

**deceptive expenses** – claiming expenses which are not valid.

**fraudulent tendering** – fraud in the procurement and tendering of contracts.

**cyber-crime** (also known as **hi-tech crime**, **computer crime** or **technology-enabled crime**) – crimes committed against computers and computer systems and/or technology being used to commit or facilitate other traditional crimes.

**Embezzlement** (sometimes called **misappropriation**) – when a person holding office in an institution, organisation or company, dishonestly and illegally appropriates, uses, or traffics the funds they have been entrusted with for personal enrichment or other activities (Transparency International 2009a).

**Falsifying documentation** – occurs when altering or modifying a document for the specific purpose of deceiving another person (Austen & Reisch 2007). The falsification of documentation can occur in relation to providing false information on tax returns, ID cards and business record-keeping, to name a few.

**Fraudulent billing** – invoicing inappropriately; that is, false invoicing, usually involving inflated billing, double billing and illegitimate expenses. Billing fraud often takes place in the form of medical insurance and the FBI estimates that this type of healthcare fraud costs US taxpayers approximately US$80 billion a year (Federal Bureau of Investigation 2013). Fraudulent billing is also a significant issue in Australia, in relation to Medicare, Australia's publicly funded healthcare system (Medicare Australia 2013).

**Deceptive expenses** – claiming expenses which are not valid. Making false and misleading claims for expenses to which one is not entitled. Businesspeople may, for example, make false claims about travelling expenses and office costs.

**Fraudulent tendering** – fraud in the procurement and tendering of contracts. This may relate to collusion among bidders, or between employees and contractors. Fraudulent tenders for contract may be issued as a scam for money; a situation that arose in Iraq, resulting in a global warning by the International Trade Association (2011).

**Cyber-crime** (also referred to as **hi-tech crime**, **computer crime** or **technology-enabled crime**) – crimes committed against computers and computer systems and/or technology being used to commit or facilitate other traditional crimes (Australian Federal Police 2013); for example, malicious hacking, destruction of data and malicious software attacks. The crime is so ubiquitous these days that agencies are working together around the world by establishing the Virtual Global Taskforce (VGT) to combat cyber-crime (Australian Federal Police 2013). For detailed discussion of cyber-crime, see Chapter 3.

**Inflating profit** – overstating profits to make profits look larger than they actually are. A recent case in India revealed the many ways a company may inflate its profits (for example, writing off expenses for reserves or revaluing assets) (see Krishnan 2009).

**Extortion** – the act of utilising, either directly or indirectly, one's access to a position of power or knowledge to demand unmerited corporate compensation as a result of coercive threats (Transparency International 2009a). Extortion consists of threatening or intimidating another person to gain some advantage from them.

A striking theme of a survey by KPMG (2013) about fraud, bribery and corruption in Australia and New Zealand was the growth of collusive behaviour; that is, perpetrators not acting alone, but in collusion with another person.

Fraud is usually made up of three dimensions, as depicted in Figure 6.2: (1) the pressure or motivation to commit the fraud; (2) the opportunity, for example, lax processes or policies; and (3) the rationalisation or reasoning that is used to justify the behaviour or action

# Ethics in the media: Embezzlement

The former Chairman of Hyundai, Chung Mong Koo, was convicted of embezzling US$110 million of company funds in 2007. He allegedly used a portion of the funds to pay off politicians and government officials (Transparency International 2009a).

**inflating profit** – overstating profits to make profits look larger than they actually are.

**extortion** – utilising, either directly or indirectly, one's access to a position of power or knowledge to demand unmerited corporation compensation as a result of coercive threats.

(Dellaportas et al. 2005). Interestingly, most fraudsters do not have a history of dishonesty, but are motivated by greed, lifestyle or personal financial pressures (KPMG 2013). Table 6.2 shows the most common characteristics of fraud.

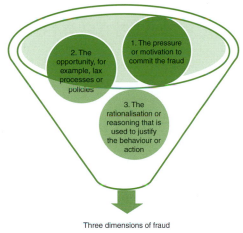

Three dimensions of fraud

**Figure 6.2:** Accounting fraud: Three dimensions of fraud

**Table 6.2**  Characteristics of fraud in Australia

Common forms of fraud:
- managers using false invoices
- employees stealing cash
- external stakeholders engaging in credit card fraud.

Common fraud motivators:
- greed
- lifestyle
- personal financial pressures.

Fraudster characteristics:
- 75% are male
- 77% act alone
- 75% are internal to the firm
- 49% of perpetrators are non-management employees.

(Adapted from: KPMG 2013)

# Ethics in practice: Fraud

A small and fast-growing company employs friends as trusted senior staff to run the company while the head focuses on growing the business. Liquidity problems uncover a series of unauthorised loans and misuse of funds by the senior staff. Even worse, before the staff resign they steal significant intellectual property (PricewaterhouseCoopers 2012).

**Questions:**
1. What are the ethical issues involved in this case?
2. How might they have been prevented?

# Ethics in practice: Fraudulent payments

Suspicious transactions led to analysis tests being performed on a company's financial system, where it was found that an employee shared the same address as a vendor; however, despite the vendor's contract being cancelled, invoices totalling US$500 million had been raised and paid to this vendor (PricewaterhouseCoopers 2012).

**Questions:**
1. What are the ethical issues involved in this case?
2. How might they have been prevented?

# Ethics in the media: Misuse of funds

In July 2012, in Singapore, a pastor of a church and five others appeared in court on charges of misusing up to US$40 million of church money to fund the music career of the pastor's flamboyant wife. The case revealed a lack of accountability and transparency ('Reaping what they sow' 2012).

# Ethics in practice: Fraud education

The homepage of the Standard Chartered website has an online game called SWAT to educate customers on fraud risk. The game illustrates risks and challenges and encourages players to minimise fraud. For example, they sift through various emails to detect fraudulent ones and rank the safety of a series of passwords (see <www.standardchartered.com/_microsites/anti-fraud/index.html>).

# Insider trading

The first prosecution for insider trading occurred in the US in 1961 when a broker used a tip from an impending dividend payout to sell stock belonging to his wife and a client. He received a US$3000 fine and suspension for 20 days from the New York Stock Exchange. However, the penalties are now becoming more frequent and more severe: the SEC brought 53 cases against 138 individuals and entities in 2010, up more than 40% on the previous year ('Tipping the scales' 2011).

**Insider trading** has been defined as an intentional disclosure of information which may be used to gain some modest benefit' ('Judge Rakoff' 2011). When testing whether insider trading is economically rational, Bhattacharya and Marshall (2012) found that a majority of executives convicted of insider trading were actually the best paid employees in the firms, indicating that friendship and ego appear to matter more than money.

> **insider trading** – the intentional disclosure of information in anticipation that it will be used for a trade in exchange for benefit.

A study of 213 business students found that men are twice as likely as women to engage in unethical behaviour, with 50% of the respondents willing to buy stock with insider knowledge (Betz, O'Connell & Shepard 2013). Insider trading has been positioned as illegal in blanket laws; however, McGee (2009) argues insider trading should be reviewed on a case-by-case basis where there are utilitarian benefits (for example, an executive who has a low base salary and supplements his income with insider trading). He argues against sanctions, and supports insider trading; a view not commonly shared.

Insider trading not only affects individuals but also financial entities. Concern of advanced notification of investors of a planned share offering is plaguing the Japanese stock market and damaging its credibility. LLC, a Japanese investment advisory company, had their licence revoked in June 2012 by the Financial Services Agency for allegedly issuing orders for trades based on non-public information (Inagaki & Dvorak 2012).

Also closely aligned to insider trading is **market manipulation**, where individuals or financial entities construct circumstances to move the market in their favour. For example, in early 2013, a 24-year-old radical, who lived at a bush campsite 500 kilometres north of

> **market manipulation** – where individuals or financial entities construct circumstances to move the market in their favour.

West Sydney, managed to wipe more than AU$300 million off the share market by using a hoax press release. The anti-coal campaigner spooked the investment community when they tricked investors and media into thinking that the firm, Whitehaven, had lost a critical AU$1.2 billion loan from the ANZ Bank. The hoax sparked a sell down as shares dropped 31 cents to AU$3.21 within minutes. While the hoaxer did not gain financially from the market manipulation, the action clearly indicated vulnerabilities (Ker & Hawthorne 2013).

# Ethics in the media: Insider trading

In the US in November 2012, the SEC accused a former portfolio manager at SAC of insider trading. It appears that the manager obtained confidential information about a clinical trial and as a consequence, reaped US$276 million in profit and avoided losses in subsequent stock market trades ('Business this week' 2012c).

# Ethics in practice: Insider trading

You are the financial controller for a listed company. Your company has a long-established policy of buying up its own shares for treasury stock, pension portfolio and executive stock options. The directors know that the value of the stock will rise dramatically when certain discoveries and innovations are announced to the public. You propose buying up as much stock as possible before the announcement.

**Question:**

1. Discuss the ethical considerations in this scenario.

## Conflict of interest

**conflict of interest** – where the primary interest of an individual may have their judgement impaired by a secondary interest.

**Conflict of interest** is a situation where the primary interest of a professional may have their judgement impaired by a secondary interest (MacKenzie & Cronstein 2006). Continuing with insider trading, there may also be conflicts of interest present, particularly where an executive has a fiduciary relationship and responsibility to a particular organisation. For example, in a high-profile case of insider trading the trial of one of America's elite business-men, Rajat Gupta, started in New York in 2012. Among other things, Mr Gupta was accused of passing sensitive information about Goldman Sachs to Raj Rajaratnam, a former hedge fund boss of Galleon Group, who was convicted of insider trading in 2011. Mr Gupta denied the charges ('Business this week' 2012a). The use of non-public information subsequently netted Mr Rajaratnam around US$840 000. The circumstances not only revealed insider trading, but was coupled with conflict of interest. Mr Gupta had a financial interest in the success of Mr Rajaratnam's hedge fund, Galleon Group ('Business this week' 2011).

Conflict of interest (© shutterstock.com/Yulia Glam)

In order to avoid conflict of interest, in October 2011 the SEC banned underwriters of asset backed securities from profiting at the expense of investors in the US ('Abacussed' 2011). In Australia, until August 2010 the Australian Securities Exchange (ASX) had oversight of regulating insider trading, but that function has now moved to the Australian Securities and Investment Commission (ASIC), to remove any potential conflict of interest from ASX as a listed company regulating other listed companies (D'Aloisio 2010).

The risk of conflict of interest also exists for financial advisers and accountants, as accountants need to have some separation from their client in order to be able to provide objective and independent advice. If they get too close to the client there is a chance that this independence will be compromised and that there will be bias, undue influence or even a potential conflict of interest. In order to assist accountants when this circumstance arises, it is advisable that they put safeguards in place, such as: withdrawing from the team; changing supervisory arrangements; terminating the financial or business relationship; ensuring that there are clear reporting lines; and ensuring transparency (International Federation of Accountants 2012).

# Tax avoidance and tax evasion

Tax avoidance and tax evasion are committed by individuals who deliberately abuse the tax system in order to obtain financial benefit by not paying what they are required to (ATO 2013). Recent high-profile cases of alleged tax abuses in Australia have included actor Paul Hogan, promoter Glen Wheatley, accountant Philip de Figueredo and, somewhat ironically, the former president of the National Institute of Accountants, Lynette Liles (Bleby 2013; El-Ansary 2010).

**tax minimisation** – when corporate structures, processes and practices are legitimately organised to reduce the amount of tax paid.

**tax avoidance** – arrangements which comply with the letter of the law but are possibly not within the spirit of the law.

**tax evasion** – unlawful actions are taken to avoid tax.

**transfer pricing** – the practice of shifting money between certain tax jurisdictions to avoid paying tax twice on the same amount.

These high-profile cases have presumably been brought to the public's attention in the hope that these examples would serve as a deterrent to taxpayers trying to evade their responsibilities.

A distinction is often undertaken between tax minimisation, tax evasion and tax avoidance. **Tax minimisation** is when corporate structures, processes and practices are legitimately organised to reduce the amount of tax paid, while **tax avoidance** is the arrangement which complies with the letter of the law but possibly not within the spirit of the law. **Tax evasion**, at the other end of the continuum, is where unlawful actions are taken to avoid tax (Dellaportas et al. 2005). Tax evasion is seen as a serious crime principally because it not only costs the government, but society at large (ATO 2013) with money being directed away from public good.

Governments are particularly active in the pursuit of unethical tax activity. In 2008, the former head of Germany's postal service was caught hiding money in the tax haven of Lichtenstein. As a consequence, Lichtenstein agreed to weakened bank secrecy proposals and encouraged exchange of tax information; however, this has resulted in Lichtenstein's bank client assets declining by 30% ('Leaky devils' 2013). In Australia, while a company's tax is usually 30%, companies involved in tax evasion can lower their tax to 3% or even eliminate it. Australia is not alone; the US, the UK and Singapore, as well as many other countries, are cracking down on tax evasion (Grant 2013).

Governments are also cooperating with each other. In June 2013, the Swiss Government proposed a bill that allowed their banks to cooperate with the US during tax evasion allegation cases ('Business' 2013b). Singapore has adopted new measures to tighten up on tax evasion. The Tax Office and the Inland Revenue Authority of Singapore will not need a court order to get information from banks and trust companies sought by foreign governments. Singapore is also planning to sign a multi-lateral treaty agreeing to share tax details, which has been created by the Organisation for Economic Co-operation and Development (Reuters 2013). Singapore has strong rules compelling financial institutions to identify accounts they strongly suspect hold the proceeds of fraudulent or wilful tax evasion, and handling the proceeds of tax evasion will become a criminal offence (Grant 2013).

# Ethics in the media: Tax minimisation

In a rare rebuke of the monarchy, the Belgian Prime Minister described Queen Fabiola's plan to try to shield some of her fortune from taxation as being legal, but ethically flawed. The Queen, who is childless, has an inheritance plan that is being widely seen as a tax dodge (O'Hare 2013).

Tax avoidance and tax evasion frequently involve offshore entities. For example, most of Google's European revenues are booked in Dublin and then shifted to a Dutch subsidiary as royalty payments, while the remaining revenue is recognised as profits by a Bermudan subsidiary, against which no income tax is levied ('Wake up and smell the coffee: corporate taxation' 2012). 61 of the top 100 companies in Australia held subsidiaries in tax havens in 2001, with the telling sign being the level of legitimate business and evidence of commercial activity (Wilkins & Butler 2013).

The accounting techniques used for tax avoidance are as follows:

- **Transfer pricing** – transfer pricing allows companies to shift money between certain tax jurisdictions to avoid paying tax twice on the same amount (Khadem 2012). It usually involves a parent company selling products or services through its subsidiaries, with costs accumulating in high-tax countries, and revenues in low-tax jurisdictions.

- **Offshore billing** – the parent company charges Australian consumers for services from its offshore tax haven subsidiary and the money goes directly to the tax haven, and not to the Australian-based company. As a consequence, the money does not form part of the Australian income and is not taxed (Taxjustice Network 2002–2005).

- **Thin capitalisation** – where the parent company loans money to its Australian subsidiary via an offshore finance arm based in a low-tax jurisdiction. The Australian company is loaded with debt and pays interest on the debt, which is tax deductible, while holding relatively few assets (ATO 2009; KPMG 2008).

- **Intangible assets** – the parent company in the tax haven owns intangible assets such as intellectual property and licenses the use of that property to the Australian operation that pays significant sums to the tax haven-based subsidiary, thereby stripping out taxable revenue from the Australian company and placing that revenue in the low-tax location (Markham 2004).

Transfer pricing (© shutterstock.com/Thomas Reichhart)

New forms of business create further difficulties for tax collection with online retailing presenting new challenges. Previously in the US, online retailers have been able to

**offshore billing** – a parent company charges consumers for services from its offshore tax haven subsidiary and the money goes directly to the tax haven; the money does not form part of the home country income and is not taxed.

**thin capitalisation** – where a parent company loans money to a subsidiary in a high-tax location via an offshore financial arm based in a low-tax jurisdiction, thereby loading debt and interest in the high-tax environment.

**intangible assets** – where a parent company in a tax haven owns intangible assets, such as intellectual property, and licenses the use of that property to their overseas operation that pays significant sums to the tax haven-based subsidiary, thereby stripping out taxable revenue from the high-tax location and placing that revenue in the low-tax location.

skirt collecting sales tax, but this may change as the Senate sets about approving a bill requiring internet merchants to collect sales tax due in states in which they operate. The legislation is called the *Market Place Fairness Act 2013*. However, life can get complicated as there are currently 9646 separate American jurisdictions that levy sales tax. eBay has resisted the legislation, urging customers and merchants to respond, indicating that collecting tax from customers will make it harder for small businesses to grow ('Tax in cyber space' 2013).

Internationally, tax authorities are also increasingly concerned about the use of sale suppression software and devices that alter cash register records. This prompted a *Report on electronic sales suppression: A threat to tax revenues*, by the Organisation for Economic Co-operation and Development (OECD) in February 2013 (see <www.oecd.org/ctp/crime/ElectronicSalesSuppression.pdf>) that outlines the problems. Figure 6.3 shows the top 10 jurisdictions Australian companies use to evade tax.

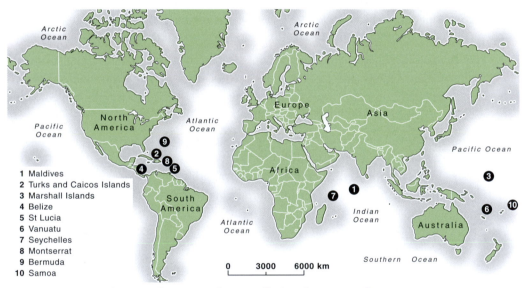

**Figure 6.3** The top 10 jurisdictions used by Australian companies for tax evasion
(Source: Data – Zirnsac 2013)

1 Maldives
2 Turks and Caicos Islands
3 Marshall Islands
4 Belize
5 St Lucia
6 Vanuatu
7 Seychelles
8 Montserrat
9 Bermuda
10 Samoa

**money laundering** – the process of concealing the origin, ownership or destination of illegally or dishonestly claimed money by hiding it within legitimate economic activities.

# Money laundering

When the transfer of funds are as a result of those funds being generated from illegal activity this is money laundering. **Money laundering** is therefore the process of concealing the origin, ownership or destination of illegally or dishonestly claimed money by hiding it within legitimate economic activities (Transparency International 2009a). A large money-laundering ring was discovered in Spain in 2005, when the 'White Whale' operation was concluded after 48 arrests of Spanish and foreign nationals was made (McIntyre 2005). The international network were accused of laundering €250 million through Costa del Sol real estate investments, having received the money through illegal activities such as blackmail, tax evasion, international arms trading and prostitution rings (Transparency International 2009a).

Money laundering (© shutterstock.com/iodrakon)

## Ethics in the media: Money laundering

An alleged US$6 billion money-laundering scheme, the biggest in history, was uncovered at Liberty Reserve, an online currency and payment processing firm. Dubbed 'Paypal for criminals', Liberty Reserve laundered illegal money including card fraud ('Liberty sell' 2013).

For additional discussion on tax evasion, transfer pricing and money laundering in the international context, see Chapter 9.

## Investment scams

**Investment scams** are also sometimes called **Ponzi schemes**, named after Charles Ponzi (1882–1949), an Italian immigrant to the US, who famously defrauded numerous investors. The scheme essentially rewards early investors by returns of funds from latter investors.

**investment scams** (also known as **Ponzi schemes**) – rewards early investors by returns of funds from later investors.

# Ethics in the media: Investment scams

Members of a Baptist church near Atlanta welcomed Ephren Taylor as a Chief Executive of a publically traded, socially conscious, company. He was, however, a fraud, and investors did not receive the 20% guaranteed returns, as they were fleeced by the 'black Bernie Madoff Ponzi scheme' ('Fleecing the flock' 2012).

Facilitated by the internet, the size and speed with which financial transactions are made today have helped spur a proliferation of investment scams, making would-be investors easy prey for such financial predators (Marquet 2011). The amounts involved in investment scams can be sizable with allegedly US$7.2 billion lost from investors in 113 countries in relation to the collapse and conviction in 2012 of the businesses of Allen Stanford. In August 2011, a South Korean pastor was indicted for misappropriating $2.4 billion Korean dollars (US$2.3 million) and in Britain, Kevin Foster's KF Concept, targeted more than 8000 individuals in South Wales ('A rise and fall' 2012). In 2013, the FBI was probing more than 1000 cases of investment scams, more than double the number outstanding in 2008. But the award for the largest investment scam to date goes to Bernie Madoff, whose victims lost an aggregate of US$20 billion. In a five-year period, 2600 Australians have been robbed of $113 million through investment scams (Oakes 2012). Table 6.3 gives more examples of recent, large-scale investment scam cases.

Charles Ponzi, after whom the term 'Ponzi schemes' is named (Source: Marquet 2011)

# Ethics on reflection: Ponzi scheme

For an interesting insight into the mind of the architect of the world's largest investment scam, read the plea allocution for Bernie Madoff (see US Department of Justice 2009, <www.justice.gov/usao/nys/madoff/madoffhearing031209.pdf>).

**Table 6.3** The largest investment scam cases

| No. | Principal | Vehicle | Perpetrator size ($ million) | Type of fraudulent investment | Year |
|-----|-----------|---------|------------------------------|-------------------------------|------|
| 1 | Bernard L Madoff | Madoff Investment Sec. | $20 000 Hedge fund | Securities trading | 2008 |
| 2 | R Allen Stanford | Stanford International | $7 200 Certificates of deposit | Certificates of deposit | 2009 |
| 3 | Thomas J Petters | Petters Group WW | $3 650 | Consumer electronics | 2008 |
| 4 | Paul Greenwood | Westridge Capital | $1 300 | Securities investments | 2009 |
| 5 | Joel Steinger | Mutual Benefits Corp. | $1 250 | Viatical and life settlements | 2009 |
| 6 | Scott Rothstein | Rothstein Rosenfeldt Adler | $1 200 | Lawsuit settlements | 2009 |
| 7 | Nevin K Shapiro | Capitol Investments | $8 80 | 'Grocery diversion' | 2010 |
| 8 | Marc S Dreier | Dreier LP | $3 80 | Promissory notes | 2008 |
| 9 | Nicholas Cosmo | Agape World | $3 70 | Commercial bridge loans | 2008 |
| 10 | Arthur G Nadel | Scoop Management | $3 60 hedge fund | Money management | 2009 |

(Source: Marquet 2011)

# Ethical investment

The **Socially Responsible Investing (SRI)** movement (also called **ethical investment**) has been growing worldwide. In the US, nearly 10% of assets are under management in SRI arrangements, equating to roughly US$2.3 trillion in both public and private markets (Social Investment Forum Foundation 2010). This growth was prompted by The United Nations Principles of Responsible Investment, which originated in 2007 and now have more than 1000 signatories and $32 trillion of funds under management, including Colonial First State and AMP. In Australia, Perpetual Ethical Fund was indicated as one of the best performing ethical funds, with a return of almost 40% during 2012 (Collett 2013).

Most SRI avoids key industries such as tobacco, gambling, alcohol and weapons, investing instead in organisations that have demonstrated significant efforts in environmental and social impact (O'Donohoe, Leijonhufvud & Saltuk 2010).

**socially responsible investing (SRI)** (also known as **ethical investment**) – avoids investment in key industries such as tobacco, gambling, alcohol and weapons, promoting investing in organisations that have demonstrated significant efforts in environmental and social impact.

# Ethics in practice: Socially responsible investing

Your elderly grandmother has an existing share portfolio of approximately AU$3 million. The share portfolio has been acquired without her intervention, through a brokerage service that her late husband commissioned. Your grandmother is now reflecting on the company shares within the portfolio, and is concerned that it does not reflect appropriate ethical investments. Provide some advice in the form of a personal email to your grandmother, in which you outline responses to the questions shown here.

**Questions:**
1. What is meant by ethical investments?
2. What would constitute unethical investments in your view?
3. What approaches you would advise her to take in order to re-cast her portfolio?

# Ethics in practice: Ethical investment

Interview a friend or family member who is over 45 years of age about what their values are that would guide their investments. Are there any companies or industries that they would, or would not, invest in? Explore their rationale, and without disclosing their identity, write this up in a paragraph. Repeat the exercise for three other individuals, and this time ensure they are of different ages and gender.

# Conclusion

Accounting, by its very nature, is quite malleable. So many investors have been ruined as a result of company failures and other business concerns that questions must be asked about moral values in this area – as practised not only by accountants in large accounting firms, but also by managers and other professionals (Ketz 2006). Examples of unethical financial institutions, such as Lehman Brothers and Goldman Sachs, show the devastating effect of cumulative unethical behaviour not only on the company and its investors but also on the market. In addition to the obvious losses, trust has been eroded.

As we have pointed out, ethical issues in accounting and finance are not just the domain of accountants, although it is important to recognise the considerable amount of effort that the professional accounting associations make to raise ethical awareness within their profession and to help their members with the ethical dilemmas they face; for example, should one be loyal to professional ethics or the company with whom one is employed? In Australia, professional bodies such as the Institute of Chartered Accountants in Australia, CPA Australia and the Institute of Public Accountants, through the Accounting Professional and Ethical Standards Board, require professional accountants to comply with certain fundamental principles: integrity; objectivity and independence; professional competence and due care (particularly in relation to diligence; timeliness; compliance; performance; technical and professional standards; confidentiality and professional behaviour (New Zealand Institute of Chartered Accountants 2013). In this chapter, we have offered a broader discipline-based perspective, in which ethical principles such as ensuring objectivity and impartiality, independence and autonomy, maintaining confidentiality and fiduciary duty, apply equally to professional and non-professional accounting practitioners.

Misrepresentation and inaccurate reporting, particularly inappropriate recognition of revenue and misstatement of earnings and hiding losses, are the more common unethical activities and given the extent of the deception potentially the most problematic to the business and investing community.

Fraud is the act of intentionally deceiving someone in order to gain an unfair or illegal advantage, which may be financial, political or otherwise. Countries consider such offences to be criminal or a violation of the civil law (Transparency International 2009a). Fraud also tends to flourish in organisational cultures where transparency is poor; and fraudulent activity in an organisation frequently highlights internal inadequacies in relation to inadequate control processes, systems and inadequate supervision while electronic transactions have provided new and plentiful challenges for fraud. PricewaterhouseCoopers (2012) have indicated an increase in economic crime in Australia, with 40% of responses reporting at least one instance of economic crime, compared with 34% globally, and 31% in the Asia–Pacific region.

One also cannot help but notice the regularity with which cases of insider trading are mentioned in the media, as well as more subtle forms of conflict of interest and tax avoidance by both organisations and individuals. With governments anxious to shore up their deficits, and tax authorities willingly assisting with finding funds for the back budget gaps, companies involved in tax evasion are now significantly under scrutiny (Wilkins & Butler 2013). Curiously, many of the companies that actively engage in tax avoidance are also likely to assert their credentials as responsible corporate citizens. For example, Starbucks, with their commitment to using fair trade coffee, have been contrasted with their ethically questionable arrangements to minimise their corporate tax liabilities ('A little integrity please' 2013).

Investment scams, or Ponzi schemes as they are more commonly known, capture many people's attention, chiefly because of the sheer audacity involved in milking large sums of money from many individuals, who are willing to part with their money because of the lure of a high return. These investors appear to be indifferent to the axiom 'if it's too good to be true, it probably isn't'.

Finally, we have briefly looked at SRI, or ethical investment, which is becoming increasingly popular as individuals and organisations are stipulating the criteria for investment. Guided by their conscience, a desire to minimise harm and to improve wellbeing, ethical investors avoid investment in specific sectors and endeavour to invest in industries that are demonstrating social and environmental mandates.

## Ethics on video

**Investment scams** – *What makes unethical behaviour contagious?* 2009, YouTube, FuquaSchOfBusiness, 29 September <https://www.youtube.com/watch?v=T4sylxCx3MA>.

**Misrepresentation and inaccurate financial reporting** – *WorldCom – what went wrong* 2008, video, Devon Hennig, 28 November, <https://www.youtube.com/watch?v=7g_d-phoUrU>.

See web material for more videos.

## Ethics at the movies

Here are a few movie suggestions that have ethical content related to accounting and finance:

\***Enron**: **The Smartest Guys in the Room** – a documentary based on the book outlining the largest business scandal in American history. *Enron – the smartest guys in the room* 2005, documentary, Gibney, A, Cuban, M, Elwood, A, Motamed, S & Kliot, J.

**The Untouchables** – Looks at tax evasion methods of Al Capone during the Prohibition. *The Untouchables* 1987, motion picture, Linson, A & Hartwick, R.

\***Author's pick**

See web material for more movies.

# Ethics on the web

**International Federation of Accountants (IFAC)**, developing all sectors of the accounting profession to protect the public interest, <www.ifac.org>.

**The International Money Laundering Information Network**, an internet-based organisation working against money laundering and terrorism financing, <www.imolin.org>.

See web material for more web references.

# Student exercises

See web material for answers to student short answer questions.

## Short answer questions

1. What behaviours would you see exhibited if one was adhering to the ethical principles of competence, confidentiality, integrity and objectivity?
2. Andrew Fastow, the former CFO of Enron, famously stated: 'Mark-to-market accounting is like crack. Don't do it.' What is mark-to-market accounting?
3. What is a contingent fee arrangement, and give an example of a contingent fee.
4. What are the key elements of a Ponzi scheme?
5. Why is insider trading unfair?
6. What role should confidentiality play for accountants as their profession has obligations to multiple stakeholders? (Cottell & Perlin 1990).
7. What does the principle of independence require of a practising accountant?
8. What is ethical investment?

## Experiential exercises

1. Select a high-profile company that has been involved in an ethical violation in accounting and finance, and provide a brief summary of the circumstances.
2. Research current ethical investment funds and identify the investment criteria, for example, companies such as Abi Life, Amit Fund, Sovereign Ethical Fund and Fellowship Trust.
3. To view an excellent, plain words short video on SRI, see <www.youtube.com/watch?v=7wrWwefzZkA>.
4. Undertake research to identify a recent example of investment fraud.

# Small case

## Case: Accounting ethics

In 2008, Olympus bought three profitless companies for the princely sum of US$800 million, and paid US$700 million in advisory fees, with payments being made to the Cayman Islands. By the end of the financial year, three-quarters of the value of these companies was written down, and the ownership and legal standing of the companies remained unclear. This accounting fraud came to light through the actions of a top executive at Olympus, who refused to be detracted from uncovering the truth, and who blew the whistle on the cover up of the investment losses that occurred in the company during the 1990s ('Paying a price for doing what's right' 2012).

**Question:**

**1.** Why is this fraud?

# Large case

## Case: Misappropriation of funds

Phosphagenics is a Melbourne-based, publicly listed company developing topically delivered pain relief medications (Urban & Boreham 2013). On 1 July 2013, Phosphagenics stood down their chief executive, Dr Esra Ogru, after their new chief financial officer (CFO), Anna Legg, noticed accounting irregularities. The outgoing CFO had left the company in January that year, having worked only one day per week (D'Angelo 2013). Phosphagenics gave Deloitte Forensic the task of undertaking an investigation of the invoicing and accounting irregularities. On 18 July 2013, Dr Ogru resigned as director of Phosphagenics (Life Scientist Staff 2013a).

The Deloitte findings, released on 24 July (Phosphagenics 2013), show irregularities dating between 2005 and 2013, with AU$5.7 million misappropriated. Indications are that the ex-CEO, Dr Ogru, and five other employees (excluding the CFO who preceded Anna Legg) were implicated. Phosphagenics states they have taken measures to recoup a significant portion of the misappropriated funds from the accused employees and will seek compensation for costs associated with the fraudulent activity (Life Scientist Staff 2013b). They have also instigated a full review of internal procedures to ensure such irregularities are not able to be replicated (Phosphagenics 2013). It was reported on 5 August that Dr Ogru sold Phosphagenics shares to the value of AU$570 000 to provide partial restitution of the misappropriated funds (*Australian Financial Review* 2013).

### Timeline

| | |
|---|---|
| 1 July 2013 | Phosphagenics stands down CEO Dr Esra Ogru; Deloitte Forensic begins investigation into irregularities. |
| 18 July 2013 | Dr Ogru resigns as a director of Phosphagenics. |

| | |
|---|---|
| 24 July | 2013 Deloitte Forensic report shows AU$5.7 million misappropriated; Dr Ogru and five other employees are implicated. |
| 5 August 2013 | Dr Ogru sells her 5.7 million shares in Phosphagenics as partial restitution of misappropriated funds. |

**Questions:**

1. Refer to the Ethics Unwrapped website <http://ethicsunwrapped.utexas.edu/video-category/concepts-unwrapped> and ascertain which concepts may have been driving the employees to misappropriate funds.

2. What were the implications for the company of the former CFO being at work only one day per week?

3. What measures would you take, as the incoming CFO and CEO, to tighten company governance and oversight at Phosphagenics?

See web material for:
- answers to short answer questions
- additional student cases
- tutor resources (tutor password required)
- additional material including Ethics at the movies, Ethics in print, Ethics on video and Ethics on the web.

# Chapter 7

## Ethical issues in financial entities

'Although gold dust is precious, when it gets in your eyes it obstructs your vision.'

Hsi-Tang Chih Tsang, 735–814,

renowned Zen master

## Chapter aim

To identify current ethical issues in financial entities.

## Chapter objectives

1.  Discuss why a large set of financial entities needs to be considered when reflecting on ethical issues in accounting and finance.
2.  Determine what some of the critical ethical concerns are in the banking sector.
3.  Identify ethical issues relevant to stockbrokers and traders.
4.  Describe the ethical issues of private equity firms and hedge funds.
5.  Express what the potential ethical pitfalls are for auditing and consulting firms.
6.  Provide examples of professional bodies and government entities that provide ethical oversight in the financial sector.

# Ethics in the media: Ethics in banking

The Hong Kong and Shanghai Banking Corporation (HSBC) were accused of ignoring state law designed to initiate talks between home owners and banks to resolve foreclosure cases by failing to file paperwork to initiate settlement talks. This comes on the back of $1.3 billion and $665 million fines in settlement of money laundering and sanction breaches (Saigol & Scannell 2013).

# Introduction

It is ironic that in 1999, in the introduction of a CD Rom on ethical practice circulated to all employees of Arthur Andersen, the international consulting and auditing firm, the managing partner noted that, 'the day we lose the public trust is the day we go out of business'. In 2002, with 85 000 employees worldwide, Arthur Andersen, one of the leading accounting firms of the times went out of business for just that; losing the trust of their customers and key stakeholders (Cooper 2013).

Accounting and finance does not operate in a vacuum and many other organisations frame the context in which accounting and finance ethical abuses occur. As a consequence, it has been recognised that rather than just looking at accountants, we ought to be investigating the practices of other relevant actors (for example, auditors, bankers and regulators) who are also on the same stage and participating in the play (Ketz 2006). Having looked at unethical practices in accounting and finance, it is now appropriate to turn to specific key financial entities.

The implication of a wider group of financial entities in unethical practices in accounting and finance has been exacerbated by the recent global financial crisis. There has been finger-pointing at a number of financial institutions in an effort to lay blame, and in a number of circumstances significant weaknesses, aggregated by a flagrant dismissal of risk and greed, have been identified as issues that need to be addressed.

According to Joseph Stiglitz (2009), author of the journal article 'The anatomy of a murder: who killed America's economy?', the main cause of the GFC was the behaviour of the banks, largely as a result of not managing risk; adopting incentive structures that induced short-term thinking; excessive remuneration for senior executives, which provided incentives for 'bad accounting', particularly extensive off balance sheet accounting.

But it is not just the banks; regulators have also been implicated. A judge allowed the Justice Department to bring a US$5 billion lawsuit against Standard and Poor's (S&P) – the worldwide rating agency – which had allegedly produced inflated ratings between 2004 and

2007 in order to please their clients and the financial industry, however, this resulted in investors being misled and proceeding with unwise investments ('Business' 2013c).

Part of the blame for the financial crisis has also been traced to poor legislation. In the US, for example, the Glass-Stegall Act was repealed in 1999 after banks argued they could not compete with securities firms and would invest in low-risk, diversified securities which would safeguard their customers (Lewis 2010). Clearly these mandates were not followed, resulting in the securitised mortgage crash in 2008, with many millions of dollars lost by investors and taxpayers, and the banks' 'too big to fail' mentality incentivising excessive risk taking (Stiglitz 2009).

In addition to a raft of ethical issues, the issue of fairness in financial institutions has been raised in recent years, and questions of whether the financial systems benefit the institutions more than the consumers they serve (Loch et al. 2012). Given the importance of the financial sector to the effective functioning of business and, more importantly in relation to the global economy as well as the myriad of players coalescing in this sector, it is appropriate to look at ethical issues related to financial entities. We also note that ethical awareness becomes even more important in an environment which is highly deregulated, as has been witnessed in recent years, particularly in the finance and banking sector.

## Banks

In their book, *The banker's new clothes: What's wrong with banking and what to do about it*, Admati and Hellwig (2013) have stated that today's banking system is dangerous and fragile. The unregulated environment in which banks have been operating has, it appears, created the opportunity for unethical actions to be easily ignored. To highlight this, embarrassing tape recordings emerged of conversations in 2008 between senior executives at the now defunct Anglo Irish Bank, which suggested that they had misled regulators about the extent of the trouble that the bank was actually in at the time it was bailed out ('No laughing matter' 2013). One of the reasons that banks are vulnerable to unethical activities is because the stakes are incredibly high with significant opportunity for personal gain. For example, Bernie Ecclestone, Chief Executive of the Formula One Group, was charged in Germany over allegedly offering a $44 million bribe to a banker in 2005. The banker was involved in the sale of the car racing championship to CVC Capital ('Business' 2013c).

**liquidity rules** – legal requirements particularly for foreign banks relating to the amount of liquid assets, essentially cash that they need to have and to be separately capitalised.

In an effort to keep banking systems safe, there is a global move occurring to apply stricter **liquidity rules** (essentially cash on hand) to foreign banks. Previously, subsidiaries of well-capitalised foreign banks were able to operate offshore without having to meet minimum capital requirements, however they are now required to ring-fence their foreign operations, and be separately capitalised. These actions have been prompted by concerns about the ability to get access to capital held abroad in the event that a subsidiary of a foreign bank fails ('The great unravelling' 2013).

Banks (© shutterstock.com/Daniilantiq)

Banks have been implicated in a number of unethical activities:

- **Improper procedures** – in January 2013, Bank of America, Citigroup, JPMorgan, JPMorgan Chase and seven other banks, agreed to an $8.5 billion settlement with regulators over improper home foreclosure procedures. Bank of America paid $11.6 billion to Fannie Mae, a government-backed mortgage company, for liabilities on toxic loans ('Business' 2013a).

- **Excessive executive compensation** – there has been much consternation about the compensation packages of bankers and whether these are equitable and truly deserved. There is an app available that enables investment bankers to compare their bonuses in New York and London, where it is common for them to earn their salary, or more, in a yearly bonus payment ('Banker app puts the onus on bonus' 2013). Compensations also take the form of exploiting loopholes in disclosure laws, with some of Australia's companies spending $1.5 billion buying shares for executives in 2012, thereby overstating operating cash flows (West 2013). Further highlighting extremely weak disclosure, 22 of the top 100 firms that bought shares for their executive incentive compensation schemes did not disclose how many shares they bought (West 2013).

- **Collusion** – more than a dozen investigations into banks were initiated, that allegedly colluded to set the LIBOR (London Inter-Bank Offered Rate) (a benchmark interest rate) in their favour. The LIBOR determines rates in $300 trillion worth of derivative contracts and other financial products. Barclays was fined in June 2012 and the Chief Executive resigned when it became clear that the bank had been involved in the manipulation ('Business this week' 2012b).

- **Money laundering** – HSBC paid penalties of US$1.9 billion, after admitting to money laundering transactions which occurred in their Mexican division ('The world this week' 2012).

- **Price manipulation** – In the US, they Federal Energy Regulatory Commission (FERC) fined Barclays Bank $453 million for manipulating electrical prices to benefit bank derivative positions in four Midwest American states, however Barclays is fighting the claim and has taken the matter to court. In a similar case, JPMorgan Chase is said to be in talks with the FERC ('Business' 2013c).

- **Violation of sanctions** – Standard Charter paid US$327 million for not taking heed of American sanctions policy effective between 2001 to 2007 in relation to Iran ('The world this week' 2012).
- **Usurious practices** – although banking institutions need to maximise shareholder returns, this should be accomplished within fair and just parameters without taking undue advantage of customers in terms of encouraging excessive debt or overly burdensome credit charges (Serrano 2010), as was the case with the US subprime mortgage crisis which began in 2008.

## Ethics in the media: Cheating

'Dude. I owe you big time. Come around after work and I'm opening a bottle of Bollinger'. This was the email a Barclays trader sent to thank his colleagues for underreporting the bank's borrowing rate. Barclays was fined US$543 million for these instances of cheating which occurred between 2005 and 2009 ('They said it' 2013).

## Ethics in practice: LIBOR scandal

The LIBOR scandal hit the banking sector in mid-2012. The LIBOR is the number that traders fix which determines the prices that people pay for loans or receive for their savings internationally, both private and commercial. The LIBOR fixes repayments of about $800 trillion of financial instruments; from home loans to complex, interest rate derivatives ('The LIBOR scandal: The rotten heart of finance' 2012). The attempts to rig LIBOR by benchmarking the interest rate not only indicated a culture of casual dishonesty but it also set the stage for lawsuits and more regulation around the globe ('The LIBOR affair: Banksters' 2012). Somewhat burnt from

its involvement with the LIBOR rate rigging scandal, Barclays' new Chief Executive issued a press release on 12 February 2013, which indicated that Barclays were going to review their operations; including improving disclosure and transparency around financial performance; embed purpose and values across Barclays; and publish an annual scorecard assessing performance (Barclays 2013).

**Question:**

1. Undertake additional research and articulate what ethical issues are involved in the LIBOR scandal.

# Stockbrokers or traders

In addition to insider trading, the press frequently presents high-profile cases of enormous losses incurred by traders involved with speculative trading with someone else's money which has resulted in severely weakened, or in some cases even prompted the demise of, the organisations they were working for. In an analysis of the Bering Bank disaster, it has been suggested that the rogue trader, Nick Leeson, was operating in a bubble in which he did not come face-to-face with the victims of his actions, allowing him to disconnect from the impending disaster as his deals involved abstract numbers and movements on the screen, making it possible for him to overlook the faces and names of the victims who suffered financial losses. They were not real people but rather just numbers on a screen (Introna 2002).

The press usually refers to these as **rogue traders**; they are traders in the stock market who operate outside of normal risk parameters, executing risky trades with the potential for heavy losses. These traders usually operate in isolation, however more recently it has been suggested that organisational pressure may tacitly endorse their risky behaviour. The USB management allegedly encouraged their traders to bring in higher profits and the Chief Executive, Oswald Grubl, who later resigned as a result of the scandal, encouraged the traders to elevate their risk levels. It also appears that a mechanism for verifying trades was mysteriously switched off until the activities of the rogue trader were exposed. It has been observed that taking smart, ambitious people and encouraging them to make as much money as possible by 'playing' with billions of dollars without sufficient oversight is a recipe for disaster ('The education of Kwekuadoboli' 2012). For an eerily similar Hollywood depiction of the USB situation, watch the film *Margin Call*.

> **rogue traders** – traders in the stock market who operate in isolation, outside of normal risk parameters with potentially heavy losses.

A stockbroker or trader (© shutterstock.com/Cartoonresource)

In addition to the usual ethical concerns of insider trading, there are concerns surrounding **churning**, the encouragement of investors to make numerous and frequent trades for the sole purpose of generating additional income for a broker. There are also circumstances of **manipulative trading** where the trader, or their organisation, deliberately manipulates the market for financial gain and exhibits predatory behaviours. These behaviours have been labelled:

> **churning** – making numerous and frequent trades for the sole purpose of generating additional income for a broker.

> **manipulative trading** – where the trader, deliberately manipulates the market for financial gain and exhibits predatory behaviours.

- **Stuffers** – overwhelm exchanges of data to slow down competitors.
- **Danglers** – sending out data that can force a squeezed trader to chase a price against their interests. Liquidity squeezers trade in ways designed to drain liquidity from distressed companies.
- **Pack hunters** – groups of traders who become aware of each other's presence, even though they do not know one another. They work in tandem to maximise the chance of triggering a cascading effect ('A close look at high frequency trading' 2012).

Deceptive reporting in the stockbroking world is not uncommon. Kwekuadoboli, the 38-year-old UBS trader who lost $2.3 billion, admitted in court proceedings that he used an account, titled 'Umbrella', to hide losses. His colleague also accessed the 'Umbrella' account, indicating this practice was commonplace ('The education of Kwekuadoboli' 2012).

In October 1987, Wall Street suffered Black Monday, when the DOW Jones industrial average fell 23% in a day. An early form of program trading called Portfolio Insurance was to blame. On 1 August 2012, Knight Capital started to use a new software program to execute their trades. Within an hour the program had caused turmoil in the market, sending errant buy and sell orders that cost Knight Capital US$440 million and also showcased their failed duty of care ('High frequency trading wait a second' 2012). The potential for conflict of interest is ever-present, and an example of conflict of interest occurred when corporate research analysts issued recommendations to buy stock in weak technology companies in an effort to gain investment banking deals for their employers. This contributed to an artificial rise, and subsequent burst, of the stock market bubble, ultimately resulting in the loss of significant money by investors (Visser et al. 2008).

## Ethics in the media: Ethics in banking

Citigroup paid a US$2 million fine following the disclosure of an analyst to a journalist, leaking details of the impending Facebook float to a blogger ('$2M' 2012).

## Investment advisers and financial planners

Consumer advocacy groups have cautioned that the financial planning industry is 'structurally corrupt' and that the financial advisory industry is driven by a conflict of interest which sees financial products promoted based on commissions, rather than on the specific benefit to the client (Chaplin 2012). But as some argue, the provision of any financial services product is better than not providing financial services ('Margin calls' 2013).

## Ethics on reflection: Conflict of interest

When you sit down with a financial planner, how do you know that the information you have been provided is accurate? For example, when the financial planner presents you with three investment options and recommends one, how do you know that that one recommendation is not entirely motivated by the fact that the commission on that recommendation is higher than the others?

In addition to honesty of information, transparency and duty of care, the primary ethical issues for financial planners are avoiding self-interest and conflicts of interest as they could steer you towards investments that benefit him or her most, rather than what is best for you.

Following a field study commissioned by the Australian Securities and Investment Commission (ASIC), the specific ethical issues identified in the Australian market in relation to investment advisers/financial planners were: an emphasis on product selling rather than tailored advice; recommendations to switch to a super fund provider paying the adviser a high commission with no obvious benefit to the client; and encouraging to borrow in order to invest mainly for the benefit of an adviser who is paid on the percentage of assets invested.

In Australia the Future of Financial Advice (FoFA) legislation, initiated in 2012, bans a number of practices, including **volume bonuses** (paid by product providers to financial adviser businesses predicated on selling a certain amount of the product in question) and **soft dollar benefits** (activities such as funding trips to overseas conferences based on sales volumes) (Chaplin 2012).

**volume bonuses** – financial bonuses paid by product providers to financial adviser businesses predicated on selling a certain amount of the product in question.

**soft dollar benefits** – activities such as funding trips to overseas conferences based on sales volumes.

## Ethics in practice: Compliance deficiencies

In January 2013, the Australian regulator, ASIC, announced that Macquarie Equities had undertaken a review of their Macquarie Private Wealth Business following a significant number of their advisers demonstrating compliance deficiencies which centred on the quality of advice and documentation for clients (Kavanagh 2013).

**Question:**

**1.** What ethical principle has been violated here?

The ASIC files provide some interesting cases in relation to investment advisers:

- Harold Moses resigned as an AMP agent in 1994 but continued to receive compulsory employment superannuation contributions from his clients until 1998. ASIC alleges that he failed to pass the contributions on to the super fund and pocketed $340 000 (ASIC 2003a).
- In 2003, a South Australian adviser, Colin Turner, was banned for promoting an unregistered investment scheme. Turner was Director of the scheme and knowingly misled investors (ASIC 2003b).
- In 2012 ASIC obtained a court order against two Queensland self-managed superannuation fund advice companies, Royale Capital and Active Super, amid concerns the companies between them had raised AU$4.75 million and had misled investors about their investments (ASIC 2012a), with the money going into shares and companies in offshore tax havens to buy distressed property in the US, but with no documents relating to these investments being lodged (ASIC 2012b).

**conflicted remuneration** – financial incentives which could influence the choice of financial product they recommend to clients.

In July 2013, new rules called the FoFA reforms, came into force for those providing financial advice in Australia. The aim of FoFA is to encourage not only more accessibility to financial advice, but also provide statutory obligation from the adviser to act in the best interest of the client. As a minimum best practice, financial advisers are banned from receiving **conflicted remuneration**, which are financial incentives which could influence the choice of financial product they recommend to clients; and there are also more stringent rules about the charging of ongoing fees and a requirement for clients to opt in every two years (Wood 2013).

# Private equity firms

A private equity firm's main role is to make money by taking over poorly managed companies, improving their performance and then selling them. Private equity firms usually charge a 2% annual fee to manage investor's capital and take 20% of the profits with private equity firms now getting approximately two-thirds of their revenue from fixed fees, regardless of performance (Metrick & Yasuda 2011). This exploitative role, while profitable, has ethical questions attached to it, yet some feel that private equity firms are unnecessarily demonised as 'vulture' capitalists who are worse than Wall Street due to plundering companies, slashing jobs, minimising taxation commitments and overcompensating executives ('Private equity' 2012).

**carried interest** – profits from tax deduction generated on interest payments of debt.

One notable ethical grey area is that equity firms can burden a company with debt and then take cash out as dividends, thus weakening the organisation with the likely outcome of bankruptcy. In addition, tax deductions can be generated on interest payments of debt, as well as taken out as cash. The profits generated from these transactions are called **carried interest** and are commonly taxed as capital gains and a lower rate than income ('Private equity' 2012).

It has been found that two years after a buy-out, employment commonly declines by 3% on average, and wages stagnate due to cost control. Although it should be recognised that it is not the mission of buyer firms to create jobs, but to produce higher risk adjusted returns ('Bain or blessing' 2012); subsequent shifts in employment may be part of a creative destruction that invigorates the economy, in which case private equity is merely facilitating this process.

"You built this with our venture capital. Now we would like our 60%."

Private equity firms (© shutterstock.com/Cartoonresource)

# Ethics in the media: Poor governance

Calpers, the largest public pension scheme in the US, had their governance questions when a third-party report found that the CEO had pressured investment staff to recommend commitments to a placement agent intermediary, who represented private equity investment opportunities, after the CEO and placement agent colluded to forge disclosure documents (Primack 2013).

# Hedge funds

What exactly is a **hedge fund**? Definitions vary depending on the jurisdiction (ASIC 2012c), but broadly, they are investment funds utilising sophisticated and risky investment techniques, which are available to institutions and individuals of meaningful wealth (BarclayHedge 2013). ASIC (2012c, p.4) notes that 'there are some characteristics that distinguish hedge funds from other managed investment schemes, such as the use of leverage, derivatives and short selling to seek returns with low correlations to equity and bond markets'. In the US, hedge funds are currently unregulated by the Securities and Exchange Commission (SEC) (BarclayHedge 2013). In Australia hedge funds are regulated by ASIC under the *Corporations Act 2001*, with regulations currently being further tightened to ensure investors are aware

**hedge funds** – investment funds utilising sophisticated and risky investment techniques, which are available to institutions and individuals of meaningful wealth.

of the risk involved in hedge fund investments, through the use of product risk disclosures statements (ASIC 2013).

An examination of hedge fund data from 2000–2010 indicated a practice called **portfolio pumping**. This is where hedge fund managers manipulate the prices of stocks they hold in order to have better returns to report to investors. How this actually occurs is that there is an increase in trading activity among some hedge funds on the last day of the month and quarter, which artificially inflates returns with as little as US$500 000 in trades. Specifically, stocks most often held by hedge funds see an average abnormal return of 0.30% on the last day of trading, with most of the increase coming in the last 20 minutes of trading. Those returns disappear just after trading opens the next day, but only after the hedge fund has reported the increase to its investors ('Some hedge funds fudge the numbers' 2013).

Conflict of interest is also a common concern. For example, it was alleged that Goldman Sachs had misled Abacus investors by failing to disclose that a hedge fund, Paulson and Company, had assisted with selecting the securities involved, which they had then bet against ('Abacussed' 2011).

In 2009, ASIC began investigating Trio Capital, a hedge fund that had deceived the trustees and investors by using a highly complex investment structure that misconstrued underlying assets and investment rates of return. This investment scheme was largely supported by self-managed superannuation funds, where investors were not necessarily well informed about the level of risk involved in the hedge fund due to low product risk disclosures, and as 'Mom and Pop' investors had unrealistic public perceptions about ASIC's ability to regulate and safeguard investments. Trio Capital freely took advantage of the inaccurate perception (Department of Treasury 2013). The relationship between the hedge funds and financial planners certainly pose a conflict of interest as there seems to be a correlation between high commissions and the recommendation of Trio Capital products. Finally, due to the Australian regulatory bodies being more stringent than some other countries (such as the US), the Trio Capital hedge fund was located overseas to overcome this limitation (Department of Treasury 2013), which resulted in diminished rules around diversification and transparency into operational workings, compared to other financial investment schemes in Australia.

**portfolio pumping** – where hedge fund managers manipulate the prices of stocks they hold in order to have better returns to report to investors.

"I'll show you my investment opportunity if you'll show me yours."

Hedge funds (© shutterstock.com/Cartoonresource)

Hedge funds prefer to operate on an opaque basis, in order to protect their intellectual property around their investment strategies (Wagner 2011), but such lack of transparency and light regulation are a recipe for 'cowboy' behaviour; ethical controls depend entirely on the nature of the hedge fund company's prevailing 'culture of compliance' (Turner 2013). Hedge fund fee structures are viewed as creating ethical problems because there is a 1.5% management fee, but also a 20% performance fee (Burgess 2013); however, when losses are experienced hedge fund managers cannot draw a performance fee. The temptation to close the non-performing fund, and start another is sometimes too great, which serves the hedge fund manager's purpose, but not the investors (Wagner 2011).

Hedge fund managers are generously compensated. Brian Hunter, a trader with the hedge fund Amaranth, who was hired in 2004, reportedly received a bonus of US$113 million. Ultimately, however, his excessive trading led to the downfall of the company in 2006.

# Ethics in the media: Securities fraud

In 2013, US Federal Prosecutors announced criminal charges against SAC Capital Advisers, a hedge fund company accused of insider trading and securities fraud (Strasburg & Rothfield 2013).

## Auditing and consulting firms

Auditors are primarily responsible for highlighting fraudulent financial reporting; that is, the intentional misrepresentation or omission of disclosures or dollar amounts with the objective to deceive financial statement readers (includes manipulation, falsification or alteration of accounting records, and misrepresentation). Auditors are also alert to misappropriation of assets – theft of company cash (embezzlement), inventory, or other assets causing distortions in the financials.

Auditors routinely assess factors that relate to the possibility of fraudulent financial reporting, misstatements and misappropriation of assets, and note the following red flag risk factors as being:

- management's compensation tied to performance
- management dominated by one individual
- disregard for regulatory authorities
- high turnover by top management
- disputes with the auditor
- large declines in customer demand
- possible bankruptcy

- lack of segregation of duties
- poor safety over cash and inventory (Calhoun, Olivero & Wolitzer 1999, p. 74).

"We've always needed an accounting magician."

Auditing and consulting firms (© shutterstock.com/Cartoonresource)

In contrast to a doctor or a lawyer, whose primary responsibility is to their patient or client, an auditor's responsibilities are wider than the client, including other stakeholders, such as investors, and society at large. However, particularly as a result of the GFC and numerous corporate collapses, attention has been directed at the quality of financial auditing reports. Critical of the accuracy of audit reports, it has been suggested that in some circumstances auditors and their auditing reports were treated like insurance, or, at its worst, PR statements in an effort to shore up confidence of analysts, bankers and investors.

The reality was that some financial accounts on which the auditor's reports were based contained errors about which the auditing firm may have been aware (although they may not have been, through deception of their clients). Litigation against auditors is fairly common, particularly in the US, where it has been found that auditors are most likely to be sued when the financial statement frauds are of a common variety, or when the frauds arise from fictitious transactions (Bonner, Palmorse & Young, 1998). It has also been found that auditors' ethical dilemmas are strongly influenced by penalties rather than affiliation sanctions, public censure or reputational damage (Ponemon & Gabhart 1990).

In June 2012, the International Auditing and Assurance Standards Board (IAASB) presented a proposal that requires auditors to include an audit general commentary to accompany audit reports. This proposal has been very contentious and the changes are unlikely to take effect until 2014–2015. The insinuation of these commentaries is that the auditor will be pushed to make comments regarding the company they are auditing over and above what the company itself was prepared to say. Auditors will essentially be in the role of shining a light on any reservations that they may have about company accounts and any shortfalls or unethical dealings that they feel may present a risk, thereby alerting potential stakeholders.

The requirement of greater scrutiny of auditing firms has come about through auditors' possible avoidance of their duty of care, and through accounting improprieties associated with collusive practices, erosion of independence and conflict of interest. Are auditors in fact able to provide an objective review of company financial statements, and to what extent can they provide accurate insights into the financial health of an organisation? In providing an opinion, an independent auditor is assuming a public duty, in a watchdog function, as they provide a supposedly unbiased opinion. For auditors, the pressures on independence come from a variety of sources (Cottell & Perlin 1990): the competition that exists among auditing firms; auditing firms where many people may work on a client; time pressures in fulfilling audit tasks; and the increasing role of management advisory services offered by auditing services. In this later circumstance, independence may be compromised when the organisation is highly dependent on the client firm for additional funds in relation to consultancy, or where the client is in its own right, extremely large, and the loss of the audit client would have an effect not only on the finances of the auditing firm, but also the career of the partner in charge.

In one year, Arthur Andersen received US$52 million from Enron; US$25 million in audit fees, and US$27 million from other services including tax and consultancy work. Andersen indicated, however, that their independence was not impaired, due to what are commonly called **double duty arrangements** (Duska & Duska 2003). See 'Ethics in practice' for more detail about Arthur Andersen.

**double duty arrangements** – the circumstance where auditing firms also provide consulting services to their clients and are thus conflicted.

# Ethics in practice: Auditing improprieties

In the 1990s, Arthur Andersen's client, Waste Management, were fraudulently reducing and depreciating charges and capitalisations that should have been expenses. Arthur Andersen raised these issues with Waste Management and decisions to amortise improper transactions were made. Later, Waste Management reneged on the deal, but Arthur

Andersen were already ethically compromised (Ketz 2006).

**Questions:**
1. Do you think this circumstance was handled well?
2. What are the pressures on Arthur Andersen?
3. How could this have been handled differently?

More recently, the accounting firm Deloitte, the auditor of the computer software firm, Autonomy, purchased by Hewlett-Packard, required a US$8.8 billion write-down because of accounting improprieties and misrepresentations. As well as auditing Autonomy, Deloitte also provided US$6.7 million in non-audited services over seven years, which included advising on executive pay ('Accountable' 2012). This raises questions regarding conflict of interest, where firms are receiving an income stream from organisations that they are auditing. One speculates that given the income generated from the client, they would be reluctant to be critical in their auditing practices. This conflict of interest could therefore undermine the integrity, objectivity and independence of the auditing process.

The close association between firm and client can also lead to insider trading. For example, in April 2003, KPMG dismissed a partner from their Los Angeles office as that office was responsible for passing sensitive corporate information about two companies to a third party for the purpose of share trading ('Business this week' 2013). Table 7.1 shows the possible ethical violations auditors may commit.

**Table 7.1**  Possible ethical violations for auditors

1. Professional fees obtained as contingent fees are where a fee is established for a service but is subject to an arrangement in which the fee will only be received if a specified finding or result is obtained, such as a successful audit.

2. When a client inappropriately influences audit judgements.

3. Prematurely signing off on audits, or signing off on audits that are knowingly inaccurate.

4. Having a direct financial interest in the audit client.

5. Violation of fiduciary responsibilities which may be related to the misappropriation of client funds and trust accounts.

6. Audit-related judgements were inappropriately influenced by the fact that relatives or independents are associated with the audit client.

7. Significant management advisory services provided to a client influence judgements due to the dependence on income from advisory services.

8. A spouse or dependent has a financial interest in the client.

9. Money has been lent to the audit client.

10. The auditor is a trustee or executor that is committed to acquiring assets or financial interests in the client.

11. The auditor has received an unsecured loan from a client.

(Adapted from: Engle & Sincich 1998)

# Ethics in the media: Duty of care

PricewaterhouseCoopers (PwC) have made a limited admission that they breached their duty of care in their auditing of Centro's multi-billion dollar debt misclassification. PwC have previously held firm against claims by shareholders that they misled or deceived investors with the Australian accounting blunder (Wood & Butler 2012).

An auditor's primary responsibility is to ferret out inaccuracies, irregularities, and potential fraud, and to report on this. To achieve this, it is imperative that an auditor remains independent of its client in order to provide an objective opinion. This independence, however, can be eroded. There are five types of threat to independence (International Federation of Accountants 2012), which apply to both professional auditors and accountants:

**Self-interest threats** – the threat that a financial or other interest will inappropriately influence professional judgement.

**Self-review threats** – the threat that a professional will not appropriately evaluate the results of a previous judgement made; usually a judgement performed by another individual within the professional's organisation.

**Advocacy threats** – the threat that a professional will promote a client's/employer's position to the point that objectivity is compromised.

**Familiarity threats** – the threat that due to a long or close relationship with a client or employer, a professional will be too sympathetic to their interest or too accepting of their work.

**Intimidation threats** – the threat that a professional will be deterred from acting objectively because of actual or perceived pressures including attempts to exercise undue influence.

# Ethics on reflection: Auditor independence

What are your thoughts on the compatibility of auditing independence and the provision of management services? Should an auditing firm be actively pursuing consulting services? How could these be properly managed so as not to erode an auditor's independence?

# Ethics in practice: Conflict of interest

Bill is currently a CPA and auditor-in-charge for a small auditing firm, which provide services to Do Good Construction Company. The Do Good CEO has asked Bill to assist with CFO recruitment. Bill would like to nominate himself for the role, as well as keep his auditor-in-charge role (Ponemon & Gabhart 1990).

**Question:**
1.  What is your advice to Bill?

**expectation gap** – the difference between what the public and other financial statement users perceive auditors' responsibilities to be and what auditors believe their responsibilities entail.

Auditors are a key part of the current corporate disclosure system with auditing firms entrusted to audit financial statements and present a true reflection of the state of the company; however, auditors may hide behind the shield of client confidentiality rather than uphold the principle of the public trust. McEnroe and Martens refer to the auditing **expectation gap**, which is the difference between public perceptions of auditors' responsibilities contrasted against what the auditor feels their responsibilities are (McEnroe & Martens 2001). If this gap widens, then the auditor's perceived role as a public watchdog is eroded. The question is, do the accounting and disclosure statements provide the transparency that is essential for the investing public?

The importance of auditor independence cannot be overstated. This requires not only objectivity of analysis and reporting, but also an assurance of financial independence from their auditing client in order that there is no element of their interaction which could impair their objectivity.

## Professional ethical oversight

The financial community, both accountants and those in financial entities, are very much responsible for the public perceptions regarding ethics in the sector. In an effort to shore up ethics in the financial sector there are numerous national and international accounting bodies (such as the International Federation of Accountants [IFAC]), which cumulatively support the operation of four independent standard setting boards; the IAASB, the International Accounting Education Standards Board (IAESB), the International Ethics Standards Board for Accountants (IESBA), and the International Public Sector Accounting Standards Board (IPSASB) (IFAC 2012).

In July 2009, the IFAC, which has oversight for the IESBA, released a revised code of ethics for professional accountants, effective from 1 January 2011. As a consequence, many national organisations were required to revise their code of ethics to ensure alignment; any organisation that failed to do so was in breach of the IFAC membership obligations (Murray & Fraser 2013).

## Ethics in practice: Professional entities

Using the country you live in as a guide, identify what the professional bodies and government entities are that provide ethical oversight in the financial sector.

To give an indication of ethical investigations and tribunal hearings, during the year ending 30 June 2012, the professional conduct team at the ICAA dealt with 297 formal complaints, or other issues, concerning the conduct of members. This was up from the previous two years, when 250 and 291 complaints were made, respectively. Of these investigations, 20 members were called to appear before the Professional Conduct Tribunal.

Such allegations usually centre on:

- failure to observe standard of professional care, skill and competency
- having committed a statutory offence
- bringing discredit on members, the institute or the profession
- adverse findings in relation to professional, or business conduct by a court, or statutory regulatory, or professional body
- breaching a charter, by laws or regulations, including ethical and professional standards
- failing to comply with direction by institute (including failure to respond to correspondence)
- member insolvency
- conduct bringing discredit on member institute or profession (Institute of Chartered Accountants Australia 2012).

Table 7.2 sets out the sanctions available for accounting bodies.

**Table 7.2**  Professional accounting body sanctions

| The common range of Professional Conduct Tribunal sanctions that can be imposed include: |
| --- |
| • membership exclusion (ultimate sanction) |
| • membership cancellation (up to five years) |
| • withdrawal of the members' right to engage in public practice |
| • fines of up to U\$100 000 can be imposed |
| • reprimands and severe reprimands (the most common sanction) |
| • imposition of remedial training or targeted quality review of the member. |

(Source: Institute of Chartered Accountants Australia 2012)

In addition to the accounting profession bodies that operate at both the national and international level, there are additional regulatory organisations and specific professional bodies. The most obvious regulators, for example, in the Australian framework are: the ASIC, which oversees auditors and liquidators, financial planners and company directors; the Tax Practitioners Board (TPB), which oversees tax practitioners; the Australian Prudential Regulation Authority (APRA), which oversees auditors and trustees of superannuation funds, directors and senior managers of insurance companies; and the Insolvency Trustee Service Australia (ITSA), which oversees trustees in bankruptcy (Institute of Chartered Accountants Australia 2012).

## Ethics in the media: Regulator reaction

The regulator, ASIC, has been criticised for taking around six months to act on information of serious misconduct inside the Commonwealth Bank's Financial Planning Unit (Wilkins 2013).

## Ethics in practice: Professional principles

Select a professional association in your country and review the principles contained in their professional code of conduct. For example, in Australia some associations are:

The Australian Financial Markets Association, <www.afma.com.au>.

Accounting Financial Planning Association, <www.fpa.asn.au>.

Financial Services Institute of Australia, <www.finsia.com>.

Accounting Professional Ethics Standards Board, <www.apesb.org.au>.

Institute of Actuaries Australia, <www.actuaries.asn.au>.

Institute of Internal Auditors, <www.theiia.org>.

# Conclusion

Clearly, ethics in accounting and finance is not just about accountants and individual mangers. It concerns a wider group of players, who are interacting in this space and who potentially collude to ensure beneficial outcomes for themselves and their organisations. Many of these actors have been complicit in the unethical operations of the business organisations that they served. For example, it was not just Enron employees who were engaged in unethical activities; their bankers were also found to have conspired with circumstances. It has been reported some banks did not record their transactions with Enron, and Citigroup, JP Morgan and Chase, engaged in sham prepaid transactions (Ketz 2006). You can see that it is therefore remiss of us to concentrate solely on the accounting profession when discussing ethical issues in relation to accounting and finance.

Given the role of banking institutions as key financiers of business operations in recent years, they have been heavily criticised for unethical behaviours that have largely arisen as a result of deregulation in the banking sector. The media provides detailed examples of questionable practices in relation to executive compensation, collusion and money laundering, to name but a few of the murky waters that some bankers have waded into.

Stockbrokers and traders have also not escaped criticism, and we have seen examples of the astonishing impact one rogue trader can have on the financial viability of a long-established bank. Investment advisers and financial planners have also not come out of recent reviews unscathed, with concern for self-interest in relation to commission-based fees being flagged as a contentious issue. Transparency appears to be an imperative in order to ensure that any inappropriate motivating factors are clearly identified, and the potential damage of self-interest is highlighted.

Private equity firms and hedge funds have the potential to engage in predatory behaviour, and the ever-present pressure to provide exemplary returns on investment can be a negative pressure for those in fund-management positions. While at auditing firms, we rely on their good judgement for investment decisions, and when that judgement is compromised in any way, our confidence and trust in the auditing process is eroded.

It is an overriding concern in the financial industry that, as became clear in investigations of the causes of the GFC, unethical behaviours arise when those in the financial industry have self-interested motivations; that is, when they are driven by competition and greed to sell products that will bring them a return, not by their users' needs. Their own self-interest, therefore, prevails over that of their clients, and the magnitude of the problems are magnified where the potential risks are ignored and the collective impact not ascertained.

Fortunately, there are numerous organisations endeavouring to uphold ethical standards for both the accounting profession and those in financial organisations. Most professional bodies have a clear mandate to maintain the standards and competency levels of their members. To achieve this, most professional organisations will have developed a code of conduct, communicated this code, and censured members who fall foul of the prescribed expectations. Some professions may perform this task better than others, but in doing so, respect and trust are generated and maintained in the sector.

## Ethics on video

**Bank scandals** – *Secret recordings: The Anglo Irish bank tapes (part 1–2)* 2013, YouTube, CelticAngloPress, 28 June, <www.youtube.com/watch?v=HyIFfxDqz84>.

**The GFC** – *Warren Buffet and Bill Gates on the economic crisis and ethics* 2009, YouTube, valueinvestingpro, 14 November, <www.youtube.com/watch?v=VTFmUuJlTZY>.

See web material for more videos.

## Ethics at the movies

Here are a few movie suggestions that have ethical content related to financial entities:

*__Margin Call__ – follows the drama at a Wall Street investment bank during the early stages of the GFC. *Margin Call* 2011, motion picture, Barnum, RO, Benaroya, M, Dodson, N, Jenckes, J, Moosa, C & Quinto, Z.

**Rogue Trader** – follows the ambitious investment banker, Nick Leeson, who singlehandedly bankrupted the UK's Barings Bank. *Rogue Trader* 1998, motion picture, Ball, C, Chapman, C, Cross, P, Day, J, Dearden, J, Frost, D, Raphael, P, Tyrer, W & Wands, AJ.

*__Author's pick__

See web material for more movies.

## Ethics on the web

**US SEC**, another US agency whose goal is to protect investors, and maintain fair, orderly, and efficient markets, and facilitate capital formation, <www.sec.gov>.

**US Commodity Futures Trading Commission** (CFTC), has a US mandate to regulate commodity futures and option markets, <www.cftc.gov/index.htm>.

See web material for more web references.

## Student exercises

See web material for answers to student short answer questions.

### Short answer questions

1. What are the key ethical issues for financial planners?
2. As a financial services professional, in practical terms how might one manage the need for independence and avoid a loss of objectivity?

## Experiential exercises

1. Finance entities have been said to be at the heart of the crash, with regulators 'asleep at the wheel' ('Crash course: the origins of the financial crisis' 2013); and financiers, irresponsible and major contributors to the global financial crisis. Undertake research to support or reject this assertion and briefly describe what role these entities played in the GFC?
2. Draw up a list of what might be the ten most common forms of unethical conduct in relation to financial advisers.

# Small cases

## Case: Financial services

Deloitte have become embroiled with Standard Charter's illicit processing transactions with Iranian banks, which have breached American sanctions. Deloitte are accused of weakening the final report about Standard Charter; omitting to mention a technique which can be used to camouflage illegal transfers ('Professional-service firms: desperately seeking scepticism' 2013).

## Case: Bank losses

Nicholas Leeson was a young derivatives trader based in Singapore in the early 1990s. Unusually, he was the Chief Trader, as well as being responsible for settling his trades – roles which are ordinarily separated. While in these positions he was responsible for a US$1.36 billion loss at Barings Bank, which led to the collapse of the 233-year-old institution a few days after Leeson fled Singapore, leaving a note apologising for the loss. The collapse was attributed to a lack of management control, and that had Barings had an effective system of management and financial and operational controls, the unauthorised positions that he took in the market would not have been condoned. Leeson was surprised at how readily the Home Office provided him with large sums of money to facilitate his trading – even more so after losing more than US$50 million in a single day – and yet the money continued to be made available (Calhoun, Olivero & Wolitzer 1999).

**Questions:**
1. What are the ethical issues involved?
2. What factors do you believe contributed to the circumstances of the Barings Bank collapse?

# Large case

## Case: Auditor independence

You were previously an auditor with a large accounting firm that had very clear policies to guide staff in relation to interactions with clients. You have, however, embarked on your own auditing practice

*cont.*

*cont.*

and are currently in the process of building, albeit slowly, your own client base. This has not been as easy as you thought it would be. While you are technically very competent you underestimated the time and skills required to build up you client base. Essentially you are not really a sales person and have difficulty getting access to potential clients and then winning them over. The upshot is that your income projection is not as good as you hoped. You could probably live with this for a while, but your partner has been putting considerable pressure on you to get married in the next year and to settle down. Your partner is very sociable, loves going out and is looking forward to a big wedding, while also looking for a house to buy.

Recently a personal contact of yours has been able to secure a meeting with a young, and very successful, entrepreneur. He is about your age and, when you met in person, you found that you got on really well and shared similar sporting interests. You are both interested in horse racing and your contact has invited you twice to the members' stand, sending you work after each occasion. It is now the racing season and, with a horse running in the Melbourne Cup, you have received an invitation to fly to Melbourne on his private plane and attend a party in his corporate tent. You know you would have a really good time and are keen to go. Your partner is ecstatic about the invitation and is really looking forward to getting dressed up and meeting a lot of new people.

**Questions:**

1. Why is this a tricky situation and what ethical principle might be eroded?
2. Of the five threats to independence described in this chapter, which threat does this situation pose?
3. What guideline would you use for determining whether to accept the hospitality?
4. What role is the partner posing?

See web material for:
- answers to short answer questions
- additional student cases
- tutor resources (tutor password required)
- additional material including Ethics at the movies, Ethics in print, Ethics on video and Ethics on the web.

# Chapter 8

## Ethical issues in entrepreneurship and small business

'When someone comes in with an idea that has never been tried, the only way you can judge is by the kind of man you are dealing with.'

Georges Doriot, 1899–1987,
father of venture capitalism

## Chapter aim

To examine the ethical issues faced by entrepreneurs and small business owners.

## Chapter objectives

1. To be cognisant of the environment within which entrepreneurs operate that may lend itself to unethical practices.
2. Review research findings in relation to the ethical characteristics of entrepreneurs.
3. Discuss the role of the entrepreneur in building an ethical culture.
4. Identify the ethical principles that more directly relate to entrepreneurs and small business owners.
5. Explore the ethical dilemmas which may confront entrepreneurs and small business owners.
6. Differentiate between sustainability, entrepreneurship and environmental entrepreneurship.
7. Explain the potential impact from social entrepreneurship.

# Ethics in the media: Entrepreneurial ethics

A budding entrepreneur lived for two months at America Online after completing a four-month start-up incubator program. Broke, he secretly lived at the internet giant's headquarters for two months until he was caught; eating at the canteen, using the gymnasium, locker and company laundromat while evading the security guards ('Teen entrepreneur squatted at AOL for two months undetected... and built a business' 2012).

## Introduction

The US Global Entrepreneurship Monitor (GEM) indicated that 29 million US adults were starting or running new businesses in 2011, and nearly 40% expected to create more than five new jobs in the next five years. The report indicated that the US experienced a more than 60% increase in entrepreneurial activity between 2010 and 2011 (Xavier et al. 2012). In the Southern Hemisphere, Australian start-ups compare well with their American counterparts. The Australian version of the GEM study indicates that Australia has high rates of entrepreneurship, second only to the US among innovation-driven economies (M Clark et al. 2013).

Entrepreneurship is highly regarded for its ability to generate individual income, produce value creation, and to enhance economic development. Companies such as Apple, Berkshire Hathaway, Google, Oracle and Starbucks, are powerful examples of founder-led companies that originated from humble beginnings to become multi-billion dollar empires. Most businesses, however, do not reach this size, and entrepreneurs settle into small to medium-sized businesses (Kopp 2013).

**entrepreneurs** – individuals who focus on the development of independent new ventures that are not sheltered by sponsoring organisations.

**Entrepreneurs** are individuals who focus on the development of independent new ventures that are not sheltered by sponsoring organisations (Clarke & Holt 2010). There are common features of the entrepreneurial environment within which entrepreneurs engage. These include uncertainty, particularly quick business growth, a scarcity of resources, a need for agility and flexibility in relation to staffing, and innovative business models in need of developing – although this innovation does not necessarily need to be particularly radical (Arnulf & Gottschalk 2012). Consequently, given the nature of this environment, questionable ethical practices may occur due to a lack of established behaviour patterns and ethical traditions (Steverson, Rutherford & Buller 2013).

The economic environment today thrusts the entrepreneur into survival mode, where a lack of resources can result in expediency, which in turn can lead to manipulating numbers to make financial statements look good and mask product or service deficiencies (Talbot 2008). It is acknowledged that small and medium-sized enterprises (SMEs) depend on their good ethical stature to survive, given that they must gain and retain the trust of their customers, supply chain partners and stakeholders, in order to enjoy sufficient legitimacy to conduct their business. However, they also face real temptations to 'change their ethics' (downward) in order to survive (Arend 2013). Specifically, entrepreneurs experience ethical problems particular to them. As noted, they typically operate in stressful environments and struggle to find time to focus on gaining perspective and achieving ethical reflection (Hannafey 2003). Fisscher et al. (2005) suggest that entrepreneurs are single-minded in their pursuit of success, to the point that they could compromise moral values when needed.

Given the role that entrepreneurs and small business owners have in new business development, job creation and economic development, they are worth examining as a group when it comes to business ethics. First, a point of clarification: the European Commission defines SMEs as those that employ fewer than 250 people; have an annual turnover not exceeding €50 million; and/or have an annual balance sheet totalling less than €43 million (Hoivik & Shankar 2011). Naturally, what constitutes an SME depends on the circumstances. For example, the Australian Bureau of Statistics (2013) defines a **small business** as an actively trading (tax-paying) business with 0–19 employees; a **micro-business** employing 0–4 employees; a **medium business** employing 20–199 employees; and a **large business** employing 200 or more people.

Entrepreneurs differ from small business owners in that entrepreneurs usually seek high growth, while small business owners appear content with generating sufficient revenue to support the owner's personal goals and lifestyle (Katz & Green 2007). Obviously, entrepreneurship can occur within large organisations involving corporate entrepreneurs, and is frequently referred to as **intrapreneurship**. For the purpose of our discussion, we will be focusing on the operation of new business ventures outside of larger organisations or corporations. We are broadly looking at independent entrepreneurs and owner managers who operate in smaller businesses, and we can also include franchise organisations and family businesses with this group. Therefore, we are using a wide, and less than subtle, distinction – hence the term 'entrepreneur' describes those involved both in start-ups and SMEs.

In order to differentiate between various types of managers and entrepreneurs, Ginsberg and Buchholtz (1989) provided a framework of entrepreneurial styles (see Table 8.1), based on two dimensions: independence, which combines a propensity for risk-taking with decision-making autonomy; and the second dimension of innovation, the propensity for creativity.

**small business** – an actively trading business with 1–19 employees.

**micro-business** – a small business with 1–4 employees.

**medium business** – a business that has 20–199 employees.

**large business** – an actively trading business with 200 or more employees.

**intrapreneur-ship** – entrepreneurial pursuits within large organisations.

**Table 8.1** A framework of entrepreneurial styles

| | Innovation | | Independence | |
|---|---|---|---|---|
| | **High** | **Low** | **High** | **Low** |
| Owner Manager | | X | X | |
| Corporate Manager | | X | | X |
| Independent Entrepreneur | X | | X | |
| Corporate Entrepreneur | X | | | X |

(Source: Ginsberg & Buchholtz 1989)

# Entrepreneurial ethics

Entrepreneurship provides a particularly rich situation for examining the role of ethics (Dunham 2010); although the ways in which entrepreneurship and ethics intersect are relatively embryonic (Harris, Sapienza & Bowie 2011). There is the potential for moral compromise (Longenecker, McKinney & Moore 1988), and it has been proposed that the ethical problems faced by entrepreneurs are notably different from those encountered by other business persons. As a result, there is a uniqueness to entrepreneurial morality (Hannafey 2003). For example, for an entrepreneur, the temptation to enhance the financial return figures can be so pressing that it stimulates behaviour that is unethical and potentially illegal. As lamented by one observer, the entrepreneurial world – and in particular the high-tech world – creates moral dilemmas. Which master do they serve? The one that makes investors feel good and gets the entrepreneur to where they want to be? Or the one that tells the story accurately, but may level out the trajectory? (Lawton 2013).

Entrepreneurial unethical behaviour has been defined as acts of omission by individuals, a group of individuals, or an organisation, which violates socially accepted norms, and/or legal structures (Khan, Tang & Zhu 2013). Entrepreneurial criminals are owners of organisations engaged in unlawful activities to generate revenue, and are categorised as working within smaller, less established companies, with less transparent governance and frequently making bigger profits (Arnulf & Gottschalk 2012). Those potentially affected by unethical entrepreneurial behaviour vary considerably, and may include:

- **investors** – where profits might be misappropriated
- **customers** – who are provided with inaccurate and deceptive information
- **governments** – who may be defrauded through tax evasion
- **innocents** – people who have not entered the business relationship, but are affected by the entrepreneur's activities (Rousseau & Telle 2010).

Although entrepreneurs have the advantage of being able to set the ethical tone of the organisation, they are still under considerable environmental pressures not conducive to ethical decision-making (Chau & Siu, 2000). While the popular press links aggressive entrepreneurial strategy to unethical activity (Neubaum, Mitchell & Schminke 2004), it appears that many entrepreneurs and small business owners clearly want to do the right thing. A survey in the US indicates that about a quarter of SMEs self-report high levels of ethics-focused capabilities (Arend 2013). The evidence is not conclusive, however, and it is worth exploring the ethical characteristics of entrepreneurs.

## Ethics in reflection: Entrepreneurial ethics

Reflect on the following questions regarding entrepreneurs and ethics.

**Questions:**

1. Should entrepreneurs be treated differently by society because of the unique task they carry out in the economy?

2. Should the ethical standards expected from entrepreneurs be different from those guiding businesspeople in established organisations?

3. How different are the ethical problems that contemporary entrepreneurs encounter, compared to managers in other types of organisation (Hannafey 2003)?

## Ethical characteristics of entrepreneurs

Many studies have assessed demographic, psychological and personality characteristics of entrepreneurs (including self-confidence, individualism and need for independence and achievement). In contrast, there is little research indicating definitive results in relation to pinpointing who will become a successful entrepreneur (Teal & Carroll 1999). Ginsberg and Buchholtz (1989) reviewed 10 studies on personality characteristics and found that entrepreneurs were typically characterised by their behaviours more than by their personalities. Entrepreneurs appear to be driven by innovation, high-risk rewards and self-interest (Longenecker, McKinney & Moore 1988). Longenecker, McKinney & Moore (1989) were among the first to investigate specifics in their study of self-employed contrasted against non-self-employed people, and concluded that entrepreneurs focus more on the direct financial benefit for themselves and demonstrate **ethical egoism**, which is commonly thought of as self-interest. It has also been suggested that entrepreneurs possess a strong 'action bias',

**ethical egoism** – self-interest.

which may inhibit them from adequately considering ethical issues and ethical considerations as they drive for outcomes rather than thinking of the means by which the outcomes are achieved (Bhide 1996).

Research in the US suggests that entrepreneurs, by their very nature, are serial rule-breakers (Zhang & Arvey 2009). Intriguingly, a positive relationship has been found between an individual's modest rule-breaking (for example, delinquency, family and school offences, drug use) in adolescence, and his or her entrepreneurial status in adulthood. The question raised subsequently is whether the adolescent rule-breaking also extends into adulthood, in terms of neglecting or bypassing social codes and ethical standards (Spence 2000). Entrepreneurs are often encouraged to break rules to take advantage of opportunities they have identified or that they can create; however, this injunction may lead entrepreneurs into any number of moral dilemmas (Brenkert 2009).

It appears that entrepreneurs with stronger **self-regulatory characteristics** are more morally aware. Self-regulatory characteristics (also known as **self-efficacy)** in the context of ethics refer to a person's self-conception in terms of moral values, virtues and standards of behaviour. In essence, it is their **moral identity** (Aquino & Reed 2002) or **moral awareness**, which is an individual's appreciation that a situation contains a moral dimension. Moral awareness assists in maintaining personal integrity and building interpersonal trust. In contrast, entrepreneurs with weaker self-regulatory characteristics appear less morally aware overall, and focus primarily on moral issues relating to failure and loss (Bryant 2008). More characteristics of Australian entrepreneurs are shown in Table 8.2.

**self-regulatory characteristics** (also known as **self-efficacy**) – in the context of ethics, it is a person's self-conception in terms of moral values, virtues and standards of behaviour. In essence, it is their moral identity.

**moral awareness** or **moral identity** – an individual's appreciation that a situation contains a moral dimension.

**Table 8.2** Characteristics of Australian entrepreneurs

| More likely | Less likely |
| --- | --- |
| Driven by opportunity | Motivated by necessity or lack of alternatives |
| Growth-oriented | |
| Prioritise research and development | |
| Business based on developing and/or sophisticated technologies | |
| University-educated | |
| Prioritise teamwork | |

(Adapted from: M Clark et al. 2013)

## Public perceptions

When investigating ethical attitudes of entrepreneurs, it has been observed that in the US people viewed individuals in small businesses as having higher ethical standards than those in positions as corporate employees and government officials (Brown & King 1982). Note that this study looked specifically at small business owners not entrepreneurs, and examines outsider perceptions of entrepreneurs. Of more relevance are the ethical attitudes of entrepreneurs themselves, and ways in which they may differ.

## Ethical attitudes

As expected, the research is not entirely conclusive but it does appear that entrepreneurs and small business owners do have strong ethical leanings (Medlin & Green 2003). Several studies examining ethical perceptions have utilised ethical dilemmas to test different groups of entrepreneurs (small business owners and managers) versus managers in larger organisations. These studies concluded that entrepreneurs demonstrate strong ethical perceptions (Hisrich & Peters 1998). Bucar and Hisrich (2001), using a variety of scenarios, found that entrepreneurs exhibited higher ethical attitudes than other managers. Interpretations of these findings are that entrepreneurs with a deep, personal engagement in their firm's activities may result in heightened sensitivity to some types of ethical issues (Hannafey 2003).

Ethical principles in entrepeneurship (© shutterstock.com/Michael D Brown)

Specifically investigating moral reasoning skills, Teal & Carroll (1999) examined the ethical reasoning of 26 entrepreneurs and discovered that entrepreneurs, while independent in their thinking, had higher levels of moral development and ethical reasoning than both middle managers and the general population. Similarly, McVea (2009) found that entrepreneurs appear to use a higher degree of moral imagination and, initially, frame a circumstance as involving a dimension of ethics; this is in contrast to MBA students who often frame a decision based around financial risk.

An extensive review of empirical studies on ethics and corporate social responsibility in entrepreneurial firms, revealed entrepreneurs and small businesspeople espouse fairly high ethical values. Many had encountered a number of ethical issues in starting and running a new venture, but had also established organisations to support the existence of an ethical climate as their firms evolved (Baucus & Cochran 2010). Comparing the attitudes of small businesspeople to the general population, Chrisman and Fry (1982) determined that small businesspeople understand corporate social responsibility better; while in another study, family firms appeared more socially responsible than non-family firms (Dyer & Whetten 2006). An exploratory study of Australian managers found that they saw considerable overlap between ethical and socially responsible behaviour, but, simultaneously, made a distinction between the ethically and socially responsible actions of companies (Cacioppe, Forster & Fox 2008). Also supporting a sound appreciation of corporate social responsibility, Fassin, Rossem and Bullens (2011) observed that small business owner–managers have a good grounding in the distinction between business ethics and corporate social responsibility, and they make sense of those concepts. This suggests that the concepts have been well introduced and disseminated in the business world, possibly by the popular media and professional associations.

## Contrasting views

In contrast, an international study of entrepreneurs observed that there was no difference in the age of entrepreneurs and their ethical attitudes, and that entrepreneurs in firms did not differ significantly from others. Managers of large firms were found to hold more ethical attitudes (Bucar, Hisrich & Glas 2003).

When investigating ethical issues faced by entrepreneurs, Longenecker, McKinney and Moore (1989) found that entrepreneurs are sometimes stricter in their ethical evaluations than others, but, at other times, are more lax in their ethical judgements, depending on the issues being considered. In contrast to non-entrepreneurs, they were more likely to approve actions that maximise personal financial rewards, even in situations where the rewards came at the expense of others. The need for financial security and the ever-present pressure for cash flow is likely to drive this behaviour. Throwing even more ambiguity into the mix, Gartner (1985) asserts that differences between individual entrepreneurs may be greater than differences between entrepreneurs and non-entrepreneurs.

# Ethics in the media: Unethical entrepreneurship

It is purported that Mark Zynga, the CEO of Zynga, the social gaming company behind Farmville, was brazen in his unethical practices. He purportedly boasted that he did every awful thing in the book just to get revenues and expand the company (Foremski 2011). See this chapter's 'Ethics on video' box.

## Contextual influence

Maintaining an ethical stance is seen as more problematic for entrepreneurs in transition economies, where they face difficulties directly linked to deficiencies in formal legal structures and under-developed financial markets (Scase 1997). Focusing specifically on entrepreneurs in a transition economy (Vietnam), it has been observed that SMEs pay more bribes than larger companies, because they lack the resources to influence public officials or pursue legal action (De Jong, Tu & Van Ees 2012). Ethical challenges facing entrepreneurs are evident in other transitional economies, such as Nigeria (Cfadahunsi & Rosa 2002). Studies undertaken in locations such as Russia, post-Soviet Ukraine, and Sri Lanka, concluded that environmental business factors have a powerful role in influencing entrepreneurial ethics (Fuxman 1997).

In a unique comparison of the ethical attitudes of entrepreneurs and managers from three different countries, Bucar, Hisrich and Glas (2003) found that Slovenian entrepreneurs and managers revealed high levels of business ethics. Conversely, ethical attitudes of Russian entrepreneurs, in some cases, were discouragingly low, particularly in relation to gifts and bribes, insider trading, ignorance of company policy or law violations. American entrepreneurs and managers revealed a high level of ethical attitudes, but there was also a sense of pragmatism, particularly in cases such as insider trading and gift-giving or bribery. However, the results of such studies can be problematic, as there is a strong distinction between knowing and doing. One can know what is right or wrong but this does not necessarily mean that person will behave accordingly.

For those moving from one culture to another, it appears that immigrant entrepreneurs adjust their beliefs, values, traditions and norms to acculturate to the host country, but still maintain links with their traditional culture (Azmat & Zutshi, 2012).

## Entrepreneurial culture

The values of the entrepreneur play a significant role in the ethical climate of a start-up (Morris et al. 2002). Often, as the owner–manager, they are in a unique position to set the moral tone of the organisation, and the people hired have a direct relationship to the founder. Others will emulate what the entrepreneur says and does, and the close dynamics coupled with a loose and emerging governance structure, will mean that the entrepreneur is the driver of the ethical environment (Ackoff 1987). Clearly, the role of the business founder has a pervasive influence on the culture and values of the organisation and their ethical conduct is, therefore, important.

The link between ethical behaviours and reputation is possibly more critical during the early phases of the business life cycle. A study of 304 individuals across 37 firms suggested that firm newness was more strongly related to ethical climate than was entrepreneurial orientation (Neubaum, Mitchell & Schminke 2004). When looking at the ethical strategies entrepreneurial firms develop as they grow, it appears the ethical climate develops in an evolutionary fashion, developing through the procedures and policies of the firm (Baucus & Cochrane, 2010). Investigating 10 successful high-growth entrepreneurial firms that had been in existence for at least five years, researchers explored whether the firms relied on legal compliance strategy, that is, following the letter of the law, or whether they evolved a more integrated strategy in regard to an ethical climate (that is, the introduction of ethical training, policies and procedures). The results indicated that all 10 of the firms exhibited a legal compliance strategy, but eight had gone further to institute more advanced integrated strategies (Joyner, Payne & Raiborn 2002).

In an effort to understand the ethical climate of entrepreneurial firms, Morris et al. (2002) proposed four distinct clusters:

- **Superlatives** – firms that place priority on ethics and have developed extensive formal and informal mechanisms to ensure ethical performance.
- **Deficients** – firms that lag in every area; while they are not inherently unethical, promoting an ethical climate is not viewed as a managerial responsibility.
- **Core proponents** – firms pursue the basic and formal elements that are legally required of them; any additional activity is seen as interventionist and is introduced as, and when, required.
- **Pain and gains** – firms do symbolic activities such as having a code of conduct. They provide no ethics training but there is ethical reinforcement, and they are doing more than the interventionist types by tying rewards and penalties to the ethical behaviour of employees while also providing role models.

## Ethicality and performance

In keeping with the truism that 'good ethics is good for business', it has been found that a firm's performance is negatively related to ethically suspect behaviours. It has also been found that entrepreneurs with better performing firms are less likely to engage in ethically suspect behaviours. From their research on Chinese entrepreneurs, Tang, Khan and Zhu (2012) found that entrepreneurs' engagement in ethically suspect behaviour impedes information acquisition, and, as it is imperative to acquire essential information to develop and grow a business, poor ethical behaviour and reputational damage can be a cost to the organisation.

# Ethical principles in entrepreneurship

Numerous ethical principles relate to entrepreneurs and small business owners. We will note the main ones here.

- **Honesty** – new venture entrepreneurs face unique ethical considerations in their quest for legitimacy, and, consequently, new entrepreneurs may attempt to both misrepresent (tell untruths) or omit key information (concealment and deception) in their attempt to gain legitimacy (Steverson, Rutherford & Buller 2013). Thus, there is the need for honesty and avoidance of over-inflated descriptions, deception or falsifications.
- **Transparency** – relates closely to the ethical principle of honesty, and for the entrepreneur; this is the need for full and accurate disclosure regarding future income projections, organisational capability and product or service capabilities.
- **Trust** – is of key importance, particularly between an entrepreneur, the business they create, the employees, customers, suppliers, and other stakeholders, and is essential for the long-term survival of a new entity.
- **Justice and fairness** – fairness or procedural justice is an important element in managing the relationships between entrepreneurs and key investors (Sapienza & Korsgaard 1996).

**honesty** – the avoidance of misrepresentation (telling untruths) or omitting important information (concealment and deception).

**transparency** – the need for full and accurate disclosure.

**trust** – the importance of trust is key, particularly between an entrepreneur, the business they create, the employees, customers, suppliers, and other stakeholders, and is essential for the long-term survival of a new entity.

**justice and fairness** – fairness and procedural justice.

Fairness is also relevant in relation to the treatment of personnel (particularly where some employees may be family members) and suppliers, when cash flow may be tight.

- **Non-maleficence** – not doing harm; for the entrepreneur this means not breaking laws, deceiving others, discriminating, or destroying trust or the natural environment.

- **Beneficence** – doing good, improving working conditions, augmenting the social fabric, as well as enhancing environmental sustainability. This is specifically the arena within which the social entrepreneur operates.

- **Conflict of interest** (also known as the **agency problem**) – this moral hazard happens when entrepreneurs (agents) act in their own interest, rather than in the best interest of the principal or investor. For the more developed entrepreneurial business, there is the concern for impropriety as a result of competing interests.

Ethical attitudes (© shutterstock.com/Sam72)

# Ethics on reflection: Posturing or deception?

Many entrepreneurs not only tell half-truths in order to win customers, but tell actual lies. This raises the question: what is the ethical difference between posturing and overt deception? (For further information, see <www.inc.com/guides/leadership_strat/20698.html>).

# Ethical issues for entrepreneurs and small businesses

As we have seen, entrepreneurial and small businesses frequently employ a relatively small number of staff and are actively managed by the owner and founder without the need to be answerable to other shareholders (although there may be additional investors to whom there

**non-maleficence** – not doing harm, which is, not breaking laws, deceiving others, discriminating, destroying trust or the natural environment.

**beneficence** – doing good, improving working conditions, augmenting social fabric as well as enhancing environmental sustainability.

**conflict of interest** – impropriety as a result of competing interests.

**agency problem** – a moral hazard where the agent (the entrepreneur) may not act in the best interests of the principal (usually the investor) after the relationship has been created, and will act in their own interest, thus creating a conflict of interest.

is some accountability). The advantage of this independence is that they are in a strong position to bring their own ethical attitudes into the business. However, there is also a downside in that the independence can also create a sense of self-justification for potentially unethical decisions (Lahdesmaki 2005), particularly when entrepreneurs are under considerable time and task pressures.

Observing that financial and operational pressures found in most entrepreneurial firms heighten the incentive to engage in expedient behaviour, and that entrepreneurs frequently confront an array of ethical dilemmas that directly affect company performance (Morris et al. 2002), it is appropriate to now look at the ethical issues entrepreneurs have to deal with.

Prior research does give some indication. It has been proposed that entrepreneurs face ethical dilemmas in relation to employee wellbeing, customer satisfaction and external accountability (Payne & Joyner 2006). Utilising a focus group of small business owners in the UK, the ethical issues identified related to impact of the owner's personality, conflicts of personal values with business needs, social responsibility, and stakeholder obligations versus responsibility to the business (Vyakarnam et al. 1997). Meanwhile, in the US, a study concluded that small business owners encountered ethical issues relating to business development, financial management, theft, and administrative decision-making (Hornsby et al. 1994).

Hannafey (2003) identifies the ethical dilemmas entrepreneurs confront related to fairness, personnel, distribution systems and customer relationships, while Sarprasatha & Suresh (2012) acknowledge personnel, pricing, distribution of wealth, environment, and corruption as key issues for entrepreneurs. More broadly, ethical issues for entrepreneurs have been trimmed down to two dimensions: those relating to administrative or instrumental circumstances and those related to profit or personal gain (Kuratko, Goldsby & Hornsby 2004).

Khan, Tang and Zhu (2013) identify the most recent typology of ethical issues that entrepreneurs and small business owners experience. Examples of entrepreneurial behaviours considered ethically suspect include:

- not fulfilling the terms of the contract
- false advertising
- inappropriate gift-giving and receiving of gifts
- bribery
- price collusion
- price discrimination and unfair pricing
- unfair treatment of employees
- cheating customers
- discriminatory hiring practices
- nepotism
- padding of expense accounts
- overselling
- unfair credit practices
- environmental pollution
- sexual harassment.

The list looks remarkably similar to ethical issues also experienced in large organisations, so it is perhaps appropriate to take a slightly different perspective and to examine morally problematic areas for entrepreneurs and small business owners within the context of new business venturing. To do this, we will use the five evolutionary stages of idea generation, venture capital generation, growth and exiting, before concluding with the increasingly popular domain of social entrepreneurship.

## 1. Idea generation

For an entrepreneur wishing to create a start-up business, the first step in the process is the initial idea generation, which is then translated into a business venture. With this step, however, come a few obvious ethical issues.

### Violation of intellectual property

Rather than generating a new and unique idea to take to market, there is always the temptation to appropriate and re-market existing intellectual property. This could involve a direct violation of intellectual property or a slight modification. In music, for example, unofficial remixes can boost sales of the original work. In a recent book, *The pirate's dilemma: How youth culture is reinventing capitalism*, Matt Mason (2008) gives the example of Nigo, a Japanese designer who took Air Force one trainers made by Nike, removed the famous 'swoosh' logo and applied his own designs. He then sold the resulting shoes in limited editions at $300 a pair under his own label, A Bathing Ape. Surprisingly, instead of suing Nigo, Nike realised he had spotted a gap in the market. Nike took a stake in his firm and launched their own premium 'remixes' of their trainers ('Look for the silver lining' 2008).

It is not uncommon to hear of individuals who have left a company taking important company property with them to facilitate the set-up of their new business venture. To prohibit the transfer of corporate knowledge, some organisations put a restraint of trade into employee contracts, thereby restricting them from operating in the sector for a period of 12 months, or more. This clause is commonplace, for example, in the recruitment industry.

Idea generation (© shutterstock.com/Sergey Nivens)

## Product safety

The pressure for profits and a lax regulatory environment can be an unhealthy combination for entrepreneurial effort, and could result in products that violate the duty of care. For example, in 2008, dairy products from over 20 Chinese companies were found to be contaminated with melamine. Distributors had used melamine to boost protein levels in milk and related products. The tainted milk scandal resulted in approximately 300 000 ill children with at least six dying. The industry took a direct hit of nearly US$232 million, while China's international reputation also plummeted (Khan, Tang & Zhu 2013).

## Overselling

**angel investor** – a wealthy individual investor.

Dave McClure, a leading **angel investor**, once asserted that perfect start-up companies need a 'hustler, a hacker, and a designer' (Foremski 2011). An entrepreneurial start-up is particularly vulnerable in that it has little history or track record upon which to trade itself to investors, distributors and customers. As a result, to inspire stakeholders to engage with the business there is the prospect of **hustling**, or so-called **overselling.** There is yet another name for this practice, **legitimacy lies** – intentional, dishonest misrepresentations told by entrepreneurs, with the goal of being granted legitimacy by stakeholders (Steverson, Rutherford & Buller 2013). Legitimacy lies for example, could be over-confidence about future market opportunities and the size and sustainability of those markets.

**legitimacy lies** (also **hustling** or **overselling**) – are intentional but dishonest misrepresentations told by entrepreneurs with the goal of being granted legitimacy by stakeholders.

A further area of legitimacy lies could be in omission. For example, a woman wanted to start her own business and leave her employer, a frozen food maker. She received many rejections; however, one organisation was happy to finance her. It then dawned on her that they were under the impression that she was representing her previous employer, when in fact she was a solo entrepreneur. She did not disavow them of their understanding and the deal went through. The business is worth US$32 million today (Steverson, Rutherford & Buller 2013). There were no untruths, but there was certainly an element of misrepresentation concerning materially relevant information.

# Ethics on reflection: Overselling

Overselling could also be in the form of outright deception or distortion. When does omission become manipulation or coercion? Additionally, what constitutes unethical distortion and deception?

## Ethical sourcing

**Ethical sourcing** is more associated with multinational companies, but the Ethical Trading Initiative point out that, while SMEs may not have the resources and leverage of large multinationals, they still bear responsibilities towards the workers involved in making their products, and should seek to source raw materials and labour ethically (McAllister 2013).

**Figure 8.1** Phases of entrepreneurial activity

## 2.  Venture capital generation

The need to finance or maintain new business start-ups can result in deceptive practices. For example, in 2010, the former chief executive of Billabong was found to have forged the signatures of his former wife and brother, in order to secure a AU\$13.5 million loan against the home held in his ex-wife's name. She claimed she was not complicit in her husband's financial dealings, as his AU\$150 million fortune disappeared after a failed investment in a Chinese supermarket chain (Calligeros 2011).

"I don't want your wallet, I want venture capital."
Venture capital generation (© shutterstock.com/Cartoonresource)

**Venture capital generation** is the acquisition of financial support from both informal (friends and family) and more formal sources (angel investors and venture capitalists) for the purpose of establishing new business (seed funding) or sustaining an existing new business venture (working capital). The ethical issues that can arise in relation to the generation of capital appear to be in two categories: investor exploitation or exploitation of entrepreneurs.

## Investor exploitation

When an investor is deceived or taken advantage of by the entrepreneur with whom they are engaged in a business venture this is deemed to be **investor exploitation**. For the investor, the difficulties may arise from the accuracy of information provided by the entrepreneur, such as the size of the potential market, the strength of competitors and product performance. Investors can also be deceived or cheated when an entrepreneur misrepresents financial or sales data, or even steals profits from investors.

**ethical sourcing** – responsibilities towards the workers involved in making their products, seeking to source raw materials and labour ethically.

**venture capital generation** – financial support from both informal and more formal sources for the purpose of establishing a new business or sustaining an existing new business venture.

**investor exploitation** – when an investor is deceived or taken advantage of by the entrepreneur with whom they are engaged in a business venture.

In order to maintain the flow of cash from outsiders, some internet companies have engaged in ethically questionable accounting practices, which have resulted in US Security Exchange Commission (SEC) investigations. They recognise issues relating to premature recognition of revenue and treating barter as revenue, and invest in companies that are also their main advertisers (Maury & Kleiner 2002). Deception and investor exploitation occurs, commonly, in relation to misrepresentation of facts or **financial puffery** with the overstatement of financial forecasts. This is obviously problematic given that, without a track record of performance, accurate evaluation of financial data is often difficult (Steverson, Rutherford & Buller 2013). Honesty in regard to communications becomes particularly important when interacting with investors, however, an ethical question that does arise is whether honesty requires complete disclosure of risks and uncertainties?

**financial puffery** – the overstatement of financial forecasts.

# Ethics in practice: Deceived investors

You are a venture capitalist who recently invested in a small business. You have since realised that the entrepreneur insinuated they were in a start-up phase, whereas, they were only in a seed phase. Even worse, the prototype they presented to you does not actually work (Sarprasatha & Suresh 2012).

**Question:**
**1.** What would you do next in this scenario?

One self-explanatory form of investor exploitation is **exploitation of family and friends**. It can involve the manipulation of emotional ties in order to attract family and friends as funders of the business. There is also the potential for deception and disappointment if promised returns are not realised and there is an inadequate return on investment, or incurred losses.

**exploitation of family and friends** – manipulation of emotional ties in order to use family and friends as investors.

## Exploitation of entrepreneurs

When looking at ethics in entrepreneurship, it is very tempting to dwell solely on the perspective of the entrepreneur and how they interact with their stakeholders. However, an alternative view should look at ethics in entrepreneurship from the point of view of the entrepreneur being exploited – given that entrepreneurs tend to 'over-trust' and are more vulnerable to the opportunistic efforts of others (Goel & Karri 2006; Karri & Goel 2008; Sarasvathy & Due 2008).

For example, Sydney Angels investigated a potential turnaround opportunity of a Bundaberg-based hotel accommodation business after the owner contacted them. The business required an urgent injection of AU$400 000 working capital, and after due diligence the investor declined to provide the financial injection, leaving the small business with an AU$10 000 bill for due diligence (Hurley 2013a).

Due diligence can be exhausting as well as costly (especially where a number of contracts are in place that require review). There are also individuals who charge introduction fees to businesses on the pretext of introducing the business to a wealthy investor, and those who charge significant due diligence fees while giving the false expectation that an investment is imminent. It has been suggested that angel investors who need to charge fees to make a living are probably not successful investors. Investors who do charge due diligence fees often follow up with a suggestion for consultancy rates to fix what they have identified as strategic flaws in the business, hence the possible distinction between an angel investor (a wealthy individual investor) and a **turnaround investor** (Hurley 2013a).

Other areas of conflict and potential ethical grey areas, where entrepreneurs feel unfairly treated by venture capitalists, occur when an investor: invests in competitors without informing them; uses false claims regarding the extent of their industry contacts; puts overt influence on the operations of the business; or tries to side-step the entrepreneur or eliminate him or her from the business (Collewaert & Fassim 2013). Similarly, according to Collewaert & Fassim (2013), actions that could also be viewed as an abuse of power occur where a venture capitalist:

- circulates rumours about the business
- eliminates minor shareholders through dubious methods (such as forcing them to sell their shares at a reduced price or blocking their investment)
- refuses to co-invest in replacing end-of-life equipment critical to the entrepreneur's business
- privileges his or her interests over the company's interests
- bills for excessive costs, or forces an early recovery of their investment.

> **turnaround investor** – investors who charge diligence fees and often follow up with a suggestion for consultancy rates to fix what they have identified as being strategic flaws in the business.

## Ethics in the media: Exploitation of entrepreneurs

One example of how entrepreneurs can be taken advantage of is that of a naïve businessman who was involved in the set-up of a boutique recruitment firm. He did not secure an ironclad shareholder agreement with full equity rights, even though he was a minority shareholder. When he was terminated, he had no recourse, as well as no job (Gardner 2012).

## 3. Growth

The pressures on entrepreneurs during the growth phase are quite immense. Khan, Tang and Zhu (2013) suggest that the powerful may compete and engage in unethical behaviour in order to stay powerful, move up, or stay in the race to and avoid dropping out. *Inc Magazine* surveyed the CEOs of companies on the *Inc* top 500 list who had grown their business with little or no capital; 14% said that they engaged in **bootstrapping**, which is defined as an unsavoury or unethical business practices. Some entrepreneurs may consider bootstrapping to be stringing out a supplier on a payment or two, while for others it means out-and-out lying (Seglin 1998).

**bootstrapping** – an unsavoury or unethical business practice.

For the small business person, it is about trying to obtain a reasonable balance between the need to survive and generate a profit, and the need to strive for ideal and ethical behaviour (Broomberg 2012). During the growth stage of a new business venture several ethical issues arise. Lahdesmaki (2005) identified six kinds of ethical business decisions:

1. Deciding whether to source raw material suppliers.
2. Deciding on the quality of production and lack of resources, including time.
3. Setting the price with considerations about competitor pricing, and the temptation to engage in price collusion.
4. The level of truthfulness in marketing and product information.
5. Employee relationships become close, making it difficult to give employees notice during economic downturns.
6. Trust, and the decision about how to collaborate with others.

Next, we will examine some of the more problematic areas for entrepreneurs in relation to the growth stage of new ventures.

## Maintaining ethical relationships

When investigating the ethical climate of small business owners, it has been found that small business owners were less likely to abuse power than other people, and are more likely to put an emphasis on caring (Welsh & Birch 1997). However, other research suggests contrasting findings (see Neubaum, Mitchell & Schminke 2004). Some entrepreneurs may have a tendency to enter instrumental or transactional relationships, which means they remain in a relationship only as long as the relationship generates benefits. Entrepreneurs will then proceed through a series of relationships, easily severing restrictive and unprofitable ones, whether with an investor, employee or others (Collins & Moore 1970). Treating people in such a way is somewhat contrary to an ethical expectation that you do not use people as a means to an end.

Partnership tensions may also be problematic, and an ethical minefield can erupt when two entrepreneurs who have gone into business together, fall out. Partnerships can be tricky at the best of times, but pressures on the relationship can create stresses resulting in deceptive practices.

## Exploitation of employees

In relation to staffing, with a limited financial base and an uncertain income stream, entrepreneurs frequently experience difficulties when hiring new staff – which may lead to potential exploitation of staff if it remains unchecked. An alternative perspective is that, given the small number of employees, a more personalised relationship can develop.

As new employees join a fledgling business, tensions can arise if there is no **value alignment.** That is, different values exist between the ethical standards of the entrepreneur and those of the newcomers (Morris et al. 2002). It has also been suggested that entrepreneurs need to develop relationships with those around them and, to do so, must also be attuned to the values, perspectives and needs of the various stakeholders in their venture (Clarke & Holt 2010).

Wellbeing can be an issue. Ensuring work–life balance is important not only for employees but also for entrepreneurs. For entrepreneurs who have put their hearts and souls into building their businesses, there is an inherent difficulty with juggling the requirements of running a business and the demands of life (Madigan 2012).

**value alignment**– the alignment of values and the ethical standards between the entrepreneur, employees, partners and other stakeholders.

## Bribery

Bribery is an ethical issue that can arise when facilitating relationships. While we are not condoning bribery, there is the suggestion that in emerging markets we tend to over-moralise bribery and overlook the benefits that may ensue. Bribery can appear to facilitate processes and increase market opportunities, specifically in transition economies, where an entrepreneur who owns the company has strong motivation to maximise company performance (performance being synonymous with personal income). Often, as entrepreneurs operate without any formal supervision, or in small groups that they oversee, the likelihood of bribery is increased. (See Chapter 7 for a more on the ethical dimensions of bribery.)

In a survey of entrepreneurs in Vietnam's transitional economy, De Jong, Tu and Van Ees (2012) propose that, to a point, bribery can have beneficial impacts on a firm's performance. In transitional economies, such as China, Russia and Vietnam, the reason that bribery is so elusive is because it is covert and beneficial to both parties; that is, to those who receive the bribe and those who experience enhanced opportunities. In addition, the opportunity for mandating against bribery is a long and slow process. While bribery allows entrepreneurs to develop and foster a network of informal relationships with public officials, and reap the accompanying benefits, it also has disadvantages, such as the inefficient allocation of resources. As De Jong, Tu and Van Ees (2012) acknowledge, bribes are also subject to the law of diminishing returns, as high levels of bribes increasingly absorb the returns on entrepreneurial activities and can distort entrepreneurial spirit and behaviour.

## Employee compensation

With limited cash flow, as a business develops, the inability to pay competitive wages can be problematic and can result in unethical actions, such as not paying staff appropriately or on time. In an effort to attract staff on limited pay, and in order to keep costs down, entrepreneurs have tried to address this problem with the promise of future financial returns, primarily through the practice of offering equity (shares or a stake in the company) to attract and incentivise talent. This practice occurred in Silicon Valley creating many overnight millionaires when businesses went public (Hurley 2013b). Normally, tax is paid when the share options are cashed, however employee share options have been treated the same as income in Australia since 2002, and the receivers of the shares are taxed on a notional valuation. Naturally, one also needs to be careful about CEOs selling large amounts of stock at opportune moments, which could unduly influence the market (Morris et al. 2002).

## Ethics in practice: Equity stakes

In recent years, start-up companies in particular have issued staff with share options (equity stakes) instead of income. Debate has arisen about whether this practice was an exercise in avoiding tax. In fairness, though, capital gains tax is payable once the shares are sold – however if the company goes bust, then employees lose their equity and no tax is paid (Hurley 2013b).

**Question**
**1.** What is your view of equity stakes?

**grossing up revenue** – claiming full gross revenue as the actual amount retained by the company, not the discounted revenue.

## Inflating revenues

Inflating revenues and revenue deception is commonplace. An issue that has arisen, particularly with internet companies, is a technique called **grossing up revenue**. For example, Maury and Kleiner (2002) cite the example of US internet company Priceline.com, reporting their gross bookings of airline tickets, hotel rooms and rental cars as their revenue. This is not indicative of their real revenue, which in fact is the difference between what the customer pays and what the companies charge for their services.

## Ethics in the media: Falsified earnings

The Japanese internet entrepreneur, Takafumi Horie, of Livdoor, was convicted of fraud in 2011 after being found to have falsified earnings using share splits in a series of fake companies. Some believe he was unfairly targeted. Livdoor is, however, still listed on the share market ('Horiemon returns' 2013).

Another means of conflating revenue involves use of **barter revenue**, where companies use an equal cash exchange scenario. That is, both companies send each other identical bills so their accounting records both reflect a revenue and an expense, creating substantial **phantom income** (Maury & Kleiner 2002).

Outright fraud can also be an ethical problem for entrepreneurs and small business owners, and it has been recognised that most small businesses fall short in putting processes and disciplines in place that are the foundation for growth. Processes such as forecasting, planning, measuring and reporting are critical for cash-flow forecasting, which is especially important during tight cash-flow periods (Kopp, 2013). Cash-flow problems can require difficult prioritisation of payments, such as determining who should be paid first: the tax office, suppliers, or employees?

## 4. Exiting

Exiting from an entrepreneurial opportunity could involve a number of alternatives, some of which are partial sale, full divestment, and closure. The same cautions regarding accurate disclosure and honesty in communication when seeking venture capital apply when proposing exit strategies.

Interestingly, it is purported that approximately 70% of family-owned businesses fail or are sold before the second generation is able to take over the business (Stalk & Foley 2012), and that only 10% of family-owned businesses are passed on to the third generation as active, privately held companies (Stalk & Foley 2012). What contributes to the high failure rates of family businesses? One factor proposed is the propensity of family-owned firms to insist that their children move into the business. The employment of friends and family is **nepotism** and often results in individuals who are not only the least qualified, but also the least interested in the role in which they have been placed.

While in some cultures it is unrealistic to avoid nepotism or to have nepotism-free family-owned businesses, to rectify the problem of nepotism some businesses use a set of guidelines in order to ensure transparency, equity and, it is hoped, the best person for the job. These guidelines may relate to the minimum age of family members applying for the job, level of tertiary education, languages spoken, and demonstrable work history and experience (Stalk & Foley 2012).

Once entrepreneur-initiated companies reach a certain size, they become attractive to larger organisations. This presents an opportunity for larger organisations to acquire a small but upcoming competitor and for the entrepreneurial firm to access greater distribution methods and finance for continued growth. However, acquisition comes at a cost, and the potential destruction of company ethos. For example, the purchase of Ben & Jerry's by Unilever eroded efforts to maintain some of the ice-cream maker's social initiatives, such as buying milk from farmers who did not use growth hormones. The acquisition resulted in an overall lack of innovation, lowered staff morale and created quality assurance issues (Hurley 2013a).

**barter revenue** – where companies exchange services but not costs in an equal cash exchange scenario. Both companies send each other identical bills so they can both record revenue and an expense.

**phantom income** – a deceptive practice where income is claimed; however, the income is not real and doesn't exist.

**nepotism** – the employment of friends and family based on relationship rather than merit.

## 5. Social entrepreneurship

In a discussion on entrepreneurship and small business, we would be remiss if we did not discuss social entrepreneurship. However, social entrepreneurship has a number of related terminologies, so let us first examine those areas before focusing on social entrepreneurship and what it entails.

### Corporate social responsibility

**corporate social responsibility (CSR)** – actions that further social good beyond the interest of the firm and that which is required by law.

Actions that further social good beyond the interest of the firm and that which is required by law, are defined as **corporate social responsibility (CSR)** (McWilliam & Siegel 2001). While an immense amount has been written on CSR, it has received little attention from entrepreneurship researchers, possibly because of the label 'corporate' in the term, which implies more established organisations (Baucus & Cochrane 2010). If we drop 'corporate' from the term, we are left with **social responsibility (SR)**, which can apply to a range of organisations, large and small. This is the approach taken by the International Organisation for Standardization (ISO). The ISO 26000 definition of SR is as follows.

**social responsibility (SR)** – responsibility of an organisation for the impacts of its decisions and activities on society and the environment, through transparent and ethical behaviour.

An organisation should be responsible for the impacts of its decisions and activities on society and the environment, by using transparent and ethical behaviour to:

- contribute to the sustainable development, health, and welfare of society
- bear in mind the expectations of stakeholders
- act in compliance with laws and international norms of behaviour
- integrate ISO Social Responsibility Standard 26000 practice in the organisation (ISO n.d.).

Many small enterprises do not implement CSR either because they do not see the market demand or because they perceive it as too expensive to implement. This is despite the push for CSR in SMEs through external factors such as the pressure from supply chain relationships, the development of legislation, international standardisation and certification of CSR, and from internal factors where CSR is linked to the ethical values and principles of owners and operators (Hoivik & Shankar 2011).

Reasons identified for not implementing SR by SMEs include:

- the limited human and financial capabilities of SMEs
- limited awareness of how CSR impacts or benefits their organisation, and a lack of expertise to prioritise and address issues
- financial limitations for implementing initiatives
- lack of bargaining power in establishing standards, especially in international arenas, and thus finding it difficult to challenge the accepted norms in the industry
- limited tools to implement CSR practices such as gaining awareness of the principles and guidelines, and making the necessary changes to management systems, training, benchmarking and reporting (Hoivik & Shankar 2011).

To overcome these limitations and to encourage engagement, Hoivik & Shankar (2011) suggest a cluster approach for SMEs to take up corporate social responsibility, thus the uptake of CSR becomes part of a network agenda of like-minded firms and the challenges of implementing CSR are minimised. By working in a cluster or using a network-based approach to implement CSR, SMEs are able to legitimise CSR engagement, overcome limitations, encourage and support each other, and motivate other SMEs who are not part of the cluster.

## Sustainability entrepreneurship

Sustainability-minded entrepreneurs seek socially, environmentally and financially stable growth for their firms. **Sustainable entrepreneurship** has been defined as entrepreneurial activity that focuses on 'the preservation of nature, life support and community, in the pursuit of apparent opportunities to create future products, processes and services for gain, where gain refers to the economic and non-economic gains to individuals, the economy and society' (Shepherd & Patzelt 2011). Interestingly, studies reveal that sustainable entrepreneurs also possess core values around continued improvement, morality, financial prudence and holistic cognition (Gagnon 2012).

## Environmental entrepreneurship

The term **environmental entrepreneurship** was developed in the mid-1980s by Groundwork Trusts UK, which aimed at regenerating urban and industrial areas in the north of England (De Jong, Tu & Van Ees 2012), and promoting positive environmental outcomes. A related term is **ecopreneurship**, which focuses on how entrepreneurial action can contribute to preserving the natural environment, biodiversity and ecosystems.

**sustainable entrepreneurship** – entrepreneurial activity that focuses on the preservation of nature, life support and community in the pursuit of perceived opportunities to bring into existence future products, processes and services for gain, where gain is broadly construed to include economic and non-economic gains to individuals, the economy and society.

**environmental entrepreneurship** – efforts that promote positive environmental outcomes.

**ecopreneurship** – focuses on how entrepreneurial action can contribute to preserving the natural environment, biodiversity and ecosystems.

## Ethics in the media: Social responsibility

Honoured in 2004 at the World Economic Forum, Martin Burt was recognised as an outstanding social entrepreneur who launched an entrepreneurial education program in 1995 to promote financial literacy for children and young people, called 'Teach a Man to Fish', equipping the poor with tools to become economically successful (Maak & Stoetter 2012).

## Ethics in the media: Social entrepreneurship

David Bussau, an inspiring social entrepreneur, retired at 35 years old, having endowed an international foundation to pioneer marketplace solutions for social problems including health, education, nutrition, water, micro-finance and leadership. David Bussau believes that wealth creation and the power of market forces can alleviate poverty and promote nation building (McHugh 2012).

## Ethics in practice: Social entrepreneurship

Undertake research in your own national environment and identify three examples of social entrepreneurship. Alternatively, look at an emerging economy and identify examples of social entrepreneurship.

## Social entrepreneurship approaches

Social entrepreneurship occurs where entrepreneurs use their business skills for addressing social problems or accelerating social change. Social entrepreneurs are driven by the desire to create value for society, whereas commercial entrepreneurs would rather capture value (Santos 2012). Specifically, **social entrepreneurship** encompasses activities and processes undertaken to realise, define and exploit opportunities in order to improve social wealth by generating new ventures, or managing existing organisations in an innovative way (Zahra et al. 2009).

Some of the higher-profile organisations that have demonstrated social entrepreneurship include companies such as Ben & Jerry's, who support a range of social causes, particularly organic agriculture and protection of the rainforest and The Body Shop, an organic body care product retailer that support a range of social and environmental programs, avoid animal testing and support Fair Trade. An example of social entrepreneurship in action in Australia is Simon Griffiths, founder of Who Gives a Crap, a toilet paper company that use their profits to build toilets in the developing world.

Social entrepreneurship may include:

- individual entrepreneurs devoted to making a difference in areas of social concern
- non-profit organisations taking on practices and processes from the profit sector
- for-profit organisations expanding their scope of impact to include social concerns
- philanthropists supporting investment in problem areas (Morris et al. 2002).

According to Mair, Battilana and Cardemas (2012), there are four clusters of social entrepreneurship:

1. organisations that address legal and human rights issues
2. organisations addressing a range of issues related to the environment, education and health
3. organisations that tackle economic issues such as poverty, poor working conditions, unemployment and lack of access to markets
4. organisations which focusing on issues related to civic engagement with the purpose of creating social change.

Social entrepreneurship is further delineated in accordance with the forms of capital that are leveraged; the common typology being social, human, and political, as well as financial capital sources (Mair, Battilana & Cardemas 2012). There is venture funding available specifically for social entrepreneurs. For example, the online bank, ING Direct, have teamed up with crowdfunding platform, StartSomeGood, to grant funding of up to AU$25 000 to projects that create positive change in the community, and have been initiated by social entrepreneurs. The projects being supported tackle homelessness, support sustainable farming and Fair Trade (Fitzsimmons 2013).

To further promote access to funding for social entrepreneurs, the UK is experimenting with **Social Impact Bonds (SIBs)**, which promises returns to private investors if social objectives are met. To give an example of how the bonds work, a bond was raised for £5 million

**social entrepreneurship** – activities and processes undertaken to discover, define and exploit opportunities in order to enhance social wealth by creating new ventures or managing existing organisations in an innovative manner.

**Social Impact Bonds (SIBs)** – government-backed bonds which promise returns to private investors if social objectives are met.

from investors to be shared between two organisations responsible for homeless people. The fund is for a three-year program, which has a number of KPIs, including once the target is met, payment flows to the investors from the Greater London Authority, which is the commissioning body for the bonds ('Commerce and conscience' 2013).

Research suggests social entrepreneurs are just like most entrepreneurs in their experience and skills. The difference lies in the fact that social entrepreneurs appear more introverted and are less organised (Spruijt 2012). However, despite their apparent disorganisation, social entrepreneurs are intent on creating positive social impact, either in the form of for-profit or non-profit organisations. What social entrepreneurs have in common is that they are seeking to address social problems such as inadequate housing, poor health, education, long-term employment and a host of other social issues that are evident in society today.

The distinction between charity and problem-solving is that social entrepreneurship is about not only caring for people, but also empowering them. With social entrepreneurship, the product or service provided is not the end in itself, but an integral part of a more complex intervention to achieve social objectives or social change (Mair, Battilana & Cardemas 2012). This could be achieved through the impact that the product or service has in itself, or the process by which it is generated (that is, being produced without harming the environment).

The question is often asked why the government is not undertaking the activities that social entrepreneurs are involved in. This is a genuine question, but, more often, social entrepreneurs are working in a space that government has not yet recognised as an emergent need. Social entrepreneurs tend to be more attuned to these growing issues and are often the first to step in. Having highlighted the problem and indicated strategies for addressing the problem, it is common for governments to then be alerted to the issue and to lend their support through funding or legislative changes (Santos 2012). Interestingly, Ashoka, the global organisation supporting social entrepreneurs, claims that over half the social entrepreneurs in their network influence national legislation within five years of launching their organisation (Sen 2007).

**collective social entrepreneurship** – social entrepreneurship that has moved away from individuals as being the leaders of social change, to looking at multiple actors collaboratively addressing social problems.

More recently, **collective social entrepreneurship** has moved away from individuals being the leaders of social change, to looking at multiple actors collaboratively addressing social problems. Habitat for Humanity's ReStore is a good example (Montgomery, Dacin & Dacin 2012), as is the partnership of Lahore-based micro-finance institution, Kashf Foundation, and the non-profit organisation Kiva, a platform dedicated to connecting global audiences through online lending. (See also the SKOLL Foundation's website at <www.skollfoundation.org> for its film series that showcasing social entrepreneurs.) Table 8.3 gives some further examples of social entrepreneurship from the international context.

**Table 8.3**  International examples of social entrepreneurship

| Organisation | Country | Social entrepreneurship example |
|---|---|---|
| Oneworld Health | US | Redesigned the pharmaceutical value chain to deliver effective drugs to fight disease in developing countries. |
| Grammen Danoe | Bangladesh | Aims to reduce malnutrition in children through the production and sale of low-cost yoghurts enriched with vitamins. |
| Yunis-Cite | France | A social enterprise founded in 1995 with the purpose of creating an opportunity for young people from different origins to perform volunteer team work for a period of one year. |
| CDI | Brazil | Launched its first information technology school in a slum in Rio Di Janeiro in 1995, in order to fight digital exclusion among poor Brazilian youth, and has spread to 1000 schools across Latin America. |
| Gram Vikas | India | A rural development organisation whose mission is to deploy running water and sanitation systems in rural villages. |
| The Barefoot College | India | Trains semi-literate people in critical areas such as irrigation and water, solar power, medicine, architecture, mechanics and accounting, and has reached approximately 600 villages in India. |
| The Body Shop | UK | Transformed the cosmetic value chain to address environmental and health issues. It is also heavily committed to social activism in the areas of human rights and animal testing. |

(Source: Pless & Appel 2012)

# Conclusion

New venture business creation is occurring with remarkable regularity. Observers note that despite tough times in the economy, economic downturns have often been a good time to start a new business. Great companies born in a recession include General Electric, Walt Disney, Burger King and Microsoft ('Start-up' 2012). We have been using the term 'entrepreneur' generically; however, we recognise that not all small businesses are started by entrepreneurs, and not all entrepreneurs run small businesses.

Research tells us that entrepreneurs are, in fact, slightly different from other people. For example, it has been suggested that entrepreneurial ethics may have their roots in the 'individualism' associated with entrepreneurial behaviour; that entrepreneurs are more autonomous thinkers who demonstrate a strong need for control, and are distrustful of others; and take independent action in preference to carrying out the directions of others (Spence 2000). Despite the environmental pressures, the challenges with developing a new business opportunity, and the many ethical dilemmas to which entrepreneurs are exposed, research suggests that entrepreneurs may actually exhibit moral reasoning skills at a higher level than middle-level managers or the general adult population (Teal & Carroll 1999). Further, some entrepreneurs are more attuned to the moral climate in their organisations, yet the research warns that the often harsh demands of the entrepreneurial environment can work to problematise ethical judgements and practices (Hannafey, 2003).

Entrepreneurs face unique and complex moral problems relating to many areas of their work, which we have aligned in this chapter to the critical stages of new venture development. For the start-up, there are potential issues involved in violation of intellectual property, product safety, overselling and ethical sourcing. Another critical area involves venture capital funding with its inherent ethical issues and their varying effects – depending on the level of engagement of the investor, the stage of the financing and the financing source used. Parties engaged in conflicts may also have different views on what is ethically acceptable or unacceptable. In a discussion of ethical issues in relation to investment, one tends to think mainly of the entrepreneur providing inflated or false information to potential investors, and, in doing so, deceiving them. However, the reality is that there is a power imbalance in an entrepreneur and investor relationship, and that potential unethical activity arises from the investor in relation to the interaction and exploitation of entrepreneurs.

Companies that are in a growth phase face many ethical issues, and we have discussed managing ethical relationships, exploitation of employees, nepotism, bribery, employee compensation and the temptation to inflate revenues. For the entrepreneur and the investor, but possibly less so for the small business owner, a critical question surrounds exit strategies, which may involve such activities as closure, divestment and selling the entity.

New forms of entrepreneurship are emerging. Sustainable entrepreneurship preserves nature and the community and supports life. Businesses of this type develop new products, or provide processes and services that provide economic and non-economic gain on an individual or societal level (Shepherd & Patzelt 2011). Social entrepreneurship is about pursuing opportunities in either a for-profit or not-for-profit arena, to deliver new and innovative products or services that advance social cohesion and social inclusion (Spruijt 2012). Social entrepreneurs are therefore seeking to enact social transformation. Some entrepreneurs operate within their existing organisational structures, while others create a separate governance structure to facilitate their social goals, such as a foundation (Santos 2012). All are essentially using entrepreneurial skills and techniques to make an impact in areas of social welfare. As Dunham (2010) notes, a wise entrepreneur:

- focuses on supporting individual and societal prosperity by creating new products, services and markets
- seeks to be virtuous
- draws on analytical, emotional, imaginative and moral capacities when pursuing entrepreneurial opportunities
- acknowledges a plurality of values embedded in options
- engages in creativity and critical thinking to find solutions.

## Ethics on video

**Entrepreneurial ethics** – *Zynga CEO I did everything horrible thing in the book just to get revenues* 2009, YouTube, Techcrunch, 5 November, <http://backtoreality.com/zynga-ceo-mark-pincus-i-did-every-horrible-th>.

**Moral virtues for successful entrepreneurs** – *Entrepreneurs and virtue ethics* 2011, YouTube, Entrepreneurial Ethic, 21 July, <www.youtube.com/watch?v=EE9KjACwvqk>.

See web material for more videos.

## Ethics at the movies

Here are a few movie suggestions that have content related to entrepreneurship and small business:

**A Small Act** – a Kenyan man, who received a scholarship as a high school student, founds a Kenyan foundation to pay forward the support he received, *A Small Act*, documentary, Lee, P & Soros, J.

\***Jerry Maguire** – stars Tom Cruise and Renee Zellweger. *Jerry Maguire* 1996, motion picture trailer, Crowe, C, Mark, L, Sakai, R & Brooks, JL.

\***Author's pick**

See web material for more movies.

## Ethics on the web

**TED**, Ideas worth spreading, <www.ted.com>.

**The Schwab Foundation for social entrepreneurship**, advances sustainable social inno-vation models, <www.schwabfound.org>.

See web material for more web references.

## Student exercises

See web material for answers to student short answer questions.

### Short answer questions

1. Is a certain amount of embellishment to be expected of entrepreneurs?
2. Social entrepreneurship is using the power of business to solve social problems or create public benefits that have a material positive impact on society and the environment. What might these impacts be?
3. What are some of the ethical issues experienced by start-ups?

### Experiential exercise

#### Exercise: Entrepreneur

Interview an entrepreneur and video or record the interview. Be sure to ask questions about the following issues.

1. What challenges did he or she face during the start-up phase of their business?
2. How did he or she protect their intellectual property?
3. Which ethical principles guided him or her in day-to-day ethical decision-making?
4. Does he or she think that entrepreneurs and small business owners are more ethical than mainstream business practitioners?
5. What ethical advice would he or she give to budding entrepreneurs?

# Small case

## Case: Investor exploitation

Business success is measured by a business's ability to make money, and earn profits. However, this has too often proven untrue in relation to dotcoms. Many internet starts-up make their money by raising money from investors and venture capitalists, with many investors yet to return a profit (Maury & Kleiner 2002).

**Question:**

**1.** Is this type of finance sustainable?

# Large case

## Case: Social entrepreneurship – The case of Grameen Danone Foods Ltd.* What factors have led to social entrepreneurial success in Bangladesh?

### Introduction

Entrepreneurship is essentially creative in nature. It is a matter of exploration, exploitation and initiation of new things, new ways of doing things, new methods of production, new use and new market for products or services. This tradition which was started by Schumpeter (1934) has been further developed and formalised in recent times in the work of Schmitz (1989) and King and Levine (1993), among others. On the contrary, social entrepreneurship is a relatively new academic field. However, the phenomenon social entrepreneurship as a practical field is not new (Dees 1998). The concept of social entrepreneurship has gained popularity over the past decades, but must still be considered as a new and emerging field academically (Short, Moss & Lumpkin 2009).

Though the academic interest in social 'entrepreneurship' is emerging (Mosher-Williams 2006), there is much that remains unresolved about the phenomena. Like entrepreneurship, which even today lacks a commonly understood and unifying definition (Shane & Venkatraman 2000), the term 'social entrepreneurship' has been defined from various perspectives (Dees 1998). In particular, the factors or considerations critical to successful 'social entrepreneurship' are not well known (Harman 2008). Like entrepreneurship in its early days as a field of scholarly endeavour, social entrepreneurship research is still largely phenomenon-driven. As a result, most of the studies in this academic area are based mainly on anecdotal evidence (Boschee 1995) or case studies (Alvord, Brown & Letts 2004). The amount of research in the area of social 'entrepreneurship' in Bangladesh is even worse.

This paper aims to develop our understanding of 'social' entrepreneurship, specifically the factors which ensure its success, using a case of 'social entrepreneurship' widely recognised as successful in Bangladesh. It seeks to answer the key question: **What are the factors associated with the success of 'social entrepreneurship' in Bangladesh?** Austin, Stevenson and Wei-Skillern's (2006) analytical framework for 'social entrepreneurship' has been used in this connection.

### Social entrepreneurship

Understanding the process of new value creation is focal to the field of entrepreneurship (Alvarez & Barney 2005). Traditional theories of entrepreneurship have focused on risk-orientation of individuals seeking profit (Kirzner 1973; Schumpeter 1942). The traditional definition of entrepreneurs ignores the large number of entrepreneurs who stay away from profits and create new organisations to bring about 'social' changes (Hibbert, Hogg & Quinn 2002; Prabhu 1999). These entrepreneurs, known as 'social' entrepreneurs, create new, viable socio-economic structures, relations, institutions, organisations and practices that bring about social benefits (Fowler 2000).

Despite increased interests in social entrepreneurship, scholarly research has been challenging in this field. Although definitions of social entrepreneurship have been developed in a number of different dimensions, e.g. not-for-profits, for-profits, the public sector, and combination of all three, a unified definition is yet to emerge (Christie & Honig 2006; Weerawardena & Mort 2006). For example, some definitions limit social entrepreneurship to non-profit organisations (Lasprogata & Cotton 2003), while others describe social entrepreneurship as for-profit companies operated by non-profit organisations (Wallace 1999), or organisations that create a firm at a financial loss (Baron 2007). Still others equate social entrepreneurship to philanthropy (Ostrander 2007), while some scholars prefer broader definitions which relate social entrepreneurship to individuals or organisations engaged in entrepreneurial activities with a social goal (Certo & Miller 2008; Van de Ven, Sapienza & Villanueva 2007).

Both the terms 'entrepreneurship' and 'social' do not easily lend themselves to clear definition. Although the field entrepreneurship is characterised by a number of definitions, it still lacks a unifying and common paradigm (Shane & Venkatraman 2000). It is generally agreed that entrepreneurship involves three elements: opportunities, enterprising individuals, and resourcefulness. Therefore, entrepreneurship involves concurrent existence of lucrative opportunities and of enterprising individuals (Venkatraman 1997) which is also an important characteristic of social entrepreneurship. In the case of social entrepreneurship, the term 'social' cannot be distinguished by labelling traditional entrepreneurial efforts as 'less social' or even 'non-social'. In fact, small businesses with less than 500 employees have generated the majority of employment in both developed and developing countries – certainly an important social achievement (US Department of Commerce 2001; Reynolds et al. 2002).

In sum, the disparity with respect to a unified definition of social entrepreneurship makes it difficult for the construct to claim legitimacy as a separate field of study (Burger & Luckman 1966; Neilsen & Rao 1987; Reed & Luffman 1986; Short, Payne & Ketchen 2008). It also hinders empirical research seeking to examine the antecedents and consequences of social entrepreneurship.

## *Theoretical framework*

A common criticism of the social entrepreneurship research, especially regarding the factors associated with its success, is that it lacks a systematic and theoretical focus (Harman 2008). In an effort to avoid this criticism, Austin, Stevenson and Wei-Skillern's (2006) analytical framework is adopted.

According to this framework, there are five components of social entrepreneurship. These are: opportunity, human resources, financial resources, contextual factors and the social value proposition. These components are interrelated and overlapping, with social value the central consideration.

Opportunity, according to Austin, Stevenson and Wei-Skillern (2006), is the 'initiating point' for social entrepreneurship. It represents the vision of a future desired state, different from the present, and the belief that this state can be achieved through a particular or credible path of change. One of the challenges for social entrepreneurship is ensuring that all parties share a common understanding of the nature of this opportunity.

Human resources and capital resources are the enabling variables for social entrepreneurship. Like commercial entrepreneurs, social entrepreneurs must understand the industry in which they are planning to attract resources and start their venture. Given the variety of stakeholders involved in social enterprises, and the restricted and short term nature of funding sources, this skill in dealing with individuals' needs, is especially important.

The context includes all those factors which are outside the control of management, yet have an effect on the nature and outcome of the opportunity. They ultimately shape the opportunities available to the entrepreneur (Austin, Stevenson and Wei-Skillern 2006). Managing and adapting to these contextual factors are critical consideration for social entrepreneurs.

According to Austin, Stevenson and Wei-Skillern (2006), the social value proposition is the integrated element at the crux of the framework. The case of social entrepreneurship is primarily about creating social value. To deliver this social value proposition, the social entrepreneur must ensure that all other components of social entrepreneurship – opportunity, human and capital resources and the context – are in a state of alignment.

## *Methodology*

This study provides an analysis of a particular case of social entrepreneurship in Bangladesh.

The study is inductive rather than deductive, designed to identify the factors associated with successful social entrepreneurship. Given the exploratory nature of the research, a case study approach is considered the most relevant. Case descriptions yield rich information and enable identification and assessment of unexpected patterns, which other methodologies may not reveal (Yin 1984). Justifying the above rationale, the researchers have chosen the case of a company which has been practicing social entrepreneurial venture since its inception. In addition, secondary sources of information were also accessed to develop an in-depth understanding about the phenomenon – social entrepreneurship, and to gather some information about the case company.

In this regard, the Grameen Danone Foods Ltd. has been selected which started its social venture in 2006. The rationale behind selecting this company case is that Grameen Danone Foods Ltd. was profiled in several reputable books and magazines, including several recent editions of Business Weeklies. Most recently, it has been featured as an example of a successful social enterprise in a publication prepared by the Grameen Dialogue – a publication of Grameen Trust. In 2006, Dr Muhammad Yunus, the founder and driving force behind the Grameen Danone Foods Ltd, was awarded the Nobel Peace Prize by Nobel Academy.

Out of the four established approaches to conducting researches including observation, focus group, survey, and experimentation (Kotler 1994); the present study primarily used the survey approach. Under the survey approach, interview techniques were adopted to collect data. Interviews can be administered by the use of either the mechanical

devices (tape recorder, video, galvanometer, etc.) or questionnaire (Kotler 1994). For this study, data was collected by using a mechanical device – tape recorder.

To conduct the in-depth interview, it was necessary to know how many of the management staff and employees of the Grammen Danone Foods Ltd. should be interviewed. For this purpose, a non-probability sampling technique was adopted in general, and 'judgement sampling' was used in particular. Based on the judgement of the researchers, a total of 50 management staff and employees of Grammen Danone Foods Ltd. (7 management staff and 43 employees) were chosen for interview. However, only 21 of them (5 from management and 16 from employees) agreed to participate in the interview process. This resulted in a response rate of only 42% for this study. In this connection, among the management staff, in-depth interviews were conducted with the Managing Director and four managers responsible for the day-to-day operations of Grameen Danone Foods Ltd. A total of 16 employees were interviewed, of which four employees were selected based on the researcher's judgement from four different functional departments of the company including: the dairy production unit, milk processing unit, accounts and finance unit, and sales and distribution unit. All the in-depth interviews were recorded on a tape recorder.

Moreover, as secondary sources of information several published and unpublished articles and reports; as well as archival material in the form of annual reports, performance reports, and other relevant organisational documents were consulted. Due to the exploratory nature of the study, the information collected from the interviews were not statistically calculated. Rather, an attempt was made to explore the areas or factors responsible for successful social entrepreneurship as the focus of the research to identify the factors associated with the success of the Grameen Danone Foods Ltd. The information collected from the interview were cross-checked with an established model

(Austin, Stevenson and Wei-Skillern 2006) of social entrepreneurship to see if the case company (Grameen Danone Foods Ltd.) could maintain and qualify the success factors (opportunity, people, financial resources, context and social value) for social entrepreneurship as proposed by Austin, Stevenson and Wei-Skillern (2006).

## Background

Grameen Danone Foods Ltd (hereinafter Grameen Danone) was established as a social business enterprise, which is neither a charity nor a regular business, but aims explicitly at social goals through business activities (Yunus 2006).

Dr. Muhammad Yunus, the founder of the Grameen Bank and winner of Nobel Peace Prize in 2006, along with the Grameen Bank, advocates that a social business enterprise should be non-loss and non-dividend to be self-sustaining and create surplus for expansion. Under this principle, Grameen Danone was undertaken by four Grameen Companies, namely, Grameen Byabosha Bikash, Grameen Kalyan, Grameen Shakti and Grameen Telecom and Group Danone of France whose objective was to help eradicate poverty by providing nutritious dairy food for children in the rural areas. Grameen Danone is registered under Companies Act of Bangladesh and its ownership is 50:50. The plant started production in April 2007.

Grameen Danone highlights four main objectives:

1. To offer a product with high nutritional value. Grameen Danone produces a yoghurt named Shokti Doi (yoghurt for power) which contains Vitamin A, iron, zinc, iodine and other micronutrients. The price of each 80 gm cup is TK5 (US$0.07) and a single cup fulfils 30% of children's daily nutritional requirements.
2. To create jobs. Grameen Danone also aims to help reduce poverty by buying the main ingredients of yoghurt, such as milk and date molasses from local producers, providing plant jobs and involving communities in marketing.

3. To protect the environment. The plant is operated by solar and biogas energy. Yoghurt packages are recyclable and made using poly lactic acid which is created from corn starch.
4. To be economically viable. Grameen Danone is a company which implements a social mission.

Since Grameen Danone was established with a view to conducting social business, it operates without the sole objective of maximising profit, but rather operates on a no-loss basis. This means that no shareholders should lose money from their participation in the business model; the business model should be profitable for each party and any profits (beyond the cost of capital) generated by the company will be reinvested in the growth and development of the business, in a manner that is mutually agreed upon by both parties in the contract.

The company was established with an authorised capital of US$3.67M and a paid-up capital of US$1.103M. Danone will take out only its initial cost of capital (US$500 000) after three years, and any surplus revenues after this return of capital, will be reinvested in the joint venture. Even after the capital amount is paid back, Grameen Danone will pay a one percent dividend annually to the shareholders.

## Social entrepreneurship: factors associated with success

In this section the researcher identifies and describes key themes relating to the factors associated with this case of successful social entrepreneurship. Those themes are organised around the analytical areas identified in the social entrepreneurship framework.

## The opportunity

Bangladesh has made significant progress in the area of human development for the last three decades. These achievements can be captured by the human development index (HDI). HDI measures the enhancement of people's quality of life through expanding opportunities. This is achieved by enhancing basic capabilities, such as the level of health, education and purchasing power. Bangladesh's HDI increased from 0.347 in 1975 to 0.547 in 2005 (UNDP 2007). However it is the second lowest in South Asia and the country's HDI rank in 2005 was 140 out of 177 countries (UNDP 2007). The index of underweight children under the age of five, which is one of the key indexes to monitor human development, shows 48% (UNDP 2007). They also lack access to healthy living conditions. This figure indicates that Bangladeshi children under the age of five are in the poorest health not only in South Asia but also in the whole world (UNDP 2007).

To alleviate this gap in nutrition of rural Bangladeshis, Dr Muhammed Yunus, the Nobel Peace Laureate 2006, proposed to form a joint venture food enterprise between Grameen group and French Food Company Danone. In 2006, a joint company named Grameen Danone Foods Ltd. launched the production of yoghurt in the Bogra district, 230 kilometers north of the capital, Dhaka. The mission was to reduce poverty by providing daily healthy nutrition to the poor.

Dr Yunus could see that opportunity would deliver benefits to the rural malnutrient children (who would consume the yoghurt), to individual job seekers (who would gain employment), to the local government (which could defer the decision and cost associated with malnutrition), to the community (who would have access to cheap but quality yoghurt), to government (who would reap the taxation benefits from the additional jobs created) and to the environment (through use of recyclable energy). The organisation, if successful, would also enhance the profile of Grameen Danone in the community and bring much needed income into the organisation. However Dr Yunus could also see that success of the organisation required the active support and inputs of these key stakeholder groups.

The organisation has been experiencing steady and managed growth. In the period between June 2008 and June 2009 growth has been steady: sales increased from 32 477 cups/day to 84 412 cups/ day in June 2009 and that has been mirrored in an increase in annual sales revenue to more than TK50M (US$0.7M). This growth has been resourced from within the organisation.

The organisation is currently planning for its next stage of growth and is aiming to establish at least 50 more factories in the next 10 years in various remote areas across the country. Such expansion will become inevitable if the plan to move into urban markets materialises. Larger set-ups will lead to economies of scale, thus cutting costs and lowering prices.

## Human resources

The social entrepreneur has the capacity to work across many diverse constituencies. From the outset, Dr Yunus has demonstrated his capacity to work with multiple, often diverse stakeholders. He has a rich network of government, business and community contacts in the area and is involved in a number of local committees and initiatives. His personal philosophy of 'never do anything alone' has underpinned his approach to Grameen Danone, and has been particularly important in terms of mobilising financial and other inputs to the organisation. This capacity to work across stakeholders is quite similar to Alvord Brown and Letts' (2002) notion of bridging capacity.

Related to this, Dr. Yunus has also demonstrated his capacity to understand the perspectives and concerns of those stakeholders whose support is critical for the initiative (similar to Austin *et al*'s (2006) political and relationship management skills). Yunus's reputation for fairness and trust may be a significant contributor to this capacity to build and then maintain strategic partnerships.

Dr Yunus's commitment has also seen him invest considerable resources into recruiting and developing the human resources of the organisation and supporting it to broaden its scope of activities where appropriate. In the past years, Dr Yunus had worked with various other social ventures on strategies to scale-up the initiative of developing the socio-economic condition of the poor. This long-term commitment is consistent with Alvord, Brown and Letts' (2002) notion of adaptive capacity.

There are others in the organisation, beyond the social entrepreneur, whose skills and knowledge are critical to successful social entrepreneurship. While much research on social entrepreneurship has focused on the role of the social entrepreneur, there are clearly others closely associated with the success of Grameen Danone. One of them is Md Imamus Sultan, Managing Director of Grameen Danone Foods Ltd. His knowledge of the workings of business, and his network of contacts, seem to have been instrumental in the success of the organisation.

## Financial resources

Organisation is financially self-sustaining. As can be expected from a Social Business Model aiming at the lowest price possible for its products, the economics of Grameen Danone are based on low margins with profitability depending highly on volume. Grameen Danone has invested around Tk 90M (Tk70 = US$1) so far into the plant, start-up costs and operating losses. 2008 was a very difficult year in terms of financials as Grameen Danone was hurt by the food crisis in Bangladesh, but 2009 started better. According to the volume acceleration since October 2008, Grameen Danone management estimates it will reach profitability of the Bogra plant in the course of 2010. The second plant will be built near Dhaka, the capital, by 2010 with sales starting in 2011.

## Context

Contextual factors have been instrumental in creating the entrepreneurial opportunity. In particular, economic and institutional factors at start-up gave impetus to the organisation. Perversely, it was the adverse contextual conditions in the early 2000s which were significant. With alarming unemployment rates in Bogra, there were insufficient jobs for those who wanted to work and levels of community concern about the impacts

of unemployment were high. Consequently, there was significant demand for, and interest in, potential solutions to the unemployment problem. Dr Yunus and key members of the organisation were able to present Grameen Danone as a sustainable way of creating new jobs in the society.

## Social value proposition

Grameen Danone has chosen to buy its milk from a milk cooperative of micro-farms; Grameen Livestock Foundation founded in 2000 and located 30km from the factory. Grameen Livestock Foundation is an original holistic model of agriculture; including fisheries and cow raising for small farmers. It is providing micro-credit, animal insurance, hygiene, feeding and veterinary advice, organising milk collection and cooling. In less than 10 years, the cooperative has 2000 cows, with a level of productivity twice as superior to Bangladesh's average. 7000 families are involved; 70% of them were below poverty line in 1989, now they earn about $150–300 per year. The Foundation is carrying a study to measure its social impact. At the same time, Grameen Danone Foods Ltd is starting to collect milk from local micro-farms around the plant.

## A job creating an environmentally-friendly mini factory

The Grameen Danone Bogra factory's yearly capacity is 3000 tons. Only 25% of the capacity of the plant is used at this time (May 2009). Priority is to reach plant capacity through proximity sales in a radius of 50km. This is in order to maximise penetration and level of consumption among local communities. And also to allow proximity transportation with rickshaw vans and small motorized vehicles with natural gas (CNG). Nevertheless in order to reach this capacity quicker, a decision was made to sell in Dhaka from November 2008. Twice a week a refrigerated truck carries the products to town.

The Grameen Danone plant in Bogra has been designed to rely on local labour rather than sophisticated machinery. This avoids expensive maintenance problems, enables the creation of 40 jobs and develops local competencies. The factory has been designed in an environmentally friendly way, to minimise the use of non-renewable resources. It is partially sourced with solar energy, it is collecting rain water, it is provided with a bio-digester that produces natural gas. This gas is reused to produce light for the factory. In the future, as factory volumes increase, it should be able to provide the surrounding houses with natural gas.

From *Table 8.4*, it is very clear that Grameen Danone Foods has been successful in excelling in all the areas of the social entrepreneurship framework proposed by Austin, Stevenson and Wei-Skillern (2006).

## *Conclusion*

This exploratory analysis identifies a number of factors associated with successful social

*cont. on next page*

**Table 8.4** Successful social entrepreneurship – the case of Grameen Danone Foods vs Austin, Stevenson and Wei-Skillern's framework

| Success factors for social entrepreneurship | Austin, Stevenson and Wei-Skillern's framework | Grameen Danone Foods Ltd | Comment |
|---|---|---|---|
| Opportunity | It is the 'initiating point' for social entrepreneurship that represents the vision of a future desired state through a particular and credible path of change. | Grameen Danone Foods came up with manufacturing a yoghurt (Shakti Doi) to mitigate the daily nutritional gap for children. This gap in children's daily nutrition has been successfully transformed into an opportunity for business with social welfare motive by Grameen Danone Foods. | Satisfactory |
| Human resources | Human resources are the people asset of an organisation who understand the organisation's business objectives and contribute attuned from different operational perspectives to attain those objectives. | Grameen Danone Foods took the challenge of meeting the daily nutritional requirement of the poor by providing a yoghurt solution, namely 'Shakti Doi'. The company experienced steady sales growth from 32 477 cups/day in June 2008 to 84 412 cups/day in June 2009. This steep growth in sales has been due to the company's ability to utilise the diversified skills of its company staff, managers inside the company and nationwide distributors – outside the company. Grameen Danone Foods has been successful in demonstrating its significant social impact in terms of growth in both revenues and employment. | Satisfactory |
| Financial resources | Financial resources are critical to social entrepreneurs since the sources of funds are restricted as the ventures are fundamentally committed to generating social value rather than maximising profit. Thus, for social entrepreneurs attracting outside investors or donors is a challenging job. | Since its inception in 2007, Grameen Danone Foods has invested US$1.3M in its plant and operating expenditure. Dr. Yunus, the founder of the company was successful in creating a joint venture with the French company Danone, to support the start-up cost of the company. Grameen Danone has also been successful with respect to availing the funding support of four different Grameen Companies – namely Grameen Byabosha Bikash, Grameen Kalyan, Grameen Telecom and Grameen Shakti. At present, Grameen Danone is operating under the Companies Act of Bangladesh with an ownership ratio of 50:50. | Satisfactory |
| Context | Context is referred to as the elements that work from outside the company that the company can exert no control over, yet they shape the opportunities for expansion available to the entrepreneur. | Grameen Danone Foods started its operation as a project in the Bogra district of Bangladesh. This region suffers from serious unemployment problems and the impact of unemployment is highly noticeable. Thus there has been a long lasting demand for job creation in the region. By establishing its plant in Bogra, Grameen Danone Foods has successfully been able to convert the adverse social context into a huge opportunity as a sustainable way of creating new jobs in the community. | Satisfactory |

*cont.*

entrepreneurship using the case of the Grameen Danone Foods Ltd. At the same time, the paper also explores the utility of Austin, Stevenson and Wei-Skillern's (2006) framework for social entrepreneurship in guiding the research process.

The research prompts a number of observations. Firstly, the framework for social entrepreneurship adopted by the researchers seem to be an appropriate lens through which social entrepreneurship and the factors related to its success can be viewed.

Although exploratory, the research provides some potential insights and guidance, both for policy makers and practitioners, around the key factors which may be associated with successful entrepreneurship.

The production of yoghurt by Grameen Danone has improved people's quality of life in Bogra. Firstly, local people, including Grameen borrowers, have started new jobs or expanded business opportunities. Second, the nutritional value of Shakti Doi has been promoted among local people. Therefore, it is suggested that Grameen Danone is playing an important role in human development in terms of viable economic activities and grass-roots nutrition and education. As a social business enterprise, Grameen Danone sets an example to follow and will be a theme for research in the future.

## Limitations

At the same time, the researchers provide a note of caution. The research is exploratory, and concentrates on one particular case of social entrepreneurship in Bangladesh. The social entrepreneurship framework of Austin, Stevenson and Wei-Skillern (2006) has been found to work only with a case company in Bangladesh. The success factors examined through the framework have been found to be efficiently applicable in the case of a company – which needs to be tested for universal effectiveness in the other parts of the world. Thus, the present paper does not claim the Austin, Stevenson and Wei-Skillern (2006) framework as the best, although [we] concede [it is] effective, in determining success factors for a social entrepreneurial venture. The researchers hope that future studies, both conceptual and empirical, in this area might answer to the unresolved question of success factors for social entrepreneurship. That is a topic for future and more extensive research.

## Questions:

1. With Grameen Danone, consider who the investors are and then think about who has the potential to exploit; the investor or the entrepreneur; and to what end?
2. Is it enough that Grameen Danone is creating employment in these communities? What measure should be taken to ensure employees are not exploited while in employment?
3. The social entrepreneurship model for Grameen Danone seems strong. Nonetheless, can you make a case to strengthen CSR, and what suggestions would you put forward to improve this category?

* Used with permission from: Ismail, Sohel & Hossain (2011: 159–73).

See web material for:
- answers to short answer questions
- additional student cases
- tutor resources (tutor password required)
- additional material including Ethics at the movies, Ethics in print, Ethics on video and Ethics on the web.

# Chapter 9

## Ethical issues in international business

'There are truths on this side of the Pyrénées which are falsehoods on the other.'

Michel de Montaigne, 1533–1592,

French essayist

## Chapter aim

To examine the ethical issues surrounding international business operations for multinational organisations.

## Chapter objectives

1. Identify the ethical principles most relevant to international business.
2. Contrast the alternative philosophical propositions of ethical relativism and ethical absolutism.
3. Recognise the current and emerging ethical issues in international business.
4. Explore in more detail the ethical issues of bribery and corruption.
5. Review a range of international bodies that have been established to provide ethical guidance to international business.
6. Describe what is meant by the concept of corporate citizenship and shared value.

# Ethics in the media: Exploitation of labour

Our love of chocolate has a dark side. In West Africa, impoverished conditions faced by families and farmers alike have resulted in a proliferation of child-trafficking and labour exploitation (World Vision Action 2012).

**globalisation –** the increasing technological and financial integration, and interdependence, of economies and business operations around the globe.

**flat world theory –** developed by Thomas Friedman, suggests that globalisation is not only occurring through countries and MNCs but now also through individuals and small groups.

**global ethics –** global issues, for example, the war on terror, drug trafficking, poverty, climate change and issues that cannot be addressed in individual nation states.

# Introduction

According to *The Economist*, the two most popular words used by business are 'global' and 'leadership' ('Davos ban and his defects' 2013), so it comes as no surprise that globalisation and the related activities of firms involved in international business activities come under constant scrutiny. In the 2012 IBM world survey of students and CEOs, of the top 10 issues, globalisation rated as the fourth most important issue for students, and ranked as number six for CEOs (Marshall & Kinser 2013). **Globalisation** is the term used to describe the ever-increasing technological and financial integration, and interdependence, of economies and business operations around the globe.

Globalisation and associated international trade activity continues exponentially, with multinational corporations (MNCs) consolidating their influence with the top 500 companies, accounting for 70% of world trade (Makwana 2006). With this growth, MNCs have been placed at the epicentre of criticism on globalisation, and are accused of exploiting workers, destroying the environment and abusing their economic power (Crane & Matten 2010).

While we frequently think of MNCs as the main agents of globalisation, the **flat world theory**, developed by Thomas Friedman (2006), suggests that globalisation occurs not only through MNCs but also through individuals and small groups. Technology, and particularly the internet, have facilitated and aided individuals to globalise and thus create a very small and flat world. So much so that it is probably cheaper, and quicker, for an American to have their tax return prepared in India, with an appropriately qualified accountant, than it is for them to have it prepared in the US. For the purpose of our discussion, however, we will be examining international business ethics from the perspective of organisations, not individuals, participating in transnational engagements and the common ethical issues surrounding managing in a global environment. Alternatively, **global ethics** concerns global issues (for example, the war on terror, drug trafficking, poverty, climate change), which cannot be addressed within individual nation states or single jurisdictions (Widdows 2012).

Individual cross-cultural ethics endeavours to describe the influence of culture on individual ethical decision-making (Jackson 2011) and how those ethical perceptions might change with a change in culture (McDonald & Kan 1996, 1997). World values survey data reveal that the worldviews of rich people differ systematically from those of low-income societies, across a wide range of political, social and religious norms. As such, both context and content can influence perceptions of rules, values, and ultimate ethical context, as described by Jackson (2011) in Figure 9.1.

**individual cross-cultural ethics** – endeavours to describe the influence of culture on individual ethical decision-making.

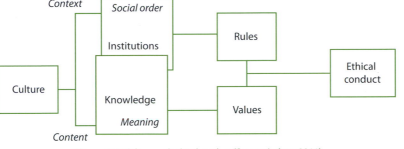

**Figure 9.1** Culture and ethical conduct (Source: Jackson 2011)

# Ethical principles in international business

There are numerous ethical principles that relate to international business; the more notable of these are:

- **Rights** – given the potential for exploitation of workers in low-wage economies, the principles of human rights and associated labour standards dominate the discussion of rights in the international context.

- **Duty of care** – closely associated with the protection of labour standards, is the duty of care that organisations have for those in their employ. This extends not only to employee health and safety but also, to international business, where there is the sensitive issue of child labour in manufacturing. Duty of care includes the safety of internationally marketed products and services.

- **Respect** – while the ethical principle of respect is commonly applied in the management of HR in global business, the principle also applies to respect for culture and associated traditions, intellectual property, respect for the environment, and the impact that a company's operations might have on ecological, social and financial infrastructures in the countries within which they operate.

- **Equity** – the desire for greater equity and fairness underpins the Fair Trade movement which endeavours to address power inequities in international trade and open access to markets on a more just and fair basis.

**rights** – the basic privileges afforded to individuals, such as basic human rights and labour standards.

**duty of care** – expectations of protection, e.g. in relation to employee health and safety.

**respect** – reference to the culture, traditions and intellectual property, and protection from ecological, social and financial damage in the country within which the multinational operates.

**equity** – fairness.

**honesty** – integrity in business operations.

**objectivity** – independence of evaluation.

**conflict of interest** – where an employee has an economic or personal interest in a transaction.

**transparency** – the need for openness in business operations.

**ethical relativism** – a school of thought that subscribes to the notion that there are no universal norms of right and wrong.

**moral relativists** – those who support the notion that what is right or wrong is decided by each person relative to the circumstances.

**anthropological relativists** – those who subscribe to the notion that what is right and wrong is determined by the moral beliefs common to that culture.

- **Honesty** – related to integrity in business operations, honesty is imperative for building trust – particularly when business is conducted between parties from significantly different cultures.
- **Objectivity** – in relation to purchasing officers, MNCs are expected to provide independent evaluations of potential worldwide suppliers in order to obtain the best possible deal for the company. The objectivity of this evaluation could, however, be compromised through inappropriate gift-giving from suppliers to purchasing officers and can create a **conflict of interest**.
- **Transparency** – the need for transparency is most notable, for example, in relation to bribery and its consequent corrupting influence. The avoidance of bribes (both the giving and receiving of facilitation payments) is imperative for an open and transparent business environment.

# Related theoretical concepts

Before embarking on a full discussion of ethical issues in the international context, it is appropriate to pause and examine the important theoretical concepts of ethical relativism versus ethical absolutism, and the related concept of hyper-norms.

## Ethical relativism

You may have heard the phrase 'when in Rome, do as the Romans do', which essentially means that when we are in another culture it is perfectly appropriate to adopt the cultural expectations and behaviours of that culture. But what if these cultural expectations involve unethical practices such as bribery, or exploitation of minors in the workplace? **Ethical relativism** is a school of thought that proposes that there are no universal norms of right and wrong. Ethicists in this camp further divide into: **moral relativists**, who support the notion that what is right and wrong is decided by each person relative to the circumstance; and **anthropological relativists**, who subscribe to the notion that what is right and wrong is determined by the moral beliefs common to that culture.

## Ethical absolutism

In complete contrast to ethical relativism is the theoretical concept of **ethical absolutism**, which is within a group of ethical theories called deontology (see Chapter 10). Supporters in this camp believe that what is right and wrong is not really up for question, as ethical decision-making is steered by moral laws that are universal, and common to us all (such as striving to be honest). Ethical absolutism suggests that there might be universal expectations that prevail across all individuals despite culture or circumstance.

Supporters of ethical absolutism point out that, despite cultural and religious differences, commonality in moral thought can be observed. For example, in Islam the term for ethics in business is *khuluq*, a term originating from the sayings and practices of Prophet Muhammad (PBUH) in the al-Qur'ân. The al-Qur'ân also uses an array of related terms which are easily aligned with moral principles such as the concepts: *khayr* (goodness), *birr* (righteousness), *adl* (justice), *haqq* (truth and right) and *taqw* (piety) (Akhter, Abassi & Umar 2011).

> **ethical absolutism** – the belief that what is right or wrong is steered by moral laws that are universal and common to all.

## Hyper-norms

Taking ethical absolutism to the next level, Painter-Morland (2008) proposes that if it were possible for all the members of a society to come together and decide what parameters or expectations should be imposed, then **hyper-norms** would represent the agreements they might develop and reasonably expect everybody to consent to. Similar to John Rawls's (1971) notion of overlapping consensus, hyper-norms, which are also sometimes called core or transcultural values, translate basic moral values into practice. Hyper-norms were initially proposed by Donaldson and Dunfee (1999), who suggest that there are global standards we all share. Hyper-norms are minute social contracts, representing the universal limits to which the members of a community agree (Painter-Morland 2008). Agreements sponsored by the United Nations (UN) or Organization for Economic Co-operation and Development (OECD), either affirming or prohibiting certain practices, are examples of the development of international hyper-norms.

> **hyper-norms** – global standards which are shared by all.

# Ethics in practice: International codes of conduct

You have recently taken on the role as CEO of a large multinational company that operates in the US, India and China. As part of your induction, you have met with the managers of all the key functional areas in your organisation. During your meeting with the Director of Global Human Resources, she brought to your attention the observation that, currently, the firm has a different code of conduct for each country in which the organisation operates. The Codes of Conduct are detailed documents that prescribe the expected ethical and professional conduct of your employees in each country location, and there is presently considerable variation across these codes.

**Question:**

1. The HR manager is interested in your views regarding whether the firm should continue this practice, or have just one code of conduct for the entire organisation. What are your thoughts?

# Ethics in practice: International bodies

Undertake an internet search and briefly summarise the main roles and missions of five of the following organisations that take your interest:
- Business for Social Responsibility (BSR)
- European Business Network for Social Cohesion (EBNSC)
- International Organisation of Employers (IOE)
- World Business Council on Sustainable Development (WBCSD)

- Prince of Wales International Business Leaders Forum (IBLF)
- Amnesty International (AI)
- Human Rights Watch (HRW)
- World Wide Fund for Nature (WWF)
- World Conservation Union (IUCN)
- World Resources Institute (WRI).

# Ethics on reflection: Live exports

Should all live animal exports from Australia be banned? What do you believe are the market implications of your views?

It is appropriate to recognise that many of the ethical issues that exist in the domestic environment also prevail in the international context. However, in the following discussion, we will focus on ethical issues that are more apparent for those operating in the international domain. Initially, we will take a broad approach by examining international governance and the issue of market collaboration, before focusing on financial considerations and product management, with a particular emphasis on corruption and bribery. We will also examine ethical issues associated with supply chain management and corporate promotion, and conclude with a descriptive discussion of corporate citizenship.

## International governance

### Cartels

The increase in internationalisation has been coupled with concerns regarding the degree of influence that large organisations may have in the countries within which they operate, and the influence they may have on the market. This influence will usually come in the form of uncompetitive behaviour such as the forming of global cartels with other players in the relevant industry, and the abuse of power. **Cartels** are agreements between two or more companies which can result in uncompetitive behaviour. For example, the airline industry has been subject to investigation by the ACCC, with a subsequent finding of wrongdoing by airlines, such as Emirates who were fined AU$10 million for participating in a freight pricing cartel with other international airlines (O'Sullivan 2012). In an effort to curb this type of activity, the ACCC has launched a campaign highlighting the dangers of collusion, particularly in the international marketplace. The campaign featured Qantas Chief Executive, Alan Joyce, whose airline was also fined both in Australia and overseas, discussing the impact of the scandal on the airline (Creedy 2012a).

> **cartel** – an agreement between two or more companies which usually results in uncompetitive behaviour.

## Abuse of power

The choking of competition might not be as orchestrated as forming a cartel, but could exist as a result of the sheer dominance of one, or a few, large and influential companies. Take, for example, Google, Apple, Facebook and Amazon, who have attracted the attention of regulators. Although it is acknowledged these big firms bring benefits to consumers and business, there is also the fear that the organisations' size overreaches, with regard to market influence, competitor acquisitions, and international market place exploitation ('Survival of the biggest' 2012). In July 2012 the European Union's Competition Commissioner was wary that Microsoft were not complying with a previous anti-trust agreement to provide consumers of new PCs with a choice of internet browsers. By offering only their own browser, Internet Explorer, Microsoft were considered to be abusing their dominant market position. They fined Microsoft US$732 million in March 2013 for this breach ('The wrong browsers' 2013).

> **abuse of power** – where a large company exerts undue influence, with the potential outcome of choking competition.

Abuse of power (© shutterstock.com/Marko Cerovac)

## Undue governmental influence

It has been questioned whether the market is truly free, or whether in fact big business and MNCs control governments (Velasquez 1998). Naturally, such influence would be moderated by the type of economy that is prevailing, whether it is an open free market economy, a command economy, or the more common mixed economy (where there is retention of

> **undue governmental influence** – the amount of influence exerted by governments.

market systems and private ownership which is modified through government regulation). In all three economic environments there is the opportunity for large MNCs to exert both political and financial pressure on governments and their agencies in order to protect their operations. This is more problematic in some sectors, such as the oil and minerals sector, where campaigners claim this industry supports predatory governments and firms who will support their position ('Corporate transparency, measuring mud' 2012).

## Ethics in practice: Bribe payer's index

The bribe payer's index, conducted by Transparency International, looks at the likelihood of firms in 19 specific sectors to engage in bribery, and exert undue influence on governments. Look up the latest Index at <http://bpi.transparency.org/bpi2011>. (Hardoon and Heinrich 2011).

**Question:**
1. Which business sectors are more prone to the practice of bribery?

## Ethics in the media: Local content censor

In a bid to secure access to global markets, Twitter has censored content where local laws are being flouted, such as in Thailand. Twitter users are disappointed by this approach which breaches freedom of expression ('Business this week' 2012b).

## Financial considerations

### Corruption and bribery

At a World Economic Forum, leaders were asked what substantial impediment developing countries faced when conducting business. They cited the biggest hurdle as corruption, with Russia leading the pack, India in second place, and China and South Africa in fifth place (Healy & Ramanna 2013). Corruption and bribery, however, are not just problems in developing nations and inexperienced transnational organisations. A 2005 internal investigation at Walmart provided evidence that executives in the company's Mexican subsidiary had paid more than US$24 million in bribes to officials, and, in 2008, Siemens settled a global corruption case for an eye-watering US$1.6 billion (Currell & Davis Bradley 2012).

In 2013, responding to criticism about lax investigations, the Australian Federal Police reopened corruption enquiries related to enforcement of anti-foreign bribery laws in Australia. Oz Minerals allegedly paid more than US$1 million to three women on the board of their joint venture partner; the women were closely related to Cambodian officials. Meanwhile, at the biomedical company Cochlear, a Portuguese newspaper suggested that seven people were involved in offering, or accepting, family holidays to Disneyland, or Italy, in exchange for influencing the decision to award an approximately US$1.2 million supply contract (Beck & Butler 2013).

# Ethics on reflection: Global corruption

For the charges and the costs of each settlement of the 10 largest global corruption cases, see <www.thefiscaltimes.com/Articles/2011/12/13/The-Ten-Largest-Global-Business-CorruptionCases>.

**Question:**
**1.** What do these cases have in common?

# Ethics in the media: Bribery

A British drugs giant had four executives, all Chinese nationals, arrested for accusations of paying nearly £500 million in bribes to doctors and officials to boost sales of the firm's treatments ('Bitter pill' 2013).

**Corruption** is commonly thought of as the misuse of entrusted powers for private gain. The term corruption, however, should be viewed as an umbrella phrase sheltering a number of undesirable business practices, of which bribery is one of the more notable activities, hence, these two terms are often coupled together. For clarity, corruption can include:

- fraud
- bribery
- conflict of interest

**corruption** – the misuse of entrusted powers for private gain.

- defalcation
- embezzlement
- nepotism
- favouritism
- trading in influence
- collusive bidding
- extortion
- illegal information brokering
- insider trading (Visser et al. 2008).

**bribery** – giving or receiving something of value to influence a transaction.

Bribery and corruption are intricately linked; the outcome of bribery is corruption, and bribery is frequently seen as a corrupt or dishonest action. Specifically, **bribery** is a practice involving payment or remuneration to a representative of a company with the specific intent to influence them into doing things that extend beyond the scope of their position or office (Adams & Maine 1998). A bribe is to offer, or even promise to offer, something of value to a person to gain an advantage. But it takes two for a bribe to take place, so, essentially, bribery is the process of giving and/or taking a bribe. Most think of a bribe as being in the form of money, but a bribe can be beyond a financial payment and could involve some element of favouritism, such as offering to facilitate employment or the entry of one's child into a good school.

**public-sector bribery** – involves government agencies and their personnel where bribes are commonly used to win public tenders, avoid regulation, speed up government processes or influence policy.

Bribery and corruption are usually examined at either the country or the individual level, with a distinction made between private and public sectors. **Public-sector bribery** involves government agencies and their personnel, where bribes are most commonly used to win public tenders, avoid regulation, speed up government processes or influence policy (Hardoon & Heinrich 2011). **Private-sector bribery** involves commercial organisations and is most commonly used to acquire new business. **Kleptocracy** is the circumstance where bribery has become the norm and is an accepted practice. The Serious Fraud Office (2013) in the UK has a list of forms of bribery that includes:

**private-sector bribery** – involves commercial organisations and is most commonly used to acquire new business.

- **illegal gratuity** – giving or receiving something of value after a transaction is completed; any acknowledgement of some influence over the transaction
- **extortion** – demanding a sum of money (or goods) with a threat of harm (physical or business) if the demand is not met
- **kickback** – a portion of the value of the contract demanded as a bribe by an official for securing the contract
- **commission/fee** – used by a company or individual to obtain the services of an agent/agency for assistance in securing a commercial contract.

**kleptocracy** – the circumstance where bribery has become the norm and is an accepted practice.

Regrettably, bribery and corruption are widespread. The Corruption Perceptions Index, conducted by Transparency International, ranks 176 countries and territories based on how corrupt their public sector is perceived to be. A country or territory's score indicates the perceived level of public-sector corruption on a scale of 0–100, where 0 means that a country is perceived as highly corrupt and 100 means it is perceived as very clean. In the 2012 study, two-thirds of the countries scored below 50, indicating a significant global problem (Transparency International 2012). Of even more relevance is the Bribe Payer's Index, also constructed by Transparency International, which ranks the likelihood of companies from 28 leading economies to win business abroad by paying bribes. Companies from Russia and China, who invested US$120 billion overseas in 2010, are seen as most likely to pay bribes abroad. Companies from the Netherlands and Switzerland are seen as least likely to bribe. The extractive industries such as oil and gas are in the business sector most prone to bribery, with companies operating in oil-rich Nigeria, having already been fined upwards of US$3.2 billion in 2010–2011 for bribery of public officials (Hardoon & Heinrich 2011).

# Ethics in practice: Consequences of bribery and corruption

Go to the Transparency International website and consider the costs and consequences of bribery and corruption. The website can be found at: <www.transparency.org/cpi2012>.

Researchers for the KPMG Global Anti-Corruption Survey 2011 (KPMG 2011), which surveyed managers in the US and UK, were alarmed to learn that seven of the 10 executives they surveyed believed that there are places in the world where business cannot be done without engaging in bribery. In a similar survey conducted by KMPG in Australia and New Zealand, very real vulnerabilities were identified, particularly in the oversight of third parties who are linked to a company and who may engage in bribery. Over half the survey respondents indicated that their organisation did not perform active monitoring of bribery and corruption payments. Almost three-quarters of respondents indicated that they do not require confirmation from foreign agents that they have complied with agency agreements in the area of bribery and corruption (KPMG 2013).

Until 1999, German companies were legally able to pay bribes abroad and to deduct bribes from their taxable income. As a consequence, the practice had become embedded in many organisational cultures and was difficult to eradicate. One such organisation, Siemens, came unstuck when they were implicated in a widespread and very public bribery scandal. The payments came to light in 2003, when auditors in a Lichtenstein bank became suspicious of an account controlled by a Siemens executive based in Greece. Siemens' offices were raided in 2006 and evidence of bribery schemes to sell power generation equipment in Italy, telecommunications infrastructure in Nigeria, and National Identity Cards in Argentina, resulted in substantial fines (Löscher 2012).

# Ethics in the media: Bribery

In 2012, the Australian Federal Police initiated an investigation into the Australian company, Tenix, in relation to its dealings in Asia between 1999 and 2008, to determine whether bribes were paid to foreign officials; specifically in relation to a government contract for six search and rescue vessels (McKenzie & Baker 2012).

The negative consequences of bribery and corruption can be felt at both the national and organisational level. *KPMG global anti-bribery and corruption survey 2011* indicated that the presence of corruption in a country can discourage foreign investment, with three in 10 companies forfeiting business in a country based on bribery and corruption issues (KPMG 2011). At the organisational level, it has been observed that bribes lead to more bribes (Surowiecki 2012) and are a financial burden for a firm. In addition, for firms found guilty of violations, the penalties can be harsh. The median fine for bribery or corruption violations under the US Foreign Corrupt Practices Act in June 2010 was US$7 million (Currell & Davis Bradley 2012). Stiff penalties also apply to persons who knowingly turn a blind eye, so it is especially important to ensure that personnel posted overseas do not become implicated in 'dodgy deals' (De Jong, Tu & Van Ees 2012). In addition to financial penalties, companies stand to lose competitiveness and employee trust. In the bigger picture, these actions diminish the value of capitalism (Healy & Ramanna 2013). Foster School of Business (2011) reports that in Karpoff, Lee and Martin's research, of the 95 US companies fined for international bribery violations, the repercussions have included: lowered market value, share price declines of 16%, increased financing costs and a higher incidence of mergers and bankruptcies.

Corruption prevention is not easy. At the international level, Business Principles for Countering Bribery were developed in 2002 by Transparency International and Social Accountability International (SAI). The 2009 edition charted new territory by placing greater emphasis on public reporting of anti-bribery systems, and recommending that enterprises commission external verification of their anti-bribery program (Transparency International 2009b). The OECD Convention established an international standard for compliance with anti-corruption, and was the first major international treaty established specifically to address 'supply-side bribery' by sanctioning the briber (Business Anti-Corruption Portal 2011). Concerned about the seriousness of the problems and threats posed by corruption to the stability and security of societies, the UN also has a Convention against Corruption (UN Global Compact 2003). The purposes of these conventions are to promote:

- measures that prevent and combat corruption more efficiently and effectively
- facilitation of international co-operation and technical assistance in the prevention of and fight against corruption, including asset recovery
- integrity, accountability and proper management of public affairs and public property.

A further international effort has involved a group of 20 leading economies (the Group of 20 or G20) committed to tackling foreign bribery by launching an anti-corruption action plan. As a result of these measures, companies are at even greater risk of legal and reputational damage resulting from failure to comply with the anti-corruption standards (Pieth, Low & Cullen 2007).

At the national level, many countries have their own anti-bribery legislation. For example, the (UK) *Bribery Act 2010* now criminalises private-sector bribery, and the US has longstanding legislation in the form of the *Foreign Corrupt Practices Act 1977* (FCPA), which legislates against bribery for all American companies regardless of their country of operation. In an effort to curb corruption, Bill Browder, an American-born financier, has proposed what is referred to as the **Magnitsky Solution**, and has run a campaign throughout the world to make it harder for individuals to benefit from the fruits of their corruption. The circumstances underpinning the changes were brought to light by a Russian lawyer, Sergei Magnitsky, who uncovered a US$230 million fraud involving suspect tax refunds, which officials had stolen from a foreign investment fund. The officials arrested Magnitsky, who afterwards died in prison in 2009. The fund's founder, Bill Browder, has named 60 people involved both in the fraud and the persecution of Magnitsky.

The campaign has gathered momentum in G20 countries. New legislation proposed in the UK suggests if evidence of wrongdoing can be produced to the crown prosecutor's office, a visa ban or asset freeze can be recommended, extending sanctions beyond national borders, and minimising corrupt officials enjoying unethical action rewards ('Visa sanctions, face control, asset freezes and visa bans give rich countries useful weapons against wrong-doers' 2012).

Encouraging the possibility of reducing corruption, in an analysis of the anti-corruption activities of 24 transition countries in the period between 1999 and 2002, Steves and Rousso (2003) observed that countries with low levels of **administrative corruption** were more likely to adopt intensive anti-corruption measures. They also suggested that by launching high-profile anti-corruption initiatives, governments may be more likely to heighten managers' perceptions of the problem rather than to actually reduce the impact of corruption on firms.

At the organisational level, policies, rules and procedures restricting bribery are reportedly increasing, with 69% of international firms in 2012 (up from 47% in 2009) having appropriate mechanisms to prevent bribery ('Corporate transparency, measuring mud' 2012). In a discussion of how integrity can be embedded in a culture in order to shape employee behaviour, particularly in relation to offering bribes or defrauding the company, Currell and Davis Bradley (2012) have observed five key factors:

1. managers take appropriate action when misconduct occurs
2. employees are encouraged to discuss misconduct and not fear retaliation
3. employees are treated with respect
4. employees are held accountable
5. a high level of trust exists.

> **Magnitsky Solution** – international changes that have seen new sanctions for corruption beyond national borders.

> **administrative corruption** – paying bribes for services in relation to the implementation of regulations.

Managing the risk of bribery is usually a combined effort of senior management, supervisors, HR and auditing departments. The most common strategies are:

- anti-bribery and corruption policies and procedures
- awareness-raising communication
- training
- whistleblower mechanisms
- ethical hotlines
- monitoring the use of third-party payments
- auditing of common corruption indicators.

# Common corruption indicators

- Abnormal cash payments
- Pressure exerted for payments to be made urgently or ahead of schedule
- Payments being made through a third-party country – for example, goods or services supplied to country 'A' but payment is being made, usually to a shell company, in country 'B'
- An abnormally high commission percentage being paid to a particular agency; it may be split into two accounts for the same agent, often in different jurisdictions
- Private meetings with public contractors or companies hoping to tender for contracts
- Lavish gifts being received
- An individual who never takes time off, even if ill, or never takes holidays, or insists on dealing with specific contractors him or herself
- Making unexpected or illogical decisions accepting projects or contracts
- The unusually smooth process of cases where an individual does not have the expected level of knowledge or expertise
- Abuse of the decision process or delegated powers in specific cases

- Agreeing to contracts not favourable to the organisation – either because of the terms or the time period
- Unexplained preference for certain contractors during tendering period
- Avoidance of independent checks on the tendering or contracting processes
- Raising barriers around specific roles or departments which are key in the tendering or contracting processes
- By-passing normal tendering or contracting procedures
- Invoices being agreed in excess of the contract without reasonable cause
- Missing documents or records regarding meetings or decisions
- Company procedures or guidelines not being followed
- Payment of, or making funds available for, high value expenses or school fees (or similar) on behalf of others
  (Source: © Serious Fraud Office)

# Ethics in the media: Bribery in India

A November 2012 poll indicated that 88% of Indians expected to pay bribes when registering a property, and 76% indicated a bribe was required to procure or renew a factory licence. The 'I Paid a Bribe' scheme (www.ipaidabribe.com) commenced in August 2010 for people in India to anonymously share bribery experiences. Within six months, some 5000 bribery reports had been logged (Healy & Ramanna 2013).

## Money laundering

The UN Convention against Corruption specifically mentions the links between corruption and other forms of crime, in particular, organised crime and economic crime – including money laundering. **Money laundering** is the process by which illegally obtained funds are given the appearance of having been legitimately obtained. It is estimated that AU$1.5 trillion worth of illegal funds are laundered worldwide each year (AU$200 billion in the Asia–Pacific region), which is more than the total output of an economy the size of the UK (AUSTRAC 2008). The funds are largely from drug trafficking, although a significant amount of corporate money, particularly from tax evasion, is included. Fake businesses known as 'fronts' are often used in the money laundering process, as are intermediaries, such as lawyers and bankers, who often play a critical role in the money laundering process. For example, in December 2012, the Hong Kong Shanghai Banking Corporation (HSBC) paid a whopping US$1.9 billion in fines for money laundering (Silver-Greenberg 2012). And, in March 2013, India's three largest private banks – ICICI Bank, HDFC Bank and Axis Bank – were accused of indulging in money laundering both within the country and outside with an online portal (Gulf News 2013).

**money laundering** – the process by which illegally obtained funds are given the appearance of having been legitimately obtained.

The Australian Transactions Reports and Analysis Centre (AUSTRAC 2008) have indicated that there are severe economic and social consequences of money laundering, including:

- financial systems are undermined as money laundering expands the black economy which undermines credibility and transparency
- crime is expanded as money laundering encourages criminal behaviour and results in illegal funds becoming legal tender through profits being reinvested into businesses
- reduced government revenue (taxation).

**tax avoidance** – the avoidance of meeting legitimate tax obligations by an organisation.

## Tax avoidance and transfer pricing

The recent global financial crisis proved that the existing arrangements for the governance of global markets are flawed, and there are serious gaps in cross-border supervision, the over-sight of global financial institutions and the monitoring of risk originating in the banking sector (Avgouleas 2012). Causing particular unease to multiple governments, is the issue of taxation and transfer pricing of firms engaged in transnational business. Google and other tech multinationals, like Apple and Microsoft, have long been criticised for accounting practices which have seen the companies wire money around the globe to ensure they pay less tax than other companies (Polites 2013). In January 2013, the UK's Prime Minister, David Cameron, indicated that aggressive tax avoidance was a problem for all countries, not just Britain, and publicly rebuked multinational organisations that are active in tax avoidance (Armitstead 2013).

# Ethics in the media: Tax evasion

Switzerland's oldest bank closed in January 2013 after pleading guilty to tax evasion of US$1.2 billion which was hidden in secret offshore accounts. Wegelin Bank agreed to pay US$57.8 million in restitution to the US authorities. They also fraudulently sold non-American clients to an Australian bank before being indicted (Neate 2013).

**transfer pricing** – the transfer of something of value, and/or the termination or renegotiation of existing commercial arrangements within a multinational enterprise group that has a dramatic impact on the allocation of a multinational's taxable profits between operating countries.

MNCs that practise tax avoidance have become more aggressive over the past decade. Some firms based in high-tax regimes, create numerous offshore subsidiaries or shell companies, each time taking advantage of the tax breaks permitted. They also claim expenses and losses in high-tax countries and declare profits in jurisdictions (tax havens) with a low or no tax rate (OECD 2013a). A study published by ActionAid indicated that 98% of the firms in the FTSE100 Index regularly use transfer pricing, and have at least one subsidiary in a tax haven. This promotes a popular strategy of transferring ownership of a multinational's main intellectual property to a subsidiary in a tax haven, such as the Cayman Islands, Bermuda or Barbados, and then charging other subsidiaries in higher tax countries for the use of that intellectual property (reported in 'Wake up and smell the coffee' 2012).

**Transfer pricing** is the general term used to describe either a transfer of value, such as assets, or the termination or renegotiation of commercial arrangements within an MNC that impacts the taxable profits of the company in the countries from which it operates (OECD n.d.). In a classic example of transfer pricing, Google has said that for their main money spinners – advertising and search products that are developed offshore – they consider it appropriate to transfer profits to where they are derived. The Federal Australian Government, however, has responded with new transfer pricing laws ('0.4%' 2012).

## Ethics in the media: Tax avoidance

In 2013, an investigation revealed that six UK water companies were avoiding millions of pounds in tax by taking high-interest loans through the Channel Islands' offshore stock exchange and loading themselves up with debt. The disclosure coincided with a public outcry about legal tax avoidance and public spending cuts (C Moore 2013).

An OECD study commissioned by the G20 to address Base Erosion and Profit Shifting (BEPS) found that some MNCs use strategies that allow them to pay as little as 5% in corporate taxes when smaller businesses are paying up to 30%. These practices enable MNCs to eliminate or reduce their taxation on income, which gives them an unfair competitive advantage over smaller businesses. In addition to the loss of public good, income tax avoidance can also hurt investment, growth and employment (OECD 2013a).

Extensive legislation governing transfer pricing exists for countries that are members of the OECD. This legislation calls for MNCs to pay a 'fairer' share of tax to the country where the service or good is used or consumed. This is a consumption tax concept found in indirect taxes such as GST or VAT. The incorporation of this concept into the international basis of allocating tax would be a significant shift, and could, however, only ever be achieved after a prolonged period of multilateral negotiation (Stacey 2013).

Help in the ethical management of tax evasion is at hand through the Association for the Taxation of Financial Transactions for the Aid of Citizens (ATTAC) which is concerned with international tax, tax havens and currency speculation. The OECD also has *Transfer Pricing Guidelines for Multinational Enterprises and Tax Administrations*, a useful tool which focuses on transfer pricing issues and the common disputes that occur between taxpayers and tax administrations (OECD 2013b). An example of one of the measures being undertaken at a global level to combat tax evasion is Project Wickenby, an international cross-agency task-force. Coordinated with agencies in the USA and UK, the taskforce sets out to find and punish those individuals committing tax evasion and significantly targets lawyers and accountants who help facilitate these crimes (Bleby 2013).

## Ethics in practice: Transfer pricing

Look up the country profiles on transfer pricing legislation and practices for OECD member countries and see what legislation exists in your geographic area. (For details of Transfer Pricing legislation, see <www.oecd.org/ctp/transfer-pricing/transferpricingcountryprofiles.htm>.)

# Supply chain management

## Ethical sourcing and Fair Trade

**ethical sourcing** – the inclusion of explicit social, ethical and or environmental criteria into supply chain management policies, procedures and programs.

MNCs are rethinking their supply chain management, as the cost of transporting goods half-way around the world has risen sharply, coupled with the accompanying environmental and equity concerns. In international business, a key competitive advantage can be gained through effective management of the supply chain, such as sourcing raw materials from low-cost providers and adding value through cheaper production in third-world locations. Supply chain management is, however, fraught with the potential for exploitation and abuse. As a consequence, **ethical sourcing** – the practice of explicit supply chain management policies covering social, ethical and/or environmental criteria (Crane and Matten 2010), as practised by businesses such as The Body Shop – has been gaining momentum with an added focus on Fair Trade.

**Fair Trade** – engaging producers, distributors and consumers in the eradication of exploitation and the pursuit of trading conducted fairly and in accordance with Fair Trade practices.

The International Federation for Alternative Trade (IFAT) (which is now called the World Fair Trade Organization (WFTO)) sees the purpose of **Fair Trade** as an international trading partnership which encourages trade using dialogue, transparency and respect. The purpose is to contribute to equitable and sustainable development though improved trading conditions for marginalised producers (WFTO 2009). Fair Trade organisations actively support producers, raise awareness, and campaign for change in conventional international business (WFTO 2009).

Fair Trade (© shutterstock.com/LHF Graphics)

The Fair Trade movement, which has been in existence for many years now, is attempting to address inequalities by modifying the structure of world trade. Originating in the Netherlands, the initiative has been replicated around the world with organisations such as:

- Fairtrade Labelling Organisations International (FLO)
- European Fair Trade Association (EFTA)
- The Fair Trade Foundation in the UK
- Max Havelaar in France
- The Fair Trade Association in Australia.

Fair Trade is rooted in ethical consumerism (Salignac 2011) and is underpinned by concepts of justice; advocating international trade exchange based on fairness and equity. While attempting to quantify Fair Trade in terms of market size is problematic (Moore 2004), there are many prominent business examples, such as the UK-based non-government organisation Oxfam, which were one of the first organisations to engage in Fair Trade, and Traidcraft, which have been active in Fair Trade since 1979. The sector is no longer niche and now offers multiple products in a variety of consumer groups, such as bananas, chocolate, coffee, tea, jewellery and clothing. Fair Trade labels are now finding themselves in competition with each other and being distributed through more traditional channels. More importantly, Fair Trade has been a catalyst for mainstreaming ethical issues within trade and business practices (Redfern & Snedker 2002). See Table 9.1 for the key principles and goals of Fair Trade.

## Ethics in practice: Fair Trade

**Question:**

**1.** What is the history of Fair Trade and who are the key players?

**Table 9.1** Key principles and goals of Fair Trade

| Principles of Fair Trade | |
|---|---|
| 1. | creating opportunities for economically disadvantaged producers |
| 2. | transparency and accountability |
| 3. | capacity building |
| 4. | payment of a fair price |
| 5. | gender equity |
| 6. | improved working conditions |
| 7. | improved environmental practices |
| **Goals of Fair Trade are to** | |
| 1. | improve equity and development opportunities for producers |
| 2. | protect human rights |
| 3. | raise consumer awareness |
| 4. | improve conventional international trade practices |

(Source: Fairtrade Diocese of London n.d.)

## Offshoring

Offshoring is where an organisation may take specific jobs or entire functions and have them undertaken in another country. The most common practice is the provision of production or services, such as call centres in the Philippines, manufacturing in China, accounting and IT in India. Also called **outsourcing** (sending work to outside contractors, both domestically and internationally) and **body shopping**, offshoring has engendered a number of sensitivities around the practice. General Electric, for example, were one of the pioneer companies of

**outsourcing** (also known as **body shopping**) – sending work to outside contractors, both domestically and internationally.

**offshoring** – where an organisation takes specific jobs or entire functions and has them conducted in another country.

**re-shoring** – the return of previously offshore activities.

**offshoring** with service centres established in India in 1998. The company has, however, since returned production to America and this **re-shoring** is evident in a number of companies including Google, Apple, Ford and Caterpillar ('Welcome Home' 2013).

The differential advantages of offshoring have narrowed, and domestically there are increasing pressures to support local labour and ethical labour practices. Some companies were initially attracted to offshoring because it involved cheaper labour, fewer workers' rights, limited environmental restrictions, and economies of scale. However, many are now rethinking the proposition due to a narrowing of the wage gap, intellectual property controls, lack of innovation, increases in transportation costs, and a hardening of expectations around offshore corporate social responsibilities. Companies such as Nike, Gap, Walmart and Disney have been in the media firing line following unseemly disclosures about supply chain practices and use of sweatshops and child labour. This has forced transnational companies to embrace social corporate responsibility as standard business practice (Redfern & Snedker 2002).

# Ethics in the media: Offshoring

The Australian discount department store, Kmart, which are part of Wesfarmers Limited, stopped production in Bangladesh with Ratul Fabrics Limited, and employees were asked to leave the premises within 70 minutes of structural defects being identified ('Kmart boycotts factory' 2013).

**ethical labour management** – the adherence to international standards for the treatment of labour.

## Ethical labour management

When MNCs operate in a number of geographic locations, disparities in human resource (HR) practices can arise. For example, in Singapore in 2012, employers welcomed mandatory paternity leave as only 50% of the companies operating there were already providing it (Sing 2012). In collaboration with Amnesty International, the Business and Human Rights Resource Centre tracks allegations and responses to misconduct in relation to labour practices in more than 3500 companies worldwide. Early in 2012 Apple was lambasted by labour activists for using the supply manufacturer Foxconn, and for failings around labour practices resulting in suicides at their facilities. The CEO of Apple promptly went on a highly-publicised tour of a Foxconn factory in China, subsequently pledging to improve workers' conditions there ('Apple' 2012).

The Fair Labour Association (FLA) undertook an independent review, discovering supply chain issues, such as the cases of 74 children under the age of 16 who were employed in one company; children using forged identity papers; young women being subjected to mandatory pregnancy tests; and bonded workers whose wages were confiscated to pay debts (Garside 2013).

However, it is not just HR practices that are involved. For example, it has been suggested that, in Bangladesh, the West's insatiable demand for cheap clothing is part of a chain that has led to cuts in standards of construction of factories, failure to audit the structural safety of buildings, and the near non-existence of labour laws for the workers and those that do exist are being less than rigorously applied ('Cheap clothing has price beyond its tag' 2013).

Interestingly, there is apparently a strong link between worker deaths from accidents and the political connectedness of corporate executives. Fisman and Wang (2013) studied corruption and cronyism (political connections) in Chinese companies and found that, on average, the rate of worker deaths is five times greater at connected companies than at other companies.

In addition to the FLA, international organisations such as Human Rights Watch (HRW), are dedicated to protecting the International Labour Organisation's (ILO) Fundamental Principles and Rights at Work (which are derived from the UN Universal Declaration of Human Rights, adopted in 1998). A useful set of guidelines for the ethical treatment of workers has been provided by the Ethical Trading Initiative Base Code. See Table 9.2.

## Ethics in the media: Unethical labour

The leader of the Bangladeshi Garment Workers, Amirul Haque Amim, was in London in 2013 to chide UK retailers for unethical behaviour. He claims that they are sourcing their products from Bangladesh, but are not paying the workers enough to lift them out of poverty ('Bangladesh workers' leader targets London Fashion Week' 2013).

## Ethics in practice: Cultural recognition

A Muslim employee wears a veil covering her face as her religious beliefs instruct her husband be the only male to see her face. Due to a former employee breaking into an office, the company requires all employees entering the building to present photo ID to the male security personnel. (Bisouq 2013).

**Question:**

**1.** What is your response to this proposal?

**Table 9.2**  Ethical treatment of labour –international standards

| | |
|---|---|
| 1. | Employment can be freely chosen with no discrimination |
| 2. | Employees have freedom of association, and the right to collective bargaining |
| 3. | Working conditions will be safe and hygienic with controlled working hours |
| 4. | No harsh or inhumane treatment is allowed |
| 5. | Child labour shall not be used |
| 6. | Living wages are paid |

(Source: Ethical Trading Initiative, n.d.)

**child labour/ child exploitation** – work that deprives children of their childhood, their potential and their dignity, and that is harmful to their physical and mental development.

## Child labour

UNICEF provides some interesting facts about child workers. For example, every day one out of every six children is involved in child labour that damages them mentally, physically, or emotionally (UNICEF 2008). Specifically, as UNICEF states:

- there are 22 000 annual deaths of children from work-related accidents
- children make up 40–50% of people in bonded labour
- whether children work in homes, or on the streets, they are not afforded legal protection
- 69% of child labourers work in agriculture, hunting, fishing, or forestry; 9% in manufacturing; 8% in retail trade and hospitality; and 7% work in community services.

**child slavery** – where children are forced into work and exposed to hazards while being denied an education.

The terms **child labour**, or **child exploitation**, are used to describe the situation where children are being used as workers and, in doing so, are sacrificing their education and childhood. **Child slavery** is considered more severe, where a child is forced into work and so denied education and often exposed to hazards. Child labour exists where children are deprived of their childhood, their future potential, and their dignity, as the work they endure tends to be physically, mentally, socially or morally harmful to their development. The work also interferes with their schooling by either depriving them totally, obliging them to leave school prematurely, or requiring them to juggle both school and work commitments (ILO 1996–2013).

MNCs that employ children, or that use suppliers which do, are culpable for charges of child labour. Obviously, these conditions are found where there are high levels of poverty and families require their children to generate money. A way of facilitating labour without child exploitation is to ensure they are of legally employable age, have safe conditions, fair wages, attend school and have limited work hours (Costello 2012).

## Ethics in the media: Child labour

In Laos, World Vision has found children tricked into working on fishing boats. One child was forced to work for 20 hours, and beaten if he did not follow orders (Costello, 2012).

The jeans company Levi Strauss is an MNC that have effectively negotiated the tension between subcontractors' use of child labour, the imperative for families to earn income through having their children in work (not allowing them to work could push them into begging or prostitution), and adherence to international standards. As there was often no proof of age, Levi's ensured their subcontractors hired a physician to identify underage children. Such children were then removed from the factory; however, they were still paid wages while attending school, and their school tuition fees, uniforms and books were paid for. Once the children met the minimum age criterion, they were rehired (Treviño & Nelson 2007).

## Dumping

In international trade, **dumping** occurs when a company exports a product to be sold at a lower price in the foreign market than the price charged in the domestic market. Depending on export volumes, it has the effect of endangering the financial viability of manufacturers or producers of local product, resulting in job losses (Investopedia 2013). While it is legal, this practice is not necessarily ethical as it is deemed to be unfair competition and encourages the use of tariffs and quotas. In Australia, manufacturers' complaints that foreign suppliers were selling goods below cost resulted in an inquiry into the need for a specialist agency to police the dumping of cheap imports by subsidiaries selling products at a loss ('Dumping enquiry' 2012).

> **dumping** – the exporting of a product by a country or company to be sold at a price that is lower in the foreign market than the price charged in the domestic market.

## Data protection

Recent years have seen growing concerns around **data protection** and the fundamental right to personal privacy. The Australian Government amended the *Privacy Act* in 2012 to respond to these concerns by limiting the personal customer information which can be sent offshore; this has had ramifications for international call centres, data processing centres, as well as cloud storage facilities (Lee & Wilkins 2012).

> **data protection** – the protection of personal by restricting companies from selling customer information offshore.

Data protection (© shutterstock.com/Slavoljub Pantelic)

The ethical issues for businesses in relation to international data protection centre on:

- technological advances resulting in the collection of new types of personal information
- the ability to not only collect information but also to have information sources that can be traced and located

- new capacities to analyse and re-contextualise personal data
- differing transnational controls and varying standards for data protection around the globe
- new opportunities for commercial use of personal data (Mendel et al. 2012).

## Ethics in practice: Data protection

In 2003, millions of Latin American residents' personal information was sourced from electronic databases by the Bush Administration (via a third-party company, ChoicePoint). It seems the information was sourced without the knowledge of the Mexican and Colombian governments, or the citizens involved (Joyce et al. 2003).

**Question:**

1. Can we argue that this happened for the betterment of society, and, by way of justification, that it was necessary in the war against drugs, or is it a case of blatantly unethical behaviour?

Organisations that are committed to protecting the online privacy of their clients are developing policies and procedures, and are likely to use a set of privacy policy principles such as those articulated by Mendel et al. (2012), which include:

- no surprises
- real choices
- sensible settings
- limited data
- user control
- trusted third parties
- user access
- security
- transparency of government sharing
- providing remedies
- privacy across the board.

## Ethics in the media: Data protection

Sony's customers had their data compromised in April 2011, when the 'Playstation Network', linked to Playstation consoles, was shut down after an attack that compromised up to 77 million customers' details. Worryingly, Sony took more than a week to inform users, and customers were unknowingly exposed on the internet for that period (Stuart 2011).

For more information on data protection and privacy, see Chapter 3.

# Product management

## Product development

 While it is anticipated that marketers will alter product features and pricing for different international markets, ethical questions begin to arise when the price differentials cannot be justified (fortunately for the consumer, internet shopping is levelling the playing field) or the product is in some way defective (that is, past its use-by date) or unsafe. Another minefield of potential exploitation is in product testing. Anxiety has been expressed surrounding the practice of pharmaceutical companies undertaking clinical trials in developing nations where, because of high levels of illiteracy, it is deemed to be easier to gain 'informed consent'. This is found to be particularly problematic in India, where evidence supports claims that doctors are being paid generous commissions by pharmaceutical companies to enlist patients. Impoverished Indians across the country are being signed up to clinical trials they do not understand and about which they remain ill-informed of potential consequences. Using illiterate people and children as guinea pigs for multinational drug companies in uncontrolled trials has resulted in the deaths of 2644 Indians since 2005, and 11 972 patients suffering adverse effects, but, appallingly, only 39 families have been compensated (Doherty 2013).

**product development** – products are differentiated for different markets, with price and quality normally being points of differentiation.

**counterfeit product** – a product manufactured with the intention of deceiving customers into believing they are purchasing the genuine article.

# Ethics in practice: Product safety

Imagine that a cure for HIV has been developed, but unfortunately it has been found that a batch of the drug is contaminated. The Minister for Health in an African country, however, is still willing to purchase the drug, knowing the side-effects, and making assurances they will disclose these side-effects to patients (Bisouq 2013).

**Question:**
**1.** What would you advise in this situation?

## Product piracy

When considering the ethical issue of product piracy, confusion may arise from the inter-related terminology such as counterfeits, look-alikes, sound-alikes, fakes, and knock-offs. There is also a large grey area surrounding unauthorised sales of overruns by legitimately contracted manufacturers. To clarify, **counterfeited products** are produced with the direct intention of deceiving a customer, while a **pirated product** is one where the consumer is aware that the product is copied and is a fake (McDonald & Roberts 1994).

**pirated products** – a product which the consumer is aware is copied and is a fake.

It has been acknowledged that counterfeits of products covered by intellectual property laws, have negatively affected international business (Globerman 1998). Intentionally copying brands to steal their product sales is **product piracy** (Jacobs, Samli & Jedlik 2001). It is, essentially, theft and has ramifications for both companies and countries. Husted (2000) found, for example, that software piracy is significantly correlated to a country's gross national product per capita, as well as income, equality and individualism. We largely think of music, software, clothing and video productions as the principal objects of product piracy; however, the practice is evident in all domains of manufacturing, including pharmaceutical items, alcohol and industrial goods as well as services. Historically, we have thought of Asia as the epicentre of product piracy, but the International Intellectual Property Alliance indicates the priority areas have shifted to:

> **product piracy** – intentionally copying the name, shape or look of another product to steal product sales.

- Ukraine
- Argentina
- Chile
- China
- Costa Rica
- India
- Indonesia
- Russian Federation (International Intellectual Property Alliance 2013).

# Ethics in practice: Product piracy

Undertake an internet search to locate statistics regarding the extent and the effect of product piracy in your country.

While alternative views of product piracy have been presented – that is, that product piracy is a precursor to economic development, facilitates the transfer of technology and satisfies market demand (McDonald & Roberts 1994) – the detrimental effects are well known. The negative effects of product piracy include:

- direct costs – loss of sales
- indirect costs – job losses
- reputational damage – brand damage from inferior products
- higher prices – incorporating the cost of monitoring
- health and safety consequences – the impacts of fake and or defective products and materials.

# Ethics in the media: Counterfeit goods

British retail giants, Sainsbury's and Boots, recalled thousands of tubes of Colgate toothpaste after discovering they were counterfeit. Although customers were assured there was no risk to their health, it was interesting to note that even Sainsbury's could be deceived, as they believed they were purchasing from a reputable source (Planer 2009).

The issue of product piracy has plagued organisations and sectors for many years and is closely linked to the issue of violation of intellectual property. Piracy is generally bad for business. It can undermine sales of legitimate products, deprive a company of valuable intellectual property and tarnish its brand ('Look for the silver lining' 2008).

According to an Ernst & Young (2008) report on product piracy, two-thirds of companies are affected and, despite the prevalence, very few companies are implementing systems to evaluate the direct and indirect damage. Fortunately, consumers are aware of the dangers, with the risk of accidents brought about by the processing of inferior quality materials identified by 67% of respondents. However, this does not appear to discourage usage because, despite these concerns, more than one in four consumers in Western Europe are purchasing counterfeited and pirated goods. Interestingly, 39% of those under the age of 35 would buy counterfeit goods, but that figure falls to just 18% for the over-55s.

# Ethics in practice: Film piracy

The Motion Picture Protection Association (2008) works internationally with government agencies to reduce film theft. Their efforts focus on local initiatives to increase consumer awareness and highlight legislative issues around the problem. View some of their public awareness campaigns at <www.mpaa.org>.

# Ethics in the media: Fake products

The Museum Plagiarius in Solingen, Germany, exhibits more than 350 product units from all sectors; that is, both the originals and their direct imitations. The museum runs guided tours, seminars and consumer events aimed at educating the industry and consumers about the extent of the problem and the dangers incurred by fakes (Aktion Plagiarius 2013).

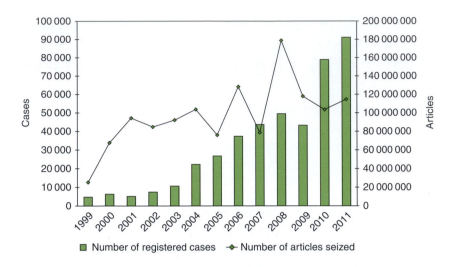

**Figure 9.2**  Number of registered cases and articles of intellectual property infringement in Europe
(Source: Taxation and Customs Union © European Union, 1995–2013)

## Intellectual property violation

**intellectual property violation** – the infringing of intellectual property rights such as trademarks, copyrights and patents.

Every year, the European Commission publishes details of the number of items suspected of infringing intellectual property rights conferred by/registered under trademarks, copyright and patents (see Figure 9.2). Statistics published in July 2012 demonstrated a clear upward trend in the number of shipments detected, with the 114 million detained articles having an estimated value of more than €1.2 billion. Alarmingly, medicines were at the top of the list of seized articles (24%), posing justified concerns over the potential risks for public health and safety (Taxation and Customs Union 2013).

**corporate espionage** – theft of trade secrets, theft of intellectual property, or copyright piracy.

Intellectual property infringement prevention is primarily concentrated on the interests of authors and inventors, but has also come to incorporate international trade interests (Kuppuswany 2009). At the extreme level, it could involve **corporate espionage** which is the use of dubious means, often online, to facilitate the theft of trade secrets and intellectual property. As with other major international ethical issues, the protection of intellectual property is managed at the international, regional, national and organisational level. International conventions for the protection of industrial property (such as the universal copyright convention) have been in existence for many years, while, at the regional and national level, statutes are more focused. In December 2012, the European parliament voted to create a unitary patent which would be automatically recognised in 25 EU countries, and be overseen by a new court. This would do away with the need to translate patents into many languages ('Yes, Ja, Oui, No, No' 2012).

At the national level in the US, there are a raft of proposed legislative statutes to regulate intellectual property violation, restrict counterfeiting and control online piracy. One of the more recent was the proposed US *Stop Online Piracy Act* (SOPA), which would have authorise the closure of whole sites hosting copied material. Opponents of SOPA support the Online Protection and Enforcement of Digitial Trade Act (OPEN). Any proposed legislation is intended to work in conjunction with the Protect Intellectual Property Bill (PIPA), an update of the Combating Online Infringment and Counterfeits Bill (COCA), which also failed to pass. PIPA aims to close down websites used to copy works (Blackwell 2012).

Intellectual property (© shutterstock.com/B-A-C-O)

# Ethics in practice: Corporate espionage

Discuss some of the more notorious cases involving big profile MNCs (see <http://imgsecurity.net/corporate-espionage-the-how/> and <www.businesspundit.com/10-most-notorious-acts-of-corporate-espionage> for cases).

**Question:**
1. What are some of the more common methods of corporate espionage/spying?

# Ethics in the media: Emerging markets

Governments in emerging markets would like their citizens to have access to better drugs; however, price points are a dilemma for the international pharmaceutical industry. A Swiss pharmaceutical company has cut the price of four drugs to the Indian market; rebranding and repackaging the product to make it more affordable ('Drugs and emerging markets' 2012).

# Ethics in practice: Cybersquatting

You are the marketing manager for a company about to embark on a major international expansion in three countries concurrently. You have just discovered that in two of those countries someone has already registered the domain names that you were intending to use. You suspect that, in one instance, the domain name holder is merely cybersquatting.

**Questions:**

1. Describe what alternative options you could pursue.
2. What is your intended future strategy.

# Corporate promotion

## International promotion

**international promotion** – the utilisation of multiple tools (i.e. advertising, public relations, etc.) to facilitate the dissemination of key messages to target audiences in more than one country.

**International promotion** could be defined as utilisation of multiple tools (that is, advertising, public relations, etc.) to spread key messages to target audiences in multiple countries, acknowledging that there are country differences in how promotional stimuli are perceived and interpreted (Douglas & Craig n.d.). It has been acknowledged that promotional tools, specifically advertising, have been useful in a cross-cultural context for creating awareness of AIDS, improving health, and promoting wellbeing. However, critics have also been quick to point out that in addition to the more obvious cultural insensitivities, advertisers are able to influence the contents and framing of mass media and messages (often Western value-based) and that this influence is substantial in countries where unsophisticated media relies on MNCs for a large portion of promotional revenue (Alozie 2011). For example, Omnicom places more than US$37 billion of advertising globally with half of their revenue coming from outside the US (Douglas & Craig n.d.).

## Advertising

**advertising** – securing the attention of the public in relation to a product or business through various means (broadcasting, print, etc.) to promote goods and services.

Consistent with many of the issues that can be identified in a national context, ethical issues in **advertising** in the international setting centre on key themes:

- **Promotion of harmful, unsafe or unhealthy products** – the introduction of fast food, the heavy hand of tobacco promotion, and apprehension around alcohol products, are all examples of ethical issues in relation to introducing products into new markets. Primary areas of concern relate to religious sensitivities, health concerns, and the spending of low levels of discretionary income.
- **False or exaggerated assertions** – deceptive claims regarding a product or service, and or deliberate miscommunication. In 2012, Qantas was fined by the US Department of Transport for their deceptive international website ads (Creedy 2012b).

- **Offensive content** – the use of sexual themes, endorsement of sexism and the use of stereotypes. In the Islamic culture it is not permissible to use emotional appeals, sex appeal, and romantic language. It has been noted that the level of offensiveness caused by advertisements of controversial products was found to be significantly associated with religious perceptions and the nature of the advertising's appeal (Akhter, Abassi & Umar 2011).
- **Culturally inappropriate content** – advertising content that is inconsistent with the cultural values or expectations of the local market, or imposes foreign values and tastes. This could also include fairly obvious translation blunders; for example, the American Dairy Association used their 'Got milk?' campaign in Mexico, only to find that the Spanish translation of that phrase meant 'Are you lactating?'
- **Inadequate labelling** – leading to product overuse or misuse through inadequate product labelling.
- **Exploitation of vulnerable individuals** – advertising to children, the elderly and the illiterate.

# Ethics in the media: International promotion

A 2009 'Dairy Milk' chocolate campaign run by Cadbury (UK) to promote the company's Fair Trade policies in Ghana was not well received. In fact, they were accused of racism and perpetuating colonial stereotypes of African people (Dugan 2009).

# Ethics in practice: Cultural blunders

Review the literature for examples of where cultural blunders have occurred when taking one advertising campaign from a specific country location to another country.

## Gift-giving

In the KPMG Global Anti-Bribery and Corruption Index, excessive **gift-giving** was seen by more than half of the respondents as an area of vulnerability (KPMG 2011). Giving or accepting a gift (a physical product, hospitality or a service) in a business setting is appropriate, so long as it does not create a sense of obligation, or the appearance of obligation (Bennett 2003). With gift-giving, there are two elements to be cognisant of: the first is overt and

**gift-giving** – usually seen as appropriate provided the gifts do not unduly influence the recipient.

excessive provision of gifts which could evoke significant external criticism and could be in violation of the legislation. The second is a more subtle form where, while unintentional, the gift could be perceived as inappropriate and could unduly influence the recipient.

Gift-giving (© shutterstock.com/The Last Word)

**inappropriate gift-giving** – offering or receiving an undue reward which goes beyond the consolidation of a business relationship, and is designed to influence the recipient to act contrary to the known rules of honesty and integrity.

**Inappropriate gift-giving** is deemed to be offering or receiving an undue reward which goes beyond the consolidation of a business relationship, and is designed to influence the recipient to act contrary to known rules of honesty and integrity (Stell 2011). Most international companies have policies surrounding gift-giving, and require declarations to ensure transparency around both the giving and receiving of gifts.

# Ethics in the media: Gift-giving

Disney's Chairman and CEO travelled to China in April 2012 to meet the Mayor of Shanghai, and the Shanghai Communist Party Secretary, where he presented them with a gold-painted model of Cinderella's castle. The US Securities Exchange Commission (SEC) issued letters to various movie studios enquiring about inappropriate gift-giving and payments (Reingold 2012).

# Ethics in practice: Gift-giving

Your organisation has a strong stand on bribery and gift-giving. However, in anticipation of a business trip to Shanghai, you spoke with a Chinese colleague. He impressed on you the importance of building relationships in China and the practice of *guanxi*. You are now somewhat caught between your corporate policies and what appears to be a common cultural phenomenon.

**Questions:**
1. What is *guanxi*?
2. How do you resolve this dilemma?
3. What are some of the policy guidelines of other international firms?
4. How does the duty of fidelity relate to gift-giving (see Table 1.1 for a definition)?

# Corporate citizenship

While not responsible for causing most of the significant world problems, business has increasingly been told that it must play a constructive role in addressing global challenges (such as poverty, hunger, child mortality, environmental degradation and AIDS); thus suggesting that business not only has a responsibility to help ameliorate many of the problems, but also that it may be the only institution capable of effectively addressing some of the issues (Smith et al. 2010). The **Base of the Pyramid (BOP) model** refers to the lowest group in the socio-economic demographic pyramid of the poorest people inhabiting the globe (estimated at 3–4 million), and there are suggestions that efforts that can be undertaken by the private sector as a means to address this profound global poverty.

Corporate citizenship (© shutterstock.com/DeiMosz)

**Impact sourcing** is an entrepreneurial means of addressing global poverty. Similar to **microfinancing**, which is common in low-income circumstances where a range of financial services are provided (for example, banking, credit, finance, insurance) for emerging small businesses, impact sourcing aspires to create meaningful work which puts money in the pockets of the people and communities most in need. In practical terms, it involves hiring people at the base or bottom of the pyramid to perform digital tasks such as transcribing auto files and editing product databases. Essentially, it outsources business processes, and boosts economic development. Companies such as Sanasourse, Digital Divide Data and Desi Crew are all organisations which act as middlemen to secure contracts for digital services from large companies by dividing the work into small tasks (micro-work) to be sourced from developing regions through a web-based interface. All tasks are done at a reduced cost while, at the same time, building skills in developing regions. Not only addressing poverty, it has also been suggested that top executives of MNCs have the power to combat emergent market corruption (Healy & Ramanna 2013).

## Shared value

The concept of **shared value** involves the creation of economic value in a way that creates value for both society and business. Essentially, rather than pitting business interests against societies, it is suggested the two can complement each other (Glasgow 2012). One example

**Base of the Pyramid model (BOP)** – refers to the lowest group in the socio-economic demographic pyramid who are the poorest people inhabiting the globe.

**impact sourcing** – the outsourcing of business processes by hiring people to perform digital tasks, such as transcribing audio files and editing product databases, where all tasks are done at a reduced cost while, at the same time, building skills in developing regions.

**microfinancing** – where a range of financial services are provided for emerging small businesses in low-income environments.

**shared value** – the creation of economic value for both society and business.

is the Australian company, Silver Chef, a kitchen equipment leasing firm founded in 1986. The business, led by their founder, Alan English, has a 35% stake in Silver Chef, of which 40% is in a foundation. The dividends on that block of shares deliver at least AU$1 million a year to philanthropic work. The intention of the foundation is to work towards stated poverty alleviation goals. There is an indication that having a purpose behind the generation of the profits has a positive effect on staff morale. Thus, embedding of motives behind profit creation throughout the business makes an example of shared value creation, rather than merely corporate responsibility. This business approach is particularly valued by the younger workers (Glasgow 2012).

## Environmentalism

**environmental-ism** – protecting the environment from pollution and destruction.

One the most pressing world problems is the need for environmental protection. Once again, this can be viewed at international, national, industry and corporate levels. At the international level are the CERES Principles, launched in 1989 by the Coalition for Environmentally Responsible Economies (CERES). They provide a 10-item code of corporate environmental conduct.

There is also the Basel Convention, an international agreement between 168 countries addressing the difficulties associated with hazardous waste. At the industry or sector level, each industry may also have its own guidelines. For example, the banking industry has the UNEP statement by banks on the environment and sustainable development, and the insurance sector has the UNEP statement of environmental commitment for the insurance industry. Multinational companies are increasingly being held accountable for the environmental impact that their operations create, and there is low tolerance for exploitative practices. However, cynicism still prevails where some MNCs are suspected of using their financial power to weaken, rather than improve environmental restrictions in the countries in which they operate.

# Conclusion

Global business activity is increasing dramatically. In 1980, the United Nations Centre for Transnational Corporations (UNCTC) published a study of the world food and beverage industries, identifying 180 companies that dominated highly-segmented markets at that time. Today, at least half of those companies occupy roughly the same market power. Twenty years ago, the top 20 pharmaceutical companies held approximately 5% of the world prescription drug trade; today, the top 10 companies control well over 40% of the market; 90% of new technologies, and product patents are controlled by global corporations; while the top 500 companies account for 70% of world trade (Judge 2001). Many think that international business is predominantly the domain of large MNCs; however, the internet has created a more level playing field where smaller businesses are now able to reach international markets with ease.

In international business, as we have seen, many ethical issues are common to the domestic environment; however, in the international context, circumstances are increasingly complex, particularly for organisations operating in underdeveloped countries where there is limited skilled labour, and financial and economic restrictions prevail (Treviño & Nelson 2007). MNCs can find themselves operating in circumstances where the logistical structure is not consistent and there are diminished expectations in regard to the treatment of products, HRs and the environment. Similarly, the cultural differences encountered could involve expatriate managers in practices that are inconsistent with their values, such as the giving of bribes.

It would be fair to say that the ethical practices of organisations operating in the international environment are under increased scrutiny, and large areas of the operations are subject to auditing, inspection and critique. Sensitive to charges of undue influence, many MNCs are now actively reporting on their operational practices and ensuring transparency in their supply chain, labour practices and political involvement.

In conclusion, conflicts can often occur between the values of home and host nations, and investing organisations need to consider whether it is possible to conduct business successfully in that environment without resorting to host practices (Macfarlane 2012). It is important to also consider the individual difficulties faced by expatriate managers adjusting to a new cultural environment and its inherent behavioural expectations (Treviño & Nelson 2007). While the extent of corporate responsibility businesses assume for transnational challenges – from pollution and currency stabilisation to AIDS, food security, environmentalism, human rights and freedom of speech – are a matter of individual company discretion, these are nevertheless significant issues that need to be addressed in a national and global context.

# Ethics on video

**Bribery** – *Black money* 2009, documentary, Frontline, 7 April, <www.pbs.org/wgbh/pages/frontline/blackmoney/view>.

**Flat world theory** – *The world is flat* 2009, YouTube, Yale University, 29 April, <www.youtube.com/watch?v=53vLQnuV9FY>.

See web material for more videos.

## Ethics at the movies

Here are a few movie suggestions that have ethical content related to international business:

*****Blood Diamond** – nominated for 5 Oscars, the film is based in Sierra Leone and revolves around the business of conflict, diamonds, and child soldiers. *Blood Diamond* 2006, motion picture trailer, Zwick, E, Herskovitz, M, King, G, Weinstein, P & Gorfil, G.

**The Chocolate Industry** – a documentary about the not so sweet side of chocolate; child labour and trafficking. *The Dark Side of Chocolate* 2012, documentary, McGraw-Herdeg, A, Denmark.

*****Author's pick**

See web material for more movies.

## Ethics on the web

**Association for the Taxation of Financial Transactions for the Aid of Citizens (ATTAC)**, an international movement working towards social, environmental and democratic alternatives in the globalisation process, <www.attac.org>.

**Ethical Trade Initiative**, an organisation working to improve the working conditions of people producing consumer goods, <www.ethicaltrade.org>.

See web material for more web references.

## Student exercises

See web material for answers to student short answer questions.

### Short answer questions

1. What are the pros and cons of globalisation?
2. Select a multinational organisation and present their code of conduct and policy guidelines in relation to their international involvements.
3. Translational issues can always be a bit of problem in international business. What are some of the more notable marketing examples demonstrating cultural insensitivity?
4. In June 2013, the US State Department released its annual report on trafficking of humans. What are some of the countries that are particularly subject to problems of illegal immigration and forced labour?

5. What are the main goals of Fair Trade?
6. What role can the Agreement on Trade Related Aspects of Intellectual Property Rights (TRIPS) agreement have in redressing inequities in the availability of drugs in developing nations?

## Experiential exercises

1. The Altagracia factory in the Dominican Republic was a former sweatshop but now pays a living wage. They have tackled not just poverty, but also increased productivity, reduced absenteeism, and boosted consumer support (Townley 2012). Undertake further research on Altagracia, at <http://altagraciaapparel.com/story/FAQ>.
2. Find some specific photographic examples of product piracy. A good starting point is <www.emap.com> and <www.stop-piracy.ch>.

# Small case

## Case: Gift-giving

You work in a branch office of a multicultural company. Your head office has quite specific rules about the giving of money or gifts to potential customers, however, you perceive that it will be difficult to conclude business in your area without giving something to those with whom you negotiate. Subsequently, you are considering appointing a sub-agent in order to assist in market development, and also to let the agents handle any of the 'under the table' activities.

### Questions:
1. What are your thoughts on this proposal?
2. Do you think it would be endorsed by your head office?
3. What are the risks you face if you proceed?

# Large case

## Case: Rolls-Royce's bribery and corruption infringements

As a global company, Rolls-Royce provide power solutions for the civil aviation, defence, aerospace, marine, and energy industries (Rolls-Royce 2013a). Until recently, Rolls-Royce; a company which is over 100 years old; have had an unblemished business record (Buss 2013).

Since 2006, however, a disgruntled former employee has made bribery and corruption allegations against Rolls-Royce in public forums under the pseudonym, 'soaringdragon', alleging bribes were paid to intermediaries in Indonesia

*cont.*

*cont.*

and China in order to secure civil aircraft engine business (Hoyos 2012). Activities include:

- Indonesia – whistleblower, Dick Taylor, claims in the early 1990s Tommy Suharto was given a Rolls-Royce car and US$20 million to secure Garuda Airlines to buy Rolls-Royce engines (Binham & Hoyos 2013)
- China – Rolls-Royce won a US$800 million contract with Air China in 2005
- China – Rolls-Royce won a US$2 billion deal with China Eastern Airlines in 2010 (Staff reporter 2013).

Despite the public allegations, Rolls-Royce only commenced an internal investigation when the Serious Fraud Office intervened in 2012 (Hoyos 2012). The results of the internal audit showed that there were indeed bribery and corruption concerns with the intermediary overseas markets (Rolls-Royce 2012). Rolls-Royce cooperated fully with the UK's Serious Fraud Office (SFO), and the US Department of Justice (DOJ) (Hoyos 2012), and, based on the inquiry, implemented the following internal changes:

- strengthened compliance procedures
- instituted a Global Ethics Code and an Intermediaries Policy
- expanded the compliance function
- appointed an independent senior figure, lawyer Lord Gold, to review compliance procedures (Rolls-Royce 2012; Rolls-Royce 2013b).

These changes were in addition to the existing frameworks put in place under the guidance of the Ethics Committee (Rolls-Royce 2010) as a response to the UK's *Bribery Act 2010*.

Just as it seemed the scandal was about to die down, in May 2013, it was reported that Mark King, President of Aerospace in Singapore, tendered his resignation. Speculation was rife there may be a link to King's departure and the bribery and corruption matter (Ruddick 2013).

Despite the scandal, in 2012, Rolls-Royce delivered record car sales; growth in the aerospace unit; a 24% rise in full-year profits (Buss 2013); and saw shares in the company rise 30% since December 2012 (Ruddick 2013). Interestingly, the scandal has seemingly had no negative repercussions on their brand. Given the stagnating European economy, it is expected that aerospace companies will be looking to the Asia–Pacific region to meet 35% of their market deliveries (Milmo 2013). It is questioned how the divisions in that region will achieve this goal if the intermediaries are no longer in use.

In the interim, Rolls-Royce still has a cloud over their heads until the matter is settled with the SFO and the US DOJ. SFO wants to sanction Rolls-Royce, but there are political sensitivities at play as Rolls-Royce are a well-respected manufacturing giant in the UK. It will be interesting to see whether the SFO will accept a civil settlement, particularly given some of the allegations are over 20 years old (Binham & Hoyos 2013).

With harsh bribery laws in both the UK and US, companies will need to think carefully about their governance to avoid future scandals. Transparency International UK (2012) believes the defence sector's global corruption costs US$20 billion per year, while revenue projections are believed to be US$500 billion.

**Questions:**

1. What actions are seen to be subverting the Bribery Act?
2. Compare and contrast the Rolls-Royce scandal to the Siemens scandal in terms of the leadership strategies and the action they implemented.

See web material for:
- answers to short answer questions
- additional student cases
- tutor resources (tutor password required)
- additional material including Ethics at the movies, Ethics in print, Ethics on video and Ethics on the web.

# PART 3

# Business Ethical Theory and Analysis

# Chapter 10

## Ethical theory

'There may be times when we are powerless to prevent injustice,
but there must never be a time when we fail to protest.'
Elie Wiesel, 1928–,
professor and political activist

## Chapter aim

To gain an appreciation of normative philosophy and ethical theory as a precursor to developing skills in ethical decision-making.

## Chapter objectives

1. Recognise the value of ethical theory in relation to ethical decision-making.
2. Defend the role of normative philosophy in the arena of business ethics.
3. Distinguish between normative ethical theory and descriptive ethical theory.
4. Describe the key theories that are deemed to be teleological/consequential theories.
5. Identify the theoretical streams within the deontological school of thought.
6. Outline the relationships between the ethical principles of duty, rights and justice.
7. Demonstrate what role virtue-based ethics has for business managers.

# Ethics in the media: Rights

An inquiry which looked at the rights of the freedom of the press and the right to privacy was undertaken in 2012–2013 by Lord Justice Leveson, in the UK. As a result, *The News of the World* closed, and it was highlighted that greater privacy protection is required (see 'Guarding the guardians' 2012).

## Introduction

There is a reason that we have left ethical theory until a later chapter in the text. It is that most people's eyes tend to glaze over and they stifle a yawn when you mention theory, but this need not be the case because ethical theory can be useful when we find ourselves face to face with an ethical situation in our own workplace. Moral philosophy acts as a pivotal theoretical foundation for our understanding of applied ethics. Ethical theories also provide a number of alternative perspectives for both evaluating and resolving ethical issues that may arise in the business context. A good way to think of the variety of ethical theories is to imagine them as different lenses through which we can view an ethical circumstance.

If you have visited the optometrist for an eye examination for new glasses, you will be familiar with the process: you wear a rather heavy frame on your face and the optometrist then slips various lenses in and out of the frame until he or she finds the combination of the left- and right-hand lenses to correct the deficiency in your sight. Each time the optometrist alters the lens, we see the lettercard in front of us in a slightly different way. Ethical theories are like the lenses used by the optometrist: each theory, or lens, will give us a slightly different perspective of what we are looking at. A good understanding of ethical theories will therefore enrich our viewing and interpretation of the ethical dilemmas we may face, in real life, through our own experiences or through those of friends and colleagues. Ethical theories also assist in the analysis and decision-making associated with hypothetical cases that have ethical content, which we may be exposed to during the course of study. It is therefore imperative that this normative foundation be examined as a prefatory step in the development of ethical decision-making. There is agreement that mastery of ethical theory provides the necessary tools to engage in intelligent personal and social analysis of moral issues (De George 1986).

An examination of moral philosophy and accompanying theoretical paradigms can help with providing:

- a historical perspective on relevant moral debates
- familiarity with concepts commonly articulated in the course of moral arguments
- sophistication in using the language of moral discourse

- assistance in the theoretical analysis of current business issues
- the ability to reflect and resolve ethical issues that we may face.

By looking at the existing body of ethical theory, we are able to gain insights into the various distinctions and categories of moral thought. The more familiar you are with ethical theory and the traditions of ethical reflection, the greater your skills will be for examining, and hopefully resolving, ethical dilemmas. It is therefore the intention of the following discussion to provide insights into the divisions and arguments within each of the theoretical foundations of ethics, and to consider how theory might be used, thereby linking theory to practice. See Table 10.1 for more on ethical theory from different perspectives.

**Table 10.1** Ethical theory from a range of perspectives

| Ethical theory perspective | Description | Type of theory |
| --- | --- | --- |
| Normative ethical theory | • Relates to thought and conduct and what ought, or should, happen<br>• What one ought to do | • Ethical egoism<br>• Utilitarianism<br>• Kantian theory<br>• Duty<br>• Rights<br>• Justice |
| Descriptive ethical theory | • Describes actual practice and theorises from this practice<br>• What is | • Kohlberg's theory of moral development<br>• Principal agency theory<br>• Stakeholder theory<br>• Social contracts theory<br>• Ethical relativism |

## Normative philosophy

For business ethics, the closest theoretical links are with normative philosophy. Broadly, **philosophy** is the study of thought and conduct, and **normative philosophy** (philosophical ethics) is the study of 'proper' thought and conduct; that is, how we all ought to behave. Why is normative philosophy more valuable to us when resolving ethical circumstances than, say, psychology? While psychology has a contribution to make, essentially, social scientists tell us *how* people feel about matters of right and wrong, whereas, the philosopher reflects on how people *ought* to feel about right and wrong.

Normative philosophy is concerned with the formulation and defence of the basic moral norms that govern the moral dimension of our lives; that is, presenting moral principles and standards that can be employed by people to follow. Normative philosophical discussions have utilised ethical theory to support these discussions and to address societal circumstances.

**Ethical theory** centres on such traditions as duties, justice, equity, truth and rights. Consequently, when we face an ethical dilemma, one's moral reasoning is facilitated by an understanding of normative philosophy and relevant ethical theory. The application of theory to specific circumstances is where theory is tested and possibly refined and improved. Applied normative philosophy and associated ethical theory are therefore

**philosophy** – is the study of thought and conduct.

**normative philosophy** (also known as **philosophical ethics**) – is the study of 'proper' thought and conduct; that is, how we all ought to behave.

**ethical theory** – centres on such traditions as duties, justice, equity, truth and rights.

concerned with assigning principles of normative philosophy to specific moral problems that appear in certain areas of human life. Such problems include those that are peculiar to individuals, to a particular profession or to particular institutions in society. Hence, normative philosophy and ethical theory can be applied by managers, those in the accounting profession, or business organisations in general. Ethical theory will not tell us specifically *what* to do, but will guide us in the deconstruction of an ethical situation, and in doing so can shed light on alternative courses of action.

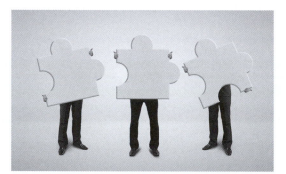

Ethical theory (© shutterstock.com/Peshkova)

# Ethics in reflection: Ethical theory

Consider the moral issue of how we distribute rewards and public recognition in society, and the potential impact it has on the social fabric of society. For example, do you consider it fair to lavish significant rewards on CEOs, who are rightfully due bonuses through contractual arrangements, as their companies go bankrupt, while ordinary workers at the same company are laid off? What is the appropriateness of athletes making millions of dollars, while nurses and teachers receive relatively low wages (Woodruff 2011), and is this fair?

**rationalist ethical theories** – theories based on rational arguments, such as utilitarianism and justice.

## Alternative perspectives of ethical theory

When we deliberate about an ethical circumstance, we can draw not only on normative philosophy but also on a wider array of theories. Given the large volume of theories, there is a natural desire find some kind of structure to help categorise them. Some make the distinction between rational and non-rational theories of ethics, with **rationalist ethical theories** being

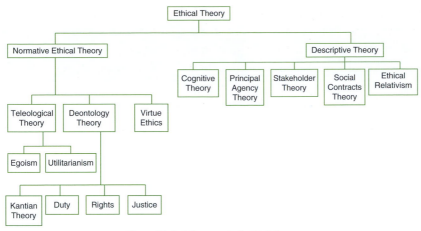

Figure 10.1 shows a framework with the following structure:

- **Ethical Theory** branches into:
  - **Normative Ethical Theory** which branches into:
    - **Teleological Theory** → Egoism, Utilitarianism
    - **Deontology Theory** → Kantian Theory, Duty, Rights, Justice
    - **Virtue Ethics**
  - **Descriptive Theory** which branches into:
    - Cognitive Theory
    - Principal Agency Theory
    - Stakeholder Theory
    - Social Contracts Theory
    - Ethical Relativism

**Figure 10.1** A framework of ethical theory

based on rational arguments (such as utilitarianism and justice), and **non-rationalist ethical theories** (such as intuitionism and feminism) incorporating other beliefs into the deliberation process (Robinson & Dowson 2012).

Alternative perspectives on ethical theory (© shutterstock.com/Cartoonresource)

Another broad categorisation that we believe would be of value and upon which this chapter is based, is the distinction between normative and descriptive theory (see Figure 10.1). **Normative ethical theory**, as alluded to above, is theory that relates to thought and conduct and what ought to, or should, happen. Examples are: ethical egoism, utilitarianism, Kantian theory, duty, rights and justice. **Descriptive ethical theory** tends to describe actual practice and theorises from this practice. Examples of descriptive ethical theory are cognitive theories such as Kohlberg's theory of moral development, principal agency theory, stakeholder theory, social contracts theory, and ethical relativism (these theories have been covered in earlier chapters). A simple way of remembering the distinction between normative and descriptive theory is: normative ethical theory is – what one ought to do; and descriptive ethical theory is – what is.

For this chapter, we will be concentrating primarily on normative ethical theory, which is best described diagrammatically (see Table 10.2).

**non-rationalist ethical theories** – theories that incorporate other beliefs, such as intuitionism and feminism, into the ethical deliberation process.

**normative ethical theory** – a theory that relates to thought and conduct and what ought to, or should, happen.

**descriptive ethical theory** – describing actual practice (referred to as 'what is'), and deriving theory from this practice.

**Table 10.2**  Overview of normative ethical theory

| Key schools and theories | Weaknesses | Key players |
|---|---|---|
| **Teleology/consequentialism: outcomes/ends-focused** | | |
| The moral worth of action is determined by the consequences of the action. | | |
| **Ethical Egoism**<br>An action is taken where the outcome will be beneficial to the individual and with self-interest prevailing. | The impact on others is de-emphasised which could result in unfair circumstances.<br>Chaotic consequences if everyone followed this approach. | Epicure<br>Aristotle<br>Thomas Hobbes |
| **Utilitarianism**<br>An action is considered morally sound where the consequences lead to the maximum benefits and minimum harm for all. | Measurement difficulties with alternatives outcomes requiring separate and time-consuming analysis of utility.<br>Decisions could be unfair. | John Locke<br>Jeremy Bentham<br>John Stewart Mill |
| **Deontology/non-consequential: means-focused** | | |
| Non-consequential, in that the outcome is not the main driver of the decision, but one's duty or principles will drive the decision. | | |
| **Kantian Theory**<br>An action is morally right if the reason is one that they would willingly have everyone act on (i.e. do unto others as you would have them do to you).<br>An action is morally right as long as you are not treating others as a means to an end. | Potentially contradictory with many counter-examples that erode universality and no priorities to guide actions.<br>Ambiguity over what is meant by a means to an end. | Immanuel Kant |
| **Duty**<br>An action is morally right which fulfils one's duty and associated obligation(s), for example, duty of care, fiduciary duty, parental duty. | Potential conflict that can develop over conflicting duties.<br>Too narrow and prescriptive | Norman Bowie |
| **Rights**<br>An individual's entitlement.<br>Rights commonly presented by moral theorists are the right to; free consent, privacy, freedom of conscience, free speech and due process. | Determining which rights prevail: legal, contractual or moral rights.<br>The need to prioritise rights to resolve in some decisions, e.g., right to life and right to choose in the abortion debate. | John Locke<br>Immanuel Kant |
| **Justice**<br>Theories of justice call upon the decision-maker to act with equity, fairness and impartiality.<br>With distributive justice/egalitarian justice, burdens and benefits are distributed fairly to all members of society. | The contrast between utility and justice. A decision outcome may be the fairest but it may not provide the best outcome for all.<br>There would be no recognition of personal effort and a dilatory individual could receive an equal share with others. | Aristotle<br>David Hume<br>John Rawls |
| **Virtue ethics** | | |
| Places the focus on the individual, rather than an outcome, and is dependent on the character traits of a virtuous individual. | | |
| **Character Values**<br>A decision-maker would refer back to the rules and values that guide their character. | There are variations in what is considered virtuous, and difficulties in determining common good. There is a long list of values to choose from.<br>Each individual decides what is right and wrong for them; that is, moral authority lies within them. | Alasdair MacIntyre |
| **Divine Command Theory**<br>One's actions and moral decisions are attributed to the will of God. | This assumes one knows the will of God. | |

# Teleological or consequential theories

The first, and most prominent, area of normative philosophy is teleological or consequential theory. Teleology is derived from the Greek word *telos*, which means a goal, result or consequence. Consequential theories hold that the moral worth of action is determined solely by the consequences of the action, subsequently, the appropriateness of an action or practice is judged by whether the consequences are good or bad.

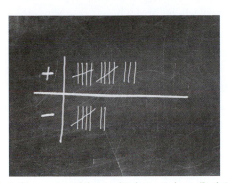

Teleological/consequential theories (© shutterstock.com/Roobcio)

## Ethical egoism

**Ethical egoism** originated in Epicure's (341–270 BC) and Aristotle's (384–322 BC) Nicomachean ethics (2009), and was later developed by Thomas Hobbes (1588–1679) (1968). In its current form, ethical egoism proposes that when a moral agent (a manager) is faced with an ethical dilemma, egoism will place oneself as the primary recipient of any beneficial outcomes that may accrue from the decision; one's duty is therefore to one's self and self-preservation. How that decision affects others is irrelevant. Normative ethics presupposes that one ought to behave in accordance with certain principles, and, with ethical egoism, this is embodied in the principle that an individual will promote their own self-interest. A manager, entrepreneur, businessperson or organisation would therefore place a lens in front of a circumstance and make a decision that is in the best interest of that individual or organisation.

Ethical egoism can come in different forms. Distinctions are made between **act egoism**, in which the egoism of a person aims to maximise utilities without limit; and **rule egoism**, where a person aims to maximise utilities through constrained cooperation with others (Mulholland 1989). This relates to the work of Adam Smith (1723–1790) (Sutherland, in Smith 1993), who suggested that self-interest actually leads to economic cooperation.

While there is clear evidence of this lens in operation, the arguments against ethical egoism as a useful decision tool rest primarily on the chaotic consequences if everybody followed this approach. It is suggested that human beings are rational enough to perceive the negative consequences if everybody pursued ethical egoism and self-interest. The outcome would be a particularly dysfunctional society and, because of this, ethical egoism should be avoided.

**ethical egoism** – where a person or entity pursues what is in their own self-interest.

**act egoism** – in which egoism of a person aims to maximise utilities without limit.

**rule egoism** – where a person aims to maximise utilities through constrained cooperation with others.

Ethical egoism, however, suggests that both parties in a conflict have a moral right to pursue their own interests exclusively. But what happens if both parties in the conflict do this? By adhering to this moral right and to ethical egoism, a conflict would never be resolved. A further question relates to who actually is the moral agent and primary recipient of this self-interest. Who is the self? Is it an individual or a company? Often, when we look at stakeholders, and particularly a variety of stakeholders such as customers, suppliers, the unions, there could be varying perspectives of self-interest. However, morally challenging situations are frequently more complicated and go beyond self-interest; so, while this theory is easy to understand, it is not particularly helpful when it comes to ethical decision-making.

## Utilitarianism

**utilitarian theory** – proposes that an action is permissible and morally sound if it leads to the greatest balance of maximum benefits and minimum harm.

**Utilitarian theory**, originating from the philosopher John Locke (1632–1702), proposes that an action is permissible and morally sound where the outcome or consequences lead to the greatest balance of maximum benefits and minimum harm. An outcome or consequence is often called happiness (writers with economic traditions tend to favour the term 'utility', or use synonymous terms such as pleasure or happiness). The net cost–benefit approach is also one that appeals to the structured approach of business decision-making. Utilitarianism, however, differs from the economic concept of cost–benefit analysis in that consideration must also be given to alternative actions such as the distribution of the cost and benefits, and the aggregate benefit of outcomes within society.

Jeremy Bentham (1748–1832) was an early and significant contributor (1970) to the theory of utilitarianism, and John Stewart Mill (1806–1873) subsequently defended it (1988). More recent contributions in utilitarianism have been made by the Australian, Peter Singer (1979). Together, these philosophers have been largely responsible for the development of **traditional utilitarianism**. The basic premise Bentham (1970) proposed is that an action is ethically correct if it produces the maximum good and the minimum harm for all concerned (including the decision-maker).

**traditional utilitarianism** – an action is ethically correct if the action produces the maximum good and the minimum harm for all concerned, including the decision-maker.

Mill also proposed that the foundation of traditional utilitarianism lay in the greatest happiness principle. The question naturally arises, for whom are we generating the greatest happiness; that is, what is our measure of the majority? An added problem is the psychological ramifications of this ethical theory, which is reliant on the essential good nature of human beings and their concern for the needs of others.

Utilitarianism is largely congruent with the reality of the business environment, and it appeals to the business sector as a logical means of moral justification because it is very closely aligned to business reasoning and decision-making. In the business environment – where managers have to maximise revenues and minimise costs, both current and future, to produce the greatest maximum benefit to shareholders, and where decisions are frequently based on quantifiable cost–benefit dimensions – utilitarianism is viewed as an attractive theory. While the methods of costs versus benefit analysis, and maximisation, might be employed by a firm, the outcome is, regrettably, not always altruistic or best for the good of society.

Take, for example, the well-known case of the Ford Pinto car in the US in 1972. Despite evidence of the risk of injury to passengers from fire resulting from the position of the petrol tank in a rear-end collision, Ford continued to market the car. Ford had conducted a detailed cost–benefit analysis that included consideration of the benefits of saving 180 burn deaths, 180 serious burn injuries, and 2100 burnt vehicles. With each saving quantified against sales and total costs, it was not until 1978, as a consequence of mounting punitive damages and public concern, that Ford issued a recall of all Pinto models produced between 1971 and 1976. It can be seen that while benefit (profit) maximisation was the concept employed, the consequential outcomes were largely adverse to the consuming public. The use of extrinsic values, such as cost or profits, which are commonly utilised in business, have continued to be criticised for ignoring the intrinsic social value of human welfare or environmental concern. The totality of outcomes and consequences would require a full examination of the impact of actions on *all* stakeholders. It is also felt that despite prevailing support for free market competition, the purpose of human action should not entirely be directed at maximising purely economic wealth.

In a business context, it has been noted that utilitarianism sometimes recommends actions that are intuitively wrong. This is exemplified by the common argument that underpaying minority employees will greatly lower costs and therefore maximise utility for the majority. But is this appropriate? Maximising utility could lead to unjust outcomes such as the exploitation of the labour force. Utilitarianism has therefore been further developed.

**Act utilitarianism** dictates that one ought to perform the action that will maximise utility for all people in that situation. As situations vary, separate and time-consuming analysis must be required for each circumstance to determine the right, moral, or correct action. Thus, if act utilitarianism were being used, for example, when faced with the temptation to break a promise, one would have to evaluate the consequences of breaking a promise in every situation when a question arose (Buchholz 1989). **Rule utilitarianism** would, however, establish a guiding principle, or rule, that would be used in each evaluative situation when determining the greater good, and this rule would be adhered to into the future.

With utilitarianism comes the responsibility of identifying and measuring the quantities of benefit and harm related to an action, to decide what the maximum utility is. To identify all the variables required, we need an understanding of all relevant factors, both current and future. But what are the values of variables such as health or life? Can we actually measure them now and into the future? Utilitarianism assumes that all benefits and costs are known and can be measured on a common scale, and can then be added, or subtracted, from each other. For example, we could pretend that there is a standard unit of pleasure, which we call a 'hedon', and a standard unit of pain, which we call a 'dolor', but it is difficult to assume that hedons and dolors are commensurate (Feldman 1978), so we are left with a fundamental confusion of apples and oranges.

To be expected, there are arguments against utilitarianism. Given the time pressures that exist when making most business decisions, there are the difficulties of anticipating all consequences in order to facilitate the determination of the alternatives; that is, arriving at an objective, quantifiable judgement of discounted current and future values of utility can be difficult and undermines utilitarianism. The calculative process therefore renders utilitarianism an impractical theory, and there are additional concerns that adherence could result in an unjust outcome.

**act utilitarianism** – dictates that one ought to perform the action that will maximise utility for all people in that situation.

**rule utilitarianism** – the use of a guiding principle, or rule, for each evaluative situation when determining the greatest good, and that rule would be adhered to into the future.

# Ethics in practice: Utilitarianism

You are an Allied leader at the end of the Second World War. Considerable effort has gone into developing expertise in deciphering the German communications codes. A collection of the brightest mathematicians has been working out of an English manor house and have been able to crack the code used by the enemy. For some time now, enemy communications have been monitored in the lead up to the D-Day invasion, which, it is hoped, will end the war. You have been recently been notified of a critically disturbing upcoming event. The enemy is planning a significant air raid on a middle-sized city in the north of England. You have the ability to send notification that would enable preparations such as evacuations to the countryside that would result in considerable saving of lives. However, in doing so, you will also be notifying the enemy that their communication code had been compromised. They would, subsequently, immediately change their code, thereby prohibiting access by the Allied forces in anticipation of the D-Day invasion. Your assistant is awaiting a decision.

**Question:**

1. Do you notify the city of the impending raid, or do you maintain the secrecy of the code?

# Deontological or non-consequential theories

**deontological ethical theory** – based on the axiom that behaviours can be morally right or wrong, regardless of their consequences.

**Deontological ethical theory** is based on the axiom that behaviours can be morally right or wrong regardless of their consequences. Deontology is based on the Greek word *deon*, meaning 'duty' or 'obligations'. Deontological theories are considered to be non-consequential, in that the outcome is not the main driver of the decision, as one's duty or principles will drive the decision. For example, in earlier times, the personal decision to go to war was rarely based on consequences, for which the likelihood is that the outcome would not be beneficial, but rather was based on one's sense of duty.

# Ethics in practice: Ethical principles

Create a list of ethical principles that might be applied in ethical decision-making, i.e. keep your promises, don't lie, don't cheat, show respect, and so on.

**Question:**

1. What ethical principles are specifically applied to the accounting profession (see Chapter 6)?

# Ethics on reflection: Deontology

The next time you see riot police in action in the face of adversity, consider what thoughts must be going through their head. Why do you think they joined up and subsequently placed themselves in a position of personal danger?

Contrasting with teleological theory is deontological theory, which is dominated by the sense of 'duty', irrespective of the consequences of the action and separate from the concept of good. Unlike utilitarians, who are concerned with the results or consequences of a decision, even at the cost of personal happiness or individual rights, deontologists are adamant that the means do not justify the end, and that, in moral decisions, consideration must be given to one's duty. For example, if a house were burning and contained two people, and a third individual had the opportunity to save only one life, would it be morally correct to save the life of his or her own child if that child were one of the two people, despite the presence of another individual who may have been of more utility or value to society (Dahl, Mandell & Barton 1988)? Parental duty would overcome utility maximisation. A similar scene was played out in the movie *I, Robot* (2004), starring Will Smith, where a robot used a rule-based rational decision-making model (weighing the cost of losing a well-trained adult versus losing a child) and, as a consequence, saved the adult (Will Smith) rather than the child, both of whom were drowning.

As the means do not justify the ends, deontologists would also view lying as always wrong, no matter the circumstances and the utility generated. The justification of an action is therefore not as a result of utility interpretations, and net value outcomes, but of the relationships that exist, and the duties within those relationships.

Similar to utilitarianism, there are also 'act' and 'rule' deontology theories. **Act deontology** states that an individual will grasp immediately what ought to be done without relying on rules or guidelines, particularly as each situation is unique. **Rule deontology** is more consistent with Kant's theory, which states that acts are right or wrong because of their conformity or non-conformity to established moral principles. A further distinction can be made between **monistic deontology** and **pluralistic deontology**. Monistic theorists advocate the supremacy of one general rule, such as the Golden Rule: Do unto others as you would expect them do unto you. Pluralistic theorists suggest that there are a number of rules that can provide simultaneous guidance, for example, the Christian belief in the 10 Commandments.

**act deontology** – in which an individual will grasp immediately what ought to be done without relying on rules or guidelines, particularly as each situation is unique.

**rule deontology** – acts are right or wrong because of their conformity or non-conformity to established moral principles.

**monistic deontology** – advocates the supremacy of one general rule such as the Golden Rule: Do unto others as you would expect them to do unto you.

**pluralistic deontology** – suggests that there are a number of rules that can provide simultaneous guidance, for example, the Christian 10 Commandments.

## Kantian theory

The principal deontological theorist is the eighteenth century philosopher, Immanuel Kant (1724–1804), who viewed duties as absolute and binding in providing moral guidance. It recognises that when making a moral judgement, one cannot base the moral worth of the decision on the intended outcomes, as they can vary enormously. Instead, the worth of a moral action should be based on the intention of the person performing the decision (Hosmer 1987).

**Categorical imperative** – Kant's principal contribution to deontology is the formulation of the categorical imperative for testing morally correct duties and action. Kant provided two principles as criteria by which one can test moral adequacy. These criteria are in two formulations.

**Categorical imperative – Kant's first formulation**: An action is morally right for a person in a certain situation if, and only if, the person's reason for carrying out the action is a reason that he or she would be willing to have every person act on, in any similar situation. The first formulation of the categorical imperative possesses both 'universality' and 'reversibility'.

- **Universality** – requires that an individual's reason for the action must be a reason that everyone could act on, at least in principle. An act or decision may be judged to be morally correct if everyone must perform the same act, or reach the same decision, given similar circumstances.

- **Reversibility** – the second component of the first formulation, questions whether, if everyone in comparable situations acted in a similar way, does the principle become a universal law? This is very close to the Golden Rule (do unto others as you would have others do unto you), although it is appropriate to mention that, despite the similarity of the phraseology, Kant explicitly rejects the view that his categorical imperative is equivalent to the Golden Rule. The main difference between the Golden Rule and the categorical imperative appears to be that the Golden Rule makes an act right if the agent would not object to having it done to him or herself. For example, with masochistic behaviour, an agent does not object to being mistreated; however, this maxim cannot be seen as a categorical imperative as the agent's action cannot be universalised; it would be inaccurate to assume everyone would think it appropriate to be mistreated (Feldman 1978).

One can easily apply the first formulation to a business setting by posing the question: how would you like a competitor to undertake the same action, say, the gaining of competitor intelligence, by deceptive means? It is at this point that the first formulation appears to have gained traction in the business environment, as many claim, 'my competitors are already doing this, and I also do this, initially in retaliation, but now it is common practice'. A degree of universality and reversibility therefore exists that would consequently condone unethical behaviour. Essentially, however, what is being said is that a moral action is an action that can be rationally followed by all individuals. For example, if everyone were to steal, there would be no ownership of property. In this scenario, stealing would be impossible and, consequently, would be seen as morally acceptable.

**categorical imperative** – views duties as absolute and binding in providing moral guidance.

**categorical imperative: Kant's first formulation** – people should be treated as ends in themselves and never solely as a means to the ends of others.

**universality** – an act or decision may be judged to be morally correct if everyone must perform the same act or reach the same decision given similar circumstances.

**reversibility** – what if everyone in comparable situations acted in a similar way? The principle becomes a universal law.

# Ethics and practice: Categorical imperative

A competitor has a new product feature that will make a big difference to their sales. The competitor plans to have a hospitality suite at the annual trade show and unveil this feature at a party thrown for dealers. You propose sending someone to this meeting hiding the fact that they work for you and pretending to be a potential client in order to gain valuable information.

**Questions:**
1. What is your view of this method of gaining competitor information?
2. Evaluate the ethical decision utilising Kant's first formulation of the categorical imperative. Does this alter your initial decision?

**Categorical imperative – Kant's second formulation:** For the second formulation, attention is directed to whether one is using people as a means to an end. Here, a decision and subsequent action is morally right if, and only if, in performing the action, the person does not treat others merely as a means for advancing his or her own interest, but also both respects and develops his or her capacity to choose freely for themselves. The concept of 'end' refers to the principle that one should not treat people as a means or object for one's own use or satisfaction. We should, however, respect the dignity and freedom of individuals, and their ability to act on the basis of their own rational judgements. Kant felt that everyone should be treated as a free person equal to everyone else; that is, everyone has a moral right to such treatment, and a correlative duty to also treat others in this way. Thus, Kant succinctly states our decisions should be guided by our duties, and that, in relation to these duties, we are further guided by fundamental moral law: that people should be treated as ends in themselves, and never solely as a means to the ends of others.

The categorical imperative has its critics, whose objections relate to the two formulations and to Kant's theorisation in general. Criticisms have been expressed with the first formulation of the categorical imperative, particularly in relation to the many different reasons why a maxim may not be able to be universal and reversible. The first criticism relates to the persuasive existence of a number of counter-examples that possibly erode the moral worth of the universality and reversibility criteria. A situation related by Hare (1965) is a case in point. Suppose that an employer discriminates against black workers, and suppose that he is fanatical in this discrimination, so much so that the employer is willing to accept the reversal proposition that, if his own skin were black, other employers should also discriminate against him. According to Kant's theory, this action would be morally correct despite the clear concern about racism. Universalism appears to require interpretation according to the situation of the individual and the action, and, while universalism is a useful method of moral reasoning, there are no priorities or degrees of importance indicated to guide actions. The categorical imperative does, however, provide some direction towards justice and equality.

> **categorical imperative: Kant's second formulation** – one ought never to act except in such a way that the maxim should become a universal law.

A difficulty that has been raised with the second formulation of the categorical impera-tive is that its meaning is not made sufficiently clear. Treating someone as a means is con-ceptually easy when one considers slaves, but what of the 20th-century workforce? Take, for example, the employer who pays only minimum wages to his or her employees and, in addition to providing poor working conditions, also refuses to provide the safety equipment they require. This employer states that in keeping with the categorical imperative, and, in particular, the second formulation, he or she is respecting the employees' capacity to freely choose for themselves; that is, they can work elsewhere if they want. Are these employees being treated as a means and also as ends, or not?

The second formulation has also been criticised for lack of evidence. How can you tell if people are being treated as a means or as ends? The motivations of individuals are rarely revealed openly. Just as it is difficult to know, except by detailed observation of communi-cation and behaviour, whether an individual is a theory 'x' or a theory 'y' manager, or pos-sesses a 'methods' or 'results' orientation, it is equally difficult to determine whether rational autonomy is, in fact, being granted. Immoral motives can lead to good consequences (for example, insider trading leading to a constructive revision of stockbroking procedures), and bad consequences can be the result of good motives (Buchholz 1989). The second formula-tion in an operational setting is therefore difficult to recognise.

As with many moral theories, the criticisms expressed are, to a certain extent, a result of the interpretive difficulties experienced by theorists in attempting to reveal and apply true meaning. With Kantian theory, the criticisms are that it is too narrow and prescriptive; that there is not enough detail to apply it practically to ethical decision-making; and that it is potentially contradictory. There are potential conflicts between moral rules, and there is a difficulty in adequately resolving these conflicts when they occur. In applying Kantian theory, one cannot lie, even if lying would bring about a better consequence. For example, there is a conflict between whether one should tell the truth and disclose damaging information, or lie to protect a person from being harmed. This situation contains two conflicting duties: (1) to tell the truth; and (2) to protect individuals from serious harm. Which duty should have priority is not always evident. If we have duties such as to do no harm, not to lie, to keep promises, to obey the law, to be loyal and to improve the lot of others, how can one prioritise universally acceptable duties? Managers have a duty to run their factories in keeping with their stewardship function, but what of the duty to prevent harm from the influence of pol-lution. Which would come first?

# Ethics in practice: Kantian theory

In the discussion of Kantian theory, we have been applying this theory to humans. Can this theory and related precepts also apply to animals? Use the guidelines within Kantian theory of the categorical imperative – first formulation and universality and reversibility, and then Kant's second formulation of 'not a means to an end' – to evaluate the moral appropriateness of animal testing.

# Duty

The theoretical concept of **duty** is associated with moral and legal obligations, as aligned to a position or role. Duties have been examined fairly extensively throughout this book, however, in addition to our understanding of the myriad of duties to which ethical decision-making may refer (for example, fiduciary duty, parental duty and legal duty), and in addition to the distinction between 'duties to others' and 'duties to oneself', we need to make one more distinction, between 'perfect' and 'imperfect' duties. A **perfect duty** is one that admits no exception in the interest of inclination; that is, one must always do that action. An **imperfect duty** is an action that, at least sometimes, will be performed when the opportunity arises, for example, charitable work where we are under no obligation to give all of our time, but choose to give some of our time (Feldman 1978). For further explanations of duty, please refer to chapters 4, 5 and 9.

**duty** – moral and legal obligation as aligned to a position or role.

**perfect duty** – a duty that we must always undertake.

**imperfect duty** – a duty to which we are under no obligation to give all of our time.

Duty (© shutterstock.com/Taeya18)

Before moving on to examine rights, a minor variation worth mentioning is **prima facie deontology**. Prima facie deontology is a more lenient and less popular theory that suggests duties have exceptions, depending on the situation. This perspective, promoted by the contemporary philosopher, Norman Bowie (1942–) (cited in Arnold, Beauchamp & Bowie 2013), has been developed in recognition of the potential conflict that can develop from conflicting duties and rules. For instance, the duty not to harm may override the duty to one's employer for an employee deciding on whether to blow the whistle on inappropriate labour practices in their company's supply chain. Historically, one can indicate circumstances that may warrant bending the rules, for example, although there is a rule about not killing another human being, we recognise the possible necessity of this occurring in self-defence, in wars, and in some countries that execute for capital crimes.

**prima facie deontology** – suggests duties have exceptions depending on the situation, for example, the duty not to harm may override the duty not to tell the truth.

"Yeah, yeah, everybody in jail is innocent of steroids."

Prima facie deontology (© shutterstock.com/Cartoonresource)

# Rights

Having examined the concept of duty, it is now appropriate to examine the correlates of duties which are in the form of rights, because, for all rights there are corresponding duties. These duties are to ensure that others will respect and not infringe on these rights. The duties that equate with a right may come in various forms, for example, the duty merely to respect the existence of a right (for example, the right of privacy). The duty might also extend to the active protection of a right (for example, the right to life). Quite simply, a **right** is an individual's entitlement to something in order that the individual may be able to pursue certain interests as well as protect those interests (Pienta & O'Neil 1989).

Rights (© shutterstock.com/Bombaert Patrick)

Rights appear to have three principal dimensions:

- The absence of restrictions that may inhibit an individual's pursuit of an interest or activity (for example, freedom to worship).
- Authorisation in that a right will empower an individual to act in a certain way (for example, the right of ownership).
- The existence of prohibitions or requirements in relation to activities (for example, the right to freedom of speech will, it is hoped, curtail individual or government restrictions on that right). The prohibitive dimension of rights therefore ensures not only the existence of that right, but also the protection of that right (Velasquez 1988).

**Types of rights** – John Locke identified three rights: the rights to life, liberty and property. In other words, we do not need permission to live, to take actions, or to acquire, hold or use peacefully the productive or creative results of our actions. We may, morally, resist (without undue force) efforts to violate or infringe upon our rights. Our rights are: (1) absolute; (2) inalienable; and (3) universal. In the business context, specifically, five rights are commonly presented by moral theorists. They are the rights to:

- free consent
- privacy
- freedom of conscience
- free speech
- due process.

But these are not the only rights that an individual could claim. In 2000, for example, the United Nations presented a global compact in support of the UN Declaration of Human Rights, directed specifically at business. The policy initiative for business outlined 10 universally accepted principles in relation to **human rights**, labour, environment and anti-corruption (see Table 10.3).

**human rights** – entitlement by virtue of being a human being.

**Table 10.3** The United Nations global compact on rights: 10 principles business should adopt

**Human rights**

1. the support and respect of human rights
2. not being complicit in human rights abuses

**Labour**

3. uphold the right to freedom of association and the right to collective bargaining
4. eliminate forced and compulsory labour
5. the abolition of child labour
6. employment or occupational discrimination should be eliminated

**Environment**

7. take a precautionary approach to environmental challenges
8. promote greater environmental responsibility
9. encourage the development and use of environmentally-friendly technologies

**Anti-corruption**

10. work against all forms of corruption

(Adapted from: UN Global Compact 2013)

# Ethics in practice: Declaration of Human Rights

Look at the United Nations Declaration of Human Rights: 10 Principles.

**Question:**

1. What are the key tenets of this declaration? Consider circumstances where worker rights might currently be abused.

In the business context, workers may claim the right to participate. As such, the right to participate not only surrounds the right to participate in, say, organised union activities, but also the right to participate in decisions. The critical question, though, is to what extent should this participation occur and, generally, in the industrial relations environment, this entails the right to be consulted and to inform the decision-making, but not necessarily to make the decision. That right remains with the employer. Participation could be looked at as a continuum (see Figure 10.2); at one point is the right to be informed, moving along to the right to consultation, and, even further along, to the right for mutually agreed decision-making. The final and most extreme case is where a decision could be delegated entirely to workers with the right to self-determination.

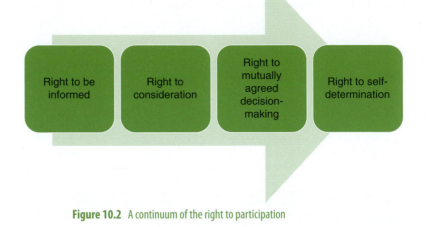

**Figure 10.2** A continuum of the right to participation

# Ethics in practice: Terrorism

Hypothetically, assume that American authorities had arrested one of the two brothers connected with the 2013 bombing of the Boston Marathon before the event. The authorities had no knowledge of the exact location of the bomb, but were aware of an impending terrorist strike.

**Question:**

1. Contrast the use of a utilitarian and a rights approach to evaluate the use of torture in order to elicit information on the location of the bomb.

# Ethics in practice: Infertility

A Sydney reproductive law expert recently called for a reciprocal arrangement in Australia whereby discounted fertility treatments could be offered to couples if they were prepared to donate leftover embryos to families, in a bid to reduce the number of unused embryos in clinic freezers and reduce the donor shortage (Marriner 2013).

**Questions:**

1. What are your thoughts on this proposal?
2. Evaluate your argument and consider what ethical lens you are using.

**legal rights** – rights assigned by the legal system and limited to specific legislative jurisdictions.

The concept of rights may be derived from different systems that assign the right for an individual to act in a certain way. Rights can therefore be classified into the categories of: (1) legal rights; (2) contractual rights; and (3) moral rights.

The legal system within which a person operates guarantees certain rights. **Legal rights** are assigned by the legal system which may, in turn, have been derived from a governing charter such as the United States Constitution. Legal rights are limited to specific legislative jurisdictions.

A further narrowing of the jurisdictional scope of rights is seen in the second category of rights, that of **contractual rights**, where limited rights and correlative duties arise as a result of an individual entering a binding agreement with another person or parties. In the business context, contractual rights dominate, and, in the simplest form, most managers have contractual agreements of employment which empower them with certain rights of administration, and the expectation that certain duties and stewardship functions will be performed which are in keeping with their managerial positions. When third parties outside the organisation are involved, the contractual situation is broadened, and one party has the contractual right, obligation, or expectation, to do what has been agreed with the other party, subject to the accepted rules that define these transactions (that is, offer and acceptance, and so on). Both parties to the agreement have a contractual duty to perform, as stipulated, in the agreement, and these duties may be attached to specific individuals or entities.

Interestingly, a common first-base argument that is often used in defence of the importance of business ethics, rests on the importance of trust and understanding, particularly in contractual arrangements, because an erosion of trust and understanding, as well as the respect for the inherent rights and duties within contractual arrangements, could weaken the entire fabric of the commercial system. Without the institution of contracts, and the rights and duties that contracts create, modern business could not operate, as virtually every business transaction at some point requires one of the parties to rely on the word of the other parties to the effect that the other party will pay later, deliver certain services, or provide goods of certain quality and quantity. Without the social institution of contracts, individuals may be unwilling to rely on the word of the other party, and transactions would never take place.

**Moral rights** originate from the systems of natural justice and normative codes. A moral right is not merely a statement of perceived entitlement; a moral right is a claim made by virtue of being a human being. These rights are also often referred to as **natural rights** and **human right**; the phrase '**God-given rights**' tends not to be used now due to the need for religious sensitivity.

Over time, rights have been formalised, as is seen in the United Nations Universal Declaration of Human Rights, which for example, stipulates the right to:

- own property
- work, have free choice of employment, have just and favourable conditions of work and to be protected against unemployment
- have just and favourable remuneration
- join trade unions
- rest and leisure, including reasonable limitations on working hard, and periodic holidays with pay.

**contractual rights** – rights as a result of entering a binding agreement with another person or parties.

**moral rights** (also known as **natural rights** and **human rights**, and formerly **God-given rights**) – rights that originate from systems of natural justice and normative codes.

# Ethics in the media: Rights

In 2012, despite Australia's harsher policies around asylum seekers, Afghan refugees were still determined to board boats from Java, ready for hazardous journeys to Australia. They were resigned to staying in detention centres certain this would lead to better opportunities, and end the terror they experienced living under the Taliban (Bachelard 2012).

**negative rights** – the right not to be interfered with, for example, the right of privacy, or not to be tortured, indicating that the duty of others is to respect the rights of others, but require no action on the part of the rights claimant.

**positive rights** – the positive duty to provide individuals with something that they are unable to provide for themselves but are entitled to by virtue of the rights they hold, as in the rights to an education, wellbeing, or shelter.

Rights have additional characteristics which can distinguish them as: (1) negative or positive rights; (2) active or passive rights; and (3) prima facie and absolute rights.

**Negative rights** are rights which stipulate the right not to be interfered with, for example, the right of privacy or the right not to be tortured. Negative rights indicate that the duty of others is a mutual respect of rights which requires no action on the part of the rights claimant. **Positive rights**, on the other hand, impose a positive duty of providing individuals with something that they are unable to provide for themselves, but are entitled to by virtue of the rights they hold, for example, the right to an education, the right to wellbeing, or the right to shelter. Positive rights appear to be more of a 20th-century phenomenon and are clearly evident in socialist and welfare states, where the duty to provide positive rights falls heavily on the governing body.

A distinction can also be drawn between an active or passive right. A **passive right** requires recognition and action by another person other than the claimant, such as the right to life, or animal rights issues, where the rights of the claimants; that is, the unborn child or animals, are protected by others. An **active right**, in contrast, is a right that will require positive action by the rights claimant; that is, the individual themselves, such as the right to free speech.

# Ethics on reflection: Passive right

A situation where one party may be exercising a passive right on behalf of another, which can create complicated and morally challenging circumstances, is the decision to sterilise a person with a disability. This situation arises when a parent argues that unborn children have moral and legal rights, and that the person with a disability is seen as incapable of parenting, thus justifying the parents' decision to sterilise, and thereby violating a basic human right; the right to bear children (Feeney 2013).

**Question:**

1. What are your views on this dilemma?

Undoubtedly, difficulties arise with the identification of what constitutes a right, and the question of supremacy of rights. Sometimes, what constitutes a moral right is not entirely clear; for example, the right of procreation is an acceptable right but so, too, is the right not to be tortured. How does one decide which right is the most important, and, in situations where rights might conflict, which right takes precedence? In attempting to resolve the dilemma of conflicting rights and absolute rights, a **prima facie right** is one where a right may be overridden in particular circumstances by more stringent competing moral demands; that is, when sufficient justification exists. If a right has an overriding status, then it is an **absolute right**. Of course, who determines absolute rights is contentious, in as much as, what absolute rights do we choose? Is it those promoted by religion, government or some other group?

**passive right** – a right that requires recognition and action by another person other than the claimant, for example, in the right to life, or animal rights issues, the rights of the claimant; that is, the unborn and the animals, are protected by others.

# Ethics on reflection: Prima facie rights

Before reading on, in the case of prima facie rights, consider in what circumstances might a right be overridden?

Some circumstances in which a right may be overridden are:

- curtailing one person's right is necessary because that person has, or will, violate the rights of others (for example, taking away the right of freedom from criminals)
- cases that arise out of conflict between equal claims to exercise the same right (for example, the separation of conjoined twins)
- in the more difficult circumstance where two equal rights conflict, and where neither can be respected or exercised (for example, war time freedom and national security) (Werhane 1985).

Some think that rights can be overridden only by another, more basic right of some kind, for example, property rights can be overridden in order to promote equality of opportunity. This argument is commonly used in defence of affirmative action in the US.

Alternatively, an absolute right is an 'indefeasible right' which is upheld without exception. The possession of human rights implies moral constraints upon others to act in certain ways. There has, in the past, been a tendency to present all rights as absolute and inviolable; that is, they provide their possessor with claims that can never, or almost never, be legitimately overridden.

**active right** – a right that will receive positive action by the rights claimant, i.e. the individual himself.

**prima facie right** – a right that overrides other competing rights in particular circumstances, because of its more stringent moral demands; that is, when sufficient justification exists.

**absolute right** – a right that has precedence over all others; an indefeasible right that is upheld without exception.

A dominant feature of rights is that they will be protected, even if a utilitarian analysis indicates that net benefits to society will be obtained if an activity governed by a right is restricted. For example, it would undoubtedly be far more productive to society if Sunday were not a day of rest or worship but a working day, yet, in contrast to the utilitarianism view, an individual's interest (the right of worship) can never rightly be sacrificed for the sake of a collective good. Rights have therefore been referred to as 'political trumps' that individuals hold, and that cannot be easily overridden for the sake of a collective good (Dworkin 1977).

# Ethics on reflection: Absolute right

The right to life could be considered an indefeasible right, or absolute right. In practice, this would mean that an intelligence agency would not be just and therefore not permitted to assassinate a ruthless tyrant, despite monumental violations of human rights and widespread suffering. Others would, however, counter that. In reality, in some cases, the interests of an individual can rightly be balanced against the good of the many and therefore morally outweighed.

**Question:**
1. What is your view?

**Eroding rights** – how might a right be eroded? Usually this happens when there are compelling additional arguments. For example, it has been argued that unwanted pregnancies have resulted in the birth of many children, and additional future demands on society's resources (such as housing, education, and possibly welfare) are costs that could have been avoided. Anti-abortion advocates, however, firmly adhere to 'the right to life' as being paramount to any utilitarian benefits or cost saving to society, and yet, when the utilitarian arguments are persuasive or powerful enough, an erosion of this right can be predicted. A classic circumstance is when the property rights of factory owners may be restricted in order to prevent damage such as environmental destruction or impacts on the health of others. The weakening of civil rights is often presented in the interest of public welfare, particularly during times of stress, for example, during strikes, civil disobedience, or a war on terror.

# Ethics in practice: Invasion of privacy

In organisations today there is a significant amount of electronic monitoring of employees, particularly how much time is spent on social media, such as Facebook, or surfing the net. This monitoring is considered by some as an invasion of privacy.

**Question:**
1. Compare an employee's right to privacy to the employer's right to ownership, and the right to pursue business in a way which is most conducive to managing a business and achieving profits.

While rights are traditionally focused on individuals in a societal context, they can easily be applied in the corporate setting. Today, the right of privacy is being applied in regard to the collection, access, maintenance and distribution of information about a potential or current employee; freedom of speech is encouraging employee whistleblowing; and the right to due process is directing greater attention to such personnel practices as recruitment and selection, performance appraisals, promotions and dismissals. Management prerogatives are being challenged with the counter-call for 'management rights', and, today, we are seeing with increasing regularity, clear evidence of individuals exercising not only their employee rights, but also their consumer rights with, for example, consumer boycotts. Stockholders are also more vocal in exercising their rights, particularly in regard to investment, portfolio composition, social and environmental issues. The overriding difficulties of working with rights in a decision-making circumstance is in determining which rights prevail, legal, contractual or moral rights, and the need to prioritise rights to resolve some decisions; for example, the right to life and the right to choose in the abortion debate.

# Ethics in practice: Conflicting rights

When Steve Jobs (1955–2011), Apple Computers' Co-founder and Chairman, left Apple to start his own computer company, NeXT Inc., he lured away eleven of Apple's finest engineers. (Jobs later returned to Apple.) Apple, facing intense competitive pressure from IBM's entry into the personal computer market, and fuelled by the suspicion that a lot of their research and development information went with their engineers, naturally filed a law suit. The conundrum, however, was what were Apple's former employees' rights to free choice of employment, and how do they co-exist with Apple's right to protect their intellectual property which was generated from their significant research investment?

**Questions:**

1. To which right do you give supremacy in this scenario?
2. How would you attempt to resolve these conflicting rights, particularly with the pressures of employment and profits?

**Justice** – rights are often grounded in what is called natural justice, which is based on an ideal standard of justice that is fixed by nature and is binding on all people. The concepts of justice and rights co-exist, and rights most often stem from basic feelings of injustice. The assertion of rights is meant to correct injustices. Quite simply, justice affirms what is morally and rightly ours. Justice is drawn from many sources such as the law and rational thought, and is an intuitive sense of fairness and equity.

The initial theoretical development of justice has been attributed to Aristotle (384–322 BC), and to David Hume (1711–1776), and with more recent, controversial developments provided by the American philosopher, John Rawls (1921–2002). Rawls (1971) notes that theories of justice call upon the decision-maker to act with 'equity, fairness and impartiality'. This extends to such activities as: the determination of policy; administration of punishment; nomination of tasks; allocation of rewards; assignment of burdens; as well as the delegation of authority. In business, problems of justice are usually more specifically manifested in matters pertaining to employee and consumer rights, fair treatment (particularly of minorities), equitable personnel policies, and the determination of structural variables. Take, for example, the equitable delegation of authority which is commonly referred to in management theory as the 'parity principle', and which stipulates that authority and accountability should always be equal. Consequently, it is morally correct from the point of view of justice that individuals should not be held responsible for matters over which they have no control.

However, perceptions of justice and fairness can be confusing. For example, an economist would contend that fair pricing is where the price has been determined by free market mechanisms. Yet, consider a situation where advanced technology in an industry, and barriers to market entry have created an oligopolistic situation in which a tacit agreement on pricing has resulted in higher prices. This could be viewed as unfair, but, as all sellers have willingly set the price, and all consumers willingly pay the price, it may be difficult to determine any injustice as the result of inequality.

Justice is the part of morality that relates most specifically to social relations and to the interpersonal relations concerned with expectations of oneself and others in society. However, morality itself appears to cover a wider domain than justice, although the precise province of justice within the field of morality is not always readily apparent. Take, for example, a scientist who falsifies results for the sake of personal advantage. Although he or she performs a blatantly unethical act, the scientist is not committing an injustice, and yet, if the action is viewed as a means of deriving acclaim and respect which is undeserved, then it may seem that there is a prima facie case for saying that questions of justice are raised.

Justice relates not only to the treatment of individuals but also to the equitable distribution of society's material outcomes, as well as burdens. All theories of justice share the same formal principle of justice: cases that are alike should be treated equally, and those that are not alike should be treated unequally. For example, it is only fair that two individuals with similar backgrounds and in similar roles be paid equally (irrespective of ethnic background, age and gender). Fairness can also extend to dissimilar circumstances as is the point of the controversy regarding excessive executive pay. Is it fair, despite the obvious differences in responsibilities, that an executive takes home an inordinate amount of money that is grossly disproportionate to the amount lower level employees receive?

The principal theories of justice can be delineated into four forms (see also Table 10.4):

**retributive justice** – ensuring that punishment matches the crime.

- **Retributive justice** which is at the core of most judicial systems involves the requirement that the punishment will match the crime. It is also important that the person receiving retributive justice did, in fact, do something wrong; that is, that due process was used in order to ascertain certitude of blame, and that the punishment is consistent and proportioned to the action in question.

- **Comparative justice** necessitates the treating of all cases alike. It should be remembered that retributive justice is not restricted merely to criminal jurisdiction; business is also naturally affected by retributive justice, commonly through the awarding of punitive damages.

- **Compensatory justice** is where people are compensated when wronged. The problematic considerations of compensatory justice are in determining: (a) the wrongdoing; and (b) in what form atonement will be made. For example, how can one be compensated for the loss of one's right arm following an industrial accident? In a practical sense, this question is easily answered by reference to worker compensation laws (where they exist) and the percentage loss of earning power that has resulted from the disability, but, in reality, how 'just' is this reparation?

- **Equal opportunity programs**, and particularly quota systems, are a form of compensatory justice, in that minority groups, as a result of unjust discrimination in the past, are now being given preferential placement in hiring, training and promotion. However, the obvious question of reverse discrimination has been raised as a potential, and contrasting, 'injustice' as a result of equal opportunity programs.

- **Procedural justice** requires equal treatment of people except if they differ significantly in relevant ways. The crux of procedural justice refers to fair decision procedures, practices or agreements, which, essentially, require equal treatment of people. It can also be seen that procedural justice is at the foundation of pay, equal opportunity, race and age discrimination legislation. The difficulty, however, arises when one attempts to interpret what is meant by 'relevant aspects' in relation to the circumstance. Relevant aspects are particularly important in pre-employment conditions and in the use of evaluative criteria for employee selection. For example, is attractiveness a relevant aspect for a client liaison person, or not? A second difficulty that arises is one of measurement, for, if we are justified in treating people dissimilarly because of relevant aspects, how does one measure the proportionality of their dissimilarity? For example, how much more valuable is six years' experience on the job in comparison to three years, or a master's degree in comparison to a first degree, in relation to an individual's pay?

- **Distributive justice** is where burdens and benefits are distributed fairly to all members of society. It should be mentioned that, as distributive justice involves the distribution of benefits and burdens, there is, as yet, no universal agreement as to what criteria should be employed to facilitate the distribution. This leads to a further discussion within distributive justice of **egalitarian justice**, which emphasises equal access to or division of primary goods, irrespective of the criteria.

**comparative justice** – treating all cases alike, so that the justice of a particular case is determined impartially by comparing it with treatment of similar relevant cases.

**compensatory justice** – an assurance that people are compensated when wronged by others.

**procedural justice** – requires equal treatment of people except if they differ significantly in relevant ways.

**distributive justice** – where burdens and benefits are distributed fairly to all members of society.

**egalitarian justice** – emphasises equal access to or division of primary goods, irrespective of other criteria.

**Table 10.4** Justice

| Different forms of justice | Description |
| --- | --- |
| Retributive | The requirement that the punishment will match the crime. |
| Compensatory | People are compensated when wronged by others. |
| Procedural | Requires equal treatment of people except if they differ significantly in relevant ways. |
| Distributive | Burdens and benefits are distributed fairly to all members of society. |

# Ethics in practice: Justice

In its simplest form, justice is often referred to as 'giving each person their due', however, this presents numerous alternatives for equitable distribution, as illustrated in the story of 30 legionnaires who steal away from the fort and fill a number of containers with water, and return safely, with a view to distributing the water 'justly'. One group, who have gone without water the longest, thinks it should be distributed according to need. A group of officers propose the division should be by rank and status.

A third group, who risked their lives getting the water, argue for a merit-based means of determining distribution. The balance of the group appeal to the notion of equality arguing the water should be evenly shared (Donaldson 1982).

**Question:**

1. What do you consider to be the fairest way of distributing the water?

While the concept of justice sounds intuitively appealing, deciding which criteria are required can be a complicated matter; for example, are we to consider greater need, effort, contribution, competence, status or merely equality? We are by no means restricted to the one evaluative criterion. For example, in developed countries, education is theoretically distributed equally, welfare payments are on the basis of need, sales commission on the basis of effort, public honour or superannuation are on the basis of prior contribution, and managerial salaries (hopefully) on the basis of competence (Hosmer 1987).

In recent years, Rawls (1971) has been the major proponent of distributive justice in a contractual form. Rawls provides a comprehensive theory of justice that is based on the assumption that conflicts involving justice should be settled by first deriving a fair method of choosing the principles by which the conflicts should be resolved. Rawls goes on to provide two principles that determine distributive justice: Principle 1, 'the principle of equal liberty', takes precedence over Principle 2(a), the 'difference principle', and 2(b), the 'principle of fair equality of opportunity'. Definitions of both principles follow.

## Principle 1

The principle of equal liberty – states that each individual (or institution) should be permitted the maximum amount of equal basic liberty compatible with similar liberties experienced by others. A corporation is just therefore if it promotes the greatest amount of basic liberty, which is compatible with 'like liberty for all'.

## Principle 2

(a) The difference principle – having assured equal basic liberty, inequalities in the distribution of social and economic primary goods (such as opportunities and income) are permitted, provided they are to the greatest benefit of the least advantaged person. In other words, the inequalities among society's members are permissible only if the inequalities raise the level of the least well-off members of society (that is why some consider differential tax systems are equitable).

(b) The principle of fair equality of opportunity – the principle of equal opportunity augments the difference principle by reiterating that inequalities among society's members are permissible only if the offices and privileges of the institutions which promote inequality are open to everyone; that is, that all individuals have equal access to these positions (for example, any qualified person can be employed by the Tax Department).

A notable corporate application of Rawlsian theory was seen at Control Data Corporation in the US, where the then Chairman, William Norris, attempted through various programs (such as 'cars for cons') to redress the inequalities in the world by raising the level of the worst-off stakeholders of Control Data. By making a profit, it was hoped the company would also be increasing the size of the pie for others.

**Egalitarian justice** (also known as **egalitarianism**) is frequently presented, conceptually, as the simplest theory of distributive justice. Egalitarians follow the view that there are no relevant differences among people by which one can justify unequal treatment (Ake 1975); that is, all human beings are equal and therefore eligible for an equal share. As expected, critics have attacked this as idealistic, by pointing out that, in reality, no two human beings are alike; we are all in the possession of differing abilities and disabilities, and also, possession of differing abilities and disabilities could fall within a wide range, for example, intelligence, or physical strength. If egalitarianism was, in fact, instigated, there would be no recognition of personal effort and a dilatory individual would receive an equal share with others.

The main concerns with justice in general are the flip side of utilitarianism and the contrast between utility and justice. A decision outcome may exhibit justice and be the fairest, but it may not provide the best outcome for all.

> **egalitarian justice** (also known as **egalitarianism**) – the simplest theory of distributive justice, proposing that all human beings are equal and therefore eligible for an equal share.

# Virtue ethics

**Virtue ethics** (also known as **non-rational ethics**), is a major strand of ethical theory. Virtue ethics does not require reference to utility calculations, or to duties, but instead the decision-maker refers back to the virtues that they value to guide their decision-making. Virtues are habits that develop into character traits. They are derived from learning how to act and practising this act. Virtue is seen as important not only to an individual, but to communities, which support virtue development and the common good (Velasquez & Andre 1998). Alasdair MacIntyre (1981) is a major advocate of virtue ethics, and character theorists could also be placed in this group. Essentially, virtue ethics places the focus on the individual rather than an action or an outcome, and is dependent on the character traits of a virtuous individual.

> **virtue ethics** (also known as **non-rational ethics**) – an ethical theory that emphasises good character and the virtues embodied in that character.

Virtue ethics (© shutterstock.com/rnl)

MacIntyre is critical of modern moral philosophy (which he estimates as commencing in the 1780s), as he believes virtue develops as a consequence of: historical narrative; narrative experiences in the actor's life; an understanding of human good; and social and political environments which link one's actions and render them understandable to others. Virtue is therefore based on historical narrative about informed moral agency, whereas, modern moral philosophy sees choice as the primary agent, with character relegated to a peripheral role. For MacIntyre, there is a natural law which is developed over time and passed between generations. His concern with moral philosophy is that it is grounded in liberalism and individualism, which support the modern state, and does not allow for conditions conducive to achieving and promoting the common good (Hauerwas 2007). The distilled element of virtue is not what you do, but what kind of person you are.

Problems naturally arise with the potential variations in what is considered virtuous and the difficulties in determining common good.

## Character values

**subjective relativism** – where each individual decides what is right and wrong for themselves.

A decision-maker would refer back to the rule and values that guide their character. This would involve **subjective relativism** where each individual decides what is right and wrong for them; seeing moral authority as lying within them. The character values entail values such as honesty, compassion, empathy, courage, respect and integrity.

## Religious values

**divine O** – indicates that one's actions and decisions should be aligned with the will of God, as prescribed by religious texts.

Theological ethical subjectivism, known as the **divine O**, indicates that one's actions and moral decisions should be aligned with the will of God, as prescribed by religious texts, whether they be Christian, Jewish, Muslim or otherwise. One would therefore subscribe to religious values aligned to a specific religion. Divine command theory has two claims: God determines what morality is; and God's commandments serve as moral obligations outlining divine will. The only difficulty here is that often these texts are subject to significant interpretation, based on the religion, with the common thread being that moral obligations lie with God (Austin 2006).

# Conclusion

Historically, discourse in ethical theory has originated from theological and philosophical traditions, with extensive examination of such issues as values, morality, rights, justice and virtue, and with each arena of discussion possessing its own crucial players in the form of theoretical proponents and critical opponents. Think of them as lenses similar to the optometrist's lenses; by putting a different lens in front of an ethical dilemma and viewing it through that lens, we are able to deconstruct the issues associated with that dilemma and gain differing perspectives to assist with ethical decision-making.

When faced with an ethical dilemma, utilitarianism would suggest that the rationale for a decision will originate from the logic associated with maximising utility. Deontology, however, focuses on a person's interior motivations and not on the consequences of one's external actions. Where do these reasons or motives originate? Deontologists purport that these motives may originate from a variety of possibilities, primarily from references to personal guiding principles, intuition and an innate knowledge of right and wrong, which then links us to virtue. Virtue ethics uses an ethical lens where the moral virtues of an individual, organisation, profession, or community are used to guide decision-making, rather than focusing on the outcome to determine the action. Similarly, the divine command theory bases one's actions and moral decisions on the will of God.

# Ethics on video

**Deontology** – *Deontology* 2008, YouTube, PHGFoundation, 8 October, <www.youtube.com/watch?v=79hOZdh4PkQ>.

**Justice** – *'Justice: What's the right thing to do?'* – *Book: Michael Sandal* 2011, YouTube, BookTV, 8 January, <www.youtube.com/watch?v=hB--71OjVEA>.

**John Rawls** – *John Rawls shares some thoughts* 2010, YouTube, Cara Gillis, 28 August, <www.youtube.com/watch?v=hCJqNrqWykU>.

**Kant on business ethics** – *Norman E. Bowie* 2010, YouTube, corporateethics, 6 October, <www.youtube.com/watch?v=RZr36ifwF2I>.

**Subjectivism** – *Chapter 3 – Ethical Subjectivism.mp4* 2012, YouTube, Alexander Miller, 14 February, <www.youtube.com/watch?v=YJdo4PCTRQM>.

**Utilitarianism** – *Utilitarianism overview* 2009, YouTube, millermanproductions, 22 July, <www.youtube.com/watch?v=knCIPpkdyVE>.

**Virtue ethics** – *Joseph R. DesJardins* 2011, YouTube, corporateethics, 11 June, <www.youtube.com/watch?v=OH7R9IfNu80>.

See web material for more videos.

# Ethics at the movies

Here are a few movie suggestions that are relevant for ethics theory:

**Horton Hears A Who!** – follows Horton the Elephant's attempts to protect a microscopic community as his neighbours refuse to believe it exists. Looks at Kantian theory. *Horton hears a who!* 2008, Gordon, B, Anderson, B & Meledandri, C.

*****Saving Private Ryan** – after a graphic portrayal of World War II's Omaha Beach assault, the film follows the United States Army Rangers' search for Private Ryan, the last surviving brother of four sons. Looks at utilitarianism. *Saving Private Ryan* 1998, Bryce, I, Gordon, M, Levinsohn, G & Spielberg, S.

*****Author's pick**

See web material for more movies.

# Ethics on the web

**Institute for Business Ethics**, based in the UK, its vision is to be the leader in knowledge and practice of corporate business ethics, <www.ibe.org.uk>.

**St James Ethics Centre**, an independent, not-for-profit organisation which provides a forum for the promotion and exploration of ethics and ethical decision-making, <www.ethics.org.au>.

See web material for more web references.

# Student exercises

See web material for answers to student short answer questions.

## Short answer questions

1.  In the discussion of Kantian Theory, we have been applying this theory to humans. Can this theory and related precepts apply also to animals and the contentious issue of animal testing?
2.  How might an organisation violate an employee's right to privacy?
3.  A question which continues to be raised and is naturally linked to the concept of rights in the business environment, is, do corporations have moral rights within the context of constitutive rules?
4.  As part of good governance, there are certain expectations that are attached to being in the role of a director; however, looking at the role from the perspective of the individual, what might be their rights?
5.  What are some the inherent difficulties with using Utilitarianism as a guide to ethical decision-making?

6. What might be the difference between compensatory and retributive justice?
7. What is Rawls's theory of distributive justice?

## Experiential exercises

1. Look up Michael Sandel's talk on 'What is the right thing to do?' online (see <www.ted.com/talks/michael_sandel_what_s_the_right_thing_to_do.html>). What scenarios challenged you the most?
2. Watch the movie *I, Robot* with Will Smith and locate the scene in which a robot undertakes a utilitarian approach to decision-making in deciding who to save from drowning.

# Small case

### Case: Product safety

You are a production supervisor in a company that provides household electrical appliances such as ovens and washing machines. You have recently become aware that one of the products that your firm makes is defective and unsafe. You have already brought this to the attention of management, but they have done nothing to remove the defect. You were considering reporting the matter to external authorities but have decided against this, as in all likelihood it would costs you your job.

**Question:**
1. Use two ethical theories as lenses through which to evaluate this situation.

# Large case

### Case: Security versus liberty

### *Background*

Normative ethical theories are used as differing perspectives from which to view an ethically charged circumstance. A skilled person will be able to use these differing perspectives to evaluate and, hopefully, resolve an ethical issue, confident that they have examined the situation from a number of moral perspectives. Let us attempt to evoke all of these theoretical perspectives in assessing a current ethical issue at the national and international level; the issue of security versus liberty.

### *National security in the US*

The circumstances should be familiar to most who are actively engaged in current affairs. In the aftermath of 11 September 2001, when Al Qaeda terrorists attacked on American soil, the US, understandably shaken, wanted to tighten national security. They rushed legislation through Congress, resulting in the Patriot Act becoming effective on 26 October 2001, which enhanced the reach of the National Security Agency (NSA). What seemed apparent was that American sentiment seemed happy to forfeit some civil liberties in exchange for potential security ('In the secret state' 2013); however, some have subsequently expressed concerns about whether American values have become causalities in the war on terror, asking whether the measures been put in place have gone too far in restricting civil liberties ('Liberties lost decade' 2013).

The ethicality of indefinite incarceration without trial; of prisoners has been raised in the instances of Guantanamo Bay, the redefinition of torture of prisoners, to categorise waterboarding and stress positions as 'enhanced interrogation'; and the degradation and abuse of Iraqi detainees at Abu Ghraib Prison in 2003 ('Liberties lost decade' 2013). These activities, as well as significant details leaked about the NSA's massive surveillance activities, including invasion into privacy to glean email and web traffic data using XKey-Score computer program, were exposed by *The Guardian* on 31 July 2013. The undertakings of the Foreign Intelligence Surveillance Act (FISA), a secret court set up in 2007 to oversee American spies, has been criticised for enabling the widespread monitoring of non-Americans ('In the secret state' 2013). Such activities have intensified rather than abating with the passing of the *FISA Amendment Act 2008*, which gives spies more freedom to monitor non-citizens abroad, including monitoring content such as email and Facebook messages.

More recently, and possibly in response to these concerns, we have seen the release of damaging military and diplomatic communications to WikiLeaks, by individuals such as Private Bradley Manning (now Chelsea Elizabeth Manning) and Edward Snowden, who have variously been named whistleblowers and traitors ('Less than treachery' 2013).

## Ethical considerations

Let us now look at the 'security versus liberty' debate through the lens of ethical normative theory. First, looking at teleological consequential theories, ethical egoism is grounded in the principle of promoting self-interest. As a consequence, most governments and organisations would feel totally justified to engage in any activity which ensures its self-protection. An erosion of civil liberties would be condoned, and regulatory bodies would actively pursue self-interest, and their own wellbeing. This type of thinking appeared prevalent immediately after the 9/11 attacks; a period through which the speedy drafting, and rapid approval of legislation, weakened civil liberties, but dramatically strengthened security measures, both nationally and internationally. Although it was acknowledged the legislation eroded personal liberties, the sacrifices were deemed irrelevant in the pursuit of self-interest and protection; and the citizens felt some measure of security by relinquishing their personal liberties, and supporting the 'war on terror'.

Now, applying the theoretical concept of utilitarianism, the focus would shift to the outcome, or the consequences, of these practices. Once again, it is likely that current practices and restrictions on civil liberties are deemed acceptable, given the belief that, while unpleasant, the unsavoury use of practices such as detention without trial or torture will lead to outcomes that, on balance, produce the maximum good for the largest number of citizens. This assumption is based on maximising the good to American citizens, but what if this was broadened to non-US citizens? Would the same utilitarian analysis therefore provide a similar result?

An evaluation on the basis of deontology, or non-consequentialism, is where it starts to get interesting, the lenses of duty and obligation are applied. If we use Kant's first formulation and principles of universality and reversibility, we could consider that an action is morally right if everyone in comparable situations acted in the same way.

In doing so, we might anticipate that it would be totally appropriate that other nations enact similar legislation and engage in similar activities, such as detention without trial.

If we consider that, since country A is doing this it is perfectly accepted and understandable, and in fact expected, that country B would also do this and would apply similar measures in similar circumstances, then the behaviour would be considered perfectly acceptable. The actions would be morally condoned. If, however, we are aghast that our enemies would use similar tactics as us, then the universality of our approach comes into question, as does the appropriateness of our practice.

If we use Kant's second formulation, it is more problematic because we must then question whether we are using people as means to an end. We would be hard pressed to say that torture with the deliberate intention of generating intelligence is not using people as a means to an end; therefore, such activities would be deemed morally inappropriate in a purely Kantian sense.

But what if we consider this case from the perspective of duty? Duty is complex, given the variation in roles from which a duty could emit. Governments will see it as their duty to protect their citizens from terrorists, and therefore actions would be deemed appropriate within the context of this duty. How about the guards at Abu Ghraib Prison? What duties do they have and, if duty of care is included, then what role does torture play?

Similarly, if we evaluative the situation using a rights perspective, we get into very sticky ground, as there are a number of rights which clearly clash, and we will need to prioritise certain ones above others, in order to arrive at a decision on the ethical worth of an action. The overarching right is the right to security as opposed to the right to privacy or liberty. But which right is more important? If you are imprisoning individuals without trial, and denying them the right to due process, then clearly the right to security has been placed above the right to liberty; however, if the right to due process is considered to have priority over the right to security, then indefinite detention would clearly be morally wrong.

Next, we might ask, what is the just thing to do? Moving away from detainees in the question of liberty versus security, we can see that justice draws on an intuitive sense of fairness and equity. For example, with widespread surveillance, one might say that all are being equally subjected to this action, therefore there is no unfairness and inequity. Further, there is no differentiation between whose privacy is being invaded, and whose is not, as all individuals are under surveillance.

Finally, what would a person of good character say of this? What would be their moral judgement? We vote political leaders into office on the basis of their personal traits, and in particular their character and integrity, in the hope that it will guide good decision-making. Once that person has the job, it is hoped that their character will provide them with the moral compass they need to make sound decisions. It is therefore not surprising that President Barack Obama, in his early speeches, heralded the need to stop torture, and yet, intriguingly, Guantanamo Bay remains open.

**Question:**
1. Which of the variety of ethical normative theories do you think is most relevant to the security versus liberty debate?.

See web material for:
- answers to short answer questions
- additional student cases
- tutor resources (tutor password required)
- additional material including Ethics at the movies, Ethics in print, Ethics on video and Ethics on the web.

# Chapter 11

## Ethical decision-making

'Real integrity is doing the right thing, knowing that
nobody is going to know whether you did it or not.'
Oprah Winfrey, 1954–,
American talk-show host and philanthropist

## Chapter aim

To investigate the 'black box' of the ethical decision-making process and to develop a set of
guidelines for effective personal ethical decision-making.

## Chapter objectives

1. Contrast two perspectives on ethical decision-making.
2. Describe the features of an interactionist model of ethical decision-making.
3. Present a six-stage model of ethical decision-making.
4. Critique the personal ramifications of whistleblowing.
5. Become familiar with a set of ethical decision-making guidelines that can be used to
   evaluate ethical dilemmas.

# Ethics in the media: Whistleblowing

In 2007, the US Internal Revenue Service awarded whistleblower Bradley Birkenfeld US$104 million for alerting them to tax evasion practices at US Bancorp (USB). Ironically, Birkenfeld was later convicted of helping a property developer avoid taxes ('The world this week' 2012a).

## Introduction

Sir Adrian Cadbury, a prominent figure in the UK and a proponent of corporate governance, tells the story that, in 1900, Queen Victoria sent a decorative tin with a bar of chocolate inside to all of her soldiers who were serving in South Africa. At the time, the order presented an ethical dilemma to Sir Adrian's grandfather, who owned and ran the second largest chocolate company in Britain. While he was anxious for the work, he was deeply and publicly opposed to the Anglo–Boer war in South Africa. How did he resolve the dilemma? He accepted the order but carried it out at cost and made no profit from what he saw as an unjust war. In doing so, his employees benefited from the additional work, the soldiers received their royal present, and Sir Adrian continues to receive the tins to this day. Interestingly, so opposed was Sir Adrian's grandfather to the South African war that he acquired, and financed, the only British newspaper that opposed it (Cadbury 1987).

Of all the chapters in this text, this one is perhaps the most important because it is here that the rubber really hits the road, and ethics changes from an abstract notion to one that requires our personal commitment. We are preparing you for the circumstance when you will be required to evaluate ethically charged situations and actually make decisions which will need to be defended. It is at this point we transfer from merely becoming aware of the ethical issues prevalent in today's business environment, and move to the more constructive and personally challenging position of evaluating ethical scenarios with an outcome in mind.

It is one thing to be aware of what the ethical issues are in a variety of dimensions of business and conversant with the ethical theory and ethical philosophies. However, it becomes more difficult when we put all of this together to move into the pragmatic realm of actual ethical decision-making. It becomes extra-challenging, when you face a real ethical dilemma, to put your knowledge of ethical issues and normative guidelines into practice in order to resolve a situation where the outcome could have significant ramifications for you personally or for a broad group of stakeholders. It may even become harder when we need to actually implement and defend our decision when you face personal reservations and organisational pressures. It is therefore particularly important that, in a text such as this, we discuss the challenges of resolving ethical dilemmas, communicating the outcomes, and defending our decisions.

You might think that the need to exercise your ethical decision-making skills is not going to happen to you. However, the reality is that all of us face ethical dilemmas and we all have the possibility of responding in appropriate or inappropriate ways, depending on our choice of alternatives. Regrettably, it is often the pressure of the circumstance, the desire for more money, the need to get ahead, the need to impress, the need to cover a mistake, or the pressing request from a senior manager, which dictates our response. According to research from the Institute of Leadership and Management (ILM) and Business in the Community (BITC), in a survey of 1000 managers across the public and private sectors, 93% said although their organisation had a value statement, more than 43% had been pressured to behave in direct violation of it; 9% of managers had been asked to break the law at some point in their career; and 10% had left a job as a result of being asked to do something that made them uncomfortable (BITC/ILM 2013).

## Ethics in practice: Decision-making

On your personal recommendation, your company or client invests considerable resources in a creative new production process. Later, you discover that the new process was by no means as effective, or cost-efficient, as you originally anticipated. This could not only be potentially embarrassing, but could reflect badly on you and impact on your career as the error is easily recognised as yours. However, if brought to the attention of others, further losses could be avoided. You propose to say nothing and hope that the error is not recognised.

**Question:**

1. What might be the consequences of this decision?

As we have just discussed, the pressure in ethical decision-making can come in a variety of forms, with lucrative consequences being the most alluring. In his 2013 book, *The Buy Side*, Turney Duff, a former stock trader, outlines moving to Galleon in 1999, just as the hedge-fund boom was starting and at a time when Galleon became one of the world's most powerful hedge-fund companies. At Galleon, he managed a US$7 billion fund where he was on the buy side, placing trades for Galleon's portfolio managers through brokerage firms. Although it was apparent the Galleon bosses lacked a moral compass, the breadth of wrongdoing was quite startling. Turney Duff did not blow the whistle, as, by his own admission, he was enjoying the results he was receiving, and, at the time, was operating in a grey ethical area, making poor ethical choices (Lattman 2013).

We may also think that the dilemma is relatively straightforward, presenting a choice between something that is right or something that is wrong (see Figure 11.1). However, it could also be that the choice is between two 'right' alternatives, such as two beneficial outcomes, and having to determine which stakeholder group wins. Take the example of a professional accountant who needs to decide who should take precedence – the

**Figure 11.1** Introduction

profession or the client? Equally, a dilemma can arise when making a decision between two 'wrong' alternatives and having to choose between two evils, hopefully selecting the alternative that has the least dire consequences. An example of this occurs during a market downturn, when decisions have to be made about whether to lay off workers and alienate employees, or significantly reduce profit expectations, thereby disappointing investors.

Ethical dilemmas are difficult because of their complexity. For example, is it better to compound a lie and keep one's job, or be scrupulously honest, maybe blow the whistle, and face possible unemployment during a recession, with all that it could mean for your family (Longstaff 1992)?

## Different perspectives of ethical decision-making

Ethical decision-making can be viewed from two perspectives:

1. **Theoretical** – models of ethical decision-making.
2. **Practical** – ethical decision-making guidelines.

In the theoretical approach, efforts have been made to look at what dimensions most significantly influence an individual, and what is going on during their decision-making process; what we are calling the black box of ethical decision-making, because it occurs in one's head and is not directly observable. Numerous **models of ethical decision-making** have been generated to provide diagrammatic representations of what might be going on, what factors are at work, and the interplay between them.

Taking a more practical perspective, ethical decision-making also focuses on how an individual might actually make a decision when you face an ethical dilemma, especially when you face compounding pressures, and possible ethical alternatives are available. How does one wade through the dimensions of the issue and arrive at an appropriate, acceptable, and ethically sound decision? The practical perspective involves **ethical decision-making guidelines** and provides assistance in the form of sequential steps that one should progress through in order to determine a morally sound outcome.

In this chapter, we will explore both perspectives and, in doing so, will develop our own six-stage model of ethical decision-making, drawing heavily on previous models which incorporate ethical decision-making guidelines that can be used for resolving ethical dilemmas.

**models of ethical decision-making** – diagrammatic representations of the cognitive decision-making process and relevant factors.

**ethical decision-making guidelines** – practical guidelines in the form of sequential steps and questions to assist in the ethical decision-making process.

# Existing models of ethical decision-making

Looking first at the theoretical perspective, and in an attempt to open up the black box of our heads to see what is actually going on, many have attempted to provide explanations of the ethical evaluation process, usually in diagrammatic form (see Wotruba 1990). These are called ethical decision-making models, a variety of which have developed over the years.

These models provide a visual representation of general theoretical abstractions associated with ethical decision-making. In other words, they attempt to describe what is actually going on. They also go further than just the traditional normative philosophical base, and draw in additional information and ideas from psychology, sociology and organisational behaviour. These models look at the interactions between a variety of dimensions, and, consequently, are commonly called **interactionist models**. In general, they attempt to describe the cognitive process decision-makers follow when you face problems containing ethical dimensions and the factors influencing ethical decision-making.

According to Ashkanasy, Windsor and Treviño (2006) and others (Pearlstein 2002; Snell 2000), recent business scandals demonstrate the need for further empirical research and the development of models which adequately encompass the multitude of factors relating to, and influencing, ethical decision-making. Ashkanasy et al. (2006) claim that ethical decision-making models tend to focus on two influences: 1) the characteristics of individuals and how they impact on a person's ethical decisions; and 2) the characteristics of organisations that influence personal ethical decisions and conduct. They argue for an extension of these two influences, and, to achieve this, draw on Treviño (1986) and Treviño and Youngblood (1990) to explore the interaction between cognitive moral development and reward and punishment expectancy.

Like Ashkanasy et al. (2006) and Husted and Allen (2008), the majority of recent literature surrounding models of ethical decision-making tends to build on the work of earlier researchers, such as Jones (1991), Treviño (1986) and Rest (1986). This continuing use of the models indicates that, although they are now dated, they still offer a sound foundation on which to build an exploration of the major factors at play in ethical decision-making.

> **interactionist models** – models that draw on a variety of dimensions to describe what is going on in ethical decision-making.

## Ethics in practice: Ethical decision-making model

When you have read this chapter, select one of the ethical decision-making models discussed here, and locate a diagrammatic representation of the model.

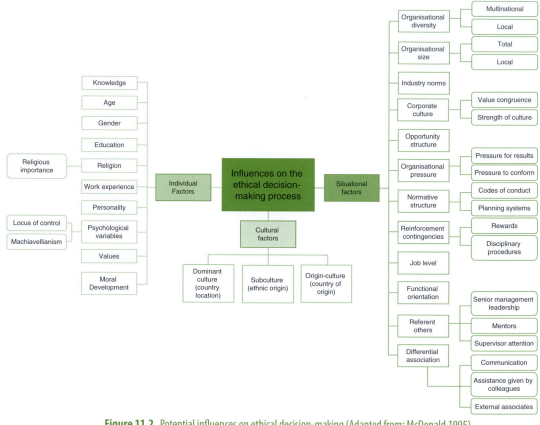

**Figure 11.2**  Potential influences on ethical decision-making (Adapted from: McDonald 1995)

From these models, a large number of factors can be observed which could be said to influence the ethical decision-making process. These influences can be broadly categorised into:

1.  individual factors
2.  organisational factors
3.  cultural factors.

Each of these three broad categories of influence contains a multitude of sub-influences as seen in Figure 11.2, for example. Individual factors could include one's prior knowledge, age, gender, level of education, religious orientation, years of work experience, psychological factors, personal values and level of moral development. Organisational factors cover a range of influences, such as: how diverse the organisation is (i.e. is it international and how many branches it has); the size of the company in terms of employee numbers; what is the industry norm; the corporate culture; and the more immediate influences, such as, opportunity for unethical action; organisational pressure; the rules and reinforcers that exist; as well as the job level at which the person operates. The influence of one's culture should be more nuanced than just looking at the dominant culture within which one resides, it should also be cognisant of the influence of one's culture of origin (that is, where you were brought up) as well as one's ethnic origins or subculture. Take, for example, a person who is living in Malaysia; the dominant culture is Malaysian, but their ethnic origin could be Indian, Chinese or Malay, yet, they could also have been brought up in, say, Australia. All of these factors will influence a person's 'ethical blue print' and their ethical decision-making.

# A six-stage model of ethical decision-making

Rest (1986, 1994) was one of the earlier theorists to assert that ethical decisions and actions are not the outcome of a single unitary decision process, but rather a combination of cognitive structures and psychological processes. Rest suggests four components critical in the decision-making process:

- **ethical sensitivity** – an initial awareness that circumstances contain ethical dimensions and that resolution of a dilemma may affect the welfare of others
- **prescriptive reasoning** – an individual's judgement of what the ideal solution would be, which can be influenced by their stage of moral development
- **ethical motivation** – the willingness to not only place ethical values, such as honesty and integrity, ahead of non-ethical values, such as security, money and power, but also demonstrating the ethical intention or willingness to comply with their ethical intention
- **ethical character** – the strength of adherence to one's ethical intention including following through with an ethical action. A strong ethical character is more likely to stay on track and implement the right decision.

A well-conceived schematic model is useful in understanding behaviour, especially in situations where an individual is subjected to multiple forces, and most of the interactionist models of ethical decision-making appear to have common elements. These models can help with the identification of an ethical issue and a decision-making process that is modified by internal and external influencing factors, leading to ethical or unethical behaviour.

In this chapter, we will build on Rest's model to develop a six-stage model of ethical decision-making, incorporating an ethical decision-making framework. The components of our model are depicted diagrammatically, in Figure 11.3, and are now discussed in more detail.

# Stage 1: Moral awareness

Our ethical decision-making model is consistent with other models, and it starts with moral awareness. **Moral awareness** is defined as a person's determination that a situation contains moral content that could be considered from a moral point of view (Reynolds 2006). Moral

**moral awareness** – sensitivity that is circumstantial and contains a moral dimension.

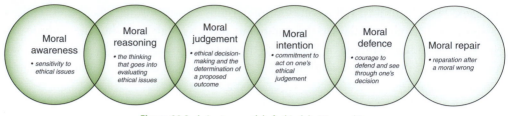

**Figure 11.3**  A six-stage model of ethical decision-making

awareness is one's sensitivity to a circumstance that contains a moral dimension and, it appears, awareness of ethical issues varies according to specific situations.

Those who have no ethical sensitivity are blissfully unaware that a particular circumstance has a moral dimension to it; a bit like not seeing the wood for the trees. These people are only aware of the personalities and facts of the situation, but cannot see which ethical principle is potentially about to be eroded, or which ethical issue is contained within the circumstance. Examples occur when: raunchy banter in the lunchroom is not seen as sexual harassment; misrepresenting oneself as a market researcher with a competitor is not seen as deception; and when awarding a large contract to a friend is not viewed as a conflict of interest. The ethical issue that unpins the details is simply not detected due to the lack of ethical awareness.

Being aware of a moral issue and its implications also involves empathy towards others and an ability to identify all relevant stakeholders. A lack of moral awareness increases the chance of unethical decision-making. An absence of moral awareness means that a person is unlikely to incorporate moral considerations into his or her deliberations, and, as a consequence, moral awareness is the foundation of moral reasoning and ethical decision-making (Bryant 2009).

# Ethics on reflection: Moral awareness

In his book, *The Folly of Fools*, biologist Robert Trivers suggests that people who are devious are often unaware of their deceit – a form of self-deception that makes it easier to manipulate others in order to get ahead. Do you believe this to be true? Is it possible for an individual to have no awareness of their deceit, and, by inference, no moral awareness or sensitivity (Trivers 2012)?

Research to date has documented the link between an individual's ethical sensitivity, level of moral development, and subsequent ethical behaviour (Cohen, Pant & Sharp 1995). It has also been noted that women tend to have greater skill at identifying ethical issues; and that training and experience can improve an individual's ethical sensitivity and ability to recognise that a decision-making situation has ethical content (Treviño, Weaver & Reynolds 2006).

Apparently, it is possible to measure one's ethical sensitivity. Rest's **defining issues test** has been used as a measure of ethical sensitivity, with studies suggesting that accounting major students consistently score lower on Rest's defining issues test than the general population, throughout and after college, which is of concern to the accounting profession (Bean & Bernardi 2007). Interestingly, it has also been found that detecting fraud increases as an individual's score on the defining issues test increases, suggesting that one's ethical sensitivity is a good precursor to fraud detection (Bernardi 1994).

**defining issues test** – a measure of ethical sensitivity.

"Maybe there's a good reason why no one else has broken into this market."

Moral awareness (© shutterstock.com/Cartoonresource)

# Ethics in practice: Moral awareness

A CEO of a struggling company reveals to the board her hidden history with chronic depression after several lengthy and unexplained absences. As Chairperson, you are now determining how to handle this situation.

**Questions:**
1. What are the ethical dimensions?
2. Who are the key stakeholders, and what are their ethical values (Pincus 2013)?

## Factors influencing moral awareness

Let's look at the factors influencing moral awareness.

**Knowledge** – the extent to which a person actually sees the moral implications in a circumstance is very much influenced by their knowledge. The more knowledge one has about the issue, as well as the consequences, the more likely they are to have sensitivities around the issue. Also, the more one is exposed to circumstances that are recognised as moral issues, the more it facilitates the recognition of moral issues (Gautschi & Jones 1998). The theory of planned behaviour proposes that for an attitude to be formed, individual factual knowledge about an issue is a pre-condition (Ajzen 1985). As an example of the link between awareness, knowledge and ultimate action, Polonsky et al.'s (2012) study of sensitivity towards environmental issues found a positive relationship between general and carbon-specific knowledge, sensitivity to the issues, and subsequent general and carbon-specific behaviours. As a consequence, it is recognised that there is a need to focus efforts on developing consumers' awareness and knowledge about environmental issues, global warming and carbon impacts in an effort to increase environmental sensitivities and influence behaviour.

**Ethical orientation** – describing a person's ethical orientation is a polite way of assessing the development of their ethical inclination or proclivity, with a documented link occurring between an individual's level of moral development and their subsequent ethical behaviour (Cohen, Pant & Sharp 1995). The best known description of moral development is **Kohlberg's stages of moral development** (Kohlberg 1969; 1981). Kohlberg's theory presents three broad stages of moral judgement, which are then delineated into six steps, with individuals irreversibly moving through and up the stages (see Chapter 1 for a discussion on Kohlberg's theory of cognitive moral development).

The three stages of Kohlberg's cognitive moral development theory are:

- **pre-conventional stage** – a childlike, self-centred stage where an individual is motivated to obey the rules in order to demonstrate obedience to authority and avoid punishment
- **conventional stage** – a more developed stage where an individual is motivated to adhere to the expectations of others. There is some recognition of duty, but largely he or she is relying on the expectations of others
- **post-conventional stage** – at this highest stage of development an individual is more independent and utilises ethical principles such as justice and rights.

Moral development has been associated with age and educational level (Rest et al. 1986). It has also been indicated that most adults sit at the conventional level, and less than 20% of American adults reach stages 5 or 6 (Rest et al. 1999). Those at the highest stage are less susceptible to contextual influences (Treviño 1986). Types of moral reasoning appear to be universal, with similar age and education trends found across cultural brackets (Treviño, Weaver & Reynolds 2006).

**Contextual issues** – it has been suggested that there are many other contextual factors that may influence moral awareness such as: the existence of a competitive framework; the issue; the magnitude of consequences; the moral language used; and the degree of social consensus around the issue (Butterfield, Treviño & Weaver 2000). That is, public outrage on an issue is evident as social consensus grows.

> **Kohlberg's stages of moral development** – three broad stages of moral development which individuals move through.

"We must lighten the load.
It's my turn to take one for the team."

Factors influencing moral awareness (© shutterstock.com/Cartoonresource)

**Self-regulation** – in relation to moral awareness, there is an aspect of social condition, termed self-regulation, which describes how people set goals and then self-direct their own thoughts and behaviour towards reaching those goals. Self-regulation is seen as an important dimension of moral awareness because being aware of the moral content of situations will influence how a person self-regulates and which moral issues they will attend to, or care about. For example, Bryant (2009) found that entrepreneurs with strong self-regulatory characteristics were more morally aware, and related such awareness with the goals of maintaining personal integrity and building interpersonal trust.

**self-regulation** – where people set goals and then self-direct their own thoughts and behaviour towards those goals.

**Psychic numbing** – but what of those circumstances we hear about where an individual, usually upon being caught, indicates that while they were brought up in a family environment that advocated moral responsibility, and would previously have claimed that they had ethical sensitivities, the circumstances they were in lulled them into not being cognisant of the moral dimensions that previously they would have been alert to? To reinforce this point, and building on Hunt and Vitell's (1993) theory of ethics and ethical sensitivity, Tenbrunsel and Messick (2004) have presented the concept of psychic numbing, which comes from being exposed to repeated circumstances where there has been ethical erosion.

**psychic numbing** – numbing that comes from being exposed to repeated circumstances where there is repeated rule-breaking or ethical violations.

The US trader Dennis Levine typifies psychic numbing and exemplifies the ethical environment in Wall Street in the 1980s. Working for Drexel Burnham, as a rising mergers and acquisitions star, he was reaping vast sums of money from insider-trading profits and depositing them into offshore bank accounts. In his book, *Inside out: An insider's account of Wall Street* (1991), Levine remarked that being offered a high-level job at Drexel Burnham was akin to stumbling on a pot of gold. He came unstuck, however, and after serving a jail term he wrote about his experiences. Intriguingly, Levine considered himself to be an ethical person brought up with strong moral values. When he reflected on why he had gone astray, he remarked that his ambition exceeded rationality and he could not find fulfilment in realistic settings. As the days passed, the deals became more critical as the scale of the finances involved grew and his desire to win increased. Drexel Burhnam, in 1986, had earned a profit of US$500 million, but four years later on 13 February 1990, the company filed for bankruptcy (Calhoun, Olivero & Wolitzer 1999).

**Moral intensity** – as we have already seen, moral awareness is a person's determination that a situation contains moral content and legitimately can be considered from a moral point of view. A lack of moral awareness increases the risk of unethical decision-making and immoral behaviour. However, it may not be a simple case of being morally aware (or not), as a person can exhibit different patterns of moral awareness in different situations (Treviño 1986) which could relate to the degree of moral intensity contained in the situation.

**moral intensity** – the degree to which an ethical circumstance contains both harm and the violation of behavioural norms.

Reynolds (2006) argues that moral awareness is stimulated by a person's attention to two characteristics of the circumstance: the presence of harm and the violation of behavioural norms. The existence of these characteristics would flag that the situation contains moral content and needs to be considered from a moral point of view. Some people are more predisposed to paying attention to both harm and violation of behavioural norms and therefore are more likely to generate moral awareness.

Jones (1991) and Leitsch (2004) provide a more detailed explanation and suggest that moral intensity is an issue which is influenced by six factors:

1. **The magnitude of the consequences** – in other words, the severity of the outcomes or the total amount of harm that could result from an action.
2. **Social consensus** – the degree of agreement by society, that is, the public consensus on the 'good' or 'bad' and what the resulting outcome could be.
3. **The probability effect** – the likelihood that an action will occur and cause harm.
4. **Temporal immediacy** – the speed in which consequences are likely to occur.
5. **Proximity** – the closer an individual is to one's actions, for example, in equities trading there is no identifiable victim who stares you in the face, so there is low proximity.
6. **The concentration of effect** – this is the number of people who will be affected as a consequence of a decision or action.

The perception of moral intensity will influence not only moral awareness but also the judgements surrounding the evaluation of ethical dilemmas and the intention to behave ethically or unethically (May & Pauli 2002).

## Stage 2: Moral reasoning

Having recognised an ethical issue, most individuals move into the next stage, in which they invoke their moral reasoning during the preceding steps towards making an ethical judgement. **Moral reasoning** refers to a person's thinking process as they grapple with an ethical dilemma and draw on guidance from known ethical principles, personal values, religious dictates, norms or rules.

**moral reasoning** – the development of the rationale and thinking process a person engages in when dealing with an ethical dilemma.

Moral reasoning is the ability to evaluate what should be considered and the development of the rationale that goes into resolving an ethical dilemma. An individual will draw on moral principles, values, rules, and any other cognitive framework that will help in thinking through the issue. If a person is aware of moral philosophy, he or she can commonly use it to provide principles in, and guidance about, personal or professional values and norms, which can shed light on the dilemma.

In the past, attempts have been made to measure ethical reasoning usually using the multi-dimensional ethics scale (MES). This instrument permits insight into the cognitive ethical reasoning process and complements the defining issues test, mentioned previously, for assessing moral awareness. In a study of financial advisers and compliance managers, Smith (2010) found that their ethical reasoning was lower than required to resolve effectively the complex ethical dilemmas often associated with the provision of advice to consumers and, thus, led to a risk of poor decision-making and unethical behaviour. LaFleur et al. (1996) observed that variations in advertisers' ethical judgements and ethical intentions were affected by the type of rules used during the evaluative process, and by the degree to which the rules are embraced. Apparently, an individual's ethical reasoning levels are significantly influenced by age and years of experience; whether the person holds a professional designation; and whether they have been previously exposed to ethics training (Smith 2010).

## Cognitive reasoning frameworks

When evaluating an ethical issue, the whole arsenal of ethical philosophy and ethical principles is available to the decision-maker, if known, to assist with ethical reasoning. For example, they could use a utilitarian analysis of maximising benefits, that is, the greatest good for the greatest number could be used in the evaluation, or the decision-maker could be guided by an overarching sense of justice and what the fair thing to do is, irrespective of consequences. Alternatively, an individual could use a different lens and consider what rights should be supported, or what his or her duty is in the circumstances (for a review of ethical theory, see Chapter 10). Philosophical frameworks and moral principles are not the only frameworks that can be used in the evaluation of ethical issues. A decision-maker could draw from their religion, psychological justifications, or even an overriding concern of being exposed, see Figure 11.4.

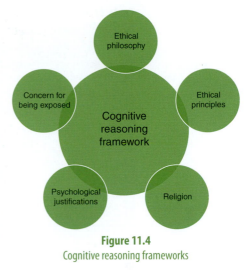

**Figure 11.4**
Cognitive reasoning frameworks

Attempts have been made to identify which **cognitive reasoning frameworks**, including utilitarian, results-based, or more rules-based approaches, are preferred by individuals (Brady & Wheeler 1996; McDonald & Pak 1996), with considerable variation being identified. Gauging which type of ethical reasoning has been used has been met with mixed findings; however, there are some indications that managers predominantly use a utilitarian approach (Premeaux & Mondy 1993; Fritzsche & Becker 1984), although it has also been recognised, and this is good to see, that individuals may use more than one philosophical framework in making an ethical judgement (Brady & Wheeler 1996; Schminke, Ambrose & Noel 1997).

Table 11.1 contains suggestions of the common cognitive frameworks used by individuals when engaged in ethical decision-making. In addition to the common philosophical cognitive frameworks, a decision-maker could draw upon their personal values, such as promise-keeping, the pursuit of excellence, loyalty and responsible citizenship (Guy 1990).

**cognitive reasoning frameworks** – philosophical frameworks, moral principles, rules, values, norms and religious dictates that may be employed during the ethical reasoning process.

# Ethics in practice: Ethical principles

Review the previous chapter and generate 10 ethical principles that could be used as part of the ethical reasoning process.

**Table 11.1** Eight cognitive reasoning frameworks

| Self-interest | Based on the teleological/consequential theory, self-interest dictates that during the reasoning process the principal evaluative concern is one of selfishly gaining the greatest degree of personal satisfaction or advantage. |
| --- | --- |
| Utilitarianism | As the flagship theory of the teleological/consequential school, utilitarianism is the reasoning process which evokes the evaluation of costs and benefits, or good and bad, in an effort to maximise utility. |
| Categorical imperative | Drawn from Immanuel Kant's contribution to deontological normative theory, ethical reasoning is based on the principle that an action is either morally right or wrong, regardless of its consequences. |
| Duty | Consideration would be given as to whether the circumstances were in keeping with, or violated, any prescribed rules of duty. |
| Justice | Concerns the question of 'fairness' and whether there has been a just distribution of benefits and burdens among all those involved. |
| Neutralisation | Drawn from the field of psychology, an individual would use justifications as part of the reasoning process. |
| Religious/philosophical conviction | When facing an ethical dilemma, the decision-maker will refer to their religious conviction. |
| Light of day | During the decision-making process, the most salient factor taken into consideration in the reasoning process by the decision-maker is in connection with the question, 'What if this information went public?' |

(Source: McDonald & Pak 1996)

## Moral disengagement

**moral disengagement** – when a person recognises that a dilemma raises ethical issues but decides not to go through an evaluative process to resolve them.

What happens when a person recognises the ethical issue but decides not to go through an evaluative process to resolve the ethical dilemma? He or she is experiencing **moral disengagement**, a term that Moore (2013) created to describe the process that enables people to behave unethically without feeling any psychological distress or believing that what they are doing is wrong. Individuals who show a high propensity to morally disengage are also more likely to justify their actions, that is, to frame their actions in morally disengaged terms, with statements such as: 'I was doing it in the best interests of the company'; 'I was looking out for shareholders'; or 'I was using best business practices'. Moore (2013) has suggested that when business leaders are morally disengaged and act unethically, they change the way other employees think about ethical decisions. Employees don't think, 'I'm going to act badly because I have to'; they actually think the behaviour is acceptable and that senior management endorse it.

## Stage 3: Moral judgement

**moral judgement** – the ethical decision-making process a person uses to evaluate an ethical dilemma.

You may have noted that in our model no final decision has yet been made. In the previous stage is where reasoning and thinking occurs and it is not until now, in the **moral judgement** stage, that we actually start to pull everything together in order to make a decision (see Figure 11.5). It is here that we have embedded ethical decision-making guidelines, which is the more practical dimension of ethical decision-making.

Moral judgement has been found to be linked to ethical conduct (Treviño & Youngblood 1990). Moral judgement has also been associated with the level of harm, and with high levels of moral judgement being exhibited when the consequences of an ethical issue are significant (Fray 2000).

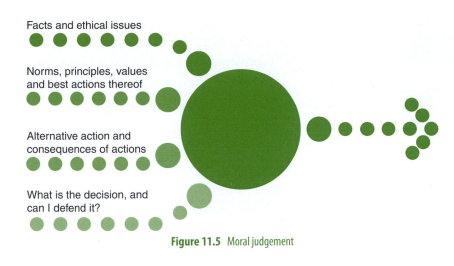

Facts and ethical issues

Norms, principles, values
and best actions thereof

Alternative action and
consequences of actions

What is the decision, and
can I defend it?

**Figure 11.5** Moral judgement

# Ethical decision-making guidelines

The theory of reasoned actions (Ajzen & Fishbein 1980) assumes that individuals are usually rational, and utilise the information that is available to them when deciding to engage in a given behaviour. For example, most people are aware that ethical or unethical behaviour leads to certain outcomes, and it is the evaluation of these outcomes in terms of their goodness or badness that will influence a decision-maker and prompt them to act or not to act. This all sounds quite reasonable, but in the circumstances of ethical decision-making, one needs to be very conscious of self-interest and pressures from other influences. In order to assist a decision-maker, the more practical provision of ethical decision-making guidelines, in the form of questions, has been proposed.

Several guidelines have been developed, and one of the more popular sets of ethical decision-making guidelines has been proposed and adopted by the American Accounting Association. It is called the **AAA model of ethical decision-making**, and it comprises a seven-step process developed by Langenderfer and Rockness (1989), in which we:

1. identify the facts
2. identify the ethical issues
3. identify the norms, principles and values related to the case
4. identify the alternative courses of action
5. identify the best course of action, consistent with step 3
6. identify the consequences of each possible course of action
7. make the decision.

The trick is to find a set of guidelines which are not overly complicated or time-consuming, but can be easily remembered and utilised when facing an ethical issue. We encourage you to look at other models and find the one with which you are most comfortable, or develop your own if you prefer. Alternatively, the AAA model provides a useful resource that can be

**AAA model of ethical decision-making** – a seven-step process designed to help with making ethical decisions.

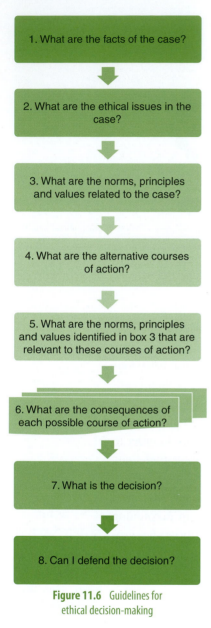

1. What are the facts of the case?

2. What are the ethical issues in the case?

3. What are the norms, principles and values related to the case?

4. What are the alternative courses of action?

5. What are the norms, principles and values identified in box 3 that are relevant to these courses of action?

6. What are the consequences of each possible course of action?

7. What is the decision?

8. Can I defend the decision?

**Figure 11.6**  Guidelines for ethical decision-making

used for real circumstances or educational cases. We will elaborate on the guidelines and add one final step in the process. Consequently, the eight steps to assist ethical decision-making as depicted in Figure 11.6 follow.

## Guidelines for ethical decision-making

1.  What are the facts of the case? In this step you are looking at one of the details of the circumstance of the case. What is the primary problem and who are the stakeholders in both the short and long term?
2.  What are the ethical issues in the case? What is the ethical issue, or issues, as there is frequently more the one ethical issue contained in the circumstance?
3.  What are the norms, principles and values related to the case? What were the principles, norms, religious dictates and rules that were considered during ethical reasoning, and are they of relevance to the case in question?
4.  What are the alternative courses of action? There are usually three courses of action which can be taken. One course of action is always to retain the status quo, that is, do nothing. Hopefully, by looking at alternative courses of action, a decision-maker can entertain extremes, and can at least put alternatives on the table for evaluation, even if some of the alternatives are not palatable to all stakeholders.
5.  What is the best course of action that is consistent with the norms, principles and values identified in step 3? In this step, the decision-maker will align their norms, principles and values against each of the alternatives and may be forced to prioritise one principle above another. This is not easy but is often necessary in order to resolve an ethical dilemma. Take, for example, the vexed issue of abortion. Here, there are two compelling principles which one could claim are of equal standing; the right to life for an unborn child, and the freedom of choice for the mother. It is not until we have prioritised one set of principles over the other that resolution is imminent. If one supports and prioritises the principle of right to life over freedom of choice, then the decision would be not to support abortion. Other principles that are often in conflict are truth versus loyalty; justice versus mercy; or even short-term versus long-term outcomes.
6.  What are the consequences of each possible course of action? Each alternative will have subsequent and ongoing impacts for a variety of stakeholders. It is advisable therefore to consider what the consequences might be, in both the short and the long term, for all stakeholders in each alternative. This evaluation should be quite exhaustive, and the deeper the evaluation undertaken at this stage, the better the chance that an appropriate decision will be made, and that risk will be minimised for the decision-maker.

7. What is the decision? Not to make a decision regarding the dilemma and to abdicate decision-making, often leads to an ethical issue festering. It is at this point the decision-maker will need to narrow down which alternative supports the ethical principle they have prioritised or value the most. For example, in their decision-making process, whistleblowers, whom we will look at in more detail later in the chapter, often face a dilemma between conflicting values of loyalty to the organisation, honesty to themselves, professional duty, and also respect for friends and colleagues which will need to be prioritised.

8. Could I publicly defend this decision? The final and additional step that we have put into this ethical decision-making guideline is to question whether you could defend your decision.

In the accounting profession, to ensure that decisions are in the public interest and that a professional accountant is acting with independence, the following questions are frequently asked:

- Are we being honest and straightforward?
- Are we compromising our judgement?
- Would another member make the same decision?
- Would a third party accept the decision we have made? Do I? Do my colleagues?
- Would we be comfortable discussing the issues with a client or a third party?
  (Adapted from Joint Accounting Bodies: CPA Australia, The Institute of Chartered Accountants in Australia & The Institute of Public Accountants 2013)

Another simple test that can be applied before we embark on a certain course of action is called the **TV test**. This test has been around for some time, but was recently given prominence when referred to by the emergency Chairman of Salomon Brothers, Warren Buffett, who appeared before a US Senate hearing regarding the improper trading of treasury bonds. Buffett suggested that the TV test be applied when asking yourself whether or not you would be happy to appear on prime-time television to be questioned about your proposed course of action by a skilled and fully informed interviewer, and knowing that your family and friends would be members of the audience. Such a test is invaluable as a rough rule of thumb (Longstaff 1992). There is also the **Mum test**: what would your mother say if she knew? Would she approve of your decision?

## Stage 4: Moral intention

It is one thing to make an ethical judgement, but it is entirely another to see that judgement through. That is, having made the right decision, do you have the full conviction, or intention to see that decision actually implemented? **Moral intention** is a person's intention to comply (or not) with an ethical judgement he or she has made that would lead to ethical behaviour. Ethical intention is influenced by **ethical motivation**, which reflects an individual's willingness to place ethical values, such as honesty, integrity, sincerity and

**TV test** – asking yourself whether you would be happy to be interviewed on TV regarding your decision-making and proposed course of action.

**Mum test** – what would your mother say if she knew about your proposed course of action?

**moral intention** – (also called ethical motivation) reflects an individual's willingness to place ethical values ahead of non-ethical values and to implement the outcome of an ethical decision.

**ethical motivation** – an individual's willingness to place ethical values above non-ethical values.

truthfulness, ahead of non-ethical values such as wealth, power, fame and recognition (Thorne 1998).

## Moral identity

**moral identity** (also known as **moral character**) – the depth to which moral values are internalised and how resilient these values are under pressure.

Our **moral identity** influences our moral intention and moral motivation. Sometimes referred to as **moral character**, moral identity can be seen as the depth to which we have internalised our moral values and how resilient these values are when under pressure. The generally held view is that moral identity has a strong oneness with moral behaviour (Aquino & Reed 2002).

Moral identity has been defined as a person's self-conception, organised around a set of fundamental values that are seen as 'good', 'worthy' and 'moral' (Taylor 1988; Narvaez & Lapsley 2009). Many theorists (see Kohlberg & Mayer 1972) have explored the issue of moral identity, and, although some question the validity of these theories for the modern day (Navaraez & Lapsley 2009; Blasi 1983, 1984, 1985, 2005), they continue to offer a useful platform from which to grasp the complexities of a moral self, character or identity.

**virtue** – describes the characteristics of the decision-maker and the increased propensity to act ethically.

Researchers have also drawn attention to the importance of **virtue**, which is closely aligned to moral identity. Virtue describes the characteristics and motivations of the decision-maker. Those who possess and exercise virtue increase their propensity to act ethically (Thorne 1998). Virtue also provides the moral intent, or moral mettle, necessary to carry out judgements according to a moral point of view (Mintz 1996).

Treviño (1986) suggests that three aspects of an **individual's moral character** affect their propensity to act ethically:

1. **Ego strength** describes one's tendency to resist impulse and follow conviction.
2. **Field dependence** describes the degree to which one uses social references as a guide for behaviour.
3. **Locus of control** reflects the extent to which one perceives that one has control over his or her own fate (Thorne 1998). There is a suggested link that the higher one's external locus of control, the higher one's moral character.

## Stage 5: Moral defence

**moral defence** – resolution to actually implement and stand by the decision.

Intention that turns into behaviour may require another strengthening of resolve, particularly when a decision is unpalatable to others. At this stage, one may be called upon to defend a decision, in what is known as **moral defence**. It has been observed that the recent financial scandals were not the result of professional accountants' lack of skill in recording transactions, but were due to a lack of courage to report problems; that is, the failures were ethical, resulting from a lack of moral courage (Brooks & Dunn 2012). Most people can intellectually work through the steps to resolve an ethical dilemma, but it often takes significant resolution to actually implement and stand by the decision. That takes courage.

## Moral courage

Courage is ubiquitously accepted as a great virtue and has been since the time of Plato and Aristotle (Miller 2005). **Moral courage** is demonstrated when a person does the right thing and holds onto their values, particularly when others look away or choose to do nothing (Miller 2005; McCain & Salter 2004). The morally courageous are people who do the right thing even when they are scared and potentially face negative consequences as a result of their actions (Coles 2000; Putnam 1997; Miller 2000).

It is important to note that an essential aspect of moral courage is action (Sekerka & Bagozzi 2007). Once a moral decision is made, an individual *must* act on that decision (Coles 2000; Miller 2005; Sekerka & Bagozzi 2007). Indeed, behaviour is necessary, as it distinguishes between moral courage and mere moral reasoning (Miller 2005).

In her book, *Giving voice to values: How to speak your mind when you know what's right*, Mary Gentile (2010) has suggested ways of actively promoting moral courage as a shift away from the 'right' answer to an ethical challenge, to how an individual can practise acting out one's values in the face of potential resentment, isolation and other pressures that a person may experience.

**moral courage** – doing the right thing and holding on to one's values, particularly when others look away or choose to do nothing.

## Ethics on reflection: Moral courage

For a discussion of the practicalities of demonstrating moral courage, watch the TED Talks video – *Creating Ethical Cultures in Business. Brook Deterline TEDx Presentation* 2012, TEDxTalks, 11 September, retrieved 31 January 2014, <www.youtube.com/watch?v=wzicXbnmllc>.

## Ethics in the media: Whistleblowing

Ex-President and CEO of Olympus Corporation, Michael Woodford, was dismissed after he brought to light an accounting scandal. He is thought to have received an out-of-court settlement valued at US$16 million for unfair dismissal ('The world this week' 2012b).

## Whistleblowing as moral courage

There is an obvious reluctance to whistleblow as the personal ramifications can be significant. According to research from the ILM and BITC, 27% of the respondents to their survey were concerned their career would suffer if they were to report an ethical breach, with **whistleblowing** fears higher among junior managers (17%) than directors (9%) (BITC/ILM 2013).

An analysis of the individual differences in whistleblowers has found that they tend to be female, tenured employees, higher performers, and those at higher job levels in an organisation (Treviño, Weaver & Reynolds 2006).

Whistleblowing (© shutterstock.com/Slavoljub Pantelic)

# Ethics in practice: Whistleblowing

Sherron Watkins was a Vice President at Enron when she wrote a memo to the company's CEO, Kenneth Lay, outlining her concerns regarding former CEO Jeffrey Skilling's abrupt departure, noting that it would raise suspicions of accounting improprieties, which were justified. She indicated that she was nervous the organisation would implode in the wake of accounting scandals. This observation was prophetic as Enron did ultimately implode and Sherron Watkins was subsequently featured on the cover of *Time* Magazine and applauded as a corporate whistleblower.

**Question:**

1. Undertake an internet search and see what you can find out about Sherron Watkins's whistleblowing actions.

# Ethics in practice: Whistleblowing

You work for a large construction company. In keeping with the industry, your company experiences high staff turnover. Recently, you have discovered that one of your most experienced employees has been cutting down pipes for resale. Your initial reaction was to report the employee, but you know that he will probably be fired if you do so. This employee is extremely valuable to you at work, and the profit he makes from the pipes is not significant.

**Question:**

1. What is the likelihood that you will take action in this case?

# Ethics in the media: Whistleblowing

Edward Snowden, America's National Security Agency whistleblower, revealed NSA had spied on the European Union's diplomatic headquarters in Brussels, to which many European countries reacted angrily, with the French calling for talks on proposed transatlantic free trade agreements to be suspended ('The world this week' 2013).

# Ethics in practice: Whistleblower resources

You have a friend who is considering blowing the whistle on financial improprieties in his company. Your friend has tried raising the issue with his immediate manager, but it has gone nowhere. Even a quiet word to one of the board directors did not generate any changes.

Have a look at the National Whistleblowers Centre (see <www.whistleblowers.org>).

**Question:**

1. What advice would you give him?

In a report into the UK Barclays LIBOR rigging scandal, it was noted that despite a number of Barclays' traders and senior executives being aware the bank was attempting to fix the inter-bank lending rate, no-one acted. In contrast, and in another circumstance, Ian Foxley, a retired Lieutenant Colonel, who was appointed in 2010 to oversee a $2 billion military communications project for GPT in Saudi Arabia, uncovered within seven months what he claims were bribes to Saudi officials, and felt compelled to blow the whistle (Monaghan & Russell 2012). Why is it that some individuals are happy to turn a blind eye to ethical transgressions, while others feel morally obligated to publicly highlight the issue and call for corrective action?

Whistleblowing has been defined as the discourse by organisational members around illegal, immoral, or illegitimate practices relating to their employers (Miceli & Near 1992); however, whistleblowing can extend well beyond one's current employer. Several issues have been identified (Seifert & Stammerjohan 2008; Allard 2012; Ethics Resource Centre 2010) as impacting on employees' decisions to blow the whistle:

- blowing the whistle would put the person in an unfavourable light
- retribution may be initiated by those directly involved with the circumstances. Forms of retribution may include being given the cold shoulder, being overlooked for promotion, and being verbally abused by their manager and other employees
- there is a risk that no corrective action would be taken
- there is a risk that the problem would not remain confidential and blow out
- the whistleblower may desire protection from harassment and pressure connected with their whistleblowing, and a reward for their action
- the whistleblower's moral identity is important.

The actions of whistleblowers are interesting because they require an immense amount of moral courage, and those who do blow the whistle frequently face retribution. Despite reprisals, the number of circumstances that arise where individuals take the bold step to blow the whistle on wrongdoing are remarkable, and these actions are occurring in both the public and private sector. One example from the private sector, is Michael Woodford, the former President of the Japanese camera company Olympus, who was dismissed after only six months in the senior role after many years with the company for blowing the whistle on the US$1.7 billion worth of transactions involving the write-down of company acquisitions and some US$700 million in 'advisory fees' that went to an entity in the Cayman Islands ('Paying a price for doing what's right' 2012).

Another example, is Andrew Wilkie, an independent member of the Australian Federal Parliament, and previously an intelligence analyst, is probably one of Australia's best known whistleblowers. He resigned in protest after he accused the then Prime Minister, John Howard, of misleading the public in regard to the Iraq war (Allard 2012).

It appears despite 'mateship' being part of Australia's national psyche, and an emphasis on personal loyalty, Australians are supportive of whistleblowers, even if it involves exposing the misconduct of a family member or friend. Disputing the perception that Australians dislike 'dobbers', that is, those who whistleblow on their mates, a survey of 1211 people found that

80% endorsed the principle that people should be supported in revealing inside information that exposed wrongdoing. It was also indicated by 87% of respondents that whistleblowers should be able to use media to draw attention to corrupt, illegal or unethical practices (Allard 2012).

Generally, there are a number of options available to a whistleblower:

- don't say anything
- raise the concern with a supervisor
- go to the next level of management above the supervisor
- write to the CEO
- speak to a member of the board
- mobilise other employees
- start a petition drive
- threaten to go public
- speak to the union
- raise the concern with a relevant professional body
- contact the appropriate regulatory agency
- meet with the local Member of Parliament
- approach the media.

## Ethics on refection: Whistleblowing

What forms of retribution do you think a whistleblower might be subjected to?

## Ethics in the media: Whistleblowing

Advocates for whistleblowing in Australia point out that the protections afforded by the *Corporations Act 2001* are weak, which discourages private sector workers from taking action (Wilkins 2013).

# Stage 6: Moral repair

The final stage of our ethical decision-making model is **moral repair** and, essentially, relates to what course of action should be taken after a moral wrong has been committed in order to repair the ethical dimensions of a relationship which has been torn to shreds (R Lucas 2012). Having made and implemented a decision, we may be required to provide reparation, or some form of restoration. The concept is not new and is closely aligned to the literature on restorative justice. It is also in keeping with Aristotle's view of the virtue of 'good temper', where it is appropriate to experience indignation, or anger, following insult, and the need to address and redress wrongdoing. The most obvious examples are what happens, or should happen, after an environmental disaster caused by poor decision-making, or where a new product has had disastrous consequences.

Moral repair (© shutterstock.com/Michael D Brown)

The concept has been well articulated by Walker (2006) in her book, *Moral repair: Reconstructing moral relations after wrongdoing*. The focus is on stakeholders who have experienced harmful acts and losses at the hands of humans who should bear responsibility for their actions, thus resulting in the need for moral repair. Moral repair, Walker argues, attempts to atone for the suffering caused to victims of offensive or harmful actions.

Walker (2006) takes a more political rather than organisational perspective, using examples of restorative justice made through South Africa's Truth and Reconciliation Commission, and East Timor's National Commission for Reception, Truth and Reconciliation, as an alternative to criminal prosecution in the domestic context. Such commissions provide the opportunity for victims of gross human rights' violations to come forward and seek public redress, while also ensuring accurate recording of historical circumstances.

In the business context, in circumstances where an ethical crisis or professional negligence has occurred, the organisation could be tempted to resist fully reflecting on who, or what, may have been damaged, and may not initiate changes or provide compensation unless forced to by the courts. They may, instead, offer up an individual or group to take the heat, to become the fall guy, and, in doing so, attempt to deflect law suits or bad publicity. Companies may try to bury the problem and any associated records in an attempt to avoid future liability ('Avoiding the fire next time' 2013). Alternatively, moral repair would involve organisations being actively involved in redressing wrongdoing resulting from inadvertent or deliberately poor ethical decision-making. Reparation could involve reimbursement, compensation or restitution at the individual, community or country level, which, it is hoped, is prompted without legal requirements.

Where there is a violation of trust, moral repair provides the opportunity for restoration. However, as Walker (2006) has found, it requires:

- both parties to agree in regard to the nature and seriousness of the violation
- that the wrongdoer, whether it be an individual or an organisation, is evidentially and truly repentant of their wrongdoing
- a reassurance that the wrongdoing will not occur again, as evidenced through the establishment of a shared set of moral rules and expectations.

## Ethics in practice: Moral repair

Select a well-known organisational circumstance in which you would expect there to be a need for moral repair.
You may wish to consider examples such as:
- the Bhopal disaster in India
- the Exxon Valdez oil spill in Alaska
- the Ford Pinto case.

**Question:**
1. Did moral repair actually occur in the case you have chosen, and in what form did it take place?

# Conclusion

In looking at ethical decision-making, we have now come to the pointy end of business ethics, where we need to clarify our own ethical identity in order to inform our ethical decision-making. This is no longer an abstract discussion, but one that involves our personal reputations and personal integrity. What do we wish to be known for, and what might the consequences be of our ethical decisions or failure to make such decisions? We have used a six-stage model of ethical decision-making as the structure for this chapter, with the notable components being: moral awareness, moral reasoning, moral intention, moral character and ethical repair.

Moral awareness, or ethical sensitivity as it is sometimes called, is an essential precursor to ethical decision-making. The first stage is for an individual to exhibit awareness of whether circumstances contain an ethical issue, or issues. Ethical sensitivity is demonstrated, essentially, by the perception and interpretation of events or circumstances, and the recognition that they contain an ethical dimension (Thorne 1998).

Moral reasoning involves drawing on ethical principles, rules and norms to inform the ethical decision-making process. Ethical judgement incorporates these principles into a more detailed evaluation of the circumstances, stakeholders, and alternatives, before arriving at a decision.

Moral intention is the intention to see an ethical decision through to action, that is, the decision-making process extends to a commitment to act and, ultimately, ethical behaviour. This commitment is strongly influenced by one's moral motivation, the ability to give priority to values with a moral dimension, and subsuming personal interest. In other words, there is an intention, and a commitment, to doing what is morally right, even if it results in personal inconvenience or sacrifice.

Moral character is closely aligned to moral motivation and moral intention. Those with moral character have significant perseverance, ego strength, and implementation skills to follow through their moral intentions.

Moral courage is required to ensure full implementation of an ethical decision and could result in the need to defend a decision in the face of opposition. Whistleblowers are a group noted for their moral courage. Given that whistleblowers invariably lose their jobs, and are very rarely considered ideal candidates for a new job, becoming a whistleblower is nothing short of an heroic action.

The final stage in our ethical model is moral repair, where restitution is recognised and instituted after previous ethical decision-making has resulted in harm. Moral repair ensures that restitution is made, and agreed moral expectations are established for the future.

At the crux of ethical decision-making is the fundamental truism that doing what is ethical is not always in the best interest of an individual or a firm. Ethical dilemmas often involve conflict, such as conflicting principles and conflicting stakeholder interests. Ensuring an appropriate resolution requires considerable airing of what the conflicts are and the prioritising of them. We have presented decision-making in a sequential and very formulaic way; however, there is much to suggest that these processes are, in fact, more complex and have greater interdependence.

It is apparent that, given enormous external pressures from shareholders and competitive environments, and internal pressures from limited resources and aspirational targets, it can be difficult for businesspeople to resist the temptation to transgress their personal ethical boundaries. It is hoped that managers do not start with a deliberate intention of being unethical. The reality is, however, that often ethical issues start with small decisions that are made on the spur of the moment or under pressure. Each decision builds the future of the businessperson and company. Reputation is formed one day at a time, and one decision at a time. Not every decision is going to be perfect, but reflecting on the outcomes and the impact of the decisions will ultimately help us to move towards a prevailing ethical climate in organisations.

# Ethics in practice: Ethical decision-making

For an informative discussion on ethical decision-making, see <http://ethicsunwrapped.utexas.edu/videos/in-it-to-win-the-story-of-jack-abramoff>.

## Ethics on video

**Moral repair** – *Stanley Hauerwas: on moral fragmentation, formation, and repair* 2012, YouTube, Pilar Timpane, 10 May, <www.youtube.com/watch?v=ADXR28YVmaA>.

**Whistleblowing** – *Should I blow the whistle* 2011, YouTube, PublicConcernAtWork, 21 September, <www.youtube.com/watch?v=3JxKepmABWg>.

See web material for more videos.

## Ethics at the movies

Here are a few movie suggestions that have ethical content in relation to ethical decision-making:

**The Informant!** – a humorous take on whistleblowing and moral defence, starring Matt Damon. *The Informant!* 2009, motion picture, Braunstein, H, Jacobs, G, Fox, J, Eichenwald, K & Jaffe, M.

*****The Insider** – a chemist becomes whistleblower on a *60 Minutes* segment about the tobacco industry. *The Insider* 1999, motion picture, Brugge, PJ & Mann, M.

*****Author's pick**

See web material for more movies.

## Ethics on the web

**Ethics Unwrapped**, The University of Texas at Austin is trying to unwrap why good people do bad things, <http://ethicsunwrapped.utexas.edu/>.

**Whistleblowers Australia**, a whistleblowing support network and resource provider, <www.whistleblowers.org.au/>.

See web material for more web references.

## Student exercises

See web material for answers to student short answer questions.

### Short answer questions

1. Describe the features of moral intensity, and explore the different dimensions of this concept.
2. One's personal values are frequently evoked when engaged in moral reasoning. What might be the values that are used?
3. What is the relationship between moral repair and trust?

### Experiential exercise

Locus of control refers to the perception of how much control an individual exerts over his/her life events. An internal locus of control believes that they have control over outcomes, whereas an external locus of control perceives that fate is largely to bear. Locus of control is a psychological trait that has been linked to moral character. Take the test at <www.queendom.com/tests/access_page/index.htm?idRegTest=704> to see what your own tendency is.

# Small case

## Case: Determining the right price

While on a holiday, you come across an antique blanket chest, which you know is valued at $2500 on the open market. The owner of the chest is unaware of its true value, and is willing to sell it for $75. You choose not to disclose its true value to him; intending to profit from information advantage.

**Question:**

**1.** Have your actions been unethical?

# Large case

## Case: Olympus – whistleblowing/accounting scandal

### Background

After 30 years of employment at Olympus, Michael Woodford was promoted to president. Within months of his promotion, facts came to light about enormous accounting anomalies within the company, and despite Woodford's best attempts to uncover the issues, the board advised him it was 'a domestic issue' and to refrain from further questioning. Woodford did not accept this position, which resulted in him being promoted to CEO, which allowed him to uncover most of the accounting scandal. Within weeks of the promotion, however, he was removed from his position by the board. Although the case highlights an accounting scandal, it also demonstrates how the decision to manage the problem from a domestic perspective does not necessarily reflect international expectations from stakeholders of a multinational corporation; which may have implications for how other multinational companies act on 'domestic issues'.

### Olympus

Olympus, a Japanese corporation, were founded in 1919. They currently have approximately 40 000 employees (Olympus Corporation 2012). They have a proud history of developing and producing precision equipment (Olympus Corporation 2012) cameras and audio equipment for private use, medical diagnostic and treatment equipment, microscopes, industrial products which provide remote visual inspections, and non-destructive product testing equipment (Olympus Corporation 2013). In April 2011, after 30 years of employment within Olympus and subsidiary companies, Michael Woodford was appointed President of Olympus by Tsuyoshi Kikukawa, Chairman and CEO. This was a notable occasion in Japan, as it was unusual for a *gaijin*

(non-Japanese) to be promoted to president, and the promotion was seen as a reward for loyalty, as well as an inclusive measure (Woodford 2012).

A few months after moving into the role, while Woodford was in Europe attending to business, he received an article written by *Facta* (a Japanese news magazine) by email, which outlined anomalies in Olympus's accounting. At this point, Woodford was unaware of the transactions mentioned in the magazine, and was confused that, as president of a large corporation, he was 'in the dark' about matters of this importance. When he returned to Japan, he began investigating the article's claims; however, he noticed he was being stonewalled by Olympus board members. Finally, the chairman told Woodford he was pursuing a 'domestic issue' (Greenfeld 2012, p. 5), and the matter was not his concern. Woodford disagreed.

Woodford actively pursued a boardroom 'shakeup', and through some tactical boardroom manoeuvres Woodford replaced Kikukawa as CEO. Woodford believed this would mean he could effectively steer the company forward from this point, but was unaware he would inherit the position in title only; Kikukawa would retain the loyalty of the board.

Despite these limitations, Woodford was keen to purge the financial scandal from the company, so, once appointed to the CEO position, he engaged PricewaterhouseCoopers to undertake an independent financial audit. The audit uncovered US$1.6 billion worth of false reporting on the company's financial statements dating from 2006, including the purchases of subsidiaries Altis, News Chef, and Humalabo, which were not visible on Olympus securities reports (Woodford 2012). Disturbed by the fraudulent activity, Woodford approached the board with the discoveries and demanded they account for the transactions, or resign. In tandem with this action he also copied in external stakeholders to ensure the fraudulent activity could not be 'buried'. To his surprise, rather than tackle the scandal, Woodford found himself fired by the board (Greenfeld 2012).

Woodford immediately left for the UK; not to retreat, but to blow the whistle on white collar crime in Olympus and as a tactic to ensure his safety. At this point he was unclear whether any 'anti-social forces' (a Japanese euphemism for organised crime) were at play resulting in the lack of action by the board (Adelstein 2012), or whether the board members were personally profiting from the fraud. He had serious concerns for his safety and actively sought publicity to cement his safety.

One wonders what conditions would lead to the accounting scandal that erupted from Olympus. To understand this, some historical financial events need to be understood as they impacted upon decisions made by the Olympus board over a 20-year period. The scandal had its roots in the 'Plaza Accord' of 1985, which saw the US dollar depreciate against five currencies at an alarming rate; including the Japanese yen (Norris 2011). This resulted in huge losses for Olympus, and, initially, their executives attempted to mitigate the losses through speculative investment; however, when the Japanese bubble burst in the 1990s, Olympus were left with even more losses, totalling some US$1 billion. A small group of executives at Olympus chose to 'bury' the losses in accounting transactions. This decision had ramifications for future boards, which became accessories to the fraud as they continued the course of action the board had begun in the 1990s. The losses were hidden until the accounting rules changed in 1997, which forced the executives to take action and get the losses off their balance sheets at book value (Olympus Corporation 2012).

In April 2000, market value accounting became effective, which once again required action from the group of executives. This time they elected to eliminate the off-balance-sheet losses by buying three domestic companies at highly inflated prices, paying for unnecessary advisory fees, and purchasing dividend preferred stock (Olympus Corporation 2012; Norris 2011). By the time Woodford was brought in as president, the group of executives felt confident that the 20-year accounting fiasco was over and dealt with in-house, and so they did not advise him of the past transactions. From their perspective, the board had spent the previous 20 years 'rectifying' the accounting anomalies, and had finally 'fixed' the problem; they were not about to encourage Woodford to undo this work and expose the fiasco.

What unfolded was not only an accounting scandal, but also a story of cultural value clashes and corporate culture impairments. Even though Woodford had been appointed as president, as a Briton he was still seen as an outsider; hence Kikukawa's decision to hide earlier events at Olympus. Interestingly, Kikukawa admitted to the Tokyo District Court that before his own appointment as president of Olympus he had not been informed of the losses, and had he been apprised, he would have declined the offer. Kikukawa further said he suggested the board announce the losses when he did find out, but former presidents had told him not to (Amano & Matsuyama 2012). For Woodford, this hierarchical servitude was problematic not just for Olympus but for Japanese business in particular (Hickey 2012), where HR policies favour 'yes men' (Wood 2011). From his perspective, the problem is so endemic that he largely sees Japanese journalists as reporting, rather than investigating (Hickey 2012). For Kikukawa, though, the course of action he took seems to have placed the value of following Confucian values above the legal obligations of the company.

Woodford's whistleblowing, the result of a domino effect from another Olympus insider's whistleblowing to *Factus* (Adelstein 2012), forced Olympus to acknowledge the scandal and implement governance and corporate culture changes. Interestingly, even though foreign shareholders wanted the roles of chairman and president to be replaced by outsiders to further solidify these changes, those concerns were not addressed. Sasa, the new President, admits the decisions made at Olympus were based on flawed decision-making that was more concerned with perception and ethical ties than the board's fiduciary obligations to shareholders (Olympus Corporation 2012). Sasa has made two pledges: (1) that corporate culture will now be 'based on fairness, transparency and good faith' through changed corporate governance and transparency measures; and (2) the 'Social IN' management philosophy will be adhered to, promoting Olympus's societal involvement and shared societal values (Olympus Corporation 2012).

Although Woodford assumed board members were lining their own pockets, it seems what was at play was a 20-year-old secret to 'save face', not only for Olympus, but also for the way Japanese companies are viewed internationally (Amano & Matsuyama 2012). Woodford notes Japanese institutional shareholders have not been vocal about the financial scandal, whereas international shareholders have been scathing (Tabuchi 2012; Tabuchi & Inoue 2012). Woodford believes that shareholders are right to be concerned about current Japanese business models, and sees the business networks as incestuous; rather than corporations fulfilling fiduciary duties, they protect members of their own business fraternity. In addition, rather than allowing businesses to fail, the banks continue to lend to worthless companies. Until there is social change within the business hierarchy, and hostile takeovers are not viewed as hostile, but as opportunities for capital injection, Woodford is grim about Japan's business future (Hickey 2012). Perhaps his comments can be dismissed as those of a disgruntled ex-employee, however, it is worth noting that Olympus is seeking to dilute international shareholder presence by increasing capital from domestic investors, and the new chairman is not only chairman of Olympus, but also has strong links

with Sumitomo Mitsui, the bank that holds an equity stake in Olympus (Tabuchi 2012). Given the common practice of cross-shareholdings in Japanese business, it does seem to support some of Woodford's claims, which paint a worrying picture of the state of affairs in Japan business.

## Ethical considerations

There is delineation between the legal aspects of the case study and the ethical decisions made by the stakeholder; legally there was no grey area, but to understand the decision-making process, understanding ethical perspectives are required.

The Japanese board members were operating from a Confucian ethical standpoint; their decisions did not necessarily reflect their personal ethical position on the matter or self-interest. They engaged in a **deontological** approach to the accounting scandal; that is, the means do not justify the end, and that, in moral decisions, consideration must be given to one's duty. This could be further unpacked as following **rule deontology** which states that acts are right or wrong because of their conformity or non-conformity to established moral principles.

Woodford operates from a utilitarian perspective; actions are morally right in proportion to their ability to promote happiness for the greatest majority. His weighting of what the ethically responsible decision would be is weighted by the degree of happiness, or utility, which can be generated from the decision. Utilitarianism and doing the greatest good for the greatest number is an intuitively appealing approach to resolving an ethical dilemma; however, it is worth noting that difficult, complex problems, and attempts to assign appropriate weighting to stakeholder groups with competing interests, can be problematic.

**Ethical issues:**
- accounting fraud
- ignoring fiduciary duties to stakeholders
- unfair dismissals.

## Timeline of events

| | |
|---|---|
| 1990s | Due to the economic bubble bursting in Japan, massive losses are incurred. |
| 1998 | Losses are moved off-balance-sheet by a small group of Olympus executives, to cover up the losses. |
| 2000 | Market value accounting becomes effective from April. |
| 2008–2010 | The small group of executives attempt to remove the losses through buying domestic companies and paying consulting fees. |
| April 2011 | Woodford is elected President and CEO. |
| July 2011 | Woodford reads *Facta* magazine articles that highlight the 2008–2010 purchases. |
| September 2011 | Woodford is elected CEO and engages PricewaterhouseCoopers as an independent auditor to investigate the accounting anomalies. |
| 14 October 2011 | Olympus board unanimously votes to dismiss Mr Woodford as President and CEO. |
| 1 November 2011 | Olympus appoints a Third-Party Committee. |
| 8 November 2011 | The Third-Party Committee reports on the accounting anomalies. |
| 7 December 2011 | Management Reform Committee, Director Management Liability Investigation Committee and Non-Director Liability Investigator Committees are formed. |
| 11 December 2011 | Japanese prosecutors raid Olympus headquarters and Kikukawa's home. |
| 14 December 2011 | Amended financial statements are submitted. |
| 21 December 2011 | Tokyo District Public Prosecutor's Office, the Tokyo Metropolitan Police Department and the Securities and Exchange Surveillance Commission raid Olympus's Tokyo headquarters. |
| 7 January 2012 | Director Management Liability Investigation Committee report is received. |
| 8 January 2012 | Olympus lodge a lawsuit for damages to establish the liability of past and current directors. |
| 16 January 2012 | Non-Director Liability Investigation Committee report is received. |
| 17 January 2012 | Olympus lodge a suit for damages seeking to establish the liability of past and present corporate auditors; the Nomination Committee is established to nominate candidate directors and corporate auditors for election at a special general meeting of shareholders. |
| 20 January 2012 | Olympus receive a listing agreement violation penalty from the Tokyo Stock Exchange, totalling ¥10 million. |
| 21 January 2012 | Olympus put on 'security on alert' by Tokyo Stock Exchange. |
| February 2012 | Yasuyuki Kimoto, a former senior managing director at Olympus main lender |

Sumitomo Mitsui Banking Corporation, is nominated as chairman; Hioyuki Sasa, a former Olympus executive officer, is nominated as president.

16 February 2012    Seven executives are arrested over Olympus accounting scandal

7 March 2012    Tokyo District Public Prosecutor's Office files charges on suspicion of fraudulent financial reporting, in violation of the *Securities and Exchange Act 1934* and *Financial Instruments and Exchange Act 2006*.

20 April 2012    A new management team is appointed at a special general meeting of shareholders; the old management team resigns (Adapted from: Olympus 2012)

21 December 2012    A Singaporean banker is arrested for assisting in Olympus' accounting fraud.

**Questions:**

**1.** It seems the Japanese board had covered up the anomalies over a 20-year-period, and were keen to keep up the ruse. Was Olympus's board 'rotten'? Is the Japanese business sector indeed grim, as Woodford suggests? Or are other factors at play? Discuss.

**2.** Using ethical principles and theory, ascertain the positions of key Olympus board members, namely Michael Woodford, Kikukawa and the balance of the board members). To better understand the ethical principles at play that led to the decision-making process of all members, you may wish to review these websites below:

Richey, J 2008–2013, 'Religion library: Confucianism: Community organization', *Patheos*, retrieved 6 September 2013, <www.patheos.com/Library/Confucianism/Ethics-Morality-Community/Community-Organization-and-Structure.html>.

Gundling, E, Sasaki, R, Dickey, D & Aoki, M 1999. 'Communicating with Japanese in business', JETRO, retrieved 6 September 2013, <www.jetro.go.jp/costarica/mercadeo/communicationwith.pdf>.

**3.** Critique Woodford's handling of the accounting scandal and his dismissal. What ethical issues were at play and what ethical perspective do his actions highlight?

See web material for:
- answer to short answer questions
- additional student cases
- tutor resources (tutor password required)
- additional material including Ethics at the movies, Ethics in print, Ethics on video and Ethics on the web.

# PART 4

# Personal Ethical Decision-Making

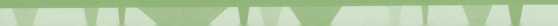

# Chapter 12

## Ethics in organisations

'We judge companies and managers by their actions,
not their pious statements of intent.'
Sir Adrian Cadbury, 1929–,
author of the Cadbury Report (1992)

## Chapter aim

To investigate organisational strategies that can be used to enhance an ethical culture.

## Chapter objectives

1. Contrast the differing perspectives of 'bad apples' versus 'bad barrels' that result in unethical behaviour.
2. Identify the features of an ethical organisational culture.
3. Determine the motivations and benefits for developing an ethical climate.
4. Prioritise the four tiers for developing a strong ethical culture.
5. Formulate the common elements of an integrated ethics program.
6. Critique the common problems as well as the characteristics of a good code of ethics.
7. Generate a profile of the different types of ethical climates which could exist in an organisation.

# Ethics in the media: Culture

## Introduction

A popular current saying in business circles is that 'culture eats strategy for breakfast'. Given the vast amount of attention that has been given to the importance of strategy and strategic planning, rather than culture, this quip attempts to redress the imbalance between strategy and culture. What is being presented is that, unless an organisation's culture is appropriately aligned, it will ultimately frustrate strategic initiatives. For example, an organisation may have an innovative strategy, but unless it has a culture that promotes creativity and risk-taking, the culture is not aligned to the strategy – the culture could eat the strategy. Similarly, an organisation may have a number of strategic initiatives to promote a moral climate in the organisation, but, if the ethical culture is one of bending the rules, and tolerance for wrongdoing, then the strategies will be useless. It is interesting to think that the basic philosophy, spirit and drive of an organisation may have far more to do with its relative achievements than its technological or economic resources, organisational structure, innovation and timing.

### Bad apples or bad barrels?

A question commonly raised, usually after a high-profile ethical scandal where an individual has been pilloried for lack of ethical judgement, is why did that happen? Was it a case of a bad apple; that is, a bad person who was in some way morally defective, who just happened to be in that company, and therefore no matter the circumstances would have come ethically unstuck? Or, is it a case of a bad barrel and the effect of a corporate culture negatively influencing essentially a good person? That is, despite having an established personal value system, supposedly fully intact, the specifics of the circumstance promoted unethical decisions. This person just happened to be in a bad barrel – an organisation where unethical decision outcomes were not just permitted, but possibly actively encouraged.

Bad apples or bad barrels? (© shutterstock.com/Oleg Iatsun)

What is also being suggested is that organisational members generally take their cues from the organisational culture before considering what the stated core organisational values are. In addition, it has been observed that the perception of peer behaviour influences the likelihood of unethical behaviour occurring more than does the individual's own beliefs (Zey-Ferrell, Weaver & Ferrell 1979), and individuals will tend to behave according to group norms, even though this may go against what they would do outside of the group setting (Bailey et al. 1991). As a warning, highly cohesive or isolated workgroups may be problematic unless led by managers who encourage the expression and consideration of diverse views (Neck & Moorhead 1995).

Building on Jennings (2006), a number of causes can contribute to the formation of bad barrels:

- pressure to meet goals, particularly financial pressures
- a culture that does not encourage open and candid conversations
- a CEO surrounded by people who agree and flatter the CEO and for whom the CEO is beyond criticism
- weak boards that do not exercise their fiduciary responsibilities and diligence
- an organisation that promotes people on the basis of nepotism and favouritism
- hubris – the arrogant belief that rules are for other people and not for us
- a flawed cost–benefit attitude which suggests that poor ethical behaviour in one area can be offset by good ethical behaviour, or corporate responsibility activities in another area
- a mistaken belief that others are also acting inappropriately which in some way condones the behaviour
- frequent statements of rationalisation
- compensation systems that reward results and not the means by which the results have been achieved.

# Ethics in reflection: Bad apples or bad barrels?

So, is unethical behaviour a case of bad apples or bad barrels? What is your view?

While some suggest that ethical behaviour is the responsibility of individuals alone, studies have shown that the overall ethical culture of an organisation (or lack of it) has a profound bearing on the people working within that organisation. Indeed, Hong Kong's Independent Commission Against Corruption (ICAC) (2000) asserts that the culture of an organisation has the power to make ethical people act unethically, and unethical people act ethically. A clear relationship has been found between the ethical climate of an organisation and the ethical decisions that employees make (Wimbush, Shepard & Markham 1997). Creating a culture of integrity is therefore important considering the impact that an organisation's culture can have not only on the behaviour of employees but also on the behaviour of those in associated entities, such as contractors and suppliers.

Given the power of organisations to influence ethical behaviour, it is therefore essential to consider several questions:

- What is an ethical organisational culture?
- What are the benefits of developing an ethical culture?
- How can organisations create an ethical culture?
- Specifically, what are some strategies and practices organisations can adopt to encourage more ethical practices and, by extension, ethical people?

## What is an ethical culture?

**organisational culture** – the glue that binds an organisation together in a common identity and action.

**Organisational culture** has usefully been described as the 'glue' that binds organisations together through a common identity and actions (Fritzsche 1991). The culture of an organisation has the capacity to influence the thoughts, feelings and behaviours of staff and also has the potential to contribute to their moral development (Treviño 1986), just as in national culture an organisation's culture is made up of collective values, beliefs, norms and traditions. A related term, often conflated with organisational culture, is that of **organisational climate**. To clarify, climate generally refers to more specific and measurable dimensions of the organisation, such as leadership, vision, strategies, structure, commitment, rewards and recognition, and is part of the organisation's culture.

**organisational climate** – the specific and measurable dimensions of the organisation, such as, leadership, vision, strategies, structure, commitment, rewards and recognition.

An **ethical culture**, by extension, is the ethical component within the corporate culture (Ferrell, Fraedrich & Ferrell 2013). An **ethical climate**, in contrast, is defined as the main perceptions of typical organisational practices and processes that have ethical content (Victor & Cullen 1987). Ethical misconduct involves, for example, insider trading, embezzlement, corporate fraud and bullying, which all implicate the influence of ethical work climates (Arnaud 2010).

As a number of writers have already done, and to make life a little easier, we shall use the terms culture and climate interchangeably, and note that what we are referring to is a shared set of norms, values and practices of organisational members regarding appropriate behaviour in the workplace (Agarwal 1999).

**ethical culture** – the ethical component within the corporate culture.

**ethical climate** – the prevailing perceptions of typical organisational practices and processes that have ethical content.

Ethical culture (© shutterstock.com/Dimitar Petarchev)

## Ethics in practice: Ethical workplace culture

View the video by Michael Josephson on creating an ethical workplace culture, <josephsoninstitute.org/business/blog/2010/11/creating-an-ethical-workplace-culture>.

### Evolution of an ethical culture

Recently, the literature has extended beyond the theoretical and observational, and moved towards the practical (McDonald 2000). This shift has taken place because there is a clear need to provide organisations and leaders with concrete advice about the strategies by which ethics can be integrated into an organisation. Recent scandals have provided the impetus for organisations to function more ethically, and work towards institutionalising an ethical culture, although naturally there are varying degrees of receptivity.

Arnold, Lampe and Sutton (1997) outline four stages in the evolution of creating an ethical culture:

1. **The absence of intention** – the firm lacks any intent to encourage ethical behaviour.
2. **Passive support** – the firm wants to encourage ethical behaviour, but has not developed a structure to support this behaviour.
3. **Active pursuit** – the firm is actively pursuing ethical behaviour.
4. **Total integration** – the firm consistently integrates ethics fully into the organisation and decision-making processes.

## Motivations for building an ethical culture

In the US, the use of ethics programs can critically reduce sentence outcomes, but for many organisations this is not necessarily the main motivation. The motivations behind developing an ethical culture appear to be varied, and figure 12.1 depicts five common drivers.

1. Risk management – the firm is primarily motivated to consider ethical strategies as a means of meeting compliance requirements as well as mitigating, or avoiding fines.
2. Peer pressure – the firm is motivated purely out of a need to adhere to industry and professional norms.
3. Organisational improvement – the firm recognises that by having an ethical culture there are benefits, for example, through the attraction and retention of staff, as well as through building the trust of customers.

**Figure 12.1** Motivations for building an ethical culture

4. Branding – the firm wishes to promote their ethical culture as part of a branding process in which they believe their approach as a responsible organisation can contribute to their positioning strategy.

5. Organisational mission – while the firm does not actively promote their ethical culture, they do; however, expect high levels of ethical performance from their employees and also key stakeholders. They see ethics as part of their corporate DNA.

"This is where you go to squawk."

Grievances (© shutterstock.com/Cartoonresource)

## The benefits of having an ethical culture

Why bother with integrating ethics into an organisational culture? As we have seen in the US through the **sentencing guidelines** which are the uniform sentencing policy for individuals and organisations convicted of felonies and serious misdemeanours in the US federal courts system, it can mitigate punishment. However, more importantly, there are also solid benefits to be gained. The benefits as identified by Reynolds (2012) are that:

- goodwill is fostered in the company and immediate community
- consistency is developed in organisational operations
- good business practices is promoted
- the organisation and its employees is protected from legal action
- unfavourable publicity is avoided.

It has also been found that ethical climates have been associated with a number of facets of satisfaction, particularly satisfaction with: promotion, co-workers, supervisors, work and overall satisfaction (Deshpande 1996). In addition to their effect on ethical behaviour, positive ethical climates have been associated with organisational commitment (Schwepker 2001), reduced stress in a role, and increased trust in supervisors (Mulki, Jaramillo & Locander 2008), as well as employee performance (Weeks et al. 2006).

In contrast, the absence of an ethical culture has costs, including: more damage claims, complaints, injuries and sick leave usage (Waring 2004), as well as turnover intentions (DeConinck, Deconinck & Banerjee 2013). It also appears that the effect of ethical climate and culture, on ethical behaviour remains consistent across cultures (Ethics and Compliance Officer Association Foundation 2006).

**sentencing guidelines** – the uniform sentencing policy for individuals and organisations convicted of felonies and serious misdemeanours in the US federal courts system.

# Building an ethical culture

Suggestions abound in the literature as to how to institutionalise ethics at an organisational level, with a particular focus on ethical codes and guidelines (McDonald 2009a; 2009b Weber 1981), as well as ethical training (McDonald & Donleavy 1995). According to Clark (2003), there are four basic components of an ethical organisation:

1. A written code of conduct.
2. Appropriate ethics training for staff at all levels.
3. Ethical advice lines.
4. Systems in place for confidential reporting.

A synthesis of the literature on building ethical climates reveals an even broader range of features, of which the following is a non-exhaustive list:

- a genuine promotion of ethics by organisational leaders
- mission statements and organisational values that stress the importance of ethics
- ethical behaviour and practice being actively promoted and modelled within the organisation
- clear and accessible policies and procedures relating to ethical conduct, which are articulated to all staff
- consistency between codes of conduct, operational policies and processes
- rewards, as well as punishments, prevail for unethical behaviour
- the inclusion of ethical roles, that is, an ethical ombudsman or the creation of formal ethical officers
- specific ethical strategies, such as, ethical training, ethical hotlines, and so on.

## Four tiers of an ethical culture

A more comprehensive approach is to consider the key components of an ethical culture in four tiers, as depicted in Figure 12.2.

- **Tier 1 – Organisational mission, values and intent**. It is at this first tier that an organisation decides what sort of organisation they want to be known as, and who they aim to be. What are the mission, values and intent of the organisation and, more importantly, does everyone believe and support them? A superficial understanding of an organisation's mission and lacklustre attempts at articulating the values will not bring about a strong culture.
- **Tier 2 – Integrated ethics program**. These are explicit strategies used as the building blocks to create an ethical climate. Each component undertakes a specific task, such as, codes of conduct, ethical leadership, ethical training programs and other related strategies.
- **Tier 3 – Supporting policies and processes**. A frequent disconnect occurs between an ethics program and the fundamental operational activities of the organisation. Therefore, it is necessary to ensure that supporting policies and processes are developed to flesh out expectations of employee behaviour in order to align the ethical code with more detailed policy. The policies include, but are not limited to, those that relate to privacy, health and safety, personal relationships and sexual harassment.

**organisational mission, values and intent** – an organisation decides what sort of organisation they want to be known as; who they aim to be.

**integrated ethics program** – a coherent set of actions directed primarily at the operational level in order to stimulate the ethical behaviour.

**supporting policies and processes** – policies and processes that flesh out the expectations regarding employee behaviour and are aligned to the ethical code of conduct, e.g., a safety and health policy, a privacy policy.

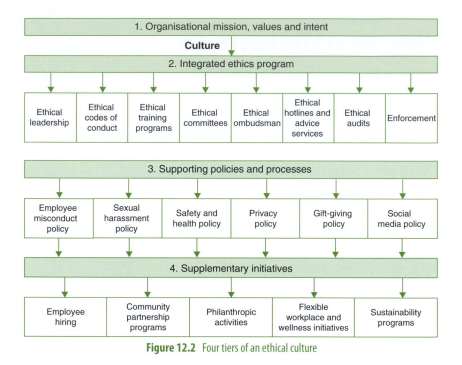

**Figure 12.2**  Four tiers of an ethical culture

**supplementary initiatives** –
related initiatives within the context of building an ethical climate, such as, organisational sustainability and philanthropic activities.

- **Tier 4 – Supplementary initiatives**. The remaining fourth tier accommodates a number of related initiatives that may occur, and places them appropriately within the context of building an ethical climate. These activities will vary considerably from organisation to organisation, but could entail significant effort and financial commitment, as is frequently seen with organisational sustainability and philanthropic activities.

# Ethics in the media: The World's Most Ethical Company award

In 2013, L'Oréal received the title of the World's Most Ethical Company for the fourth time by the international organisation, the Ethisphere Institute. L'Oréal Chairman and CEO, Jean-Paul Agon, said striving for ethical excellence was a source of inspiration that helped shape their internal and external identity (L'Oréal 2013).

# An integrated ethics program

Culture appears to be the primary driver of employee behaviour and cultures are greatly influenced by numerous facets from the more macro dimensions of an organisational mission, through to supplementary initiatives. The multiple tiers of an ethical culture highlight that there needs to be stronger forces at work than just a code of conduct and an ethics training program. In order to try and remain as focused as possible, we will be concentrating on Tier 2, and the key components of an integrated ethics program. An integrated ethics program is a coherent set of actions directed primarily at the operational level in order to stimulate the ethical behaviour of those working within a particular organisation (McDonald & Nijhof 1999) and the organisation is cognisant of the pressures of power and politics on its employees. Actions taken within an integrated ethics program can be administered by the CEO's office, the human resources department, the audit unit, or in larger organisations, an ethics office or division.

Given the centrality of the integrated ethics program for encouraging an ethical climate, we will now examine each of the constituents that could be utilised to make up an integrated ethics program. It should be noted that not every organisation will include every component suggested, but the more building blocks that are present, the greater the likelihood an ethical culture will develop.

## Ethics on reflection: Integrated ethics program

For some insight into what characterises an integrated ethics programs, see Treviño's explanation at: <www.youtube.com/watch?v=BmAlKP3SNSk&list=PLF088ACD0FD75F9EE>. Note that the video rolls on into other segments which you may also find interesting.

## Ethical leadership

Despite limited studies to the contrary (Murphy, Smith & Daley 1992; Zey-Ferrell et al. 1979), the behaviour of leaders and managers in organisations has been found to significantly influence the ethical behaviour of staff. In fact, Lysons (1989) found that the conduct of managers is one of the key determinants of unethical conduct in organisations. The 'tone at the top' from leaders, in terms of ethicality, can have a profound impact on staff (Ferrell, Fraedrich & Ferrell 2013). Both the formal and informal statements a CEO issues in support of ethical behaviour have been found to result in more ethical decisions being made by staff (Hegarty & Sims, 1979), and an extensive study by ICAC (2000) concluded that staff who work for ethical leaders are more committed and loyal.

"We're getting back to first principles ... which means we're going to have some."

Ethical leadership (© shutterstock.com/Cartoonresource)

Aspects of ethical conduct are undoubtedly learnt from others, hence the need to consider the behaviour modelling process which takes place with leaders. Staff are more likely to do what they see their supervisors and leaders doing, particularly their senior managers, than to adhere to written ethical policy (Andrews 1989). Moore (2013) suggests that when business leader's act unethically they also change the way employees think about ethical decisions. Most employees don't think, 'I'm going to act badly because I have to', rather, they actually think the behaviour is okay and condoned by their boss. Hence the term **moral disengagement**, which refers to a process that enables people to behave unethically without feeling any psychological distress or belief that what they are doing is wrong.

**moral disengagement** – the process that enables people to behave unethically without feeling any psychological distress or believe what they are doing is wrong.

Unfortunately, bad leadership can have a compounding effect. If managers at the top of the organisation are demonstrating unethical behaviour, they are more likely to recruit, socialise and promote employees similar to themselves, who exhibit similar ethical values. Conversely, employees who do not match the managers' level of moral reasoning ability will be unable to fit in, or adapt, to the moral culture of the firm, thereby having little hope of career advancement, with the consequence that they will likely become frustrated and leave the firm for another opportunity (Dellaportas et al. 2005).

A manager's cognitive moral development has been found to be related to their subordinates' perceptions of them as transformational leaders. So, subordinates perceive leaders who are able to frame an ethical issue, have insight into its complexity, and demonstrate developed cognitive and moral reasoning abilities as transformative, while leaders who have lower levels of moral reasoning were found to depress group performance, as well as the group's average level of moral reasoning (Turner et al. 2002).

## Strategies to create ethical leaders

So, what can organisations do to create genuine ethical leaders? Neck and Moorhead (1995) propose a range of features. They claim that 'closed' and 'directive' leaders increase the risk of unethical decision-making. These leaders are said to: not foster staff participation; prioritise their own opinions; not be open to different ideas; and not openly stress the importance of ethical decisions and conduct. In contrast, 'open' leaders were found to promote ethical conduct and decision-making in staff. These 'open' leaders were found to: relinquish control; be open to criticism, objections and feedback; act as advisers and facilitators; and allow staff to speak freely and raise concerns.

Suggested strategies that can help to develop ethical leaders include:

- recognising and using the behaviour of leaders as a critical part of setting an ethical tone
- practising role modelling throughout the organisation's management structure
- being careful around crisis situations, which is where leaders are most vulnerable
- frequently assessing the quality of the organisation's leaders
- providing developmental opportunities and ensuring that processes are in place to foster and encourage ethical leadership (for example, include ethics training in leadership programs)

- keeping an eye on hiring and firing to reduce the risk of hiring 'yes' people or removing those who may have a critical voice
- welcoming and encouraging feedback from staff
- developing open lines of communication so that ethical conduct is discussed and behaviour critiqued
- spending time on recognising and reaffirming the organisational mission and core values
- encouraging leaders to make the hard calls to reinforce ethical behaviour, although that might mean losing both people and money.

# Ethics in the media: Core values (the good)

Tony Hsieh, CEO of Zappos, the online shoe retailer (now a unit of Amazon), didn't initially have a foundation of values for the company, but as the company expanded, he recognised the need. In the end, Zappos' core values didn't come from any one individual; Hsieh listened to his employees and moulded their personal values into what ultimately became the 'Zappos family core values'. With more than 3000 employees, Zappos are the largest online shoe store in the US, thanks to their company culture and core values (Buchanan 2013).

# Ethics on reflection: Core values (the bad)

Bernard Ebbers, the former chairman and CEO of WorldCom, was convicted and sentenced to 25 years in prison for fraud and conspiracy. WorldCom were at the centre of one of the world's largest accounting scandals with a loss of US$100 billion to investors. He has the dubious award from *Time* magazine of being the tenth most corrupt CEO of all time ('Top 10 crooked CEOs' 2009).

**Questions:**
1. Undertake an internet search for 'Bernard Ebbers' and 'WorldCom'.
2. Consider the organisational wrongdoings committed by the organisation and its leader.

# Ethics in practice: Core values (the ugly)

The case of Enron was one of the most publicised recent corporate collapses caused by organisational wrongdoing. The former president of Enron, Jeffrey Skilling, was found guilty of multiple felony charges and sentenced to a 24-year prison sentence.

**Questions:**

1. Undertake an internet search for 'Enron' and 'Skilling' and identify what you perceive to be the major ethical wrongdoings they committed.

2. What personal and organisational pressures – for example, personal ambition, a performance recognition system, profit targets or other factors – do you believe would have been in play within Enron before their collapse?

## A company code of ethics

**code of ethics**
(also known as a **code of conduct**)
– a declaration clarifying an organisation's principles, values, ethics and overall standards relating to conduct and practice punishments.

In creating an ethical organisation, the first step many companies undertake is to develop a code of ethics. A **code of ethics** (sometimes called a **code of conduct**) is a declaration clarifying an organisation's principles, values and overall standards relating to conduct and practice (Langlois & Schlegelmilch 1990). This means that all of the expectations relating to ethical conduct and decision-making are documented and accessible for all members of staff in order to both govern and guide. The code may cover areas such as:

- the importance of ethics
- employment practices
- conflicts of interest
- bribery, gifts and entertainment policies
- health and safety
- customer relations
- relations with suppliers/contractors
- respect for the environment
- responsibilities to shareholders/community
- monitoring and compliance
- disciplinary outcomes for non-compliance
- avenues for further information.

# Ethics on reflection: Volvo's code of conduct

For a brief review of the contents of Volvo's code of conduct, view the video – *VOLVO Group code of conduct – a short introduction* 2012, <www.youtube.com/watch?v=ZRA_GJ9Yx38>.

Alternatively, organisations can take a less prescriptive or rules-based approach, and propose key values, such as respect, honesty and accountability, which they believe should guide behaviour and decision-making in all circumstances. Supplemented with examples, a values-based approach can provide flexibility in a rapidly changing work environment and allow for personal discretion when an individual evaluates potential ethical issues.

The intentions which prompt an organisation to develop a code of ethics vary significantly and are complex. The most common drivers for adopting a code of ethics, identified within the literature, are seen to be (McDonald 2009a):

- ensuring compliance with statutory requirements
- making clear and formalising the company's expectations for appropriate conduct
- minimising risk
- ensuring consistency across global networks
- fostering trust and confidence in stakeholders
- enhancing the reputation of the organisation.

"Have you hammered out the new rule book yet?"
Company code of ethics (© shutterstock.com/Cartoonresource)

Over the past 10 years, there has been a significant increase in the popularity of the adoption of codes of ethics around the world. Organisations in countries such as the UK, USA, Japan, Australia, Canada, Spain, Sweden and South Africa, to name a few, are seeing the benefits of the adoption of codes. It is unfortunate, however, that a large number of companies simply borrow a model code from another organisation rather than taking an individualised approach (Snell, Chak & Chu 1996; Svensson & Wood 2007).

Employees of organisations that adopt and enforce a corporate policy and ethical codes have been found to be more sensitive to ethical dilemmas and are more likely to choose ethical outcomes in their decision-making. Needless to say, there are those who doubt the capability of a code of ethics to improve ethical behaviour (Bavaria 1991; Hyman et al. 1990); however, for the most part, it is commonly accepted that a corporate code of ethics does have a positive impact on ethical attitudes and, potentially, on the behaviour of employees.

## Characteristics of a good code of ethics

Calhoun, Olivero and Wolitzer (1999) suggest that the characteristics of a good code of ethics are that the code should be:

- easy to read
- outline the company's vision
- up to date
- accurate and authentic
- easy to apply
- positive
- aligned with the code of conduct.

McDonald (2009a) proposes five key components which determine the effectiveness and usefulness of a code of ethics:

- it should, ideally, reflect the culture of the organisation
- it should clearly articulate the core values of the organisation
- it must have full support from the leadership team
- it should make the responsibilities of staff and the organisation clear to all
- it should make appropriate channels of communication available (particularly for handling ethical dilemmas, whistleblowing and instances of ethical violations).

For a code of ethics to be effective, ICAC (2000) also recommend that:

- it undergo regular review (to ensure core values are actionable and in line with the company's vision)
- staff knowledge of the code is actively promoted
- it is promoted outside the organisation (including to clients and the community)
- it is part of a larger training and development plan.

# Ethics on reflection: Codes and unethical culture

Why might an organisation have a detailed code of ethics and yet still suffer from an unethical culture? Discuss the issues involved.

## Problems with codes of ethics

1. **Inadequate coverage** – what should be, and what isn't, covered in a code can be problematic as, clearly, a code needs to engage, and a wide sweep of every likely misdemeanour is going to create a very long and tedious document. Nestlé is aware of this problem and announced at the onset of their Code of Business conduct that the code is not intended to cover all possible situations, but acts as a framework of expectation.

2. **An emphasis on risk** – the problem with many codes of conduct introduced by organisations to create an ethical culture, is that they concentrate on risk rather than ethics (Ferrell, Fraedrich & Ferrell 2013), which, as Stevens (1996) maintains, does not engender a guiding or visionary tone. Schwartz (2000), similarly, contends that ethical codes are most often used by organisations to ensure compliance as part of a control system and can be entirely devoid of ethical content. It is for these reasons, among others, that some doubt the impact that codes have on corporate behaviour (Akaah & Riordan 1989; Callan 1992; Cleek & Leonard 1998; Matthews 1987).

3. **Misalignment with other policies and practices** – a further problem occurs when there is a misalignment between what the code is saying and what is actually happening in practice, that is, the values actually being demonstrated, the leadership behaviour being exhibited, and what is being recognised and rewarded. When we see exceptions to the code being granted for high-performing employees (Burkus 2011), or violations of the code not being addressed, such actions will render the code virtually useless.

4. **Not user-friendly** – the language of codes can be problematic. Snell and Herndon (2004) point to the need for a code of ethics to be reader-friendly, deal with relevant ethical issues, encourage open discussion, be applicable to everyone, match an organisation's fundamental values and encompass broader issues pertaining to social responsibility. When codes adequately meet these requirements, they have been found to improve ethical perceptions and standards in organisations (Hunt, Chonko & Wilcox 1984; Murphy, Smith & Daley 1992; Weeks & Nantel 1992).

5. **Not communicated or enforced** – it is beneficial to have a well-crafted code of ethics, but it will have little effect if it is not communicated to new and existing staff. The use of induction processes can be useful for new staff, as can multiple touch points in the form of a written booklet, electronic communication, videos, training sessions, staff meetings, contracts of employment and performance reviews.

## Ethics in practice: International codes

You have been approached by a company that expanded rapidly and operates in a number of different countries. The senior management of the company are now deliberating as to whether they should have one code of conduct to reflect the consistent brand and values of the company, or maintain a series of independent codes that reflect the culture and customs of the countries within which they currently operate.

**Question:**
1. What advice would you give them?

# International codes of conduct

Differing cultural factors can lead to problems in global operations. For example, for a multinational public accounting firm, the notion of independence from client pressures when conducting an audit might be perceived differently by auditors from a more collectivist society such as Japan, than by auditors from a more individualistic society such as Australia (Cohen, Pant & Sharp 1993). The scenario where a company needs to decide on one or multiple codes is not uncommon. Companies operating in more than one geographic location need to grapple with the need for multiple national variations, or the adoption of a single code of conduct for the whole organisation. As a consequence, firms in this circumstance will need to spend time reflecting on their organisation and what the expectations of employees and contractors are, irrespective of where the business is conducted.

It has been noted that establishing an ethical culture for a multinational company requires far greater effort than for a standard domestic culture (Jackson 1997). Where a standard code of conduct is used across all areas of the operation, it not only establishes expectations of behaviour, but also communicates the company identity, and how it operates, irrespective of what country acts as the primary interface. In many ways, the code also reinforces the brand of who the company is, and how they do business. To promote their standard code, Shell Corporation's code of conduct is available in 15 different languages.

Obviously, the primary difficulty in the development of an international code of ethics lies in trying to reconcile ethical views across international borders (Robertson & Fadil 1998; Smeltzer & Jennings 1998). In an attempt to do just this, international businesses may tend towards an approach based on principles or common values. For example, Schwartz (2005) established six universal moral values by which corporate codes of ethics can be constructed and evaluated: 1) trustworthiness; 2) respect; 3) responsibility; 4) fairness; 5) caring; and 6) citizenship.

Ethical theory provides a particularly useful platform from which to consider international codes. Donaldson (1992) proposes there are different languages of ethics, including: 1) virtue and vice; 2) self-protection through to self-control; 3) maximisation of human welfare; 4) avoidance of human harm; 5) rights and duties as well as legal constraints; and 6) social contracts.

Going one step further, eight governing ethical principles have been developed, which, when taken together are called, the **Global Business Standards Codex** (Paine et al., 2005). These eight principles, the defining features of which are shown here, can be used to create, or evaluate, a code of conduct:

**Global Business Standards Codex** – eight governing ethical principles which can be used to build or evaluate a code of conduct.

1. The fiduciary principle (diligence, loyalty).
2. The property principle (protection, theft).
3. The reliability principle (contracts premises, commitments).
4. The transparency principle (truthfulness, deception, disclosure, candour, objectivity).
5. The dignity principle (respect for the individual, health and safety, privacy and confidentiality, use of force, association and expression, learning and development, employment security).
6. The fairness principle (fair dealing, fair treatment, fair competition, fair process).

7. The citizenship principle (law and regulation, public good, cooperation with authorities, political non-involvement, civic contribution).

8. The responsiveness principle (addressing concerns, public involvement).

An international code has been found to be most useful, not just with an organisation's own employees, but also when global operations require the use of subcontractors. Levi Strauss and Company were the first multinational to establish sourcing operational guidelines, which are applicable and consistently applied in more than 60 countries.

## Ethics in practice: Codes of conduct

Undertake an internet search of some publicly available company codes of conduct. Consider and reflect on the commonalities and differences between the codes.

## Corporate ethics training programs

Ethical training programs are said to have multiple objectives. A synthesis of the literature reveals that ethical programs will, ideally:

- create awareness of standards and ethical conduct
- enhance understanding of ethical expectations
- underscore the importance of ethics in organisations
- help staff apply ethical decision-making in the workplace.

It has been observed that, for ethical programs to be successful in organisations, there needs to be strategic input from the organisation's leaders as well as support from all members of the management team. It is not enough to have a single champion or program run solely by the HR department. The creation of an ethical climate, and the success of ethical training, necessitates a top-down approach, which management at all levels support.

"It's flying time."

Corporate ethics training programs (© shutterstock.com/Cartoonresource)

There are several strategies for ensuring the effectiveness of ethical training:

1. A commitment by organisational leaders to the importance of the training (it is not uncommon to have an introductory video message from the CEO setting the rationale behind the emphasis on ethics).
2. A collective approach is taken, and the responsibility for an ethical culture is shared.
3. The company's own (local) employees are used as facilitators, rather than outside consultants.
4. The objectives of the training are made clear.
5. The training is underpinned by the code of conduct and related policies and processes.
6. The relevance, genuineness and reality of the training are emphasised, with numerous examples drawn from the experience of the company and the sector, within which the organisation operates, with discussion of past violations of ethical codes and standards.
7. Sessions are highly interactive, experiential (for example, using board games, case studies and media-rich digital content).
8. Where there are language variations in the organisation, training is conducted in the local language of the attendees.
9. Training sessions and workshops are not treated as an opportunity for organisational gripe sessions. Discussion should be redirected to the topic at hand.
10. Employees who have ethics-related roles and responsibilities are identified and their contact details circulated (this would include ethics officers, the ombudsman and audit staff).
11. Consequences for ethical violations are spelled out.
12. Access to further information and support is provided.

# An ethical ombudsman

**ethical ombudsman** – a designated person who maintains a hands-on focus for receiving and resolving ethical issues.

An **ethical ombudsman** is a designated person within an organisation who maintains a 'hands-on' focus for receiving and investigating concerns regarding unethical behaviour. Generally speaking, the ethical ombudsman most often acts as a third party in the resolution of ethical disputes (Dunfee & Werhane 1997). Despite the title, an ombudsman can be either male or female. An ombudsman is usually a person with significant depth and breadth of experience, who has been with the company for a number of years and is committed to integrity in the workplace. The ombudsman should be easily approachable to employees, even over geographic distance and have the authority to undertake preliminary independent reviews. In smaller organisations, this could be an additional role with a time allocation given to an existing staff member, or, in larger organisations, it could be a full-time position, or even a department. More recently, in some companies, the role has a broader brief in order to be available not only to employees of the company, but also to related business entities (contractors) and stakeholders (suppliers and customers).

Common roles of an ethical ombudsman include:

- providing counselling and advice
- responding to allegations of wrongdoing
- investigating disputes

- maintaining independence, confidentiality and impartiality
- providing in-depth knowledge of the organisation's corporate policy and value system
- determining appropriate resolution and advice
- advising senior management of current or emerging ethical risks.

As an example, Covidien, an international provider of healthcare products, have an internal Office of the Ombudsman, who is described as an employee who is an independent and impartial resource for employees, suppliers, investors, or customers, who want to address ethics and compliance concerns. It is the intention that the ombudsman does not replace local resources for resolving issues (such as human resources, line management, environmental, health and safety, legal or quality) but is an additional resource (Covidien 2013). See Table 12.1.

**Table 12.1**  Dos and don'ts of an ombudsman

| The ombudsman will: |
| --- |
| listen to understand concerns that staff may have |
| keep information as confidential as possible |
| remain impartial |
| endeavour to reframe the issue |
| help the staff to evaluate options |
| assist individuals with bringing their concerns forward |
| provide information and coaching, as required |
| facilitate informal review and resolution |
| strive towards successful outcomes consistent with fair treatment |
| identify issues that require systemic change. |
| The ombudsman will not: |
| be partial to any one side |
| be party to the formal investigations |
| determine policy or binding decisions |
| be in an organisational role that conflicts with ombudsman status |
| create records or reports for the organisation |
| substitute formal channels. |

(Source: Covidien 2013)

# Ethics on reflection: Ethical Ombudsman

To gain an understanding of the role of an ethical ombudsman, view these videos:
- *The role of the Ombusman.M4V*, <www.youtube.com/watch?v=vJsy8u4Hysg>.
- *Rockwell Collins Ombudsman – Committed to integrity*, <www.youtube.com/watch?v=1JwqikT3cKY>.

## An ethics committee

**ethics committee**
– a formal group of individuals assigned to the specific task of undertaking ethical decision-making and promoting ethical behaviour.

An **ethics committee** is a formal group of individuals assigned to the specific task of ensuring ethical decision-making in an organisation. Deloitte, for example, maintain that the purpose of their social and ethics committee is to give voice to and help the business behave as, a socially responsible corporate citizen (Deloitte 2012).

Ethics committees are used by organisations that wish to ensure that an ethical issue is handled correctly. When left to an individual, there is the possibility that they may cave to prevailing power and politics or self-interest will rule; however, by handing over an ethical issue to an ethics committee, the organisation can be assured that the issue will be reflected upon, relevant ethical principles and decision processes applied and that the decision, even if it is unpalatable or costly to the organisation, will be endorsed and actioned.

The predominant benefit of having a formal ethics committee is that it allows an objective review and resolution of ethical issues when they arise and, as ethical committees are made up of different people with varied individual values and stances on ethics issues, this variety of perspectives can work to ensure a range of alternatives are considered (Ferrell, Fraedrich & Ferrell 2013).

## Ethics in practice: Ethics committee

BP operate an ethics committee (BP 2012) (see <www.bp.com/content/dam/bp/pdf/investors/BP_Annual_Report_and_Form_20F_2012.pdf>).

**Question:**
1. What appears to be the main focus of this committee?

## Ethics on reflection: Social and ethics committee

Download Deloitte's social and ethics committee resource guide at: <www.deloitte.com/assets/Dcom-SouthAfrica/Local%20Assets/Documents/social_ethics_resource_guide2.pdf>. Read over and reflect on, the duties of the committee as outlined on pages 15–16 of the resource guide.

## An ethical advice service or hotline

Ensuring that there are open lines of communication relating to ethical issues is a central component of an ethical organisation. A strategy adopted to achieve this goal is the creation

**Table 12.2** Ethical advice and hotline services in Australia

| Company | Ethical advice or hotline service | Website |
|---|---|---|
| Ernst & Young (EY) | EY operate an ethics hotline but, naturally, encourage employees to speak to their immediate manager first. | <www.ey.com/AU/en/About-us/EY-Ethics-hotline> |
| Lockheed Martin | Lockheed Martin employees can communicate with the ethics office by: talking to their ethics officer, calling the Corporate Ethics HelpLine, or sending an email to corporate ethics. | <www.lockheedmartin.com.au/us/who-we-are/ethics/culture-ethics.html> |
| BP | BP have an independent ethical hotline called OpenTalk helpline, available for staff to report ethical infringements confidentially. | <www.bp.com/en/global/corporate/sustainability/our--people-and-values/our-code-of-conduct/speaking-up.html> |
| Metcash | One of Australia's leading wholesale distribution and marketing companies, Metcash have an ethics hotline. | <www.metcash.com/corporate-governance/ethics-hotline> |
| Covidien | Covidien's 'Integrity Helpline' is open seven days a week, 24 hours a day, not just to employees but also to suppliers, customers or others who may have concerns. | <www.covidien.com/covidien/pages.aspx?page=contact/businessethics> |

of an ethical hotline. **Ethical advice**, or **ethical hotlines** as they are sometimes called, are a service provided to staff who wish to discuss or report unethical conduct, or who seek assistance when facing an ethical dilemma. Ethical hotlines enable staff to make calls confidentially about ethical issues. Having the option of a hotline has been shown to give staff members a sense of support and confidence that assistance and advice are available when needed. Table 12.2 gives some examples of Australian companies that currently run such a service.

While we have used the phrase 'ethics hotline', some companies, such as Covidien, call theirs the 'Integrity Helpline'. For smaller firms there is the possibility of outsourcing the hotline. For example, Deloitte Touche Tohmatsu manage an ethics hotline on behalf of Australian Airservices.

The mechanism of advice or hotlines can also operate by email, with IT infrastructure ensuring the sender is able to maintain their anonymity. Organisations might also periodically collate the key issues and locations from which concerns are originating and communicate this information to senior management as part of a regular reporting outcome. The establishment of such hotlines demonstrates the commitment of an organisation to ethical practice and to the creation of an ethical culture. However, ethical hotlines should not operate in isolation because, without supporting codes and training programs, they will not be as effective.

**ethical advice** (sometimes called **ethical hotlines**) – a service provided to staff who wish to discuss or report unethical conduct.

## Whistleblowing

The balance required between supporting staff with advice on how to resolve an ethical dilemma and providing staff with the opportunity to blow the whistle on unacceptable pressures or unethical behaviour enacted by another employee, can never be predicted. In recent years there has possibly been a shift more towards hotlines providing the opportunity for staff to highlight a concern before it goes public. In a case described in PricewaterhouseCoopers' global economic survey (2012), a whistleblower hotline was the key to obtaining key information to unravel a complex case against an executive from an ASX200 company. Initially, the whistleblower provided fragmentary information; however, it was enough to commence an investigation. Later, the informant's information was verified through organisational evidence and interviews, thus unravelling a fraudulent (achieved through manipulating inventory and assets via a third-party supplier) and corrupt ('kickbacks') workplace.

The challenge is to create an environment where whistleblowing is encouraged, but also protected. In order to stimulate engagement in the US, whistleblowers are offered up to 30% of any fine that results from information they receive (Monaghan & Russell 2012), which most certainly motivates their participation. Companies like BHP, Rio Tinto, Leighton Holdings, Qantas and Transfield have responded to a global regulatory crackdown by establishing ethics units, policies and hotlines to protect their reputation and assets, particularly as they expand into Asia (Durkin 2013).

# Ethics in the media: Whistleblowers

A law in Utah pays whistleblowers up to 30% of recoveries and the Securities and Exchange Commission (SEC) operates a similar scheme for cases larger than US$1 million ('Ponzi schemes' 2012).

## An ethical audit

**ethical audit**
– measures the degree to which an organisation's performance and operations align with its values and codes.

An **ethical audit** measures the degree to which an organisation's daily performance and operation aligns with it values and codes. Ethical audits can be conducted to hone and refine an organisation's core values and ethics and it should be treated as the opportunity to heighten ethical awareness rather than a control mechanism. The ideal audit will create open dialogue and discussion and enable all staff (and possibly also key stakeholders) to reflect on their own performance as well as the organisation's.

Various mechanisms to audit an organisational culture have been developed, such as: Cameron and Quinn's (2006) Organisational Culture Assessment Inventory; ethical climate scales (Babin, Boles & Robin 2000; Schwepker 2001); practical advice (Ingram 2013); and guidance as to how audits relate to other dimensions of ethics programs (Metzger, Dalton & Hill 1993).

For international firms, audits have been extended to include their supply chain following criticisms of labour and safety abuse and, for some years now, consumer product and retail companies have been fending off sweatshop critics by hiring auditors (preferably independent of the company), to inspect their overseas factories for labour violations. In 2010, Woolworths made changes to their ethical audit program, demanding that all of their suppliers complete an audit of their workplace standards. Woolworths attributed the changes to their audit program to increasing concerns from the community about ensuring the products they are purchasing are from a trustworthy source. These community concerns prompted Woolworths to institute the changes to the audit program to guarantee their suppliers are not using harmful chemicals, or child labour. Not surprisingly, the changes have received criticism from suppliers (Hall 2010).

Since June 2003, in a move towards greater transparency, companies that belong to the Fair Labor Association (FLA), such as Nike and Reebok, have made public their labour audits on the FLA's website. Audits can be conducted by the organisation themselves, or undertaken through **Fair Labor Association Audits**, which provide for independent monitoring and verification to ensure that the FLA's Workplace Standards are upheld. Apple has audited every final assembly factory in their supply chain each year since 2006 and, in February 2012, announced that the FLA would conduct special voluntary audits of Apple's final assembly suppliers. As part of its independent assessment, the FLA interviewed thousands of employees about working and living conditions, including health and safety, compensation, working hours and communication with management (Apple Inc. 2012).

> **Fair Labor Association Audits** – the Fair Labor Association (FLA) conducts independent monitoring and verification to ensure that its Workplace Standards are upheld.

# Ethics in the media: Ethical audits

Significant criticism surrounds systems for auditing the complex and constantly changing, supply chain for global firms. Walmart, Gap and Nike all acknowledge that audits alone are not doing enough to improve safety ('Avoiding the fire next time' 2013).

## Enforcement of ethical expectations

For ethical policies and codes to be effective in an organisation they must be successfully implemented. Implementation requires that ethical codes and policies be integrated into everyday organisational activities on a systematic basis and it has been observed that without this stringent approach to implementation, the impact on improving ethical behaviour is limited (Ferrell & Pride 1981). A significant factor of successful implementation lies in the enforcement of ethical policy. In practice, enforcement means that employees guilty of ethical violations should be identified and disciplined.

The importance of enforcement has been noted in the literature and is commonly accepted as a key factor in the adoption and overall effectiveness, of codes (Adams, Tashchian & Shore 2001). Enforcement as a factor contributing to the effectiveness of codes is best examined from the perspective of expectancy theory, which includes not only punishments, but also rewards.

### Rewards and punishments

It has been noted that differing rewards and penalties for ethical and unethical behaviour have a significant bearing on employee behaviour. Knouse and Giacolone (1992) claim that, where

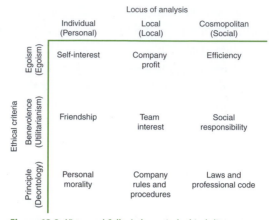

**Figure 12.3**  Victor and Cullen's theoretical ethical climate types
(adapted from: Victor & Cullen 1988)

certain conduct leads directly and consistently to rewards, strong motivation towards ethical behaviour is generally produced. Four incentives that work as rewards for ethical conduct are: 1) recognition; 2) appreciation; 3) commendation; and 4) monetary rewards. Of course, it is imperative that organisations ensure that such rewards are the result of desired ethical behaviours, rather than rewards for financial performance or cost savings (Kerr 1995).

On the flip side, the threat of punishment for those failing to behave ethically ensures that staff make more effort to understand and follow ethical guidelines and codes (Logsdon & Yuthas 1997). Codes alone do not stop unethical behaviour; they must be accompanied by clearly proposed sanctions if they are to minimise the likelihood of unethical behaviour (Laczniak & Inderrieden 1987). The threat of punishment has been found to be an effective deterrent to unethical behaviour (Hegarty & Sims 1978). Similarly, top management reprimands have been found to decrease the perception of ethical problems in an organisation (Chonko & Hunt 1985). Punishment can come in the form of: 1) verbal censure; 2) written warning; 3) demotion; or 4) dismissal.

There are those, however, who warn against an over-reliance on reward and punishment as such an environment can translate into staff operating at lower levels of moral reasoning. The reward and punishment of ethical and unethical behaviour, ideally, operates in an environment that is premised on ethics, where employees are trusted to make ethical decisions, rather than in a control system heavily reliant on reward and punishment (Baucus & Beck-Dudley 2005).

## Differing ethical climates

During the preceding discussion we have been referring to the development of a single ethical climate; however, it has been proposed that an organisation may exhibit a number of different types of ethical climate (Victor & Cullen 1988). In an effort to identify the different ethical climates, Victor and Cullen (1988) developed a 3x3 matrix with multiple climates

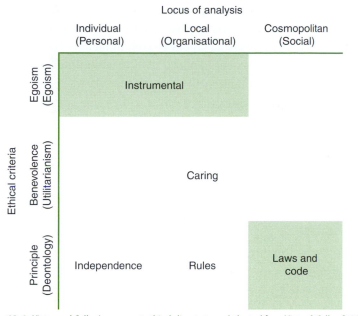

**Figure 12.4**  Victor and Cullen's emergent ethical climate types (adapted from Victor & Cullen [1988])

(see Figure 12.3). The left axis provides three ethical criteria (note the alignment to ethical theory): egoism (egoism), benevolence (utilitarianism) and principle (deontology); the horizontal axis, called the locus of analysis, describes the referent group one would consult when considering ethical issues: individual (personal), local (organisational) and cosmopolitan (social). The outcomes describe nine possible ethical climate types.

While there has been minor criticism that the typology does not have a universal dimension, the framework has been defended as robust (Fritzsche 2000). The typology has also been used to develop the Victor and Cullen Ethical Climate Questionnaire (Cullen, Victor & Bronson 1993) which has been used in many subsequent research studies (Simha & Cullen 2012). It has also been noted that ethical climates change over the life cycle of an organisation (Belak & Mulej 2009).

While the nine climates are all possible, five ethical climates have been found to occur more frequently (see Figure 12.4).

- **Instrumental climates** – encourage an egoistic perspective with self-interest prevailing in decision-making (Cullen, Parboteeah & Victor 2003).
- **Caring climates** – are benevolent and are concerned with the wellbeing of all.
- **Independence climates** – decision-makers refer back to their personal moral beliefs and values.
- **Rules climates** – decision-making is made with reference to local rules and standards and local organisational codes.
- **Law and codes climates** – predictably, decision-making is based on legality, professional codes, universal codes and religious dictates.

To summarise, a benevolent climate emphasises looking after the interests of the broadest group of people. An egoist ethical climate focuses on maximising an individual's self-interest. Not surprisingly, it has been found that employee commitment is positively associated with an employee's perception of the extent to which their organisational climate is benevolent/ caring and, in contrast, their commitment is negatively related, that is, less commitment exists when the organisational climate is deemed to be egoist (Vline, Cullinan & Farrar 2008).

A positive association has been found between caring and rules climates and job satisfaction (Wang & Hsieh 2012). Egoistic climates tend to have a higher frequency of unethical behaviour (Peterson 2002a), dysfunctional behaviour (Martin & Cullen 2006), higher risk-taking (Saini & Martin 2009) and to encourage employee turnover (DeConinck 2010). In contrast, principled/rules and benevolent/caring climates, appear to reduce employee turnover intentions (Stewart et al. 2011), reduce bullying behaviours (Bulutlar & Oz 2009), and are negatively associated with unethical behaviours (Smith, Thompson & Iacovou 2009). Benevolent or caring climates have also been found to have a positive association with employees' willingness to blow the whistle (Rothwell & Baldwin 2007).

# Conclusion

Appropriate ethical behaviour is at the heart of an organisation's ability to generate and retain the trust of key stakeholder groups, not only customers and clients. As we suspect, the ability to see ethical issues, and respond ethically, may be related more to attributes of the corporate culture and climate than to the attributes of individual employees (Chen, Sawyer & Williams 1997). By ethical culture we are referring to the shared perceptions of what behaviour is right, and what behaviour the organisation expects, from its members, as well as what is considered to be ethically correct behaviour, and how ethical issues should be handled (Victor & Cullen 1987).

A clear relationship has been found between the ethical climate of an organisation and the ethical decisions that employees make (Wimbush, Shepard & Markham 1997) and, as we have seen, positive ethical cultures have been linked to reduced role conflict, employee job satisfaction, commitment to quality, reduced role stress, increased trust in supervisors and employee performance (Mulki, Jaramillo & Locander 2008; Weeks et al. 2006); Appelbaum, Deguire & Lay 2005. Given the positive benefits and the inherent advantages, there are several strategies that can be used to build an ethical culture.

The most powerful of all the available strategies to ensure ethics is the influence of managers. The values and behaviour of senior leadership have been found to be especially influential in shaping an ethical culture (Dickson et al. 2001), with ethics higher in organisations where a leader's norms, as well as their behaviour, encourage ethical conduct and where ethical conduct is rewarded while unethical conduct is punished.

The development of a code of ethics is frequently seen as the most common action undertaken to create an ethical organisation. Many organisations have been found to have looked at older, more established companies in an attempt to develop an appropriate code for use, particularly when operating in the international arena. While this may prove a useful starting point, it is imperative that companies reflect on their own values as they attempt to determine the standards of practice that they feel are operational and enforceable. By 'enforceable', we mean that there are organisational sanctions for wrongdoing. Laczniak and Inderrieden (1987) found that when unethical behaviour receives a negative reaction and punishment, it is less likely to be repeated. The ethical culture of an organisation is, thus, best served by a code of ethics which includes clearly stated disciplinary measures.

Codes on their own are not enough and, ideally, an ethical training program will follow the introduction of a code to ensure all staff are aware of the importance of ethics, and the dimensions of the code will be clearly articulated to all. Further strategies can also be utilised. Ethical advice or ethical hotlines open up a specific channel of communication and can be electronic as well as telephonic. Some companies go to great lengths to provide anonymity to employees, while others require personal identification. It is also not uncommon for the issues raised through this service to be aggregated in a report to senior management and the board.

Organisations that have an ethical ombudsman's office usually rely on direct contact or information from ethical hotlines. As a consequence of being alerted to some form of transgression, they will undertake a preliminary review and, if deemed appropriate, an internal investigation will usually work with the functional areas within the organisation. If necessary, the matter could be escalated to senior management.

The creation of ethical committees is another strategy used by organisations to help employees make ethical decisions and to provide consistency with past decisions. Committees are responsible for making and disseminating clear guidelines for ethical actions. An over-arching activity is conducting an ethics audit (not to be confused with an accounting audit), which can be carried out by the organisation themselves, or, more appropriately, by ethics auditors external to the company. Prompted by a sweatshop monitoring group started in 1997, with the help of the US Clinton administration, a number of high-profile international companies are now going public with the audits of their supply chains. By putting these reports in the public domain, a huge incentive is created for companies to remedy the problems identified.

To conclude, these strategies do not generally operate in isolation and are part of a complex interaction of organisational policies and processes which entail hiring practices and specific programs in key areas. However, the overall resolve is for the organisation to commit to, and fulfil, its intent to be an ethical organisation and maintain an ethical culture.

## Ethics on video

**Decision-making** – *Business ethics keynote speaker Chuck Gallagher shares straight talk about ethics* 2013, YouTube, Chuck Gallagher, 27 January 2013, <www.youtube.com/watch?v=gUJ00vNGCPE>.

**Ethical culture** – *The education of a reluctant businessman, Yves Chouinard* 2008, YouTube, University of California Television (UCTV), 7 February, <www.youtube.com/watch?v=NVfy2T0rzMc>.

See web material for more videos.

## Ethics at the movies

Here are a few movie suggestions that have ethical content in relation to ethics in organisations:

*Invictus** – starring Morgan Freeman, Matt Damon and Tony Kgoroge whose characters show the essence of what inspirational leadership is, and what it can achieve. *Invictus* 2009, motion picture, Neufeld, M, Lorenz, R, Eastwood, C and McCreary, L.

**Remember the Titans** – Denzel Washington is assigned as coach to a football team and has the task of uniting a racially-divided football team through team culture. *Remember the Titans* 2000, motion picture, Oman, C & Bruckheimer, J.

*Author's pick**

See web material for more movies.

# Ethics on the web

**Ethical culture building**, Dreamworks' creative culture building – see Grose, J 2013, 'The animated workplace: Dreamworks' "six pack" approach to building a culture of creativity', *Fast Company & Inc*, 15 March, <www.fastcocreate.com/1682550/the-animated-workplace-dreamworks-six-pack-approach-to-building-a-culture-of-creativity>.

**International Ombudsman Association** supports international organisational ombudsmen, <www.ombudsassociation.org/about-us/code-ethics>.

See web material for more web references.

# Student exercises

See web material for answers to student short answer questions.

## Short answer questions

1. Contrast a prescriptive/rules-based approach versus a values-based approach to a code of conduct.
2. What are the benefits of having an ethical culture?

## Experiential exercise

1. You believe that establishing an ethical hotline in your company is a worthwhile initiative. What do you believe should be the key features? Make up a flyer to promote the ethics hotline.

## Small case

### Case: An integrated ethics program

Rocked by a recent ethical scandal involving a low-level employee in your company the Board of Directors have requested a proposal at the next board meeting for the introduction of an integrated ethics program.

**Question:**

1. Describe what is an integrated ethics program and the common elements contained in such a program. Sketch out the notes in preparation for your proposal.

# Large case

## Enron – a barrel of bad apples

### Background

In the 1990s, Enron were the darling of Wall Street; seen as innovative and well-managed, even winning *Fortune's* best-managed company award in 2000. Although this now seems ironic, at the time Enron were the poster child for good management practice – they were involved in corporate social responsibility (CSR) programs, environmental programs, ethics programs and philanthropy. In 2001, though, Enron went into bankruptcy, with 20 000 staff losing their jobs and pensions and hundreds of thousands of investors losing their investments (Collins 2009). How did this happen?

### The Enron collapse

Rondal and Brinkmann (2003) believe that the issue is the company used corporate artifacts to promote an ethical facade, that is, although Enron had an ethical code of conduct and an ethics officer, this did not mean the company embraced ethical behaviour or that ethical behaviour was embedded in the corporate culture. By all accounts, in the early days the company did embrace the code of conduct, before Jeffrey Skilling's rise to the top (he was initially the chairman of Enron Gas Services Co., but he quickly rose to be Ken Lay's second-in-charge and became CEO when Lay resigned). However, as Skilling became more influential in the company, he eroded the corporate culture and encouraged an individualistic mentality in employees.

In the early days of Enron, in the late 1980s, they were a struggling company. Deregulation of the energy power market in 1988 allowed them to change direction and move the company from being an energy delivery company to an energy broker company – Enron essentially took the risk between buyers and sellers of natural gas reserves. By 1990,

Skilling was employed by the head of Enron, Ken Lay, and the company culture started changing as Skilling became focused on maximising his bonus and encouraged employees to add value and innovate at all costs – this was a prerequisite to surviving and thriving at the company. Employees were rewarded for their innovative ways to increase profits, regardless of questionable ethical considerations (Rondal & Brinkmann 2003).

In 1991, Skilling floated the idea of Enron changing from traditional accounting methods to a 'mark-to-market' method, which would better reflect the impressive results the Gas Bank division was receiving and showcase the guaranteed future revenue streams they had generated. Initially the SEC rejected the suggestion, however with some backing from Arthur Andersen, and Enron's board, the mark-to-market method was introduced in 1992. This notion of seeing numbers as purely an accounting procedure initially bolstered Enron's returns and reduced their balance sheet debt levels, however this practice would later be their undoing (Collins 2009).

Another innovative technique Enron used was introduced by Andrew Fastow, who eventually became the chief financial officer. Enron stock was transferred into non-consolidated special purpose entities (SPEs), which took Enron's debt off the balance sheet and gave Enron an injection of cash (Rondal & Brinkmann 2003). This was not an illegal activity, but the regulations set by the SEC around second SPEs in a securitisation transaction required that the second SPE be owned and operated independently from the company originating the deal. To meet with the SEC's arm's-length regulation, the SPE had to have 3% equity from outside investors and meet certain legal obligations. Enron's accounting firms made sure Enron met the legal regulation in order to qualify, however in reality, they were subsidiaries, run by existing and former Enron officials, including Andrew Fastow and Michael Kopper. Anything but arm's length, and clearly a conflict of interest with both people, and their families, financially benefiting from the 'partnership' companies. Even less of an arm's length was one SPE in particular, Chewco, which were run by Kopper and 99% funded by Enron (Collins 2009). This meant the 3% independent equity requirement was breached (Schwarcz 2001).

The premise behind making SPEs work was that Enron stock had a solid history of rising stock prices, which made the company feel secure that the likelihood of them having to pay on the guarantee was remote. Unfortunately, when Enron stock hit a snag and fell, then so did the SPEs and Enron were required to pay the guarantee payments, which then negatively affected Enron's balance sheet and triggered further stock price falls (Schwarcz 2001).

The accounts at Enron were so complex that the left hand didn't seem to know what the right hand was doing. The conflicts of interest and accounting breaches did not end with the 'partnership' SPEs; the men running the partnerships were making enormous sums of money, which clouded their decision-making process about where to draw the ethical line (Rondal & Brinkmann 2003; Collins 2009).

These clever accounts were overseen by Arthur Andersen auditors, who must have realised the idea was likely to fall like a pack of cards – however the auditors were from the same company that received significant consulting business from Enron (in one year Arthur Andersen were paid $35 million in audit fees and $27 million in consultancy fees) – to query the problem and pursue it to the natural end would result in the loss of consulting business, something both Skilling and Fastow reminded auditors about if too many questions were asked (Collins 2009). It is hard not to view this arrangement as a conflict of interest; however, Arthur Andersen indicated that their independence was not impaired from the double-duty arrangements (Duska & Duska 2003).

In 2001, Skilling took over from Lay as CEO of Enron. Skilling predicted a massive rise in stocks; however, this never happened, and in fact the stock started to slide. Some of the reasons were that: trade analysts came to the conclusion the stocks must be over-priced; Arthur Andersen was embroiled in an accounting fraud scandal with another client, and was looking more closely at the books; Fastow's SPE arrangements were exposed in a *Wall Street Journal* article and some employees began a class action against Enron for insider trading. By 20 November, 2011, Enron's stock was worthless, and a month later Enron were delisted from the Stock Exchange.

## Questions:

1. What key ethical issues led to the demise of Enron?
2. Milton Friedman promotes the notion that businesses' primary social responsibility is to maximise profits, and in turn the taxes would benefit communities. Enron certainly worked on the premise of maximising profits. What warnings would a business ethicist give a company following this approach?
3. Which tier of ethical culture did Enron adopt?
4. Explain what the term moral disengagement is and how you believe the behaviour came about at Enron.
5. If Enron had survived, what suggestions would you put in place to turn the company's ethical program around?

See web material for:
- answers to short answer questions
- additional student cases
- tutor resources (tutor password required)
- additional material including Ethics at the movies, Ethics in print, Ethics on video and Ethics on the web.

# References

'0.4%' 2012, *Business Review Weekly*, 29 November–6 December, p. 11.

'$2M' 2012, *Business Review Weekly*, 1–7 November, p. 11.

'A close look at high frequency trading' 2012, *Biz/Ed*, September/October, p. 55.

'A fistful of dollars' 2012, *The Economist*, 4 February, p. 9.

'A knight in digital armour' 2012, *The Economist Technology Quarterly*, 1 September, p. 1.

'A little integrity please' 2013, *The Times Higher Education*, 13 June, pp. 14–15.

'A new social movement. Marks & Spencer' 2013, *Harvard Business Review*, March, p. 89.

'A rise and fall' 2012, *The Economist*, 10 March, p. 74.

AAP 2012, 'American Express fined US$27.5', *Couriermail.com.au*, 2 October, retrieved 4 February 2013, <www.couriermail.com.au/news/breaking-news/american-express-fined-us275m/story-e6freoo6–1226486223322>.

'Abacussed' 2011, *The Economist*, 1 October, p. 75.

ABC News 2011, 'Milk inquiry hears claims of price collusion', *ABC News*, 10 March, retrieved 5 February 2013, <www.abc.net.au/news/2011–03–10/milk-inquiry-hears-claims-of-price-collusion/2662974>.

——2013, 'Barack Obama pledges changes to restore trust in NSA surveillance programs', 10 August, retrieved 12 August 2013, <www.abc.net.au/news/2013–08–10/obama-pledges-changes-to-restore-trust-in-nsa-spying/4877886>.

Accord on Fire and Building Safety in Bangladesh 2013, 'FAQs', *Accord on Fire and Building Safety In Bangladesh*, retrieved 17 January 2014, <www.bangladeshaccord.org/faqs>.

'Accountable' 2012, *The Economist*, 8 December, p. 67.

Ackoff, RL 1987, 'Business ethics and the entrepreneur', *Journal of Business Venturing*, vol. 2, pp. 185–91.

Adage 2013, 'Ask Heidi', *Adage*, retrieved 12 February 2013, <www.adage.com.au>.

Adams, D & Maine, E 1998, *Business Ethics for the 21st Century*, Mayfield Publishing Company, Mountview, California.

Adams, JS, Tashchian, A & Shore, TH 2001, 'Codes of ethics as signals for ethical behaviour', *Journal of Business Ethics*, vol. 29, pp. 199–211.

Adelstein, J 2012, 'What Michael Woodford saw at Olympus', *The Atlantic Wire*, 21 December, retrieved 14 June 2013, <www.theatlanticwire.com/global/2012/12/what-michael-woodford-saw-olympus/60259>.

Adikaram, AS, Gunawardena, C & Perea, T 2011, 'Sexual harassment in the workplace: the effect of perpetrator attributes and recipient attributes in the judgement of sexual harassment incidences', *Sri Lankan Journal of Management*, vol. 16, nos 3–4, July–December, pp. 63–88.

Admati, A & Hellwig, M 2013, *The Banker's New Clothes: What's Wrong with Banking and What to Do about It*, Princeton University Press, Oxfordshire, UK.

Advertising Standards Authority New Zealand 2010, 'Children's Code for Advertising Food', Advertising Standards Authority New Zealand, retrieved 10 July 2013, <www.asa.co.nz/code_children_food.php>.

Advertising Standards Board 2012, 'Diageo Australia Ltd', Australian Standards Board, 11 July, Case report no. 0272/12, retrieved 19 February 2013, <www.adstandards.com.au/casereports/determinations/standards>.

Aflac 2013, 'Aflac makes Ethisphere's annual world's most ethical companies list', media release, 6 March, retrieved 14 October 2013, <www.aflac.com/aboutaflac/pressroom/pressreleasestory.aspx?rid=1792995>.

Agarwal, J 1999, 'Ethical work climate dimensions in a not for profit organisation: An empirical study', *Journal of Business Ethics*, vol. 20, pp. 1–14.

Agence France-Presse 2012, 'Apple denies e-book pricing collusion', *The Australian*, April 13, retrieved 5 February 2013, <www.theaustralian.com.au/australian-it/apple-denies-e-book-pricing-collusion/story-e6frgakx-1226325835522>.

Aid, M 2012, 'Will the senate renew the FISA amendment act?', *Matthewaid.tumblr.com*, 9 December, retrieved 12 August 2013, <http://matthewaid.tumblr.com/post/37635658102/will-the-senate-renew-the-fisa-amendments-act>.

Ajzen, I 1985, 'From intentions to actions: a theory of planned behaviour', in NJ Kuhl & J Beckman (eds), *Action Control: From Cognition to Behaviour*, Springer, Heidelberg, Germany, pp. 11–39.

Ajzen, I & Fishbein, M 1980, *Understanding Attitudes and Predicting Social Behaviour*, Prentice Hall, New Jersey, USA.

Akaah, IP & Riordan, EA 1989, 'Judgements of marketing professionals about ethical issues in marketing research: A replication and extension', *Journal of Marketing Research* vol. 26, no. 1, pp. 112–20.

——1990, 'The incidence of unethical practices in marketing research: An empirical investigation', *Journal of Academy of Marketing Science*, vol. 18, no. 2, pp. 143–52.

Ake, C 1975, *Justice and Equality, Philosophy and Public Affairs*, Fall, vol. 5, no. 1, pp. 69–89.

Akhter, W, Abassi, AS and Umar, S 2011, 'Ethical issues in advertising in Pakistan: An Islamic perspective', *World Applied Sciences Journal*, vol. 13, no. 3, pp. 444–52.

Aktion Plagiarius 2013, 'Negative award 'Plagiarius' sheds public light on unscrupulous counterfeits!', *Aktion Plagiarius*, 15 February, media release, retrieved 21 April 2013, <www.plagiarius.com/img/pressrelease_plagiariusaward_2013.pdf>.

Allard, T 2012, 'Strong support for whistleblowers', *The Age*, 6 June, p. 8.

Alliance for Bangladesh Worker Safety 2014, 'About the Alliance for Bangladesh Worker Safety', Alliance for Bangladesh Worker Safety, retrieved 17 January 2014, <www.bangladeshworkersafety.org/about>.

Alozie, EC (ed.) 2011, *Advertising in Developing and Emerging Countries: The Economic, Political and Social Context*, Gower Publishing, retrieved 22 April 2013, <www.ashgate.com/pdf/samplepages/advertising-in-developing-and-emerging-countries-intro.pdf>.

Alpert, LI & Sonne, P 2013, 'Snowden still stuck at airport, but looking forward to seeing Russia', *Wall Street Journal*, 24 July, retrieved 12 August 2013, <http://online.wsj.com/news/articles/SB10001424127887323610704578625531841511870>.

Alvarez, S & Barney JB 2005, 'Discovery and creation: Alternative theories of entrepreneurial action', working paper, Department of Management and Human Resources, Fisher College of Business, Ohio State University, 2005.

Alvord, SH 2004, 'Social entrepreneurship and societal transformation', *Journal of Applied Behavioral Science*, vol. 40, no. 3, pp. 260–82.

——Brown, LD & Letts, CW 2002, 'Social entrepreneurship and social transformation: an exploratory study', Hauser Center for Nonprofit Organizations, Working Paper no. 15.

Amano, T & Matsuyama, K 2012, 'Ex-Olympus chairman says stopped from disclosing losses', *Bloomberg*, 20 November, retrieved 15 June 2013, <www.bloomberg.com/news/2012–11–19/ex-olympus-chairman-says-stopped-from-disclosing-losses.html>.

Amber Alert GPS 2012, 'Amber alert GPS device fact sheet', *Amber Alerts*, retrieved 18 February 2013, <www.amberalertgps.com/press>.

American Marketing Association 2013a, 'Definition of marketing', American Marketing Association, retrieved 10 February 2013, <www.marketingpower.com/AboutAMA/Pages/DefinitionofMarketing.aspx>.

——2013b, 'Ethical values', American Marketing Association, retrieved 4 February 2013, <www.marketingpower.com/AboutAMA/Pages/Statement%20of%20Ethics.aspx>.

——2013c, 'Marketing power', American Marketing Association, retrieved 10 February 2013, <www.marketingpower.com/AboutAMA/Pages/AboutMarketingPower.aspx>.

Andreasen, A 2003, 'Ethics in social marketing', *Australasian Marketing Journal*, vol. 11, no. 1, pp. 100–10.

Andrews, KR 1989, 'Ethics in practice', *Harvard Business Review*, September–October, pp. 99–104.

Appelbaum, SH, Deguire, KJ & Lay, M 2005, 'The relationship of ethical climate to deviant workplace behaviour', *Corporate Governance*, vol. 5, no. 4, pp. 43–55.

'Apple: a good cook' 2012, *The Economist*, 25 August, p. 52.

Apple Inc. 2012, 'Fair labor association begins inspections of Foxconn', Apple Inc., media release, 13 February, retrieved 26 November 2013, <www.apple.cpm/pr/library 2012/02/13 fair-labor-association-begins inspection-of -foxconn.html>.

Aquino, K & Reed, A 2002, 'The self-importance of moral identity', *Journal of Personality and Social Psychology*, vol. 83, no. 6, pp. 1423–40.

Arend, RJ 2013, 'Ethics-focused dynamic capabilities: A small business perspective', *Small Business Economics*, vol. 4, no. 1, pp. 1–24.

Areni, C 2010–2011, 'Teaching ethics: Marketing principles and ethical dilemmas in marketing', Business and Professional Ethics Group, The University of Sydney Business School, *The University of Sydney*.

Aristotle 2009 [1861], in L Brown *The Nicomachean Ethics*, (ed.), Oxford University Press, New York.

Armitstead, L 2013, 'Cameron lashes tax avoiders', *Saturday Age*, 26 January, p. 9.

Arnaud, A 2010, 'Conceptualizing and measuring ethical work climate: Development and validation of the ethical climate index', *Business and Society*, vol. 49, no. 2, pp. 345–58.

Arnold, DG, Beauchamp, TL & Bowie, NL 2013, *Ethical Theory and Business*, 9th edn, Pearson Higher Education, USA.

Arnold, F, Lampe, JC & Sutton, SG 1997, 'Understanding the factors underlying ethical organisations: Enabling continuous improvement', *Journal of Applied Business Research*, vol. 15, no. 3, pp. 1–18.

Arnulf, JK & Gottschalk, P 2012, 'Principals, agents and entrepreneurs white-collar crime: An empirical typology of white-collar criminals in a National sample', *Journal of Strategic Management Education*, vol. 8, no. 3, pp. 1–22.

Arup, T 2013, 'Global greenhouse gas emissions reach record level', *The Age*, 20 November, p. 4.

Arutunyan, A & Stanglin, D 2013, 'Snowden remains stuck at Moscow airport', *USA Today*, 24 July, retrieved 12 August 2013, <www.usatoday.com/story/news/world/2013/07/24/edward-snowden-russia-moscow-airport/2582189>.

Ashkanasy, NM, Windsor, CA & Treviño, LK 2006, 'Bad apples and bad barrels revisited: Cognitive moral development, just world beliefs, rewards, and ethical decision making', *Business Ethics Quarterly*, vol. 16, no. 4, pp. 449–73.

Associated Press 2008, 'US supreme court allows lawsuits over 'light' cigarettes', 15 December, *The Guardian*, retrieved 4 February 2013, <www.guardian.co.uk/world/2008/dec/15/supreme-court-smoking-altria-reynolds>.

Austen, LA & Reisch, JT 2007, 'Documentation insights from the auditing profession', *Commercial Lending Review*, July–August, p. 36.

Austin, J, Stevenson, H & Wei-Skillern, J 2006, 'Social and commercial entrepreneurship: Same, different, or both?', *Entrepreneurship Theory and Practice*, vol. 30, no. 1, pp. 1–22.

Austin, MW 2006, 'Divine Command Theory', *Internet Encyclopedia of Philosophy*, retrieved 10 June 2013, <www.iep.utm.edu/divine-c>.

Australian Bureau of Statistics (ABS) 2008, 'One in five Australians have a mental illness: ABS', media report, 23 October, retrieved on 21 February 2013, <www.abs.gov.au/ausstats/abs@.nsf/Latestproducts/4326.0Media%20Release12007?opendocument&tabname=Summary&prodno=4326.0&issue=2007&num=&view=>.

——2012, 'Education differences between men and women', *ABS*, 10 December, retrieved 21 February 2013, <www.abs.gov.au/AUSSTATS/abs@.nsf/Lookup/4102.0Main+Features20Sep+2012>.

——2013, ABS website, accessed 1 October 2013, <www.abs.gov.au>.

Australian Competition and Consumer Commission (ACCC) 2009, 'ACCC alleges price fixing by Queensland construction companies', Australian Competition and Consumer Commission, media release, 21 September, retrieved 4 February 2013, <www.accc.gov.au/content/index.phtml/itemId/893715>.

——2012a, 'ACCC accepts informal undertaking for alleged misleading carbon price claims', Australian Competition and Consumer Commission, media release, 5 July, retrieved 19 February 2013, <www.accc.gov.au/media-release/accc-accepts-informal-undertaking-for-alleged-misleading-carbon-price-claims>.

——2012b, 'Cathay Pacific and Singapore Airlines to pay $23 million in penalties for price fixing', Australian Competition and Consumer Commission, media release, 7 December, retrieved 19 February 2013, <www.accc.gov.au/content/index.phtml/itemId/1092802/fromItemId/142?pageDefinitionItemId=16940>.

——2013a, 'Identity theft', Scamwatch, retrieved 10 February 2013, <www.scamwatch.gov.au/content/index.phtml/tag/identitytheft>.

——2013b, 'Using social media to promote your business', Australian Competition and Consumer Commission, retrieved 19 February 2013, <www.accc.gov.au/content/index.phtml/itemId/1091193>.

Australian Federal Police 2013, 'Cybercrime', Commonwealth of Australia, retrieved 4 August 2013, <www.afp.gov.au/policing/cybercrime.aspx>.

Australian Financial Review 2013, 'Ex-CEO of Phosphagenics sells shares to repay biotech', *The Australian Financial Review*, 5 August, retrieved 9 August, 2013, <www.afr.com/p/business/companies/ex_ceo_of_phosphagenics_sells_shares_QR2sdHhhDwe8bs6jEjuwBN>.

Australian Human Resource Institute (AHRI) 2013, 'HR Practices Day 2013', retrieved 12 November 2013, <www.hrpractices.ahri.com.au/home>.

Australian Human Rights Commission n.d., *Young People Case Studies*, Australian Human Rights Commission, retrieved 20 February 2013, <www.humanrights.gov.au/complaints_information/young_case_studies.html>.

——2012, *Review into the Treatment of Women in the Australian Defence Force: Phase 2 Report*, Australian Human Rights Commission, retrieved 12 November 2013, < http://defencereview.humanrights.gov.au/sites/default/files/adf-front.pdf l>.

Australian Institute of Management 2012, *Managing in a flexible work environment white paper*, retrieved 21 February 2012, <www.aim-nsw-act.com.au/managing-flexible-work-environment-white-paper#.USX3Dld5dyM>.

Australian Securities & Investments Commission (ASIC) 2003a, '03–361 Former AMP agent jailed', Australian Securities & Investments Commission, media release, 13 November, retrieved 16 July 2013, <www.asic.gov.au/asic/asic.nsf/byheadline/03–361+Former+AMP+agent+jailed?openDocument>.

——2003b, '03–018 South Australian investment advisers banned', Australian Securities & Investments Commission, media release, 17 January, retrieved 16 July 2013, <www.asic.gov.au/asic/asic.nsf/byheadline/03–018+South+Australian+investment+advisers+banned+?openDocument>.

——2012a, '12–161 MR ASIC obtains court orders against Queensland-based self-managed super advice companies', Australian Securities & Investments Commission, media release, 12 July, retrieved 16 July 2013, <www.asic.gov.au/asic/asic.nsf/byheadline/12–161MR+ASIC+obtains+court+orders+against+Queensland-based+self-managed+super+advice+companies?OpenDocument&Click=>.

——2012b, '12–289MR ASIC acts against offshore companies', Australian Securities & Investments Commission, media release, 19 November, retrieved 16 July 2013, <www.asic.gov.au/asic/asic.nsf/byheadline/12–289MR+ASIC+acts+against+offshore+companies?openDocument>.

——2012c, 'Regulation impact statement: Hedge funds: improving disclosure', Australian Securities & Investments Commission, September, retrieved 19 July 2013, <www.asic.gov.au/asic/pdflib.nsf/LookupByFileName/RIS-hedge-funds-published-18-September-2012.pdf/$file/RIS-hedge-funds-published-18-September-2012.pdf>.

——2013, '134–117MR ASIC to further improve hedge fund disclosure', Australian Securities & Investments Commission, media release, 23 May, retrieved 19 July 2013, <www.asic.gov.au/asic/asic.nsf/byheadline/13–117MR+ASIC+to+further+improve+hedge+fund+disclosure?openDocument>.

Australian Taxation Office (ATO) 2009, 'Thin capitalisation: Why you need to know', Commonwealth of Australia, 6 November, QC16458, retrieved 15 July 2013, <www.ato.gov.au/Business/Thin-capitalisation/In-detail/Overview/Thin-capitalisation---what-you-need-to-know>.

——2013, 'Tax evasion and crime', Commonwealth of Australia, retrieved 4 August 2013, <www.ato.gov.au/General/Tax-evasion-and-crime>.

Australian Transaction Reports and Analysis Centre (AUSTRAC) 2008, 'Introduction to money laundering', Australian Government, 12 December, retrieved 19 April 2013, <www.austrac.gov.au/elearning/pdf/intro_amlctf_money_laundering.pdf>.

Avgouleas, E 2012, *Governance of Global Financial Markets: The Law, the Economics, the Politics*, Cambridge University Press, Cambridge.

'Avoiding the fire next time' 2013, *The Economist*, 4 May, retrieved 2 October 2013, <www.economist.com/news/business/21577078-after-dhaka-factory-collapse-foreign-clothing-firms-are-under-pressure-improve-working>.

Azmat, F & Zutshi, A 2012, 'Influence of home country culture and regulatory environment on corporate social responsibility perceptions: A case of Sri Lankan immigrant entrepreneurs', *Thunderbird International Business Review*, vol. 54, no. 1, January/February, pp. 15–27.

Babin, BJ, Boles, JS & Robin, DP 2000, 'Representing the perceived ethical work climate among marketing employees', *Journal of the Academy of Marketing Science*, vol. 28, no. 3, pp. 345–58.

Bachelard, M 2012, 'We're still coming: Boat people won't be deterred', *National Times*, 15 August, retrieved 6 June 2013, <www.smh.com.au/opinion/political-news/were-still-coming--boat-people-wont-be-deterred-20120814–246vt.html>.

'Back to the drawing board' 2012, *The Economist*, 3 November.

Bailey, JE, Schermerhorn, JR, Hunt, JG, & Osborn, RN 1991, *Managing Organisational Behaviour*, John Wiley & Sons, Brisbane.

'Bain or blessing', 2012, *The Economist*, 28 January, p. 65–66, retrieved 27 August 2013, <www.economist.com/privateequity12>.

Bakir, A, & Vitell, S 2010, 'The ethics of food advertising targeted toward children: Parental viewpoint', *Journal of Business Ethics*, vol. 91, no. 2, pp. 299–311.

'Bangladesh workers' leader targets London Fashion Week' 2013, *Dunstans Publishing*, retrieved 7 October 2013, <www.ethicalperformance.com/article/790>.

Banjo, S, Zimmerman, A & Kapner, S 2013, 'Wal-Mart goes solo on safety', *Wall Street Journal*, p. 23.

'Banker app puts the onus on bonus' 2013, *Business Review Weekly*, 24–30 January, p. 37.

BarclayHedge 2013, 'What is a hedge fund?', *BarclayHedge*, retrieved 17 July 2013, <www.barclayhedge.com/research/educational-articles/hedge-fund-strategy-definition/what-is-a-hedge-fund.html>.

Barclays 2013, 'Barclays announces the outcome of its strategic review and sets out commitment for 2015', Barclays, media release, 12 February, retrieved 13 March 2013, <http://group.barclays.com.

Barling, J, Dupré, KE, & Kelloway, EK 2009, 'Predicting workplace aggression and violence', *Annual Review of Psychology*, vol. 60, pp. 671–92.

Baron, DP 2007, 'Corporate social responsibility and social entrepreneurship', *Journal of Economics & Management Strategy*, vol. 16, no, 3, pp. 683–717.

Baron, J 1996, 'Do no harm', in DM Messick & AE Tenbrunsel (eds), *Codes of Conduct: Behavioural Research into Business Ethics*, Russell Sage Foundation, New York, pp. 197–213.

Bateman, C 2010, 'A colossal fracking mess', *Vanity Fair*, 21 June, retrieved 19 December 2013, <www.vanityfair.com/business/features/2010/06/fracking-in-pennsylvania-201006>.

Battersby, L 2012, 'What's in a domain name? Today we find out', *The Age Business Day*, 14 June, p. 4.

Baucus, MS & Beck-Dudley, CL 2005, 'Designing ethical organisations: Avoiding the long-term negative effects of rewards and punishments', *Journal of Business Ethics*, vol. 56, pp. 355–70.

Baucus, MS & Cochran, PL 2010, 'USA: An overview of empirical research on ethics in entrepreneurial firms within the United States', in LJ Spence & M Painter-Morland (eds), *Ethics in Small and Medium Sized Enterprises*, The International Society of Business, Economics and Ethics, Book Series 2, Springer Science Plus Business Medium, pp. 99–119.

Bavaria, S 1991, 'Corporate ethics should start in the boardroom', *Business Horizons*, January–February, pp. 9–12.

BBC News South Asia 2011, 'India TV channels told not to air sexy deodorant ads', *BBC News South* Asia, 26 May, retrieved 4 February 2013, <www.bbc.co.uk/news/world-south-asia-13562182>.

Bean, DF & Bernardi, RA 2007, 'A proposed structure for an accounting ethics course', *Journal of Business Ethics Education*, vol. 4, pp. 27–54.

Beck, M & Butler, B 2013, 'Police reopen bribery cases', *Sunday Age*, 13 January, p. 17.

Becker, K 2012, 'Workplace Bullying', *Mink Hollow Media, Ltd.*, 29 March, retrieved 12 February 2013, <www.minkhollow.ca/becker/doku.php?id=ethics:bullying>.

Beckett, C & Ball, J 2012, *WikiLeaks: News in the Network Era*, Polity Press, Cambridge, UK.

Belak, J & Mulej, M 2009, 'Enterprise ethical climate changes over life-cycle stages', *Kyberbetes*, vol. 38, pp. 1377–98.

Benard, S 2012, 'Why his merit raise is bigger than hers', *Harvard Business Review*, April, p. 26.

Bennett, C 2003, *Ethics in Business*, SouthWestern, Thompson Learning, Mason, OH.

Bentham, J 1970 [1789], *An Introduction to the Principles of Morals and Legislation*, Athlone Press, London.

Bernardi, LM n.d., 'Bullying in the workplace', *Bernardi Human Resources Law*, retrieved 12 February 2013, <www.hrlawyers.ca/pdf/employment_law/bullying_in_the_workplace.pdf>.

Bernardi, RA 1994, 'Fraud detection: The effect of client integrity and confidence and auditor cognitive style', *Auditing: Journal of Practice and Theory*, vol. 13, pp. 68–84.

Best, K 2006, 'Visceral hacking or packet wanking? The ethics of digital code', *Culture, Theory & Critique*, vol. 47, no. 2, pp. 213–35.

Better Health Channel 2012, 'Work–related fatalities', State Government of Victoria, retrieved 11 February 2013, <www.betterhealth.vic.gov.au/bhcv2/bhcarticles.nsf/pages/Work_related_fatalities>.

Betz, M, O'Connell, L & Shepard, JM 2013, 'Gender differences in proclivity for unethical behaviour', *Citation Classics from the Journal of Business Ethics, Advances in Business Ethics Research*, vol. 2, Springer, The Netherlands, pp. 427–32.

Bhattacharya, U & Marshall, C 2012, 'Do they do it for the money?' *Journal of Corporate Finance*, vol. 18, pp. 92–104.

Bhide, A 1996, 'The question every entrepreneur must answer', *Harvard Business Review*, vol. 74, pp. 120–30.

'Big trouble in Tokyo: The Olympus scandal' 2011, *The Economist*, 12 November, p. 70.

Binham, C & Hoyos, C 2012, 'SFO weighs deal to end Rolls-Royce probe', *Financial Times*, 22 March, retrieved 30 May 2013, <www.ft.com/intl/cms/s/0/ff136074–931e-11e2-b3be-00144feabdc0.html>.

Biron, CL 2013, 'Walmart, Gap seek separate safety standards for Bangladesh factories', Inter Press Service, 31 May, retrieved 17 January 2014, <www.ipsnews.net/2013/05/walmart-gap-seek-separate-safety-standards-for-bangladesh-factories>.

Bisouq, T 2013, 'Business through an ethics lens', *BizEd*, January/February, p. 28–34.

'Bitter pill' 2013, *The Economist*, 20 July, p. 56.

Blackwell, A 2012, 'Union joins white coat revolution', *Campus Review*, 6 March, p. 6.

Blasi, A 1983, 'Moral cognition and moral action: A theoretical perspective', *Developmental Review*, vol. 3, pp. 178–210.

——1984, 'Moral identity: Its role in moral functioning', in WM Kurtines & JJ Gewitz (eds), *Morality, Moral Behaviour and Moral Development*, John Wiley & Sons, New York, pp. 128–39.

——1985, 'The moral personality: reflections for social science and education', in MW Berkowitz & F Oser (eds), *Moral Education: Theory and Application*, Wiley, New York, pp. 433–43.

——2005, 'Moral character: A psychological approach', in DK Lapsley & FC Power (eds), *Character Psychology and Character Education*, University of Notre Dame Press, Notre Dame, USA.

Bleby, M 2012, 'Pumping up the volume', *Business Review Weekly*, 2–8 August, pp. 26–7.

——2013, 'Project Wickenby: Wealthy and their advisors on ATO's tax haven hitlist', *Business Review Weekly*, 10 May, retrieved 4 August 2013, <www.brw.com.au/p/professions/project_wickenby_wealthy_and_their_axliFs1u9GVMiva9v1u5AN>.

Boehm, E 2010, 'Pennsylvania still only state without natural gas severance tax', *Watchdog*, 21 October, retrieved 19 December 2013, <http://watchdog.org/7026>.

Bonner, SE, Palmorse, ZV & Young, SM 1998, 'Fraud type and auditor litigation: An analysis of SEC accounting and auditing enforcement releases', *Accounting Review*, vol. 73, no. 4, p. 502–32.

Borenstein, J 2010, 'Computing ethics work life in the robotic age', *Communications of the ACM*, vol. 53, no. 7, July, pp. 30–1.

Boschee, J 1995, Social entrepreneurship, *Across the Board*, vol. 32, no. 30, pp. 20–5.

'Bosses under fire' 2012, *The Economist*, January 14, p. 11.

Bowen, H 1953, *Social Responsibilities of the Businessman*, Harper & Row, New York.

Bowker, GC & Knobel, C 2011, Values and Design, *Communications of the Association for Computing Machinery*, vol. 54, no. 7, pp. 26–8.

Brady, N 2012, 'Empathy tactic fails on worst bullies', *Sunday Age*, 19 August, p. 8.

Brady, FN & Wheeler, GE 1996, 'An empirical study of ethical predisposition', *Journal of Business Ethics*, vol. 16, pp. 927–40. p. 8.

Branson, R 2012, 'Richard Branson on love in the workplace', *Business Review Weekly*, 23 February–4 April, p. 14.

Brenkert, GG 2009, 'Innovation, rule breaking and the ethics of entrepreneurship', *Journal of Business Venturing*, vol. 24, pp. 448–64.

Brey, P 2000, 'Disclosive computer ethics', *Computer and Society*, vol. 30, no. 4, pp. 10–16.

Brightman, HJ 2009, *Today's White-Collar Crime: Legal, Investigative, and Theoretical Perspectives*, Routledge, New York.

Brooks, LJ & Dunn, P 2012, *Business and Professional Ethics for Directors, Executives and Accountants*, SouthWestern Cengage Learning, USA.

Broomberg, SE 2012, 'Small business ethics', *Business Ethics*, 29 April, retrieved 29 April 2013, <www.businessethics.net>.

Brown, D & King, J 1982, 'Small business ethic: Influences and perceptions', *Journal of Small Business Management*, vol. 20, no. 1, pp. 11–18.

Brown, RMC 2011, 'The simple message of ethics', *Charter*, August, retrieved 18 July 2013, <www.charteredaccountants.com.au/News-Media/Charter/Charter-articles/Financial-advisory-services/2011–11-Robert-Brown-The-Simple-Message-of-Ethics.aspx>.

Brunner, PW & Costello, ML 2003, 'When the wrong woman wins: Building bullies and perpetuating patriarch', *Advancing Women*, retrieved 12 February 2013, <www.advancingwomen.com/awl/spring2003/BRUNNE~1.HTMLU>.

Bryant, P 2008, 'Self-regulation and moral awareness among entrepreneurs', *Journal of Business Venturing*, vol. 24, pp. 505–18.

——2009, 'Self-regulation and moral awareness among entrepreneurs', *Journal of Business Venturing*, vol. 24, pp. 505–18.

Bucar, B & Hisrich, RD 2001, 'Ethics of business managers vs. entrepreneurs', *Journal of Developmental Entrepreneurship*, vol. 6, no. 1, pp. 59–82.

——Hisrich, RD & Glas, M 2003, 'Ethics and entrepreneurs: An international study', *Journal of Business Venturing*, vol. 18, pp. 261–81.

Buchanan, C 2013, 'How Zappos turns personal values into company values', *The Company Ethicist*, 13 June, retrieved 14 October 2013, <www.convercent.com/company-ethicist/how-zappos-turned-personal-values-into-company-values>.

Buchholz, R 1989, *Fundamental Concepts and Problems in Business Ethics*, Prentice-Hall, Englewood Cliffs, NJ.

Bully Busters 2011, 'Campaign against workplace bullying', retrieved 12 February 2013, <www.bullybusters.org>.

Bulutlar, F, & Oz, EU 2009, 'The effects of ethical climates on bullying behavior in the workplace', *Journal of Business Ethics*, vol. 86, no. 3, pp. 273–95.

Burgess, M 2013, 'Debunking the hedge fund myths', *Kardinia Capital*, 7 May, retrieved 19 July 2013, <www.bennfundsmanagement.com.au/views/64/debunking-the-hedge-fund-myths#.Uejmt23IuSo>.

Burger PL, Luckman T 1966, *The Social Construction of Reality*, Anchor Books, New York.

Burkus, D 2011, 'The tale of two cultures: Why culture trumps core values in building ethical organizations', *Journal of Values-Based Leadership*, vol. 4, no. 1, retrieved 14 October 2013, <www.valuesbasedleadershipjournal.com/issues/vol4issue1/tale_2culture.php>.

Burrell, A 2013, 'Korab boss admits to suing shareholder', *The Australian*, 25 July, p. 21.

'Business' 2011, *The Economist*, 14 July, p. 7.

'Business' 2012, *The Economist*, 20 October, p. 9.

'Business' 2013a, *The Economist*, 12 January, p. 8.

'Business' 2013b, *The Economist*, 1 June, p. 8.

'Business' 2013c, *The Economist*, 20 July, p. 7.

Business Anti-Corruption Portal 2011, retrieved 14 February 2013, <www.oecd.org/corruption>.

Business in the Community/Institute of Leadership and Management (BITC/ILM) 2013, *Added Values: The Importance of Ethical Leadership*, Institute of Leadership and Management, London.

'Business this week', 2011, *The Economist*, 29 October, p. 76.

'Business this week' 2012a, *The Economist*, 26 May, p. 8.

'Business this week' 2012b, *The Economist*, 29 September, p. 10.

'Business this week' 2012c, *The Economist*, 12 November, p. 10.

'Business this week' 2013, *The Economist*, 13 April, p. 8.

Businessdictionary.com 2013, 'Fiduciary duty', *WebFinance Inc.*, retrieved 5 August 2013, <www.businessdictionary.com/definition/fiduciary-duty.html>.

Buss, D 2013, 'Rolls-Royce hires top BP exec to help amid bribery probe', *brandchannel*, 15 February, retrieved 30 May 2013, <www.brandchannel.com/home/post/2013/02/15/Rolls-Royce-BP-021513.aspx>.

Butler, AB & Skattebo, A 2004, 'What is acceptable for women may not be for men: The effect of family conflicts with work on job-performance ratings', *Journal of Occupational and Organizational Psychology*, vol. 77, pp. 553–64.

Butterfield, KD, Treviño, LK & Weaver, GR 2000, 'Moral awareness in business organizations: Influences of issue-related and social context factors', *Human Relations*, vol. 53, pp. 981–1018.

Cacioppe, R, Forster, M & Fox, M 2008, 'A survey of managers' perceptions of corporate ethics and social responsibility and actions that may affect companies' success', *Journal of Business Ethics*, vol. 82, pp. 681–700.

Cadbury, A 1987, 'Ethical managers make their own rules', *Harvard Business Review*, September/October, pp. 69–73.

Cade, V 2011, 'Welcome to bully free at work', *Bully Free at Work*, retrieved 1 February 2013, <http://bullyfreeatwork.com/blog>.

Calhoun, CH, Olivero, ME & Wolitzer, P 1999, *Ethics and the CPA*, John Wiley & Sons, New York.

Callan, VJ 1992, 'Predicting ethical values and trading needs in codes of ethics', *Journal of Business Ethics*, vol. 11, no. 10, pp. 761–9.

Calligeros, M 2011, 'High-flying entrepreneur seduced by dreams of foreign market riches', *Sydney Morning Herald*, 24 September, retrieved 29 April 2013, <www.smh.com.au/business/highflying-entrepreneur-seduced-by-dreams-of-foreign-market-riches-20110923–1kp6h.html>.

Cameron, KS & Quinn, RE 2006, *Diagnosing and Changing Organisational Culture: Based on a Competing Values Framework*, Jossey-Bass, San Francisco, CA.

Campbell, P 2012, 'We're living in the age of augmented reality when worlds collide', *Geelong Advertiser*, 13 August, p. 13.

'Capitalism with a value-added face' 2012, *Business Review Weekly*, 29 November–6 December, p. 35.

Carl, R 2012, 'Are you on call 24/7? There is a way to achieve a better work/life balance', *Health and Fitness*, retrieved 29 August, 2012, <www.itbdigital.com/tools-of-the-trade/2012/08/23/work-life-balance-business-professionals>.

Carroll, AB 1991, 'The pyramid of corporate social responsibility: Towards the moral management of organisational stakeholders', *Business Horizons*, July–August, pp. 39–48.

Carter, W 2009, 'Next week in the Judiciary committees, shields and cyberbullies', *Point of Law*, <www.pointoflaw.com/archives/2009/09/next-week-in-th.php>.

Cassidy, J 2013, 'Why Edward Snowden is a hero', *New Yorker*, 10 June, retrieved 2 July 2013, <www.newyorker.com/online/blogs/johncassidy/2013/06/why-edward-snowden-is-a-hero.html>.

Certo, ST & Miller, T 2008, 'Social entrepreneurship: Key issues and concepts', *Business Horizons*, vol. 51, no. 4, pp. 267–71.

Cfadahunsi, A & Rosa, P 2002, 'Entrepreneurship and illegality: Insights from the Nigerian cross-border trade', *Journal of Business Venturing*, vol. 17, pp. 397–429.

Chadwick, V 2012, 'Mobile apps allow analysts to view private information', *The Age*, 19 September, p. 212.

Chambers, R 1892, *Chambers' Encyclopaedia: A Dictionary of Universal Knowledge, new edn, vol. IV*.

Chaplin, D 2012, 'Corrupt advice on notice', *Business Review Weekly*, 1 November, p. 40.

Chau, LL & Siu, W 2000, 'Ethical decision making in corporate entrepreneurial organisations', *Journal of Business Ethics*, vol. 23, pp. 365–75.

'Cheap clothing has price beyond its tag' 2013, *The Age*, 28 April, retrieved 7 October 2013,

<www.theage.com.au/federal-politics/editorial/cheap-clothing-has-a-price-beyond-its-tag-20130427–2ilip.html#ixzz2SOeIuTsT%29>.

Chen, AYS, Sawyer, RB & Williams, PF 1997, 'Reinforcing ethical decisions through corporate culture', *Journal of Business Ethics*, vol. 16, pp. 855–65.

Chess, DM, Palmer, CC & White, SR 2003, 'Security in an autonomic computing environment', *IBM Systems Journal*, vol. 42, issue 1, pp. 107–18.

Chonko, LB & Hunt, SD 1985, 'Ethics and marketing management: An empirical examination', *Journal of Business Research*, vol. 13, pp. 339–59.

Chrisman, JJ & Fry, FL 1982, 'Public versus business expectations: Two views on social responsibility for the small business', *Journal of Small Business Management*, vol. 20, no. 1, pp. 19–26.

Christensson P 2013, 'Computer ethics', *TechTerms.com*, retrieved 6 February 2013, <www.techterms.com/definition/computerethics>.

Christie M & Honig, B 2006, 'Social entrepreneurship: new research findings', *Journal of World Business*, vol. 41, no. 1, pp. 1–5.

Cialdina, R, Petrova, P & Goldstein, N 2004, 'The hidden cost of organisational dishonesty', *MIT Sloan Management Review*, vol. 45, no. 3, Spring, pp. 67–73.

Clark, M 2003, 'Corporate ethics programs make a difference, but not the only difference', *HR Magazine*, 1 July, p. 36.

Clark, M, Eaton, M, Meek, D, Pye, E & Tuhin, R 2013, 'Australian small business: key statistics and analysis', Department of Industry, Innovation, Science, Research and Tertiary Education, December, Canberra.

Clark, WH, Biddle, D, Reath, LLP & Vranka, L 2013, *White paper: the need and rationale for the benefit corporation: Why it is that legal form that best addresses the needs of social entrepreneurs, investors, and ultimately, the public*, Benefit Corp, 18 January, retrieved 5 January 2014, <http://benefitcorp.net/for-attorneys/benefit-corp-white-paper>.

Clarke, F & Dean, G 2007, *Indecent Disclosure: Gilding the Corporate Lily*, Cambridge University Press, Port Melbourne, Australia.

——Dean, G & Oliver, K 2003, *Corporate Collapse: Accounting, Regulatory and Ethical Failure*, 2nd edn, Cambridge University Press, Port Melbourne, Australia.

Clarke, J 2012, 'Price discrimination', *Australian Competition Law*, retrieved 4 February 2013, <www.australiancompetitionlaw.org/law/pricediscrimination.html>.

——& Holt, R 2010, 'Reflective judgement: Understanding entrepreneurship as ethical practice', *Journal of Business Ethics*, vol. 92, pp. 317–31.

Clarkson, MBE 1995, 'A stakeholder framework for analysing and evaluating corporate performance', *Academy of Management Review*, vol. 20, no. 1, pp. 92–117.

Cleek, MA & Leonard, SL 1998, 'Can corporate codes of ethics influence behaviour?' *Journal of Business Ethics*, vol. 17, no. 9, pp. 619–30.

Cohen, A 2001, 'Internet Security', *Time* Magazine, 2 July, pp. 35–41.

Cohen, JR, Pant, L & Sharp, D 1993, 'Culture-based ethical conflicts confronting multi-national accounting firms', *Accounting Horizons*, vol. 7, September, pp. 1–13.

——1995, 'An international comparison of moral constructs underlying auditors' ethical judgements', *Research on Accounting Ethics*, vol. 1, pp. 97–126.

Coles, R 2000, *Lives of Moral Leadership*, Random House, New York.

Collett, J 2013, 'Perpetual ethical fund tops performance as share funds rebound', *The Age*, 16 January, p. 18.

Collewaert, V & Fassim, Y 2013, 'Conflicts between entrepreneurs and investors: The impact of perceived unethical behaviour', *Small Business Economics*, vol. 40, pp. 635–49.

Collins, D 2009, 'Case study: Enron: The good, the bad, and the really ugly', in Gini, A & Marcoux, AM (eds), *Case Studies in Business Ethics*, 6th edn, Prentice Hall, Upper Saddle River, NJ.

Collins, O & Moore, DG 1970, 'The organisation makers: A behavioural study of independent entrepreneurs', *Appleton Century Cross*, New York.

'Commerce and conscience' 2013, *The Economist*, 23 February, p. 67.

Compaine, B 2001, *The Digital Divide: Facing a Crisis or Creating a Myth*, MIT Press, Cambridge, MA.

'Companies' moral compasses' 2013, *The Economist*, 2 March, retrieved 17 December 2013, <www.economist.com/news/business/21572748-some-ideas- restoring-faith-firms-companies-moral-compasses>.

'Complete disaster in the making' 2012, *The Economist*, 15 September, p. 67.

'Computer viruses: A thing of threads and patches' 2012, *The Economist*, 25 August, p. 63.

Cone Communications 2012, 'Cause marketing remains strong: 2010 core cause evolution', retrieved 23 December 2012, <www.conecomm.com/cause-marketing-remains-strong>.

Connor, M 2010, 'Toyota recall: Five critical lessons', *Business Ethics: The Magazine of Corporate Responsibility*, 31 January, retrieved 5 February 2013, <http://buness-ethics.com/2010/01/31/2123-toyota-recall-five-critical-lessons>.

Conservation Voters of Pennsylvania 2011, 'Natural gas industry gives $7.175 million to Pennsylvania politicians', Conservation Voters of Pennsylvania, 10 May, retrieved 19 December 2013, <www.conservationpa.org/news/natural-gas-industry-gives-7–175-million-to-pennsylvania-politicians>.

Consumer Goods Forum 2012, 'Sustainability', January, retrieved 5 January 2014, <http://sustainability.mycgforum.com/the-glossary.html>.

Cooper, BJ 2013 'Investigation and discipline: is the accounting profession doing enough?', paper presented at Institute of Chartered Accountants of the Caribbean, 2013 Annual Conference, Barbados, 28 June 2013.

'Copyright and the internet: Letting the baby dance' 2012, *The Economist*, 1 September, p. 51.

'Corporate transparency, measuring mud' 2012, *The Economist*, 14 July, p. 56.

Costello, T 2012, 'What can we do about child slavery?' *The Age*, 27 September, p. 20.

Cottrell, PG & Perlin, TM 1990, *Accounting Ethics: A Practical Guide for Professionals*, Quorum Books, Westport, CT.

Covidien 2013, 'Business ethics', *Covidien*, retrieved 26 November 2013, <www.covidien.com/covidien/pages.aspx?page=contact/businessethics>.

Crane, A & Matten, D 2010, *Business Ethics*, 3rd edn, Oxford University Press, Oxford.

'Crash course: The origins of the financial crisis' 2013, *The Economist*, 7 September, p. 64–5.

Creedy, S 2012a, '$10 million Emirates fine "a warning on cartels"', *Weekend Australian*, 13–14 October, p. 27.

——2012b, 'US fines Qantas for deceptive website ads', *The Australian*, 6 March, retrieved 22 April 2013, <www.theaustralian.com.au/business/aviation/us-fines-qantas-for-deceptive-website-ads/story-e6frg95x-1226289869389>.

'Cromme comes a cropper' 2013, *The Economist*, 6 March, p. 9.

*Crossing the line: Ordinary people committing extraordinary crimes* 2013, YouTube, HeliosDigital, 29 March, retrieved 7 August 2013, <www.youtube.com/watch?v=QIwH5E7nX-A>.

'CSR offers no "halo effect"' 2012, *Biz/Ed*, September/October, p. 54.

Cullen, JB, Parboteeah, KP & Victor, B 2003, 'The effects of ethical climate on organisational commitment: A two study analysis', *Journal of Business Ethics*, vol. 46, pp. 127–41.

——, Victor, B, & Bronson, JW 1993, 'The ethical climate questionnaire: An assessment of its development and validity', *Psychological Reports*, vol. 73, pp. 667–74.

Currell, D & Davis Bradley, T 2012, 'Greased palms, giant headaches', *Harvard Business Review*, September, pp. 21–3.

Curry, E, Guyon, B, Sheridan, C, & Donnellan, B 2012, 'Developing a sustainable IT capability: Lessons from Intel's journey', *MIS Quarterly Executive*, vol. 11, no. 2, June, pp. 61–74.

'Cyber warfare seek and hide' 2012, *The Economist*, 9 June, p. 60.

Dach, L 2013, 'Don't spin a better story. Be a better company', *Harvard Business Review*, October, p. 42.

Dahl, JG, Mandell, MP & Barton, ME 1988, 'Ethical frameworks of tomorrow's business leaders', *International Journal of Value Based Management*, vol. 1, no. 2, pp. 65–81.

D'Aloisio, T 2010, 'Insider trading and market manipulation', Chairman's speech presented at the Supreme Court of Victoria Law Conference, Melbourne, 11 August.

D'Angelo, L 2013, 'More biotech woes', *Business Review Weekly*, 1 August, p. 36.

D'Angelo Fisher, L 2012a, 'Can we afford the weekend?' *Business Review Weekly*, 18–24 October, retrieved

11 February 2013, <www.brw.com.au/p/sections/features/can_we_afford_the_weekend_1jPqZu3CiDQZmj0Ma7o2UL?hl>.

——2012b, 'Give workers reason to stay', *Business Review Weekly*, 18–24 October, p.32.

Danish, J, Muhammad, N & Ali, K 2011, 'Is ethical hacking ethical?' *International Journal of Engineering Science and Technology*, vol. 3, no. 5, pp. 3758–63.

Danna, A & Gandy, OH 2002, 'All that glitters is not gold: digging beneath the surface of data mining', *Journal of Business Ethics*, vol. 40, pp. 373–86.

'Data privacy out of shape' 2012, *The Economist*, 21–27 July, p. 15.

'Davos ban and his defects' 2013, *The Economist*, 26 January, p. 59.

De George, RT 1986, *Business Ethics*, 2nd edn, Macmillan, New York.

De Jong, G, Tu, PA & Van Ees, H 2012, 'Which entrepreneurs bribe and what do they get from it? Exploratory evidence from Vietnam', *Entrepreneurship Theory and Practice*, vol. 36, no. 2, pp. 323–45.

DeConinck, JD 2010, The influence of ethical climate on marketing employees' job attitudes and behaviours, *Journal of Business Research*, vol. 63, no. 4, pp. 384–91.

——, DeConinck, MB & Banerjee, D 2013, 'Outcomes of an ethical work climate among salespeople', *International Journal of Business Administration*, vol. 4, no. 4, pp. 1–7.

Dees, JG 1998, 'The meaning of "social entrepreneurship"', occasional paper, Centre for the Advancement of Social Entrepreneurship, Fuqua School of Business, Duke, USA.

Dellaportas, S, Gibson, K, Alagiah, R, Hutchinson, M, Leung, P & Van Homrigh, D 2005, *Ethics, Governance and Accountability: A Professional Perspective*, John Wiley & Sons Australia, Brisbane.

Deloitte 2012, 'The Social and Ethics Committee and the management of the ethics performance of the company', Deloitte, retrieved 26 November 2013, <www.deloitte.com/assets/Dcom-SouthAfrica/Local%20Assets/Documents/NED_Social_Ethics.pdf>.

Denizet-Lewis, B 2006, 'The man behind Abercrombie & Fitch', *Salon*, 24 January, retrieved 15 August 2013, <www.salon.com/2006/01/24/jeffries>.

Dent, G & D'Aangelo Fisher, L 2012, 'Managers more likely to lie about qualifications', *Business Review Weekly*, 5–11 July 2012, p. 37.

Department of Treasury 2013, 'Review of the Trio Capital fraud and assessment of the regulatory framework', Commonwealth of Australia, 26 April, ACT, retrieved 19 July 2013, <www.treasury.gov.au/~/media/Treasury/Publications%20and%20Media/Publications/2013/Trio%20Capital%20fraud%20review/Downloads/PDF/Trio_Capital_Fraud_Review.ashx>.

Deshpandé, SP 1996, 'The impact of ethical climate types on facets of job satisfaction: An empirical investigation', *Journal of Business Ethics*, vol. 15, pp. 655–60.

Dickson, M, Smith, D, Grojean, M & Ehrhart, M 2001, 'An organizational climate regarding ethics: The outcome of leader values and the practices that reflect them', *Leadership Quarterly*, vol. 12, no. 2, pp. 197–217.

Direct Selling Association of Malaysia 2013, 'What is pyramid selling?', Direct Selling Association of Malaysia, retrieved 10 February 2013, <www.dsam.org.my/industry/what-is-pyramid-selling>.

'Disaster at Rana Plaza' 2013, *The Economist*, 4 May, p. 10.

Doherty, B 2013, 'Indian girls pay the price for our fashion choices', *Saturday Age*, 19 October, p. 18.

Donaldson, J 1992, *Business Ethics: A European Casebook*, Academic Press, London.

Donaldson, T 1982, *Corporations and Morality*, Prentice Hall, Englewood Cliffs, NJ.

——2001, *Ethics in Cyberspace: Have we Seen this Movie Before?* Bentley College: Center for Business Ethics, pp. 4–24.

Donaldson, T & Dunfee, TW 1994, 'Toward a unified conception of business ethics', *Academy of Management Review*, vol. 19, pp. 252–71.

—— & DunFee TW 1999, *Ties that Bind: A Social Contracts Approach to Business Ethics*, Harvard Business School Press, Boston.

—— & Preston, LE 1995, 'The stakeholder theory of the corporation: Concepts, evidence and implications', *Academy of Management Review*, vol. 20, no. 1, pp 65–9.

Donnelly, B 2013, 'Contender for world's worst parking fine', *The Age*, 25 July, p. 14.

'Don't hate me because I'm beautiful' 2012, *The Economist*, 31 March, p. 71.

Dooley, R 2013, 'The perverse brilliance of Abercrombie & Fitch's CEO', *Forbes*, 16 May, retrieved 15 August 2013, <www.forbes.com/sites/rogerdooley/2013/05/16/abercrombie-ceo>.

Douglas, G 2012, 'Fraud is worldwide', *Australian Business Review Weekly*, 17–23 May, p. 12.

Douglas, SP & Craig, C n.d., 'International advertising', Stern School of Business, New York University, retrieved 22 April 2013, <http://people.stern.nyu.edu/sdouglas/rpubs/intad.html>.

Drape, J 2013, 'Snowden thanks Russia for asylum', *Courier Mail*, 2 August, retrieved 2 August 2013, <www.couriermail.com.au/news/breaking-news/snowden-thanks-russia-for-asylum/story-fnihsg6t-1226689893267>.

Drencheva, A 2012, 'Mobile phones for social good: the case of Africa, *Sustainable Life Media*, 9 May, retrieved on 8 February 2013, <www.sustainablebrands.com/news_and_views/may2012/mobile-phones-social-good-case-africa>.

'Drugs and emerging markets' 2012, *The Economist*, 8 September, p. 14.

Duff, T 2013, *The Buy Side: A Wall Street Trader's Tale of Spectacular Excess*, Crown Business, New York.

Dugan, E 2009, 'Cadbury accused of racial stereotyping in chocolate advert', *The Independent*, 11 October, retrieved 5 February 2013, <www.independent.co.uk/news/media/advertising/cadbury-accused-of-racial-stereotyping-in-chocolate-advert-1801020.html>.

'Dumping enquiry: Business today', *The Age*, 5 July, p. 3.

Dunfee, TW & Werhane, P 1997, 'Report on business ethics in North America', *Journal of Business Ethics*, vol. 16, no. 14, pp. 1589–1596.

Dunham, LC 2010, 'From rational to wise action: Recasting our theories of entrepreneurship', *Journal of Business Ethics*, vol. 92, pp. 513–30.

Dunphy, D, Griffiths, A & Benn, S 2003, *Organizational Change for Corporate Sustainability: A Guide for Leaders and Change Agents of the Future*, Routledge, London.

Durkin, P 2013, 'Ethics managers: who needs them?', *Australian Financial Review*, 13 March, p. 8.

Duska, R 2007, 'Whistleblowing and employee loyalty', *Contemporary Reflections on Business Ethics*, pp 139–47.

—— & Duska, BS 2003, *Accounting Ethics*, Blackwell Publishing, Oxford.

Dworkin, R 1977, *Taking Rights Seriously*, Harvard University Press, Cambridge, MA.

Dyer, WG & Whetten, DA 2006, 'Family firms and social responsibility: Preliminary evidence from the S&P500', *Entrepreneurship Theory and Practice*, vol. 30, no. 6, pp. 785–802.

Eagle, L 2009, *Social Marketing Ethics: Report Prepared for the National Social Marketing Centre*, National Social Marketing Centre, University of the West of England, retrieved 5 February 2013, <http://eprints.uwe.ac.uk/54>.

Eccles, RG & Serafeim, G 2013, 'The performance frontier', *Harvard Business Review*, May, pp. 50–6.

Eccles, RG & Ioannou, I & Serafeim, G 2012, 'Is sustainability now the key to corporate success?' *The Guardian*, 17 January, retrieved 23 January 2014, <www.theguardian.com/sustainable-business/sustainability-key-corporate-success>.

——, 2013, 'The impact on corporate behaviour and performance', *Harvard Business School*, working paper 12–035, 29 July, <www.hbs.edu/faculty/Publication%20Files/12–035_a3c1f5d8–452d-4b48–9a49–812424424cc2.pdf>.

'Eco-labels can muddle the message' 2013, *BizEd magazine*, Jan/Feb, p. 60.

Edgerton, J 2011, 'Altmire, Critz & Shuster Write Pro-Shale Drilling Letter', PoliticsPA, 27 June, retrieved 19 December 2013, <www.politicspa.com/altmire-critz-shuster-write-pro-shale-drilling-letter/25707>.

Edwards, J 2011, 'Time for Abbott to come clean about its deceptive baby formula', CBS MoneyWatch, 7 February, retrieved 10 February 2013, <www.cbsnews.com/8301–505123_162–42847330/time-for-abbott-to-come-clean-about-its-deceptive-baby-formula-research>.

EEOC 2010, 'Abercrombie & Fitch sued for religious discrimination', US Equal Employment Opportunity Commission, media release, 1 September, retrieved 19 February 2013, <www.eeoc.gov/eeoc/newsroom/release/9–1–10.cfm>.

El-Ansary, Y 2010, 'Project Wickenby on the lookout for those who do the wrong thing by our community', *The Australian*, 20 September, retrieved 5 August

2013, <www.theaustralian.com.au/business/opinion/
project-wickenby-on-the-lookout-for-those-who-
do-the-wrong-thing-by-our-community/story-
e6frg9if-1225926420899>.

Elkington, J 1994, 'Towards the sustainable corporation:
Win-win-win business strategies for sustainable
development', *California Management Review*, vol. 36,
no. 2 pp. 90–100.

Elliott, C 2012, 'Security breaches shake confidence in
credit card safety', *The Newsweek Magazine*, 9 April,
retrieved 27 June 2013, <www.thedailybeast.com/
newsweek/2012/04/08/security-breaches-shake-
confidence-in-credit-card-safety.html>.

'Email destruction policy revealed in hacking case' 2012,
*Saturday Age*, 25 February, p. 11.

Engle, TJ & Sincich, TL 1998, 'The loss of auditor independence', *Research on Accounting Ethics*, vol. 4,
pp. 167–84.

Ernst & Young 2008, 'Pirates of the 21st Century: the
consumer goods industry under attack', Ernst &
Young, retrieved 21 April 2013, <www.markenverband.
de/english_/europe-international/piracy>.

Ethical Performance 2012a, 'Unethical practices
"common in UK workplaces" finds ILM/BITC study',
Dunstans Publishing, retrieved 16 December 2013,
<www.ethicalperformance.com/news/article/7722>.

——2012b, 'Toyota tops best green brand report',
Dunstans Publishing, retrieved 5 January 2014,
<http://ethicalperformance.com/news/article>.

——2012c, 'Dell upgrades to waste-free packaging',
Dunstans Publishing, retrieved 5 January
2014, <http://ethicalperformance.com/news/
article/7721>.

——2013a, 'Budweiser brewer extends environmental
goals', *Ethical Performance Newsletter*, September,
retrieved 1 January 2013, <http://ethicalperformance.
com/news/article/7720>.

——2013b, 'MillerCoors raises glass to decreased water
usage', *Ethical Performance Newsletter*, September,
retrieved 1 January 2013, <http://ethicalperformance.
com/news/article/7902>.

——2013c, 'General Mills makes strides in sustainable
sourcing', *Ethical Performance Newsletter*, 13
September, retrieved 5 January 2013, <www.
ethicalperformance.com>.

Ethical Trading Initiative n.d., 'The Ethical Trading
Initiative base code', The Ethical Trading Initiative,
retrieved 20 April 2013, <www.ethicaltrade.org/sites/
default/files/resources/ETI%20Base%20Code%20
-%20English_0.pdf>.

Ethics and Compliance Officer Association Foundation
2006, *Ethical Culture Building: A Modern Business
Imperative*, Ethics Resource Center, retrieved 26
November 2013, <www.ethics.org/files/u5/ECOA-
Report-FINAL.pdf>.

Ethics Resource Centre 2010, 'Blowing the whistle on
workplace misconduct', Ethics Resource Centre,
December, retrieved 2 October 2013, <www.ethics.
org/files/u5/WhistleblowerWP.pdf>.

——2011, *National Business Ethics Survey®: Workplace
Ethics in Transition*, retrieved 16 December 2013,
<www.ethics.org/nbes/findings.html>.

——2013, *Generational differences in workplace
ethics: A supplementary report of the 2011 National
Business Ethics Survey*, retrieved 16 December 2013,
<www.ethics.org/nbes/files/2011GenDiffFinal.
pdf>.

'Europe launches "board ready" database' 2013, *Biz/Ed*,
March/April, p. 63.

European Commission 2009, 'Airline ticket selling
websites – EU enforcement results. Questions and
answers', European Commission, media release
memo/09/238, 14 May, retrieved 22 February 2013,
<http://europa.eu/rapid/press-release_MEMO-
09–238_en.htm?locale=en>.

Evans, M 2013, 'In Bangladesh's garment trade
empowerment comes at $20 a week: The
growing power of Bangladesh's female garment
workers', *CBC News*, 18 June, retrieved 8 July
2014, <www.cbc.ca/news/world/in-bangladesh-
s-garment-trade-empowerment-comes-at-20-a-
week-1.1321640>.

Fairtrade Diocese of London n.d., 'Principles and goals of
Fairtrade', The Fairtrade Diocese of London, retrieved
20 April 2013, <http://fairtrade.london.anglican.org/
Main%20pages/FTPandG.htm>.

Fair Work Commission 2013, *Unfair Dismissal: Guide 3*,
brochure, Fair Work Commission, Commonwealth of
Australia, retrieved 3 December 2013, <www.fwc.gov.
au/index.cfm?pagename=resourcefactsunfair>.

'Fake ID cards, identity crisis' 2012, *Economist*, 11 August, p. 52, retrieved on 8 February 2013, <www.economist.com/node/21560244>.

*Fashion Victims: Four Corners* 2013, television program, Australian Broadcasting Corporation, Sydney, 24 June, retrieved 17 January 2014, <www.abc.net.au/4corners/stories/2013/06/25/3785918.htm>.

Fassin, V, Rossem, AV & Bullens, M 2011, 'Small business owner managers' perceptions of business ethics and corporate social responsibility related concepts', *Journal of Business Ethics*, vol. 98, pp. 425–53.

Fazey, M 2012, 'Human resource development and career management', in P Nel, A du Plessis, M Fazey, R Erwee, S Pillay, BH Mackinnon, R Wordsworth & B Millet (eds), *Human Resource Management in Australia and New Zealand*, Oxford University Press, South Melbourne, Australia.

Federal Bureau of Investigation (FBI) 2013, 'Medicare fraud strike force charges 89 individuals for approximately $223 million in false billing', US Department of Justice, media release, 14 May, retrieved 7 August 2013, <www.fbi.gov/news/pressrel/press-releases/medicare-fraud-strike-force-charges-89-individuals-for-approximately-223-million-in-false-billing>.

Federal Trade Commission 2012, 'Sketchers will pay $40 million to settle FTC charges that it deceived consumers with ads for "toning shoes"', Federal Trade Commission, media release, 16 May, retrieved 19 February 2013, <http://ftc.gov/opa/2012/05/consumerrefund.shtm>.

——2013, 'Google agrees to change its business practices to resolve FTC competition concerns in the markets for devices like smart phones, games and tablets, and in online search', Federal Trade Commission, media release, 2 January, retrieved 19 February 2013, <http://ftc.gov/opa/2013/01/google.shtm>.

Feeney, K 2013, 'Sterilising people with disabilities: Eugenics or common sense?', *Brisbane Times*, 3 April, retrieved 10 June 2013, <www.brisbanetimes.com.au/queensland/sterilising-people-with-disabilities-eugenics-or-common-sense-20130402-2h4u5.html>.

Fein, B & Snowden, L 2013, 'Edward Snowden's father writes open letter to NSA whistleblower in Moscow', *The Guardian*, 3 July, retrieved 1 August 2013, <www.theguardian.com/world/2013/jul/02/edward-snowden-father-open-letter?guni=Article:in%20body%20link>.

Feldman, F 1978, *Introductory Ethics*, Prentice-Hall, Englewood Cliffs, NJ.

Fenwick & West LLP 2009, 'Fenwick employment brief – May 14 2009', *Fenwick West LLB*, 14 May, retrieved 13 August 2013, <www.fenwick.com/publications/Pages/Fenwick-Employment-Brief-May-14–2009.aspx#3.4>.

Ferrell, OC & Pride, WM 1981, 'Management must practise support and enforce usable ethical policies', *Marketing News*, vol. 1, p. 11.

——Fraedrich, J & Ferrell, L 2013, *Business Ethics: Ethical Decision Making and Cases*, 9th edn, SouthWestern, Cengage Learning, OH.

Finklea, KM 2012, *Identity Theft: Trends and Issues*, Congressional Research Service Report for Congress to Members and Committees of Congress, 15 February, USA, retrieved 8 February 2013, <www.fas.org/sgp/crs/misc/R40599.pdf>.

'First public service ad campaign in forty years targets recycling' 2013, *Ethical Performance*, 10 August, retrieved 5 January 2014, <http://ethicalperformance.com/news/article/7833>.

Fisman, R & Wang, Y 2013, 'The unsafe side of Chinese crony capitalism', *Harvard Business Review*, January/February, p. 24.

Fisscher, O, Frenkel, D, Lurie, Y & Nijhof, A 2005, 'Managerial perceptions of marketing performance: Efficiency, adaptability, effectiveness and satisfaction', *Journal of Business Ethics*, vol. 60, no. 3, pp. 207–9.

Fitzsimmons, C 2013, 'ING banks on doing good', *Business Review Weekly*, 21–27 February, p. 49.

'Fleecing the flock' 2012, *The Economist*, 28 January, p. 55.

Floyd, E 2012, *1001 Little Healthy Eating Miracles*, Carlton Books Limited, Victoria.

'Food' 2013, *Time Magazine*, May 20, p. 9.

Foremski, T 2011, 'Questionable ethics and the next generation of entrepreneurs', *Silicon Valley Watcher*, retrieved 19 April 2013, <www.siliconvalleywatcher.com/mt/archives/2011/04/unethical_found.php>.

Forester, T & Morrison, P 1990, *Computer Ethics: Cautionary Tales and Ethical Dilemmas in Computing*, MIT Press, Cambridge, MA.

Foster School of Business 2011, 'Bribery penalties sting less than penalties for other financial misconduct', University of Washington, 23 May, retrieved 19 April 2013, <www.foster.washington.edu/centers/facultyresearch/Pages/bribery.aspx>.

Fowler, A 2000, 'NGDO's as a moment in history: beyond aid to 'social entrepreneurship' of civic innovation?', *Third World Quarterly*, vol. 21 no. 4, pp. 637–54.

Fox, J 2013, 'What we've learnt from the financial crisis', *Harvard Business Review*, November, pp. 94–101.

Fray, BF 2000, 'The impact of moral intensity of decision making in a business context', *Journal of Business Ethics*, vol. 26, pp. 181–95.

Freeman, RE 1984, *Strategic Management: A Stakeholder Approach*, Pitman, Boston.

French, P 1984, *Collective and Corporate Responsibility*, Columbia University Press, New York.

Frey, BS & Osterloh, M 2012, 'Stop tying paid performance', *Harvard Business Review*, January/February, p. 51.

Friedman, M 1970, 'The social responsibility of business is to increase its profits', *New York Times Magazine*, 13 September, retrieved 14 January 2014, <www.colorado.edu/studentgroups/libertarians/issues/friedman-soc-resp-business.html>.

Friedman, TL 2006, *The World is Flat: The Globalised World in the Twenty-First Century*, Penguin, Camberwell, Victoria.

Fritzsche, DJ 1991, 'A model of decision making incorporating ethical values', *Journal of Business Ethics*, vol. 10, pp. 841–52.

——2000, 'Ethical climates and the ethical dimension of decision making', *Journal of Business Ethics*, vol. 24, pp. 125–40.

—— & Becker, H 1984, 'Linking management behaviour to ethical philosophy – an empirical investigation', *Academy of Management Journal*, vol. 27, no. 1, pp. 166–75.

Froehlich, T 2004, 'A brief history of information ethics', Facultat de Biblioteconomia i Documentació, Universitat de Barcelona, Barcelona, December, no. 13, retrieved 8 February 2013, <www.ub.edu/bid/13froel2.htm>.

Fullerton, T 2009, 'Garuda investigated for alleged price-fixing', *Lateline Business*, 2 September, retrieved 4 February 2013, <www.abc.net.au/lateline/business/items/200909/s2674954.htm>.

Fuxman, L 1997, 'Ethical dilemmas of doing business in post-Soviet Ukraine', *Journal of Business Ethics*, vol. 16, pp. 1273–82.

Gagnon, MA 2012, 'Sustainable minded entrepreneurs: Developing and testing a value-based framework', *Journal of Strategic Innovation and Sustainability*, vol. 8, no. 1, pp. 9–25.

Gardner, J 2012, 'Start-up stalled in legal stoush', *Business Review Weekly*, 1–7 November, p. 34.

Garside, J 2013, 'Audit reveals 100+ cases of child labour in Apple's production chain', *Sunday Age*, 27 January, p. 18.

Gartner, WD 1985, 'Framework for describing the phenomenon of new venture creation', *Academy of Management Review*, vol. 10, no. 4, pp. 696–707.

Gautschi, FH & Jones, TM 1998, 'Enhancing the ability of business students to recognise ethical issues: An empirical assessment of the effectiveness of a course in business ethics', *Journal of Business Ethics*, vol. 17, pp. 206–16.

Gender Bias Learning Project 2013, 'Maternal wall', Centre for Worklife Law, retrieved 24 June 2013, <www.genderbiasbingo.com/maternalwall.html>.

Gentile, MC 2010, *Giving Voice to Values: How to Speak your Mind when you Know What's Right*, Yale University Press, CJ.

Gibney, E 2012, 'Research Intelligence – for all their sakes, and science's too', *Times Higher Education*, 31 May, pp. 22–3.

GIIRS 2012, 'Powered by B Lab', *GIIRS*, retrieved 5 January 2014, <http://giirs.org/powered-by-b-lab>.

Ginsberg, A & Buchholtz, A 1989, 'Are entrepreneurs a breed apart? A look at the evidence', *Journal of General Management*, vol. 15, pp. 32–40.

Glasgow, W 2012, 'The business of sharing', *Business Review Weekly*, 29 November–6 December, pp. 34–5.

Globerman, S 1998, 'Addressing international product piracy', *Journal of International Business Studies*, vol. 19, no. 3, pp. 497–504.

'Go away payments: Face the sack' 2012, *Business Review Weekly*, 18–24 October, p. 4.

Goel, S & Karri, R 2006, 'Entrepreneurs, effectual logic and over-trusting', *Entrepreneurship Theory in Practice*, vol. 8, no. 4, pp. 477–93.

Goldacre, B 2012, *Bad Pharma: How Drug Companies Mislead Doctors and Harm Patients?* Harper-Collins, London.

GoodCorporation 2012, 'Does running a business ethically add value or cost?', GoodCorporation Ltd., September, retrieved 21 November 2013, <www.goodcorporation.com/business-ethics-debates/does-running-a-business-ethically-add-value-or-cost>.

Goodpaster, KF 1983, 'The concept of corporate moral responsibility', *Journal of Business Ethics*, vol. 2, no. 1, pp. 1–22.

Goree, K 2007, *Ethics in the Workplace*, 2nd edn, SouthWestern Cengage Learning, OH.

Gorniak-Kocikowska, K 2007, 'From computer ethics to the ethics of global ICT society', *Library Hi Tech*, vol. 25, no. 1, pp. 47–57.

Gotterbarn, D 1990, 'Computer ethics: Responsibility regained', paper presented at the Computers and Quality of Life Conference, 16 September, Washington, DC.

Gottschalk, P 2011, 'Actions and suspicion of white-collar crime in business organisations: An empirical study of intended responses by Chief Financial Officers', *Professional Issues in Criminal Justice*, vol. 6, nos 1&2, pp. 41–51.

Gough, D 2012, 'Children lured to unhealthy food', *The Age*, 26 December, p. 5.

'Government surveillance' 2012, *The Economist*, 21–27 July, pp. 29–30.

Government of Western Australian Public Sector Commission 2009, *Learning from Leaving: A Guide to Exit Interviews for the Western Australian Public Sector*, Public Sector Commission, March, retrieved 21 February 2013, <www.publicsector.wa.gov.au/sites/default/files/documents/learning_from_leaving.pdf>.

Grace, D & Cohen, S 2010, *Business Ethics*, 4th edn, Oxford University Press, Melbourne.

Graduate Careers Australia 2012, 'GradStats', Graduate Careers Australia, December, retrieved 12 February 2013, <www.graduatecareers.com.au/wp-content/uploads/2011/12/GCA-GradStats-2012_FINAL1.pdf>.

Grant, J 2013, 'Singapore tightens tax evasion measures', *Financial Times*, 30 June, retrieved 5 August 2013, <www.ft.com/cms/s/0/452495a6-e14e-11e2-b796-00144feabdc0.html#axzz2b3gSrclB>.

Greenfeld, KT 2012, 'The story behind the Olympus scandal', *Bloombergbusinessweek*, 16 February, retrieved 8 July 2014, <www.businessweek.com/articles/2012-02-16/the-story-behind-the-olympus-scandal>.

Greenhouse, S & Yardley, J 2013, 'Big retailers back Bangladesh safety pact', *International Herald Tribune*, 15 May, p. 4.

Greenwald, G 2013a, 'NSA collecting phone records of millions of Verizon customers daily', *The Guardian*, 6 June, retrieved 2 September 2013, <www.theguardian.com/world/2013/jun/06/nsa-phone-records-verizon-court-order>.

——2013b, 'Xkeyscore: NSA tool collects 'nearly everything a user does on the internet', *The Guardian*, 31 July, retrieved 2 September 2013, <www.theguardian.com/world/2013/jul/31/nsa-top-secret-program-online-data>.

——2013c, 'Email service used by Snowden shuts itself down, warns against using US-based companies', *The Guardian*, 9 August, retrieved 12 August 2013, <www.theguardian.com/commentisfree/2013/aug/09/lavabit-shutdown-snowden-silicon-valley>.

—— & MacAskill, E 2013, 'NSA Prism program taps in to user data of Apple, Google and others', *The Guardian*, 7 June, retrieved 2 July 2013, <www.theguardian.com/world/2013/jun/06/us-tech-giants-nsa-data>.

——, MacAskill, E, Poitras, L, Ackerman, S & Rushe, D 2013, 'How Microsoft handed the NSA access to encrypted messages', *The Guardian*, 12 July, retrieved 2 September, <www.theguardian.com/world/2013/jul/11/microsoft-nsa-collaboration-user-data>.

Grennblat, E 2013, 'Target left wearing fake cosmetics as US supplier vanishes'. *The Age*, 6 May, pp. 25, 29.

Grove, L 2012, 'How to spot a workplace crazy: The warning signs of office mayhem', *Newsweek*, 3 September, vol. 160, no. 10, p. 5.

'Guarding the guardians' 2012, *The Economist*, 4 February, p. 45.

Guilliatt, R 2011a, 'Workers at war', *The Australian*, 26 November, retrieved 12 February 2013, <www.theaustralian.com.au/news/features/workers-at-war/story-e6frg8h6-1226202193068>.

——2011b, 'Spurious cases mean genuine bullying in workplace is ignored', *The Weekend Australian*, 26 November, retrieved 12 November 2013, <www.theaustralian.com.au/national-affairs/spurious-cases-mean-genuine-bullying-in-workplace-is-ignored/story-fn59niix-1226206556225#sthash.Z365Uvtx.dpuf>.

Guilti, J 2009, 'Creative destruction and destructive creations: environmental ethics and planned obsolescence', *Journal of Business Ethics*, vol. 89, no. 1, pp. 19–28.

Gulf News 2013, 'RBI Governor for corrective steps to prevent money laundering', *Gulf News*, 24 March, retrieved 20 April 2013, <http://gulfnews.com/business/banking/rbi-governor-for-corrective-steps-to-prevent-money-laundering-1.1162127>.

Guy, M 1990, *Ethical Decision Making in Everyday Work Situations*, Quorum Books, New York.

Haanaes, K, Michel, D, Jurgens, J, & Rangan, S 2013, 'Making sustainability profitable', *Harvard Business Review*, March.

Hadfield, S 2011, 'Rivers chief Philip Harry Goodman sued in office sex case', *Daily Telegraph*, 4 November, retrieved 30 May 2013, <www.news.com.au/business/rivers-chief-philip-harry-goodman-sued-in-office-sex-case/story-e6frfm1i-1226186320811>.

Hales, L 2013, 'Global water scarcity predicted to rise by 40%', *Sydney Morning Herald*, 18 December, retrieved 1 January 2014, <www.smh.com.au/environment/water-issues/global-water-scarcity-predicted-to-rise-by-40–20131218–2zke9.html>.

Hall, C 2010, 'Woolworths rejects changes to ethics audits', *The World Today*, 1 March, retrieved 25 November 2013, <www.abc.net.au/worldtoday/content/2010/s2833058.htm>.

Hall, K 2013, 'Bank in $13B toxic loans payout', *The Age*, 21 November, p. 16.

Hanley, G 2003, 'Don't do what I say – just bloody well do what I say! The workplace bullying experience of Australian academics', working paper series, Monash University, Faculty of Business and Economics, Melbourne.

Hannafey, FT 2003, 'Entrepreneurship and ethics: A literature review', *Journal of Business Ethics*, vol. 46, pp. 99–110.

Hansegard, J & Lahiri, T 2013, 'No seamless approach to factory safety', *Wall Street Journal*, p. 20.

Hansen, M, Ibarra, H, & Peyer, U 2013, 'The best performing CEOs in the world', *Harvard Business Review*, January/February, pp. 81–96.

Hardoon, D & Heinrich, F 2011, 'Bribe payers index', *Transparency International*, retrieved 17 April 2013, <www.http://bpi.transparency.org/bpi2011>.

Hare, R 1965, review of von Wright 1963, *The Philosophical Quarterly*, 15, pp. 172–5.

Harman, J 2008, 'Successful social entrepreneurship: The case of the EagleHawk recycle shop, *Journal of Services Research*, vol. 201.

Harris, JD, Sapienza, HJ & Bowie, NE 2011, 'Ethics in entrepreneurship', *Journal of Ethics and Entrepreneurship*, vol. 1, no. 1, pp. 7–26.

Hastings, L 2013, 'Not tweet in love, war', *Capital City Daily*, p. 3.

Hastings, R 2012, 'Facebook founder's hacking past', *The Independent*, 19 May, p. 11.

Hauerwas, S 2007, 'The virtues of Alasdair MacIntyre', *First Things*, October, retrieved 8 June 2013, <www.firstthings.com/article/2007/09/004-the-virtues-of-alasdair-macintyre-6>.

Havenstein, H 2008, 'One in five employers uses social networks in hiring process', *Computerworld*, 12 September, retrieved 12 February 2013, <www.computerworld.com/s/article/9114560/One_in_five_employers_uses_social_networks_in_hiring_process>.

Healy, P & Ramanna, K 2013, 'When the crowd fights corruption', *Harvard Business Review*, January/February, pp. 122–9.

Heard, H 2011, 'Assault payout', *Sunday Herald Sun*, 13 November, retrieved 3 June 2013, <www.nowickicarbone.com.au/mediaupload/News%20in%20the%20Hun%20131111.pdf>.

Heathcoat, A 2013, 'Waste not, want not', *Business Review Weekly*, 21–27 March, pp. 17–20.

Hegarty, WH & Sims, HP 1978, 'Some determinants of unethical behaviour: An experiment', *Journal of Applied Psychology*, vol. 63, no. 4, pp. 451–7.

——1979, 'Organisational philosophy, policies and objectives related to unethical decision behaviour: A laboratory experiment', *Journal of Applied Psychology*, vol. 64, no. 3, pp. 331–8.

Henning, J 2009, 'Perspectives on financial crimes in Roman-Dutch law: Bribery, fraud, and the general crime of falsity', *Journal of Financial Crime*, vol. 16, no. 4, pp. 295–304.

Heuer, M 2011, 'Sustainability governance across time and space: Connecting environmental stewardship in the firm with the global community', *Business Strategy and the Environment*, vol. 21, no. 2, pp. 86–97.

Hibbert, SA, Hogg, G & Quinn, T 2002, 'Consumer response to "social" entrepreneurship: the case of the big issue in Scotland', *International Journal of Nonprofit & Voluntary Sector Marketing*, vol. 7, no. 3, pp. 288–301.

Hickey, D 2012, 'Michael Woodford: Japan's whistle-blower supreme speaks out', *Japan Times*, 2 December.

Higgs, B & Milner L 2005, 'Portrayals of cultural diversity in Australian television commercials: a benchmark study', ANZMAC 2005 Conference, Perth, 5–7 December 2005, retrieved 5 February 2013, <http://vuir.vu.edu.au/877/1/1-Higgs.pdf>.

'High frequency trading wait a second' 2012, *The Economist*, 11 August, p. 10.

'Hiring hotties' 2012, *The Economist*, 21–27 July, p. 31, retrieved 12 February 2013, <www.economist.com/node/21559357>.

Hisrich, RD., & Peters, M P 1998, *Entrepreneurship: Starting, Developing, and Managing a New Enterprise*, 4th edn, Irwin/McGraw-Hill, Burr Ridge, IL.

Hobbes, T 1968, *Leviathan*, ed. CB Macpherson, Penguin Books, Middlesex.

Hoivik, H & Shankar, D 2011, 'How can SMEs in a cluster respond to global demands for corporate responsibility', *Journal of Business Ethics*, vol. 101, no. 2, pp. 175–95.

'Honestly unvarnished' 2012, *The Economist*, 8 December, p. 61.

'Horiemon returns' 2013, *The Economist*, 6 April, p. 63.

Hornsby, JS, Kuratko, DF, Naffziger, DW, LaFollette, WR & Hodgetts, RM 1994, 'The ethical perceptions of small business owners: A factor analytic study', *Journal of Small Business Management*, vol. 32, no. 4, pp. 9–16.

Hosmer, LT 1987, *The Ethics of Management*, Irwin Publishers, Homewoo,d IL.

*How money laundering works* 2011, YouTube, Ronnie Darko, 10 May, retrieved 8 January 2014, <www.youtube.com/watch?v=pGocvqSKi4k>.

Hoyos, C 2012, 'Rolls-Royce bribery claims date to 2006', *Financial Times*, 9 December, retrieved 30 May 2013, <www.ft.com/intl/cms/s/0/75aa410e-4229–11e2–979e-00144feabdc0.html>.

Hsu, T 2012, 'eBay Bans Supernatural Sales of magic spells, potions, hexes', *Los Angeles Times*, 16 August, retrieved 9 July 2013, <http://articles.latimes.com/2012/aug/16/business/la-fi-mo-ebay-supernatural-ban-20120816>.

Hunt, SD & Vitell, S 1993, 'The general theory of marketing ethics: a retrospective and revision', in N Craig Smith & JA Smith (eds), *Ethics in Marketing*, Chicago, IL, USA.

——, Chonko, LB & Wilcox, JB 1984, 'Ethical problems of marketing researchers', *Journal of Marketing Research*, vol. 21, August, pp. 309–24.

Huq, R 2013, 'Letter from a Bangladesh factory', *Wall Street Journal*, p. 12.

Hurley, B 2013a, 'Dropping dollars', *Business Review Weekly*, 28 February-3 March, pp. 31–3.

——2013b, 'Entrepreneurs start-ups lose their options', *Business Review Weekly*, 4–10 April, pp. 34–6.

Husted, BW 2000, 'The impact of national culture on software piracy', *Journal of Business Ethics*, vol. 26, pp. 197–211.

—— & Allen, DB 2008, 'Toward a model of cross-cultural business ethics: the impact of individualism and collectivism on the ethical decision-making process', *Journal of Business Ethics*, vol. 82, no. 2, pp. 293–305.

Hyman, MR, & Skipper, R & Tansey, R 1990, 'Ethical codes are not enough', *Business Horizons*, March–April, pp. 15–22.

——, Tansey, R & Clark, JW 1994, 'Research on Advertising Ethics: Past, Present and Future', *Journal of Advertising*, vol. 23, no. 3, pp. 2–15.

'I spy, with my big eye' 2012, *The Economist*, 28 April, pp. 56, 68.

'Identifying women for corporate boards' 2012, *BizEd*, September/October, p. 12.

'In search of honesty' 2002, *The Economist*, 15 August, retrieved 17 July 2013, <www.economist.com/node/1284261>.

'In the secret state' 2013, *The Economist*, 3 August, p. 31.

Inagaki, K & Dvorak, P 2012, 'Behind insider leaks, a quest for favor – salespeople in Japan offered gossip, cryptic talk to good clients; investors learned to piece together hints', *Asian Wall Street Journal*, 17 August, p. 15.

Independent Commission against Corruption (ICAC) 2000, *What is an ethical culture? Key issues to consider in building an ethical organisation*, summary report, ICAC, pp. 1–39, retrieved 25 November 2013, <www.icac.nsw.gov.au/documents/doc_download/1670-what-is-an-ethical-culture-key-issues-to-consider-in-building-an-ethical-organisation--summary-report>.

IndiaCSR 2013, 'PsU failed to bridge the social responsibility gap', *IndiaCSR*, 8 February, retrieved 5 January 2014, <www.indiacsr.in/en/?p=9652>.

Ingram, D 2013, 'How to conduct an ethical audit', Hearst Communications, retrieved 25 November 2013, <http://smallbusiness.chron.com/conduct-ethical-audit-16101.html>.

Injured Worker Support 2013, 'Rivers boss fights sex harassment cases', The Injured Workers Support Network, 10 February, 31 May 2013, <www.injuredworkerssupport.org.au/?p=5239>.

Institute of Chartered Accountants Australia 2012, 'Professional Conduct Report', Institute of Chartered Accountants Australia, August, retrieved 30 October 2013, <www.charteredaccountants.com.au/search-results.aspx?keywords=Professional%20Conduct%20Report%E2%80%99>.

International Ethics Standards Boards for Accountants 2012, *Handbook of the Code of Ethics for Professional Accountants*, International Federation of Accountants, July, New York.

International Federation of Accountants (IFAC) 2005, 'Revised codes of conduct – completed', June, retrieved 8 January 2014, <www.ifac.org/ethics/projects/revised-code-ethics-completed>.

——2012, *International Ethics Standards Board for Accountants: Handbook of the Code of Ethics for Professional Accountants*, International Federation of Accountants, July, , New York.

International Intellectual Property Alliance 2013, 'The 2013 Special 301 Report on Property Protection', International Intellectual Property Alliance, retrieved 20 April 2013, <www.iipa.com/special301.html>.

International Labour Organisation (ILO) 1996–2013, 'What is child labour?', International Labour Organisation, retrieved 20 April 2013, <www.ilo.org/ipec/facts/lang--en/index.htm>.

International Organisation for Standardization (ISO) n.d., 'ISO 26000 Social responsibility', ISO, retrieved 29 April 2013, <www.iso.org/iso/home/standards/iso26000.htm>.

International Trade Association 2011, 'Fraud warning: Re Iraqi procurement', Iraq Investment and Reconstruction Task Force, Market Access and Compliance, International Trade Administration, US Department of Commerce, 21 January, retrieved 5 August 2013, <www.trade.gov/static/iraq_pdf_fraud.pdf>.

'Internet freedom' 2012, *The Economist*, 6 October, p. 60.

'Internet freedom: Plus ça change', *The Economist*, 8 September 2012, p. 30.

'Internet piracy' n.d., *PCMag.com*, retrieved 10 February 2013, <www.pcmag.com/encyclopedia_term/0%2C1237%2Ct%3DInternet+piracy&i%3D63907%2C00.asp>.

InterOrganization Network (ION) 2013, *2013 Annual status report*, ION, retrieved 5 January 2014, <www.ionwomen.org/wp-content/uploads/2013/09/ION_StatusReport_2013_FINAL.pdf>.

Introna, LD 2002, 'The (im)possibility of ethics in the information age', *Information and Organisation*, vol. 12, p. 71–84.

Investopedia 2013, 'Dumping', *Investopedia US*, retrieved 20 April 2013, <www.investopedia.com/terms/d/dumping.asp>.

Ismail, KB, Sohel, MH & Hossain, MJ 2011, 'Successful social entrepreneurship-the case of Grameen Danone Foods Ltd', in J Meuller, R Franklin & DD Warrick (eds), *Lessons for Worldwide Best Practice Cases: Non-Profit Excellence*, RossiSmith Academic Publishing, Oxford pp. 159–73.

Jackson, KT 1997, 'Globalizing corporate ethics programs: Perils and prospects', *Journal of Business Ethics*, vol. 16, pp. 1227–35.

Jackson, T 2011, *International Management Ethics: A Critical, Cross-Cultural Perspective*, Cambridge University Press, Cambridge.

Jacobs, L, Samli, AC & Jedlik, T 2001, 'The nightmare of international product piracy: exploring defensive strategies', *Industrial Marketing Management*, vol. 30, no. 6, August, pp. 499–509.

James, D 2012, 'Remuneration under the microscope', *Business Review Weekly*, 16–22 February, p. 34–5.

Janssen, C 2012a, 'Internet worm', *Techopedia*, retrieved 10 February 2013, <www.techopedia.com/definition/7786/internet-worm>.

——2012b, 'Rootkit', *Techopedia*, retrieved 10 February 2013, <www.techopedia.com/definition/4088/rootkit>.

——n.d., 'Virus', *Techopedia*, retrieved 10 February 2013, <www.techopedia.com/definition/4157/virus>.

Jawahar, IM & McLaughlin, GL 2001, 'Toward a descriptive stakeholder theory: An organisational life-cycle approach', *Academy of Management Review*, vol. 26, pp. 397–414.

Jennings, M 2006, *The Seven Signs of Ethical Collapse: How to Spot Moral Meltdowns in Companies Before It's Too Late*, St Martin's Press, New York.

Jennings, PD & Zandbergen, PA 1995, 'Ecologically sustainable organizations: An institutional approach', *Academy of Management Review*, vol. 20, no. 4, pp. 1015–52.

Johns, G & Saks, AM 2004, *Organizational Behaviour: Understanding and Managing Life at Work*, 6th edn, Pearson/Prentice Hall, Ontario, Canada.

Johnson, D 2000, 'Democratic values', in D Langford (ed.), *Ethics and the Internet*, Macmillan, UK.

Joint Accounting Bodies: CPA Australia Ltd, The Institute of Chartered Accountants in Australia & The Institute of Public Accountants 2013, *Independence Guide*, Joint Accounting Bodies, 4th edn, February, Joint Accounting Bodies.

Jones, SC & Hall, DV 2006, 'Ethical issues in social marketing' in University of Newcastle Research Online: *Proceedings of the 3rd Australasian Non-profit and Social Marketing Conference*, Newcastle, 10–11 August 2006.

Jones, TM 1991, 'Ethical decision making by individuals in organizations: An issue-contingent model', *Academy of Management Review*, vol. 16, no. 2, pp. 366–95.

Joyce, D, Blackshaw, B, King, C & Muller, L 2003, 'Codes of conduct for computing professionals: An international comparison', in *16th Annual NACCQ conference*, S Mann & A Williamson (eds), Palmerston North, New Zealand.

Joye, C 2013, 'Edward Snowden: Whistleblower or traitor', *Australian Financial Review*, 15 June, retrieved 2 July 2013, <www.afr.com/p/national/edward_snowden_whistleblower_or_EiC9zP9DQbBs4VxGfAK5XL>.

Joyner, BE, Payne, D & Raiborn, CA 2002, 'Building values, business ethics and corporate responsibility into the developing organisation', *Journal of Developmental Entrepreneurship*, vol. 7, no. 1, pp. 113–31.

Judge, A 2001, 'The global compact of the United Nations', *Laetus in Praesens*, retrieved 19 November 2013, <http://laetusinpraesens.org/docs/globcomp/globcom2.php>.

'Judge Rakoff: A hot bench' 2011, *The Economist*, 9 June, p. 73.

Jurkiewicz, CL & Brown, R 2000, 'The P/E ratio that really counts', *Journal of Power and Ethics, HighBeam Research*, no. 1.

Kaliski, BS (ed.) 2001, *Encyclopaedia of Business and Finance*, Macmillan, Sydney.

Kan, M 2013, 'China fines Samsung, LG and four others in LCD price-fixing scheme', *PC World Australia*, 4 January, retrieved 5 February 2013, <www.pcworld.idg.com.au/article/445578/china_fines_samsung_lg_four_others_lcd_price-fixing_scheme>.

Kant, I [1785] 2010, *Groundwork of the Metaphysics of Morals*, eds M Gregor & J Timmermann (eds), Cambridge University Press, Cambridge.

Karena, C 2012, 'Lifting the fog of cloud adoption', *The Age*, Tuesday 25 September, pp. 2–3.

Karri, R & Goel, S 2008, 'Effectuation and over-trust: response to Sarasvathy and Due', *Entrepreneurship Theory and Practice*, vol. 32, no. 4, pp. 739–48.

Kassane, K 2012, 'Generation lost?', *Saturday Age*, 8 September, p. 15.

Katz, JA & Green, RP 2007, *Entrepreneurial Small Business*, McGraw-Hill Irwin, New York.

Kavanagh, J 2013, 'Beware the mask of deception', *Sunday Age*, 3 March, p. 14.

Kenny, G 2013, 'The stakeholder or the firm? Balancing the strategic framework', *Journal of Business Strategy*, vol. 34, no. 3, pp. 33–9.

Kenny, R, Pierce, J & Pye, G 2012, 'Ethical considerations in guidelines in web analytics and digital marketing: A retail case study', *Conference Proceedings of the 6th Australian Institute of Computer Ethics Conference*, Shona Leitch & Matthew Warren (eds), Melbourne, 13 February 2012.

Ker, P & Hawthorne, N 2013, 'Whitehaven: A siren call for a host of hoaxes', *Saturday Age*, 12 January, pp. 6–7.

Kerr, P 2012, 'The brave new shadowy world of eavesdropping', *The Age Business Day*, 14 June, p. 6.

Kerr, S 1995, 'On the folly of rewarding A while hoping for B', *Academy of Management Executive*, February, pp. 7–19.

Kershaw, A 2012, 'Big rise in students who plagiarise applications', *Independent* [UK], 19 May, p. 5.

Ketz, JE 2006, *Accounting Ethics: Critical Perspectives on Business and Management*, vol. 1, Routledge, UK.

——(ed.) 2006, 'Auditing failures and their associated auditing firms', *Accounting Ethics: Critical Perspectives on Business and Management*, vol. 1, Routledge, New York.

Khadem, N 2012, 'ATO to be investigated', *Business Review Weekly*, 25 October–21 November, p. 69.

Khan, SA, Tang, J & Zhu, R 2013, 'The impact of environmental, firm, and relational factors on entrepreneurs' ethically suspect behaviors', *Journal of Small Business Management*, vol. 51, no. 4, pp. 637–57.

'Kid gloves' 2012, *The Economist*, 9 June, p. 63.

Kidder, R 2009, 'Sexting and our moral future', *Ethics Newsline*, April, <www.globalethics.org/newsline/2009/04/20/sexting-2>.

Kieseker, R & Marchant, T 1999, 'Workplace bullying in Australia: a review of current conceptualisations and existing research', *Australian Journal of Management & Organisational Behaviour*, vol. 2, no. 5, p. 61–75.

King, RG & Levine, R 1993, 'Finance, entrepreneurship and growth, theory and evidence', *Journal of Monetary Economics*, vol. 32, no. 4, pp. 513–42.

Kirpich, J 2013, 'Abercrombie & Fitch: Solid marketing or marketing faux pas?', *Grafik*, 13 May, retrieved 8 July 2014, <www.grafik.com/abercrombieandfitch>.

Kirzner, IM 1973, *Competition and 'Entrepreneurship'*, University of Chicago Press, Chicago.

'Kmart boycotts factory' 2013, *The Age*, 25 May, p. 3.

Knouse, SB & Giacolone, RA 1992, 'Ethical decision making in business: Behavioural issues and concerns', *Journal of Business Ethics*, vol. 11, pp. 369–78.

Knowlton, B 2013, 'Edward Snowden's father to visit Russia, urging fugitive son to return to US', *Sydney Morning Herald*, 12 August, retrieved 13 August 2013, <www.smh.com.au/world/edward-snowdens-father-to-visit-russia-urging-fugitive-son-to-return-to-us-20130812-2rqq8.html>.

Koehn, D 2001, 'Ethical issues connected with multi-level marketing schemes', *Journal of Business Ethics*, vol. 29, nos. 1/2, pp. 153–60.

Kohlberg, L 1963, 'Moral development and identification', in HW Stevenson (ed.), J Kagan (Col), C Spiker (Col); NB Henry (ed.) & HG Richey (ed.), *Child Psychology: The Sixty-Second Yearbook of the National Society for the Study of Education, Part 1*, National Society for the Study of Education, Chicago, & University of Chicago Press, Chicago, pp. 277–332.

——1969, 'Stage and sequence: The cognitive development approach to socialisation', in ND Gosling (ed.), *Handbook of Socialisation Theory*, Rand McNally, Chicago, USA, pp. 347–480.

——1981, *The Philosophy of Moral Development: Moral Stages and the Idea of Justice*, Harper and Row, San Francisco, CA.

——& Mayer, R 1972, 'Development as the aim of education', *Harvard Educational Review*, vol. 42, no. 4, pp. 449–96.

Kopp, M 2013, 'Buck must stop at feet of the SME founder', *Business Review Weekly*, 28 March–1 May, p. 55.

Kotler, P 1994, *Marketing Management: Analysis, Planning, Implementation, and Control*, 8th edn, Prentice Hall, NJ.

KPMG 2008, 'Tax in focus', KPMG, retrieved 15 July 2013, <www.kpmg.com.au/newsletters/Tax/2008/Dec/23/KPMGBrief40.pdf>.

——2009, *KPMG International Survey of Corporate Responsibility Reporting* 2008, KPMG, London.

——2011, *Global anti-bribery and corruption survey 2011*, KPMG International Cooperative, retrieved 18 April 2013, <www.kpmg.com/au/en/issuesandinsights/articlespublications/pages/global-anti-bribery-and-corruption-survey-2011.aspx>.

——2013, *A survey of fraud, bribery and corruption in Australia and New Zealand* 2012, KPMG Forensic, February, retrieved 5 August 2013, <www.kpmg.com/AU/en/IssuesAndInsights/ArticlesPublications/Fraud-Survey/Documents/fraud-bribery-corruption-survey-2012v2.pdf>.

Krim, NSA, Zamzuri, NHA & Nor, YN 2009, 'Exploring the relationship between Internet ethics in university students and the big five model of personality', *Computers and Education*, vol. 53, pp. 86–93.

Krishnan, R 2009, 'A dozen ways of inflating profits, valuations', *Live Mint & the Wall Street Journal*, January 25, retrieved 5 August 2013, <www.livemint.com/Home-Page/EF9PWxvDbyJK2sBQ9TvpQI/A-dozen-ways-of-inflating-profits-valuations.html>.

Kuddus 2013, 'US to impose sanctions on any country that protects Snowden', *DigitalJournal*, 25 July, retrieved 12 August 2013, <http://digitaljournal.com/article/355181>.

Kuppuswany, C 2009, 'The ethics of intellectual property rights: the impact of traditional knowledge and health on International Intellectual Property Law', *Asian Medicine*, vol. 5, no. 2, pp. 340–62.

Kuratko, DF, Goldsby, MG & Hornsby, JS 2004, 'The ethical perspectives of entrepreneurs: An examination of stakeholder salience', *Journal of Applied Management and Entrepreneurship*, vol. 9, no. 4, pp. 19–42.

Lacy, P, Haines, A & Hayward, R 2012, 'Developing strategies and leaders to succeed in a new era of sustainability: Findings and insights from the United Nations Global Compact Accenture CEO study', *Journal of Management Development*, vol. 31, no. 4, pp. 346–57.

Laczniak, GR & Inderrieden, EJ 1987, 'The influence of stated organizational concern upon ethical decision making, *Journal of Business Ethics*, vol. 6, pp. 297–307.

—— & Murphy, PE 2006, 'Normative perspectives for ethical and socially responsible marketing', *Journal of Micromarketing*, vol. 26, no. 2, pp. 154–77.

Ladd, J 1981, 'Physicians and society: Tribulations of power and responsibility', in SF Spicker, JM Healey & HT Englehardt (eds), *The Law-Medicine Relation: A Philosophical Exploration*, Kluwer, Netherlands.

LaFleur, EK, Reidenbac, RE, Robin, DP & Forrest, PJ 1996, 'An exploration of rule configuration effects on the ethical decision process of advertising professionals', *Journal of Academy Marketing Science*, vol. 24, no. 1, pp. 66–76.

LaFrenz, C 2013, 'Phosphagenics former CEO named in fraud', *Australian Financial Review*, 25 July, p. 23.

Lahdesmaki, M 2005, 'When ethics matters-interpreting the ethical disclosure of small nature-based entrepreneurs', *Journal of Business Ethics*, vol. 61, pp. 55–68.

Lallo, M 2012, 'The problem with oversharing: why burglars like you using Facebook', *Sunday*, 10 June, p. 4.

Langenderfer, HQ & Rockness, JW 1989, 'Integrating ethics into the accounting curriculum: Issues, problems and solutions', *Issues in Accounting Education*, vol. 4, no. 1, pp. 58–69.

Langlois, CC & Schlegelmilch, BB 1990, 'Do corporate codes of ethics reflect national character? Evidence from Europe and the United States', *Journal of International Business Studies*, Fourth Quarter, pp. 519–39.

Lasprogata G & Cotton, M 2003, 'Contemplating 'enterprise': The business and legal challenges of social entrepreneurship', *American Business Law Journal*, vol. 41, no. 1, pp. 67–114.

Lattman, P 2013, 'A tale of Wall Street excess', *New York Times*, 3 June, retrieved 31 October 2013, <http://dealbook.nytimes.com/2013/06/03/a-tale-of-wall-st-excess/?_r=0>.

Laux, V & Stocken, PC 2012, 'Managerial reporting, over-optimism and litigation risk', *Journal of Accounting and Economics*, vol. 53, pp. 577–91.

Lawton, J 2013, 'Ethics and the entrepreneur', Ewing Marion Kauffman Foundation, retrieved 28 April

2013, <www.entrepreneurship.org/resource-center/ethics-and-the-entrepreneur.aspx>.

Le Menestrel, M, Hunter, M, & De Bettignies, HC 2002, 'Internet ethics in confrontation with an activist's agenda. Yahoo! on trial', *Journal of Business Ethics*, vol. 39, pp. 135–44.

Leadership Management Australasia 2012, 'Diversity in the workplace – survey suggests lip-service, but why?', *L.E.A.D. Survey News*, 28 June, retrieved 20 February 2013, <www.leadershipmanagement.com.au/lead-survey-news/diversity-in-the-workplace-survey-suggests-lip-service-but-why>.

'Leaky devils' 2013, *The Economist*, 13 April 13, p. 67.

Lee, J & Wilkins, G 2012, 'Coalition joins fight against privacy law reform', *The Age*, 21 September, p. 3.

Leitsch, DL 2004, 'Differences in the perception of moral intensity and the moral decision process: an empirical examination of accounting students', *Journal of Business Ethics*, vol. 53, pp. 313–23.

'Less than treachery' 2013, *The Economist*, 3 August, p. 32.

'Let them eat cake' 2012 *The Economist*, 4 February, p. 56.

Leveson, NG & Turner, CS 1993, 'An investigation of the Therac-25 accidents', *IEEE Computer*, July, vol. 26, no. 7, pp. 18–41.

Levine, DB 1991, *Inside Out: An Insider's Account of Wall Street*, GP Putnam's Sons, New York.

Levinson, S 2013, 'Abercrombie & Fitch's CEO explains why he hates fat chicks', *Elite Daily*, 3 May, retrieved 15 August 2013, <http://elitedaily.com/news/world/abercrombie-fitch-ceo-explains-why-he-hates-fat-chicks>.

Levy, S 1984, *Hackers: Heroes of the Computer Revolution*, Double Day, USA.

Lewis, M 2010, *The Big Short: Inside the Doomsday Machine*, WW Norton and Company, New York.

Lewis, P 1985, 'Defining business ethics: Like nailing jello to a wall', *Journal of Business Ethics*, vol. 4, pp. 377–83.

'Liberties lost decade' 2013, *The Economist*, 3 August, p. 12.

'Liberty sell', *The Economist*, 1 June, p. 8.

Life Scientist Staff 2013a, 'Phosphagenics CEO steps down', *Australian Life Scientist*, 22 July, retrieved 9 August 2013, <http://lifescientist.com.au/content/biotechnology/news/phosphagenics-ceo-steps-down-1339591385>.

——2013b, 'Phosphagenics releases results of investigation', *Life Scientist*, 24 July, retrieved 9 August, <http://lifescientist.com.au/content/biotechnology/news/phosphagenics-releases-results-of-investigation-547656692>.

Life Without Plastic Wholesale 2014, 'Products', Life Without Plastic Wholesale, retrieved 5 January 2014, <https://sanctusmundo.com/products/ethical-sourcing>.

'Little peepers everywhere' 2012, *The Economist*, 21–27 July, pp. 29–30.

Loch, CH, Sting, FJ, Huchzermeier, A & Decker, C 2012, 'Finding the profit in fairness', *Harvard Business Review*, September, p. 111–15.

Lockheed Martin 2013, 'Polishing our ethics performance', Lockheed Martin, retrieved 14 October 2013, <www.lockheedmartin.com.au/us/who-we-are/ethics/culture-ethics.html>.

Logsdon, JM & Yuthas, K 1997, 'Corporate social performance, stakeholder orientation and organisational moral development', *Journal of Business Ethics*, vol. 16, pp. 1213–26.

Long, MD & Rao, S 1995, 'The wealth effects of unethical business behaviour', *Journal of Economics and Finance*, vol. 19, no. 2, Summer, pp. 65–75.

Longenecker, JG, McKinney, JA & Moore, CW 1988, 'Egoism and independence: Entrepreneurial ethics', *Organisational Dynamics*, vol. 16, pp. 64–72.

——1989, 'Ethics in small business', *Journal of Small Business*, vol. 27, January, pp. 27–31.

Longstaff, S 1992, 'Ethics of the accounting profession: Staying out of the disciplinary committee', Paper presented at the CPA Australia conference, retrieved 15 April 2013, <www.ethics.org.au/ethics-articles/ethics-accounting-profession>.

'Look for the silver lining' 2008, *The Economist*, 17 July, retrieved 29 April 2013, <www.economist.com/node/11750492>.

L'Oréal 2013, 'L'Oréal is named to Ethisphere's 2013 World's Most Ethical Companies list', L'Oreal, 6 March, retrieved 25 November 2013, <www.loreal.com/who-we-are/awards-recognitions/loreal-is-named-to-ethispheres-2013-worlds-most-ethical-companies-list.aspx>.

Löscher, P 2012, 'The CEO of Siemens on using a scandal to drive change', *Harvard Business Review*, November, pp. 39–42.

Lotich, P 2011, 'Ethics in business – 6 examples of business ethics and integrity', *The Thriving Small Business*, 4 October, retrieved 17 December 2013, <www.thethrivingsmallbusiness.com/examples-of-business-ethics-and-integrity>.

Lovegrove, N & Thomas, M 2013, 'Triple-strength leadership', *Harvard Business Review*, September, 2013, pp. 47–56.

Lowe, A 2012a, 'Facebook joins cyberbullying fight', *Australian Age*, 14 June, p. 8.

——2012b, 'Software to protect children online', *The Australian Age*, 14 June, p. 8.

Lucas, C 2012, 'Laws are failing bullying victims', *The Age*, 10 July, p.5.

Lucas, R 2012, 'After things go wrong', *Conference Proceedings of 6th Australian Institute of Computer Ethics Conference*, Melbourne, S Leitch and M Warren (eds), 13 February 2012, pp. 38–41.

Lysons, CK 1989, *Purchasing*, Pitman, London.

Maak, T & Stoetter, N 2012, 'Social entrepreneurs as responsible leaders: Fundacion Paraguaya and the case of Martin Burt', *Journal of Business Ethics*, vol. 111, pp. 413–30.

Mace, W 2012, 'Two Bridgecorp directors facing prison', *Saturday Age*, April 6–7, p. 3.

MacDonald, C 2010, 'The MBA Oath helps remind graduates of their ethical obligations', *Canadian Business*, 8 November, retrieved 8 July 2014, <www.canadianbusiness.com/business-strategy/the-mba-oath-helps-remind-graduates-of-their-ethical-obligations>.

Macfarlane, B 2012, 'Packing a moral compass when branching out or risk losing your way', *Times Higher Education*, 18 October, p. 31.

MacIntyre, AC 1981, *After Virtue: A Study in Moral Theory*, 2nd edn, Duckworth, London.

MacKenzie, CR, & Cronstein, BN 2006, 'Conflict of interest', *HSS Journal*, vol. 2, no. 2, pp. 198–201, retrieved 10 July 2013, <www.ncbi.nlm.nih.gov/pmc/articles/PMC2488162>.

Madigan, N 2012, 'The guilt of the father', *Business Review Weekly*, 1–7 November, p. 32.

Maher, K 2011, 'Gas drilling bringing jobs to Pennsylvania, but how many?', *Wall Street Journal*, 2 August, retrieved 19 December 2013, <http://online.wsj.com/news/articles/SB100014240531119042334045764625433762265l6>.

Maiolo, A 2012, 'Trying to outsmart Google', *Campus Review*, vol. 22, no. 13, 10 July, p. 3.

Mair, J, Battilana, J & Cardemas, J 2012, 'Organising for society: A typology of social entrepreneuring models', *Journal of Business Ethics*, vol. 111, pp. 353–73.

Makwana, R 2006, 'Multinationals (MNCs) beyond the profit motive', Share the World's Resources: Sustainable Economics to End Poverty, 3 October, retrieved 17 April 2013, <www.stwr.org/multinational-corporations/multinational-corporations-mncs-beyond-the-profit-motive.html>.

Maldonado, A 2012, 'Chicken & soda: Power and stereotypes in advertisements', UT Austin Sociology, April 13, retrieved 8 February 2013, <http://sites.la.utexas.edu/utaustinsoc/2012/04/13/chicken-soda-power-and-stereotypes-in-advertisements>.

Malik, A & Jenkins, C 2013, 'New company law to change CSR landscape', *LiveMint and the Wall Street Journal*, 12 August, retrieved 2 January 2014, <www.livemint.com/Companies/tOGwGAPjhQs1QautjL4GEI/New-company-law-to-change-CSR-landscape.html>.

Marcellus Shale Coalition 2011, retrieved 2 August 2011, <http://marcelluscoalition.org>.

Marcus, J 2012a, 'A lot of help from its friends', *Times Higher Education*, 8 March, p. 17.

——2012b, 'In cyberspace everyone can hear all about your misdeeds', *Times Higher Education*, 11 October, retrieved 15 February 2013, <www.timeshighereducation.co.uk/story.asp?storycode=421430>.

'Margin calls' 2013, *The Economist*, 16 February, p. 64.

Marion, AM 2001, 'Ethics in marketing', *eNotes*, retrieved 4 February 2013, <www.enotes.com/ethics-marketing-reference>.

Markham, MA 2004, 'Transfer pricing of intangible assets in the US, the OECD and Australia: Are profit-split methodologies the way forward?' *University of Western Sydney Law Review*, vol. 8, pp. 55–78.

Marks, R & Moon S 1995, 'Professional attitudes concerning the ethics of comparative advertising', *Journal of Professional Services Marketing*, vol. 12, no. 1, pp. 107–16.

Marquet, CT 2011, *The Marquet report on Ponzi schemes: A white-collar fraud study of major Ponzi-type investment fraud cases revealed from 2002–2011*, Marquet International, 2 June, retrieved 2 August 2013, <www.marquetinternational.com/pdf/marquet_report_on_ponzi_schemes.pdf>.

Marriner, C 2013, 'Call to discount IVF for embryo donors', *Sydney Morning Herald*, 20 January, retrieved 4 June 2013, <www.smh.com.au/national/health/call-to-discount-ivf-for-embryo-donors-20130119–2d00k.html>.

Marshall, A and Kinser, C 2013, 'Connected generation perspectives from tomorrow's leaders in a digital world. Insights from the 2012 IBM Global Student Study', *IBM Institute for Business Value, IBM Global Business Services, Executive Report 2012,* retrieved 17 April 2013, <http://public.dhe.ibm.com/common/ssi/ecm/en/gbe03530usen/GBE03530USEN.PDF>.

Martin, KD & Cullen, JB 2006, 'Continuities and extensions of ethical climate theory: A meta-analytic review', *Journal of Business Ethics*, vol. 69, pp. 175–94.

Mason, M 2008, *The Pirate's Dilemma: How Youth Culture is Reinventing Capitalism*, Free Press, New York.

Mastria, L 2012, 'Digital advertising alliance gives guidance to marketers for Microsoft IE10 "Do Not Track" default settings', Digital Advertising Alliance, media release, 9 October, retrieved 22 February 2013, <www.aboutads.info/blog/digital-advertising-alliance-gives-guidance-marketers-microsoft-ie10-%E2%80%98do-not-track%E2%80%99-default-set>.

Matthews, MC 1987, 'Codes of ethics: Organisational behaviour and misbehaviour', in WC Frederick & LE Preston (eds), *Research in Corporate Social Performance and Policy*, JIA Press, Greenwich, CT, pp. 107–30.

Mauboussin, MJ 2012, 'The true measures of success', *Harvard Business Review*, October, pp. 48–56.

Maury, MD & Kleiner, DS 2002, 'E-commerce, ethical commerce?' *Journal of Business Ethics*, vol. 36, pp. 21–31.

May, DR & Pauli, KP 2002, 'The role of moral intensity in ethical decision making', *Business and Society*, vol. 41, no. 1, pp. 84–117.

'Mayer culpa' 2013, *The Economist*, 2 March, p. 12.

Mazzella, C, Durkin, K, Cerini, E & Buralli, P 1992, 'Sex role stereotyping in Australian television advertisements', *Sex Roles,* vol. 26, nos 7–8, pp. 243–59.

McAllister, P 2013, 'You have nothing to fear but fear itself', *Ethical Trading Initiative*, 6 March, retrieved 29 April 2013, <www.ethicaltrade.org/news-and-events/blog/peter-mcallister/nothing-to-fear-on-ruggie-but-fear-itself>.

McCabe, P & Hardman, L 2005, 'Attitudes and perceptions of workers to sexual harassment', *Journal of Social Psychology*, vol. 6, pp. 719–40.

McCain, J & Salter, M 2004, *Why Courage Matters*, Random House, New York.

McClaren, N 2012, 'The personal selling and sales management ethics research', *Journal of Business Ethics*, vol. 112, no. 1, pp. 101–125, retrieved 1 February 2012, <http://link.springer.com/article/10.1007%2Fs10551–012–1235–4>.

McClymont, K 2012, 'Magnate tried to mislead ASX on Obeid', *The Age*, 8 December, p. 4.

McDonald, C 2012, 'Complexities in the ethics in informatics, research and innovation', *Conference Proceedings of 6th Australian Institute of Computer Ethics Conference*, 13 February, Leitch, S & Warren, M (eds), Melbourne, pp. 270–31.

McDonald, GM 1995, Business ethics: A cross-cultural comparison in the Asia Pacific region, unpublished PhD thesis, The London School of Economics and Political Science.

——2000, 'Business ethics: Practical proposals for organisations', *Journal of Business Ethics*, vol. 19, no. 2, pp. 143–58.

——2009a, 'An anthology of codes of ethics', *European Business Review*, vol. 21, no. 4, pp. 344–72.

——2009b, 'Codes of ethics', in G Svensson & G Wood (eds), *Business Ethics: Through Time and Across Contexts*, Studentlitteratur AB, pp. 113–35.

McDonald, GM & Donleavy, GD 1995, 'Objections to the teaching of business ethics', *Journal of Business Ethics*, vol. 14, pp. 839–53.

McDonald, GM & Kan, PC 1996, Ethical acculturation of expatriate managers in a cross-cultural context, *Cross-Cultural Management*, vol. 3, no. 3, pp. 9–30.

——1997, Ethical perceptions of expatriate and local managers in Hong Kong, *Journal of Business Ethics*, vol. 16, pp. 1605–23.

McDonald, GM & Nijhof, A 1999, 'Beyond codes of ethics: An integrated framework for stimulating morally responsible behaviour in organisations', *Leadership and Organisation Development Journal*, vol. 20, no. 3, pp. 133–46.

McDonald, GM & Pak CK 1996, 'It's all fair in love, war and business: Cognitive philosophies in ethical decision-making', *Journal of Business Ethics*, vol. 15, pp. 973–66.

McDonald, GM & Roberts, C 1994, 'Product piracy: The problem that will not go away', *Journal of Product and Brand Management*, vol. 3, no. 4, pp. 55–65.

McEnroe, JE & Martens, SC 2001, 'Auditor's and investor's perceptions of the expectation gap', *Accounting Horizons*, vol. 15, no. 4, pp. 345–58.

McGee, RW 2009, 'Analysing insider trading from the perspective of utilitarian ethics and rights theory', *Journal of Business Ethics*, vol. 91, no. 1, pp. 65–82.

McGonigal, J 2012, 'Building resilience by wasting time', *Harvard Business Review*, October, p. 38.

McHugh, M 2012, 'Largest, longest, tallest, widest', *Mind Food*, 12 October, pp. 129–31.

McIntyre, O 2005, 'Police smash Costa crime', *Andulucia Com S.L.*, 22–28 September, retrieved 12 December 2013, <www.andalucia.com/news/cdsn/2005–09–28.htm>.

McKenzie, N & Baker, R 2012, 'Executive says he faced bribe threat over ship deal', *Saturday Age*, 29 September, p. 7.

McWilliam, A & Siegel, D 2001, 'Corporate social responsibility: A theory of the firm's perspective', *Academy of Management Review*, vol. 26, no. 1, pp. 117–27.

McVea, JF 2009, 'A field study of entrepreneurial decision-making and moral imagination', *Journal of Business Venturing*, vol. 24, pp. 491–504.

Medicare Australia 2013, 'Fraud', Commonwealth of Australia, retrieved 2 August 2013, <www.medicareaustralia.gov.au/provider/business/audits/fraud.jsp>.

Medlin, B, Green, KG 2003, 'Ethics in small business: Attitudes and perceptions of owner managers. *Academy of Entrepreneurship Journal*, vol. 9, pp. 113–32.

Mendel, R, Puddephatt, A, Wagner, B, Hawtin, D & Torres, N 2012, 'Global survey on internet privacy and freedom of expression: UNESCO series on internet freedom', UNESCO Publishing, retrieved 21 April 2013, <http://unesdoc.unesco.org/images/0021/002182/218273e.pdf>.

Merritt, M 2013, 'Bots and botnets: A growing threat', retrieved 6 February 2013, <http://au.norton.com/botnet/promo>.

Metrick, A & Yasuda, A 2011, 'Venture capital and other private equity: A survey', *European Financial Management*, vol. 17, no. 4, pp. 619–54.

Metzger, N, Dalton, DR & Hill, JW 1993, 'The organisation of ethics and the ethics of organisations: The case of expanded organisational ethics audits', *Business Ethics Quarterly*, January, vol. 3, no. 1, pp. 27–43.

Miceli, MP & Near, JP 1992, *Blowing the Whistle: The Organisational and Legal Implications for Companies and Employees*, Books, Lexington, New York.

Mill, JS [1806] 1998, in R Crisp (ed.), *Utilitarianism*, Oxford University Press, Oxford.

Miller, R 2005, 'Moral courage: definition and development', Ethics Resource Centre, pp. 1–34, retrieved 2 October 2013, <www.ethics.org/files/u5/Moral_Courage_Definition_and_Development.pdf>.

Miller, S & Weckett, J 2000, 'Privacy, the workplace and the internet', *Journal of Business Ethics*, vol. 28, pp. 255–65.

Miller, WI 2000, *The Mystery of Courage*, Harvard University Press, Cambridge, MA.

Milmo, D 2013, 'Rolls-Royce accused of bribing a Chinese airline executive', *The Guardian*, 6 January, retrieved 30 May 2013, <www.guardian.co.uk/business/2013/jan/06/rolls-royce-accused-bribing-chinese>.

Mintz, S 1996, 'The role of virtue in accounting education', *Accounting Education*, vol. 1, no. 1, pp. 67–91.

Mirkinson, J 2013, '*The Guardian* blocked by the army after NSA stories', *Huffington Post*, 28 June, retrieved 2 July 2013, <www.huffingtonpost.com/2013/06/28/army-blocks-the-guardian_n_3515374.html>.

Mitchell, RK, Agle, BR & Wood, DJ 1997, 'Towards a theory of stakeholder identification and salience: Defining the principle of who and what really counts', *Academy of Management Review*, vol 24, no. 2, pp. 222–7.

Mokoena, N 2008, 'National integrity framework: consolidating the fight against corruption', *Report of proceedings of the Third National Anti-Corruption Summit*, South Africa, 4–5 August 2008, retrieved 8 February 2013, <www.nacf.org.za/anti-corruption-summits/third_summit/UnitedNationsReport_summit3_Chapter7.pdf>.

Monaghan, A 2013, 'Rolls-Royce tries to clear the air as prized executive steps down', *The Observer*, 5 May, retrieved 17 November 2013, <www.theguardian.com/business/2013/may/05/rolls-royce-clear-air-executive-resigns>.

Monaghan, A & Russell, J 2012, 'Whistle blowers join forces to set up support organisation', *Daily Telegraph*, 27 August, p. 83.

Monash University 2003, 'Sexual harassment: the 'reasonable persons' test', Monash University, retrieved 10 September 2013, <www.monash.edu.au/equity-diversity/discriminationharassment/onlinetraining/sexual-harassment/sexual-harassment-reasonable-person.html>.

'Money for nothing' 2012, *The Economist*, 14 January, p. 51.

Montero, K 2012, 'When brands brawl: 5 digital ad wars', *iMediaConnection*, 9 March, retrieved 4 February 2013, <www.imediaconnection.com/printpage/printpage.aspx?id=31182>.

Montgomery, AW, Dacin, PA & Dacin, MT 2012, 'Collective social entrepreneurship: Collaboratively shaping social good', *Journal of Business Ethics*, vol. 111, pp. 375–88.

Moon, J 2013, 'Corporate Social Responsibility', Gourlay Professional Presentation, Deakin University, 19 November, Melbourne.

——, Crane, A & Matten, D 2005, 'Can corporations be citizens? Corporate citizenship as a metaphor for business participation in society', *Business Ethics Quarterly*, vol. 15, no. 3, July, pp. 429–53.

Moor, JH 1985. 'What is computer ethics?' *Metaphilosophy*, vol. 16, no. 4, October, pp. 266–75.

Moore, C 2013, 'Solving the ethics puzzle', *BizEd*, January/February, p. 56.

Moore, G 2004, 'The Fair Trade movement: Parameters, issues and future research', *Journal of Business Ethics*, vol. 53, no. 1–2, pp. 73–86.

Moore, J 2013, 'Now water companies are caught avoiding tax', *The Independent*, 14 February, retrieved 20 April 2013, <www.independent.co.uk/money/tax/exclusive-now-water-companies-are-caught-avoiding-tax-8496162.html>.

'Morals and the machine – As robots grow more autonomous societies need to develop rules to manage them' 2012, *The Economist*, 2 June, p. 13.

Morici, P 2013, 'Hail Edward Snowden, public servant: Economist', *CNBC*, 13 June, retrieved 2 July 2013, <www.cnbc.com/id/100810632>.

Morris, MH, Schindehutte, M, Walton, J & Allen, J 2002, 'The ethical context of entrepreneurship: Proposing and developing a developmental framework', *Journal of Business Ethics*, vol. 40, pp. 331–61.

Moses, A 2012, 'Fake online reviews mean cash-for-comment is rife', *Sydney Morning Herald*, 28 September, retrieved 10 February 2013, <www.smh.com.au/technology/technology-news/fake-online-reviews-mean-cashforcomment-is-rife-20120928–26p4e.html>.

Mosher-Williams, R 2006, 'Much more to do: Issues for further research on 'social entrepreneurship', in R Mosher-Williams (ed.), *Research on 'Social' Entrepreneurship: Understanding and Contributing to an Emerging Field*, ARNOVA Occasional Paper Series 1:3.

Motion Picture Association of America 2008, 'Public awareness campaigns', Motion Picture Association of America, retrieved 22 April 2013, <www.mpaa.org/contentprotection/public-service-announcements>.

Mukherji, S & Rickling, N 2013, 'The Dhaka factory fire: Who is responsible', Santa Clara University, 22 January, retrieved 17 January 2014, <www.scu.edu/ethics-center/ethicsblog/globaldialog.cfm?c=15006>.

Mulholland, L 1989 'Egoism and morality', *Journal of Philosophy*, vol. 86, no. 10, pp. 542–50.

Mulki, JP, Jaramillo, JF & Locander, WB 2008, 'Effect of ethical climate on turnover intention: Linking attitudinal and stress theory', *Journal of Business Ethics*, vol. 78, pp. 559–74.

Murphy, PR, Smith, JE & Daley, JM 1992, 'Executive attitudes, organizational size and ethical issues: Perspectives on a service industry', *Journal of Business Ethics*, vol. 11, pp. 11–19.

Murray, TH 1997, 'Ethical issues in human genome research' in K Shrader-Frechette & L Westra (eds), *Technology and Values*, Rowan and Littlefield Publishers, Oxford.

Murray, Z & Fraser, M 2013, 'Revision of NZCIA's code of ethics', New Zealand Institute of Chartered Accountants, May, p. 10.

Namie, G 2003, 'Workplace bullying: Escalated incivility', *Ivey Business Journal*, vol. 68, no. 2, pp. 1–6.

—— & Namie, R 2000, *The Bully at Work: What you Can Do to Stop the Hurt and Reclaim your Dignity on the Job*, Sourcebooks, Naperville, IL.

Narvaez, D & Lapsley, DK 2009, 'Moral identity, moral functioning, and the development of moral character', in DM Bartels, CW Bauman, LJ Skitka & DL Medin (eds), *The Psychology of Learning and Motivation*, vol. 50, Academic Press, Burlington, USA, pp. 237–74.

'Nasty, but rarer sexual harassment' 2011, *The Economist*, 12 November, p. 70.

Nazarkina, L 2012, 'How sustainable are the growth strategies of sustainability entrepreneurs?', in G. Mennillo, T Schlenzig & E Friedrick (eds), *Balanced Growth: Finding Strategies for Sustainable Development*, Springer-Verlag, Berlin, pp. 105–21.

Neate, R 2013, 'Oldest Swiss bank Wegelin to close after admitting aiding US tax evasion', *The Guardian*, 6 January, p. 8, retrieved 20 April 2013, <www.guardian. co.uk/world/2013/jan/04/swiss-bank-wegelin-close-tax-evasion>.

Neck, CP & Moorhead, G 1995, 'Groupthink remodelled: The importance of leadership, time pressure, and methodical decision-making procedures', *Human Relations*, vol. 48, pp. 537–57.

Neilsen, EH & Rao, MVH 1987, 'The strategy-legitimacy nexus: a thick description', *Academy of Management Review*, vol. 12, no. 3, pp. 523–33.

Neubaum, DO, Mitchell, MS & Schminke, M 2004, 'Firm newness, entrepreneurial orientation and ethical climate', *Journal of Business Ethics*, vol. 52, pp. 335–47.

New Zealand Institute of Chartered Accountants 2013, 'Invitation to comment and exposure draft on code of ethics (revised)', Professional Standards Board of the New Zealand Institute of Chartered Accountants, 8 March, pp. 10–14.

'News Corporation: An old new scandal' 2012, *The Economist*, 31 March 31, <www.economist.com/node/21551536>.

'#newscrashrecover' 2013, *The Economist*, 27 April, p. 60.

Nittle, NK 2013, 'What is a stereotype?' *About.com*, retrieved 4 February 2013, <http://racerelations.about.com/od/understandingrac1/a/WhatIsaStereotype.htm>.

'No laughing matter' 2013, *The Economist*, 29 June, p. 8.

Norris, F 2011, 'Deep roots of fraud at Olympus', *New York Times*, 8 December.

'Not very evil' 2012, *The Economist*, 12 May, p. 7.

NSW Government Fair Trading 2012, 'Special offer and competitions', State of New South Wales through NSW Fair Trading NSW Government, 26 September, retrieved 10 February 2013, <www.fairtrading.nsw. gov.au/Businesses/Advertising_and_marketing/Special_offers_and_competitions.html>.

Oakes, D 2012, 'Criminals buying personal details for frauds', *The Age*, 9 July, p. 3.

O'Donohoe, N, Leijonhufvud, C & Saltuk, Y 2010, *Report on Impact Investing: An Emerging Asset Class*, JP Morgan, 29 November, retrieved 7 August 2013, <www.rockefellerfoundation.org/uploads/files/2b053b2b-8feb-46ea-adbd-f89068d59785-impact.pdf>.

OECD 2013a, 'OECD urges stronger co-operation on corporate tax', OECD, 12 February, retrieved 20 April 2013,<www.oecd.org/newsroom/oecd-urges-stronger-international-co-operation-on-corporate-tax.htm>.

——2013b, 'Addressing base erosion and profit shifting', OECD Publishing, retrieved 20 April 2013, <http://dx.doi.org/10.1787/9789264192744-en>.

——n.d., 'About transfer pricing', OECD, retrieved 20 April 2013, <www.oecd.org/ctp/transfer-pricing/abouttransferpricing.htm>.

O'Hare, 2013, 'Belgian former Queen criticised by her own PM over legal tax dodge as the country's economy struggles', *Mail Online*, 12 January, retrieved

5 August 2013, <www.dailymail.co.uk/news/article-2260736/Belgiums-Dowagen-Queen-Fabiola-criticised-PM-legal-tax-dodge-countrys-economy-struggles.html>.

Olympus Corporation 2012, 'Olympus CSR report 2012 special edition: Rebuilding trust: The first 100 days', Olympus Corporation, December, retrieved 14 June 2013, <www.olympus-global.com/en/common/pdf/csr_confidence_2012.pdf>.

——2013, 'Business overview', Olympus Corporation, retrieved 14 June 2013, <www.olympus-global.com/en/corc/company/medical/index.jsp>.

'On public companies, trolleyology, written knowledge' 2012, *The Economist*, 9 June, p. 20.

'One child policy raises multiple issues' 2013, *Monash Magazine*, June, p. 18.

Ostrander, SA 2007, 'The growth of donor control: Revisiting the social relations of philanthropy', *Non-profit and Voluntary Sector Quarterly*, vol. 36, no. 2, pp. 356–72.

O'Sullivan, M 2012, 'Emirates fined $10 million for cartel', *Saturday Age*, 13 October, p. 3.

'Out of office', *AFR Boss*, 12 October, p. 10.

'Out of sight, out of mind' 2012, *The Economist*, 13 October, p. 74.

'Oxfordshire pensioner spends life savings on junk mail' 2012, BBC News Oxford, 17 March, retrieved 10 July 2013, <www.bbc.co.uk/news/uk-england-oxfordshire-17399179>.

Paine, L, Deshpandé, R, Margolis, JD & Bettcher, KE 2005, 'Up to code: Does your company's conduct meet world-class standards?' *Harvard Business Review*, December, pp. 122–33.

Painter-Morland, M 2008, *Business Ethics as Practice*, Cambridge University Press, Cambridge.

Painter-Morland, M & Ten Bos, R 2011, *Business Ethics and Continental Philosophy*, Cambridge University Press, Cambridge.

Parker, L 2012, 'Life's big decisions', *The Age*, 21 November, pp. 6–7.

Parrish, JL 2010, 'PAPA knows best: principles for the ethical sharing of information on social networking sites', *Ethics and Information Technology*, vol. 12, no. 2, pp. 187–93.

Pash, A 2011, 'A guide to sniffing out passwords and cookies (and how to protect yourself against it)', Gawker Media, 26 October, retrieved on 8 February 2013, <http://lifehacker.com/5853483/a-guide-to-sniffing-out-passwords-andcookies>.

Pavlo, W 2013, 'The anonymous SEC whistle-blower award of $14 million is a game-changer', *Forbes* 3 October, retrieved 17 December 2013, <www.forbes.com/sites/walterpavlo/2013/10/03/the-anonymous-sec-whistleblower-award-of-14m-is-a-game-changer>.

'Paying a price for doing what's right' 2012, *The Economist*, 24 November, pp. 80–1.

Payne, D & Joyner, B 2006, 'Successful US entrepreneurs: Identifying ethical decision making and social responsibility behaviours', *Journal of Business Ethics*, vol. 65, pp. 203–17.

Pearlstein, S 2002, 'In blossoming scandal, culprits are countless', *Washington Post*, 28 June, p. A1.

Perry, W 2012, Cyber security is mission critical, *BizEd*, July/August, pp. 36–41.

Peterson, DK 2002a, 'Computer ethics: the influence of guidelines in universal moral beliefs', *Information Technology and People*, vol. 15, no. 4, pp. 346–61.

——2002b, 'The relationship between unethical behaviour and the dimension of the ethical climate questionnaire', *Journal of Business Ethics*, vol. 41, pp. 313–26.

Pfitzer, M, Bockstette, V & Stamp, M 2013, 'Innovating for shared values: Companies that deliver both social benefit and business value rely on five mutually reinforcing elements', *Harvard Business Review*, September, pp. 101–7.

Phosphagenics 2013, 'Phosphagenics Limited; invoicing and accounting irregularities, Phosphagenics, market announcement', 24 July, retrieved 9 August 2013, <www.phosphagenics.com/site/DefaultSite/filesystem/documents/2013%20Jul%2024%20Invoicing%20and%20Accounting%20Misappropriations%20Investigation.pdf>.

Pickert, K 2012, '2 Doing good by texting', *Time Magazine*, 27 August, p. 25.

Pienta, DA & O'Neil, RF 1989, 'Value based management: Can it be quantified?' *International Journal of Value Base Management*, vol. 2, no. 1, pp. 93–102.

Pierce, M & Henry, J 1996, 'Computer ethics: The role of personal, informal and formal codes', *Journal of Business Ethics*, vol. 15, pp. 425–37.

Pieth, M, Low, LA and Cullen, PJ 2007, *The OECD Convention on Bribery*, Cambridge University Press, Cambridge.

Pimple, KD 2011, 'Computing ethics surrounded by machines: a chilling scenario portends a possible future', *Communications of the ACM*, March, vol. 54, no. 3, pp. 29–31.

Pincus, JD 2013, 'The seminar that worked', *BizEd*, May/June, p. 43.

Planer, B 2009, 'Product piracy – five examples from China and Europe', *Planet Retail*, 16 February, retrieved 21 April 2013, <http://blog.emap.com/boris/2009/02/16/product-piracy-%E2%80%93-five-examples-from-china-and-europe>.

Pless, NM & Appel, J 2012, 'In pursuit of dignity and social justice: Changing lives through 100% inclusion – how Gram Vikas fosters sustainable development', *Journal of Business Ethics*, vol. 111, pp. 389–411.

Polites, H 2013, 'ATO finds Google other multinational tax practices to be "commercially realistic"', *Business Spectator*, 23 January, retrieved 19 April 2013, <www.technologyspectator.com.au/ato-finds-google-other-multinationals-tax-practices-be-commercially-realistic>.

Polonsky, M, Vocino, A, Grau, S, Garma, R & Shahriar, A 2012, 'The impact of general and carbon-related environmental knowledge on attitudes and behaviour of US consumers', *Journal of Marketing Management*, vol. 28, nos 2–4, pp. 238–63.

Ponemon, LA & Gabhart, DL 1990, 'Auditor independence judgements: A cognitive-developmental model and experimental evidence', *Contemporary Accounting Research*, vol. 7, no. 1, pp. 227–51.

'Ponzi schemes: fleecing the flock' 2012, *The Economist*, 28 January, p. 55.

Portelli, E 2013, 'Rivers boss settles sexual harassment suit against designer after judge allows two other women to testify', *Herald Sun*, 3 September, retrieved 10 September 2013, <www.heraldsun.com.au/news/law-order/rivers-boss-settles-sexual-harassment-suit-against-designer-after-judge-allows-two-other-women-to-testify/story-fni0fee2-1226709321463>.

Powell, P 2011, 'Social elements of TBL (triple bottom line) reporting', *Relational Research*, retrieved 6 January 2014, <www.relationshipsglobal.net/Web/OnlineStore/Product.aspx?ID=37>.

Prabhu, GN 1999, 'Social entrepreneurial leadership', *Career Development International*, vol. 4, no. 3, pp. 140–5.

Premeaux, SR & Mondy, RW 1993, 'Linking management behaviour to ethical philosophy', *Journal of Business Ethics*, vol. 12, pp. 349–57.

'Press regulation: guarding the guardians' 2012, *The Economist*, 4 February, p. 45.

PricewaterhouseCoopers (PwC) 2012, *Cybercrime: Out of Obscurity and into Reality, 6th PwC Global Economic Crime Survey*, PricewaterhouseCoopers, March, retrieved 2 August 2013, <www.pwc.com.au/consulting/assets/risk-controls/global-economic-crime/Global-Economic-Crime-AU-Mar11.pdf>.

Pride in Diversity 2012, 'Top 10 employers 2012: The Australian workplace equality index', Pride in Diversity, retrieved 8 November 2013, <www.prideindiversity.com.au/awei>.

Primack, D 2013, 'Where is Calpers's governance when you need it?', *Fortune*, 20 May, p. 39.

'Private equity: Monsters, Inc?' 2012, *The Economist*, 28 January, p. 10–11.

Productivity Commission 2009, *Executive remuneration in Australia – Productivity Commission inquiry report*, Commonwealth of Australia, 19 December, no. 49, retrieved 21 August 2013, <www.pc.gov.au/__data/assets/pdf_file/0008/93590/executive-remuneration-report.pdf>.

'Professional-service firms: Desperately seeking scepticism' 2013, *The Economist*, 22 June, p. 69.

PRSA 2009–2013, 'Ethical Guidance for Public Relations Practitioners' 2009–2013, *Public Relations Society of America*, retrieved 11 February 2013, <www.prsa.org/AboutPRSA/Ethics>.

Pryor, P 2012, 'How to beat the web of deceit', *Sunday Age*, 26 February, p. 6.

PsychTests 2013, 'Integrity and work ethic test', PsychTests AIM Inc., retrieved 18 December 2013, <http://testyourself.psychtests.com/testid/3090>.

Putnam, D. 1997. 'Psychological courage', *Philosophy, Psychiatry and Psychology*, vol. 4, no. 1, pp. 1–11.

Quinn, M 2012, *Ethics in the Information Age*, 4th edn, Addison Wesley, Boston.

Rainey, DL 2006, *Sustainable Development: Inventing the Future through Strategy, Innovation and Leadership*, Cambridge University Press, Cambridge.

Ralph, S 2013, 'Abercrombie & Fitch only sells to popular people. Ethical? #fitchthehomeless', *Morally Marketed Ltd*, 27 May, retrieved 15 August 2013, <www.morallymarketed.com/case-studies/abercrombie-fitch-only-sells-to-popular-people-ethical-fitchthehomeless>.

Raman, S 2011, 'India cap on text messages to deter tele-marketers', BBC News, 27 September, retrieved 10 February 2013, <www.bbc.co.uk/news/world-south-asia-15071086>.

Rawls, J 1971, *A Theory of Justice*, Harvard University Press, Cambridge, MA.

'Reaping what they sow' 2012, *The Economist*, 4 August, p. 22.

Redfern, A & Snedker P 2002, 'Creating market opportunities for small enterprises: experiences of the Fair Trade movement', International Labour Office, SEED Working Paper No.30, Geneva, retrieved 20 April 2013, <www.european-fair-trade-association.org/efta/Doc/2002-Market-op.pdf>.

Redrup, V 2013, 'Rivers boss in court over more sexual harassment allegations', *SmartCompany*, 27 August, retrieved 10 September 2013, <www.smartcompany.com.au/legal/057193-rivers-boss-in-court-over-more-sexual-harassment-allegations.html>.

Reed, R & Luffman, GA 1986, 'Diversification: The growing confusion', *Strategic Management Journal*, vol. 7, no. 1, pp. 29–35.

Reingold, J 2012, 'The fun king', *Fortune Pacific Asia Pacific Edition*, 21 May, no. 7, pp. 68–74.

'Research needed on women on boards' 2013, *Australian Financial Review*, 6 May, p. 43.

Rest, J 1986, *Moral Development: Advances in Research and Theory*, Praeger Publishers, New York.

——1994, 'Background: theory and research', in J Rest & D Narvaez (eds), *Moral Development in the Professions*, Lawrence Erlbaum Associates, Hillsdale, NJ, pp. 1–126.

Rest, JR, Bebeau, MJ & Thoma, SJ 1999, *Postconventional Moral Thinking: A Neo-Kohlbergian Approach*, Psychology Press, UK.

Rest, J, Thoma, SJ, Moon, YL & Getz, I 1986, 'Different cultures, sexes, and religion', in J Rest (ed.), *Moral Development: Advances in Research and Theory*, Praeger, New York, pp. 89–132.

Reuters 2013, 'Singapore to take steps against foreign tax evaders', *New York Times*, 14 May, p.17.

Reynolds, GW 2012, *Ethics in Information Technology*, 4th edn, Cengage Learning, USA.

Reynolds, PD, Bygrave, WD, Autio, E, Cox, LW & Hay, M 2002, 'GEM global 2002 executive report', Global Entrepreneurship Monitor, Babson College, London.

Reynolds, SJ 2006, 'Moral awareness and ethical predispositions: Investigating the role of individual difference in the recognition of moral issues', *Journal of Applied Psychology*, vol. 91, no. 1, pp. 233–43.

Right Management Consultants 2013, 'Thought leadership', Right Management Inc., retrieved 18 December 2013, <www.rightmanagement.ca/en/thought-leadership/default.aspx>.

Riley, J 2012, 'Ethical marketing', Tutor2u, retrieved on 4 February 2013, <www.tutor2u.net/business/gcse/marketing_ethics.html>.

Rintoul, S 2013, 'Burger off!' *Good Weekend*, 28 September, pp. 31–2.

Riser, G 2010, 'The 12 least ethical companies in the world: Covalence's rankings', *Huffington Post* 30 March, retrieved 16 December 2013, <www.huffingtonpost.com/2010/01/28/the-least-ethical-compani_n_440073.html?slidenumber=0ZHHXzV%2FaPE%3D&slideshow>.

Robertson, C & Fadil, PA 1998, 'Developing corporate codes of ethics in multinational firms: Bhopal revisited', *Journal of Managerial Issues*, vol. 9, no. 4, Winter, pp. 454–68.

Robinson, S & Dowson, P 2012, *Business Ethics in Practice*, Chartered Institute of Personnel Development (CIPD), UK.

Rolfe, J & Lentini, R 2011, 'TVI express a pyramid scam, a Federal Court finds', *Daily Telegraph*, 29 November, retrieved 4 February 2013, <www.dailytelegraph.com.au/money/tvi-travel-offer-really-a-pyramid-scam-federal-court-finds/story-e6frezc0–1226209159301>.

Rolls-Royce plc 2010, 'Ethics committee report', retrieved 30 May 2013, <www.rolls-royce.com/reports/2010/governance/ethics-committee-report.shtml>.

——2012, 'Rolls-Royce reports to the SFO', media release, 6 December, retrieved 30 May 2013, <www.rolls-royce.com/news/press_releases/2012/121206_reports_sfo.jsp>.

——2013a, 'Our corporate story', retrieved 30 May 2013, <www.rolls-royce.com/about/index.jsp>.

——2013b, 'Rolls-Royce announces the appointment of Lord Gold', media release, 10 January, retrieved 30 May 2013, <www.rolls-royce.com/news/press_releases/2013/100113_lord_gold.jsp>.

Rondal, RS & Brinkmann, J 2003, 'Enron ethics: Culture matters more than codes', *Journal of Business Ethics*, vol. 45, no. 3, p. 243.

Rosenbach, M, Stark, H & Stock, J 2013, 'Prism exposed: Data surveillance with global implications', *Spiegelonline*, 10 June, retrieved 2 July 2013, <www.spiegel.de/international/world/prism-leak-inside-the-controversial-us-data-surveillance-program-a-904761.html>.

Ross, JK, Stutts, MA & Patterson, L 1991, 'Tactical considerations for the effective use of cause-related marketing', *Journal of Applied Business Research*, vol. 7, no. 2, pp. 58–65.

Rothwell, GR & Baldwin, JN 2007, 'Ethical climate agencies in the state of Georgia', *Journal of Business Ethics*, vol. 70, no. 4, pp. 341–61.

Rouse M 2005, 'Flaming', *TechTarget*, retrieved 10 February 2013, <http://searchsoa.techtarget.com/definition/flaming>.

——2009, 'Cybersquatting', *TechTarget*, retrieved 8 February 2013, <http://searchsoa.techtarget.com/definition/cybersquatting>.

——2010, 'Cybersecurity', *TechTarget*, retrieved 8 February 2013, <http://whatis.techtarget.com/definition/cybersecurity>.

——2011, 'What is spyware', *TechTarget*, retrieved 10 February 2013, <http://whatis.techtarget.com/reference/What-is-spyware>.

——2012, 'Botnet (zombie army)', *TechTarget*, retrieved 6 February 2013, <http://searchsecurity.techtarget.com/definition/botnet>.

Rousseau, S & Telle, K 2010, 'On the existence of the optimal fine for environmental crime', *International Review of Law and Economics*, vol. 30, no. 4, pp. 329–37.

Ruddick, G 2013, 'Rolls-Royce aerospace head quits as bribery fears mount', *Telegraph*, 4 May, retrieved 30 May 2013, <www.telegraph.co.uk/finance/newsbysector/industry/10037809/Rolls-Royce-aerospace-head-quits-as-bribery-fears-mount.html>.

Saigol, L & Scannell, K 2013, 'HSBC sued over home loan failures', *Financial Times*, 5 June, p. 14.

Saini, A & Martin, K 2009, 'Strategic risk-taking propensity: The role of ethical climate and marketing output control', *Journal of Business Ethics*, vol. 90, pp. 593–606.

Salignac, F 2011, 'The Fair Trade movement: Reconciling profit-seeking with ethical behaviour', Business and Professional Ethics Group 2010–2011, University of Sydney Business School, The University of Sydney, pp. 19–20.

Samala CM 2012, 'The good stuff – episode 1: Take THAT, plastic bags', The story of stuff project, retrieved 10 February 2013, <www.storyofstuff.org/2012/01/22/take-that-plastic-bags>.

'Samsung slapped for price-fixing' 2009, CBS News, 11 February, retrieved 4 February 2013, <www.cbsnews.com/news/samsung-slapped-for-price-fixing>.

Samuelson, JF 2013, 'Putting pinstripes in perspective', *Biz/Ed*, May/June, pp. 66–7.

'Sandoz recalls some Introvale birth control pills' 2012, Reuters, 6 June, retrieved 10 February 2013, <www.reuters.com/article/2012/06/06/us-novartis-sandoz-recall-idUSBRE8551IK20120606>.

Santos, FN 2012, 'A positive theory of social entrepreneurship', *Journal of Business Ethics*, vol. 111, pp. 335–351.

Sapienza, HJ & Korsgaard, A 1996, 'Procedural justice in entrepreneur/investor relations', *Academy of Management Journal*, vol. 39, no. 3, pp. 544–74.

Sar, RK, Al-Saggaf, Y & Zia, T 2012, 'You are what you type: Privacy in online social networks', *Conference Proceedings of 6th Australian Institute of Computer Ethics Conference*, Melbourne, 13 February, pp. 13–17.

Sarasvathy, S & Due, N 2008, 'Effectuation and over-trust: Debating Goel and Karri', *Entrepreneurship Theory in Practice*, vol. 32, no. 4, pp. 727–37.

Sarprasatha, J & Suresh, J 2012, 'Do attitudes influence situational ethics?' *International Journal of Management*, vol. 3, no. 2, May-August, pp. 144–49.

Satter, R 2012, 'UK's top court backs extradition of Assange', *China Daily*, Thursday 31 May, p. 12.

Savage, GT, Nix, TW, Whitehead, CJ & Blair, JD 1991, 'Strategies for assessing and managing stakeholders', *Academy of Management Executive*, vol.5, no. 2, pp. 61–75.

Scase, R 1997, 'The role of small businesses in the economic transformation of Eastern Europe: Real but relatively unimportant', *International Small Business Journal*, vol. 16, pp. 113–21.

Schenker, JL 2003, 'Look out inside the PC! It's the killer worm', *Time Magazine*, 10 February, pp. 56–7.

Schminke, M, Ambrose, ML & Noel, TW 1997, 'The effects of ethical frameworks on perceptions of organisational justice', *Academy of Management Journal*, vol. 40, pp. 1190–1207.

Schmitz, JA 1989, 'Imitation, entrepreneurship and long-run growth', *Journal of Political Economy*, vol. 97, pp. 721–39.

Schneiders, B 2010, 'Workplace bullying case "worst ever seen"', *The Age*, 29 April, retrieved 12 February 2013, <www.theage.com.au/small-business/managing/workplace-bullying-case-worst-ever-seen-20100428-tshs.html>.

——2012, 'Explainer: What is sexual harassment?' *The Age*, 29 April, p. 5.

Schumpeter, JA 1934, *The Theory of Economic Development*, Harvard University Press, Cambridge, MA.

——1942, *Capitalism, Socialism and Democracy*, Harper, New York.

Schumpeter, J 2012a, 'The mummy track', *The Economist*, 25 August, p .55.

——2012b, 'Corporate burlesque', *The Economist*, 3 November, p. 66.

Schwarcz, SL 2001, 'Enron and the use and abuse of special purpose entities in corporate structures', *University of Cincinnati Law Review*, vol. 70, pp. 1309–18, retrieved 13 January 2014, <http://heinonline.org/HOL/Page?handle=hein.journals/ucinlr70&div=46&g_sent=1>.

Schwartz, M 2000, 'Why ethical codes constitute an unconscionable regression', *Journal of Business Ethics*, vol. 21, pp. 173–84.

—— & Carroll, A 2003, 'Corporate social responsibility: A three domain approach', *Business Ethics Quarterly*, vol. 13, no. 4, pp. 503–30.

Schwartz, MS 2005, 'Universal moral values for corporate codes of ethics', *Journal of Business Ethics*, vol. 59, pp. 27–44.

Schwepker, CH 2001, 'Ethical climate's relationships to job satisfaction, organisational commitment and turnover in the sales force', *Journal of Business Research*, vol. 54, no. 1, pp. 39–52.

Segal, MN & Giabobbe, RW 2011, 'Prioritising ethical concerns for the Australian marketing research profession', *Alliance Journal of Business Research*, 16 June, pp. 17–32.

Seglin, J 1998, 'True lies', *Inc Magazine*, 15 October, retrieved 29 April 2013, <www.inc.com/magazine/19981015/1107.html>.

Seifert, DL & Stammerjohan, WW 2008, 'Moral identity as a moderator of perceived whistle-blowing under threat of retaliation, no protection and no reward', *Research on Professional Responsibility and Ethics in Accounting*, Emerald Group Publishing, vol. 13, pp. 41–66.

Sekerka, LE & Bagozzi, RP 2007, 'Moral courage in the workplace: Moving to and from the desire and decision to act', *Business Ethics: A European Review*, vol. 16, no. 2, pp. 132–49.

Sen, P 2007, 'Ashoka's big idea: Transforming the world through social entrepreneurship', *Futures*, vol. 39, pp. 534–53.

Serious Fraud Office (SFO) 2013, 'Bribery & corruption', UK Serious Fraud Office, retrieved 18 April 2013, <www.sfo.gov.uk/bribery--corruption/bribery--corruption.aspx>.

Serrano, RS 2010, 'Ethical issues facing the banking industry', Fidelis International Institute, January, retrieved 15 July 2013, <www.fidelisinstitute.org/article.php?se=13&ca=22>.

Sethi, SP 1979, 'A conceptual framework for environmental analysis of social issues and evaluation of business response patterns, *Academy of Management Review*, January, vol. 4, pp. 63–74.

'Sex, drugs and hope: How big business fought aids in South Africa', *The Economist*, 13 April, p. 63.

Shah, A 2001, 'Terminator technology', *Global Issues*, 14 July, retrieved 18 February 2013, <www.globalissues.org/article/194/terminator-technology>.

Shane, S & Venkatraman, S 2000, 'The promise of entrepreneurship as a field of research', *Academy of Management Review*, vol. 25, no. 1, pp. 217–26.

Shaw, C 2012, 'Don't count on a silver bullet', *Times Higher Education*, 19 January, p. 7.

Shepherd, DA & Patzelt, H 2011, 'A new field of sustainable entrepreneurship: Studying entrepreneurial action linking 'what is to be sustained?' with 'What is to be developed?'', *Entrepreneurship Theory in Practice*, vol. 35, pp. 137–63.

SHL 2010, 'HR leader – employers beware: one third of job applicants lying', media release, July 30, SHL, retrieved 20 February 2013, <www.shl.com/uk/news-item/news/hr-leader-employers-beware-one-third-of-job-applicants-lying1>.

Short, JC, Moss, TW & Lumpkin, GT 2009, 'Research in social entrepreneurship: Past contributions and future opportunities', *Strategic Entrepreneurship Journal*, vol. 3, pp. 161–94.

——, Payne GT & Ketchen DJ 2008, 'Research in configurations: Past accomplishments and future challenges', *Journal of Management*, vol. 34, pp. 1053–79.

Short, N 2012, 'Playing nice in the social media sandpit', *Saturday Age*, 8 September, p. 21.

Shrader-Frechette, K & Westra, L 1997, *Technology and Values*, Rowan and Littlefield, Oxford.

Silver-Greenberg, J 2012, 'HSBC to pay record fine to settle money laundering charges', *New York Times*, 11 December, retrieved 19 April 2013, <http://dealbook.nytimes.com/2012/12/11/hsbc-to-pay-record-fine-to-settle-money-laundering-charges>.

——2013, 'JP Morgan sons and daughters probe extends to Asia Pacific', *The Age*, 4 November, p. 28.

Simha, A & Cullen, JB 2012, 'Ethical climates and their effects on organizational outcomes: Implications from the past and prophecies for the future', *Academy of Management Perspectives*, vol. 26, no. 4, pp. 20–34.

Sing, M 2012, 'Paternity leave already prevalent', *Business Times*, 28 August, p. 2.

Singer, P 1979, *Practical Ethics*, Cambridge University Press, Cambridge.

——2013, 'The spying game', *Project Syndicate*, 5 July, retrieved 29 July 2013, <www.project-syndicate.org/commentary/edward-snowden-s-service-to-democracy-by-peter-singer>.

'Six degrees of mobilisation' 2012, *The Economist Technology Quarterly*, 1 September, p. 7.

Skeptical Raptor's Blog 2013, 'GlaxoSmithKline fined $3 billion by FDA for improper marketing and unethical behavior', Skeptical Raptor's Blog, retrieved 5 February 2013, <www.skepticalraptor.com/skepticalraptorblog.php/glaxosmithkline-fined-3-billion-fda-improper-marketing-unethical-behavior>.

Slaper, TF & Hall, TJ 2011, 'The triple bottom line: What is it and how does it work', *Indiana Business Review*, vol. 86, no. 1, retrieved 2 January 2014, <www.ibrc.indiana.edu/ibr/2011/spring/article2.html>.

Smeltzer, LR & Jennings, MM 1998, 'Why an international code of business ethics would be good for business', *Journal of Business Ethics*, vol. 17, pp. 57–66.

Smith, A 1993, *An Inquiry into the Nature and Causes of the Wealth of Nations*, ed. K Sutherland, Oxford University Press, Oxford.

Smith, C, Bhattacharya, CB, Vogel, D, & Levine, DI (eds) 2010, *Global Challenges in Responsible Business*, Cambridge University Press, Cambridge.

Smith, F 2012a, 'Time to tackle age bias', *Business Review Weekly*, 18–24 October.

——2012b, 'Why bullies rule at work', *Business Review Weekly*, 30 August–3 October, pp. 48–9.

Smith, HJ, Thompson, RL & Iacovou, CL 2009, 'The impact of organisational climate on reporting behaviours in information systems projects', *Journal of Business Ethics*, vol. 90, pp. 577–91.

Smith, J 2010, *Ethics and Financial Advice: The Final Frontier*, Argyle Lawyers Pty Ltd & Victoria University, Melbourne.

Smith, P 2012, 'Cyber battle front line of global war', *Australian Financial Review*, 23 January 2012, p. 42.

Smith, SE 2012, 'What is password sniffing?' *WiseGEEK*, <www.wisegeek.org/what-is-password-sniffing.htm>.

Smithers, R 2013, 'John Lewis puts lifetime electricity cost on product labels', *The Guardian*, 10 September, retrieved 5 January 2013, <www.theguardian.com/environment/2013/sep/09/john-lewis-product-label-scheme-energy-efficiency>.

Snell, RS 2000, 'Studying moral ethos using an adapted Kohlbergian model', *Organization Studies*, vol. 21, pp. 267–95.

Snell, RS & Herndon Jr, NC 2004, 'Hong Kong's code of ethics initiative: Some differences between theory and practice', *Journal of Business Ethics*, vol. 51, pp. 75–89.

——, Chak, AM-K & Chu, JW-H 1996, 'Codes of ethics in Hong Kong: Espousal, evidence and impact', in *ANZAM 96 Conference, Diversity and Change: Challenges for Management into the 21st Century*, Wollongong, NSW.

Soares, R, Marquis, C & Lee, M 2011, 'Gender and corporate social responsibility: It's a matter of sustainability', Catalyst Inc., 16 November, retrieved 5 January 2014, <www.catalyst.org/knowledge/gender-and-corporate-social-responsibility-its-matter-sustainability>.

Social Investment Forum Foundation 2010, *2010 Report on Socially Responsible Investing Trends in the United States*, Social Investment Forum Foundation, retrieved 6 August 2013, <www.ussif.org/files/Publications/10_Trends_Exec_Summary.pdf>.

Sojka, J & Spangenberg, ER 1994, 'Ethical concerns in marketing research' in CT Allen & DR John (eds), *NA-Advances in Consumer Research*, vol. 21, Association for Consumer Research, pp. 392–6.

'Solar stoush' 2013, *The Age*, 9 May, p. 13.

'Some hedge funds fudge the numbers' 2013, *BizEd*, May/June, p. 56.

Spence, L 2000, 'Priorities, practice and ethics in small firms', Institute of Business Ethics, London.

Spinello, RA 2000, 'Information integrity' in D Langford, (ed.), *Internet Ethics*, Macmillan, London, pp. 158–80.

—— 2003, *Case Studies in Information Technology Ethics*, 2nd edn, Prentice-Hall, NJ.

Spruijt, J 2012, 'Experience, skills and intentions of social entrepreneurs towards innovation', in S Smyczek (ed.), *Technology Driven Promotion for NGO: Experiences against Social Exclusions*, University of Economics in Katowice Publishing House, Katowice, Poland.

Stacey, P 2013, 'The tax treatment of multinationals', The Institute of Chartered Accountants in Australia, 11 February, retrieved 20 April 2013, <https://www.charteredaccountants.com.au/secure/myCommunity/blogs/548042/tax-blogs/330/the-tax-treatment-of-multinationals>.

Staff reporter 2013, 'Rolls-Royce probed for China bribe scandal, suspect a 'scapegoat', *Want China Times*, 20 January, retrieved 30 May 2013, <www.wantchinatimes.com/news-subclass-cnt.aspx?id=20130120000100&cid=1103>.

Stalk, G & Foley, H 2012, 'Avoid the traps that can destroy family businesses', *Harvard Business Review*, January/February, pp. 25–7.

Standard Chartered 2013, 'The secure web action team (S.W.A.T.)', Standard Chartered, retrieved 7 August 2013, <www.standardchartered.com/_microsites/anti-fraud/index.html>.

Starr, B & Yan, H 2013, 'Man behind NSA leaks say he did it to safeguard privacy, liberty', *CNN.com*, 23 June, retrieved 2 July 2013, <http://edition.cnn.com/2013/06/10/politics/edward-snowden-profile>.

'Start-up: Taking the plunge' 2012, *The Economist*, 13 October, p. 94.

State Services Commission 2000, 'Protecting New Zealand's infrastructure from cyber threats', E-Government Unit: State Services Commission, December, retrieved 10 February 2013, <www.ssc.govt.nz>.

Steiner, GA 1972, 'Social policies for business', *California Management Review*, Winter, pp. 17–24.

Stell, T 2011, 'The ethics of giving or receiving – Bribery Act 2010', *Human Resources Management Support*, retrieved 22 April 2013, <www.hrmanagementsupport.com/employlaw/the-ethics-of-gift-giving-or-receiving-bribery-act-2010>.

Stevens, B 1996, 'Using the competing values framework to assess corporate ethical codes', *Journal of Business Communication*, vol. 33, no. 1, January, pp. 71–84.

Steverson, BK, Rutherford, MW & Buller, PF 2013, 'New venture legitimacy, lies and ethics: An application of social contract theory', *Journal of Ethics and Entrepreneurship*, vol. 3, no. 1, pp. 73–92.

Steves, F & Rousso 2003, 'Anti-corruption programmes in post-communist transition countries and changes in the business environment, 1999–2002', European Bank for Reconstruction and Development, working paper no. 85, October, retrieved 22 April 2013, <www.ebrd.com/downloads/research/economics/workingpapers/wp0085.pdf>.

Stewart, R, Volpone, D, Avery, DR & McKay, P 2011, 'You support diversity, but are you ethical? Examining the interactive effects of diversity and ethical climate perceptions on turnover intentions', *Journal of Business Ethics*, vol. 100, pp. 581–93.

Stiglitz, JE 2009, 'The anatomy of a murder: Who killed America's economy', *Critical Review: A Journal of Political Politics and Society*, vol. 21, p. 329–39.

Strasburg, J & Rothfield, N 2013, 'US redies SAC charges', *Wall Street Journal*, 24 July, retrieved 29 October 2013, <http://stream.wsj.com/story/latest-headlines/SS-2–63399/SS-2–284717>.

'Stress levels rising' 2012, *Business Review Weekly*, 4–10 October, p. 31.

Stuart, I & Stuart, B 2004, *Ethics in the Post-Enron Age*, Thomson SouthWestern, OH.

Stuart, K 2011, 'PlayStation network hack: what every user needs to know', *The Guardian*, retrieved March 27, <www.guardian.co.uk/technology/gamesblog/2011/apr/27/psn-security-advice>.

Sujuan, W 2012, 'E-publishers talk copyright protection', *China Daily*, 30 May, p. 24.

Surowiecki, J 2012, 'Invisible hand, greased palm', *New Yorker*, 14 May, retrieved 14 February 2013, <www.newyorker.com/talk/financial/2012/05/14/120514ta_talk_surowiecki>.

'Survival of the biggest' 2012, *The Economist*, 1 December p. 130.

Susquehanna River Basin Commission 2010, *2010 State of the Susquehanna Report*, Susquehanna River Basin Commission, Harrisburg, Pennsylvania, retrieved 19 December 2013, <www.srbc.net/stateofsusq2010/documents/SOS%20Report_FINAL_10_18_10_low%20res.pdf>.

Svensson, G & Wood, G 2007, 'Strategic approaches of corporate codes of ethics in Australia: A framework for classification and empirical illustration', *Corporate Governance*, vol. 7, no. 1, pp. 93–101.

Tabuchi, H 2012, 'With Olympus managers still entrenched, an ousted chief drops his sword', *New York Times*, 6 January.

—— & Inoue, M 2012, 'Olympus shareholders shake-off scandal', *New York Times*, 20 April.

Talbot, F 2008, 'The entrepreneur, economics and ethics', *Biznik*, 18 October, retrieved 28 April 2013, <www.biznik.com/articles/the-entrepreneur-economics-and-ethics>.

Tang, J, Khan, SA & Zhu, R 2012, 'Entrepreneurs, ethically suspect behaviours and effective information acquisition: The moderating effects of impression management', *Journal of Developmental Entrepreneurship*, vol. 7, no. 4, pp. 1–23.

Tavani, HT 2000, 'Privacy and security', in Langford, D (ed.), *Internet Ethics*, Macmillan Press, Basingstoke, UK.

——2007, *Ethics and Technology: Ethical Issues of Information and Communication Technology*, 2nd edn, John Wiley & Sons, NJ.

'Tax in cyber space' 2013, *The Economist*, 4 May, retrieved 5 August 2013, <www.economist.com/news/business/21577071-online-retailers-may-soon-have-collect-sales-tax-amazon-oddly-gloating-tax>.

Taxation and Customs Union 2013, 'Facts and figures', European Commission, 14 March, retrieved 22 April 2013, <http://ec.europa.eu/taxation_customs/customs/customs_controls/counterfeit_piracy/statistics>.

Taxjustice Network 2002–2005, 'Tax havens cause poverty', Taxjustice Network, retrieved 15 July 2013, <www.taxjustice.net/cms/front_content.php?idcat=2#3>.

Taylor, C 1988, *Sources of the Self: The Making of Modern Identity*, Harvard University Press, Cambridge MA.

——2002, 'What spies beneath', *Time*, 7 October, p. 63.

Teal, EJ & Carroll, AB 1999, 'Moral reasoning skills: Are entrepreneurs different?', *Journal of Business Ethics*, vol. 19, pp. 229–40.

'Teen entrepreneur squatted at AOL for two months undetected…and built a business' 2012, *Sydney Morning Herald*, 28 May, retrieved 29 April 2013, <www.smh.com.au/action/printArticle?id=3331050>.

Tenbrunsel, AE & Messick, DM 2004, 'Ethical fading: The role of self-deception in ethical behaviour', *Social Justice Research*, vol. 17, no. 2, pp. 223–36.

Tennyson, EG 2012, 'The FDA's recall powers and the McNeil "Phantom Recall"' controversy, *Iowa Law Review*, vol. 97, pp. 1839–49.

The Antarctic Circle 2011, 'Shackleton quote', The Antarctic Circle, retrieved 4 February 2013, <www.antarctic-circle.org/advert.htm>.

'The digital divide, ICT and the 50 x 15 initiative' 2012, Miniwatts Marketing Group, 27 October, retrieved 10 February 2013, <www.internetworldstats.com/links10.htm>.

'The education of Kwekuadoboli' 2012, *The Economist*, 24 November, p. 12.

*The ethics of business: Where and why it can go wrong* 2013, YouTube, Professional Development Training, 26 September, retrieved 14 October 2013, <www.youtube.com/watch?v=vKWNFAiQHG8>.

'The great unravelling: The Balkanised banking' 2013, *The Economist*, 20 April, p. 66–7.

'The hidden costs of unethical behavior' 2004, *Josephson Institute Reports*, retrieved 17 December 2013, <http://josephsoninstitute.org/pdf/workplace-flier_0604.pdf>.

'The LIBOR affair: Banksters' 2012, *The Economist*, 7 July, p. 12.

'The LIBOR scandal: The rotten heart of finance' 2012, *The Economist*, 7 July, p. 23–25.

'The price of reputation' 2013, *The Economist*, 23 February, p. 60.

'The value of friendship' 2012, *The Economist*, 4 February, pp. 19–21.

'The week in higher education' 2013, *Times Higher Education*, 21 March, p. 4.

'The world this week' 2012, *The Economist*, 14 January–15 December.

'The world this week' 2013, *The Economist*, 22 June–9 November.

'The wrong browsers' 2013, *The Economist*, 9 March, p. 10.

'They said it' 2013, *Business Review Weekly*, 13 December–30 January, p. 14.

Thompson, D 2012, *The Fix*, Collins, UK.

Thorne, L 1998, 'The role of virtue in auditors' ethical decision making: An integration of cognitive/development and virtue/ethics perspectives', *Research on Accounting Ethics*, vol. 4, pp. 291–308.

Thornton, LF 2010, 'Planned obsolescence: Is it ethical? No. Can we still have the newest gadgets? Yes!', *Leading in Context*, 30 June, retrieved 8 July 2014, <http://leadingincontext.com/2010/06/30/planned-obsolescence-is-it-ethical>.

'Tipping the scales' 2011, *The Economist*, 15 October, retrieved 5 August 2013, <www.economist.com/node/21532280>.

Tomazin, F 2013, 'State moved to crack down on doctored ads', *Sunday Age*, 7 July, retrieved 17 December 2013, <www.theage.com.au/victoria/state-move-to-crack-down-on-doctored-ads-20130706–2piv9.html>.

'Top 10 crooked CEOs' 2009, *time Magazine*, retrieved 25 November 2013, <http://content.time.com/time/specials/packages/article/0,28804,1903155_1903156_1903160,00.html>.

*Top banks in record fine* 2013, video, Reuters, 5 December, retrieved 16 December 2013, <http://nz.finance.yahoo.com/video/top-banks-record-fine-154825136.html>.

'Tracking of iPad illegal' 2012, *Saturday Age*, 8 September, p. 7.

Transparency International 2009a, *The Anti-Corruption Plain Language Guide*, Transparency International, 28 July, p. 17, retrieved 5 August 2013, <www.transparency.org/whatwedo/pub/the_anti_corruption_plain_language_guide>.

——2009b, 'Business principles for countering bribery: a multi-stakeholder intiative led by transparency international', Transparency International, retrieved 22 April 2013, <http://archive.transparency.org/global_priorities/private_sector/business_principles>.

——2012, 'Corruption perceptions index 2012', Transparency International, retrieved 18 April 2013, <http://issuu.com/transparencyinternational/docs/cpi_2012_report/8>.

Transparency International UK 2012, 'Media advisory: Are defence companies doing enough to prevent corruption?', 28 September, retrieved 30 May 2013, <www.transparency.org/news/pressrelease/media_advisory_are_defence_companies_doing_enough_to_prevent_corruption>.

Treviño, LK 1986, 'Ethical decision making in organizations: A person-situation interactionist model', *Academy of Management Review*, vol. 11, pp. 601–17.

Treviño, LK & Nelson, KA 2007, *Managing Business Ethics: Straight Talk about How to Do it Right*, 4th edn, John Wiley and Sons, NJ.

Treviño, LK & Youngblood, SA 1990, 'Bad apples in bad barrels: A causal analysis of ethical decision-making behaviour', *Journal of Applied Psychology*, vol. 75, no. 4, pp. 378–85.

Treviño, LK, Weaver, GR & Reynolds, SJ 2006, 'Behavioural ethics in organisations: A review', *Journal of Management*, vol. 32, pp. 951–90.

Trivers, R 2012, *The Foley of Fools: The Logic of Deceit and Self-Deception in Human Life*, Basic Books, New York.

Turner, J 2013, 'SEC has three words for hedge funds: 'Culture of compliance'. But what do they mean?', Thomson Reuters, 3 April, retrieved 19 July 2013, <http://blogs.reuters.com/financial-regulatory-forum/2013/04/03/sec-has-three-words-for-hedge-funds-culture-of-compliance-but-what-do-they-mean>.

Turner, N, Baling, J, Epitropako, O, Butcher, B. & Milner, C 2002, 'Transformational leadership and moral reasoning', *Journal of Applied Psychology*, vol. 87, pp. 304–11.

Tysver, D & Mawhood, J 2000, 'Law and the internet', in Langford, D (ed.), *Internet Ethics*, Macmillan, Basingstoke, UK.

Uddin, S & Newland, J 2013, 'Bangladeshi garment factory owners on defensive, fear losing "lifeline"', *NBC News*, 25 May, retrieved 17 January 2014, <http://worldnews.nbcnews.com/_news/2013/05/25/18297608-bangladeshi-garment-factory-owners-on-defensive-fear-losing-lifeline?lite>.

'UK – the world leader in cybercrime' 2012, *The Independent*, 19 May, p. 2.

UN Global Compact 2013, 'The ten principles', retrieved 4 June 2013, <www.unglobalcompact.org/AboutTheGC/TheTenPrinciples/index.html>.

UNDP 2007, *Human Development Report 2007/2008: Fighting Climate Change: Human Solidarity in a Divided World*, Palgrave Macmillan, Basingstoke, UK.

UNICEF 2008, 'Facts about child labour', UNICEF, retrieved 20 April 2013, <www.unicef.org.nz/page/138/Factsaboutchildlabour.html>.

United Nations 2003, '*United Nations Convention against Corruption*', United Nations, 31 October, retrieved 22 April 2013, <http://treaties.un.org/doc/source/RecentTexts/Corruption_E.pdf>.

Urban, R & Boreham, T 2013, 'Biotech implicates five more in fraud', *Wall Street Journal*, 25 July, retrieved 8 July 2014, <www.theaustralian.com.au/business/companies/biotech-implicates-five-more-in-fraud/story-fn91v9q3-1226684615412?nk=cd6ad09cc72389f7f2a2bcfbc9a09111>.

US Department of Commerce 2001, Bureau of the Census.

US Department of Justice 2009, 'United States of America v. Bernad L Madoff', US Department of Justice, 12 March, retrieved 7 August 2013, <www.justice.gov/usao/nys/madoff/madoffhearing031209.pdf>.

Valdes, M 2012, 'Job seekers get asked for Facebook passwords', Associated Press, 20 March.

Van de Ven AH, Sapienza HJ & Villanueva J 2007, 'Entrepreneurial pursuits of self – and collective interests', *Strategic Entrepreneurship Journal*, vol. 1, nos 3–4, pp. 353–70.

van der Ploeg 2012, 'When biometrics fail: Gender, race, and technology of identity', *Times Higher Education*, 31 May, p. 50.

Van Narrewijk 2003, 'Concepts and definitions of CSR and corporate sustainability: Between agency and communion', *Journal of Business Ethics*, vol. 44, pp. 95–110.

Varadarajan, PR & Menon, A 1988, 'Cause-related marketing: A coalignment of marketing strategy and corporate philanthropy', *The Journal of Marketing*, vol. 52, no. 3, pp. 58–74.

'Vatican website attacked' 2012, *The Age*, 8 March, p. 14.

Vega, T & Kaufman, L 2013, 'The distasteful side of social media puts advertisers on their guard', *International Herald Tribune*, 5 June, p. 16.

Velasquez, MG 1988, *Business Ethics: Concepts and Cases*, 2nd edn, Prentice Hall, Englewood Cliffs, NJ.

Velasquez, MG & Andre, C 1998, 'Ethics and virtue', *Issues in Ethics*, vol. 1, no. 3.

Venkatraman, S 1997, 'The distinctive domain of entrepreneurship research: an editor's perspective', in J Katz & R Brockhaus (eds), *Advances in*

*Entrepreneurship, firm Emergence and Growth*, vol. 3, JAI Press, CT, pp. 119–38.

Verada, V 2006, *Blank world map with blue oceans*, world map, Wikimedia Commons, 25 July, retrieved 22 July 2013, <http://commons.wikimedia.org/w/index.php?title=File:A_large_blank_world_map_with_oceans_marked_blue.svg&oldid=77396135>.

Verschoor, C 1998, 'A study of the link between a corporation's financial performance and its commitment to ethics', *Journal of Business Ethics*, vol. 17, no. 13, pp. 1509–16.

'Very personal finance' 2012, *The Economist*, 2 June.

Victor, B & Cullen, JB 1987, 'A theory and measure of ethical climate in organisations', in WC Frederick (ed.), *Research in Corporate Social Performance and Policy*, vol. 9, JAI Press, Greenwich, CT pp. 51–7.

——1988, 'The organizational bases of ethical work climates', *Administrative Science Quarterly*, vol. 33, pp. 101–25.

Victoria Legal Aid 2012, 'Workplace bullying policy and procedures', Victoria Legal Aid, retrieved 1 February 2013, <www.legalaid.vic.gov.au/find-legal-answers/discrimination-harassment-and-bullying/workplace-bullying-and-discrimination>.

Victorian Equal Opportunity & Human Rights Commission 2012, 'Workplace rights and responsibilities', retrieved 21 February 2013, <www.humanrightscommission.vic.gov.au/index.php/employer-responsibilities/liability>.

'Visa sanctions, face control, asset freezes and visa bans give rich countries useful weapons against wrong-doers. Campaigners want them used' 2012, *The Economist*, 21–27 July, pp. 49–50.

Visser, W, Matten, D, Pohl, M & Tollhurst, N 2008, *The A–Z of Corporate Social Responsibility*, John Wiley & Sons, West Sussex.

Vline, DM & Cullinan, CP & Farrar, R 2008, 'Ethical climate and organisational commitment among management accountants', *Research on Professional Responsibility and Ethics in Accounting*, vol. 13, pp. 67–86.

von Weltzien Høivik, H & Shankar, D 2011, 'How can SMEs in a cluster respond to global demands for corporate responsibility?', *Journal of Business Ethics*, vol. 101, no. 2, pp. 175–95.

Vyakarnam, S, Bayley, A, Myers, A & Vernett, D 1997, 'Towards an ethical understanding of ethical behaviour in small firms', *Journal of Business Ethics*, vol. 16, pp. 1625–36.

Wagner, R 2011, 'Hedge funds', *Seven Pillars Institute for Global Finance & Ethics*, 19 April, retrieved 19 July 2013, <http://sevenpillarsinstitute.org/case-studies/hedge-funds>.

'Wake up and smell the coffee: Corporate taxation' 2012, *The Economist*, 15 December, p. 58.

Walker, MU 2006, *Moral Repair: Reconstructing Moral Relations after Wrongdoing*, Cambridge University Press, New York.

Wallace, SL 1999, 'Social entrepreneurship: The role of social purpose enterprises in facilitating community economic development', *Journal of Developmental Entrepreneurship*, vol. 4, pp. 153–74.

Wang, YD & Hsieh, HH 2012, 'Toward a better understanding of the link between ethical climate and job satisfaction: A multilevel analysis', *Journal of Business Ethics*, vol. 105, pp. 535–45.

Ward, D 2002, 'Reserves being misused to boost earnings', *Los Angeles Times*, 12 August, retrieved 6 August 2013, <http://articles.latimes.com/2002/aug/12/business/fi-account12>.

Waring, C 2004, 'Measuring ethical climate risk', *The Internal Auditor*, December, no. 1, pp. 71–5.

Watkin, D 2011, 'Are insurance referral fees a racket?', *BBC News*, 5 July, retrieved 10 February 2013, <www.bbc.co.uk/news/business-14028214>.

Weber, J 1981, 'Institutionalizing ethics into the corporation', *MSU Business Topics*, vol. 29, Spring, pp. 47–52.

Webley, S & More, E 2003, 'Does business ethics pay?' *Institute of Business Ethics*, London.

Weckert, J 2000, 'What is new or unique about Internet activities?' in D Langford (ed.), *Internet Ethics*, Macmillan, Basingstoke, UK.

Weeks, WA & Nantel, J 1992, 'Corporate codes of ethics and sales force behaviour: A case study', *Journal of Business Ethics*, vol. 11, pp. 671–8.

——, Loe, T, Chonko, L, Martinez, C & Wakefield, K 2006, 'Cognitive moral development and the impact of perceived organisational ethical climate on the search for sales force excellence: A cross-cultural study', *Journal of Personal Selling and Sales Management*, vol. 26, no. 2, pp. 205–17.

Weerawardena J & Mort GS 2006, 'Investigating social entrepreneurship: A multidimensional model', *Journal of World Business*, vol. 41, no. 1, pp. 21–35.

'Welcome Home', 2013, *The Economist*, 19 January, pp. 11–12.

Wells, PE 2013, *Business Models for Sustainability*, Edward Elgar Publishing, MA.

Welsh, DHB & Birch, NJ 1997, 'The ethical orientation of US small business decision makers: A preliminary study', *Journal of Small Business Strategy*, vol. 2, pp. 41–51.

Werhane, PH 1980, 'Formal organizations, economic freedom and moral agency', *Journal of Value Inquiry*, vol. 14, pp. 43–50.

——, 1985, *Person's Rights and Corporations*, Prentice-Hall, Englewood Cliffs, NJ.

West, M 2013, 'Share bonanza for executives as companies exploit loopholes', *The Age*, 27 March, pp. 23–9.

'What is unlawful discrimination?' 2013, *A Whole New Approach*, retrieved 11 February 2013, <www.antidiscriminationaustralia.com.au>.

Widdows, H 2012, *Global Ethics: An Introduction*, Polity Press, Cambridge.

Wikileaks 2013, 'Wikileaks press conference on Edward Snowden's exit from Hong Kong' retrieved 2 July 2013, <https://wikileaks.org/Transcript-of-WikiLeaks-Press.html>.

Williams, JC & Cuddy, A 2012, 'Will working mothers take your company to court?', *Harvard Business Review*, September, pp. 95–9.

Williams, J & Elson, RJ 2010, 'Improving ethical education in the accounting program: A conceptual course', *Academy of Educational Leadership Journal*, vol. 14, no. 4, pp. 107–16.

Willingham, R 2013, 'Five journalists facing charges make plea on source protection', *The Age*, 2 April, retrieved 19 December 2013, <www.theage.com.au/victoria/five-journalists-facing-charges-make-plea-on-source-protection-20130402-2h4dr.html>.

Willison, R 2006, 'Understanding the perpetration of employee computer crime in the organisational context', *Information and Organisation*, vol. 16, pp. 304–24.

Wilkins, G 2013, 'Banking industry distances itself from ASIC enquiry', *The Age*, 21 June, p. 23.

Wilkins, G & Butler B 2013, 'Island allure: The tax secrets of big business', *Saturday Age*, 25 May, p. 10–11.

Wilson, N 2012, 'Former Commonwealth bank Chief Sir Ralph Norris owed $9.6m for five months' work', *Herald Sun*. 21 August 2012, retrieved 8 November 2013, <www.heraldsun.com.au/business/former-commonwealth-bank-chief-sir-ralph-norris-owed-96m-for-five-months-work/story-fn7j19iv-1226454455432>.

Wimbush, J, Shepard, J, & Markham, S 1997, 'An empirical examination of the relationship between ethical climate and ethical behavior from multiple levels of analyses', *Journal of Business Ethics*, vol. 16, no. 16, pp. 1705–16.

Witbourn, M 2013, 'Social media ban on bosses in push to protect privacy', *Saturday Age*, 12 October, p. 6.

'Women in business' 2012, *The Economist*, 10 March, p. 65.

'Women of influence' 2012, *Biz/Ed*, March/April, p. 52–3.

Wood, DJ 2011, 'Japan's corporate "yes" culture', *New York Times*, 21 December.

Wood, G 2013, 'Five minutes with an advisor', *Private World: NAB Private Wealth Magazine*, issue 12, July, p. 27.

Wood, L & Butler, B 2012, 'Centro breach admitted', *The Age*, 17 April, p. 6.

Woodford, M 2012, *Exposure: Inside the Olympus Scandal: How I went from CEO to Whistleblower*, Portfolio/Penguin, New York.

Woodruff, P 2011, *The Ajaxdil Dilemma: Justice, Fairness and Rewards*, Oxford University Press, New York.

Woodward, S 2011, 'Controversy at UQ deepens', *Campus Review*, 15 November, pp. 1–4.

Workplace Gender Equity Agency 2012a, 'Women on boards but not in pipeline to leadership', media release, 27 November, Workplace Gender Equity Agency, retrieved 12 November 2013, <www.wgea.gov.au/content/women-boards-not-pipeline-leadership>.

——2012b, 'Gender pay gap short-changes women $250.50 a week', media release, Workplace Gender Equity Agency, 18 May, retrieved 12 November 2013, <www.wgea.gov.au/content/gender-pay-gap-short-changes-women-25050-week>.

——2013, 'GradStats-starting salaries', Workplace Gender Equality Agency, retrieved 12 November 2013,

<www.wgea.gov.au/sites/default/files/2013–01–07_GradStats_factsheet_tag.pdf>.

WorkPro 2008, 'Australian workplaces rife with bullying survey finds', media release, 14 August, WorkPro, retrieved 21 February 2013, <www.workpro.com.au/downloads/pdf/media/releases/14th_Aug_2008_Australian_workplace_rife_with_bullying_survey_finds.pdf>.

World Fair Trade Organization (WFTO) 2009, 'What is Fair Trade?', World Fair Trade Organization, 7 November, retrieved 20 April 2013, <www.wfto.com/index.php?option=com_content&task=blogcategory&id=11&Itemid=12>.

World Vision Action 2012, 'Our guilty pleasure; Exploitative child labour in the chocolate industry', World Vision Australia, January, retrieved 17 April 2013, <www.worldvision.com.au/Libraries/DTL_Demand_Ethical_Chocolate/FINAL_Our_Guilty_Pleasure_Summary_Version_09_02_2012.pdf>.

Wotruba, TR 1990, 'Comprehensive framework for the analysis of ethical behaviour, with a focus on sales organisations', *Journal of Personal Selling and Sales Management*, vol. 10, pp. 29–42.

Wu, RWS 2002, 'The new Hong Kong domain name dispute resolution policy: A comparative analysis', *International Review of Law, Computers & Technology*, vol. 16, no. 3, pp. 251–63.

Xavier, SR, Kelley, D, Kew, J, Herrington, M & Vorderwülbecke, A 2012, 'Global Entrepreneurship Monitor (GEM) 2012 Global Report', Global Entrepreneurship Research Association, retrieved 28 April 2013, <www.babson.edu/academics/centers/blank-center/global-research/gem/pages/reports.aspx>.

Yeates, C 2012, 'Ex-premier Brumby to head probe into dumping', *The Age*, 4 July, retrieved 15 November 2013, <www.theage.com.au/business/expremier-brumby-to-head-probe-into-dumping-20120704–21gm0.html>.

'Yes, ja, oui, no, no' 2012, *The Economist*, December 15, p. 58.

Yin, R 1984, *Case Study Research: Design and Methods*, Sage Publications, Beverly Hills, CA.

Young, JR 2012, 'Online classes see cheating go hi-tech', *Chronicle of Higher Education*, 3 June, <http://chronicle.com/article/online-classes-see-cheating-go/132093>.

YourMorals.Org n.d., 'Explore your morals', YourMorals.org, retrieved 18 December 2013, <www.yourmorals.org/explore.php>.

'You've been sacked – the world this week' 2012, *The Economist*, 3 November, p. 7.

Yunus, M 2006, ''We can put poverty into museums' Nobel lecture by Muhammad Yunus', Nobelprize.org, Nobel Media A, 10 December, retrieved 7 Nov 2013, <www.nobelprize.org/nobel_prizes/peace/laureates/2006/yunus-lecture-en.html>.

Zahra, SA, Gedaglovic, E, Neubaum, DO & Shulman, JM 2009, 'Apology of social entrepreneurs: Motives, search processes and ethical challenges', *Journal of Business Venturing*, vol. 24, no. 5, pp. 519–32.

Zakaria, T & Hosenball, M 2013, 'Edward Snowden charged with espionage over NSA leaks', *Huffington Post*, 21 June, retrieved 2 July 2013, <www.huffingtonpost.com/2013/06/21/edward-snowden-charged_n_3480984.html>.

Zey-Ferrell, M, Weaver, KM & Ferrell, OC 1979, 'Predicting unethical behaviour among marketing practitioners', *Human Relations*, vol. 32, no. 7, pp. 557–69.

Zhang, Z & Arvey, RD 2009, 'Rule breaking in adolescents and entrepreneurial status: An empirical investigation', *Journal of Business Venturing*, vol. 24, pp. 436–47.

Zirnsak, M 2013, *Secrecy, Jurisdiction, the ASX100 and Public Transparency*, report for Justice & International Mission, Uniting Church in Australia, Synod of Victoria and Tasmania, May, Victoria, retrieved 22 July 2013, <http://wr.victas.uca.org.au/assets/5463/ASX100_and_secrecy_jurisdiction_report_May_2013.pdf>.

Zuel, B 2012, 'Home of the illegal track', *The Age*, Wednesday 19 September, p. 3.

Zumbo, F 2009, 'Collapse of Kleenmaid should ring warning bells', *The Age*, 23 June, retrieved 29 April 2013, <www.theage.com.au/small-business/franchising/collapse-of-kleenmaid-should-ring-warning-bells-20090619-cr00.html>.

# Index